From **AARON** *to* **ZOE**

From **AARON** *to* **ZOE**

15,000 *Great Baby Names*

DANIEL AVRAM RICHMAN

Little, Brown and Company
Boston Toronto London

To those who gave me my name and, by their example and guidance, have helped me try to live up to it

Special thanks for their editorial assistance to Glen Berger, Lana Hart, Suzanne Maynard, Laurie D. Rubin, Peggy Stafford, Jane E. Starr, and Laura K. Utterback; and for her patience and support, to Joy.

The names in this book are also available in a computer program that gives you six browsers, all usable at the same time, as well as other features to help you find the perfect name. BABY-NAMER! is available for DOS or Macintosh at most software stores. Or call 800-228-4078 to order.

First Edition

Library of Congress Cataloging-in-Publication Data
Richman, Daniel A.
From Aaron to Zoe: 15,000 great baby names/Daniel Avram Richman.—1st ed.
p. cm.
Includes bibliographical references.
ISBN 0-316-74444-1 (pbk.)
1. Names, Personal—Dictionaries. I. Title.
CS2377.R5 1993
929.4'4'03—dc20 92-44632

10 9 8 7 6 5 4 3 2 1

MV-NY

Design by Barbara Werden
Illustrations by Bob Barner

Published simultaneously in Canada by Little, Brown & Company (Canada) Limited

Printed in the United States of America

Contents

Introduction

What are you going to name the baby?

Do you want to name him or her after a family member, famous artist, or renowned author? Would you like your child's name to have a specific meaning, such as "strength" or "beloved"? Should it be popular or rare? Should it reflect a certain ethnicity?

Whether you're ready to give a name at the instant of arrival or prefer to let your first impressions of the child guide you, you'll undoubtedly spend many hours considering the possibilities.

You'll become hypersensitive to names around you, and an expert on definitions. On being introduced to a new colleague, you'll automatically spout that his or her name means "one who eats paste." Associations will turn up from your past. You'll reject names with explanations along the lines of "a kid with that name threw up on me." Family and cultural traditions, aesthetics, namesakes, and nicknames will all factor in.

But before the process begins to seem altogether too overwhelming and you start desperately picking names from road signs, RELAX. The user-friendly organization of *From Aaron to Zoe* will help you find the perfect name for your bundle of joy.

I've included more than 15,000 names (the right one is in here somewhere), lively and detailed origins and definitions, and an accessible cross-referencing system called browsers. The browsers organize names in significant categories, so you can pick a name on the basis of language or ethnicity, popularity, meaning, or namesakes from various occupations and activities. And once you've culled preferences from the browsers, you can turn to the boys' and girls' alphabetical sections for more details: place of origin, meaning, relative rarity, historical or contemporary namesakes, nicknames, and alternative spellings.

My material is based on extensive research and reliable studies, so you can feel confident that if you choose a name because it means "powerful," it won't turn out down the road to mean "porpoise." With your own ideas and the counsel offered here, you'll have all the tools you'll need to make a thoughtful choice.

Happy naming!

From **AARON** *to* **ZOE**

Naming Considerations

ASSOCIATIONS AND STEREOTYPES

Who hasn't liked the sound of a name but avoided it because "I knew a guy in the third grade who had that name, and he used to get beat up all the time"?

Not only personal associations but historical events and personalities influence a name's popularity. For example, the number of children named Adolf declined rapidly during World War II, and the number of Glenns increased dramatically after John Glenn's space flight. One recent book noted that "it usually takes three generations for a name to shed its moldy skin."

But really, associations and history are a pretty flimsy basis for a naming decision. After all, most names have been borne by a wide range of people, from heroes to scoundrels.

So try to get that third-grade wimp out of your mind when considering a name. Ask others — especially your partner — what associations the name has for them. And look to the browsers for meaning and occupations/activities for more sense of what baggage, good or bad, a name carries.

POPULARITY

Closely related to a name's associations and stereotypes is its popularity. It's been shown repeatedly in studies that at any given time, the names people prefer tend to be those that are most popular. For example, the more popular a man's name, the more likely both men and women are to rate it "strong," "active," and "good." Yet many names go through distinct cyclical vogues.

Over time, when names become too familiar to be desirable, parents choose less familiar names, until those names become too familiar, when a new cycle of popularity begins.

A number of studies have examined whether having an "unusual" name harms or helps a child. But as some of the studies have noted, not all unusual names have the same effect — either positive or negative.

For example, the unusual male names McKinley and Talmadge are perceived quite differently from each other. The first is seen as more upper-class, overconfident, intolerant, and cold, and the second as more lower-class, weak, stupid, and unattractive.

Similarly, the unusual female names Courtney and Berleana have different associations. The first is seen as stronger, smarter, more upper-class and attractive; the second falls at the bottom of the desirability scale.

Some studies say a rare name may put a child at a disadvantage. One, for example, found that boys aged eight to twelve have a favorable stereotype of common names and a somewhat unfavorable stereotype of uncommon names.

Another study concluded that boys with "peculiar" names had a significant tendency to become more severely emotionally disturbed than boys with other names. Girls with "peculiar" names showed no such tendency. "Peculiar" was defined as occurring at most twice in the sample of 1,682 subjects and as having "something of an odd or aberrant sound in our culture." The study emphasized, though, that it didn't find a cause-and-effect relationship between a name's peculiarity and emotional disturbance.

Female college students are less likely to graduate with honors if they bear unusual names, while males show no such tendency, according to one study.

Still other studies say having an unusual name is harmless. In a large sampling (over 11,000 subjects), high school students with unusual names scored no differently than others in academic performance, leadership, and initiative, or on tests measuring IQ, creativity, and achievement. Asked to speculate about the academic prowess of their incoming classes, teachers studied before the beginning of the school year didn't think their unusually named students would fare worse than the others. The teachers also tended to think of unusually named students as coming from families of higher socioeconomic status.

And to balance matters out, some studies indicate that having an unusual name can actually benefit a child. Although college men with unusual names scored no differently from other men on an eighteen-point personality inventory, unusually named college women scored significantly higher than their conventionally named classmates in five areas: capacity for status, sociability, social presence, self-acceptance, achievement via conformance, and psychological-mindedness. College women with unusual names (names that occurred only once among the student population of 1,749) had a higher sense of uniqueness and self-esteem than did their more commonly named classmates. Men did, too, but to a lesser extent.

Male psychologists with unusual names (occurring only once among the sample of 284) were more likely to be honored as Fellows, to be interested in esoteric areas of research or practice, to be cited in textbooks, and to be consulted as journal-article reviewers.

One study found that having an unusual name may influence a child's career choice. It concluded that children with unusual names tend to become bookish early in life and, perhaps as a direct consequence, frequently end up as professors. The fancier the unusual name, the more likely it is that its bearer will teach drama or art, that study concluded.

So what's the upshot of these contradictory studies? Obviously, it's your choice. Your own attitude toward your baby's name is going to have more impact on the child than any other factor. So cast a wide net and find the name that feels inevitable and perfect — regardless of how rare or popular it is.

SOUND

A name's sound may be the most important consideration to you — even more important than its meaning. But what "sounds good" is far from universally agreed upon. One good idea is to speak aloud each first name and family name you are considering using, in all possible combinations.

You should pay attention to the first letter or sound and the last letter or sound. Consider the effect of repeating initial sounds, as in Marilyn Monroe and James Joseph Jefferson, or how a name sounds if its last letter is repeated in the last name's first letter, as in Alexandra Allen and Norman Nash. A name's last letter may determine its "feeling." For example, names ending with the letter *o* have been characterized as "friendly, breezy, but not lightweight; strong." You may like the sound made by combining first and last names that have similar endings: Janice Wallace, Brendan Nolan.

In trying out names, you should also be mindful of the full name's rhythm and experiment with syllables. One suggestion often given is that if the family name is short, the first name should be long (multisyllabic), and vice versa. Consider, for example, how the name Eleanor Brown sounds more pleasing than Nell Brown, or Nell Brownington more than Eleanor Brownington. If you're choosing both a first and a middle name, one should be short and the other long. But which should be which ought to be determined by the rhythmic patterns the names form when combined. For instance, the rhythmic pattern in the names Barbara Joan and Roberta Sue is smoother than those in Joan Barbara and Sue Roberta.

Also take into account that hard-sounding family names such as Becker and Pratt may sound best with soft names such as Arthur or Ellen, and be alert for rhyming names, such as Jane Crane or Lawrence Torrence. Listen carefully to the overall sound — your child will be hearing it all his or her life.

MEANING

You may want your child's name to reflect some quality you admire and want him or her to have, or to echo a feeling or experience you associate with the child. Using this book's entries, you can evaluate the meanings of your favorite names, and the meanings browser can help you choose a name on the basis of specific meanings.

ETHNIC NAMING PRACTICES

The names we choose for our young — and the reasons we choose them — reveal much about our values as a culture. Most English names come from the Judeo-Christian tradition. Indeed, the number of biblical names commonly used today illustrates the enormous role religion plays in our history and our lives. The following is a brief survey of some of the customs and sources for naming in other cultures. You may decide to pay tribute to your heritage and assimilate some of these traditions, or these practices may give you inspiration for sources or methods.

African

Although the size and diversity of cultures on the African continent are daunting, some commonalities among naming traditions can be discerned. For example, many African children are given two names, one at the moment of birth and the other at a later-celebrated date.

In Nigeria, newborn members of the Yoruba community are given an *oruku,* which describes the specific circumstances of their birth (for example, the name Ige means "delivered feet-first"), as well as an *oriki,* or praise name, which suggests the expectations and hopes for the child (for example, Bolanile, "the wealth of this house").

Similarly, among Swahili speakers in certain Kenyan tribes, the first, or birth, name (called the *jina la utotoni*) is chosen by an elderly relative. It usually refers to the child's appearance. Up to forty days later, the *jina la ukubwani,* or adult name, is picked by the parents or paternal grandparents.

Totems play an important role in the choice of an African name. Members of tribes or clans try to keep these symbolic emblems (usually in the form of an animal, plant, or object image) in mind as they give names to their young. A proper name should reflect the totem, and thus the values, of the community.

Another commonality among some African peoples is the practice of naming ceremonies. For Akan speakers in Ghana, this event takes place seven days after the birth. It is here that the father chooses the name of a distinguished relative for the child, who is then expected to manifest the same desirable characteristics as his or her namesake.

Nigerian Yorubas celebrate by touching the newborn's mouth with salt, oil, and other substances representing power, prosperity, happiness, and a strong character.

African "born-to-die" names sound morbid but are intended to shield newborns from malignant spirits intent on causing their death.

Chinese

In China, parents sometimes give boys plain or meaningless names in an attempt to trick evil spirits into overlooking them. Girls receive more elaborate names, or names that represent a graceful natural object, such as Li Hua ("pear blossom") or Jing-wei ("small bird").

Chinese names are designed to be highly individual, so that each is shared by no more than a few others. The unique meaning of a name may be known only to the parents. A person may, however, be given a different or more common name at some later stage of life, such as marriage or the beginning of college.

One notable Chinese naming custom is the use of generational names. Every member of a generation has one name in common, usually a word from a poem. The subsequent generations take a different name from the same poem, creating a kind of poetic record of the ancestral lineage.

Greek

Traditional Greeks, naming their children on the seventh or tenth day after birth, use the paternal grandfather's name for the first-born male and the paternal grandmother's name for the first daughter. Other relatives' names are often used for the later children.

The Greek Orthodox church is also a strong influence; popular saints' names have historically been Greek favorites. Greek names often connote moral or intellectual characteristics, as in Sophia ("wisdom").

Many Greek names have been used significantly in other languages but are no longer popular among Greeks themselves.

Hispanic Countries

The influence of the Roman Catholic church is so prevalent in most Spanish-speaking countries that the name Maria, in honor of the Virgin Mary, is a part of most girls' names. Often Maria will serve as a prefix to another name that's used every day, as in Maria de la Lucita ("Mary of the Light"), where Lucita is the name used regularly. Religious events are also common sources for female names, such as Natividad ("nativity") or Milagros ("miracles").

Although boys are sometimes given pet names or nicknames emphasizing their physical attributes or peculiarities, they too may receive religious names, as in Manuel ("God is with us") or Cristobal ("Christ-bearer"). Jesus is a very popular name for newborn Mexican boys, though not for Puerto Ricans, who consider it too holy.

For most Spanish-speakers, a personal name celebrates and secures family ties, reserving an indisputable spot for the bearer on the extended family tree. For their full names, Spanish-speaking children often adopt not only their father's family name but their mother's and even their grandmothers' family names as well. Add to that the given names and a confirmation name chosen by the individual, and the result is the verbose yet fluid string of names that is characteristically Spanish — for example, Maria de la Luz Magdalena Cordova Rodriquez Torres y Gonzales.

The order of these names is as follows: The given names (first and middle), the confirmation name, the father's family name, the mother's maiden name, the paternal grandmother's maiden name, and the maternal grandmother's maiden name. This leaves little question as to the nameholder's family lineage.

Indian (Hindu)

In Hinduism, God is thought to be a part of every object in the world—a flower, a cat. God is thought to be present even in concepts, such as peace and intelligence. Children are often named after such objects and concepts, and every time their names are spoken, the speaker in effect speaks the name of God. It is believed that this brings the speaker nearer to spiritual wholeness.

It is more common, however, to assign a child the name of a particular god — such as Vishnu, Siva, Ramya, or Sakti — or of some quality associated with a god. This is not as difficult a task as it would be in the West, where the names for God are somewhat limited. There are countless Hindu manifestations and names that are divine. Siva, the god of destruction, for example, has more than a thousand names.

Like the Chinese and some Africans, Hindus sometimes bestow an undesirable name upon a child in an effort to make the demons think that the child's presence is bothersome or a matter of indifference. Thus some children receive names like Pollyam ("goddess of the plague") or Kirwa ("worm"). Traditionally, it is the grandparents who choose the child's name.

Italian

The majority of popular baby names in Italy are derived from the names of saints of the Roman Catholic church. Often, local patron saints are used as namesakes in the surrounding community. Romolo, for example, is a common name in Rome and environs but is seldom used throughout the rest of the country.

Modern Italian, unlike most other European languages, borrows very little from other cultures' names. Once a name has carved out a place for itself in Italian tradition, it usually enjoys a long and busy life; the Italian reverence for tradition runs deep.

Japanese

A significant number of Japanese girls' names extol the quiet virtues of their culture. Names like Ko ("filial piety") and Kazu ("obedient") have literal meanings, while others imply a virtue, like Miyuki ("deep snow"), suggestive of the stillness that follows a snowfall. Boys' names are far less inventive or moral, often reflecting number or order of birth. Taro ("first-born male") and Jiro ("second-born male") are among the most common. Higher numbers connote the hopes for a long life, while the largest numbers, such as Chi ("thousand"), are traditional good omens.

Jewish

The most common Jewish naming practice is to honor a relative by naming a child after him or her. A dichotomy has emerged between the two geographical groups of Jews — Sephardim and Ashkenazim — regarding which relatives to honor.

The Sephardic Jews, hailing from Spain, Portugal, North Africa, and the Middle East, name their young after living relatives, believing that this will augment the years of the elder's life. More often than not, the eldest children are given the names of their same-sex paternal grandparents. Later children are given the names of their maternal grandparents, aunts, and uncles.

Ashkenazic Jews — those from Eastern and central Europe — have adopted the Egyptian custom of using the names of deceased relatives, intended to ensure that the memory of that ancestor will live on. This group believes that to name a child after a living person would rob that person of his or her own unique spirit.

Bestowing a deceased relative's exact Hebrew or Yiddish name on a child is still popular among Orthodox Jews, while it's more common among Reform Jews to use only the first letter of the deceased relative's name, with the understanding that newborn Samantha's name is in memory of Aunt Sarah. Some Jewish parents prefer using a more modern Jewish name that shares a similar or identical meaning with the relative's name.

Double-naming is also a favorite Jewish custom today. Originally, gentile names were given to Jewish boys to be used during interaction with non-Jews. It eventually became customary to prescribe one name for use in everyday business life and another Hebrew or Yiddish name for religious purposes and celebrations. Reform Jews often honor this tradition by assigning a gentile or Americanized first name and a more traditionally Jewish middle name.

North American Indian

Nature is to North American Indian names what the Roman Catholic church is to Hispanic names: all-pervasive in its influence. Although the diversity among North American Indian cultures and languages is vast, it is clear that each tribe celebrates nature in the names it chooses for its young.

Typical are descriptive names such as Mituna ("wrapping a salmon with willow stems and leaves after catching it") and Tukuli ("caterpillar traveling down a tree") from the Miwok tribe of California, and Odahingum ("ripple on the water") from the language of the Chippewas.

Other sources for naming include tribal symbols, totems, religious or spiritual images, and events, such as a war or a hunt. In many tribes, names are inherited from older relatives, usually deceased. A child's physical or mental characteristics are also instrumental in the creation of names, as in the Sioux names Howahkan ("mysterious voice") and Kohana ("swift").

NICKNAMES

Do recognize that despite your careful choice of your child's name, a nickname may be appropriated or attached over time. Look at the nicknames provided in the definitions and decide whether they would be pleasant alternatives. A name with several variations lets a child change his or her name as he or she grows up — for example, Betsy when she is young, Liz or Lizzy when she is older, and Elizabeth when she is an adult. In contrast, a name with no nicknames tends to be less flexible and more formal.

SPECIAL CONSIDERATIONS

Some parents these days debate whether a child should bear the father's family name, the mother's, or a hyphenated combination of the two. If one name is chosen over another, the name not selected can be used as the child's middle name.

Sometimes parents contemplate giving children their own names. Most often, boys are given their father's name. A boy may be given his father's name plus "Jr." out of the father's wish to perpetuate himself in his son, to have his son emulate him, and to retain a superior role himself. The son may feel this as a burden laid on him, a pressure to comply with the paternal desires and to mold his personality and career accordingly. You might consider using "II" rather than "Jr." Students with names ending with "II" scored higher in capacity for status, well-being, responsibility, socialization, self-control, and tolerance than those with names ending in "Jr." Of course, much depends on how you handle the designation.

Another consideration is the choice of a unisex name. Many names today are unisex. The use of a name for both sexes tends to be unstable and of brief duration. Although evolution does occur in both directions, names tend to evolve from masculine to unisex and from unisex to feminine, rather than the other way around. That trend may reflect a preference for giving a masculine name to a girl rather than a feminine name to a boy. In this book the names in the listings are broken down into those that currently tend to be used either principally for girls or principally for boys. Unisex names are listed under both genders, but complete information for those names appears only under the gender for which they're most commonly used.

The number of factors and the weight of the choice may seem daunting, but relax, keep these considerations in mind as you explore the selection, and you'll find the perfect name. Years from now your child's name will be such a natural part of his or her identity that you'll wonder how you could have agonized so over it.

Language/ Ethnicity BROWSER

This browser organizes names by the language or ethnic group from which they originated. More than sixty languages and ethnic groups, from Acadian to Yiddish, are included. Experts often disagree on a name's language or ethnicity and on that of its root name. For example, Aaron is thought by some to be Egyptian and by others to be Hebrew. In such cases, I have tried to determine which is the best authority and listed the name accordingly. If a name occurs in two or more languages or cultures, its meaning in both is noted in the definitions in the main section of the book. The usual gender of a particular name is noted with an "M" for male or "F" for female in parentheses after the name. Finally, names that are categorized as "created" are those for which no definition or origin can be located. However, the fact that these names have been made up by parents in no way diminishes their legitimacy or appeal.

Names of English origin are not included here, as their inclusion would require repeating most of the names in the Girls' and Boys' Names sections. Uniquely American names, however, are listed here.

Acadian

Imma (F)

African

Aba (F)
Abana (F)
Abasi (M)
Abdalla (M)
Abena (F)
Abina (F)
Abmaba (F)
Adeben (M)
Adia (F)
Adom (M)
Ajua (F)
Ajuji (F)
Akon (M)
Akosua (F)
Akron (M)
Aleela (F)
Alila (F)
Alile (F)
Ama (F)
Amadika (F)
Annan (M)
Apangela (F)
Ashon (M)
Asiza (F)
Ayondela (F)
Aziza (F)
Balala (F)
Banjoko (F)
Batini (F)
Bello (M)
Bem (M)
Bene (F)
Binti (F)
Blom (F)
Bodua (M)
Bour (M)
Bron (M)
Caimile (F)
Cakusola (F)
Catava (F)
Chane (M)
Chiriga (F)
Chuma (M)
Cilehe (F)
Cilombo (M)
Cinofila (F)
Ciyeva (F)
Cohila (F)
Dabir (M)
Danladi (M)
Daudi (M)
Dede (F)
Delu (F)
Dinka (F)
Dumaka (M)
Durosimi (F)
Durosomo (F)
Efua (F)
Ekua (F)
Essien (M)
Fynn (M)
Garai (M)
Gyasi (M)
Hadiya (F)
Hakim (M)
Hasina (F)
Jahi (M)
Jimoh (M)
Jina (F)
Jumah (M)
Kalere (F)
Kaluwa (F)
Kamali (F)
Kamaria (F)
Kameke (F)
Kanene (F)
Kanika (F)
Kapuki (F)
Kaseko (M)
Kasinda (F)
Kateke (F)
Katura (F)
Kerel (M)
Kesi (F)
Kesse (M)
Kessie (F)
Kissa (F)
Kito (M)
Kizza (M)
Koffi (F)
Kokudza (M)
Kontar (M)
Kosoko (F)
Kruin (M)
Kudio (F)
Kwabina (F)
Kwaku (M)
Kwamin (M)
Kwashi (F)
Kwau (F)
Kwesi (M)
Lado (M)
Liu (M)
Livanga (F)
Luister (M)
Magara (F)
Makadisa (F)
Malomo (F)
Mandisa (F)
Mansa (M)
Manu (M)
Marar (M)
Marara (M)
Marini (F)
Masika (F)
Matanmi (F)
Matope (M)
Mosi (M)
Moswen (M)
Mundan (M)
Musenda (M)
Nassor (M)
Neema (F)
Nuru (M)
Odinan (M)
Odissan (M)
Ohin (M)

Okon (M)
Olisa (F)
Onani (M)
Paka (F)
Paki (M)
Pedzi (F)
Pemba (F)
Penda (F)
Pili (M)
Pita (F)
Poni (F)
Ramadan (M)
Ramla (F)
Rance (M)
Rudo (M)
Sandeep (F)
Sanura (F)
Senwe (M)
Shaka (M)
Shani (F)
Siko (F)
Siti (F)
Sudi (M)
Sukoji (F)
Sultan (M)
Tabia (F)
Tanno (M)
Tano (M)
Tawia (F)
Thema (F)
Tisa (F)
Topwe (M)
Ulan (M)
Uzoma (M)
Vatusia (F)
Visolela (F)
Winda (F)
Zahur (M)
Zareb (M)
Zawadi (F)
Zesiro (M)
Zina (F)
Zuri (F)

American

Aesha (F)
Aiesha (F)
Aisha (F)
Aisia (F)
Anaca (F)
Anaka (F)
Anecky (F)
Anika (F)
Anikee (F)
Annaka (F)
Annik (F)
Anthjuan (M)
Antjuan (M)
Areta (F)
Aretha (F)
Aretta (F)
Ashanta (F)
Ashante (F)
Ashanti (F)
Ashaunta (F)
Ashuntae (F)
Autumn (F)
Ayshea (F)
Chanel (F)
Chantal (F)
Chante (F)
Charmaine (F)
Chevy (M)
Concetta (F)
Concetto (M)
Cornell (M)
Cortez (M)
Dakota (M)
Danetta (F)
Danette (F)
Danica (F)
Danice (F)
Danyelle (F)
Darnell (M)
Deborha (F)
Deborrah (F)
Delmar (M)
Denyce (F)
Ebony (F)
Elbert (M)
Elberta (F)
Elbertine (F)
Elbie (F)
Elroy (M)
Floy (F)
Ieasha (F)
Ieashia (F)
Iesha (F)
Ivory (F)
Jajuan (M)
Jamille (F)
Joi (F)
Jonelle (F)
Julas (M)
Julias (M)
Kenda (F)
Kia (F)
Kiana (F)
King (M)
Kismet (F)
Kizzy (F)
Lafayette (M)
Lamont (M)
Laticia (F)
Lavon (F)
Lavonne (F)
Quiana (F)
Rasheda (F)
Rashida (F)
Renaldo (M)
Renauld (M)
Rinaldo (M)
Samaria (F)
Samarie (F)
Samarthur (F)
Samella (F)
Samentha (F)
Samuela (F)
Saundra (F)
Shaaron (F)
Shan (F)
Shanta (F)
Shantae (F)
Shantelle (F)
Shari (F)
Sharice (F)
Sharma (F)
Sharmine (F)
Sharona (F)
Sharonda (F)
Sharone (F)
Sharren (F)
Sharronda (F)
Shavonne (F)
Shawn (M)
Shawnee (F)
Shayla (F)
Sheri (F)
Sherice (F)
Sherissa (F)
Shervan (F)
Shivohn (F)
Shyvonia (F)
Simona (F)
Stella (F)
Stevi (F)
Sylvia (F)
Tanish (F)
Tanisha (F)
Timaula (F)
Tyesha (F)

Arabic

Abdelgalil (M)
Abdul (M)
Abdulaziz (M)
Abdullah (M)
ʿAbu Kamāl (M)
ʿĀdil (M)
ʿAfaʾf (F)
Ahkeel (M)
Ahmed (M)
Akeel (M)
Akil (M)
Akilah (F)
ʿAlā (M)
Alasid (M)
Alea (F)
Aleah (F)
Aleser (M)
Alhena (F)
Alim (M)
Alima (F)
Almira (F)
Altair (M)
Alzubra (F)
Amāl (M)
Amina (F)
Aminah (F)
Amineh (F)
Amir (M)
Amit (M)
Antuwain (M)
Antwan (M)
Anwar (M)
Asʿad (M)
Asadel (M)
Asha (F)
Ashia (F)
Aswad (M)
Ayasha (F)
Azeem (M)
ʿAzīz (M)
Barika (F)
Basimah (F)
Ben-Ahmed (M)
Bibi (F)
Bilal (M)
Cemal (M)
Chardae (F)
Charde (F)
Coman (M)
Dawud (M)
Dayana (F)
Dekel (M)
Emmali (F)
Fāḍil (M)
Faizah (F)
Fath (M)
Fāṭima (F)
Fatma (F)
Fatmeh (F)
Gadi (M)
Gadiel (M)
Genna (F)
Ghādah (F)
Ghassān (M)
Ḥabīb (M)
Ḥabibah (F)
Hadad (M)
Ḥaidar (M)
Ḥakīm (M)
Halim (M)
Hamal (M)
Hamdrem (M)
Hamdun (M)
Hamid (M)
Hammad (M)
Hanif (M)
Harb (M)
Ḥarith (M)
Ḥarithah (M)
Harun (M)
Hāshim (M)
Ḥassan (M)
Hilel (M)
Humayd (M)
Hussein (M)
Ibn-Mustapha (M)
Ibrāhīm (M)
Imān (F)
Imran (M)
Iskandar (M)
Jaʾfar (M)
Jalīla (F)
Jamaal (M)
Jamaine (M)
Jamal (M)
Jamel (M)
Jamell (F)
Jamila (F)
Jarita (F)
Jawhar (M)
Jessenia (F)
Kadar (M)
Kade (M)
Kadin (M)
Kadir (M)
Kaela (F)
Kaelyn (F)
Kailey (F)
Kalb (M)
Kaleela (F)
Kalil (M)
Kalila (F)
Kalilla (F)
Kaliq (M)
Kalyn (F)
Kamāl (M)
Kāmil (M)
Kamila (F)
Kamilah (F)
Kamillah (F)
Kardal (M)
Kareem (M)
Karida (F)
Kasib (M)
Kasim (M)
Kaylene (F)
Kayley (F)
Kaylil (F)
Kaylin (F)
Kedar (M)
Kelila (F)
Khadījah (F)
Khālid (M)
Khalīl (M)
Kilab (M)
Latavia (F)
Lilith (F)
Maḥmūd (M)
Maimun (M)
Malik (M)
Manṣūr (M)
Marid (M)
Mariyah (F)
Marwan (M)
Maryam (F)
Masʿud (M)
Māzin (M)
Medina (F)
Mehemet (M)
Mohamet (M)
Mohammad (M)
Mohammadi (M)
Mohammed (M)
Mustapha (M)
Nabīl (M)
Najīb (M)
Nasser (M)
Nepa (F)
Noura (F)
Numa (M)
Numair (M)
Nusair (M)
Qabil (M)
Qadim (M)
Qadir (M)
Qamar (M)
Qiturah (F)
Rabiah (F)
Rafì (M)
Rahman (M)
Rayhan (M)
Riḍa (F)
Rihana (F)
Saddam (M)
Saʿīd (M)
Salama (F)
Salih (M)
Salīm (M)
Sameh (F)
Samein (M)
Samīr (M)
Samman (M)
Sanā (F)
Seif (M)
Shahar (F)
Shammara (F)
Sharīf (M)
Shatara (F)
Sherika (F)
Sofian (M)
Syed (M)
Syreeta (F)
Ṭāhir (M)
Takia (F)
Talib (M)
Tayib (M)
Timin (M)

Wattan (F)
Wazir (M)
Yaella (F)
Yaḥya (M)
Yardan (M)
Yasar (M)
Yasir (M)
Yazid (M)
Yesenia (F)
Yiesha (F)
Yusef (M)
Zada (F)
Zafina (F)
Zahid (M)
Zahira (F)
Zahra (F)
Zaida (F)
Zaim (M)
Zaki (M)
Zakia (F)
Zara (F)
Zarifa (F)
Zayn (M)
Zimraan (M)

Aramaic

Cephas (M)
Shera (F)
Talman (M)

Armenian

Arpiar (M)
Hovhannes (M)
Kaloosh (M)
Margarid (F)
Seda (F)
Shoushan (F)
Takoohi (F)
Vartan (M)

Australian

Kye (F)
Kylene (F)
Kylie (F)
Narelle (F)
Nyree (F)

Bulgarian

Agnessa (F)
Alekko (M)
Aleksandŭr (M)
Aleksi (F)
Alisa (F)
Andreĭ (M)
Andrey (M)
Artur (M)
Avram (M)
Benedikt (M)
Ceciliia (F)
Danil (M)
Devora (F)
Dimitr (M)
Elena (F)
Emilia (F)
Feliks (M)
Feodor (M)
Franc (M)
Gavril (M)
Gedeon (M)
Georg (M)
Georgi (M)
Grigoi (M)
Grigor (M)
Henri (M)
Henrim (M)
Ioan (M)
Isak (M)
Judita (F)
Kaiser (M)
Karl (M)
Kazimir (M)
Kir (M)
Kira (F)
Kiril (M)
Klara (F)
Lucine (F)
Marketa (F)
Mateĭ (M)
Mihail (M)
Moisei (M)
Neron (M)
Nikolas (M)
Paulina (F)
Petr (M)
Piotr (M)
Rahil (F)
Reveka (F)
Samuil (M)
Stefan (M)
Suzana (F)
Tereza (F)
Timotei (M)
Viktor (M)
Viktoria (F)
Vilhelm (M)
Yosif (M)

Burmese

Yon (F)

Chinese

Ah Kum (F)
Ah Lam (F)
Bao (M)
Chaoxing (F)
Chen (M)
Chu Hua (F)
Chun (F)
De (M)
Dewei (M)
Dingbang (M)
Ho (M)
Howin (M)
Hu (M)
Hua (F)
Jin (M)
Jing-Quo (M)
Jun (M)
Kuai Hua (F)
Lei (M)
Li (F)
Li Hua (F)
Lian (F)
Liang (M)
Lien (F)
Lien Hua (F)
Like (M)
Liko (M)
Long (M)
Manchu (M)
Mani (F)
Mu Lan (F)
Mu Tan (F)
Shaiming (M)
Shing (M)
Shu (F)
Tao (F)
Ushi (F)
Wei-Quo (M)
Xiang (F)
Yong (M)
Yul (M)
Zhen (F)

Czech

Ada (F)
Adamec (M)
Adamko (M)
Adela (F)
Adelka (F)
Agnesa (F)
Agneska (F)
Albertik (M)
Albinek (M)
Aleš (M)
Alica (F)
Alžběta (F)
Anastazia (F)
Anděla (F)
Andrej (M)
Andula (F)
Andulka (F)
Aneska (F)
Anežka (F)
Anicka (F)
Antek (M)
Antonín (M)
Anuška (F)
Arno (M)
Artis (M)
Aurel (M)
Bandi (F)
Bára (F)
Barbora (F)
Barborka (F)
Bartek (M)
Barto (M)
Bartz (M)
Baruška (F)
Bazil (M)
Bedřich (M)
Bedřiška (F)
Bela (M)
Benedikt (M)
Bernek (M)
Berno (M)
Berty (M)
Běta (F)
Bětka (F)
Betuška (F)
Blanka (F)
Blaza (F)
Blazena (F)
Bobek (M)
Bobina (F)
Brandeis (M)
Brandt (M)
Broňa (F)
Cecilie (F)
Celestin (M)
Celestyna (F)
Christofer (M)
Cile (F)
Cilka (F)
Crystina (F)
Dagmara (F)
Dalibor (M)
Damek (M)
Danko (M)
Dano (M)
Dasa (F)
Davidek (M)
Dela (F)
Dita (F)
Ditka (F)
Doma (F)
Domek (M)
Dominik (M)
Dora (F)
Dorka (F)
Dorota (F)
Dumin (M)
Durko (M)
Edita (F)
Edko (M)
Edo (M)
Edus (M)
Edvard (M)
Elena (F)
Elenka (F)
Eliska (F)
Eman (M)
Emilek (M)
Emilie (F)
Emilka (F)
Erich (M)
Ervin (M)
Eugen (M)
Evička (F)
Evka (F)
Evuška (F)
Fedor (M)
Fela (F)
Franca (F)
Francka (F)
Fridrich (M)
Gabko (M)
Gabo (M)
Gabris (M)
Gabys (M)
Gitka (F)
Gituska (F)
Gizela (F)
Gustav (M)
Gustik (M)
Gusty (M)
Hana (F)
Hanicka (F)
Hanka (F)
Hanuš (M)
Hedvick (F)
Hedvika (F)
Hela (F)
Helenka (F)
Heluska (F)
Herma (F)
Hermina (F)
Hinrich (M)
Holic (M)
Honza (M)
Hubertek (M)
Ianos (M)
Iduska (F)
Ilja (M)
Imrich (M)
Irenka (F)
Irka (F)
Izabella (F)
Izak (M)
Jakub (M)
Jan (M)
Jana (F)
Janco (M)
Janica (F)
Janka (F)
Jano (M)
Jenda (M)
Jenka (F)
Jindra (M)
Jindraska (F)
Jindřich (M)
Jirca (F)
Jiři (M)
Jiřina (F)
Jitka (F)
Johanka (F)
Johanna (F)
Jokubas (M)
Josef (M)
Jula (F)
Julca (F)
Juliana (F)
Juliska (F)
Julka (F)
Jur (M)
Juraz (M)
Jurik (M)
Jurko (M)
Juro (M)
Jusa (M)
Justyn (M)
Karel (M)
Karla (F)
Karlicka (F)
Karlik (M)
Karlinka (F)
Karol (M)
Karola (F)
Karolina (F)
Kaspar (M)
Kata (F)
Katarina (F)
Kateřina (F)
Katica (F)
Katuska (F)
Kazimir (M)
Klara (F)
Klema (M)
Klement (M)
Klemo (M)
Konrad (M)
Kovar (M)
Krispin (M)
Krista (F)
Kristinka (F)
Kristof (M)
Krystina (F)
Kuba (M)
Kubes (M)
Kubik (F)
Kubo (M)
Květa (F)
Květka (F)
Leksik (M)
Lekso (M)
Lenka (F)
Leosko (M)
Leska (F)
Lexa (F)
Lukáš (M)
Magda (F)
Magdelena (F)

Marca (F)
Marek (M)
Marenka (F)
Margita (F)
Marienka (F)
Marka (F)
Markéta (F)
Marko (M)
Marticka (F)
Martinka (M)
Matek (M)
Matus (M)
Matylda (F)
Maxi (M)
Maxim (M)
Michal (M)
Milada (F)
Milka (F)
Milko (M)
Misa (M)
Misko (M)
Miso (M)
Natalia (F)
Natasa (F)
Nikula (M)
Nikulas (M)
Noach (M)
Noe (M)
Olina (F)
Olunka (F)
Oluska (F)
Ondro (M)
Otik (M)
Oto (M)
Pavla (F)
Pavlina (F)
Pepa (M)
Pepik (M)
Rajmund (M)
Rebeka (F)
Reza (F)
Rezka (F)
Risa (M)
Roba (F)
Rubert (M)
Ruda (M)
Rudek (M)
Rusalka (F)
Ruza (F)
Růžena (F)
Ruzenka (F)
Ryba (F)
Salamun (M)
Samko (M)
Samo (M)
Slane (M)
Stano (M)
Stasa (F)
Staska (F)
Stefan (M)
Stefania (F)
Stefka (F)
Tadeas (M)
Tedik (M)
Teodor (M)
Teodora (F)
Teodus (M)
Terezia (F)
Terezie (F)
Terezka (F)
Tomáš (M)
Tonda (M)
Tonik (M)
Trava (F)
Tylda (F)
Tyna (F)
Tynek (M)
Tynko (M)
Valtr (M)
Vanda (F)
Vasil (M)
Věrka (F)
Verona (F)
Veronka (F)
Viktorie (F)
Viktorka (F)
Vila (M)
Vilek (M)
Viliam (M)
Vilko (M)
Vilma (F)
Vilous (M)
Vincenc (M)
Vinco (M)
Vladko (M)
Vorsila (F)
Waltr (M)
Zelenka (F)
Zenda (M)
Zofia (F)
Zofie (F)
Žofka (F)
Zusa (F)
Zuzana (F)
Zuzanka (F)
Zuzka (F)

Danish

Bardo (M)
Christoffer (M)

Clemens (M)
Edvard (M)
Ejnar (M)
Frants (M)
Jensine (F)
Karen (F)
Knud (M)
Knute (M)
Kristan (F)
Lauritz (M)
Malena (F)
Niels (M)
Poul (M)
Svend (M)

Dutch

Aleen (F)
Alene (F)
Alleen (F)
Aloys (M)
Aloysia (F)
Ate (M)
Barth (M)
Bram (M)
Gerrit (M)
Gustaff (M)
Jan (M)
Jeremias (M)
Johan (M)
Laurens (M)
Marielle (F)
Mena (F)
Nicolaas (M)
Pieter (M)
Rip (M)
Saskia (F)
Schuyler (M)
Skylar (M)
Valdemar (M)
Zeeman (M)

Egyptian

Keb (M)
Nen (M)
Nenet (F)
Sef (M)
Shen (M)

Eskimo

Hiti (F)
Kirima (F)
Meriwa (F)
Sedna (F)

Esperanto

Amara (F)

Estonian

Aleksander (M)
Artur (M)
Betti (F)
Daggi (F)
Elisabet (F)
Elli (F)
Elts (F)
Etti (F)
Hele (F)
Jaan (M)
Johan (M)
Juku (M)
Juri (M)
Katharina (F)
Kati (F)
Krista (F)
Kristian (M)
Kristjan (M)
Krists (M)
Leena (F)
Leks (M)
Lenni (F)
Liisa (F)
Liisi (F)
Marga (F)
Mari (F)
Marye (F)
Matt (M)
Meeri (F)
Mihkel (M)
Mikk (M)
Nikolai (M)
Olli (F)
Peet (M)
Peeter (M)
Reet (F)
Riki (M)
Riks (M)
Rolli (M)
Tilda (F)
Toomas (M)
Ulli (F)
Urmi (F)
Welsh (M)

Finnish

Aila (F)
Aili (F)
Annikki (F)
Arto (M)
Frans (M)
Hannes (M)
Hanni (F)
Hannu (M)
Helli (F)
Henrik (M)
Janne (M)
Jeremias (M)
Joosef (M)
Jooseppi (M)
Juhana (M)
Juho (M)
Jukka (M)
Jussi (M)
Kaarina (F)
Kosti (M)
Kristia (F)
Lusa (F)
Maija (F)
Maijii (F)
Maikki (F)
Margarete (F)
Marja (F)
Marjatta (F)
Mikko (M)
Mirjam (F)
Nilo (M)
Reku (M)
Risto (M)
Sakari (M)
Tapani (M)
Tauno (M)
Timo (M)
Tuomas (M)
Tuomo (M)
Vaino (M)
Valma (F)
Viljo (M)

French

Abrial (F)
Absalon (M)
Adèle (F)
Adrien (M)
Adrienne (F)
Agathe (F)
Agnies (F)
Alain (M)
Albertine (F)
Aletta (F)
Alette (F)
Alexandre (M)
Alexandrie (F)
Alexius (F)
Alix (F)
Allain (M)
Aloin (M)
Alphonse (M)
Alphonsine (F)
Aluin (M)
Amand (M)
Amandine (F)
Amélie (F)
Amice (F)
Amie (F)
Anastasie (F)
André (M)
Angele (F)
Angeline (F)
Angélique (F)
Annette (F)
Antoine (M)
Antonie (F)
Aralt (M)
Archaimbaud (M)
Archambault (M)
Arette (F)
Ariane (F)
Armine (F)
Armond (M)
Arnaud (M)
Arry (M)
Aubert (M)
Aubin (M)
Audric (M)
Aurèle (M)
Aurore (F)
Bale (M)
Barbe (F)
Barnabe (M)
Barthélmy (M)
Bartholome (M)
Bartholomieu (M)
Basile (M)
Baudier (M)
Bayard (M)
Beatrix (F)
Benoist (M)
Benoît (M)
Benoîte (F)
Bergette (F)
Bernadette (F)
Bernardin (M)
Bette (F)
Blaisot (M)
Boyce (M)
Brigide (F)
Brigitta (F)
Brigitte (F)
Camille (F)
Carole (F)
Carvel (M)
Catant (F)
Cateline (F)
Cecile (F)
Cecilie (F)
Céleste (F)
Celestine (F)
Célie (F)
Céline (F)
Cerise (F)
Charlotte (F)
Charlotty (F)
Chérie (F)
Cherise (F)
Chev (M)
Chevalier (M)
Chevi (M)
Chimene (F)
Christine (F)
Christophe (M)
Clairette (F)
Clarette (F)
Clarisse (F)
Claude (M)
Claudelle (F)
Claudette (F)
Claudine (F)
Clotilda (F)
Colar (M)
Coletta (F)
Colette (F)
Colletta (F)
Collette (F)
Conrade (M)

Coralie (F)
Corinne (F)
Crepin (M)
Crestienne (F)
Damien (M)
Daniell (F)
Delphine (F)
Demetre (M)
Denis (M)
Didier (M)
Dione (M)
Dominique (M)
Domonique (F)
Donois (M)
Doralice (F)
Dorette (F)
Dorolice (F)
Dorothee (F)
Edgard (M)
Édouard (M)
Elaine (F)
Elisa (F)
Élise (F)
Esdras (M)
Étienne (M)
Eugénie (F)
Eulalie (F)
Evaine (F)
Fabert (M)
Fabien (M)
Fiipote (F)
Flavere (F)
Flavian (M)
Flavie (F)
Flavien (M)
Flore (F)
Francette (F)
Franchesca (F)
Franchot (M)
François (M)
Françoise (F)
Frédérique (F)
Gaspard (M)
Gautier (M)
Gedeon (M)
Genève (F)
Geoffroie (F)
Geoffroy (M)
Georgette (F)
Georgienne (F)
Géraud (M)
Germain (M)
Gervais (M)
Gervaise (F)
Gilles (M)
Grazielle (F)
Grégoire (M)
Guilette (F)
Guillaume (M)
Guillaums (M)
Gunter (M)
Gustav (M)
Guy (M)
Héloïse (F)
Henri (M)
Henriette (F)
Hercule (M)
Hippolyte (M)
Honorine (F)
Ide (F)
Ignace (M)
Isabeau (F)
Ivette (F)
Jacques (M)
Jacquet (M)
Jean (M)
Jean-François (M)
Jean-Michel (M)
Jean-Phillipe (M)
Jeanne (F)
Jeannot (M)
Jeoffroi (M)
Joëlle (F)
Joie (F)
Jonas (M)
Josephe (M)
Josette (F)
Josue (M)
Jourdain (M)
Judithe (F)
Jules (M)
Julien (M)
Julienne (F)
Juliette (F)
Justine (F)
Laron (M)
Lasimonne (M)
Laure (F)
Laurent (M)
Laurette (F)
Lauriane (F)
Lienard (M)
Lissette (F)
Lissie (F)
Lolotte (F)
Louis (M)
Lourdes (F)
Luce (M)
Lucette (F)
Lucie (F)
Lucien (M)
Lucrece (F)
Lydie (F)
Lynette (F)
Madeleine (F)
Mahaut (F)
Manette (F)
Manon (F)
Marce (F)
Marcel (F)
Marcelle (F)
Marguerite (F)
Marianne (F)
Marie (F)
Marielle (F)
Marthe (F)
Martine (F)
Maslin (M)
Mathieu (M)
Matilde (F)
Matthieu (M)
Maxime (M)
Mertin (M)
Michau (M)
Michelle (F)
Michon (M)
Moïse (M)
Monique (F)
Nadine (F)
Nathalie (F)
Nathaniel (M)
Neron (M)
Nicolás (M)
Nicolette (F)
Noë (M)
Odelette (F)
Odette (F)
Odile (F)
Ödön (M)
Olery (M)
Olivier (M)
Othon (M)
Pascal (M)
Pascale (F)
Patrice (M)
Perceval (M)
Pernelle (F)
Peronelle (F)
Philippel (M)
Philippine (F)
Pierre (M)
Pierrot (M)
Quennel (M)
Questa (F)
Quiterie (F)
Rachelle (F)
Rainier (M)
Raoul (M)
Raoule (F)
Rapier (M)
Raymonde (F)
Rebeque (F)
Reine (F)
Reinette (F)
Renault (M)
Rene (M)
Renée (F)
Robers (M)
Robinet (M)
Rodolphe (M)
Rodrique (M)
Roi (M)
Rolande (F)
Romain (M)
Romaine (F)
Rosalie (F)
Rosemarie (F)
Rousse (M)
Salaun (M)
Salomon (M)
Sarotte (F)
Sébastien (M)
Sebastienne (F)
Serge (M)
Si (M)
Sidon (M)
Sidonie (F)
Siffre (M)
Sigfroi (M)
Silvain (M)
Silvaine (F)
Simion (M)
Simone (F)
Sinclair (M)
Sophie (F)
Souline (F)
Soulle (F)
Stanislas (M)
Stéphane (M)
Stéphanie (F)
Susette (F)
Suszanne (F)
Suzetta (F)
Sy (F)
Sylvie (F)
Tenille (F)
Teppo (M)
Tereson (F)
Thadee (M)
Thérèse (F)
Thomas (M)
Tiennot (M)
Tite (M)
Toinon (F)
Trinnette (F)
Trista (F)
Tristen (F)
Urbaine (M)
Ursule (F)
Venise (F)
Verdun (M)
Verenice (F)
Verlie (M)
Vernon (M)
Verone (F)
Véronique (F)
Victoir (M)
Victoire (F)
Victorine (F)
Vincenz (M)
Violette (F)
Virginie (F)
Vitus (M)
Wilhelm (M)
Wilhelmine (F)
Willi (M)
Willy (M)
Yolanda (F)
Yolane (F)
Yves (M)
Yvette (F)
Yvon (M)
Yvonne (F)
Zacharie (M)
Zaidee (F)
Zeno (M)

Frisian

Elsbet (F)

German

Abalard (M)
Abelard (M)
Abilard (M)
Adal (M)
Adelicia (F)
Adolph (M)
Adolphus (M)
Adriane (F)
Ahren (M)
Alaric (M)
Albrecht (M)
Alder (M)
Alexia (F)
Alexis (F)
Alexius (F)
Alois (M)
Aloisa (F)
Alwin (M)
Amalia (F)
Anastacie (F)
Andreas (M)
Angelika (F)
Anitte (F)
Annchen (F)
Anneli (F)
Arius (M)
Aurelius (M)
Babette (F)
Baldwin (M)
Barthel (M)
Bartol (M)
Basle (M)
Beatrix (F)
Benedikt (M)
Beppi (M)
Berend (M)
Berta (F)
Bertel (M)
Betti (F)
Bettina (F)
Blasi (M)
Blasius (M)
Bridgette (F)
Brigette (F)
Brigitta (F)
Bruns (M)
Cäcilia (F)
Charlotte (F)
Christa (F)
Christiane (F)
Christoforus (M)
Christoph (M)
Chrystel (F)
Cilli (F)
Clarissa (F)
Claus (M)
Conny (M)
Constanz (F)
Cordula (F)
Deboran (F)
Dieter (M)
Dionysus (M)
Dominik (M)
Dorchen (F)
Dore (F)
Dorle (F)
Dorlisa (F)
Editha (F)
Elis (F)
Elisabet (F)
Elisavet (F)
Elke (F)
Elli (F)
Elman (M)
Elsbeth (F)
Elschen (F)
Else (F)
Elvire (F)
Emrick (M)
Erich (M)
Eugen (M)
Eugenius (M)
Evchen (F)
Evgenios (M)
Evy (F)
Faber (M)
Faxon (M)
Franz (M)
Franze (F)
Franziska (F)
Franzl (M)
Fredi (F)
Frida (F)
Frieda (F)
Friedel (M)
Friederike (M)
Friedrich (M)
Fritz (M)
Fritzchen (M)
Fritze (F)

Fritzinn (F)
Georgina (F)
Georgine (F)
Gottfried (M)
Gratia (F)
Greeta (F)
Gretal (F)
Gretchen (F)
Grete (F)
Gretel (F)
Grethal (F)
Guenther (M)
Gunter (M)
Gusta (F)
Gustav (M)
Hanne (F)
Hannele (F)
Hanni (F)
Hans (M)
Hansel (M)
Heiner (M)
Heinrich (M)
Heinz (M)
Helmine (F)
Hetta (F)
Hinrich (M)
Hrodohaidis (F)
Humbert (M)
Idette (F)
Ilse (F)
Inglebert (M)
Irma (F)
Isaak (M)
Jeorg (M)
Jeremias (M)
Jockel (M)
Johann (M)
Johanna (F)
Josef (M)
Josua (M)
Jupp (M)
Jürgen (M)
Just (M)
Justus (M)
Jutta (F)
Kaese (M)
Karal (M)
Karl (M)
Karla (F)
Karoline (F)
Kasch (M)
Kase (M)
Kaspar (M)
Kasper (M)
Kass (M)
Katchen (F)
Katharina (F)
Katrina (F)
Kazimir (M)
Keelby (M)
Kelby (M)
Kellby (M)
Klarissa (F)
Klaus (M)
Konni (M)
Konrad (M)
Konstanze (F)
Korb (M)
Kornelia (F)
Krischan (M)
Krispin (M)
Kriss (M)
Lene (F)
Lenore (F)
Leonhard (M)
Leopold (M)
Liesa (F)
Lieschen (F)
Liesel (F)
Lili (F)
Linchen (F)
Linfred (M)
Lise (F)
Lothar (M)
Lottchen (F)
Lotte (F)
Lotti (F)
Loudon (M)
Ludwig (M)
Luzi (F)
Malkin (F)
Margret (F)
Martel (M)
Mathe (M)
Mathias (M)
Mathilde (F)
Matthaus (M)
Matthias (M)
Maximalian (M)
Mena (F)
Menz (M)
Meta (F)
Meyer (M)
Milo (M)
Monika (F)
Natalia (F)
Nele (F)
Nettchen (F)
Nicolaus (M)
Otfried (M)
Otho (M)
Ottocar (M)
Ottomar (M)
Parzival (M)
Patricius (M)
Patrizius (M)
Pepi (M)
Pepin (M)
Philipp (M)
Rahel (F)
Raimund (M)
Raimunde (F)
Rainer (M)
Rebekka (F)
Regine (F)
Reinold (M)
Resel (F)
Resi (F)
Richart (M)
Roderich (M)
Rosalinde (F)
Rüdiger (M)
Rudland (M)
Rudolf (M)
Ruland (M)
Rupert (M)
Ruprecht (M)
Rutz (M)
Sacharja (M)
Salomo (M)
Seifert (M)
Seifried (M)
Sepp (M)
Sergius (M)
Siegfried (M)
Siegmund (M)
Sigismund (M)
Sigmund (M)
Simmy (M)
Stanislau (M)
Stefan (M)
Steffel (M)

Stephanine (F)
Stoffel (M)
Susann (F)
Tewdor (M)
Thaddaus (M)
Theodor (M)
Theodoric (M)
Therese (F)
Thoma (M)
Timotheus (M)
Tresa (F)
Trescha (F)
Trinchen (F)
Trine (F)
Ulbrecht (M)
Ulla (F)
Ulrich (M)
Verona (F)
Veronike (F)
Vincenz (M)
Walther (M)
Waltli (M)
Wolfgang (M)
Woolf (M)
Xaver (M)
Zacharia (M)
Zamiel (M)
Zella (F)

Greek

Adara (F)
Agamemnon (M)
Agathi (F)
Alala (F)
Aleka (F)
Alekos (M)
Alexandros (M)
Alexiou (F)
Alike (F)
Aludra (F)
Alverta (F)
Alvertos (M)
Amyntas (F)
Andonios (M)
Andonis (M)
Andreas (M)
Angelica (F)
Angeliki (F)
Annas (M)
Archelaus (M)
Arete (F)
Arethi (F)
Ariadne (F)
Aristides (M)
Aristotle (M)
Athanasios (M)
Athena (F)
Athene (F)
Avel (M)
Bambis (M)
Basilios (M)
Belen (M)
Berek (F)
Berenike (F)
Binkentios (M)
Calliope (F)
Charis (F)
Charissa (F)
Charisse (F)
Charmian (F)
Christianos (M)
Christina (F)
Christos (M)
Cipriana (F)
Clio (F)
Constantinos (M)
Costa (M)
Darius (M)
Darrius (M)
Demetrois (M)
Dimitrios (M)
Dimos (M)
Dinos (M)
Dionusios (M)
Dionysia (F)
Dorothea (F)
Dwora (F)
Eirini (F)
Elena (F)
Eleni (F)
Elenitsa (F)
Eleutherios (M)
Elias (M)
Eliasz (M)
Enrikos (M)
Euclid (M)
Evadne (F)
Evadnie (F)
Evagelos (M)
Evathia (F)
Fotina (F)
Georgios (M)
Giannes (M)
Giannis (M)
Giannos (M)
Giorgis (M)
Giorgos (M)
Gogos (M)
Gregorios (M)
Grigorios (M)
Haralpos (M)
Hericlea (F)
Hermes (M)
Hippolyta (F)
Hrisoula (F)
Hypatia (F)
Iakobos (M)
Iakov (M)
Iakovos (M)
Icarus (M)
Ilias (M)
Ioanna (F)
Ioannes (M)
Ioannis (M)
Iosif (M)
Ioudith (F)
Isaak (M)
Joannes (M)
Judas (M)
Kalica (F)
Kalie (F)
Kalliope (F)
Kalyca (F)
Karlotta (F)
Kassandra (F)
Katerini (F)
Katina (F)
Khambis (M)
Kharlambos (M)
Konstandinos (M)
Konstantinos (M)
Korudon (M)
Kosta (F)
Kostas (M)
Kostatina (F)
Kotsos (M)
Kristo (M)
Kristos (M)
Lazarus (M)
Leonidas (M)
Lilika (F)
Linus (M)
Litsa (F)
Loukas (M)
Lukas (M)
Makis (M)
Margareta (F)
Margaritis (F)
Margaro (F)
Marika (F)
Marina (F)
Marinos (M)
Markos (M)
Maroula (F)
Martinos (M)
Matthaios (M)
Melantha (F)
Mihail (M)
Mikhail (M)
Mikhalis (M)
Mikhos (M)
Mimis (M)
Mitsos (M)
Moisis (M)
Nani (F)
Nicodemus (M)
Nikolaos (M)
Nikolos (M)
Nikos (M)
Nitsa (F)
Noe (M)
Noula (F)
Obelia (F)
Omega (F)
Orestes (M)
Panayiotos (M)
Panos (M)
Pavlos (M)
Pelagia (F)
Pelegia (F)
Pelgia (F)
Petros (M)
Philander (M)
Phillipos (M)
Phthisis (M)
Pinelopi (F)
Pipitsa (F)
Pirro (M)
Plato (M)
Pol (M)
Popi (F)
Rasia (F)
Rena (F)
Reveka (F)
Rihardos (M)
Ritsa (F)
Roula (F)

Rouvin (M)
Roxane (F)
Samouel (M)
Sema (F)
Semon (M)
Socrates (M)
Socratis (M)
Sofi (F)
Sophia (F)
Sophoon (F)
Sophronia (F)
Stamatios (F)
Stamos (M)
Stavros (M)
Stefanos (M)
Stefos (M)
Stephanos (M)
Takis (M)
Tassos (F)
Thalia (F)
Thanos (M)
Theodosia (F)
Theophila (F)
Theophilus (M)
Theron (M)
Theta (F)
Thetis (F)
Timotheos (M)
Titos (M)
Titus (M)
Tonis (M)
Triphena (F)
Tryphana (F)
Tryphena (F)
Tryphene (F)
Tryphenia (F)
Tryphina (F)
Urania (F)
Urian (M)
Vasilios (M)
Vasilis (M)
Vasilos (M)
Vassos (M)
Voska (F)
Xanthe (F)
Xanthippe (F)
Xenia (F)
Xenos (M)
Xylia (F)
Xylina (F)
Xylon (M)
Yannis (M)
Yiannis (M)
Zacceus (M)
Zacchaeus (M)
Zaccheus (M)
Zenobia (F)
Zēnōn (M)
Zoë (F)
Zoee (F)
Zoey (F)
Zoie (F)
Zowie (M)

Gypsy

Baul (M)
Bavol (M)
Bersh (M)
Besh (M)
Beti (F)
Beval (M)
Brishen (M)
Cam (M)
Camlo (M)
Cappi (M)
Chal (M)
Chik (M)
Choomia (F)
Danior (M)
Dudee (F)
Dukker (M)
Durriken (M)
Durril (M)
Emalia (F)
Fordel (M)
Garridan (M)
Gillie (M)
Jal (M)
Jibben (M)
Ker (M)
Kerey (M)
Kistur (M)
Lash (M)
Lashi (M)
Lasho (M)
Lel (M)
Lennor (M)
Lutherum (M)
Mander (M)
Merripen (M)
Mestipen (M)
Miri (F)
Narilla (F)
Narrila (F)
Nav (M)
Nicabar (M)
Patia (F)
Patrin (M)
Pattin (M)
Pias (M)
Pov (M)
Rawnie (F)
Romany (F)
Shuri (F)
Simen (M)
Stiggur (M)
Tas (M)
Tawnie (F)
Tawno (M)
Tem (M)
Tobbar (M)
Yarb (M)

Hawaiian

Ahulani (F)
Akela (F)
Akoni (M)
Alamea (F)
Alani (F)
Alaula (F)
Alika (F)
Aloha (F)
Alohi (F)
Alohilani (F)
Amaui (F)
Anabela (F)
Ane (F)
Anela (F)
Ani (F)
Aolani (F)
Aulii (F)
Babara (F)
Balaniki (F)
Bane (M)
Cristian (M)
Dorisa (F)
Edena (F)
Edi (F)
Elese (F)
Emele (F)
Ezera (M)
Gladi (F)
Hale (M)
Hoku (M)
Hokulani (F)
Inoa (F)
Iwalani (F)
Kai (M)
Kakaulani (F)
Kalama (F)
Kale (M)
Kama (F)
Kanani (F)
Kanoa (F)
Kapua (F)
Kaula (F)
Kaulana (F)
Keahi (M)
Kekoa (M)
Kekona (F)
Kelii (M)
Kiele (F)
Kieley (F)
Kieli (F)
Kikilia (F)
Kini (F)
Konane (M)
Lahela (F)
Laka (F)
Lani (M)
Lehua (F)
Leilani (F)
Lekeke (M)
Lileana (F)
Lilia (F)
Liliha (F)
Lio (M)
Liona (F)
Loe (M)
Lokelani (F)
Lola (F)
Lono (M)
Lulani (M)
Mahina (F)
Makana (F)
Makani (M)
Malia (F)
Malulani (F)
Mamo (F)
Mana (F)
Mauli (M)
Nahele (M)
Nani (F)
Okalani (F)
Oliana (F)
Palani (M)
Palila (F)
Peke (F)
Pililani (F)
Pilis (F)
Pilisi (F)
Pualani (F)
Puni (F)
Rahela (F)
Roselani (F)
Silivia (F)
Suke (F)
Suse (F)
Ulani (F)
Vegenia (F)

Hebrew/ Israeli

Abia (M)
Abiah (M)
Abiatha (M)
Abiathar (M)
Abiather (M)
Abiel (M)
Abigal (F)
Abijah (M)
Abimelech (M)
Abira (F)
Abishag (F)
Alma (F)
Almon (M)
Alona (F)
Alpheus (M)
Aluma (F)
Alumice (F)
Alumit (F)
Alvah (F)
Alvan (M)
Amariah (M)
Amaris (F)
Amiel (M)
Amira (F)
Amissa (F)

Abital (F)
Absalom (M)
Adah (F)
Adeana (F)
Aderes (F)
Aderet (F)
Adie (F)
Adiella (F)
Adina (F)
Adine (F)
Adir (M)
Adira (F)
Adiv (M)
Admon (M)
Adrial (M)
Adriel (M)
Ahava (F)
Ahe (M)
Ahouva (F)
Ahuda (F)
Akeem (M)
Akiba (M)
Akiva (M)
Aleeza (F)
Alitza (F)
Aliya (F)
Aliza (F)
Amnon (M)
Amon (M)
Anais (F)
Ardon (M)
Arel (M)
Areli (M)
Arella (F)
Ari (M)
Ariel (F)
Ariella (F)
Arielle (F)
Ariza (F)
Armoni (M)
Arna (F)
Arnice (F)
Arnina (F)
Arnit (F)
Arnon (M)
Arza (F)
Arzice (F)
Arzit (F)
Asa (M)
Asher (M)
Asiel (M)
Asisa (F)
Astera (F)
Asteria (F)
Astra (F)
Atara (F)
Ataret (F)
Atida (F)
Atira (F)
Avi (M)
Avidan (M)
Avidor (M)
Aviel (M)
Avital (M)
Aviv (M)
Aviva (F)
Avivi (F)
Avivice (F)
Avner (M)
Avniel (M)
Avraham (M)
Avram (M)
Avrit (F)
Ayelet (F)
Ayla (F)
Azaria (F)
Azariah (M)
Azriel (M)
Baram (M)
Barth (M)
Baruch (M)
Basia (F)
Bathia (F)
Batia (F)
Batsheva (F)
Behira (F)
Benzi (M)
Bethel (M)
Bethell (M)
Bethia (F)
Betula (F)
Bina (F)
Bithia (F)
Bona (F)
Bracha (F)
Carmel (M)
Carmela (F)
Carmeli (F)
Carmi (F)
Carmia (F)
Carmiel (F)
Carna (F)
Carnit (F)
Chaim (M)
Chanah (F)
Chanoch (M)
Chava (F)
Chaya (F)
Dagan (F)

Dagana (F)
Dagania (F)
Dagon (M)
Dalice (F)
Dalilah (F)
Dalit (F)
Dalya (F)
Dani (F)
Dania (F)
Danit (F)
Danya (F)
Dar (M)
Deedee (M)
Denae (F)
Deroit (F)
Deror (M)
Derora (F)
Derori (M)
Derorice (F)
Devorah (F)
Dickla (F)
Didi (F)
Diklice (F)
Diklit (F)
Dina (F)
Ditzah (F)
Diza (F)
Dodie (F)
Dor (M)
Dorit (F)
Dotan (M)
Dothan (M)
Dov (M)
Dovev (M)
Dur (M)
Elah (M)
Elanit (F)
Eleazar (M)
Eleora (F)
Eli (M)
Eliana (F)
Elihu (M)
Elisha (F)
Elisheba (F)
Elisheva (F)
Elkan (M)
Elkanah (M)
Eloy (M)
Elrad (M)
Ely (M)
Elza (F)
Emuna (F)
Ephraim (M)
Ezra (M)
Ezraella (F)
Ezrela (F)
Gada (F)
Gafna (F)
Gal (F)
Gali (F)
Galice (F)
Galya (F)
Gana (F)
Ganice (F)
Ganit (F)
Ganya (F)
Gavriel (M)
Gavrilla (F)
Gazit (F)
Geela (F)
Geva (F)
Gibor (M)
Gidon (M)
Gilad (M)
Gilada (F)
Ginton (M)
Gisa (F)
Gissa (F)
Givon (M)
Goel (M)
Gozal (M)
Gur (M)
Gurice (F)
Gurit (F)
Hadassah (F)
Hagia (F)
Hagice (F)
Hagit (F)
Ham (M)
Hanan (M)
Hania (F)
Haniya (F)
Harel (M)
Haviva (F)
Hedia (F)
Heman (M)
Hephsibah (F)
Hephzabah (F)
Hephzibah (F)
Hepzabah (F)
Hepzibah (F)
Hiram (M)
Hod (M)
Huldah (F)
Ilan (M)
Ilana (F)
Ilanit (F)
Ira (M)
Ishmael (M)
Ismael (M)
Ivria (F)
Ivrit (F)
Jaffa (F)
Jaffice (F)
Jafit (F)
Jametta (F)
Japheth (M)
Jardena (F)
Jaren (M)
Jaron (M)
Jehu (M)
Jephtha (M)
Jezebel (F)
Joab (M)
Joachim (M)
Joah (M)
Jona (F)
Jonati (F)
Jonina (F)
Jonit (F)
Jora (F)
Jotham (M)
Jubal (M)
Kaija (F)
Kalanit (F)
Kan (M)
Kaniel (M)
Kanny (M)
Karniela (F)
Karniella (F)
Karnis (F)
Karnit (F)
Kedem (M)
Kenaz (M)
Kenya (F)
Kerenhappuch (F)
Keturah (F)
Ketzi (F)
Ketzia (F)
Kezi (F)
Kezia (F)
Keziah (F)
Kissie (F)
Kiva (M)
Kivi (M)
Laban (M)
Lavi (M)
Leah (F)
Leeba (F)
Leib (M)
Leibel (M)
Leor (M)
Leron (M)
Levana (F)
Levi (M)
Levia (F)
Levona (F)
Lirit (F)
Livana (F)
Livia (F)
Livona (F)
Lot (M)
Mahir (M)
Mahira (F)
Mahlah (F)
Malka (F)
Manasseh (M)
Mangena (F)
Margalit (F)
Marganit (F)
Marni (F)
Marnin (M)
Matana (F)
Mazal (F)
Mehetabel (M)
Mehira (F)
Meir (M)
Menachem (M)
Mendel (M)
Menora (F)
Merab (F)
Mered (M)
Miri (F)
Mordechai (M)
Moria (F)
Moriel (F)
Morit (F)
Moselle (F)
Moshe (M)
Mozelle (F)
Nagid (M)
Nagida (F)
Namir (M)
Napthali (M)
Nasya (F)
Natan (M)
Nava (F)
Navice (F)
Navit (F)
Nechama (F)
Nediva (F)
Nehemiah (M)
Neta (F)
Netia (F)
Nili (M)
Nimrod (M)
Nirel (F)
Nissan (M)
Nissim (M)
Nitza (F)
Nitzana (F)
Nizana (F)
Noach (M)
Noga (F)
Noy (M)
Nur (M)
Nuri (M)
Nuria (F)
Nurice (F)
Nuriel (F)
Nurit (F)
Nurita (F)
Obadiah (M)
Odeda (F)
Odelia (F)
Odera (F)
Ofira (F)
Omar (M)
Ophira (F)
Ora (F)
Oralee (F)
Oren (M)
Orit (F)
Orli (F)
Orlice (F)
Orna (F)
Ornice (F)
Ornit (F)
Orpah (F)
Orpha (F)
Orphy (F)
Paza (F)
Pazia (F)
Pazice (F)
Pazit (F)
Peninah (F)
Peninit (F)
Pinchas (M)
Pninah (F)
Rabbi (M)
Rachamim (M)
Ranice (F)
Ranit (F)
Ranita (F)
Ranon (M)
Raviv (M)
Raz (M)
Razi (M)
Raziel (M)
Razilee (F)
Reuven (M)
Rimon (M)
Rimona (F)
Rivka (F)
Ronel (M)
Roni (M)
Ronia (F)
Ronice (F)
Ronit (F)
Ronli (F)
Sabra (F)
Selah (M)
Selima (F)
Seth (M)
Shalom (M)
Shamir (M)
Shamira (F)
Sharai (F)
Shaul (M)
Shem (M)
Shilo (F)
Shimon (M)
Shira (F)
Shiri (F)
Shlomo (M)
Shmuel (M)
Shoshanah (F)
Shulamit (F)
Sima (M)
Simpson (M)
Sivan (M)
Talia (F)
Tamar (F)
Telem (M)
Teman (M)
Temira (F)
Teva (M)
Thirza (F)
Timora (F)
Timur (M)
Tivon (M)
Tivona (F)
Tobit (F)
Tov (M)
Tovah (F)
Tovi (M)
Tzipora (F)
Tzvi (M)
Uri (M)
Uzziah (M)
Uzziel (M)
Vardice (F)
Vardit (F)
Vered (M)
Yaakov (M)
Yachne (F)
Yadid (M)
Yadin (M)
Yael (F)
Yaffa (F)
Yarin (M)
Yarkona (F)
Yechezkel (M)
Yehoshua (M)
Yehuda (M)
Yehudi (M)
Yehudit (F)
Yemina (F)
Yisrael (M)
Yitzchak (M)
Yochanan (M)
Yonah (M)
Yonatan (M)
Yonina (F)
Yonit (F)
Yonita (F)
Yosef (M)
Yovela (F)
Yoyi (M)
Zahava (F)
Zamir (M)
Zared (M)
Zayit (F)
Ze'ev (M)
Zebulon (M)
Zedekiah (M)
Zephaniah (M)
Zera (F)
Zia (M)
Zilah (F)
Zillah (F)

Zilpah (F)
Zimri (M)
Zoheret (F)
Zora (F)
Zorah (F)
Zylpha (F)

Hispanic

Abrahán (M)
Abrán (M)
Acquila (M)
Adelita (F)
Agustín (M)
Alano (M)
Alejandra (F)
Alejandrina (F)
Alejandro (M)
Alejo (M)
Aleta (F)
Aletea (F)
Alfonso (M)
Alfredo (M)
Alicia (F)
Alida (F)
Alita (F)
Aloisia (F)
Aloisio (M)
Alonzo (M)
Alroy (M)
Aluino (M)
Amada (F)
Amado (M)
Amalia (F)
Amando (M)
Amata (F)
Amato (M)
Anda (F)
Andrés (M)
Angelita (F)
Anica (F)
Anita (F)
Antonina (F)
Antonio (M)
Antuca (F)
Aquila (M)
Archibaldo (M)
Arlo (M)
Armando (M)
Arrio (M)
Arturo (M)
Asela (F)
Balta (M)
Barnebas (M)
Barto (M)
Bartoli (M)
Bartolo (M)
Bartolomé (M)
Basilio (M)
Beatriz (F)
Bebe (F)
Belia (F)
Belica (F)
Belicia (F)
Belita (F)
Benedicta (F)
Benedicto (M)
Beni (M)
Benicia (F)
Benita (F)
Benitín (M)
Benito (M)
Benja (M)
Bernabé (M)
Bernardel (M)
Bernardina (F)
Bernardo (M)
Bertín (M)
Berto (M)
Betina (F)
Blanca (F)
Blas (M)
Brigida (F)
Cachi (M)
Calida (F)

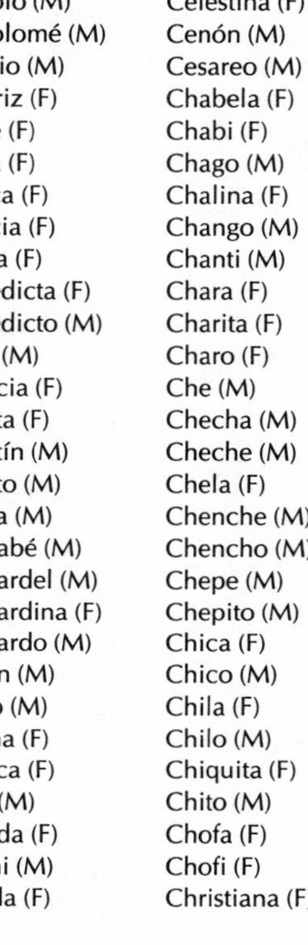

Camila (F)
Carlo (M)
Carlos (M)
Carlota (F)
Carmen (F)
Carmencita (F)
Cashi (M)
Casimiro (M)
Castel (M)
Catalina (F)
Catón (M)
Cecilla (F)
Celestina (F)
Cenón (M)
Cesareo (M)
Chabela (F)
Chabi (F)
Chago (M)
Chalina (F)
Chango (M)
Chanti (M)
Chara (F)
Charita (F)
Charo (F)
Che (M)
Checha (M)
Cheche (M)
Chela (F)
Chenche (M)
Chencho (M)
Chepe (M)
Chepito (M)
Chica (F)
Chico (M)
Chila (F)
Chilo (M)
Chiquita (F)
Chito (M)
Chofa (F)
Chofi (F)
Christiana (F)
Chumin (M)
Chumina (F)
Chuminga (M)
Chumo (M)
Cicerón (M)
Cirilo (M)
Ciro (M)
Cisco (M)
Clareta (F)
Clarisa (F)
Clarita (F)
Cleme (M)
Clemen (M)
Clemente (M)
Clemento (M)
Conrado (M)
Constancia (F)
Constanza (F)
Consuela (F)
Cordero (M)
Crispo (M)
Cristian (M)
Cristiano (M)
Cristino (M)
Cristóbal (M)
Cristy (F)
Curcio (M)
Currito (M)
Curro (M)
Damita (F)
Danilo (M)
Dario (M)
Demetrio (M)
Diego (M)
Dionis (M)
Dionisio (M)
Dolorcitas (F)
Doloritas (F)
Domicio (M)
Dominga (F)
Domingo (M)
Dorotea (F)
Edgardo (M)
Edmundo (M)
Elenor (F)
Eleonor (F)
Elisa (F)
Elsa (F)
Elvira (F)
Emilio (M)
Eneas (M)
Engracia (F)
Enrique (M)
Enriqueta (F)
Esdras (M)
Esmarelda (F)
Esmerelda (F)
Estanislao (F)
Estéban (M)
Estevao (M)
Eugenio (M)
Evita (F)
Farruco (M)
Federico (M)
Federoquito (M)
Felipe (M)
Felipino (M)
Felo (M)
Fernando (M)
Fico (M)
Filipo (M)
Flavio (F)
Francisca (F)
Francisco (M)
Franco (M)
Frasco (M)
Frascuelo (M)
Frederico (M)
Fredo (M)
Galeno (M)
Gaspar (M)
Gencho (M)
Genoveva (F)
Georgina (F)
Geraldo (M)
Gianina (F)
Gidita (F)
Gil (M)
Gina (F)
Ginata (F)
Ginia (F)
Gisela (F)
Gitana (F)
Godofredo (M)
Gofredo (M)
Gracia (F)
Graciana (F)
Guadalupe (M)
Gualberto (M)
Gualterio (M)
Guido (M)
Guilla (F)
Guillerma (F)
Guillermo (M)
Gustavo (M)
Gutierre (M)
Haraldo (M)
Heriberto (M)
Huberto (M)
Hubi (M)
Iban (M)
Incencio (M)
Inés (F)
Inesita (F)
Inigo (M)
Inocente (M)
Irenea (F)
Isabelita (F)
Jacinda (F)
Jacinta (F)
Jacinto (M)
Jacobo (M)
Jada (F)
Jaimito (M)
Jandina (F)
Jandino (M)
Jando (M)
Javier (M)
Jayme (M)
Jeremias (M)
Jesús (M)
Jesusa (F)
Joaquín (M)
Jobo (M)
Jonas (M)
Jorge (M)
Jorgina (F)
Jorrín (M)
José (M)
Josecito (M)
Josée (F)
Joseito (M)
Joselito (M)
Josue (M)
Joyita (F)
Juan (M)
Juana (F)
Juanch (M)
Juancho (M)
Juanita (F)
Juanito (M)
Julián (M)
Juliana (F)
Julieta (F)
Julio (M)
Junita (F)
Justino (M)
Justo (M)
Kika (F)
Kiki (M)
Lando (M)
Lao (M)
Laureana (F)
Laurencio (M)
Lázaro (M)
Lencho (M)
Leni (F)
Leonardo (M)
Leonor (F)
Leya (F)
Licha (F)
Lici (F)
Lico (M)
Lilia (F)
Liliosa (F)
Liseta (F)
Lolita (F)
Lorenza (F)
Lorenzo (M)
Lucila (F)
Lucio (M)
Lucita (F)
Luis (M)
Luisa (F)
Luz (F)
Magaly (F)
Magda (F)
Magola (F)
Maita (F)
Mando (M)
Mango (M)
Manny (M)
Manolón (M)
Manue (M)
Manuel (M)
Manuela (F)
Marcos (M)
Margara (F)
Margarita (F)
Margarite (F)
Mari (F)
María (F)
Mariquita (F)
Marita (F)
Martina (F)
Martiniano (M)
Marto (M)
Maruca (F)
Maruja (F)
Mateo (M)
Matías (M)
Matilde (F)
Matusha (F)
Matuxa (F)
Maxi (M)
Maximiliano (M)
Maximino (M)
Máximo (M)
Mega (F)
Melosa (F)
Mema (F)
Mercedes (F)
Micho (M)
Miguel (M)
Migui (M)
Miki (M)
Mincho (M)
Minel (M)
Mingo (M)
Mique (M)
Mora (F)
Morena (F)

Mundo (M)
Nana (F)
Napier (M)
Natacha (F)
Natal (M)
Natan (M)
Necha (F)
Necho (F)
Nelia (F)
Nelo (M)
Neneca (F)
Neper (M)
Neron (M)
Nesho (F)
Neto (M)
Neva (F)
Nicanor (M)
Nicho (M)
Nicolás (M)
Ninita (F)
Nita (F)
Noe (M)
Nuela (F)
Oalo (M)
Olo (M)
Ordando (M)
Orlando (M)
Orlo (M)
Osmundo (M)
Otilio (M)
Otman (M)
Oto (M)
Otón (M)
Pablo (M)
Paca (F)
Paco (M)
Pacorro (M)
Paloma (F)
Pancha (F)
Panchita (F)
Panchito (M)
Pancho (M)
Paquita (F)
Paquito (M)
Patricio (M)
Paulino (M)
Paulita (F)
Paulo (M)
Paz (M)
Pedrín (M)
Pedro (M)
Pepe (M)
Pepillo (M)
Pepin (M)
Pepita (F)

Pepito (M)
Pequin (M)
Perequin (M)
Perico (M)
Petronio (M)
Peyo (M)
Pilar (M)
Pipo (M)
Piti (M)
Pitin (M)
Pito (M)
Platón (M)
Querida (F)
Queta (F)
Quico (M)
Quinto (M)
Quiqui (M)
Quito (M)
Rafael (M)
Rafaela (F)
Rafì (M)
Raimundo (M)
Ramón (M)
Raquel (F)
Raúl (M)
Reina (F)
Rey (M)
Ría (F)
Ricardo (M)
Riccardo (M)
Richi (M)
Rico (M)
Riel (M)
Riqui (M)
Rita (F)
Rober (M)
Roberto (M)
Rodas (M)
Rodolfo (M)
Rodrigo (M)
Rodriguez (M)
Rogelio (M)
Rogerio (M)
Rolando (M)
Roldán (M)
Rollon (M)
Rolo (M)
Rolon (M)
Rosita (F)
Rudi (M)
Rufo (M)
Ruperta (F)
Ruy (M)
Salamón (M)
Salvador (M)

Sanchia (F)
Sanson (M)
Santana (F)
Santiago (M)
Santo (M)
Sarita (F)
Saritia (F)
Sarito (M)
Senón (M)
Sevilla (F)
Seville (F)
Shaba (F)
Shem (M)
Sidonio (M)
Sigfrido (M)
Sigifredo (M)
Sofia (F)
Soficita (F)
Solana (F)
Stancio (M)
Suela (F)
Suelita (F)
Tabo (M)
Tadeo (M)
Tanix (M)
Tano (M)
Tasia (F)
Teb (M)
Techa (F)
Teodomiro (M)
Teodoro (M)
Tere (F)
Teresita (F)
Teté (F)
Tia (F)
Tiago (M)
Tiana (F)
Tiara (F)
Ticha (F)
Ticho (M)
Tilo (M)
Timoteo (M)
Tino (M)
Tita (F)
Tito (M)
Tobal (M)
Tobalito (M)
Toli (M)
Tomás (M)
Tona (F)
Trella (F)
Turi (M)
Tuto (M)
Urbano (M)
Ursulina (F)

Valeriana (F)
Vicente (M)
Victoriana (F)
Victorina (F)
Victorino (M)
Victorio (M)
Vincente (M)
Virida (F)
Vitin (M)
Vito (M)
Vitoria (F)
Waterio (M)
Wilfredo (M)
Ximen (M)
Ynesita (F)
Ynez (F)
Yoli (F)
Ysabel (F)
Zacarias (M)
Zarita (F)
Zenon (M)
Zita (F)

Hungarian

Adél (M)
Ádorjan (M)
Agi (F)
Ágota (F)
Agotha (F)
Alexa (F)
Aliz (F)
Alizka (F)
Amalia (F)
Anci (F)
Andor (M)
András (M)
Andris (M)
Anikó (F)
Annus (F)
Annuska (F)
Antal (M)
Anti (M)

Arrow (M)
Artur (M)
Ballas (M)
Bandi (M)
Barna (M)
Barta (M)
Bazel (M)
Bela (M)
Bence (M)
Benci (M)
Benedek (M)
Benedik (M)
Benke (M)
Beno (M)
Bernat (M)
Bertalan (M)
Berti (M)
Bódog (M)
Boske (F)
Boski (F)
Bözsi (F)
Cezar (M)
Dacso (M)
Damján (M)
Daneil (M)
Dani (F)
Darda (F)
Deco (M)
Demeter (M)
Dénes (M)
Dennes (M)
Dome (M)
Domó (M)
Domokos (M)
Domonkos (M)
Domotor (M)
Donahue (M)
Duci (F)
Edgard (M)
Edit (F)
Edvard (M)
Elek (M)

Endre (M)
Erinn (F)
Evi (F)
Evike (F)
Ferike (F)
Franci (F)
Frici (F)
Fülöp (M)
Gábor (M)
Gáspár (M)
Gellart (M)
Gitta (F)
Gizi (F)
Gizike (F)
Gizus (F)
Gottfrid (M)
Gracia (F)
Gruzia (F)
Gyorci (F)
Henrik (M)
Ila (F)
Ilka (F)
Ilona (F)
Ilonka (F)
Iluska (F)
Imrus (M)
Iren (F)
Irenka (F)
Isti (M)
István (M)
Jakab (M)
Jancsi (M)
Janika (M)
Jano (M)
János (M)
Jenci (M)
Jensi (M)
Johanna (F)
Jolán (F)
Jolanka (F)
Joli (F)
Jóska (M)
Juci (F)
Jucika (F)
Judit (F)
Julianna (F)
Julinka (F)
Juliska (F)
Jutka (F)
Kálmán (M)
Kamila (F)
Károly (M)
Kata (F)
Katinka (F)
Kató (F)

Katoka (F)
Katone (M)
Katus (F)
Kázmér (M)
Kelemen (M)
Kerestel (M)
Klarika (F)
Kobi (M)
Konrad (M)
Kriska (F)
Krispin (M)
Kristof (M)
Lekszi (F)
Lenci (F)
Lenci (M)
Lidi (F)
Lilike (F)
Linka (F)
Liszka (F)
Loránd (M)
Lóránt (M)
Lorinc (M)
Maco (M)
Magdolna (F)
Maks (M)
Makszi (M)
Malcsi (F)
Máli (F)
Malika (F)
Mano (M)
Mara (F)
Marci (M)
Marcilka (M)
Marcilki (M)
Marcsa (F)
Margit (F)
Mariska (F)
Márkus (M)
Martino (M)
Martus (F)
Martuska (F)
Máté (M)
Maxi (M)
Micu (M)
Mihal (M)
Mihály (M)
Miki (M)
Miksa (M)
Misi (M)
Miska (M)
Mózes (M)
Natan (M)
Neci (F)
Niki (M)
Niklos (M)

Ninacska (F)
Noe (M)
Nusi (F)
Odi (M)
Ödön (M)
Onella (F)
Orbán (M)
Pál (M)
Pali (M)
Palika (M)
Rebeka (F)
Rendor (M)
Rez (M)
Rezi (F)
Rezső (M)
Riczi (M)
Rikard (M)
Riza (F)
Rizus (F)
Robi (M)
Rodrigo (M)
Rogerios (M)
Roza (F)
Rozalia (F)
Rozsi (F)
Ruzsa (F)
Salamon (M)
Samie (M)
Samu (M)
Sándor (M)
Sanyi (M)
Sarika (F)
Sarolta (F)
Sasa (F)
Szigfrid (M)
Tabor (M)
Tade (M)
Tamás (M)
Teca (F)
Tercsa (F)
Teresa (F)
Terez (F)
Terezia (F)
Terike (F)
Teruska (F)
Timót (M)
Tivadar (M)
Todor (M)
Tomi (M)
Toni (M)
Treska (F)
Vazul (M)
Vencel (M)
Vica (F)
Vidor (M)
Viktor (M)
Vili (M)
Vilmos (M)
Vinci (M)
Zacharias (M)
Zako (M)
Zigana (F)
Zigfrid (M)
Zizi (F)
Zoltán (M)
Zsa Zsa (F)
Zsanett (F)

Icelandic

Arni (F)
Falda (F)
Gleda (F)
Jonas (M)
Katrin (F)
Olafur (M)
Pall (M)
Sofronia (F)
Sula (F)

Indonesian

Kersen (M)

Indo-Pakistani

Aditi (F)
Adri (M)
Adya (F)
Agni (M)
Aja (F)
Ajay (M)
Almiron (M)
Amandeep (M)
Amar (M)
Ambarish (F)
Ambika (F)
Amin (M)
Amitan (M)
Amma (F)
Anala (F)
Anand (M)
Ananda (F)
Anila (F)
Artha (F)
Asoka (F)
Atman (M)
Baka (F)
Bakula (F)
Bali (M)
Balin (M)
Ballabh Das (M)
Bel (F)
Chana (F)
Chanda (F)
Chandi (F)
Chandra (F)
Channa (F)
Chhaya (F)
Daksh (M)
Dalal (M)
Daru (F)
Deva (F)
Devaki (F)
Devi (F)
Durva (F)
Elamma (F)
Ellama (F)
Ganesa (F)
Gauri (F)
Girisa (F)
Gurpreet (M)
Hanuman (M)
Hara (F)
Hardeep (M)
Hari (M)
Harpreet (M)
Hasin (M)
Hastin (M)
Jaspal (M)
Jaspreet (F)
Javas (M)
Jibon (F)
Jivin (M)
Josha (M)
Jyoti (F)
Kakar (M)
Kala (M)
Kaleenda (F)
Kali (F)
Kalinda (F)
Kalindi (F)
Kalkin (M)
Kalpana (F)
Kama (F)
Kantu (M)
Kanya (F)
Kapildev (M)
Karma (F)
Karuna (F)
Kasi (F)
Kaveri (F)
Kavindra (F)
Kera (F)
Kerani (F)
Kers (M)
Kery (F)
Kesava (F)
Kesin (M)
Kiritan (M)
Kirsi (F)
Kistna (M)
Kistnah (M)
Kona (F)
Krishna (M)
Krishnah (M)
Kumuda (F)
Kusa (F)
Lais (M)
Lakya (F)
Lal (M)
Lalita (F)
Lota (F)
Mahesa (M)
Mamta (F)
Mandara (F)
Matrika (F)
Maya (F)
Mehtar (M)
Mela (F)
Mesha (F)
Minda (F)
Mohan (M)
Nandin (M)
Narain (M)
Natesa (F)
Navin (M)
Nehru (M)
Nipa (F)
Nirveli (F)
Nutan (F)
Padma (F)
Pandita (F)
Pausha (F)
Pinga (F)
Pollyam (F)
Pramod (M)
Prem (M)
Rani (F)
Ratri (F)
Ravi (M)
Rekha (F)
Reva (F)
Risha (F)
Rohana (F)
Rohin (M)
Roi (M)
Ruana (F)
Ruchi (F)
Rudra (F)
Sadhana (F)
Sagara (F)
Sahen (M)
Sakari (F)
Sakti (F)
Sala (F)
Salmalin (M)
Santosh (M)
Sanya (F)
Sarad (M)
Sarngin (M)
Sarojin (M)
Saura (F)
Sharad (M)
Sita (F)
Siva (M)
Soma (F)
Sumati (F)
Sundeep (M)
Surata (F)
Suri (F)
Surya (F)
Tirtha (F)
Trina (F)
Trisha (F)
Tula (F)
Tulsi (F)
Tulsidas (M)
Uma (F)
Vadin (M)
Valin (M)
Vasin (M)
Veda (F)
Vikas (M)
Vinay (M)
Vinod (M)
Yasiman (F)
Yasmine (F)

Irish

Aibhlin (F)
Aidan (M)
Ailan (M)
Ailis (F)
Aindrea (M)
Aingeal (F)
Aisling (F)
Aislinn (F)
Aithne (F)
Allsun (F)
Alsandair (M)
Anntoin (M)
Arlen (M)
Artur (M)
Ashling (F)
Ashlyn (F)
Baird (M)
Beathag (F)
Bedelia (F)
Biddie (F)
Bidelia (F)
Blane (M)
Bow (M)
Bowen (M)
Bowie (M)
Brigid (F)
Brigit (F)
Caitlin (F)
Caitria (F)
Caitriona (F)
Callum (M)
Car (M)
Carlin (M)
Carling (M)
Carney (M)
Carthach (M)
Catlin (M)
Cearbhall (M)
Ciara (F)
Ciarra (F)
Ciera (F)
Clancy (M)
Clodagh (F)
Coleman (M)
Colm (M)
Colum (M)
Columba (M)
Columbina (F)
Conan (M)
Connor (M)
Cowan (M)
Cristiona (F)
Darrie (M)
Decla (F)
Declan (M)
Delaney (M)
Delano (M)
Denis (M)
Dermod (M)
Dermot (M)
Derry (M)
Dev (M)
Devlin (M)
Diarmuid (M)
Donohue (M)
Dooriya (F)
Dooya (F)
Dymphna (F)
Dympna (F)
Eamonn (M)
Egan (M)
Eibhlin (F)
Eilis (F)
Eimile (F)
Eion (M)
Eithne (F)
Ena (F)
Eoghan (M)
Ethna (F)
Ethne (F)
Ethnea (F)
Eveleen (F)
Falon (F)
Farrar (M)
Farrell (M)
Farrow (M)
Fidelma (F)
Filib (M)
Finella (F)
Finola (F)
Flurry (M)
Garrett (M)
Grady (M)
Grainne (F)
Grainnia (F)
Grania (F)
Hanraoi (M)
Heneage (M)
Hogan (M)
Hurley (M)
Ina (F)
Ita (F)
Keara (F)

Kearney (M)
Keary (M)
Keegan (M)
Keenan (M)
Keon (M)
Kern (M)
Kerry-Anne (F)
Kier (M)
Kieran (M)
Kiran (F)
Kyrie (F)
Labhras (M)
Lanty (M)
Liam (M)
Lon (M)
Mab (F)
Mabyn (F)
Mackenzie (M)
Macmurray (M)
Maeve (F)
Maire (F)
Mairona (F)
Malachy (M)
Maura (F)
Maureen (F)
Mavin (F)
Megan (F)
Moira (F)
Moss (M)
Moyne (F)
Muire (F)
Nappy (F)
Nev (M)
Nevin (M)
Nevins (M)
Nial (M)
Oona (F)
Oonagh (F)
Oonie (F)
Oran (M)
Orla (F)
Orlagh (F)
Padraic (M)
Pilib (M)
Quillan (M)
Quinley (M)
Quinlin (M)
Quinn (M)
Rafe (M)
Rafer (M)
Raff (M)
Raffer (M)
Rafferty (M)
Redmond (M)
Riobard (M)
Rohan (M)
Rois (M)
Roisin (M)
Ronan (M)
Rosaleen (F)
Seamus (M)
Sean (M)
Shamus (M)
Shanahan (M)
Sheehan (M)
Sile (F)
Sina (F)
Sinead (F)
Siobhan (F)
Siobhian (F)
Somhairle (M)
Sorcha (F)
Sosanna (F)
Sullivan (M)
Tiomoid (M)
Torin (M)
Torrence (M)
Uilliam (M)

Italian

Abrahamo (M)
Abramo (M)
Adamo (M)
Adele (F)
Adelina (F)
Adriana (F)
Adriano (M)
Agne (F)
Agnella (F)
Agnesca (F)
Agnese (F)
Agnesina (F)
Agnola (F)
Alberto (M)
Albino (M)
Alda (F)
Aldo (M)
Alessandra (F)
Alessandro (M)
Alessio (F)
Alfredo (M)
Alonso (M)
Alphonse (M)
Alphonsine (F)
Alvino (M)
Amadea (F)
Amadeo (M)
Amalia (F)
Amica (F)
Amico (M)
Aminta (F)
Amintor (M)
Angelo (M)
Annetta (F)
Annina (F)
Antonia (F)
Antonieta (F)
Antonino (M)
Antonio (M)
Araldo (M)
Aranne (M)
Armando (M)
Aroldo (M)
Arrigo (M)
Arturo (M)
Aurelio (M)
Basilio (M)
Beatrice (F)
Benedetta (F)
Benedetto (M)
Beniamino (M)
Bernardina (F)
Bernardino (M)
Bernardo (M)
Betta (F)
Bettina (F)
Betto (M)
Biagio (M)
Briano (M)
Brigada (F)
Brigida (F)
Camilla (F)
Camillo (M)
Caprice (F)
Carina (F)
Carita (F)
Carla (F)
Carlino (M)
Carlo (M)
Carlotta (F)
Carmela (F)
Carmelo (M)
Carmilla (F)
Carmine (M)
Carolo (M)
Caterina (F)
Cathe (F)
Celestina (F)
Cella (F)
Chiara (F)
Cirillo (M)
Clarice (F)
Clarissa (F)
Claudia (F)
Claudio (M)
Clemente (M)
Clemenza (F)
Cola (M)
Concettina (F)
Conrado (M)
Constantia (F)
Constanza (F)
Cosimo (M)
Cosmo (M)
Crispino (M)
Cristiano (M)
Cristoforo (M)
Damiano (M)
Daniela (F)
Daniele (M)
Davida (F)
Davide (M)
Demetrio (M)
Detta (F)
Dionigi (M)
Dionisio (M)
Domenico (M)
Donaldo (M)
Donatello (M)
Donati (M)
Donato (M)
Edetta (F)
Edgardo (M)
Edita (F)
Edmondo (M)
Eduardo (M)
Elba (M)
Elisa (F)
Elisabetta (F)
Eloisa (F)
Emilia (F)
Emilio (M)
Enrico (M)
Enzio (M)
Enzo (M)
Erico (M)
Ezio (M)
Fabiano (M)
Fabio (M)
Federico (M)
Filippa (F)
Filippina (F)
Filippo (M)
Filomena (F)
Flavio (M)
Francesca (F)
Francesco (M)
Gabriela (F)
Gabriele (M)
Gabrielli (M)
Gabriello (M)
Geraldo (M)
Geremia (M)
Gessica (F)
Gia (F)
Giacobbe (M)
Giacomo (M)
Giacopo (M)
Giamo (M)
Gian (M)
Giancarlo (M)
Gianetto (M)
Gianna (F)
Gideone (M)
Ginevra (F)
Gino (M)
Gioffredo (M)
Giona (M)
Giordana (M)
Giosia (M)
Giotto (M)
Giovanna (F)
Giovanni (M)
Giraldo (M)
Gisela (F)
Giulia (F)
Giuseppe (M)
Giustino (M)
Grazia (F)

Graziosa (F)
Gregorio (M)
Gualtiero (M)
Guido (M)
Guntero (M)
Gustavo (M)
Iago (M)
Imelda (F)
Inés (F)
Isabella (F)
Leonardo (M)
Letizia (F)
Liliana (F)
Lisettina (F)
Lorenza (F)
Lorenzo (M)
Loretto (M)
Luca (F)
Lucia (F)
Luciano (M)
Lucrezia (F)
Lugia (F)
Luigi (M)
Maddalena (F)
Marcello (M)
Marco (M)
Margarita (F)
Margherita (F)
Maria (F)
Mariella (F)
Mario (M)
Marta (F)
Martino (M)
Masaccio (M)
Massimiliano (M)
Massimo (M)
Matelda (F)
Matteo (M)
Maurizio (M)
Menico (M)
Michaelle (F)
Natale (M)
Natalia (F)
Nataniele (M)
Nerone (M)
Nicola (M)
Nicoletta (F)
Nicolo (M)
Noe (M)
Olinda (F)
Olindo (M)
Orlando (M)
Orsino (M)
Otello (M)
Ottone (M)
Paolina (F)
Paolo (M)
Patrizia (F)
Patrizio (M)
Paulo (M)
Peppe (M)
Peppo (M)
Pero (M)
Piero (M)
Pietro (M)
Pino (M)
Pippa (F)
Raimondo (M)
Ranieri (M)
Reina (F)
Renzo (M)
Roberto (M)
Rocco (M)
Rodolfo (M)
Rodrigo (M)
Rolando (M)
Rosario (M)
Rosetta (F)
Rosina (F)
Ruberto (M)
Rudolfo (M)
Rudolpho (M)
Ruggerio (M)
Ruperto (M)
Salomone (M)
Salvatore (M)
Samuele (M)
Sansone (M)
Santo (M)
Saverio (M)
Savina (F)
Sergio (M)
Sigefriedo (M)
Sofia (F)
Stanislao (M)
Stefano (M)
Taddeo (M)
Taro (M)
Tazio (M)
Teodoro (M)
Teresa (F)
Teresina (F)
Thaddeo (M)
Timoteo (M)
Tito (M)
Tomaso (M)
Urbano (M)
Valencia (F)
Venezia (F)
Vicenzo (M)

Vincenzo (M)
Violetta (F)
Vittore (M)
Vittoria (F)
Vittorio (M)
Viviana (F)
Zaira (F)
Zola (F)

Japanese

Akako (F)
Aki (F)
Akio (M)
Akira (M)
Anzu (F)
Ayame (F)
Azami (F)
Botan (M)
Chidori (F)
Chika (F)
Chikako (F)
Chizu (F)
Chizuko (F)
Dai (F)
Gina (F)
Goro (M)
Hama (F)
Hana (F)
Haru (F)
Hiroshi (M)
Hisa (F)
Hisae (F)
Hisako (F)
Hisayo (F)
Hisoka (M)
Hoshi (F)
Hoshiko (F)
Hoshiyo (F)
Isas (M)
Ishi (F)
Ishiko (F)
Ishiyo (F)
Jiro (M)
Jo (M)
Joji (M)
Kagami (F)
Kameko (F)
Kami (F)
Kei (F)
Kichi (F)
Kiku (F)
Kimi (F)
Kimiko (F)
Kimiyo (F)
Kin (M)
Kishi (F)
Kita (F)
Kiwa (F)
Kiyoshi (M)
Koko (F)
Koto (F)
Kuma (F)
Kumi (F)
Kuni (F)
Kuniko (F)
Kuri (F)
Machi (F)
Masago (F)
Matsu (F)
Michi (F)
Michiko (F)
Midori (F)
Mika (F)
Miki (F)
Mikiyo (F)
Mineko (F)
Mio (F)
Miwa (F)
Miwako (F)
Miya (F)
Miyo (F)
Miyoko (F)
Miyuki (F)
Mura (F)
Nara (F)
Nari (F)
Nariko (F)
Nishi (F)
Nori (F)
Oki (F)
Ori (F)
Orino (F)
Osen (F)
Raiden (M)
Raku (F)
Ren (F)
Rin (F)
Ringo (M)
Ruri (F)
Saburo (M)
Sachi (F)
Sada (F)
Saki (F)
Sakura (F)
Samaru (M)
Sato (F)
Sawa (F)
Sayo (F)
Seki (F)
Sen (M)
Shika (F)
Shina (F)
Shino (F)
Shiro (M)
Shizu (F)
Shizuka (F)
Shizuko (F)
Shizuyo (F)
Sugi (F)
Suki (F)
Sumi (F)
Suzu (F)
Suzuki (F)
Suzuko (F)
Taka (F)
Takara (F)
Taki (F)
Tama (F)
Tamaki (F)
Tamako (F)
Tamayo (F)
Tamika (F)
Tamiko (F)
Tamiyo (F)
Tanaka (F)
Tani (F)
Tatsu (F)
Tazu (F)
Tetsu (F)
Toki (F)
Tokiwa (F)
Tomo (F)
Tora (F)
Tori (F)
Toshi (M)
Toshie (F)
Toshiko (F)
Toshio (M)
Toshiyo (F)
Ume (F)
Umeko (F)
Umeyo (F)
Washi (F)
Yachi (F)
Yachiko (F)
Yachiyo (F)
Yasu (F)
Yasuko (F)
Yasuyo (F)
Yemon (M)
Yoi (F)
Yoko (F)
Yori (F)
Yoshi (M)
Yoshie (F)
Yoshiko (F)
Yoshino (F)
Yoshiyo (F)
Yuki (F)
Yukiko (M)
Yukio (M)

Korean

Cho (F)
Chul (M)
Eun (F)
Gi (M)
Hye (F)
In (F)
Ja (M)
Kwan (M)
Sook (F)

Laotian

Margita (F)

Latin

Camillus (M)
Caractacus (M)
Carola (F)
Claudius (M)
Cornelius (M)
Crispina (F)
Crispus (M)
Damaras (F)
Damaress (F)
Damaris (F)
Damris (F)
Decima (F)
Decimus (M)
Dionysius (M)
Dulcibel (F)
Dulcibella (F)
Faustina (F)
Fortunatus (M)
Honoria (F)
Julián (M)
Julianus (M)
Julius (M)
Lelia (F)
Leo (M)
Lucretia (F)
Marcellus (M)
Mariabella (F)
Marius (M)
Maxima (F)
Melodia (F)
Modesta (F)
Modestus (F)
Neptune (M)
Nero (M)
Octavia (F)
Octavius (M)
Oriana (F)
Orion (M)
Peregrine (M)
Petronella (F)
Radolphus (M)
Renātus (M)
Roxana (F)
Septima (F)
Septimus (M)
Sidra (F)
Silas (M)
Silva (F)
Silvania (F)
Stephanus (M)
Tatiānus (M)
Tatius (M)
Tersia (F)
Tertius (M)
Ursa (F)
Venetia (F)
Venice (F)
Venus (F)
Verna (F)
Vesta (F)
Viola (F)
Violante (F)
Zacharias (M)
Zea (F)

Latvian

Alberts (M)
Albins (M)
Ansis (M)
Antons (M)
Anya (F)
Anyuta (F)
Armands (M)
Asenka (F)
Aska (F)
Asya (F)
Beatrise (F)
Berngards (M)
Bernhard (M)
Bernhards (M)
Brencis (M)
Brigita (F)
Cecilija (F)
Daniels (M)
Edgars (M)
Edite (F)
Edmunds (M)
Elizabete (F)
Eriks (M)
Ervins (M)
Fabius (M)
Filips (M)
Gerda (F)
Gizela (F)
Gotfrids (M)
Gregors (M)
Grieta (F)
Gustavs (M)
Haralds (M)
Henriette (F)
Irka (F)
Irusya (F)
Jana (F)
Janina (F)
Jazeps (M)
Jeks (M)
Jeska (M)
Judite (F)
Justins (M)
Justs (M)
Kamila (F)
Karina (F)
Karlen (M)
Karlene (F)
Karlens (M)
Karlis (M)
Kola (M)
Kriss (M)
Krista (F)
Kristine (F)
Krists (M)
Krisus (M)
Labrencis (M)
Leonhards (M)
Leons (M)
Liene (F)
Lisbete (F)
Lizina (F)
Lucija (F)
Lukas (M)
Mare (F)
Margrieta (F)
Martins (M)
Marts (M)
Mikelis (M)
Miks (M)
Mikus (M)
Milkins (M)
Nadina (F)
Nastasya (F)
Nastka (F)
Nastusya (F)
Niklavs (M)
Nikolais (M)
Pauls (M)
Pavils (M)
Richards (M)
Rihards (M)
Roberts (M)
Rudolfs (M)
Sarlote (F)
Stasya (F)
Stefans (M)
Tasenka (F)
Taska (F)
Tasya (F)
Urzula (F)
Valter (M)
Valters (M)
Zanna (F)
Zigfrids (M)

Lithuanian

Adomas (M)
Agniya (F)
Ale (F)
Aliute (F)
Andrius (M)
Anikke (F)
Annze (F)
Antavas (M)
Bernardas (M)

Danukas (M)
Dovidas (M)
Elzbieta (F)
Haroldas (M)
Janina (F)
Jecis (M)
Jekebs (M)
Jonelis (M)
Jonukas (M)
Jonutis (M)
Jurgis (M)
Justas (M)
Justinas (M)
Justukas (M)
Kofryna (F)
Leonas (M)
Liutas (M)
Margarita (F)
Marija (F)
Martinas (M)
Moze (M)
Nastasya (F)
Nastka (F)
Nastusya (F)
Ona (F)

Petras (M)
Petrelis (M)
Petrukas (M)
Raulas (M)
Raulo (M)
Risardas (M)
Rosertas (M)
Roze (F)
Rozele (F)
Rozyte (F)
Samuelis (M)
Solomonas (M)
Stasya (F)
Tasenka (F)
Taska (F)
Tasya (F)
Tomas (M)
Tomelis (M)
Vacys (M)
Vanda (M)
Vandele (M)
Waldemar (M)

Malaysian

Norazah (F)
Norhaneza (F)
Norlaili (F)
Normah (F)

Native American

Adoette (F)
Ahanu (M)
Ahdik (M)
Ahmik (M)
Aiyana (F)
Akando (M)
Akule (M)
Alameda (F)
Alaqua (F)
Algoma (F)
Alkas (F)
Alnaba (F)
Altsoba (F)
Amayeta (F)
Anaba (F)
Anevay (F)
Angeni (F)
Anoki (M)
Aponi (F)
Aquene (F)
Awan (M)
Awanata (F)
Awanta (F)
Awendela (F)
Awenita (F)
Ayita (F)
Bena (F)
Bly (M)
Chenoa (F)
Chesmu (M)
Cheyenne (F)
Chilali (F)
Chimalis (F)
Chitsa (F)
Cholena (F)
Chumana (F)
Cocheta (F)
Dasan (M)
Delsin (M)
Delsy (M)
Demothi (M)
Dena (F)
Dezba (F)
Dichali (M)
Doba (F)
Dohosan (M)
Dyami (M)
Dyani (F)
Elan (M)
Elia (M)
Elki (M)
Elsu (M)
Enli (M)
Enola (F)
Etenia (F)
Etu (M)
Etumu (F)
Etumuye (F)
Eyota (M)
Gosheven (M)
Guyapi (M)
Hahnee (M)
Hakan (M)
Halian (M)
Halona (F)
Hateya (F)
Hausu (F)
Helaku (M)
Helki (F)
Heltu (F)
Hesutu (M)
Heta (F)
Hinun (M)
Hoho (M)
Hola (F)
Honon (M)
Honovi (M)
Hototo (M)
Howi (M)
Huata (F)
Hulwema (M)
Huslu (M)
Hute (M)
Igasho (M)
Imala (F)
Inteus (M)
Iskemu (M)
Istas (F)
Istu (M)
Ituha (F)
Iuana (F)
Iye (M)
Izusa (F)
Jacy (M)
Jolon (M)
Kachina (F)
Kaga (M)
Kahsha (F)
Kaliska (F)
Kamata (F)
Kanda (F)
Kasa (F)
Kasha (F)
Kaya (F)
Kele (M)
Kenda (F)
Kibbe (M)
Kijika (M)
Kimama (F)
Knoton (M)
Kolenya (F)
Kono (M)
Kulya (F)
Kutattoa (F)
Kutcuyak (F)
Kuzih (M)
Kwam (M)
Kwanita (F)
Langundo (M)
Lanu (M)
Lenno (M)
Leotie (F)
Liluye (F)
Liseli (F)
Lissilma (F)
Litonya (F)
Liwanu (M)
Loiyetu (F)
Lokni (M)
Lolotea (F)
Lomasi (F)
Lonato (M)
Luna (F)
Lupetu (F)
Lusela (F)
Lusio (M)
Lusita (F)
Luyu (M)
Magena (F)
Malila (F)
Malkuyu (F)
Manaba (F)
Manco (M)
Manipi (M)
Mansi (F)
Maska (M)
Mato (M)
Mausi (F)
Meda (F)
Melvern (M)
Membta (F)
Migina (F)
Miltaiye (M)
Minal (F)
Mingan (M)
Minowa (F)
Misu (M)
Mituna (F)
Moemu (F)
Mojag (M)
Momuso (M)
Motega (M)
Muata (M)
Muliya (F)
Mulya (F)
Muna (F)
Muraco (M)
Nahma (M)
Nalren (M)
Namid (M)
Nashota (F)
Nasnan (F)
Nata (F)
Natane (F)
Nawat (M)
Nayati (M)
Neka (F)
Netis (M)
Niabi (F)
Nibaw (M)
Nida (F)
Nigan (M)
Nita (F)
Nitis (M)
Nituna (F)
Nodin (M)
Nokonyu (M)
Noksu (F)
Nolcha (F)
Notaku (F)
Noton (M)
Nuna (F)
Ogin (F)
Ohanko (M)
Olathe (F)
Omusa (F)
Onatah (F)
Onawa (F)
Onida (F)
Orenda (F)
Otadan (M)
Ouray (M)
Oya (F)
Paco (M)
Pallaton (M)
Papina (F)
Patakasu (M)
Patamon (M)
Pati (F)
Patwin (M)
Pay (M)
Payat (M)
Pelipa (F)
Peni (F)
Pillan (M)
Posala (F)
Powa (M)
Raini (M)
Rozene (F)
Sadzi (F)
Sahale (M)
Sakima (M)
Sakuna (F)
Sanuye (F)
Sapata (F)
Satinka (F)
Sewati (M)
Shada (F)
Shappa (F)
Shasta (F)
Shuma (F)
Shumana (F)
Sihu (F)
Sipeta (F)
Sisika (F)
Siwili (M)
Songan (M)
Sora (F)
Soso (F)
Suletu (F)
Suni (F)
Sunki (F)
Sutki (F)
Suzamni (F)
Taci (F)
Tadan (M)
Tadewi (F)
Tadi (M)
Tadita (F)
Tadzi (M)
Taima (F)
Taipa (F)
Tait (M)
Takala (F)
Takenya (F)
Tala (F)
Talasi (F)
Talli (M)
Tallulah (F)
Tasida (F)
Tate (M)
Tiimu (M)
Tiktu (M)
Tiponya (F)
Tiwa (F)
Tiwolu (F)
Tohon (M)
Tolikna (F)
Toloisi (F)
Toski (F)
Totsi (F)
Tuketu (M)
Tukuli (M)
Tunu (M)
Tupi (M)
Tusa (F)
Tuwa (F)
Tyee (M)
Uhubitu (M)
Una (F)
Utatci (M)
Utina (F)
Waban (M)
Wakanda (F)
Wakiza (M)
Waneta (F)
Wapi (M)
Wemilat (M)
Wemilo (M)
Wenonah (F)
Wenutu (M)
Wichado (M)
Wilanu (M)
Wilny (M)
Wilu (M)
Winema (F)
Wingi (M)
Winona (F)
Wuliton (M)
Wunand (M)
Wuyi (M)

Wyanet (F)
Wynono (M)
Yakecen (M)
Yakez (M)
Yaluta (F)
Yamka (F)
Yana (M)
Yanaba (F)
Yancy (M)
Yelutci (M)
Yenene (F)
Yepa (F)
Yoki (F)
Yoluta (F)
Yotimo (M)
Yottoko (M)
Yuma (M)
Yutkiye (F)
Yuttciso (F)
Yutu (M)
Zaltana (F)
Zihna (F)

Nigerian

Abebi (F)
Abeni (F)
Abiona (F)
Adamma (F)
Adesina (F)
Agu (M)
Ahkeen (M)
Akanke (F)
Akeen (M)
Akin (M)
Akisatan (F)
Alake (F)
Aleeka (F)
Alika (F)
Alike (F)
Amoke (F)
Aniweta (F)
Apara (F)
Asabi (F)
Atuanya (M)
Ayoka (F)
Azi (M)
Chi (M)
Ega (F)
Fayola (F)
Femi (F)
Gowon (M)
Hasana (F)
Ilom (M)
Iniko (M)
Kalechi (M)
Kayin (M)
Kwako (M)
Nnamdi (M)
Nwa (M)
Nwake (M)
Oba (F)
Odion (M)
Ogun (M)
Ogunkeye (M)
Ogunsanwo (M)
Ogunsheye (M)
Oko (M)
Olorun (M)
Olufemi (M)
Olujimi (M)
Olukayode (M)
Olushegun (M)
Olushola (M)
Oni (F)
Orji (M)
Orunjan (M)
Ottah (M)
Sarauniya (F)
Tomi (M)
Tor (M)

Norwegian

Arkin (M)
Artur (M)
Arve (M)
Åsta (F)
Aud (F)
Audr (M)
Birgit (F)
Bodil (M)
Dag (M)
Dagny (F)
Donalt (M)
Dorte (F)
Dreng (M)
Dyre (M)
Einar (M)
Fredrika (F)
Galt (M)
Gressa (F)
Gunda (F)
Karena (F)
Katla (F)
Krist (M)
Kristine (F)
Leif (M)
Matteus (M)
Mikkel (M)
Nicolai (M)
Odo (M)
Petter (M)
Rane (F)
Salamon (M)
Signe (F)
Sigrid (F)
Sigvard (M)
Siurt (M)
Terese (F)
Thordis (F)
Tor (M)

Persian

Nard (M)
Sadira (F)
Soraya (F)
Vashti (F)
Xerxes (M)
Zahreh (F)
Zel (F)

Phoenician

Feliks (M)

Polish

Adas (M)
Adelaida (F)
Adok (M)
Aga (F)
Agatka (F)
Agnieszka (F)
Ala (F)
Albek (M)
Albertyna (F)
Albin (M)
Albinka (F)
Aleksander (M)
Aleska (F)
Alka (F)
Amalia (F)
Amelcia (F)
Ania (F)
Aniol (M)
Anka (F)
Anta (F)
Antek (M)
Antoni (M)
Antonin (M)
Antonina (F)
Antos (M)
Arek (M)
Aronek (M)
Artek (M)
Artur (M)
Atanazy (M)
Atek (M)
Atka (F)
Aurek (M)
Aureli (M)
Barnaby (M)
Bartek (M)
Bartos (M)
Bazek (M)
Bendek (M)
Benek (M)
Beniamin (M)
Bernarda (F)
Bernardyn (M)
Blazek (M)
Bryga (F)
Brygida (F)
Brygitka (F)
Casimir (M)
Cecylia (F)
Cela (F)
Celek (F)
Celinka (F)
Celka (F)
Cesia (F)
Cezar (M)
Cezary (M)
Cezek (M)
Chaimek (M)
Chrystian (M)
Crystek (M)
Daga (F)
Danek (M)
Danielka (F)
Danka (F)
Dawid (M)
Dobry (M)
Dodek (M)
Dominik (M)
Donat (M)
Donek (M)
Dorek (M)
Dorka (F)
Dorosia (F)
Dorota (F)
Dymek (M)
Dymitry (M)
Dyzek (M)
Edda (F)
Edek (M)
Edka (F)
Edyta (F)
Edzio (M)
Ela (F)
Eliza (F)
Elka (F)
Elsbietka (F)
Elżbieta (F)
Elzunia (F)
Emilian (M)
Erwinek (M)
Ewa (F)
Fabek (M)
Fela (F)
Felcia (F)
Felka (F)
Fil (M)
Filipa (F)
Filipek (M)
Filpina (F)
Fotfryd (M)
Fraka (F)
Franciszka (F)
Franek (M)
Frania (F)
Franio (M)
Franus (M)
Fredek (M)
Fryda (F)
Garek (M)
Genek (M)
Genio (M)
Gerik (M)
Gita (F)
Hana (F)
Hanka (F)
Henia (F)
Heniek (M)
Henier (M)
Henka (F)
Henrieta (F)
Heronim (M)
Himeronim (M)
Holleb (M)
Honok (M)
Ignac (M)
Inek (M)
Inka (F)
Inok (F)
Itka (F)
Iwan (M)
Iwona (F)
Iwonka (F)
Iza (F)
Izabel (F)
Izabella (F)
Jaga (F)
Jakubek (M)
Jalu (M)
Jan (M)
Jana (F)
Janek (M)
Jankiel (M)
Jarek (M)
Jas (M)
Jasia (F)
Jasio (M)
Jedrek (M)
Jedrus (M)
Joanka (F)
Joasia (F)
Jola (F)
Jolanta (F)
Jula (F)
Julcia (F)
Jurek (M)
Justek (M)
Kamila (F)
Kamilka (F)
Karol (M)
Karolek (M)
Karolina (F)
Karolinka (F)
Kasia (F)
Kasienka (F)
Kasin (F)
Kaska (F)
Kassia (F)
Kazek (M)
Kazik (M)
Kazio (M)
Klara (F)
Klemens (M)
Klimek (M)
Krys (M)
Krysia (F)
Krysta (F)
Krystian (M)
Krystka (F)
Krystyna (F)
Krystynka (F)
Kubus (M)
Ladislaus (M)
Laurka (F)
Leonek (M)
Leos (M)
Letycia (F)
Lida (F)
Lidka (F)
Lilka (F)
Linek (M)
Lodoiska (F)
Lopa (F)
Lorenz (M)
Lucya (F)
Ludka (F)
Ludwika (F)
Łukasz (M)
Machas (M)
Macia (F)
Magda (F)
Magia (F)
Makimus (M)
Maksymilian (M)
Mandek (M)
Manka (F)
Marcia (F)
Marcin (M)
Margisia (F)
Margita (F)
Maryla (F)
Maryna (F)
Masia (F)
Matyas (M)
Mela (F)
Melcia (F)
Melka (F)
Michak (M)
Michal (M)
Michalek (M)
Mietek (M)
Mikolai (M)
Milek (M)
Milla (F)
Minka (F)

Moshe (M)
Mosze (M)
Moszek (M)
Mundek (M)
Nacia (F)
Nardek (M)
Nata (F)
Natalia (F)
Natan (M)
Natka (F)
Nela (F)
Nelek (M)
Nelka (F)
Ola (F)
Olek (M)
Olés (M)
Olesia (F)
Onek (M)
Osmanek (M)
Otek (M)
Otton (M)
Patek (M)
Paulin (M)
Paweł (M)
Pawlina (F)
Pela (F)
Pelcia (F)
Penelopa (F)
Pictrus (M)
Pietrek (M)
Piotrek (M)
Pola (F)
Polcia (F)
Rebeka (F)
Renia (F)
Rita (F)
Rolek (M)
Rye (M)
Rysio (M)
Ryszard (M)
Salamen (M)
Salcia (F)
Serg (M)
Sergiusz (M)
Sewek (M)
Slawek (M)
Stanisław (M)
Stanisława (F)
Stasiek (M)
Stasio (M)
Stefa (F)
Stefan (M)
Stefania (F)
Stefcia (F)
Stefka (F)
Tadek (M)
Tadeusz (M)
Tadzio (M)
Tanek (M)
Tawia (F)
Telek (M)
Teodor (M)
Teodorek (M)
Teos (M)
Terenia (F)
Tereska (F)
Tesa (F)
Tesia (F)
Tila (F)
Titek (M)
Tola (F)
Tolek (M)
Tolsia (F)
Tomcio (M)
Tomek (M)
Tomislaw (M)
Tonek (M)
Tosia (F)
Truda (F)
Tymek (M)
Tymon (M)
Tytus (M)
Wala (F)
Waleria (F)
Wandzia (F)
Wera (F)
Wicek (M)
Wicent (M)
Wicus (M)
Wiera (F)
Wiercia (F)
Wierka (F)
Wiktor (M)
Wira (F)
Wirke (F)
Wisia (F)
Witek (M)
Zannz (F)
Zewek (M)
Zocha (F)
Zofia (F)
Zosha (F)
Zusa (F)
Zuzana (F)
Zuzanka (F)
Zuzia (F)
Zuzka (F)
Zygfryd (M)
Zygi (M)
Zytka (F)

Portuguese

Abrao (M)
Adão (M)
Agueda (F)
Ailinn (F)
Alao (M)
Alexio (M)
Alwin (M)
Basilio (M)
Beatriz (F)
Bernardina (F)
Branca (F)
Carlota (F)
Catarina (F)
Celestina (F)
Conrado (M)
Cristao (M)
Cristiano (M)
Cristovão (M)
Dario (M)
Davi (M)
Diani (F)
Domingos (M)
Duarte (M)
Eduardo (M)
Emilio (M)
Erico (M)
Gaspar (M)
Graca (F)
Gregorio (M)
Haroldo (M)
Henrique (M)
Humberto (M)
Ivone (F)
Jaco (M)
Jayme (M)
Jeremias (M)
João (M)
Joaquim (M)
Josef (M)
Judite (F)
Leão (M)
Leonardo (M)
Lourenco (M)
Marcos (M)
Margarida (F)
Martinho (M)
Mateus (M)
Maximiliano (M)
Mel (M)
Moises (M)
Natalia (F)
Nicolau (M)
Patricio (M)
Raimundo (M)
Raquel (F)
Rebeca (F)
Sansão (M)
Siguefredo (M)
Simão (M)
Tereza (F)
Timoteo (M)
Tomas (M)
Tomaz (M)
Tome (M)
Urbano (M)
Vanda (F)
Vitor (M)
Vitoria (F)
Zacarias (M)
Zetta (F)
Zeusef (M)

Romanian

Amalia (F)
Andrei (M)
Anicuta (F)
Artur (M)
Aurelian (M)
Dic (M)
Dol (F)
Dorotthea (F)
Elica (F)
Elisabeta (F)
Ema (F)
Enric (M)
Francise (F)
Geofri (M)
Godoired (M)
Gustav (M)
Iancu (M)
Ioan (M)
Ionel (M)
Iosua (M)
Irini (F)
Iulia (F)
Jenica (F)
Maricara (F)
Mihail (M)
Mihas (M)
Noe (M)
Petar (M)
Petru (M)
Rafael (M)
Reimond (M)
Reveca (F)
Simion (M)
Ursule (F)
Vasile (M)

Russian

Adamka (M)
Adeliya (F)
Adrik (M)
Afon (M)
Afonya (M)
Agafia (F)
Agasha (F)
Akim (M)
Albin (M)
Aleksandr (M)
Aleksasha (F)
Aleksei (M)
Aleksey (F)
Alena (F)
Alenka (F)
Alexandr (M)
Alina (F)
Alisa (F)
Alya (F)
Amaliya (F)
Andreian (M)
Andrey (M)
Andreyan (M)
Andreyka (M)
Andri (M)
Andrik (M)
Andriyan (M)
Angelina (F)
Anhelina (F)
Anja (F)
Anninka (F)
Annuska (F)
Anouska (F)
Antin (M)
Antinko (M)
Antonette (F)
Antonina (F)
Anya (F)
Arina (F)
Arinka (F)
Armen (M)
Aronos (M)
Artur (M)
Asenka (F)
Asya (F)
Aurel (M)
Avreliy (M)
Beatriks (F)
Beatrisa (F)
Benedikt (M)
Benedo (M)
Berdy (M)
Berngards (M)
Betti (F)
Cela (F)
Celestyn (F)
Celestyna (F)
Cesia (F)
Cheslav (M)
Christofer (M)
Christoff (M)
Damian (M)
Daniela (F)
Danikla (F)
Danila (F)
Danilka (F)
Danya (M)
Danylets (M)
Danylo (M)
Dasha (F)
Daveed (M)
Dema (M)
Denis (M)
Denka (M)
Denya (M)
Dima (M)
Dimitri (M)
Dimka (M)
Dmitrik (M)
Dodya (M)
Dominika (F)
Domka (F)
Dorka (F)
Doroteya (F)
Dosya (F)
Duscha (F)
Dusya (F)
Dwora (F)
Edgard (M)
Edik (M)
Edmond (M)
Egor (M)
Elena (F)
Elisavetta (F)
Eriks (M)
Eugeni (M)
Fabi (M)
Fabiyan (M)
Faddei (M)
Fanya (F)
Fayina (F)
Fedinka (M)
Fedor (M)
Feeleep (M)
Feliks (M)
Feodor (M)
Feodora (F)
Filipp (M)
Filya (M)
Foma (M)
Fomka (M)
Fonya (M)
Fridrich (M)
Galina (F)
Galinka (F)
Galka (F)
Galya (F)
Garald (M)
Garolds (M)
Gasha (F)
Gashka (F)
Gaspar (M)
Gavril (M)
Gelya (F)
Genka (M)
Genya (M)
Georgina (F)
Georgiy (M)
Gina (F)
Gotfrid (M)
Halina (F)
Hedeon (M)
Igor (M)
Inessa (F)
Inka (F)
Ioakim (M)
Ioann (M)
Ioanna (F)

Iosif (M)
Iov (M)
Irena (F)
Irina (F)
Irisa (F)
irisha (F)
Iryna (F)
Isak (M)
Iustin (M)
Ivan (M)
Ivanchik (M)
Ivanna (F)
Ivano (M)
Ivas (M)
Ivona (F)
Izabele (F)
Izabella (F)
Jakiv (M)
Jakov (M)
Jasha (M)
Jelena (F)
Jeremija (M)
Jereni (F)
Jov (M)
Jurgi (M)
Karina (F)
Karine (F)
Karl (M)
Karlen (M)
Karlin (M)
Karyna (F)
Katenka (F)
Katerinka (F)
Katinka (F)
Katka (F)
Katryna (F)
Katya (F)
Kazimir (M)
Kenya (M)
Kesar (M)
Kesha (M)
Khaim (M)
Kharald (M)
Khristina (F)
Khristya (F)
Kisa (F)
Kiska (F)
Klara (F)
Klemet (M)
Klim (M)
Kliment (M)
Klimka (M)
Kolya (M)
Konrad (M)
Konstantin (F)
Kostenka (F)
Kostya (F)
Kostyusha (F)
Kotik (F)
Kotinka (F)
Labrentsis (M)
Larka (M)
Larochka (F)
Larya (M)
Lavr (M)
Lavra (F)
Lavrik (M)
Lavro (M)
Leka (F)
Lelya (F)
Lenka (F)
Lenora (F)
Leonid (M)
Lera (F)
Lerka (F)
Lesya (F)
Lev (M)
Levko (M)
Lida (F)
Lidka (F)
Lidochka (F)
Lili (F)
Liolya (F)
Lisenka (F)
Lizanka (F)
Lizka (F)
Lorka (F)
Luchok (M)
Luiza (F)
Luka (M)
Lukash (M)
Lukasha (M)
Lukyan (M)
Luyiza (F)
Luzija (F)
Madelina (F)
Magda (F)
Magdalina (F)
Mahda (F)
Maksim (M)
Maksimka (M)
Maksym (M)
Manka (F)
Manuil (M)
Manya (F)
Mara (F)
Maria (F)
Marina (F)
Marinka (F)
Mariya (F)
Marka (M)
Markusha (M)
Martyn (M)
Maruska (F)
Marya (F)
Masha (F)
Mashenka (F)
Mashka (F)
Matfei (M)
Matvey (M)
Mayfey (M)
Melana (F)
Melaniya (F)
Melanka (F)
Melanya (F)
Melashka (F)
Melasya (F)
Michail (M)
Mika (M)
Mika (F)
Mikhail (M)
Mikhalka (M)
Milya (F)
Misha (M)
Mishca (M)
Mishka (M)
Moisey (M)
Mosya (M)
Motka (M)
Motya (M)
Nada (F)
Nadenka (F)
Nadia (F)
Nadina (F)
Nadiya (F)
Nadja (F)
Nadka (F)
Nadya (F)
Nastasya (F)
Nastka (F)
Nastusya (F)
Nata (F)
Natalka (F)
Natalya (F)
Natan (M)
Natasha (F)
Natashia (F)
Nelya (F)
Nessia (F)
Nika (F)
Nikita (M)
Nikolai (M)
Nil (M)
Nilya (M)
Noi (M)
Nyura (F)
Nyusha (F)
Oleksa (F)
Oleksandr (M)
Olena (F)
Olenko (F)
Oles (M)
Olesko (M)
Olesya (F)
Olga (F)
Olka (F)
Olya (F)
Olyusha (F)
Opanas (M)
Orina (F)
Orlenda (F)
Orya (F)
Oryna (F)
Osip (M)
Osya (M)
Palasha (F)
Panas (M)
Panya (F)
Pasha (M)
Pashka (M)
Pavel (M)
Pavla (F)
Pavlik (M)
Pavlina (F)
Pavlinka (F)
Pavlo (M)
Pawl (M)
Pelageya (F)
Perka (M)
Petinka (M)
Petr (M)
Petro (M)
Petruno (M)
Petrusha (M)
Pyotr (M)
Raina (F)
Rakhil (F)
Rakhila (F)
Rashel (F)
Revekka (F)
Rostik (M)
Rostislav (M)
Rostya (M)
Rurich (M)
Ruvim (M)
Ruzha (F)
Sacha (M)
Sachar (M)
Samuil (M)
Samvel (M)
Sarka (F)
Sasa (F)
Sascha (M)
Sasha (F)
Sashenka (M)
Sashka (M)
Selinka (F)
Sergei (M)
Sergey (M)
Sergeyka (M)
Sergie (M)
Sergo (M)
Sergunya (M)
Serhiy (M)
Serhiyko (M)
Serzh (M)
Shura (F)
Shurik (M)
Shurka (F)
Slava (M)
Slavik (M)
Slavka (M)
Sofka (F)
Sofya (F)
Sonja (F)
Stas (M)
Stashko (M)
Staska (M)
Stasya (F)
Stefan (M)
Stefania (F)
Stenya (M)
Stepa (F)
Stepan (M)
Stepanida (F)
Stepanya (M)
Stepanyda (F)
Stepka (M)
Stesha (F)
Steshka (F)
Susanka (F)
Svetlana (F)
Syarhey (M)
Tadey (M)
Tama (F)
Tamara (F)
Tamarra (F)
Tammara (F)
Tammera (F)
Tamra (F)
Tamyra (F)
Tana (F)
Tanas (M)
Tania (F)
Tanja (F)
Tanka (F)
Tannia (F)
Tanya (F)
Tarnia (F)
Tarnya (F)
Tasenka (F)
Tasha (F)
Tashia (F)
Tashina (F)
Tashka (F)
Taska (F)
Tasya (F)
Tata (F)
Terezilya (F)
Tima (M)
Timka (M)
Timofei (M)
Timofey (M)
Timok (M)
Tisha (M)
Tishka (M)
Todor (M)
Todos (M)
Tomas (M)
Tomochka (F)
Tonya (F)
Tosha (F)
Tosky (F)
Tosya (F)
Tuska (F)
Tusya (F)
Urvan (M)
Ustin (M)
Valka (F)
Valya (F)
Vanda (F)
Vanek (M)
Vania (F)
Vanka (M)
Vanya (M)
Varenka (F)
Varka (F)
Varvara (F)
Varya (F)
Vas (M)
Vasilak (M)
Vasilek (M)
Vasili (M)
Vasiliy (M)
Vaska (M)
Vassili (M)
Vassily (M)
Vasya (M)
Vasyl (M)
Vava (F)
Vavka (F)
Venedict (M)
Venedikt (M)
Venka (M)
Venya (M)
Vera (F)
Verasha (F)
Verinka (F)
Verka (F)
Verusya (F)
Vika (F)
Vikent (M)
Vikenti (M)
Vikesha (M)
Viktor (M)
Viktoria (F)
Vilma (F)
Vitenka (M)
Vitka (M)
Vitya (M)
Vladimir (M)
Vladlen (M)
Vlas (M)
Volya (M)
Vova (M)
Vovka (M)
Yanka (M)
Yarina (F)
Yaryna (F)

Yashko (M)
Yegor (M)
Yekaterina (F)
Yelena (F)
Yelisabeta (F)
Yelizaveta (F)
Yeremey (M)
Yerik (M)
Yeska (M)
Yesya (M)
Yeva (F)
Yevgenyi (M)
Yevka (F)
Yov (M)
Yudif (F)
Yudita (F)
Yula (F)
Yulinka (F)
Yuliya (F)
Yulka (F)
Yulya (F)
Yura (M)
Yurchik (M)
Yuri (M)
Yurik (M)
Yurko (M)
Yusha (M)
Yusif (M)
Yusts (M)
Yustyn (M)
Yusup (M)
Yuzef (M)
Zakhar (M)
Zheka (M)
Zhenka (M)
Zhorka (M)
Zigfrids (M)
Zilya (F)
Zinon (M)

Sanskrit

Zudora (F)

Scandinavian

Agna (F)
Agneta (F)
Agnetta (F)
Alvis (M)
Anders (M)
Aren (M)
Arne (M)
Arney (M)
Arnie (M)
Assa (F)
Assi (F)
Astri (F)
Astrid (F)
Astrud (F)
Astyr (F)
Atti (F)
Audun (M)
Axel (M)
Axell (M)
Bengt (M)
Bengta (F)
Bent (M)
Bjorn (M)
Borg (M)
Brede (M)
Burr (M)
Dagmar (F)
Davin (M)
Erik (M)
Franzen (M)
Gala (F)
Georg (M)
Gerda (F)
Gerhard (M)
Goran (M)
Gunnar (M)
Haakon (M)
Hako (M)
Hakon (M)
Harald (M)
Helga (F)
Hilmar (M)
Hulda (F)
Inga (F)
Ingamar (M)
Ingar (M)
Inge (F)
Ingeberg (F)
Ingeborg (F)
Ingemar (M)
Inger (M)
Ingmar (M)
Ingrid (F)
Ingvar (M)
Isak (M)
Ivar (M)
Jakob (M)
Jan (M)
Jens (M)
Joergen (M)
Johan (M)
Jorgen (M)
Josef (M)
Judit (F)
Justinus (M)
Kalle (M)
Karin (F)
Karr (M)
Kelda (F)
Kirsten (F)
Knut (M)
Kristin (F)
Lang (M)
Lars (M)
Larse (M)
Laurans (M)
Leontes (M)
Lorens (M)
Lunt (M)
Margreta (F)
Margrete (F)
Marna (F)
Nisse (F)
Noak (M)
Norna (F)
Odin (M)
Olaf (M)
Olav (M)
Olavus (M)
Olay (M)
Ole (M)
Olef (M)
Olle (M)
Olof (M)
Olov (M)
Oluf (M)
Peder (M)
Ragnar (M)
Rakel (F)
Rikard (M)
Roald (M)
Rolf (M)
Rolfe (M)
Rolph (M)
Royd (M)
Sakarias (M)
Sakarja (M)
Sigurd (M)
Sonja (F)
Sven (M)
Tait (M)
Tate (M)
Thor (M)
Thorbjorn (M)
Thorleif (M)
Thorvald (M)
Thyra (F)
Timoteus (M)
Tomas (M)
Tyra (F)
Viktoria (F)
Zakris (M)

Scottish

Adair (M)
Adhamh (M)
Aenea (F)
Aeneas (M)
Ailsa (F)
Aindreas (M)
Ainslie (M)
Alaister (M)
Alastair (M)
Aley (F)
Alistar (M)
Alpin (M)
Alpine (M)
Anders (F)
Andra (F)
Angus (M)
Angusina (F)
Anndra (M)
Artair (M)
Athol (M)
Aulay (M)
Barclay (M)
Baubie (F)
Beatham (M)
Bonar (M)
Boyd (M)
Broderick (M)
Brody (M)
Cailean (M)
Cailin (F)
Campbell (M)
Chalmer (M)
Chalmers (M)
Daveen (F)
Davelle (F)
Davena (F)
Davida (F)
Devene (F)
Dougal (M)
Douglasina (F)
Drummond (M)
Dugald (M)
Durell (M)
Egidia (F)
Egidius (M)
Eilidh (F)
Eirene (F)
Elsa (F)
Elspet (F)
Elspeth (F)
Elspie (F)
Ewan (M)
Farquhar (M)
Feargus (M)
Fergus (M)
Ferguson (M)
Fife (M)
Forbes (M)
Gavin (M)
Gillean (M)
Gilleasbuig (M)
Gordan (M)
Graeme (M)
Gregor (M)
Hamish (M)
Harailt (M)
Hughina (F)
Ian (M)
Innes (M)
Innis (M)
Iona (F)
Ishbel (F)
Isla (F)
Jacobina (F)
Jessie (F)
Johan (F)
Kameron (M)
Keddy (M)
Kentigern (M)
Kerr (M)
Labhruinn (M)
Lachlan (M)
Lachlanina (F)
Lachunn (M)
Lawrie (M)
Lennox (M)
Lilias (F)
Lorn (M)
Lorna (F)
Lorne (M)
Macaulay (M)
Macdonald (M)
Macdougal (M)
Mairi (F)
Maisie (F)
Manius (M)
Marsail (F)
Mata (M)
Maxwell (M)
Mazie (F)
Mhairie (F)
Michaela (F)
Micheil (M)
Moira (F)
Morag (F)
Moray (F)
Morna (F)
Morven (M)
Muir (M)
Muire (F)
Mungo (M)
Munroe (M)
Murdo (M)
Murdoch (M)
Murnia (F)
Murray (M)
Myrna (F)
Mysie (F)
Nairne (M)
Nessie (F)
Ninian (M)
Padruig (M)
Parlan (M)
Peadair (M)
Rab (M)
Raby (M)
Ranald (M)
Richie (M)
Robertina (F)
Rossalyn (F)
Rosslyn (F)
Ruthven (F)
Sawney (M)
Senga (F)
Seonaid (F)
Seumas (M)
Sheena (F)
Sheona (F)
Shiona (F)
Sholto (M)
Shonah (F)
Shone (F)
Siusan (F)
Tamarka (F)
Tammas (M)
Tammy (F)
Tatiana (F)
Tavis (M)
Tevis (M)
Tevish (M)
Torquil (M)

Serbian

Blaz (M)
Bogomir (M)
Dusan (M)
Josip (M)
Jozhe (M)
Jula (F)
Juliana (F)
Liljana (F)
Loman (M)
Mara (F)
Stane (M)
Taman (M)
Vika (F)

Slavic

Amalia (F)
Antonetta (F)
Boris (M)
Brodny (M)
Dani (F)
Dragomira (F)
Elza (F)
Iva (F)
Ivanka (F)
Jaroslav (M)
Jerney (M)
Jovan (M)
Kasimir (M)
Kristian (M)
Lala (F)
Lucika (F)
Lucka (F)
Ludmila (F)
Mila (F)
Milena (F)
Milica (F)
Neda (F)
Neza (F)

Radinka (F)
Radman (M)
Radmilla (F)
Radomil (M)
Rude (M)
Rurik (M)
Stanislav (M)
Tavo (M)
Timkin (M)
Toni (M)
Tota (F)
Tynka (F)
Vanda (F)
Varina (F)
Veta (F)
Yarmilla (F)
Zelimir (M)
Ziv (M)
Ziven (M)
Zorana (F)
Zorina (F)

Swedish

Alicia (F)
Alrik (M)
Anneka (F)
Annika (F)
Antonetta (F)
Arram (M)
Arriet (F)
Artur (M)
Arvid (M)
Barbro (F)
Barthelemy (M)
Basilius (M)
Basle (M)
Birgitta (F)
Bittan (F)
Blanka (F)
Blenda (F)
Brita (F)
Britt (F)
Britta (F)
Celia (F)
Chresta (M)
Edvard (M)
Elsa (F)
Frederik (M)
Freja (F)
Fritz (M)
Gries (M)
Gustaf (M)
Hadrian (M)
Hans (M)
Hansel (M)
Jeremia (M)
Jonam (M)
Jonas (M)
Josua (M)
Kajsa (F)
Kersten (F)
Klara (F)
Kolina (F)
Konrad (M)
Kornelis (F)
Krister (M)
Kristina (F)
Kristoffer (M)
Laris (M)
Lauris (M)
Lotta (F)
Lukas (M)
Malin (F)
Mathias (M)
Mihalje (M)
Mikael (M)
Niklas (M)
Nils (M)
Per (M)
Rickard (M)
Rika (F)
Rolle (M)
Simson (M)
Sofi (F)
Stefan (M)
Viktor (M)
Vilhelm (M)
Ville (M)
Vilma (F)
Wandja (F)
Wera (F)
Wilhelm (M)

Swiss

Beck (M)
Imelda (F)

Syrian

Adar (M)

Turkish

Abi (M)
Acar (M)
Adem (M)
Adli (M)
Ahir (M)
Akar (M)
Anka (M)
Areef (M)
Arif (M)
Arslan (M)
Asker (M)
Azad (M)
Azize (F)
Basir (M)
Berk (M)
Bitki (F)
Cahil (M)
Cari (F)
Duman (M)
Elma (F)
Halil (M)
Hasad (M)
Kabil (M)
Kahil (M)
Kerem (M)
Kiral (M)
Meryem (F)
Ohannes (M)
Onan (M)
Onur (M)
Rahmet (M)
Rashid (M)
Saril (F)
Sevilen (M)
Sofya (F)
Tabib (M)
Umay (F)
Uner (M)
Yucel (M)
Yunus (M)
Zeheb (M)
Zeki (M)
Zerdali (F)
Zeynep (F)

Ukrainian

Bogdashka (M)
Bohdan (M)
Fadey (M)
Fayina (F)
Mihailo (M)
Zofia (F)
Zorya (M)

Vietnamese

Am (F)
An (M)
Anh (M)
Bay (M)
Bian (F)
Binh (M)
Bua (F)
Cadao (M)
Cai (F)
Cham (M)
Chim (M)
Dinh (M)
Duoc (M)
Gan (M)
Ha (F)
Hai (M)
Hieu (M)
Hoa (F)
Hoang (M)
Hong (F)
Hung (M)
Huong (F)
Huy (M)
Lap (M)
Ngu (F)
Tai (M)
Thanh (F)
Thao (F)
Thi (F)
Thien (M)
Thuy (F)
Tin (M)
Truc (F)
Tuan (M)
Tung (M)
Tuyen (F)
Tuyet (F)

Welsh

Alun (M)
Alys (F)
Aneirin (M)
Angharad (F)
Anwen (F)
Arfon (M)
Bevan (M)
Bevin (M)
Blanchefleur (F)
Blodwen (F)
Blodwyn (F)
Blodyn (F)
Bronwen (M)
Bronwyn (F)
Bryn (F)
Brynmor (M)
Cade (M)
Cadel (M)
Cai (M)
Caio (M)
Caius (M)
Caradog (M)
Caron (F)
Carrone (F)
Carys (F)
Catrin (F)
Catriona (F)
Caw (M)
Ceinwen (F)
Ceredig (M)
Ceretic (M)
Ceri (F)
Ceridwen (F)
Cerri (F)
Cerrie (F)
Cerys (F)
Cledwyn (M)
Colwyn (M)
Dafydd (M)
Delwyn (F)
Delyth (F)
Derren (F)
Derron (F)
Dewi (M)
Dilwyn (M)
Eifion (M)
Eifiona (F)
Eiluned (F)
Eilwen (F)
Eilwyn (M)
Eira (F)
Eiralys (F)
Eirian (F)
Eirlys (F)
Eirwen (F)
Elin (F)
Elined (F)
Eluned (F)
Elwin (M)
Elwina (F)
Emrys (M)
Eryl (F)
Ev (M)
Evan (M)
Evans (M)
Gaius (M)
Gawain (M)
Gerwyn (M)
Geth (M)
Gethin (M)
Glyndwr (M)
Gwenda (F)
Gwenllian (F)
Gwilym (M)
Gwladys (F)
Gwynedd (F)
Gwynfa (F)
Gwynfor (M)
Gwynne (F)
Haydn (M)
Heulwen (F)
Hew (M)
Huw (M)
Iago (M)
Idris (M)
Idwal (M)
Iestin (F)
Iestyn (M)
Ieuan (M)
Ifor (M)
Iola (F)
Iolo (M)
Iorwerth (M)
Ithel (M)
Jestina (F)
Jone (M)
Llewellyn (M)
Llinos (F)
Luned (F)
Lynwen (F)
Mair (F)
Mairwen (F)
Maldwyn (M)
Megan (F)
Meirionfa (F)
Meirionwen (F)
Merfin (M)
Merion (M)
Meurig (M)
Morfydd (F)
Morgan (M)
Morwenna (F)
Mostyn (M)
Myfannwy (F)
Nerys (F)
Nest (F)
Nesta (F)
Newlin (M)
Nye (M)
Olwen (F)
Owain (M)
Owena (F)
Peredur (M)
Reese (M)
Rhett (M)
Rhian (F)
Rhiannon (F)
Rhodri (M)
Rhonwen (F)
Rhys (M)
Rice (M)
Romney (M)
Ronwen (F)
Siân (F)
Siarl (M)
Siôn (M)
Sulwen (F)
Sulwyn (M)
Taliesin (M)
Tegan (F)
Tegwen (F)
Trefor (M)
Tudor (M)
Winne (F)
Yestin (M)

Yiddish

Adi (M)
Aizik (M)
Alein (M)
Avrum (M)
Blum (F)
Bluma (F)
Dawid (M)
Dowid (M)
Dwora (F)
Fischel (M)
Gisela (F)
Gita (F)
Hersz (M)
Hinda (F)
Icek (M)
Immanuel (M)
Isaak (M)
Ita (F)
Josef (M)
Kayle (F)
Kelula (F)
Kuper (M)
Kyla (F)
Leben (M)
Mendeley (M)
Moises (M)
Moshe (M)
Mózes (M)
Raizel (F)
Rebekah (F)
Rifka (F)
Ruchel (F)
Schmuel (M)
Shaina (F)
Shelomoh (M)
Shemuel (M)
Velvel (M)
Welfel (M)
Welvel (M)
Wolf (M)
Yousef (M)

Popularity BROWSER

Records kept by the health departments of several states make it possible to determine how often a name has been given to newborns since fairly early in this century. This browser lists the ten most popular boys' and girls' names in the country by decade from 1930 to 1970, then by five-year period from 1970 to 1990.

The most popular names of 1990, the most recent year for which complete information is available, are also listed.

1930*s*

	Female		***Male***
1.	Mary	1.	John
2.	Betty	2.	James
3.	Maria	3.	William
4.	Dorothy	4.	Robert
5.	Billie	5.	Charles
6.	Doris	6.	George
7.	Wanda	7.	Billie
8.	Helen	8.	José
9.	Joyce	9.	Billy
10.	Margaret	10.	Thomas

1940*s*

	Female		***Male***
1.	Mary	1.	James
2.	Maria	2.	John
3.	Linda	3.	Robert
4.	Barbara	4.	William
5.	Patricia	5.	Charles
6.	Betty	6.	David
7.	Sandra	7.	Jerry
8.	Carolyn	8.	Thomas
9.	Gloria	9.	Richard
10.	Martha	10.	José

1950s

Female	Male
1. Linda	1. James
2. Mary	2. Robert
3. Maria	3. John
4. Patricia	4. David
5. Barbara	5. Michael
6. Deborah	6. William
7. Sandra	7. Charles
8. Brenda	8. Larry
9. Sharon	9. José
10. Carolyn	10. Gary

1960s

Female	Male
1. Mary	1. Michael
2. Susan	2. David
3. Lisa	3. James
4. Karen	4. John
5. Linda	5. Robert
6. Deborah	6. William
7. Kimberly	7. Mark
8. Donna, Patricia	8. Richard
9. Maria, Teresa	9. Jeffrey
10. Cynthia, Michelle	10. Charles, Joseph, Thomas

1970–74

Female	Male
1. Jennifer	1. Michael
2. Michelle	2. John
3. Lisa	3. James
4. Melissa	4. Christopher
5. Kimberly	5. David
6. Christine	6. Robert
7. Amy	7. William
8. Angela	8. Brian
9. Mary	9. Joseph
10. Nicole	10. Jeffrey

1975–79

Female	Male
1. Jennifer	1. Michael
2. Melissa	2. Jason
3. Jessica	3. Christopher
4. Amy	4. David
5. Heather	5. John
6. Christine	6. James
7. Michelle	7. Brian
8. Nicole	8. Matthew
9. Sarah	9. Robert
10. Angela	10. Joseph

1980–84

Female	Male
1. Jennifer	1. Michael
2. Jessica	2. Christopher
3. Amanda	3. Matthew
4. Melissa	4. David
5. Sarah	5. Jason
6. Nicole	6. John
7. Christine	7. James
8. Ashley	8. Joshua
9. Stephanie	9. Robert
10. Heather	10. Daniel

1985–89

Female	Male
1. Jessica	1. Michael
2. Ashley	2. Christopher
3. Amanda	3. Matthew
4. Jennifer	4. Joshua
5. Sarah	5. Daniel
6. Brittany	6. Andrew
7. Nicole	7. David
8. Stephanie	8. James
9. Lauren	9. Joseph
10. Samantha	10. John

The Most Popular Baby Names of 1990

Female		Male	
1. Ashley	26. Alyssa	1. Michael	26. Steven
2. Jessica	27. Laura	2. Christopher	27. Timothy
3. Amanda	28. Hannah	3. Matthew	28. Jordan
4. Brittany	29. Victoria	4. Joshua	29. Cody
5. Sarah	30. Jasmine	5. David	30. Aaron, Alexander
6. Samantha	31. Kimberly	6. Andrew	31. Adam, Brian
7. Stephanie	32. Alexandra	7. James	32. Richard
8. Megan	33. Mary	8. Daniel	33. Stephen
9. Jennifer	34. Sara	9. John	34. Charles
10. Elizabeth	35. Kelsey	10. Justin	35. Patrick
11. Lauren	36. Erin	11. Joseph	36. Jeremy
12. Emily	37. Erica	12. Ryan	37. Benjamin
13. Kayla	38. Kelly	13. Robert	38. Sean
14. Rachel	39. Kristen	14. Nicholas	39. Travis
15. Amber	40. Crystal	15. William	40. Samuel
16. Courtney	41. Amy	16. Brandon	41. Jeffrey
17. Rebecca	42. Taylor	17. Jonathan	42. Mark
18. Christine	43. Andrea, Anna, Maria	18. Zachary	43. José
19. Heather	44. Caitlin, Jordan	19. Jacob	44. Nathan
20. Nicole	45. Allison	20. Anthony	45. Jason
21. Melissa	46. Lindsey	21. Tyler	46. Dustin, Juan
22. Katherine	47. Cassandra	22. Eric	47. Gregory
23. Tiffany	48. Brittney	23. Thomas	48. Jesús
24. Danielle	49. Shelby	24. Kevin	49. Austin
25. Chelsea, Michelle	50. Morgan	25. Kyle	50. Kenneth, Luis

Meanings BROWSER

Some names carry strong associations based on their root or meaning: Sophia for wisdom, Alexander for strength, Amanda for beloved. In this browser names are listed according to meanings, so if you're interested in finding a name that conveys a certain spirit or association, you can look under the heading that most closely approximates it.

The following list shows every heading in this browser. Following each is a series of words and phrases that either describe the heading or are examples of meanings represented by the names under that heading. Some words or phrases may appear under more than one heading, reflecting the different contexts in which they occur.

CHARM: attract, courteous, dancing, delicate, fragrance, grace, graceful, magic, pettable, playful, poetry, smooth, sweet, tender, to tame, yielding

GOD AND RELIGION: biblical, blessed, current religious beliefs or gods, devoted to God, enlightened, heavenly, holy, idol, on the upward path, pilgrim, prophet, source, spirituality, supernatural, true believer, watcher

GRATITUDE: asked-for, borrowed all, gracious, hope, incense, may he expand, praise, praised, prayer, request, reverence, wish, wished-for, words of a prayer

HELP-GIVING: charity, counsel, friend, friendly, generosity, healer, healing, listener, physician, servant, strengthened, teacher, willing

HONOR: above, celebrated, chief, chosen, crown, distinguished, duke, earl, esteem, exalted, fame, famous, fit to be admired, glory, grand, great, greatest, guest, head of the household, hero, honor, king, knight, lady, lord, man of the people, master, mistress of the house, names of kings, noble, one, praiseworthy, preeminence, prince, respect, spoken well of, stature, superior, throne, worthy of reverence

INTELLECT: alert, creativity, dreams, imagination, memory, philosopher, prudent, remember, scholar, seeker, understanding, vision, wisdom

JOY: amusement, bliss, blithe, chosen, delight, fame, fanciful, fortunate, fortune, free, freedom, fulfillment, glory, good fortune, good news, happiness, laughter, liberty, lively, lover of nature, luck, merry, poetry, resurrection, smiling, success, to rejoice, triumph, victory

LIFE: age, ancient, be thou there, breath, destiny, elderly, fate, fertile, fertility, fresh, fruitful, full of life, going, growth, he is so, healthy, honey, hoary, humanity, immortal, lively, living, longevity, mature, new, old, old one, order, propagator, reincarnation, self, somebody, sower, the unknown, times of life, to touch, to dispose, universal, vigor, vivacity, young, young man, youth

LIGHT: better, brightness, brilliance, burning, chaste, chastity, clear, darkness, dawn, day, enlightened, evening, fire, forgiving, good, goodness, maiden, marvelous, modest, night, perfect, pure, purity, radiance, refined, shadow, shining, splendid, splendor, sunny, sunshine, temperance, twilight, virtuous, visible, wonder, wonderful

LOVE: ardent, beloved, companion, desire, devotion, girlfriend, heart, kiss, sweetheart

MUSIC AND SOUNDS: babble, bell, cymbal, harmony, harp player, horn, instruments, loud, messenger, prattle, quiet, sighs, silence, song, speech, stammerer, stuttering, thunder, voice, whisper

PEACE: alone, amiable, blessed, calm, comfort, compassion, consolation, dignity, envy-free, fellowship, finished, forgiveness, gentle, gentleness, gracious, home, hospitable, kind, mercy, mild, obedient, patience, pity, pleasantness, politeness, quiet, redeemed, relieved, resting place, safety, satisfaction, security, settle down, sleep, slumber, smooth, sublime, unity, vindicated, welcome

POWER: able, action, bold, brave, captain of a ship, champion, commanding, conqueror, constancy, courage, defender, disciplinarian, efficient, enduring, expert, fiery, firm, fleetness, great leaper, guard, hard, headstrong, healthy, holding fast, host, independent, industrious, intense, iron, judicious, leader, long-lasting, lord, manly, mighty, moderate, obstinate, of iron, protector, quick, rebel, resistor, resolute, rugged, rule, ruler, runner, self-control, self-disciplined, shield, skill, solid, steadfast, stern, strength, striving, strong, swift, unswaying, valor, vigorous, watchful, will, wrestler

RICHES: add, all, benefits, beyond price, bounty, bronze, dear, diamond, excellent quality, gift, glorious, gold, heir, inheritor of property, jewelry, my fine one, ornament, plenty, possessions, precious, precious and semiprecious stones, prize, rare, talents, treasure, wealth, wealthy

Charm

Akanke (F)
Amoke (F)
Anais (F)
Anna Mary (F)
Annaleisa (F)
Annalisa (F)
Annamarie (F)
Anne-Marie (F)
Anneliese (F)
Annelisa (F)
Annmaria (F)
Annmarie (F)
Arete (F)
Barrie Anne (F)
Beth Ann (F)
Betty Ann (F)
Carissa (F)
Carol Ann (F)
Carrie Ann (F)
Ceridwen (F)
Charis (F)
Charissa (F)
Charisse (F)
Cory Anne (F)
Curcio (M)
Curtis (M)
Dalilah (F)
Damian (M)
Damiano (M)
Damien (M)
Damján (M)
Damon (M)
Delilah (F)
Dema (M)
Dowsabel (F)
Dulcibel (F)
Dulcibella (F)
Dulcie (F)
Dulcinea (F)
Engracia (F)
Eula (F)
Eulalia (F)
Eulalie (F)
Florann (F)
Gayna (F)
Gaynor (F)
Genevra (F)
Genn (F)
Gennifer (F)
Ghādah (F)
Ginevra (F)
Ginnifer (F)
Graca (F)
Grace (F)
Gracia (F)
Graciana (F)
Gracie (F)
Gratia (F)
Grazia (F)
Grazielle (F)
Graziosa (F)
Guinevere (F)
Gyasi (M)
Hye (F)
Ja (M)
Jenelle (F)
Jenn (F)
Jenna (F)
Jennafer (F)
Jennifer (F)
Jenny (F)
Kanda (F)
Kelly-Ann (F)
Kenda (F)
Kerri-Ann (F)
Kerrianne (F)
Kerry-Anne (F)
Laka (F)
Lalita (F)
Lian (F)
Lori Ann (F)
Louann (F)
Luann (F)
Mandisa (F)
Marianne (F)
Mary-Ann (F)
Maryann (F)
Maryanna (F)
Melosa (F)
Mercedes (F)
Mignon (F)
Mignonette (F)
Nat (M)
Natan (M)

Natane (F)
Nate (M)
Nathan (M)
Natty (M)
Orenda (F)
Paulann (F)
Pollyann (F)
Pollyanna (F)
Qiturah (F)
Rae Ann (F)
Ruthanne (F)
Sakari (F)
Sally-Ann (F)
Sarann (F)
Satinka (F)
Selby-Ann (F)
Shani (F)
Suzamni (F)
Wakanda (F)
Wakenda (F)
Winsome (F)
Xiang (F)
Ysanne (F)
Zarifa (F)
Zihna (F)

God and Religion

Abasi (M)
Abbot (M)
Abdalla (M)
Abdelgalil (M)
Abdul (M)
Abdulaziz (M)
Abdullah (M)
Abia (M)
Abiatha (M)
Abiathar (M)
Abiel (M)
Abijah (M)
Adeliza (F)

Aditi (F)
Adlai (M)
Adoette (F)
Adom (M)
Adri (M)
Adriel (M)
Agni (M)
Ahmed (M)
Ahulani (F)
Aingeal (F)
Akeem (M)
Akim (M)
Almiron (M)
Alpha (F)
Alžběta (F)
Amadea (F)
Amadeo (M)
Amado (M)
Amanda-Jane (F)
Amando (M)
Amariah (M)
Amaris (F)
Ambarish (F)
Ambika (F)
Amias (M)
Amiel (M)
Amma (F)
Amos (M)
Amyas (M)
Ana (F)
Anala (F)
Anci (F)
Anděla (F)
Andula (F)
Andulka (F)
Ane (F)
Anela (F)
Anetta (F)
Anette (F)
Anežka (F)
Angel (F)
Angela (F)

Angèle (F)
Angelia (F)
Angelic (F)
Angelica (F)
Angelika (F)
Angeliki (F)
Angelina (F)
Angeline (F)
Angélique (F)
Angelita (F)
Angelo (M)
Angeni (F)
Angie (F)
Anhelina (F)
Ania (F)
Anibal (M)
Anica (F)
Anicka (F)
Anicuta (F)
Anikke (F)
Anikó (F)
Anila (F)
Anita (F)
Anitte (F)
Aniweta (F)
Anja (F)
Anjelica (F)
Anka (F)
Ann (F)
Anna (F)
Annah (F)
Annaleisa (F)
Annalie (F)
Annalisa (F)
Annas (M)
Annchen (F)
Anne (F)
Anneka (F)
Anneli (F)
Anneliese (F)
Annelisa (F)
Anneth (F)
Annetta (F)
Annette (F)
Annie (F)
Annika (F)
Annikki (F)
Annina (F)
Anninka (F)
Annus (F)
Annuska (F)
Annze (F)
Anouska (F)
Ansel (M)
Anselm (M)

Anselma (F)
Ansis (M)
Anuška (F)
Anya (F)
Anyuta (F)
Arel (M)
Areli (M)
Arella (F)
Ariadne (F)
Ariane (F)
Arianna (F)
Arianne (F)
Ariel (F)
Ariella (F)
Arielle (F)
Arkin (M)
Asenka (F)
Asiel (M)
Aska (F)
Assa (F)
Assi (F)
Åsta (F)
Astri (F)
Astrid (F)
Astrud (F)
Astyr (F)
Asya (F)
Atti (F)
Avi (M)
Avidan (M)
Avidor (M)
Aviel (M)
Avniel (M)
Azaria (F)
Azariah (M)
Azriel (M)
Ballabh Das (M)
Banjoko (F)
Barrie Jane (F)
Basia (F)
Bathia (F)
Bathsheba (F)
Bathshua (F)
Batia (F)
Batsheva (F)
Beathag (F)
Bel (F)
Belia (F)
Belica (F)
Belicia (F)
Belita (F)
Bella (F)
Beppi (M)
Bersaba (F)
Bess (F)

Bessie (F)
Běta (F)
Beth (F)
Beth Ann (F)
Bethel (M)
Bethell (M)
Bethia (F)
Bethsabee (F)
Bethsheba (F)
Betina (F)
Bětka (F)
Betsy (F)
Bett (F)
Betta (F)
Bette (F)
Betti (F)
Bettina (F)
Bettine (F)
Betty (F)
Betty Ann (F)
Betty Jo (F)
Betty Lou (F)
Betty Mae (F)
Betty Sue (F)
Betuška (F)
Biddy (F)
Billie Jean (F)
Billy Joe (M)
Bithia (F)
Bobbi-Jo (F)
Bobby Joe (M)
Boski (F)
Bözsi (F)
Bron (M)
Buffa (F)
Cam (F)
Camila (F)
Camilla (F)
Camille (F)
Camillo (M)
Camillus (M)
Cammi (F)
Chabela (F)
Chabi (F)
Chanah (F)
Chavon (F)
Che (M)
Cheche (M)
Chepe (M)
Chepito (M)
Chevon (F)
Chi (M)
Chresta (M)
Chris (M)
Chrisanda (F)

Chrissie (F)
Christa (F)
Christal (F)
Christeen (F)
Christel (F)
Christen (F)
Christian (M)
Christiana (F)
Christiane (F)
Christiann (F)
Christianna (F)
Christianos (M)
Christina (F)
Christine (F)
Christmas (M)
Christofer (M)
Christoff (M)
Christoffer (M)
Christoforus (M)
Christoph (M)
Christophe (M)
Christopher (M)
Christos (M)
Christy (F)
Chrys (F)
Chrystal (F)
Chrystel (F)
Chrystian (M)
Chumin (M)
Chumina (F)
Chuminga (M)
Concetta (F)
Concetto (M)
Connor (M)
Conway (M)
Crestienne (F)
Cristao (M)
Cristian (M)
Cristiano (M)
Cristino (M)
Cristiona (F)
Cristoforo (M)
Cristovão (M)
Cristy (F)
Crystal (F)
Crystek (M)
Crystina (F)
Crystol (F)
Cymon (M)
Dacso (M)
Dan (M)
Danae (F)
Danal (M)
Daneen (F)
Danek (M)

Danetta (F)
Danette (F)
Dani (F)
Dani (M)
Dania (F)
Danica (F)
Danice (F)
Danie (F)
Daniel (M)
Daniela (F)
Daniele (M)
Danielka (F)
Daniell (F)
Daniella (F)
Danielle (F)
Daniels (M)
Danika (F)
Danikla (F)
Danil (M)
Danila (F)
Danilka (F)
Danilo (M)
Danise (F)
Danit (F)
Danita (F)
Danka (F)
Danko (M)
Danne (F)
Danny (M)
Dano (M)
Danukas (M)
Danya (M)
Danya (F)
Danyele (F)
Danyelle (F)
Danylets (M)
Danylo (M)
Dasha (F)
Dayana (F)
Dayne (M)
Deanna (F)
Deanne (F)
Deco (M)
Delsie (F)
Deva (F)
Devaki (F)
Devi (F)
Di (F)
Diana (F)
Diane (F)
Diani (F)
Dina (F)
Dinah (F)
Dode (F)
Dol (F)

Doll (F)
Dolly (F)
Dom (M)
Doma (F)
Dome (M)
Domek (M)
Domenico (M)
Domicio (M)
Dominga (F)
Domingo (M)
Domingos (M)
Domini (F)
Dominic (F)
Dominica (F)
Dominick (M)
Dominik (M)
Dominika (F)
Dominique (M)
Domka (F)
Domó (M)
Domokos (M)
Domonique (F)
Domonkos (M)
Donek (M)
Donna Michelle (F)
Donois (M)
Dora (F)
Doralice (F)
Dorchen (F)
Dore (F)
Dorek (M)
Doretha (F)
Dorette (F)
Dorinda (F)
Dorka (F)
Dorle (F)
Dorlisa (F)
Dorolice (F)
Doron (M)
Dorosia (F)
Dorota (F)
Dorotea (F)
Doroteya (F)
Dorothea (F)
Dorothee (F)
Dorothia (F)
Dorothy (F)
Dorotthea (F)
Dorrit (F)
Dorte (F)
Dosi (F)
Dosya (F)
Dot (F)
Dottie (F)
Dumin (M)
Durva (F)
Dusan (M)
Ean (M)
Eilis (F)
Eiluned (F)
Eion (M)
Elamma (F)
Eleazar (M)
Eleora (F)
Elga (F)
Eli (M)
Elia (M)
Eliana (F)
Elias (M)
Elie (M)
Elihu (M)
Elijah (M)
Elin (F)
Elined (F)
Eliora (F)
Elis (F)
Elisa (F)
Elisabet (F)
Elisabeta (F)
Elisabeth (F)
Elisabetta (F)
Elisavet (F)
Elisavetta (F)
Élise (F)
Elisha (F)
Elisheba (F)
Elisher (M)
Elisheva (F)
Elisie (F)
Elison (M)
Elisveta (F)
Eliza (F)
Elizabete (F)
Elizabeth (F)
Elka (F)
Elkan (M)
Elkanah (M)
Ellama (F)
Ellis (M)
Eloy (M)
Elrad (M)
Elsbet (F)
Elsbeth (F)
Elsbietka (F)
Elschen (F)
Elsi (F)
Elspet (F)
Elspeth (F)
Elspie (F)
Elts (F)
Eluned (F)
Ely (M)
Elya (M)
Elyse (F)
Elyssa (F)
Elza (F)
Elžbieta (F)
Elzunia (F)
Eman (M)
Emanuel (M)
Emanuela (F)
Emek (M)
Gabriella (F)
Gabrielle (F)
Gabrielli (M)
Gabriello (M)
Gabris (M)
Gaby (F)
Gabys (M)
Galya (F)
Ganesa (F)
Ganya (F)
Gavriel (M)
Gavril (M)
Gedeon (M)

Er (M)
Eryl (F)
Estrid (F)
Etti (F)
Ev (M)
Evan (M)
Evans (M)
Ezekiel (M)
Ezraella (F)
Ezrela (F)
Feargus (M)
Fedinka (M)
Fedor (M)
Fedora (F)
Feodor (M)
Feodora (F)
Feodore (M)
Fergus (M)
Fifi (F)
Gab (M)
Gabby (M)
Gabe (M)
Gabko (M)
Gabo (M)
Gábor (M)
Gabriel (M)
Gabriela (F)
Gabriele (M)
Gelya (F)
Geremia (M)
Gerome (M)
Gessica (F)
Gian (M)
Giancarlo (M)
Gianetta (F)
Gianetto (M)
Gianina (F)
Gianna (F)
Giannis (M)
Gideon (M)
Gideone (M)
Gidon (M)
Gillean (M)
Gilleasbuig (M)
Gillespie (M)
Gino (M)
Giosia (M)
Giovanna (F)
Giovanni (M)
Girisa (F)
Giuseppe (M)
Glenda (F)
Glenwys (F)
Glenys (F)
Godfrey (M)
Godwin (M)
Goel (M)
Gurpreet (M)
Gussy (M)
Gustaf (M)
Gustaff (M)
Gustav (M)
Gustava (M)
Gustave (M)
Gustavo (M)
Gustavs (M)
Gustik (M)
Gustus (M)
Gusty (M)
Hadad (M)
Hallewell (M)
Hana (F)
Hanan (M)
Handel (M)
Hanicka (F)
Hanif (M)
Hanka (F)
Hannah (F)
Hanne (F)
Hannele (F)
Hannes (M)
Hanni (F)
Hannu (M)
Hans (M)
Hansel (M)
Hanuš (M)
Hara (F)
Hardeep (M)
Harel (M)
Hari (M)
Harpreet (M)
Haskel (M)
Hedeon (M)
Hedia (F)
Helga (F)
Helliwell (M)
Hezekiah (M)
Hinun (M)
Honza (M)
Hovhannes (M)
Ian (M)
Iancu (M)
Ianos (M)
Iban (M)
Ieuan (M)
Ignac (M)
Ikia (F)
Ilias (M)
Ilja (M)
Ilse (F)
Immanuel (M)
Imran (M)
Ioakim (M)
Ioan (M)
Ioann (M)
Ioanna (F)
Ioannis (M)
Ionel (M)
Iosif (M)
Iosua (M)
Iov (M)
Isa (F)
Isabeau (F)
Isabelita (F)
Isabella (F)
Isabelle (F)
Isaiah (M)
Ishbel (F)
Ishmael (M)
Ismael (M)
Isobel (F)
Israel (M)
Issi (F)
Iva (F)
Ivan (M)
Ivanchik (M)
Ivanka (F)
Ivanna (F)
Ivano (M)
Ivas (M)
Iwan (M)
Iza (F)
Izabel (F)
Izabele (F)
Izabella (F)
Jaan (M)
Jack (M)
Jackie (M)
Jan (M)
Jan (F)
Jana (F)
Janae (F)
Janco (M)
Jancsi (M)
Jane (F)
Janean (F)
Janek (M)
Janella (F)
Janelle (F)
Janene (F)
Janeska (F)
Janessa (F)
Janet (F)
Janeta (F)
Janetta (F)
Janica (F)
Janice (F)
Janie (F)
Janika (M)
Janina (F)
Janine (F)
Janita (F)
Janka (F)
Jankiel (M)
Janna (F)
Janne (M)
Jannetta (F)
Jannine (F)
Jano (M)
János (M)
Jansen (M)
Janson (M)
Jantzen (M)
Jany (F)
Janyte (F)
Janzen (M)
Jas (M)
Jasen (M)
Jasia (F)
Jasio (M)
Jason (M)
Jayna (F)
Jayne (F)
Jaynell (F)
Jaynie (F)
Jayson (M)
Jazeps (M)
Jean (M)
Jean (F)
Jean-François (M)
Jean-Michel (M)
Jean-Phillipe (M)
Jeana (F)
Jeane (F)
Jeanetta (F)
Jeanette (F)
Jeani (F)
Jeanie (F)
Jeanine (F)
Jeanna (F)
Jeanne (F)
Jeannetta (F)
Jeannette (F)
Jeannie (F)
Jeannine (F)
Jeannot (M)
Jed (M)
Jedediah (M)
Jedidiah (M)
Jehan (M)
Jehu (M)

Jena (M)
Jenae (F)
Jenda (M)
Jenet (F)
Jenetta (F)
Jenette (F)
Jenica (F)
Jenine (F)
Jenka (F)
Jenkin (M)
Jenkyn (M)
Jennet (F)
Jennett (F)
Jennetta (F)
Jennette (F)
Jennica (F)
Jennine (F)
Jens (M)
Jensine (F)
Jephtha (M)
Jeramie (M)
Jeramy (M)
Jere (M)
Jereme (M)
Jeremey (M)
Jeremia (M)
Jeremiah (M)
Jeremias (M)
Jeremie (M)
Jeremija (M)
Jeremy (M)
Jerimiah (M)
Jermey (M)
Jerome (M)
Jeromy (M)
Jeron (M)
Jerrome (M)
Jesica (F)
Jess (F)
Jessalyn (F)
Jesse (M)
Jesseca (F)
Jessey (M)
Jessi (F)
Jessica (F)
Jessie (M)
Jessie (F)
Jessika (F)
Jessy (M)
Jesús (M)
Jesusa (F)
Jinni (F)
Jinny (F)
Jo (M)
Jo (F)
Jo Anna (F)
Joab (M)
Joachim (M)
Joah (M)
Joan (F)
Joana (F)
Joani (F)
Joanka (F)
Joann (F)
Joanna (F)
Joannah (F)
Joanne (F)
Joannes (M)
João (M)
Joaquim (M)
Joaquín (M)
Joasia (F)
Jobo (M)
Jock (M)
Jocko (M)
Joe (M)
Joeann (F)
Joeanne (F)
Joel (M)
Joela (F)
Joella (F)
Joëlle (F)
Joellen (F)
Joellyn (F)
Joey (M)
Johan (M)
Johan (F)
Johana (F)
Johanka (F)
Johann (M)
Johanna (F)
Johannes (M)
John (M)
Johnathan (M)
Johnathon (M)
Johnie (M)
Johnna (F)
Johnnie (M)
Johnny (M)
Johnson (M)
Jojo (M)
Jolean (F)
Joleen (F)
Jolene (F)
Jolinda (F)
Joline (F)
Jolyn (F)
Jolynne (F)
Jon (M)
Jonam (M)
Jonathan (M)
Jonathen (M)
Jonathon (M)
Jone (M)
Jonelis (M)
Jonella (F)
Jonelle (F)
Joni (F)
Jonie (F)
Jonna (F)
Jonni (M)
Jonnie (M)
Jonny (M)
Jonothan (M)
Jonothon (M)
Jonukas (M)
Jonutis (M)
Jony (F)
Joosef (M)
Jooseppi (M)
José (M)
Josecito (M)
Josee (F)
Josef (M)
Joseito (M)
Joselito (M)
Joseph (M)
Josepha (F)
Josephe (M)
Josephene (F)
Josephina (F)
Josephine (F)
Josephus (M)
Josette (F)
Josh (M)
Joshua (M)
Joshuah (M)
Josiah (M)
Josie (F)
Josip (M)
Jóska (M)
Josua (M)
Josue (M)
Jotham (M)
Jov (M)
Jovan (M)
Jozhe (M)
Juan (M)
Juana (F)
Juanch (M)
Juancho (M)
Juanita (F)
Juanito (M)
Juda (M)
Judah (M)
Judas (M)
Judd (M)
Jude (M)
Judson (M)
Juhana (M)
Juho (M)
Jukka (M)
Junita (F)
Jupp (M)
Jussi (M)
Jutta (F)
Kachina (F)
Kalechi (M)
Kali (F)
Kalkin (M)
Kaloosh (M)
Kama (F)
Kami (F)
Kamila (F)
Kamilka (F)
Kantu (M)
Kanya (F)
Kapildev (M)
Kasi (F)
Katone (M)
Kaula (F)
Kaveri (F)
Keirstan (F)
Kera (F)
Kerani (F)
Kerby (M)
Kerestel (M)
Kerie (F)
Kersten (F)
Kersti (F)
Kerstie (F)
Kerstine (F)
Kery (F)
Kesava (F)
Kester (M)
Khālid (M)
Khristina (F)
Khristya (F)
Kia (F)
Kiana (F)
Kiersten (F)
Kini (F)
Kirby (M)
Kiritan (M)
Kirk (M)
Kirsta (F)
Kirsteen (F)
Kirsten (F)
Kirsti (F)
Kirstie (F)
Kirstien (F)
Kirstin (F)
Kirstine (F)
Kirston (F)
Kirsty (F)
Kirstyn (F)
Kirton (M)
Kistna (M)
Kistnah (M)
Kit (M)
Kitt (M)
Kona (F)
Kosti (M)
Kris (M)
Krischan (M)
Krishna (M)
Krishnah (M)
Kriska (F)
Kriss (M)
Krissi (F)
Krissie (F)
Krissy (F)
Krist (M)
Krista (F)
Kristal (F)
Kristan (F)
Kristel (F)
Kristen (F)
Krister (M)
Kristi (F)
Kristia (F)
Kristian (M)
Kristie (F)
Kristin (F)
Kristina (F)
Kristine (F)
Kristinka (F)
Kristjan (M)
Kristo (M)
Kristof (M)
Kristofer (M)
Kristoffer (M)
Kristofor (M)
Kristol (F)
Kristoph (M)
Kristopher (M)
Kristos (M)
Krists (M)
Kristy (F)
Kristyn (F)
Krisus (M)
Krys (M)
Krysia (F)
Krysta (F)
Krystal (F)
Krystek (M)
Krystel (F)
Krysten (F)
Krysti (F)
Krystian (M)
Krystin (F)
Krystina (F)
Krystka (F)
Krystle (F)
Krystyna (F)
Krystynka (F)
Kusa (F)
Kwam (M)
Kwanita (F)
Kyrsty (F)
Lal (M)
Lalita (F)
Lanu (M)
Lázaro (M)
Lazarus (M)
Lehua (F)
Leilani (F)
Lemmie (M)
Lemmy (M)
Lemuel (M)
Lemy (M)
Libby (F)
Liesa (F)
Lieschen (F)
Liesel (F)
Liisa (F)
Liisi (F)
Like (M)
Liko (M)
Lilith (F)
Linet (F)
Linetta (F)
Linette (F)
Linnette (F)
Lisa (F)
Lisa-Jane (F)
Lisa-Marie (F)
Lisanne (F)
Lisbete (F)
Lise (F)
Lisel (F)
Lisenka (F)
Liseta (F)
Lisettina (F)
Lissa (F)
Lissette (F)
Lissie (F)
Liszka (F)
Liz (F)
Liza (F)
Lizabeth (F)
Lizanka (F)
Lizanne (F)
Lizbeth (F)
Lizina (F)
Lizka (F)
Lizzy (F)
Lloyd (M)
Lokelani (F)
Lolotea (F)
Lono (M)
Lota (F)
Loyd (M)
Luned (F)
Lusa (F)
Luz (F)
Lynetta (F)
Lynette (F)
Lynnet (F)
Lynnette (F)
Machas (M)
Maco (M)
Maheesa (F)
Mahesa (M)
Mahisa (F)
Makis (M)
Malachi (M)
Malachy (M)
Malcolm (M)

Malcom (M)
Malulani (F)
Mana (F)
Mango (M)
Manny (M)
Mano (M)
Manolón (M)
Manṣūr (M)
Manue (M)
Manuel (M)
Manuela (F)
Manuil (M)
Manuyil (M)
Mat (M)
Mata (M)
Máté (M)
Mateĭ (M)
Matek (M)
Mateo (M)
Mateus (M)
Matfei (M)
Mathe (M)
Mathew (M)
Mathia (M)
Mathias (M)
Mathieu (M)
Matías (M)
Matrika (F)
Matt (M)
Matteo (M)
Matteus (M)
Matthaios (M)
Matthaus (M)
Matthew (M)
Matthia (M)
Matthias (M)
Matthieu (M)
Mattias (M)
Mattie (M)
Mattmias (M)
Matty (M)
Matus (M)
Matvey (M)
Matyas (M)
Maya (F)
Mayfey (M)
Meda (F)
Mehetabel (M)
Mela (F)
Menico (M)
Micael (M)
Micaela (F)
Michael (M)
Michaela (F)
Michaella (F)
Michaelle (F)
Michail (M)
Michak (M)
Michal (M)
Michal (F)
Michala (F)
Michalek (M)
Michau (M)
Micheal (M)
Micheil (M)
Michel (M)
Michel (F)
Michela (F)
Michele (M)
Michele (F)
Michell (F)
Michelle (F)
Micho (M)
Michon (M)
Mick (M)
Mickala (F)
Mickel (M)
Mickey (M)
Micki (F)
Mickie (M)
Micky (M)
Mietek (M)
Miguel (M)
Migui (M)
Mihail (M)
Mihailo (M)
Mihal (M)
Mihalje (M)
Mihály (M)
Mihas (M)
Mihkel (M)
Mika (M)
Mika (F)
Mikael (M)
Mike (M)
Mikel (M)
Mikelis (M)
Mikhail (M)
Mikhalis (M)
Mikhalka (M)
Mikhos (M)
Miki (M)
Mikk (M)
Mikkel (M)
Mikko (M)
Miks (M)
Mikus (M)
Milkins (M)
Milla (F)
Minel (M)
Mingo (M)
Mique (M)
Misa (M)
Mischa (M)
Misha (M)
Mishca (M)
Mishka (M)
Misi (M)
Miska (M)
Misko (M)
Miso (M)
Mitch (M)
Mitchel (M)
Mitchell (M)
Mitchelle (F)
Miya (F)
Mohan (M)
Monica (F)
Monika (F)
Monique (F)
Moria (F)
Moriah (F)
Moriel (F)
Morit (F)
Motka (M)
Motya (M)
Mycala (F)
Myckala (F)
Mykela (F)
Nacia (F)
Nan (F)
Nana (F)
Nance (F)
Nanci (F)
Nancy (F)
Nandin (M)
Nanette (F)
Nani (F)
Nanna (F)
Nannie (F)
Nanny (F)
Narain (M)
Nasia (F)
Nasya (F)
Nata (F)
Natacha (F)
Natal (M)
Natala (F)
Natale (M)
Natalee (F)
Natalia (F)
Natalie (F)
Natalina (F)
Nataline (F)
Natalka (F)
Natalya (F)
Nataniele (M)
Natasa (F)
Natasha (F)
Natashia (F)
Natelie (F)
Natesa (F)
Nathalia (F)
Nathalie (F)
Nathaniel (M)
Nati (F)
Natie (F)
Natka (F)
Natti (F)
Nattie (F)
Neda (F)
Nehemiah (M)
Nelo (M)
Nettchen (F)
Nev (M)
Nevan (M)
Nevin (M)
Nevins (M)
Nika (F)
Nina (F)
Ninacska (F)
Ninetta (F)
Ninette (F)
Ninnetta (F)
Ninnette (F)
Nirel (F)
Nissim (M)
Nita (F)
Niven (M)
Noel (F)
Noela (F)
Noeleen (F)
Noelene (F)
Noeline (F)
Noella (F)
Noëlle (F)
Noleen (F)
Noula (F)

Novella (F)
Nowell (M)
Nur (M)
Nuri (M)
Nuria (F)
Nuriel (F)
Nusi (F)
Nyura (F)
Obadiah (M)
Obe (M)
Obed (M)
Obie (M)
Odelia (F)
Ogun (M)
Ogunkeye (M)
Ogunsanwo (M)
Ogunsheye (M)
Ohannes (M)
Oko (M)
Olga (F)
Olia (F)
Olina (F)
Olisa (F)
Olka (F)
Olli (F)
Olly (F)
Olorun (M)
Olufemi (M)
Olujimi (M)
Olukayode (M)
Olunka (F)
Olushegun (M)
Olushola (M)
Oluska (F)
Olva (F)
Olya (F)
Olyusha (F)
Ona (F)
Orunjan (M)
Osbern (M)
Osbert (M)
Osbon (M)
Osborn (M)
Osborne (M)
Osbourn (M)
Osburn (M)
Oscar (M)
Osgood (M)
Osip (M)
Osman (M)
Osmand (M)
Osmanek (M)
Osmen (M)
Osmond (M)
Osmund (M)
Osmundo (M)
Oswald (M)
Oswall (M)
Oswell (M)
Oswin (M)
Oswold (M)
Osya (M)
Oz (M)
Ozzi (M)
Ozzie (M)
Ozzy (M)
Palmer (M)
Pepa (M)
Pepe (M)
Pepik (M)
Pepillo (M)
Pepin (M)
Pepita (F)
Pepito (M)
Peppe (M)
Peppo (M)
Pilan (M)
Pillan (M)
Pinga (F)
Pino (M)
Pipo (M)
Pollyam (F)
Prescot (M)
Prescott (M)
Priestley (M)
Priestly (M)
Prior (M)
Pry (M)
Pryor (M)
Pualani (F)
Puni (F)
Quiana (F)
Quianna (F)
Rabbi (M)
Rafael (M)
Rafaela (F)
Rafi (M)
Raiden (M)
Raini (M)
Raphael (M)
Raphaela (F)
Ratri (F)
Ravi (M)
Rayhan (M)
Reva (F)
Riḍa (F)
Riel (M)
Risto (M)
Rohin (M)
Romeo (M)
Roselani (F)
Rudra (F)
Saba (F)
Sachar (M)
Sacharja (M)
Sadhana (F)
Saint (F)
Sakari (M)
Sakarias (M)
Sakarja (M)
Salvador (M)
Salvatore (M)
Sam (M)
Samanntha (F)
Samantha (F)
Samara (F)
Samaria (F)
Samarie (F)
Samarthur (F)
Samaru (M)
Sameh (F)
Samein (M)
Samella (F)
Samentha (F)
Samie (M)
Samko (M)
Sammel (M)
Sammi (F)
Sammie (M)
Sammy (M)
Samo (M)
Samouel (M)
Samu (M)
Samuel (M)
Samuela (F)
Samuele (M)
Samuelis (M)
Samuella (F)
Samuil (M)
Samvel (M)
Sancha (F)
Sanchia (F)
Sancia (F)

Sandeep (F)
Santana (F)
Santiago (M)
Santo (M)
Sara-jane (F)
Sarah-Jane (F)
Sarah-jayne (F)
Sarngin (M)
Sarojin (M)
Saul (M)
Saura (F)
Schmuel (M)
Sean (M)
Seann (M)
Sedna (F)
Sef (M)
Seif (M)
Selah (M)
Selma (F)
Sem (M)
Sema (F)
Semon (M)
Seonaid (F)
Sepp (M)
Seth (M)
Shadrach (M)
Shadrack (M)
Shaine (M)
Shan (F)
Shana (F)
Shanae (F)
Shanan (F)
Shanay (F)
Shandi (F)
Shandra (F)
Shane (M)
Shann (F)
Shanna (F)
Shannah (F)
Shannan (F)
Shannen (F)
Shannie (F)
Shannon (F)
Shanon (F)
Shaul (M)
Shaun (M)
Shauna (F)
Shaunda (F)
Shaune (F)
Shauneen (F)
Shaunette (F)
Shaunna (F)
Shavon (F)
Shavone (F)
Shavonne (F)
Shawn (M)
Shawna (F)
Shawnda (F)
Shawnee (F)
Shawni (F)
Shawnna (F)
Shayn (M)
Shayne (M)
Sheba (F)
Sheena (F)
Sheenagh (F)
Sheenah (F)
Shem (M)
Shemuel (M)
Shena (F)
Sheona (F)
Shervan (F)
Shevon (F)
Shevonne (F)
Shimon (M)
Shiona (F)
Shivohn (F)
Shivon (F)
Shmuel (M)
Shona (F)
Shonagh (F)
Shonah (F)
Shone (F)
Shuna (F)
Shyvonia (F)
Siân (F)
Sim (M)
Simao (M)
Simeon (M)
Simion (M)
Simm (M)
Simmina (F)
Simms (M)
Simmy (M)
Simon (M)
Simona (F)
Simone (F)
Simonia (F)
Simonne (F)
Sina (F)
Sinah (F)
Sinead (F)
Sinjon (M)
Sinjun (M)
Siobahn (F)
Sioban (F)
Siobhan (F)
Siobhian (F)
Siôn (M)
Siva (M)
Somhairle (M)
St. John (M)
Stina (F)
Stine (F)
Stoffel (M)
Sundeep (M)
Surya (F)
Symantha (F)
Symon (M)
Tabo (M)
Takia (F)
Tasha (F)
Tashia (F)
Tashina (F)
Tashka (F)
Tavo (M)
Ted (M)
Tedd (M)
Teddie (M)
Teddy (M)
Tedik (M)
Teena (F)
Tena (F)
Teodomiro (M)
Teodor (M)
Teodora (F)
Teodorek (M)
Teodoro (M)
Teodus (M)
Teos (M)
Tesia (F)
Tetty (F)
Tewdor (M)
Thea (F)
Theadora (F)
Thekla (F)
Theo (M)
Theodor (M)
Theodora (F)
Theodore (M)
Theodosia (F)
Theophila (F)
Theophilus (M)
Tiernan (F)
Tierney (F)
Tifani (F)
Tiff (F)
Tiffaney (F)
Tiffani (F)
Tiffanie (F)
Tiffany (F)
Tiffiney (F)
Tiffini (F)
Tiffiny (F)
Tiffney (F)
Tiffy (F)
Tim (M)
Tima (M)
Timaula (F)
Timi (F)
Timie (F)
Timka (M)
Timkin (M)
Timmi (F)
Timmie (M)
Timmothy (M)
Timmy (M)
Timo (M)
Timofei (M)
Timofey (M)
Timok (M)
Timon (M)
Timót (M)
Timotei (M)
Timoteo (M)
Timoteus (M)
Timothea (F)
Timothee (M)
Timotheos (M)
Timotheus (M)
Timothey (M)
Timothy (M)
Tina (F)
Tinah (F)
Tine (F)
Tiomoid (M)
Tisha (M)
Tishka (M)
Tivadar (M)
Tobal (M)
Tobalito (M)
Tobey (M)
Tobi (F)
Tobias (M)
Tobie (M)
Toby (M)
Todor (M)
Todos (M)
Tolek (M)
Tudor (M)
Tull (M)
Tulley (M)
Tullie (M)
Tully (M)
Tulsidas (M)
Tuyen (F)
Tymek (M)
Tymon (M)
Tyna (F)
Uma (F)
Urena (F)
Uri (M)
Uria (M)
Uriah (M)
Urias (M)
Urie (M)
Uriel (M)
Urina (F)
Uzziah (M)
Uzziel (M)
Vanek (M)
Vanka (M)
Vanya (M)
Vasin (M)
Veda (F)
Veta (F)
Wazir (M)
Wellington (M)
Winefred (F)
Winefride (F)
Winefriede (F)
Winiefrida (F)
Winifred (F)
Winifreda (F)
Winifrede (F)
Winifrid (F)
Winifride (F)
Winifryde (F)
Winn (F)
Winnafred (F)
Winnefred (F)
Winnie (F)
Winniefred (F)
Winnifred (F)
Winnifrid (F)
Wunand (M)
Wynifred (F)
Yadin (M)
Yael (F)
Yanka (M)
Yannis (M)
Yechezkel (M)
Yehoshua (M)
Yehuda (M)
Yehudi (M)
Yelisabeta (F)
Yelizaveta (F)
Yeremey (M)
Yerik (M)
Yeska (M)
Yesya (M)
Yiannis (M)
Yisrael (M)
Yochanan (M)
Yonatan (M)
Yosef (M)
Yosif (M)
Yousef (M)
Yov (M)
Ysabel (F)
Ysanne (F)
Yusef (M)
Yusif (M)
Yusuf (M)
Yusup (M)
Yuzef (M)
Zacariah (M)
Zacarias (M)
Zacceus (M)
Zacchaeus (M)
Zaccheus (M)
Zach (M)
Zacharia (M)
Zachariah (M)
Zacharias (M)
Zacharie (M)
Zachary (M)
Zachery (M)
Zack (M)
Zackary (M)
Zackery (M)
Zakaria (M)
Zakhar (M)
Zako (M)

Zakris (M)
Zamiel (M)
Zane (M)
Zanna (F)
Zannz (F)
Zechariah (M)
Zedekiah (M)
Zeke (M)
Zelma (F)
Zeusef (M)
Zizi (F)
Zsanett (F)

Gratitude

Abebi (F)
Abeni (F)
Adia (F)
Ahmed (M)
Amāl (M)
Amara (F)
Annas (M)
Ansis (M)
Arabella (F)
Atira (F)
Bede (M)
Chavon (F)
Chevon (F)
Dusya (F)
Ean (M)
Eion (M)
Esperance (F)
Esperanza (F)
Ev (M)
Evan (M)
Evans (M)
Gian (M)
Gianetta (F)
Gianetto (M)
Gianina (F)
Gianna (F)
Giannis (M)
Gino (M)
Giovanna (F)
Giovanni (M)
Giulia (F)
Hamdrem (M)
Hamdun (M)
Hamid (M)
Hammad (M)
Hanan (M)
Hannes (M)
Hannu (M)
Hans (M)
Hansel (M)
Hanuš (M)

Honza (M)
Hope (F)
Hovhannes (M)
Humayd (M)
Ian (M)
Iancu (M)
Ianos (M)
Iban (M)
Ieuan (M)
Ignac (M)
Ioan (M)
Ioann (M)
Ioanna (F)
Ioannis (M)
Ionel (M)
Ioudith (F)
Iva (F)
Ivan (M)
Ivanchik (M)
Ivanka (F)
Ivanna (F)
Ivano (M)
Ivas (M)
Iwan (M)
Jack (M)
Jackie (M)
Jan (M)
Jan (F)
Jana (F)
Janae (F)
Janco (M)
Jancsi (M)
Jane (F)
Janean (F)
Janek (M)
Janella (F)
Janelle (F)
Janene (F)
Janeska (F)
Janessa (F)
Janet (F)
Janeta (F)
Janetta (F)
Janica (F)
Janice (F)
Janie (F)
Janika (M)
Janina (F)
Janine (F)
Janita (F)
Janka (F)
Jankiel (M)
Janna (F)
Janne (M)
Jannetta (F)
Jannine (F)
Jano (M)
János (M)
Janson (M)
Jany (F)
Japheth (M)
Jas (M)
Jasia (F)
Jasio (M)
Jayna (F)
Jaynell (F)
Jean (M)
Jean (F)
Jeane (F)
Jeanetta (F)
Jeanette (F)
Jeanna (F)
Jeanne (F)
Jeannie (F)
Jeannine (F)
Jeannot (M)
Jena (M)
Jenda (M)
Jenet (F)
Jenette (F)
Jenica (F)
Jenka (F)
Jenkin (M)
Jenkyn (M)
Jennett (F)
Jennetta (F)
Jennica (F)
Jens (M)
Jensine (F)
Jessie (F)
Jinni (F)
Jitka (F)
Joab (M)
Joan (F)
Joani (F)
Joanka (F)
Joanna (F)
Joanne (F)
Joannes (M)
João (M)
Joasia (F)
Jock (M)
Jocko (M)
Jodie (F)
Johan (M)
Johan (F)
Johana (F)
Johanka (F)
Johann (M)
Johanna (F)
John (M)
Johnie (M)
Johnnie (M)
Johnny (M)
Johnson (M)
Jonam (M)
Jone (M)
Jonelis (M)
Jonella (F)
Jonelle (F)
Joni (F)
Jonie (F)
Jonna (F)
Jonnie (M)
Jonny (M)
Jonukas (M)
Jonutis (M)
Jovan (M)
Juan (M)
Juana (F)
Juanch (M)
Juancho (M)
Juanita (F)
Juanito (M)
Juci (F)
Jucika (F)
Judah (M)
Judas (M)
Judd (M)
Jude (M)
Judit (F)
Judita (F)
Judite (F)
Judith (F)
Judithe (F)
Judson (M)
Judy (F)
Juhana (M)
Juho (M)
Jukka (M)
Junita (F)
Jussi (M)
Jutka (F)
Jutta (F)
Kalechi (M)
Kei (F)
Keturah (F)
Kini (F)
Kwam (M)
Kwanita (F)
Levona (F)
Livona (F)
Macia (F)
Maḥmūd (M)
Mahomet (M)
Maija (F)
Maijii (F)
Maikki (F)
Mair (F)
Maire (F)
Mairi (F)
Mairona (F)
Mairwen (F)
Malia (F)
Mally (F)
Mame (F)
Mamie (F)
Manette (F)
Mani (F)
Manka (F)
Manon (F)
Manya (F)
Mara (F)
Marca (F)
Marcsa (F)
Mare (F)
Maren (F)
Marenka (F)
Maretta (F)
Marette (F)
Mari (F)
María (F)
Mariae (F)
Mariam (F)
Mariana (F)
Maricara (F)
Marice (F)
Maridel (F)
Marie (F)
Mariel (F)
Mariela (F)
Mariella (F)
Marielle (F)
Marienka (F)
Marietta (F)
Mariette (F)
Marija (F)
Marika (F)
Marilee (F)
Marilyn (F)
Marinda (F)
Marinka (F)
Marion (F)
Mariquita (F)
Marisa (F)
Marise (F)
Marisha (F)
Mariska (F)
Marita (F)
Mariya (F)
Mariyah (F)
Marja (F)
Maroula (F)
Maruca (F)
Maruja (F)
Maruska (F)
Mary (F)
Maryam (F)
Marye (F)
Maryla (F)
Maryna (F)
Masha (F)
Mashenka (F)
Mashka (F)
Maura (F)
Maureen (F)
Meri (F)
Meryem (F)
Mhairie (F)
Mia (F)
Mimi (F)
Miram (F)
Miri (F)
Miriain (F)
Miriam (F)
Miriama (F)
Mirjam (F)
Mirrian (F)
Mitzi (F)
Mohammed (M)
Moira (F)
Moll (F)
Molly (F)
Morena (F)
Moya (F)
Moyra (F)
Muire (F)
Nada (F)
Nadena (F)
Nadenka (F)
Nadia (F)
Nadina (F)
Nadine (F)
Nadja (F)
Nadka (F)
Nata (F)
Nissim (M)
Odelia (F)
Ohannes (M)
Pepi (M)
Pepin (M)
Poll (F)
Polley (F)
Rance (M)
Rancel (M)
Roula (F)
Saul (M)
Sean (M)
Seonaid (F)
Shaine (M)
Shan (F)
Shana (F)
Shanae (F)
Shandi (F)
Shandra (F)
Shane (M)
Shaul (M)
Shaun (M)
Shauna (F)
Shaunda (F)
Shauneen (F)
Shaunette (F)
Shavonne (F)
Shawn (M)
Shawnee (F)
Shayn (M)
Shea (M)
Sheena (F)
Shelah (F)
Sheona (F)
Shervan (F)
Shevon (F)
Shiona (F)
Shivohn (F)
Shona (F)
Shonah (F)
Shone (F)
Shuna (F)
Shyvonia (F)
Siân (F)
Sina (F)
Sinead (F)
Siobhan (F)
Siobhian (F)
Siôn (M)
Umay (F)
Vanek (M)
Vanka (M)
Vanya (M)
Yachne (F)
Yanka (M)
Yehuda (M)
Yehudi (M)
Yehudit (F)
Yiannis (M)
Yochanan (M)
Yudif (F)
Yudita (F)
Zane (M)
Zanna (F)
Zannz (F)
Zsanett (F)

Help-giving

Aaron (M)
Abiatha (M)
Abiathar (M)
Adom (M)
Ailwyn (M)
Albin (M)
Albreda (F)
Alden (M)
Aldred (M)
Aldreda (F)
Aldwyn (M)
Alf (M)
Alfie (M)
Alfred (M)
Alfreda (F)
Alfredo (M)
Aloin (M)
Althea (F)
Aluin (M)
Aluino (M)
Alured (M)
Alvedine (F)
Alvena (F)
Alverdine (F)
Alvie (F)
Alvin (M)
Alvine (F)

Alvino (M)
Alwin (M)
Alwyna (F)
Alwynne (F)
Amica (F)
Amice (F)
Amico (M)
Amicus (M)
Amissa (F)
Aranne (M)
Arek (M)
Aronek (M)
Aronos (M)
Aubary (M)
Aubree (F)
Aubrey (M)
Avery (M)
Azaria (F)
Azariah (M)
Azriel (M)
Bail (M)
Bailey (M)
Baldwin (M)
Bea (F)
Beathag (F)
Beatrice (F)
Beatriks (F)
Beatrisa (F)
Beatrise (F)
Beatrix (F)
Beatriz (F)
Beattie (F)
Bebe (F)
Bello (M)
Berger (M)
Bertín (M)
Berwin (M)
Blaza (F)
Blazena (F)
Bud (M)
Buddy (M)
Cam (F)
Camila (F)
Camilla (F)
Camille (F)
Camillo (M)
Camillus (M)
Cammi (F)
Carita (F)
Cater (M)
Charity (F)
Cherelle (F)
Cherilyn (F)
Cherry (F)
Cheryl (F)
Cherylene (F)
Chi (M)
Comfort (F)
Con (M)
Conn (M)
Conni (M)
Conny (M)
Conrad (M)
Conrade (M)
Conrado (M)
Cort (M)
Curt (M)
Dabir (M)
Dafydd (M)
Darwin (M)
Dave (M)
Daveed (M)
Daveen (F)
Davelle (F)
Davena (F)
Davi (M)
David (M)
Davida (F)
Davide (M)
Davidek (M)
Davon (M)
Davy (M)
Dawid (M)
Dawūd (M)
Delvin (M)
Devene (F)
Dewi (M)
Divina (F)
Divinia (F)
Dodya (M)
Dovidas (M)
Dowid (M)
Dumaka (M)
Ebbaneza (M)
Eben (M)
Ebenezer (M)
Edwin (M)
Edwina (F)
Elan (M)
Eldred (M)
Eldreda (F)
Eldridge (M)
Eleazar (M)
Elvie (F)
Elvin (M)
Elvina (F)
Elwin (M)
Elwina (F)
Erwin (M)
Erwinek (M)

Esdras (M)
Esra (M)
Ethelwin (M)
Ethelwyn (M)
Ethelwyne (M)
Ethelwynne (M)
Ezekiel (M)
Ezera (M)
Ezra (M)
Fāḍil (M)
Friend (M)
Friendship (M)
Galen (M)
Galena (F)
Galeno (M)
Gildero (M)
Gilday (M)
Gildrey (M)
Gildroy (M)
Gillean (M)
Gilroy (M)
Godwin (M)
Halil (M)
Harun (M)
Haskel (M)
Hildred (F)
Hiroshi (M)
Ikia (F)
Inek (M)
Irwin (M)
Isaiah (M)
Ithel (M)
Kadin (M)
Kalil (M)
Kamila (F)
Kamilka (F)
Kareem (M)
Khalīl (M)
Konni (M)
Konrad (M)
Kurt (M)
Ladd (M)
Laddy (M)
Lancelot (M)
Launce (M)
Launclet (M)
Lázaro (M)
Lazarus (M)
Lewin (M)
Luister (M)
Maldwyn (M)
Mander (M)
Manṣūr (M)
Miles (M)
Milessa (F)
Mileta (F)
Milla (F)
Milo (M)
Monica (F)
Monika (F)
Monique (F)
Moria (F)
Moriel (F)
Morit (F)
Myer (M)
Myers (M)
Mylie (F)
Mylinda (F)
Nediva (F)
Netis (M)
Nitis (M)
Obadiah (M)
Obed (M)
Obie (M)
Ogunsanwo (M)
Ophelia (F)
Oswin (M)
Padget (M)
Page (F)
Paget (M)
Paige (F)
Radmilla (F)
Radolphus (M)
Rafael (M)
Rafaela (F)
Rafi (M)
Raimondo (M)
Raimund (M)
Raimunde (F)
Raimundo (M)
Rajmund (M)
Ralph (M)
Ralphie (M)
Ralphina (F)
Ralphine (F)
Ramón (M)
Ramona (F)
Ranald (M)
Raoul (M)
Raoule (F)
Raphael (M)
Raphaela (F)
Raúl (M)
Ray (M)
Raymond (M)
Raymonde (F)
Redmond (M)
Reg (M)
Reginald (M)
Reimond (M)
Reinold (M)
Renaldo (M)
Renauld (M)
Renault (M)
Reynold (M)
Rinaldo (M)
Ron (M)
Ronald (M)
Ronna (F)
Ronnette (F)
Ronney (M)
Ronni (M)
Ronnie (M)
Ronny (M)
Serg (M)
Serge (M)
Sergei (M)
Sergey (M)
Sergeyka (M)
Sergie (M)
Sergio (M)
Sergius (M)
Sergiusz (M)
Sergo (M)
Sergunya (M)
Serhiy (M)
Serhiyko (M)
Serzh (M)
Sewek (M)
Sherilyn (F)
Sherryll (F)
Spence (M)
Spencer (M)
Steward (M)
Stuart (M)
Syarhey (M)
Tabib (M)
Ticha (F)
Tris (F)
Trissie (F)
Trissina (F)
Trixie (F)
Veda (F)
Vida (M)
Vidette (F)
Warren (M)
Wichado (M)
Winfred (M)
Wingi (M)
Winthrop (M)
Yadid (M)
Yechezkel (M)

Honor

Abimelech (M)
Ada (F)
Adal (M)
Adalheid (F)
Adaline (F)
Adar (M)
Adda (F)
Addie (F)
Adél (M)
Adela (F)
Adelaida (F)
Adelaide (F)
Adelbert (M)
Adele (F)
Adelia (F)
Adelicia (F)
Adelina (F)
Adeline (F)
Adelita (F)
Adeliya (F)
Adeliza (F)
Adelka (F)
Adella (F)
Adelle (F)
ʿĀdil (M)
Adir (M)
Admiral (M)
Adolph (M)
Adolphus (M)
Aenea (F)
Aeneas (M)
Aethelthryth (F)
Agusta (F)
Agustín (M)
Agustus (F)
Ailis (F)
Akela (F)
Alaric (M)
Albert (M)
Alberta (F)
Albertik (M)
Albertina (F)
Albertine (F)
Alberto (M)
Alberts (M)
Albertyna (F)
Albie (M)
Albrecht (M)
Alby (M)
Alea (F)
Aleah (F)
Aleesha (F)
Aletha (F)
Aley (F)
Ali (M)
Ali (F)
Alia (F)
Alica (F)
Alice (F)
Alicia (F)
Alida (F)
Alika (F)
Alike (F)
Alina (F)
Aline (F)
Alis (F)
Alisa (F)
Alisanne (F)
Alise (F)
Alissa (F)
Alita (F)
Alix (F)
Aliz (F)
Alizka (F)
Allison (F)
Allsun (F)
Almira (F)
Alpheus (M)
Alroy (M)
Alverta (F)
Alvertos (M)
Alys (F)
Alysanne (F)
Alyshia (F)
Alysoun (F)

Amir (M)
Amit (M)
Amor (M)
Amory (M)
Aneirin (M)
Anevay (F)
Arch (M)
Archaimbaud (M)
Archambault (M)
Archibald (M)
Archibaldo (M)
Archie (M)
Aren (M)
Arkin (M)
Art (M)
Artair (M)
Artek (M)
Artheia (F)
Arthelia (F)
Arthene (F)
Arthur (M)
Arthuretta (F)
Arthurina (F)
Arthurine (F)
Artie (M)
Artina (F)
Artis (F)
Artis (M)
Artlette (F)
Arto (M)
Artrice (F)
Artur (M)
Arturo (M)
Arvid (M)
Atara (F)
Ataret (F)
Athanasios (M)
Athelstan (M)
Atrice (F)
Atur (M)
Auberon (M)
Aubert (M)

Audey (F)
Audra (F)
Audreen (F)
Audrey (F)
Audria (F)
August (M)
Augusta (F)
Augustia (F)
Augustin (M)
Augustina (F)
Augustine (M)
Augustus (M)
Austen (M)
Aylmer (M)
Bale (M)
Baron (M)
Bas (M)
Basil (M)
Basile (M)
Basilia (F)
Basilie (F)
Basilio (M)
Basilios (M)
Basilius (M)
Basle (M)
Bazek (M)
Bazel (M)
Bazil (M)
Beatham (M)
Bela (M)
Ben (M)
Beniamin (M)
Beniamino (M)
Benja (M)
Benjamin (M)
Benjamon (M)
Benjy (M)
Benna (F)
Bennie (M)
Benny (M)
Beno (M)
Benzi (M)

Bertín (M)
Bertina (F)
Bertine (F)
Berto (M)
Bibi (F)
Bob (M)
Bobbette (F)
Bobbi (F)
Bobby (M)
Bobek (M)
Bobina (F)
Brencis (M)
Cachi (M)
Candace (F)
Candy (F)
Captain (M)
Case (M)
Casey (M)
Cashi (M)
Casimir (M)
Casimiro (M)
Castimer (M)
Chalmer (M)
Chalmers (M)
Charita (F)
Chencho (M)
Chev (M)
Chevalier (M)
Chevi (M)
Chevy (M)
Cirillo (M)
Cirilo (M)
Ciro (M)
Colonel (M)
Coman (M)
Corydon (M)
Coryell (M)
Cuthbert (M)
Cy (M)
Cyril (M)
Cyrus (M)
Daga (F)
Daggi (F)
Dagmar (F)
Dagmara (F)
Dai (F)
Damita (F)
Dasa (F)
Dela (F)
Della (F)
Delle (F)
Delroy (M)
Der (M)
Derek (M)
Derrie (M)

Dirk (M)
Dob (M)
Dolphus (M)
Donna (F)
Donna Maria (F)
Donna Marie (F)
Donna Michelle (F)
Dragomira (F)
Duke (M)
Earl (M)
Earlene (F)
Earlina (F)
Earlinda (F)
Edeline (F)
Effam (F)
Effie (F)
Ela (F)
Elbert (M)
Elberta (F)
Elbertina (F)
Elbertine (F)
Elbie (F)
Elese (F)
Elica (F)
Elice (F)
Elicia (F)
Eliska (F)
Elita (F)
Elke (F)
Ellice (F)
Ellie (F)
Elmer (M)
Elroy (M)
Elsa (F)
Else (F)
Elsie (F)
Elza (F)
Eneas (M)
Eppie (F)
Esma (M)
Esme (M)
Esmee (F)
Estéban (M)
Estevao (M)
Ethel (F)
Ethelbert (M)
Ethelberta (F)
Etheldreda (F)
Ethelena (F)
Ethelind (F)
Ethelinde (F)
Etheline (F)
Ethelle (F)
Ethelwin (M)

Ethelwyn (M)
Ethelwyne (M)
Ethelwynne (M)
Ethylinda (F)
Étienne (M)
Euphan (F)
Euphemia (F)
Eyota (M)
Fayola (F)
Feargus (M)
Fergus (M)
Freja (F)
Freya (F)
Gab (M)
Gabby (M)
Gabe (M)
Gabko (M)
Gabo (M)
Gábor (M)
Gabriel (M)
Gabriela (F)
Gabriele (M)
Gabriella (F)
Gabrielle (F)
Gabrielli (M)
Gabriello (M)
Gabris (M)
Gaby (F)
Gabys (M)
Gavriel (M)
Gavrii (M)
Geremia (M)
Gia (F)
Gibor (M)
Gomer (M)
Grady (M)
Gus (M)
Gusta (F)
Gwynfa (F)
Gwynfor (M)
Haakon (M)
Hako (M)
Heidi (F)
Hieu (M)
Hilmar (M)
Hopkin (M)
Howell (M)
Humbert (M)
Humberto (M)
Hypatia (F)
Ichabod (M)
Idris (M)
Idwal (M)
Ingemar (M)
Iola (F)

Iolo (M)
Iorwerth (M)
Isas (M)
Isti (M)
István (M)
Ithel (M)
Jalīla (F)
Jeramie (M)
Jeramy (M)
Jere (M)
Jeremia (M)
Jeremiah (M)
Jeremias (M)
Jeremija (M)
Jeremy (M)
Jerimiah (M)
Jermey (M)
Jethro (M)
Kacey (M)
Kaci (F)
Kandace (F)
Kandi (F)
Kareem (M)
Kasey (M)
Kasie (F)
Kasimir (M)
Katone (M)
Kaulana (F)
Kaycee (F)
Kayin (M)
Kazek (M)
Kazik (M)
Kazimir (M)
Kazio (M)
Kázmér (M)
Kelii (M)
Kendrick (M)
Kenrick (M)
Kentigern (M)
Keon (M)
Kerem (M)
Kerrick (M)
Kimball (M)
Kimi (F)
Kimiko (F)
Kimiyo (F)
Kingston (M)
Kinston (M)
Kir (M)
Kira (F)
Kiral (M)
Kiril (M)
Kiritan (M)
Kiryl (M)
Korudon (M)

Kyra (F)
Labhras (M)
Labhruinn (M)
Labrencis (M)
Labrentsis (M)
Lady (F)
Lando (M)
Lanty (M)
Laris (M)
Larka (M)
Larry (M)
Lars (M)
Larya (M)
Laurence (M)
Laurencio (M)
Laurens (M)
Laurent (M)
Laurentia (F)
Laurice (F)
Lauricia (F)
Laurie (F)
Laurina (F)
Lauris (M)
Lauritz (M)
Laurus (M)
Lavr (M)
Lavrik (M)
Lavro (M)
Lawrance (M)
Lawrence (M)
Lawrie (M)
Lencho (M)
Lenci (M)
Leroy (M)
Licha (F)
Lici (F)
Loe (M)
Loránd (M)
Lóránt (M)
Lord (M)
Lorence (M)
Lorens (M)
Lorenz (M)
Lorenza (F)
Lorenzo (M)
Loretto (M)
Lorin (M)
Lorinc (M)
Loris (F)
Louann (F)
Louella (F)
Lourenco (M)
Luann (F)
Luther (M)
Magnus (M)

Maheesa (F)
Mahesa (M)
Mahisa (F)
Maita (F)
Malik (M)
Malka (F)
Manco (M)
Manius (M)
Mansa (M)
Maranda (F)
Marcia (F)
Marta (F)
Martha (F)
Marthe (F)
Marthena (F)
Marticka (F)
Martina (F)
Martus (F)
Martuska (F)
Marv (M)
Marvin (M)
Marvine (M)
Masia (F)
Mehtar (M)
Melicent (F)
Meliscent (F)
Mellicent (F)
Mellisent (F)
Melvern (M)
Meredith (F)
Merfin (M)
Meridith (F)
Merri (F)
Merrill (M)
Milley (F)
Millicent (F)
Milliestone (F)
Mincho (M)
Miranda (F)
Mona (F)
Morag (F)
Morgan (M)
Morganetta (F)
Morganne (F)
Moyna (F)
Mustapha (M)
Nabīl (M)
Nagid (M)
Nagida (F)
Najīb (M)
Nediva (F)
Nerys (F)
Noble (M)
Nolan (M)
Norbert (M)
Nye (M)
Oberon (M)
Ogunkeye (M)
Ogunsheye (M)
Ohin (M)
Oleda (F)
Oleta (F)
Olo (M)
Ordando (M)
Orla (F)
Orlagh (F)
Orland (M)
Orlando (M)
Orlo (M)
Osten (M)
Owain (M)
Owen (M)
Owena (F)
Paddy (M)
Padraic (M)
Padruig (M)
Panya (F)
Pat (M)
Patek (M)
Patrice (M)
Patricia (F)
Patricio (M)
Patricius (M)
Patrick (M)
Patrizia (F)
Patrizio (M)
Patrizius (M)
Patsy (F)
Pattey (F)
Patti (F)
Pharoah (M)
Phemie (F)
Pol (M)
Prin (F)
Prince (M)
Princess (F)
Queen (F)

Queena (F)
Queenation (F)
Queeneste (F)
Queenette (F)
Queenie (F)
Rab (M)
Raby (M)
Rae Louis (F)
Rafi (M)
Raina (F)
Raine (F)
Rane (F)
Rani (F)
Raulas (M)
Raulo (M)
Rawnie (F)
Reggi (F)
Reggie (F)
Regina (F)
Regine (F)
Reginna (F)
Reina (F)
Reine (F)
Reinette (F)
Renia (F)
Renzo (M)
Rex (M)
Rey (M)
Rhonda (F)
Riel (M)
Riobard (M)
Roald (M)
Rob (M)
Roba (F)
Robbi (M)
Robbie (F)
Robby (M)
Rober (M)
Robers (M)
Robert (M)
Roberta (F)
Robertina (F)
Roberto (M)
Roberts (M)
Robi (M)
Robin (M)
Robin (F)
Robina (F)
Robinet (M)
Robinette (F)
Robinia (F)
Robyn (F)
Roddy (M)
Roderich (M)
Roderick (M)
Rodge (M)
Rodman (M)
Rodrigo (M)
Rodrique (M)
Rog (M)
Rogelio (M)
Roger (M)
Rogerio (M)
Rogerios (M)
Roi (M)
Roland (M)
Rolande (F)
Rolando (M)
Roldán (M)
Rolek (M)
Rolla (M)
Rolle (M)
Rollie (M)
Rollins (M)
Rollo (M)
Rolly (M)
Rolon (M)
Rosertas (M)
Rowe (M)
Royal (M)
Royalyn (F)
Royce (M)
Rubert (M)
Ruberto (M)
Rüdiger (M)
Rudland (M)
Ruggerio (M)
Ruland (M)
Rupert (M)
Ruperta (F)
Ruperto (M)
Ruprecht (M)
Rurich (M)
Rurik (M)
Rutger (M)
Ruy (M)
Ryan (M)
Ryne (M)
Sadella (F)
Sadie (F)
Sahale (M)
Saida (F)
Sakima (M)
Salcia (F)
Sally (F)
Sally-Ann (F)
Sarah (F)
Sarah-Jane (F)
Sarai (F)
Sarann (F)
Sarauniya (F)
Sarena (F)
Sarene (F)
Saretta (F)
Sarette (F)
Sari (F)
Sarika (F)
Sarita (F)
Saritia (F)
Sarka (F)
Sarolta (F)
Sarotte (F)
Sarra (F)
Sasa (F)
Sharai (F)
Sir (M)
Siti (F)
Squire (M)
Stamatios (F)
Stamos (M)
Starling (F)
Stavros (M)
Stef (M)
Stefa (F)
Stefan (M)
Stefania (F)
Stefanie (F)
Stefano (M)
Stefans (M)
Stefcia (F)
Steffel (M)
Steffi (F)
Stefka (F)
Stefos (M)
Stenya (M)
Stepa (F)
Stepan (M)
Stepania (F)
Stepanida (F)
Stepanie (F)
Stepanya (M)
Stepanyda (F)
Steph (M)
Stepha (F)
Stephan (M)
Stephana (F)
Stéphane (M)
Stéphanie (F)
Stephanine (F)
Stephanos (M)
Stephanus (M)
Stephen (M)
Stephena (F)
Stephene (F)
Stepka (M)
Stesha (F)
Steshka (F)
Steve (M)
Stevena (F)
Stevens (M)
Stevenson (M)
Stevi (F)
Stevie (M)
Stevy (M)
Sultan (M)
Taka (F)
Takoohi (F)
Tana (F)
Tania (F)
Tanis (F)
Tanka (F)
Tapani (M)
Tarnia (F)
Tata (F)
Tatiana (F)
Tatiānus (M)
Tatius (M)
Tawnya (F)
Tazio (M)
Teb (M)
Teppo (M)
Thanos (M)
Thema (F)
Theodoric (M)
Tiara (F)
Ticho (M)
Tiennot (M)
Tierra (F)
Tino (M)
Tor (M)
Torin (M)
Tricia (F)
Trish (F)
Turi (M)
Tuska (F)
Tusya (F)
Tyee (M)
Ulbrecht (M)
Ulric (M)
Ulrica (F)
Ulrich (M)
Uner (M)
Unique (F)
Unita (F)
Unity (F)
Valda (F)
Vasil (M)
Vasile (M)
Vasilek (M)
Vasili (M)
Vasilios (M)
Vasilis (M)
Vasily (M)
Vasin (M)
Vazul (M)
Velda (F)
Wemilo (M)
Willimar (M)
Winema (F)
Wylmer (M)
Xenos (M)
Yaella (F)
Yardan (M)
Yeremey (M)
Yerik (M)
Yorath (M)
Zahira (F)
Zaidee (F)
Zaira (F)
Zara (F)
Zaria (F)
Zarita (F)
Zebulon (M)
Zimraan (M)
Zimri (M)

Intellect

Ahkeel (M)
Aisling (F)
Aislinn (F)
Akeel (M)
Akil (M)
Akilah (F)
Akio (M)
Akira (M)
Aldric (M)
Aldrich (M)
Aldridge (M)
Alim (M)
Aloysius (M)
Alvis (M)
Ambarish (F)

Areef (M)
Arif (M)
Ashling (F)
Ashlyn (F)
Ashlynn (F)
Audric (M)
Basir (M)
Batini (F)
Berdy (M)
Billy Ray (M)
Bina (F)
Bobby Ray (M)
Cassidy (F)
Cato (M)
Catón (M)
Channing (M)
Chanoch (M)
Chofa (F)
Chofi (F)
Darda (F)
Eloisa (F)
Eloise (F)
Eloisia (F)
Elric (M)
Enoch (M)
Ganesa (F)
Ḥakīm (M)
Hardeep (M)
Héloïse (F)
Hew (M)
Hobart (M)
Hubbard (M)
Hube (M)
Huber (M)
Hubert (M)
Hubertek (M)
Huberto (M)
Hubi (M)
Hudson (M)
Huey (M)
Hugh (M)
Hughes (M)
Hughie (M)
Hughina (F)
Hugo (M)
Hutchinson (M)
Huw (M)
Kaliq (M)
Kalpana (F)
Kassidy (F)
Kaya (F)
Manasseh (M)
Maya (F)
Mendel (M)
Michiko (F)
Minda (F)
Minerva (F)
Minivera (F)
Miwa (F)
Miwako (F)
Oma (F)
Omar (M)
Onawa (F)
Oona (F)
Oonagh (F)
Oonie (F)
Ophelia (F)
Pandita (F)
Parzival (M)
Peni (F)
Perceval (M)
Percival (M)
Peredur (M)
Phineas (M)
Pru (F)
Prudence (F)
Prue (F)
Quinn (M)
Rabbi (M)
Sachar (M)
Sacharja (M)
Sakari (M)
Sakarias (M)
Sakarja (M)
Schuyler (M)
Shanahan (M)
Silence (F)
Sill (M)
Skye (F)
Skylar (M)
Sofi (F)
Sofia (F)
Soficita (F)
Sofka (F)
Sofya (F)
Sonja (F)
Sophia (F)
Sophie (F)
Sophoon (F)
Sophy (F)
Sunya (F)
Tab (M)
Tace (F)
Tacey (F)
Talib (M)
Thanh (F)
Tin (M)
Tomo (F)
Una (F)
Vadin (M)
Veda (F)
Wilbert (M)
Wisdom (F)
Yarin (M)
Zacarias (M)
Zacchaeus (M)
Zach (M)
Zacharia (M)
Zachariah (M)
Zacharias (M)
Zacharie (M)
Zachary (M)
Zack (M)
Zakaria (M)
Zakhar (M)
Zako (M)
Zakris (M)
Zechariah (M)
Zeke (M)
Zeki (M)
Zocha (F)
Zofia (F)
Zofie (F)
Žofka (F)
Zosha (F)

Joy

Abagail (F)
Abagil (F)
Abby (F)
Abigail (F)
Abigal (F)
Abigel (F)
Abigil (F)
Aditi (F)
Ahanu (M)
Aida (F)
Aizik (M)
Ajay (M)
Aleeza (F)
Alitza (F)
Aliya (F)
Aliza (F)
Allegra (F)
Anand (M)
Ananda (F)
Anastace (F)
Anastacia (F)
Anastacie (F)
Anastasia (F)
Anastasie (F)
Anastatia (F)
Anastazia (F)
Anastice (F)
Anisha (F)
Anissa (F)
Annice (F)
Annis (F)
Anstice (F)
Asher (M)
Ayoka (F)
Azad (M)
Barika (F)
Basimah (F)
Bea (F)
Beatrice (F)
Beatriks (F)
Beatrisa (F)
Beatrise (F)
Beatrix (F)
Beatriz (F)
Beattie (F)
Bebe (F)
Berenice (F)
Berenike (F)
Bernice (F)
Bilal (M)
Blaza (F)
Blazena (F)
Blythe (F)
Bobby Lee (M)
Bobby Ray (M)
Bódog (M)
Boniface (M)
Bow (M)
Bowen (M)
Bowie (M)
Broňa (F)
Cai (M)
Cailean (M)
Cailin (F)
Caio (M)
Caius (M)
Cappi (M)
Caprice (F)
Car (M)
Carney (M)
Caw (M)
Chance (M)
Charmian (F)
Claus (M)
Cola (M)
Colan (M)
Colar (M)
Cole (M)
Colena (F)
Coletta (F)
Colin (M)
Colina (F)
Collett (F)
Colletta (F)
Collette (F)
Collins (M)
Cosette (F)
Coulson (M)
Delice (F)
Delicia (F)
Delisa (F)
Delise (F)
Delys (F)
Delysia (F)
Deroit (F)
Deror (M)
Derora (F)
Derori (M)
Derorice (F)
Ditzah (F)
Diza (F)
Edena (F)
Edna (F)
Eleutherios (M)
Elza (F)
Estanislao (F)
Eunice (F)
Evadne (F)
Evangeline (F)
Faizah (F)
Fath (M)
Faustina (F)
Fayola (F)
Fela (F)
Felcia (F)
Felica (F)
Felice (F)
Felicia (F)
Felicity (F)
Feliks (M)
Felix (M)
Felka (F)
Felo (M)
Fortuna (F)
Fortunatus (M)
Fortune (F)
Free (M)
Freedom (M)
Freeman (M)
Gada (F)
Gail (F)
Gaila (F)
Gaius (M)
Gay (F)
Gaye (F)
Gaylord (M)
Geela (F)
Gilada (F)
Gleda (F)
Gloria (F)
Gloris (F)
Glory (F)
Gwynedd (F)
Gwyneth (F)
Gwynneth (F)
Hagia (F)
Hagice (F)
Hagit (F)
Halona (F)
Happy (F)
Hasin (M)
Hephsibah (F)
Hephzabah (F)
Hephzibah (F)
Hephzibeth (F)
Hepsey (F)
Hepsie (F)
Hepsy (F)
Hepzabah (F)
Hepzibah (F)
Hilarie (F)
Hilary (F)
Hilery (F)
Hillary (F)
Hillery (F)
Hrodohaidis (F)
Icek (M)
Ike (M)
Ikey (M)
Isaac (M)
Isak (M)
Izak (M)
Jephtha (M)
Joi (F)
Joie (F)
Joy (F)
Joya (F)
Joyce (F)
Joycelyn (F)
Kanoa (F)
Kantu (M)
Karney (M)
Kavindra (F)
Kearney (M)
Kei (F)
Kichi (F)
Kistna (M)
Klaus (M)
Kola (M)
Kolya (M)
Krishna (M)
Laetitia (F)
Lal (M)
Lao (M)
Lara (F)
Larisa (F)
Larissa (F)
Larochka (F)
Laticia (F)
Leda (F)
Ledah (F)
Leeta (F)
Leta (F)
Letitia (F)
Letizia (F)
Lettice (F)
Lettitia (F)
Letty (F)
Letycia (F)
Liberty (F)
Lucky (F)
Mab (F)
Machi (F)
Maimun (M)
Marni (F)
Marnin (M)
Masʿud (M)
Mazal (F)
Mestipen (M)
Micu (M)
Miki (M)
Mikolai (M)

Milek (M)
Minnehaha (F)
Mohan (M)
Naomi (F)
Naomia (F)
Nasser (M)
Nassor (M)
Nastasya (F)
Nastka (F)
Nastusya (F)
Nicanor (M)
Nichol (F)
Nicholas (M)
Nicholyn (F)
Nick (M)
Nicki (F)
Nicky (M)
Nicodemus (M)
Nicol (M)
Nicola (F)

Nicola (M)
Nicolaas (M)
Nicolai (M)
Nicolás (M)
Nicolau (M)
Nicolaus (M)
Nicole (F)
Nicoletta (F)
Nicolette (F)
Nicoli (F)
Nicolina (F)
Nicoline (F)
Nicolo (M)
Niels (M)
Niki (M)
Nikita (M)
Nikita (F)
Nikky (M)
Niklas (M)
Niklavs (M)
Niklos (M)
Nikola (F)
Nikolai (M)
Nikolais (M)
Nikolaos (M)
Nikolas (M)
Nikolia (F)
Nikolos (M)
Nikos (M)
Nikula (M)
Nikulas (M)
Nils (M)
Numa (M)
Nykola (F)
Olukayode (M)
Olushegun (M)
Osen (F)
Phylicia (F)
Pias (M)
Pitin (M)
Pito (M)
Pleasance (F)
Pleasant (F)
Pramod (M)
Radman (M)
Raku (F)
Ranice (F)
Ranit (F)
Ranita (F)
Ranon (M)
Risa (F)
Ronel (M)
Roni (M)
Ronia (F)
Ronice (F)
Ronit (F)
Ronli (F)
Sachi (F)
Sagar (M)
Sa'īd (M)
Seifert (M)
Seifried (M)
Seth (M)
Seward (M)
Shani (F)
Shing (M)
Siegfried (M)
Siegmund (M)
Siffre (M)
Sig (M)
Sigefriedo (M)
Sigfrid (M)
Sigfrido (M)
Sigfroi (M)
Sigifredo (M)
Sigismund (M)
Sigmund (M)
Signe (F)
Sigrid (F)
Siguefredo (M)
Sigurd (M)
Sigvard (M)
Siurt (M)
Slavik (M)
Stacia (F)
Stacy (F)
Stana (M)
Stando (M)
Stane (M)
Stanislao (M)
Stanislas (M)
Stanislau (M)
Stanislaus (M)
Stanislav (M)
Stanisław (M)
Stanisława (F)
Stano (M)
Stas (M)
Stasa (F)
Stashko (M)
Stasiek (M)
Stasio (M)
Staska (M)
Staska (F)
Stasya (F)
Sudi (M)
Surata (F)
Syed (M)
Szigfrid (M)
Tait (M)
Tanix (M)
Tano (M)
Tasenka (F)
Tasia (F)
Taska (F)
Tasya (F)
Tate (M)
Tatum (F)
Ticha (F)
Tilo (M)
Tish (F)
Tisha (F)
Tivon (M)
Tivona (F)
Tris (F)
Trissie (F)
Trissina (F)
Trixie (F)
Ulani (F)
Unice (F)
Vic (M)
Vicki (F)
Victoir (M)
Victoire (F)
Victor (M)
Victoria (F)
Victoriana (F)
Victorina (F)
Victorine (F)
Victorino (M)
Victorio (M)
Victory (F)
Vidor (M)
Vika (F)
Viktor (M)
Viktoria (F)
Viktorie (F)
Viktorka (F)
Vinod (M)
Visolela (F)
Vitenka (M)
Vitin (M)
Vitka (M)
Vito (M)
Vitor (M)
Vitoria (F)
Vittore (M)
Vittoria (F)
Vittorio (M)
Vitya (M)
Wapi (M)
Wiktor (M)
Wisia (F)
Witek (M)
Wuliton (M)
Yachi (F)
Yachiko (F)
Yachiyo (F)
Yitzchak (M)
Yovela (F)
Zada (F)
Zafina (F)
Zahreh (F)
Zaida (F)
Zigfrid (M)
Zigfrids (M)
Zygfryd (M)
Zygi (M)

Life

Abel (M)
Aesha (F)
Afon (M)
Afonya (M)
Agusta (F)
Agustín (M)
Agustus (F)
Aiesha (F)
Aisha (F)
Aisia (F)
Alda (F)
Aldo (M)
Aldous (M)
Aldred (M)
Aldreda (F)
Aldwyn (M)
Amar (M)
Ambrose (M)
Ambrosina (F)
Ambrosine (F)
Anda (F)
Arius (M)
Arno (M)
Asha (F)
Ashia (F)
Atanazy (M)
Atek (M)
Atman (M)
August (M)
Augusta (F)
Augustia (F)
Augustín (M)
Augustina (F)
Augustine (M)
Augustus (M)
Austen (M)
Ava (F)
Aveen (F)
Avel (M)
Aviv (M)
Aviva (F)
Awan (M)
Ayasha (F)
Ayesha (F)
Ayshea (F)
Azi (M)
Baka (F)
Burr (M)
Buster (M)
Cahil (M)
Cenón (M)
Chaim (M)
Chaimek (M)
Chava (F)
Chaya (F)
Chizu (F)
Chizuko (F)
Chloe (F)
Cilla (F)
Cocheta (F)
Cosimo (M)
Cosmo (M)
Delano (M)
Delsin (M)
Delsy (M)
Destiny (F)
Earnest (M)
Ebba (F)
Eldred (M)
Eldreda (F)
Eldridge (M)
Emrys (M)
Enid (F)
Ephraim (M)
Erna (F)
Ernest (M)
Ernestina (F)
Ernestine (F)
Ernestino (M)
Ernesto (M)
Ernie (M)
Eustace (M)
Eustacia (F)
Eva (F)
Evaine (F)
Evangelia (F)
Evangelina (F)
Evathia (F)
Evchen (F)
Eve (F)
Evi (F)
Evička (F)
Evie (F)
Evike (F)
Evita (F)
Evka (F)
Evuška (F)
Evy (F)
Ewa (F)
Ewan (M)
Ewen (M)
Floyd (M)
Fonya (M)
Geraint (M)
Ghādah (F)
Gus (M)
Gusta (F)
Hayyim (M)
Hebe (F)
Helki (F)
Hogan (M)
Hyam (M)
Hyman (M)
Ida (F)
Idalia (F)
Idalina (F)
Idaline (F)
Ide (F)
Idella (F)
Idelle (F)
Idette (F)
Iduska (F)
Ieasha (F)
Ieashia (F)
Iesha (F)
In (F)
Irma (F)
Ita (F)
Itka (F)
Iwilla (F)
Jibben (M)
Jibon (F)
Jivin (M)
Junior (M)
Kahil (M)
Kaija (F)
Kameko (F)
Karma (F)
Kasib (M)
Kedem (M)
Keenan (M)
Kerel (M)
Khaim (M)
Kishi (F)
Kismet (F)
Kokudza (M)
Leben (M)
Lissilma (F)
Litsa (F)
Masago (F)
Mazal (F)
Mel (M)
Merab (F)
Merripen (M)
Navin (M)
Neto (M)
Nnamdi (M)

Nova (F)
Nutan (F)
Opanas (M)
Osten (M)
Panas (M)
Priscilla (F)
Priss (F)
Prissy (F)
Qadim (M)
Renata (F)
Renātus (M)
Rene (M)
Renée (F)
Renelle (F)
Renita (F)
Rennie (F)
Senón (M)
Shanan (F)
Shann (F)
Shannah (F)
Shannan (F)
Shannie (F)
Shannon (F)
Shanon (F)
Shawni (F)
Sholto (M)
Sven (M)
Svend (M)
Tanas (M)
Tanek (M)
Tansy (F)
Thetis (F)
Tilden (M)
Tino (M)
Vian (M)
Vica (F)
Vikas (M)
Vitalis (M)
Viv (F)
Viva (F)
Vivia (F)
Vivian (F)
Viviana (F)
Vivie (F)
Vivien (F)
Vyvian (M)
Vyvyan (M)
Yaḥya (M)
Yamka (F)
Yeva (F)
Yevka (F)
Yiesha (F)
Young (M)
Zeno (M)
Zēnōn (M)
Zera (F)
Zewek (M)
Zinon (M)
Ziv (M)
Ziven (M)
Zoe (F)
Zoltán (M)
Zowie (M)

Light

Abna (M)
Abner (M)
Acar (M)
Adelbert (M)
Aden (M)
Adin (M)
'Afa'f (F)
Ag (F)
Aga (F)
Agafia (F)
Agasha (F)
Agata (F)
Agatha (F)
Agathe (F)
Agathi (F)
Agatka (F)
Aggie (F)
Agi (F)
Agna (F)
Agne (F)
Agnella (F)
Agnes (F)
Agnesa (F)
Agnesca (F)
Agnese (F)
Agnesina (F)
Agneska (F)
Agnessa (F)
Agneta (F)
Agneti (F)
Agnetta (F)
Agnies (F)
Agnieszka (F)
Agniya (F)
Agnola (F)
Ágota (F)
Agotha (F)
Agueda (F)
Aibhlin (F)
Aidan (M)
Aila (F)
Aileen (F)
Aili (F)
Ailie (F)
Ailinn (F)
Aithne (F)
Alaula (F)
Albert (M)
Alberta (F)
Albertik (M)
Albertina (F)
Albertine (F)
Alberto (M)
Alberts (M)
Albertyna (F)
Albie (M)
Albrecht (M)
Alby (M)
Ale (F)
Aleen (F)
Aleena (F)
Aleene (F)
Alena (F)
Alene (F)
Alenka (F)
Aliute (F)
Alohi (F)
Alohilani (F)
Aludra (F)
Alva (F)
Alvah (F)
Alverta (F)
Alvertos (M)
Amandeep (M)
Anala (F)
Aneska (F)
Anesse (F)
Anice (F)
Anis (F)
Annes (F)
Anwar (M)
Areta (F)
Aretha (F)
Arethi (F)
Aretta (F)
Arette (F)
Aristotle (M)
Arpiar (M)
Asia (F)
Atka (F)
Aubert (M)
Aurea (F)
Aurora (F)
Aurore (F)
Avner (M)
Balder (M)
Barnett (M)
Barta (F)
Bartha (F)
Baudier (M)
Behira (F)
Bela (M)
Berdy (M)
Berta (F)
Bertha (F)
Berthold (M)
Berti (M)
Bertina (F)
Bertine (F)
Berto (M)
Bertram (M)
Bertrand (M)
Berty (M)
Betula (F)
Birt (M)
Bob (M)
Bobbette (F)
Bobbi (F)
Bobby (M)
Bobek (M)
Bobina (F)
Bonnie (F)
Breana (F)
Breann (F)
Brian (M)
Briano (M)
Brie (F)
Brieanne (F)
Bryant (M)
Bunni (F)
Caitlin (F)
Caitlon (F)
Caitria (F)
Caitrin (F)
Caitriona (F)
Caren (F)
Carey (M)
Carina (F)
Cassi (F)
Catalina (F)
Catant (F)
Catarina (F)
Catarine (F)
Cateline (F)
Caterina (F)
Catharina (F)
Cathe (F)
Cathelina (F)
Catherina (F)
Catherine (F)
Catherleen (F)
Cathleen (F)
Cathy (F)
Catlin (M)
Catrin (F)
Catrina (F)
Catrine (F)
Catriona (F)
Cayla (F)
Caylee (F)
Chasity (F)
Chassidy (F)
Chastity (F)
Chhaya (F)
Chiara (F)
Claire (F)
Clairette (F)
Clairine (F)
Clara (F)
Clarence (M)
Clareta (F)
Clarey (F)
Claribel (F)
Clarice (F)
Clarina (F)
Clarinda (F)
Claris (F)
Clarisa (F)
Clarissa (F)
Clarisse (F)
Clarita (F)
Cora (F)
Coralee (F)
Coralie (F)
Corella (F)
Corene (F)
Coretta (F)
Corette (F)
Corin (F)
Corina (F)
Corinna (F)
Corinne (F)
Corissa (F)
Correen (F)
Corrina (F)
Corrinna (F)
Cuthbert (M)
Davin (M)
Dawn (F)
Dawna (F)
Dawnetta (F)
Dawnielle (F)
Dawnysia (F)
Dayton (M)
De (M)
Delbert (M)
Delia (F)
Delya (F)
Dewei (M)
Dob (M)
Dobry (M)
Dudee (F)
Edan (M)
Egan (M)
Egbert (M)
Eibhlin (F)
Eileen (F)
Eiley (F)
Eilidh (F)
Eily (F)
Eithne (F)
Elah (M)
Elaina (F)
Elaine (F)
Elana (F)
Elbert (M)
Elberta (F)
Elbertina (F)
Elbertine (F)
Elbie (F)
Eleana (F)
Eleanor (F)
Elena (F)
Elene (F)
Eleni (F)
Elenitsa (F)
Elenka (F)
Elenora (F)
Eleora (F)
Elina (F)
Ellen (F)
Elli (F)
Ellie (F)
Elliner (F)
Elnora (F)
Elon (F)
Ena (F)
Engelbert (M)
Ethelbert (M)
Ethelberta (F)
Ethna (F)
Ethne (F)
Ethnea (F)
Fordel (M)
Galina (F)
Galinka (F)
Galka (F)
Galya (F)
Gasha (F)
Gashka (F)
Gilbert (M)
Gilberta (F)
Gilberto (M)
Gita (F)
Glenda (F)
Gwenda (F)
Haidee (F)
Halina (F)
Hasina (F)
Haydn (M)
Hela (F)
Helaku (M)
Hele (F)
Helen (F)
Helena (F)
Helene (F)
Helenka (F)
Helenor (F)
Hellenor (F)
Helli (F)
Heluska (F)
Herbert (M)
Heriberto (M)
Heulwen (F)
Ho (M)
Hobart (M)
Hod (M)
Hopkin (M)
Hubbard (M)
Hube (M)
Huber (M)
Hubert (M)
Hubertek (M)
Huberto (M)
Hubi (M)
Huey (M)

Ila (F)
Ilena (F)
Ilene (F)
Iliana (F)
Ilka (F)
Ilona (F)
Ilonka (F)
Iluska (F)
Imogen (F)
Imogene (F)
Ina (F)
Incencio (M)
Inés (F)
Inesita (F)
Inessa (F)
Inglebert (M)
Inocente (M)
Iram (M)
Jaga (F)
Jaspal (M)
Jaspreet (F)
Jelena (F)
Jezebel (F)
Joela (F)
Joellen (F)
Junella (F)
Jyoti (F)
Kaarina (F)
Kady (F)
Kaitlin (F)
Kajsa (F)
Kalama (F)
Kaleenda (F)
Kalinda (F)
Kamāl (M)
Kāmil (M)
Kamila (F)
Kanya (F)
Kara (F)
Karen (F)
Karena (F)
Karida (F)
Karina (F)
Karine (F)
Karyn (F)
Karyna (F)
Kasia (F)
Kasienka (F)
Kasin (F)
Kaska (F)
Kassia (F)
Kata (F)
Katarina (F)
Katchen (F)
Kate (F)

Katenka (F)
Kateřina (F)
Katerini (F)
Katerinka (F)
Katharaine (F)
Katharina (F)
Katheline (F)
Kathereen (F)
Katherina (F)
Katherine (F)
Katheryn (F)
Katheryne (F)
Kathleen (F)
Kathlyn (F)
Kathrene (F)
Kathy (F)
Kati (F)
Katia (F)
Katica (F)
Katie (F)
Katina (F)
Katinka (F)
Katka (F)
Katla (F)
Katleen (F)
Katlin (F)
Kató (F)
Katoka (F)
Katrin (F)
Katrina (F)
Katrine (F)
Katriona (F)
Katryna (F)
Kattrina (F)
Katus (F)
Katuska (F)
Katya (F)
Kay (F)
Kayla (F)
Keahi (M)
Keegan (M)
Ken (M)
Kenaz (M)

Kenenza (F)
Kenia (F)
Kenna (F)
Kenneth (M)
Kennice (F)
Kennie (M)
Kenny (M)
Kenya (M)
Kenza (F)
Kesha (M)
Kibbe (M)
Kiska (F)
Kitteen (F)
Kitty (F)
Klara (F)
Klarika (F)
Klarissa (F)
Kofryna (F)
Kolina (F)
Konane (M)
Kora (F)
Koreen (F)
Koren (F)
Kori (F)
Korina (F)
Kotinka (F)
Laine (F)
Lambard (M)
Lambert (M)
Lavina (F)
Laviner (F)
Lavinia (F)
Lavinie (F)
Leanora (F)
Leanore (F)
Leena (F)
Leila (F)
Leilia (F)
Leka (F)
Lela (F)
Lelya (F)
Lena (F)
Lenci (F)

Lene (F)
Lenka (F)
Lenni (F)
Lenor (F)
Lenora (F)
Lenorah (F)
Lenore (F)
Leonor (F)
Leonora (F)
Leonore (F)
Leor (M)
Leora (F)
Levener (F)
Levenia (F)
Liang (M)
Liene (F)
Lila (F)
Lili (F)
Liolya (F)
Lovenah (F)
Loveviner (F)
Luce (F)
Lucetta (F)
Lucette (F)
Lucia (F)
Lucian (M)
Luciana (F)
Luciano (M)
Lucida (F)
Lucie (F)
Lucien (M)
Lucienne (F)
Lucija (F)
Lucika (F)
Lucila (F)
Lucilla (F)
Lucille (F)
Lucina (F)
Lucinda (F)
Lucine (F)
Lucio (M)
Lucita (F)
Lucius (M)
Lucka (F)
Lucy (F)
Lucya (F)
Lugia (F)
Lusita (F)
Luz (F)
Luzi (F)
Luzija (F)
Manchu (M)
Manipi (M)
Meir (M)
Meira (F)

Meliora (F)
Mellear (F)
Melyor (F)
Menora (F)
Merial (F)
Merilyn (F)
Meriol (F)
Merrilee (F)
Merrill (M)
Meryl (F)
Mirabel (F)
Mirabella (F)
Modesta (F)
Modestina (F)
Modestine (F)
Modestus (F)
Modesty (F)
Morgan (M)
Morganetta (F)
Morganne (F)
Morwenna (F)
Muriel (F)
Necha (F)
Necho (F)
Nell (F)
Nella (F)
Nellie (F)
Nelya (F)
Nesa (F)
Nesho (F)
Ness (F)
Nessa (F)
Nessi (F)
Nessia (F)
Nessie (F)
Nest (F)
Nesta (F)
Neysa (F)
Neza (F)
Nitsa (F)
Noga (F)
Nolcha (F)
Nora (F)
Norazah (F)
Noreen (F)
Noreena (F)
Norhaneza (F)
Norlaili (F)
Normah (F)
Noura (F)
Nur (M)
Nuri (M)
Nuria (F)
Nuriel (F)
Nuru (M)

Nyusha (F)
Okon (M)
Olena (F)
Olenko (F)
Onella (F)
Ora (F)
Oralee (F)
Oralia (F)
Orelda (F)
Orelle (F)
Oriana (F)
Orion (M)
Orit (F)
Orlann (F)
Orlene (F)
Orli (F)
Orlice (F)
Osbert (M)
Osgood (M)
Oz (M)
Ozzy (M)
Parthenia (F)
Parthina (F)
Parthine (F)
Pathania (F)
Pathena (F)
Peke (F)
Pheba (F)
Phobe (F)
Phoebe (F)
Phoeboe (F)
Rab (M)
Raby (M)
Ratri (F)
Rhian (F)
Riobard (M)
Rob (M)
Roba (F)
Robbi (M)
Robbie (F)
Robby (M)
Rober (M)
Robers (M)
Robert (M)
Roberta (F)
Robertina (F)
Roberto (M)
Roberts (M)
Robi (M)
Robin (M)
Robin (F)
Robina (F)
Robinet (M)
Robinette (F)
Robinia (F)

Robyn (F)
Rosamond (F)
Rosamund (F)
Rosertas (M)
Roxana (F)
Roxane (F)
Roxanna (F)
Roxanne (F)
Roxianne (F)
Roxy (F)
Rubert (M)
Ruberto (M)
Rupert (M)
Ruperta (F)
Ruperto (M)
Ruprecht (M)
Sada (F)
Sakti (F)
Ṣāliḥ (M)
Sanā (F)
Sandeep (F)
Sayo (F)
Sebert (M)
Senga (F)
Shatara (F)
Shera (F)
Sherburne (M)
Shina (F)
Shizu (F)
Shizuka (F)
Shizuko (F)
Shizuyo (F)
Sook (F)
Sorcha (F)
Sue Ellen (F)
Sumi (F)
Sundeep (M)
Sunshine (F)
Tab (M)
Ṭāhir (M)
Taliesin (M)
Tasarla (F)
Tayib (M)
Thanh (F)
Thi (F)
Thorbert (M)
Tobi (F)
Tobias (M)
Tobie (M)
Tobit (F)
Tov (M)
Tovah (F)
Tovi (M)
Trina (F)
Trinchen (F)

Trine (F)
Trinita (F)
Trinnette (F)
Twyla (F)
Urena (F)
Uri (M)
Uriah (M)
Urias (M)
Uriel (M)
Vinia (F)
Vinnie (F)
Winne (F)
Wybert (M)
Wyn (F)
Yekaterina (F)
Yelena (F)
Ynesita (F)
Ynez (F)
Yoi (F)
Zahira (F)
Zaki (M)
Zakia (F)
Zhen (F)
Zilah (F)
Zillah (F)

Love

Adeana (F)
Adina (F)
Adine (F)
Ahava (F)
Ahouva (F)
Ahuda (F)
Alma (F)
Aloha (F)
Amabel (F)
Amada (F)
Amadea (F)
Amadeo (M)
Amadika (F)
Amado (M)
Amand (M)
Amanda (F)
Amanda-Jane (F)
Amandine (F)
Amando (M)
Amata (F)
Amato (M)
Ami (F)
Amia (F)
Amias (M)
Amica (F)
Amice (F)
Amico (M)
Amicus (M)
Amie (F)
Amorous (M)
Amy (F)
Amyas (M)
Anabela (F)
Anabella (F)
Angharad (F)
Annabella (F)
Annabelle (F)
Annaple (F)
Cakusola (F)
Calida (F)
Cam (M)
Cara (F)
Caractacus (M)
Caradog (M)
Caron (F)
Carron (F)
Carrone (F)
Cartage (M)
Carthach (M)
Carthage (M)
Carys (F)
Ceri (F)
Cerri (F)
Cerrie (F)
Cerys (F)
Cher (F)
Chereen (F)
Chérie (F)
Cherish (F)
Chika (F)
Chikako (F)
Choomia (F)
Connor (M)
Cordelia (F)
Cordula (F)
Dafydd (M)
Dalilah (F)
Darla (F)
Darlene (F)
Darwin (M)
Daudi (M)
Dave (M)
Daveed (M)
Daveen (F)
Davelle (F)
Davena (F)
Davi (M)
David (M)
Davida (F)
Davide (M)
Davidek (M)
Davon (M)
Davy (M)
Dawid (M)
Dawūd (M)
Deedee (M)
Delilah (F)
Delpha (F)
Delphe (F)
Delphia (F)
Demeter (M)
Demetre (M)
Demetria (F)
Demetrio (M)
Demetrius (M)
Devene (F)
Dewi (M)
Didi (F)
Dima (M)
Dimitr (M)
Dimitri (M)
Dimitrios (M)
Dimos (M)
Divina (F)
Divinia (F)
Dmitrik (M)
Doda (F)
Dodie (F)
Dodya (M)
Domotor (M)
Dovidas (M)
Dowid (M)
Duscha (F)
Dymek (M)
Dymitry (M)
Dyzek (M)
Ema (F)
Emma (F)
Erasmus (M)
Fancy (F)
Farquhar (M)
Feeleep (M)
Felipe (M)
Felipino (M)
Femi (F)
Fiance (M)

Fiipote (F)
Fil (M)
Filib (M)
Filip (M)
Filipa (F)
Filipek (M)
Filipo (M)
Filipp (M)
Filippa (F)
Filippina (F)
Filippo (M)
Filips (M)
Filomena (F)
Filpina (F)
Filya (M)
Fischel (M)
Fülöp (M)
Gan (M)
Gerwyn (M)
Grainne (F)
Grainnia (F)
Grania (F)
Ḥabīb (M)
Ḥabībah (F)
Haviva (F)
Idris (M)
Jed (M)
Jedediah (M)
Jedidiah (M)
Kaela (F)
Kaelyn (F)
Kailey (F)
Kaleela (F)
Kalila (F)
Kalyn (F)
Kama (F)
Karah (F)
Karenza (F)
Kayle (F)
Kaylene (F)
Kayley (F)
Kaylil (F)
Kaylin (F)
Kelila (F)
Kelula (F)
Kerensa (F)
Kyla (F)
Leeba (F)
Leif (M)
Lewin (M)
Love (F)
Ludmila (F)
Mabel (F)
Mamta (F)
Manda (F)
Mandaline (F)
Mandy (F)
Maybelle (F)
Maybull (F)
Mila (F)
Milada (F)
Mimis (M)
Mitsos (M)
Morna (F)
Murnia (F)
Myrna (F)
Olufemi (M)
Oni (F)
Onida (F)
Pelipa (F)
Penda (F)
Phil (M)
Philadelphia (F)
Philander (M)
Philemon (M)
Philip (M)
Philipp (M)
Philippa (F)
Philippel (M)
Philippine (F)
Phillie (F)
Phillipina (F)
Phillipos (M)
Phillips (M)
Philomena (F)
Philomene (F)
Philomina (F)
Pilib (M)
Pilis (F)
Pippa (F)
Pippy (F)
Prem (M)
Querida (F)
Reese (M)
Rhett (M)
Rhys (M)
Rice (M)
Ruchi (F)
Rudo (M)
Ruth (F)
Ruthalma (F)
Ruthanne (F)
Ruthella (F)
Ruthetta (F)
Ruthie (F)
Ruthina (F)
Ruthine (F)
Sadhana (F)
Seraphina (F)
Seraphine (F)
Serofina (F)
Sevilen (M)
Shereen (F)
Shereena (F)
Sheri (F)
Shericia (F)
Sherie (F)
Sherina (F)
Sherita (F)
Sherree (F)
Sherry (F)
Sheryl (F)
Sofian (M)
Suki (F)
Syreeta (F)
Tanita (F)
Tanith (F)
Tanitha (F)
Tesia (F)
Theophila (F)
Theophilus (M)
Thorleif (M)
Veda (F)
Venus (F)
Vida (M)
Vidette (F)
Yadid (M)

Music and Sounds

Aaron (M)
Alima (F)
Allegra (F)
Amira (F)
Aranne (M)
Arek (M)
Arnina (F)
Aronek (M)
Aronos (M)
Baird (M)
Ballas (M)
Biagio (M)
Blaise (M)
Blaisot (M)
Blas (M)
Blasi (M)
Blasius (M)
Blaze (M)
Blazek (M)
Cadao (M)
Carna (F)
Carniella (F)
Carnis (F)
Carnit (F)
Ciyeva (F)
Clotilda (F)
Cornalia (F)
Cornelia (F)
Cornelie (F)
Cornelius (M)
Cornella (F)
Cornelle (F)
Cornelus (M)
Cornie (F)
Cornilear (F)
Crowther (M)
Cymon (M)
Demothi (M)
Dichali (M)
Dovev (M)
Echo (F)
Eula (F)
Eulalia (F)
Eulalie (F)
Gala (F)
Geneva (F)
Genève (F)
Genevieve (F)
Genoveva (F)
Ginetta (F)
Ginette (F)
Ginnette (F)
Harmony (F)
Harper (M)
Harun (M)
Hedia (F)
Hototo (M)
Inoa (F)
Ishmael (M)
Ismael (M)
Jaren (M)
Jaron (M)
Jubal (M)
Karniela (F)
Karniella (F)
Karnis (F)
Karnit (F)
Kera (F)

Kerani (F)
Kery (F)
Kijika (M)
Kiyoshi (M)
Kornelia (F)
Kornelis (F)
Koto (F)
Kuzih (M)
Lalage (F)
Lallie (F)
Lei (M)
Leron (M)
Liluye (F)
Lirit (F)
Liu (M)
Liwanu (M)
Lyra (F)
Lyris (F)
Malachi (M)
Malachy (M)
Mangina (F)
Marnin (M)
Melodia (F)
Melody (F)
Minowa (F)
Mojag (M)
Nari (F)
Nariko (F)
Nasnan (F)
Nata (F)
Nele (F)
Nelia (F)
Odelette (F)
Oma (F)
Omar (M)
Preston (M)
Ranice (F)
Ranit (F)
Ranita (F)
Ranon (M)
Ruana (F)
Sam (M)
Samantha (F)
Samaria (F)
Samarie (F)
Samarthur (F)
Samaru (M)
Samein (M)
Samella (F)
Samentha (F)
Samie (M)
Samko (M)
Sammel (M)
Sammi (F)
Sammie (M)

Sammy (M)
Samo (M)
Samouel (M)
Samu (M)
Samuel (M)
Samuela (F)
Samuele (M)
Samuelis (M)
Samuella (F)
Samuil (M)
Samvel (M)
Saril (F)
Schmuel (M)
Seda (F)
Selah (M)
Sem (M)
Semon (M)
Shappa (F)
Shem (M)
Shemuel (M)
Shimon (M)
Shira (F)
Shiri (F)
Shizu (F)
Shizuka (F)
Shizuko (F)
Shizuyo (F)
Shmuel (M)
Siko (F)
Silence (F)
Sill (M)
Sim (M)
Simao (M)
Simion (M)
Simm (M)
Simmina (F)
Simms (M)
Simmy (M)
Simon (M)
Simona (F)
Simone (F)
Simonia (F)
Simonne (F)
Somhairle (M)
Sora (F)
Suzu (F)
Suzuki (F)
Suzuko (F)
Tace (F)
Tacey (F)
Taima (F)
Tait (M)
Tate (M)
Thorald (M)
Torquil (M)
Vadin (M)
Vlas (M)
Wilny (M)
Wilu (M)
Yakecen (M)
Yaluta (F)
Yoshi (M)
Yoshie (F)
Yoshiko (F)
Yoshiyo (F)
Zamiel (M)
Zamir (M)
Zel (F)
Zimri (M)

Peace

Absalom (M)
Absalon (M)
Ace (M)
Adeana (F)
Adina (F)
Adine (F)
Adiv (M)
Alein (M)
Alleen (F)
Amandeep (M)
Amina (F)
Aminah (F)
An (M)
Anh (M)
Aquene (F)
Arina (F)
Arinka (F)
Arriet (F)
Aspasia (F)
Axel (M)
Bambis (M)
Bane (M)
Barn (M)
Barna (M)
Barnabas (M)
Barnabe (M)
Barnaby (M)
Barnebas (M)
Barney (M)
Baruch (M)
Beata (F)
Bedřich (M)
Bedřiška (F)
Bem (M)
Bena (F)
Benci (M)
Bendek (M)
Bendix (M)
Benedek (M)
Benedetta (F)
Benedetto (M)
Benedict (M)
Benedicta (F)
Benedicto (M)
Benedik (M)
Benedikt (M)
Benedo (M)
Benek (M)
Bengt (M)
Bengta (F)
Beni (M)
Benicia (F)
Benita (F)
Benitín (M)
Benito (M)
Benke (M)
Bennett (M)
Benni (F)
Benoist (M)
Benoît (M)
Benoîte (F)
Bent (M)
Bernabé (M)
Betto (M)
Binnie (F)
Bogomir (M)
Bonar (M)
Bracha (F)
Chenoa (F)
Chimene (F)
Clem (M)
Cleme (M)
Clemen (M)
Clemence (F)
Clemency (F)
Clemens (M)
Clement (M)
Clemente (M)
Clementia (F)
Clementina (F)
Clementine (F)
Clemento (M)
Clemenza (F)
Clemmons (M)
Clemmy (M)
Codi (F)
Cody (M)
Consuela (F)
Denae (F)
Dermod (M)
Detta (F)
Diarmuid (M)
Dinh (M)
Doba (F)
Dor (M)
Dulcinea (F)
Eden (F)
Eirena (F)
Eirene (F)
Eirini (F)
Elysia (F)
Emerson (M)
Emory (M)
Emrick (M)
Enrico (M)
Enrieta (F)
Enrikos (M)
Enrique (M)
Enriqueta (F)
Enzio (M)
Ettie (F)
Farrah (F)
Federico (M)
Federoquito (M)
Ferdinand (M)
Fernando (M)
Fico (M)
Fotfryd (M)
Fred (M)
Fredalena (F)
Fredaline (F)
Freddie (F)
Freddy (M)
Fredek (M)
Frederica (F)
Frederick (M)
Frederickina (F)
Frederico (M)
Frederik (M)
Frederine (F)
Frédérique (F)
Fredi (F)
Fredith (F)
Fredo (M)
Fredora (F)
Fredricia (F)
Fredwick (M)
Freeda (F)
Frici (F)
Frida (F)
Fridrich (M)
Frieda (F)
Friedel (M)
Friederike (M)
Friedrich (M)
Fritz (M)
Fritzchen (M)
Fritze (F)
Fritzinn (F)
Fryda (F)
Galen (M)
Galena (F)
Galeno (M)
Galya (F)
Gareth (M)
Gent (M)
Gentle (M)
Geoffery (M)
Geoffrey (M)
Geoffroie (F)
Geoffroy (M)
Geofri (M)
Gioffredo (M)
Giotto (M)
Godfrey (M)
Godofredo (M)
Godoired (M)
Gofredo (M)
Gotfrid (M)
Gotfrids (M)
Gottfrid (M)
Gottfried (M)
Gwyn (M)
Gwynne (F)
Hagan (M)
Hal (M)
Halcyon (F)
Halim (M)
Hania (F)
Haniya (F)
Hank (M)
Hanraoi (M)
Haralpos (M)
Harmony (F)
Harriet (F)
Harrietta (F)
Harry (M)
Hattie (F)
Heber (M)
Heiner (M)
Heinrich (M)
Heinz (M)
Hendrik (M)
Heneretta (F)
Henia (F)
Heniek (M)
Henier (M)
Henka (F)
Henri (M)
Henrieta (F)
Henriete (F)
Henrietta (F)
Henriette (F)
Henrik (M)
Henrika (F)
Henrim (M)
Henrique (M)
Henry (M)
Henryk (M)
Hericlea (F)
Hersz (M)
Hettie (F)
Hinrich (M)
Hoa (F)
Hoang (M)
Holleb (M)
Honok (M)
Humphrey (M)
Imrich (M)
Imrus (M)
Iren (F)
Irena (F)
Irene (F)
Irenea (F)
Irenka (F)
Irin (F)
Irini (F)
Irisha (F)
Irka (F)
Irusya (F)
Iryna (F)
Jahi (M)
Jeff (M)

Jefferson (M)
Jeffrey (M)
Jeoffroi (M)
Jereni (F)
Jindraska (F)
Jindřich (M)
Josha (M)
Karuna (F)
Katura (F)
Kelemen (M)
Ker (M)
Kerem (M)
Kerey (M)
Kermit (M)
Khambis (M)
Kharlambos (M)
Kika (F)
Kiki (M)
Kiyoshi (M)
Klema (M)
Klemens (M)
Klement (M)
Klemet (M)
Klemo (M)
Klim (M)
Klimek (M)
Kliment (M)
Klimka (M)
Knud (M)
Kody (M)
Langundo (M)
Lasimonne (M)
Latavia (F)
Lico (M)
Linfred (M)
Lono (M)
Lutherum (M)
Magara (F)
Mahala (F)
Mahalar (F)
Mahalia (F)
Mahela (F)
Mahelea (F)
Mahlah (F)
Manfred (M)
Mega (F)
Mehala (F)
Mehalia (F)
Menachem (M)
Mendeley (M)
Menz (M)
Mercedes (F)
Mercy (F)
Merry (F)
Mildred (F)
Miles (M)
Milessa (F)
Mileta (F)
Milley (F)
Milo (M)
Morna (F)
Mungo (M)
Murnia (F)
Mylie (F)
Mylinda (F)
Myrna (F)
Nalren (M)
Nechama (F)
Nehemiah (M)
Ngu (F)
Noach (M)
Noah (M)
Noak (M)
Noe (M)
Noi (M)
Onur (M)
Orina (F)
Orya (F)
Oryna (F)
Patience (F)
Patient (F)
Paz (M)
Peace (F)
Phineas (M)
Queta (F)
Quinto (M)
Quiqui (M)
Quiterie (F)
Rachamim (M)
Radomil (M)
Rahman (M)
Rahmet (M)
Reenie (F)
Rena (F)
Rene (F)
Rocco (M)
Rosanna (F)
Rosanne (F)
Rozanna (F)
Sal (F)
Salama (F)
Salamen (M)
Salamon (M)
Salamun (M)
Salaun (M)
Salīm (M)
Salom (M)
Saloma (F)
Salome (F)
Salomo (M)
Salomon (M)
Salomone (M)
Sameh (F)
Santosh (M)
Seifert (M)
Seifried (M)
Selim (M)
Selima (F)
Serena (F)
Serenah (F)
Shalom (M)
Sheehan (M)
Shelomoh (M)
Shlomo (M)
Sholom (M)
Shu (F)
Shulamit (F)
Siegfried (M)
Siffre (M)
Sig (M)
Sigefriedo (M)
Sigfrid (M)
Sigfrido (M)
Sigfroi (M)
Sigifredo (M)
Siguefredo (M)
Sigvard (M)
Siurt (M)
Sol (M)
Solly (M)
Soloman (M)
Solomon (M)
Solomonas (M)
Suela (F)
Suelita (F)
Sumati (F)
Szigfrid (M)
Terza (F)
Thao (F)
Thersa (F)
Thersea (F)
Thien (M)
Thirza (F)
Thuy (F)
Truc (F)
Tuan (M)
Tull (M)
Tully (M)
Tung (M)
Venedict (M)
Venka (M)
Venya (M)
Vinay (M)
Wilfred (M)
Wilfredo (M)
Wilfrida (F)
Winefride (F)
Winefriede (F)
Winfred (M)
Winiefrida (F)
Winifred (F)
Winifreda (F)
Winn (F)
Winnie (F)
Xena (F)
Xenia (F)
Ximen (M)
Yarina (F)
Yaryna (F)
Yasu (F)
Yasuko (F)
Yasuyo (F)
Yetta (F)
Yette (F)
Yoshi (M)
Yoshie (F)
Yoshiko (F)
Yoshiyo (F)
Yucel (M)
Zelimir (M)
Zigfrid (M)
Zigfrids (M)
Zilpah (F)
Zina (F)
Zygfryd (M)
Zygi (M)
Zylpha (F)

Power

Abalard (M)
Abasi (M)
Abelard (M)
Abilard (M)
Abira (F)
Adar (M)
Adira (F)
Aethelthryth (F)
Agamemnon (M)
Ahkeen (M)
Aimil (F)
Aindrea (M)
Aindreas (M)
Akeen (M)
Akin (M)
Al (M)
ʿAlā (M)
Alaister (M)
Alastair (M)
Alastor (M)
Aldric (M)
Aldrich (M)
Aldridge (M)
Alec (M)
Aleister (M)
Alejandra (F)
Alejandrina (F)
Alejandro (M)
Alejo (M)
Aleka (F)
Alekko (M)
Alekos (M)
Aleks (F)
Aleksander (M)
Aleksandr (M)
Aleksandŭr (M)
Aleksasha (F)
Aleksei (M)
Aleksey (F)
Aleksi (F)
Aleš (M)
Aleska (F)
Alessandra (F)
Alessandro (M)
Alessio (F)
Alester (M)
Alexa (F)
Alexander (M)
Alexandr (M)
Alexandra (F)
Alexandraeana (F)
Alexandre (M)
Alexandrea (F)
Alexandrena (F)
Alexandrene (F)
Alexandrie (F)
Alexandros (M)
Alexena (F)
Alexene (F)
Alexi (F)
Alexia (F)
Alexina (F)
Alexine (F)
Alexio (M)
Alexiou (F)
Alexis (M)
Alexis (F)
Alexius (F)
Alistair (M)
Alistar (M)
Alix (F)
Aljexi (F)
Alka (F)
Alli (F)
Almena (F)
Alrik (M)
Alsandair (M)
Alya (F)
Amali (F)
Amalia (F)
Amaliya (F)
Amelcia (F)
Ameldy (F)
Amelia (F)
Amélie (F)
Amelina (F)
Amelita (F)
Amella (F)
Amilia (F)
Amilie (F)
Andera (F)
Anders (M)
Anders (F)
Andor (M)
Andra (F)
András (M)
André (M)
Andrea (F)
Andrean (F)
Andreana (F)
Andreas (M)
Andree (F)
Andrei (M)
Andrej (M)
Andrés (M)
Andrette (F)
Andrew (M)
Andrewina (F)
Andrey (M)
Andreyka (M)
Andria (F)
Andriana (F)
Andrienne (F)
Andrietta (F)
Andrik (M)
Andris (M)
Andrius (M)
Andy (M)
Aniol (M)
Anndra (M)
Araldo (M)
Aralt (M)
Arch (M)
Archaimbaud (M)
Archambault (M)
Archelaus (M)
Archibald (M)
Archibaldo (M)
Archie (M)
Aric (M)
Arnaud (M)
Arnold (M)
Aroldo (M)
Arriet (F)
Arrigo (M)
Arry (M)
Atalanta (F)
Audey (F)
Audie (M)
Audra (F)
Audreen (F)
Audrey (F)
Audria (F)
Audric (M)
Azeem (M)
ʿAzīz (M)
Baldwin (M)
Bali (M)
Balin (M)
Bambis (M)
Bandi (F)
Bandi (M)
Barzillai (M)
Bedelia (F)
Bedřich (M)
Bedřiška (F)
Berek (F)
Berend (M)
Bergette (F)

Bergit (F)
Berk (M)
Bern (M)
Berna (F)
Bernadette (F)
Bernadina (F)
Bernadine (F)
Bernal (M)
Bernard (M)
Bernarda (F)
Bernardas (M)
Bernardel (M)
Bernardette (F)
Bernardin (M)
Bernardina (F)
Bernardine (F)
Bernardino (M)
Bernardo (M)
Bernardyn (M)
Bernarr (M)
Bernat (M)
Bernek (M)
Bernel (M)
Bernetta (F)
Bernette (F)
Berngards (M)
Bernhard (M)
Bernhards (M)
Bernie (F)
Bernita (F)
Berno (M)
Berthold (M)
Biddie (F)
Bidelia (F)
Bill (M)
Billie (F)
Billie Jean (F)
Billy (M)
Billy Joe (M)
Billy Ray (M)
Bink (M)
Binkentios (M)
Birgit (F)
Birgitta (F)
Bittan (F)
Blaz (M)
Boaz (M)
Bodil (M)
Bogdan (M)
Bogdashka (M)
Bohdan (M)
Bour (M)
Bride (F)
Bridget (F)
Bridgette (F)
Bridie (F)
Brietta (F)
Brigada (F)
Brigette (F)
Brigid (F)
Brigida (F)
Brigide (F)
Brigit (F)
Brigita (F)
Brigitta (F)
Brigitte (F)
Brita (F)
Britt (F)
Britta (F)
Brydie (F)
Bryga (F)
Brygida (F)
Brygitka (F)
Cachi (M)
Carlin (M)
Carling (M)
Casandra (F)
Casandrey (F)
Case (M)
Casey (M)
Cashi (M)
Casie (F)
Casimir (M)
Casimiro (M)
Casson (F)
Cassondra (F)
Castimer (M)
Chad (M)
Chenche (M)
Chul (M)
Cirillo (M)
Cirilo (M)
Comfort (F)
Con (M)
Concettina (F)
Conn (M)
Conni (M)
Connie (F)
Conny (M)
Conrad (M)
Conrade (M)
Conrado (M)
Constance (F)
Constancia (F)
Constancy (F)
Constant (M)
Constanta (F)
Constantia (F)
Constantine (M)
Constantinos (M)
Constanz (F)
Constanza (F)
Cort (M)
Costa (M)
Curt (M)
Custance (M)
Cyril (M)
Daksh (M)
Dante (M)
Dare (M)
Daria (F)
Dario (M)
Darren (M)
Dasan (M)
Dev (M)
Devi (F)
Devlin (M)
Dic (M)
Dick (M)
Dicken (M)
Dickon (M)
Dicky (M)
Dimka (M)
Dingbang (M)
Dinos (M)
Don (M)
Dona (F)
Donal (M)
Donald (M)
Donalda (F)
Donaldina (F)
Donaldo (M)
Donaleen (F)
Donalt (M)
Donelda (F)
Donella (F)
Donellia (F)
Donette (F)
Doni (F)
Donie (F)
Donita (F)
Donnelle (F)
Donny (M)
Dontae (M)
Dreng (M)
Drew (M)
Drina (F)
Duarte (M)
Eamonn (M)
Ed (M)
Eddie (M)
Eddye (F)
Edek (M)
Edik (M)
Edko (M)
Edmee (F)
Edmond (M)
Edmondo (M)
Edmund (M)
Edmundo (M)
Edmunds (M)
Edo (M)
Édouard (M)
Edric (M)
Edrice (F)
Eduardo (M)
Edus (M)
Edvard (M)
Edward (M)
Edzio (M)
Elek (M)
Elfrida (F)
Elfride (F)
Elmena (F)
Elric (M)
Em (F)
Emalia (F)
Emele (F)
Emelia (F)
Emelina (F)
Emelita (F)
Emera (F)
Emerson (M)
Emila (F)
Emilia (F)
Emilka (F)
Emillia (F)
Emily (F)
Emmali (F)
Emmy (F)
Emory (M)
Emrick (M)
Endre (M)
Enric (M)
Enrico (M)
Enrieta (F)
Enrikos (M)
Enrique (M)
Enriqueta (F)
Enzio (M)
Enzo (M)
Eric (M)
Erica (F)
Erich (M)
Erick (M)
Erico (M)
Erik (M)
Eriks (M)
Esmond (M)
Etheldreda (F)
Ettie (F)
Evagelos (M)
Everard (M)
Everett (M)
Ezraella (F)
Ezrela (F)
Faddei (M)
Fadey (M)
Farrell (M)
Federico (M)
Federoquito (M)
Ferdinand (M)
Fernando (M)
Fico (M)
Finlay (M)
Finley (M)
Finn (M)
Flint (M)
Forbes (M)
Fred (M)
Fredalena (F)
Fredaline (F)
Freddie (F)
Freddy (M)
Fredek (M)
Frederica (F)
Frederick (M)
Frederickina (F)
Frederico (M)
Frederik (M)
Frederine (F)
Frédérique (F)
Fredi (F)
Fredith (F)
Fredora (F)
Fredricia (F)
Fredwick (M)
Freeda (F)
Frici (F)
Fridrich (M)
Friedel (M)
Friederike (M)
Friedrich (M)
Fritz (M)
Fritzchen (M)
Fritze (F)
Fritzinn (F)
Fryda (F)
Garald (M)
Gari (M)
Garner (M)
Garolds (M)
Garret (M)
Garrett (M)
Garrick (M)
Gary (M)
Gautier (M)
Gavrilla (F)
Gazit (F)
Gedeon (M)
Gellart (M)
Gerald (M)
Geralda (F)
Geraldine (F)
Geraldo (M)
Geralyn (F)
Gerard (M)
Géraud (M)
Gerda (F)
Gerrie (M)
Gerrit (M)
Gerry (F)
Gertina (F)
Gertrude (F)
Gerty (F)
Gi (M)
Gideon (M)
Gideone (M)
Gidita (F)
Gidon (M)
Giraldo (M)
Gisa (F)
Gissa (F)
Gosheven (M)

Greer (F)
Greg (M)
Grégoire (M)
Gregor (M)
Gregorio (M)
Gregorios (M)
Gregors (M)
Gregory (M)
Gries (M)
Griffith (M)
Grigoi (M)
Grigor (M)
Gualberto (M)
Gualterio (M)
Gualtiero (M)
Guilette (F)
Guilla (F)
Guillaume (M)
Guillaums (M)
Guillerma (F)
Guillermo (M)
Gutierre (M)
Gwilym (M)
Hagan (M)
Hakan (M)
Ḥakīm (M)
Hal (M)
Hale (M)
Hank (M)
Hanraoi (M)
Harailt (M)
Harald (M)
Haralda (F)
Haraldo (M)
Haralds (M)
Haralpos (M)
Hardy (M)
Harold (M)
Haroldas (M)
Haroldene (F)
Haroldo (M)
Harriet (F)
Harrietta (F)
Harry (M)
Hāshim (M)
Hateya (F)
Hattie (F)
Hector (M)
Hedeon (M)
Heiner (M)
Heinrich (M)
Heinz (M)
Helma (F)
Helmi (F)
Helmine (F)

Hendrik (M)
Heneretta (F)
Henia (F)
Heniek (M)
Henier (M)
Henka (F)
Henri (M)
Henrieta (F)
Henriete (F)
Henrietta (F)
Henriette (F)
Henrik (M)
Henrika (F)
Henrim (M)
Henrique (M)
Henry (M)
Henryk (M)
Hericlea (F)
Heronim (M)
Hersz (M)
Hettie (F)
Hezekiah (M)
Hilma (F)
Himeronim (M)
Hinrich (M)
Hisa (F)
Hisae (F)
Hisako (F)
Hisayo (F)
Hod (M)
Honok (M)
Honovi (M)
Hung (M)
Igor (M)
Ilma (F)
Ima (F)
Imala (F)
Imrich (M)
Imrus (M)
Inga (F)
Inge (F)
Ingeberg (F)
Ingeborg (F)
Ingvar (M)
Inteus (M)
Iskandar (M)
Israel (M)
Jandina (F)
Jandino (M)
Jando (M)
Jarrell (M)
Javas (M)
Jedrek (M)
Jedrus (M)
Jerald (M)

Jeraldine (F)
Jerilyn (F)
Jerri (F)
Jerry (M)
Jindra (M)
Jindraska (F)
Jindřich (M)
Jing-Quo (M)
Juku (M)
Kacey (M)
Kadar (M)
Kade (M)
Kama (F)
Kami (F)
Kanda (F)
Karma (F)
Kasandra (F)
Kasey (M)
Kasie (F)
Kasimir (M)
Kassandra (F)
Kassie (F)
Kavindra (F)
Kaycee (F)
Kazek (M)
Kazik (M)
Kazimir (M)
Kazio (M)
Kázmér (M)
Kedar (M)
Kenda (F)
Kendra (F)
Kenelm (M)
Khambis (M)
Kharald (M)
Kharlambos (M)
Kika (F)
Kiki (M)
Kindra (F)
Kiril (M)
Kiryl (M)
Konni (M)
Konrad (M)
Konstantin (F)
Konstantinos (M)
Konstanze (F)
Kosta (F)
Kostas (M)
Kostatina (F)
Kostenka (F)
Kostya (F)
Kostyusha (F)
Kotik (F)
Kotsos (M)
Kurt (M)

Kwan (M)
Kyra (F)
Ladislaus (M)
Lanny (M)
Lap (M)
Lekeke (M)
Leks (M)
Leksik (M)
Lekso (M)
Lekszi (F)
Lel (M)
Len (M)
Lenda (F)
Leneen (F)
Lenette (F)
Lenia (F)
Lenna (F)
Lenny (M)
Leonard (M)
Leonardo (M)
Leonek (M)
Leonhard (M)
Leonhards (M)
Leonid (M)
Leons (M)
Leontes (M)
Leopold (M)
Lera (F)
Lerka (F)
Leska (F)
Lesya (F)
Lex (M)
Lexa (F)
Lexi (F)
Lexine (F)
Liam (M)
Lico (M)
Lienard (M)
Like (M)
Linek (M)
Llewellyn (M)
Lon (M)
Magnus (M)
Mahir (M)
Mahira (F)
Major (M)
Makimus (M)
Maks (M)
Maksim (M)
Maksimka (M)
Maksymilian (M)
Makszi (M)
Malcsi (F)
Maldwyn (M)
Máli (F)

Malika (F)
Malulani (F)
Mana (F)
Manius (M)
Manley (M)
Maska (M)
Massimiliano (M)
Massimo (M)
Mato (M)
Max (M)
Maxi (M)
Maxie (M)
Maxim (M)
Maxima (F)
Maximalian (M)
Maxime (M)
Maximilian (M)
Maximiliano (M)
Maximino (M)
Máximo (M)
Maxina (F)
Maxine (F)
Maxy (M)
Maynard (M)
Mehira (F)
Melcia (F)
Melia (F)
Mellicent (F)
Mellisent (F)
Mema (F)
Mena (F)
Miksa (M)
Mildred (F)
Milica (F)
Milka (F)
Milley (F)
Millicent (F)
Milliestone (F)
Min (F)
Mina (F)
Minetta (F)
Minette (F)
Minka (F)
Minna (F)
Minnie (F)
Miwa (F)
Miwako (F)
Mundek (M)
Mundo (M)
Nagid (M)
Nardek (M)
Nayati (M)
Nealie (F)
Neci (F)
Ned (M)

Neda (F)
Neddy (M)
Neil (M)
Neilla (F)
Nels (M)
Neneca (F)
Nero (M)
Neron (M)
Nerone (M)
Nial (M)
Nibaw (M)
Nigel (M)
Nil (M)
Niles (M)
Nili (M)
Nilo (M)
Nilya (M)
Nimrod (M)
Nuela (F)
Odeda (F)
Odi (M)
Ödön (M)
Ola (F)
Olek (M)
Oleksa (F)
Oleksandr (M)
Olery (M)
Oles (M)
Olesia (F)
Olesko (M)
Olesya (F)
Ondro (M)
Osmanek (M)
Osmond (M)
Osmundo (M)
Oswald (M)
Oswell (M)
Palladin (M)
Pallaton (M)
Pepi (M)
Pepin (M)
Platón (M)
Pry (M)
Pryor (M)
Qabil (M)
Qadir (M)
Queta (F)
Quinley (M)
Quinlin (M)
Quinto (M)
Quiqui (M)
Radinka (F)
Ragnar (M)
Ragnor (M)
Raimondo (M)

Raimund (M)
Raimunde (F)
Raimundo (M)
Rainer (M)
Rainier (M)
Rajmund (M)
Ramón (M)
Ramona (F)
Ranald (M)
Rancie (M)
Rand (M)
Randall (M)
Randee (F)
Randey (M)
Randi (M)
Randie (M)
Randolph (M)
Randy (M)
Ranieri (M)
Ransom (M)
Ranson (M)
Rapier (M)
Ray (M)
Raymond (M)
Raymonde (F)
Rayner (M)
Rea (F)
Redmond (M)
Reg (M)
Reginald (M)
Reimond (M)
Reinold (M)
Reku (M)
Renaldo (M)
Renauld (M)
Renault (M)
Rendor (M)
Reynold (M)
Rhodri (M)
Ricard (M)
Ricardo (M)
Rich (M)

Richard (M)
Richarda (F)
Richards (M)
Richart (M)
Richenda (F)
Richenza (F)
Richi (M)
Richie (M)
Richmal (F)
Rick (M)
Rickard (M)
Rickert (M)
Rickie (M)
Ricky (M)
Rico (M)
Riczi (M)
Rihardos (M)
Rihards (M)
Rika (F)
Rikard (M)
Riki (M)
Rikki (F)
Riks (M)
Riley (M)
Rinaldo (M)
Riqui (M)
Risa (M)
Risardas (M)
Ritchie (M)
Ritsa (F)
Roald (M)
Roddy (M)
Roderich (M)
Roderick (M)
Rodrigo (M)
Rodrique (M)
Rolli (M)
Ron (M)
Ronald (M)
Ronna (F)
Ronnette (F)
Ronney (M)

Ronni (M)
Ronnie (M)
Ronny (M)
Rostik (M)
Rostislav (M)
Rostya (M)
Rurich (M)
Rurik (M)
Ruy (M)
Rye (M)
Rysio (M)
Ryszard (M)
Sacha (M)
Samara (F)
Sande (M)
Sander (M)
Sanders (M)
Sanderson (M)
Sándor (M)
Sandra (F)
Sandrea (F)
Sandrell (F)
Sandrina (F)
Sandy (F)
Sanyi (M)
Sasa (F)
Sascha (M)
Sasha (F)
Sashenka (M)
Sashka (M)
Saundra (F)
Sawney (M)
Seki (F)
Shad (M)
Shura (F)
Shurik (M)
Shurka (F)
Skip (M)
Skipper (M)
Skippy (M)
Slava (M)
Slavin (M)
Slavka (M)
Slevin (M)
Sloan (M)
Soffrona (F)
Sofronia (F)
Sondra (F)
Songan (M)
Sophronia (F)
Stancio (M)
Stannard (M)
Steele (M)
Sunki (F)
Tad (M)
Taddeo (M)
Taddy (M)
Tade (M)
Tadeas (M)
Tadek (M)
Tadeo (M)
Tadeusz (M)
Tadey (M)
Tadita (F)
Tadzio (M)
Tauno (M)
Temperance (F)
Tetsu (F)
Thaddaus (M)
Thaddeo (M)
Thaddeus (M)
Thaddy (M)
Thadee (M)
Thelma (F)
Theobald (M)
Thormond (M)
Thorvald (M)
Tokiwa (F)
Truda (F)
Trudie (F)
Trudy (F)
Uilliam (M)
Uzziah (M)
Uzziel (M)
Vacys (M)
Val (F)
Valaria (F)
Valdemar (M)
Valence (F)
Valencia (F)
Valene (F)
Valentia (F)
Valentina (F)
Valentine (M)
Valeria (F)
Valeriana (F)
Valerie (F)
Valery (F)
Valin (M)
Valka (F)
Vallie (F)
Valma (F)
Valry (F)
Valter (M)
Valters (M)
Valtr (M)
Valya (F)
Vanda (M)
Vandele (M)
Vas (M)
Vasilak (M)
Vaska (M)
Vassos (M)
Vasya (M)
Vasyl (M)
Velma (F)
Velvel (M)
Vic (M)
Vicente (M)
Vicenzo (M)
Victoir (M)
Victoire (F)
Victor (M)
Victorino (M)
Victorio (M)
Vikent (M)
Vikenti (M)
Vikesha (M)
Viktor (M)
Vila (M)
Vilek (M)
Vilhelm (M)
Vili (M)
Viliam (M)
Viljo (M)
Vilko (M)
Ville (M)
Vilma (F)
Vilmos (M)
Vilous (M)
Vin (M)
Vince (M)
Vincenc (M)
Vincent (M)
Vincente (M)
Vincentia (F)
Vincenz (M)
Vincenzo (M)
Vincetta (F)
Vinci (M)
Vinco (M)
Vint (M)
Virtue (F)
Vitenka (M)
Vitin (M)
Vitka (M)
Vito (M)
Vitor (M)
Vittore (M)
Vittorio (M)
Vitya (M)
Vladimir (M)
Vladko (M)
Vladlen (M)
Volya (M)
Vova (M)
Vovka (M)
Wakanda (F)
Wakiza (M)
Wala (F)
Walburga (F)
Waldemar (M)
Waldo (M)
Waleria (F)
Wally (M)
Walt (M)
Walter (M)
Walther (M)
Waltli (M)
Waltr (M)
Waneta (F)
Warren (M)
Wat (M)
Waterio (M)
Watkin (M)
Wei-Quo (M)
Welfel (M)
Welvel (M)
Wicek (M)
Wicent (M)
Wicus (M)
Wiktor (M)
Wilbert (M)
Wiletta (F)
Wilette (F)
Wilfred (M)
Wilfredo (M)
Wilfrida (F)
Wilhelm (M)
Wilhelmina (F)
Wilhelmine (F)
Wilkinson (M)
Will (M)
Willa (F)
Willard (M)
Willey (M)
Willi (M)
Willi (F)
William (M)
Williamson (M)
Willimar (M)
Willis (M)
Wilma (F)
Wilmette (F)
Wilmotina (F)
Wilmott (M)
Wilson (M)
Witek (M)
Wolf (M)
Wylmer (M)
Xerxes (M)
Yael (F)
Yanaba (F)
Yazid (M)
Yemina (F)
Yemon (M)
Yetta (F)
Yette (F)
Yisrael (M)
Yong (M)
Zandra (F)
Zareb (M)
Zedekiah (M)
Zenobia (F)
Zephaniah (M)

Riches

Adah (F)
Adair (M)
Adia (F)
Adie (F)
Adiella (F)
Adlai (M)
Agate (F)
Ah Kum (F)
ʿAlā (M)
Alamea (F)
Amber (F)
Amberetta (F)
Amberly (F)
Amor (M)
Amory (M)
Aneirin (M)
Ardon (M)
Artha (F)
Arve (M)
Asadel (M)
Audr (M)
Aziza (F)
Azize (F)
Bao (M)
Beppi (M)
Betty Mae (F)
Bo (M)
Bobbi-Jo (F)
Bobby Joe (M)
Cara (F)
Cash (M)
Caspar (M)
Cass (M)
Cedric (M)
Ceinwen (F)
Che (M)
Cheche (M)
Chepe (M)
Chepito (M)
Cressida (F)
Dar (M)
Dara (F)
Darda (F)
Darius (M)
Dasha (F)
Diamond (F)
Dita (F)
Ditka (F)
Diverous (M)
Divers (M)
Dives (M)
Dode (F)
Dodek (M)
Dol (F)
Doll (F)
Dolly (F)
Donat (M)
Donatello (M)
Donati (M)
Donato (M)
Donatus (M)
Dora (F)
Doralice (F)
Doran (M)
Dorchen (F)
Dore (F)
Dorek (M)
Doretha (F)
Dorette (F)
Dorinda (F)
Doritt (F)
Dorka (F)
Dorle (F)
Dorlisa (F)
Dorolice (F)
Dorosia (F)
Dorota (F)
Dorotea (F)
Doroteya (F)
Dorothea (F)
Dorothee (F)
Dorothy (F)
Dorotthea (F)
Dorrit (F)
Dorte (F)
Dosi (F)
Dosya (F)
Dot (F)
Dottie (F)
Duci (F)
Dyre (M)
Eamonn (M)
Eda (F)
Edda (F)
Edetta (F)
Edgar (M)
Edgard (M)
Edgardo (M)
Edgars (M)
Edi (F)
Edie (F)
Edit (F)
Edita (F)
Edite (F)
Edith (F)
Editha (F)
Ediva (F)
Edka (F)
Edmee (F)
Edmond (M)
Edmondo (M)
Edmund (M)
Edmundo (M)
Edmunds (M)
Edwin (M)
Edwina (F)
Edwy (M)
Edyta (F)
Eirian (F)
Elidi (F)
Ella (F)
Ellaline (F)

Emerald (F)
Esmarelda (F)
Esmerelda (F)
Esmond (M)
Etenia (F)
Eudora (F)
Eun (F)
Fedinka (M)
Fedor (M)
Fedora (F)
Feodor (M)
Feodora (F)
Fifi (F)
Gadi (M)
Gadiel (M)
Garek (M)
Garnet (M)
Garnett (M)
Garnetta (F)
Gáspár (M)
Gaspard (M)
Gem (F)
Gemma (F)
Gerik (M)
Gessica (F)
Gina (F)
Gita (F)
Gitka (F)
Gitta (F)
Gituska (F)
Giuseppe (M)
Greeta (F)
Greta (F)
Gretal (F)
Gretchen (F)
Grete (F)
Gretel (F)
Grethal (F)
Grieta (F)
Gwen (F)
Gwendolen (F)
Gwennie (F)
Hadiya (F)
Hrisoula (F)
Huy (M)
Hyacinth (F)
Iola (F)
Iolo (M)
Iorwerth (M)
Iosif (M)
Isadora (F)
Isidora (F)
Isidore (M)
Ivory (F)
Izzy (M)
Jada (F)
Jade (F)
Jasper (M)
Jawhar (M)
Jazeps (M)
Jemma (F)
Jessalyn (F)
Jessi (F)
Jessica (F)
Jewel (F)
Jin (M)
Jo (M)
Jo (F)
Jōbo (M)
Joe (M)
Joey (M)
Jojo (M)
Jolene (F)
Jolinda (F)
Joline (F)
Jolyn (F)
Jonathan (M)
Joosef (M)
Jooseppi (M)
José (M)
Josecito (M)
Josée (F)
Josef (M)
Joselito (M)
Joseph (M)
Josepha (F)
Josephe (M)
Josephina (F)
Josephine (F)
Josephus (M)
Josette (F)
Josie (F)
Josip (M)
Jóska (M)
Joyita (F)
Jozhe (M)
Jupp (M)
Kāmil (M)
Kamila (F)
Kamilah (F)
Kamillah (F)
Karah (F)
Kaspar (M)
Kasper (M)
Kin (M)
Kito (M)
Lolotea (F)
Louella (F)
Mag (F)
Maggie (F)
Maidie (F)
Maisie (F)
Majorie (F)
Makana (F)
Manci (F)
Marella (F)
Marelle (F)
Marga (F)
Margalit (F)
Margara (F)
Margaret (F)
Margarete (F)
Margaretha (F)
Margarid (F)
Margarida (F)
Margarita (F)
Margarite (F)
Margaritis (F)
Margaro (F)
Margeretta (F)
Margerite (F)
Marget (F)
Margherita (F)
Margie (F)
Margisia (F)
Margit (F)
Margita (F)
Margret (F)
Margreta (F)
Margrete (F)
Margrieta (F)
Margrita (F)
Marguerite (F)
Mari (F)
Marjatta (F)
Marjorie (F)
Marka (F)
Markéta (F)
Marsail (F)
Mata (M)
Matana (F)
Máté (M)
Mateĭ (M)
Matek (M)
Mateo (M)
Mateus (M)
Matfei (M)
Mathe (M)
Mathia (M)
Mathias (M)
Mathieu (M)
Matías (M)
Matt (M)
Matteo (M)
Matteus (M)
Matthaios (M)
Matthaus (M)
Matthew (M)
Matthia (M)
Matthias (M)
Matthieu (M)
Mattias (M)
Mattmias (M)
Matty (M)
Matus (M)
Matvey (M)
Matyas (M)
Mayfey (M)
Maysie (F)
Mazie (F)
Medora (F)
Meeri (F)
Meg (F)
Megan (F)
Meggie (F)
Mehetabel (M)
Meta (F)
Motka (M)
Motya (M)
Mundek (M)
Mundo (M)
Myfannwy (F)
Mysie (F)
Nagida (F)
Nat (M)
Natan (M)
Natane (F)
Nataniele (M)
Nate (M)
Nathan (M)
Nathaniel (M)
Natty (M)
Neema (F)
Nye (M)
Odette (F)
Odi (M)
Odile (F)
Odo (M)
Ödön (M)
Ofira (F)
Olujimi (M)
Onan (M)
Onek (M)
Opal (F)
Ophira (F)
Osip (M)
Osya (M)
Otadan (M)
Otek (M)
Otello (M)
Otfried (M)
Otho (M)
Othon (M)
Otik (M)
Otilio (M)
Otis (M)
Otman (M)
Oto (M)
Otón (M)
Otto (M)
Ottocar (M)
Ottomar (M)
Otton (M)
Ottone (M)
Pearl (F)
Pearla (F)
Pearlena (F)
Pearline (F)
Peg (F)
Peggetty (F)
Peggotty (F)
Peggy (F)
Peninah (F)
Peninit (F)
Pepa (M)
Pepe (M)
Pepik (M)
Pepillo (M)
Pepin (M)
Pepita (F)
Pepito (M)
Peppe (M)
Peppo (M)
Perlie (F)
Pino (M)
Pipo (M)
Pninah (F)
Powa (M)
Precious (F)
Purly (F)
Rafe (M)
Rafer (M)
Raff (M)
Rafferty (M)
Reet (F)
Reta (F)
Rita (F)
Rubina (F)
Ruby (F)
Ruri (F)
Sapphire (F)
Segel (M)
Sepp (M)
Shamir (M)
Shamira (F)
Shina (F)
Sima (M)
Sterling (M)
Stirling (M)
Tabia (F)
Tadan (M)
Tai (M)
Takara (F)
Tama (F)
Tamaki (F)
Tamako (F)
Tamayo (F)
Ted (M)
Teddy (M)
Tedik (M)
Teodomiro (M)
Teodor (M)
Teodora (F)
Teodorek (M)
Teodoro (M)
Teodus (M)
Teos (M)
Tewdor (M)
Thalia (F)
Thea (F)
Theo (M)
Theodor (M)
Theodora (F)
Theodore (M)
Theodosia (F)
Thurston (M)
Tita (F)
Tivadar (M)
Todor (M)
Todos (M)
Tolek (M)
Tonek (M)
Tudor (M)
Ula (F)
Ulbrecht (M)
Wemilat (M)
Yasar (M)
Yasir (M)
Yeska (M)
Yesya (M)
Yonatan (M)
Yorath (M)
Yosef (M)
Yosif (M)
Yousef (M)
Yusef (M)
Yusif (M)
Yusup (M)
Zahava (F)
Zawadi (F)
Zayn (M)
Zeheb (M)
Zeusef (M)
Zeynep (F)

Occupation/ Activity BROWSER

This browser lets you choose a name associated with a particular occupation or endeavor because of famous or notable people who have worked in that field.

Namesakes were selected on the basis of their fame or their unusual achievements. Obviously, the more common the name, the more likely it is to have been borne by someone in every field imaginable.

The list below shows every heading in this browser. Following each one is a series of words and phrases that either describe the heading or are examples of professions or activities you'll find under this heading. Some words or phrases may appear under more than one heading, reflecting the different contexts in which they occur.

ARTISTRY: architect, art critic, boat builder, choreographer, clothing designer, collector, craftsman, dancer, fashion designer, harpsichord maker, illustrator, interior designer or decorator, landscape designer, lithographer, orator, painter, photographer, printer (before twentieth century; otherwise under Journalism), rhetorician, sculptor, silversmith, subject of any of these, textile designer

BIBLE AND RELIGION: apostle, archbishop, clergyman, founder of religion, martyr, missionary, pope, preacher, rabbi, saint, theologian

BUSINESS AND FINANCE: founder of business, industrialist, merchant, philanthropist

FICTION AND LITERATURE: cartoonist, character in, editor of, novels, short stories, translator of, writer of

FOLKLORE AND MYTH: figure in, Roman and Greek gods and goddesses. Not used if gods are worshiped today by any significant following.

HISTORY AND POLITICS: cabinet member, explorer, military leader, officeholder, politician, royalty, statesman

JOURNALISM AND PUBLISHING: columnist, editor, editorial cartoonist, print journalist, printer (if twentieth-century; otherwise under Artistry), publisher. Not TV or radio.

LAW: jurist, law professor, lawyer, Supreme Court Justice

MEDICINE: dentist, nurse, physician, researcher

MOVIES: actor, actress, character in movies, director, producer, screenplay writer, star

MUSIC: character in a musical work, composer, instrument maker, librettist, lyricist, musician, singer

POETRY: character in poem, critic, poet

SCIENCE: astronaut, astronomer, botanist, cartographer, engineer, forester, geographer, geologist, horticulturist, inventor, mathematician, meteorologist, naturalist, ornithologist, physicist, speliologist, zoologist

SHOW BIZ: circus performer, circus-animal trainer, comedian, magician, nightclub entertainer

SOCIAL SCIENCE: anthropologist, archaeologist, criminologist (includes Law), economist, Egyptologist, ethnologist, geographer, historian, linguist, Orientalist, philologist, political scientist, psychoanalyst, psychologist, sociologist

SPORTS AND GAMES: aviator, bridge, chess, figure in, mountain climber

THEATER: actor, actress, character in play, drama critic, playwright, puppeteer, set designer, theater owner

TV AND RADIO: actor/actress usually working here rather than on screen or stage, broadcast journalist, character in program, figure in field, newsreader

Artistry

Abraham (M)
Addison (M)
Adeline (F)
Adolph (M)
Agnes (F)
Albertina (F)
Albrecht (M)
Aldo (M)
Aleksandr (M)
Alessandro (M)
Alicia (F)
Allegra (F)
Alonso (M)
Aloys (M)
Alphonse (M)
Alvar (M)
Anders (M)
André (M)
Andreas (M)
Andrey (M)
Andy (M)
Angelica (F)
Anna (F)
Anna Mary (F)
Ansel (M)
Anthony (M)
Antoine (M)
Anton (M)
Antonello (M)
Antonia (F)
Antonin (M)
Antonio (M)
Archibald (M)
Asher (M)
Aston (M)
Aubrey (M)
August (M)
Augusta (F)
Augustin (M)
Augustus (M)
Barnett (M)
Barth (M)
Bartolomé (M)
Basil (M)
Ben (M)
Benedetto (M)
Bernardino (M)
Bernardo (M)
Bertel (M)
Bertram (M)
Betsy (F)
Blanche (F)
Brooks (M)
Caius (M)
Calvert (M)
Calvin (M)
Camillo (M)
Candace (F)
Carlotta (F)
Caspar (M)
Cass (M)
Catherine (F)
Christian (M)
Christophe (M)
Cicero (M)
Ciro (M)
Clark (M)
Claude (M)
Claudio (M)
Claus (M)
Colin (M)
Colonel (M)
Conni (M)
Constant (M)
Cristóbal (M)
Cynthia (F)
Damian (M)
Dan (M)
Daniel (M)
Dante (M)
Debbie (F)
Demetrius (M)
Dennis (M)
Diane (F)
Diego (M)
Dirk (M)
Domenico (M)
Dominique (M)
Donald (M)
Donatello (M)
Donato (M)
Doris (F)
Dorothea (F)
Duncan (M)
Edie (F)
Édouard (M)
Eduardo (M)
Edward (M)
Edwin (M)
Elie (M)
Elihu (M)
Elsa (F)
Elsie (F)
Emanuel (M)
Emily (F)
Enoch (M)
Enrico (M)
Enrique (M)
Eugen (M)
Faith (F)
Ferdinand (M)
Filippo (M)
Ford (M)
Francesca (F)
Francesco (M)
Francisco (M)
François (M)
Frank (M)
Frans (M)
Fred (M)
Frederik (M)
Gabriel (M)
Galina (F)
Garfield (M)
Gari (M)
Gaspard (M)
Gavin (M)
Gene (M)
Genevieve (F)
Geoffroy (M)
George (M)
Georgia (F)
Gerard (M)
Germain (M)
Gerrit (M)
Giacomo (M)
Gifford (M)
Gil (M)
Gilbert (M)
Ginger (F)
Gino (M)
Giotto (M)
Giovanni (M)
Giselle (F)
Gloria (F)
Gottfried (M)
Graham (M)
Grant (M)
Guido (M)
Gustave (M)
Harald (M)
Heidi (F)
Hendrik (M)
Herbert (M)
Hercules (M)
Hermes (M)
Hester (F)
Hiram (M)
Homer (M)
Humphrey (M)
Ibrāhīm (M)
Imogen (F)
Inigo (M)
Isabella (F)
Isadora (F)
Jacinto (M)

Jackson (M)
Jacob (M)
Jan (M)
Jean (M)
Jean-François (M)
Jens (M)
Jerome (M)
Jo (M)
Joaquín (M)
Johann (M)
Joni (F)
Josef (M)
Joshua (M)
Juan (M)
Julien (M)
Juliet (F)
Julio (M)
Julius (M)
Jürgen (M)
Karel (M)
Kazimir (M)
Konrad (M)
Kristoffer (M)
Lancelot (M)
Laura (F)
Laurent (M)
Lauritz (M)
Leonardo (M)
Leone (M)
Lev (M)
Lisa (F)
Lorenzo (M)
Louis (M)
Louisa (F)
Luca (M)
Lucas (M)
Lucia (F)
Luis (M)
Madeleine (F)
Malvina (F)
Mariana (F)
Marianne (F)
Marie (F)
Mark (M)
Mary (F)
Mateo (M)
Mathilde (F)
Matteo (M)
Matthaus (M)
Maurice (M)
Maya (F)
Miguel (M)
Mikhail (M)
Mincho (M)
Moira (F)
Morgan (M)
Myron (M)
Nathaniel (M)
Nicholas (M)
Nicola (F)
Nicolás (M)
Nikolai (M)
Norman (M)
Olga (F)
Othon (M)
Pablo (M)
Palmer (M)
Paris (M)
Patience (F)
Paula (F)
Pedro (M)
Peter (M)
Philipp (M)
Piero (M)
Pierre (M)
Pieter (M)
Pietro (M)
Pirro (M)
Quentin (M)
Rachel (F)
Ragnar (M)
Randolph (M)
Raoul (M)
Reginald (M)
Reuben (M)
Rex (M)
Reza (F)
Rodolphe (M)
Roland (M)
Rosa (F)
Rose (F)
Rowena (F)
Royal (M)
Salomon (M)
Salvador (M)
Salvatore (M)
Santiago (M)
Saskia (F)
Sébastien (M)
Serge (M)
Shen (M)
Simon (M)
Simone (F)
Sonia (F)
Stanford (M)
Stanley (M)
Stanton (M)
Stefan (M)
Stefano (M)
Stuart (M)
Suzanne (F)
Suzuki (F)
Taddeo (M)
Thomas (M)
Tommy (M)
Tori (F)
Twyla (F)
Vernon (M)
Vicenzo (M)
Viljo (M)
Vincent (M)
Vincenzo (M)
Vinnie (F)
Violet (F)
Vittore (M)
Walker (M)
Washington (M)
Wolf (M)
Wyatt (M)
Wyndham (M)
Yekaterina (F)
Yevgenyi (M)
Yves (M)

Bible and Religion

Aaron (M)
Abdul (M)
Abel (M)
Abigail (F)
Abijah (M)
Abimelech (M)
Abishag (F)
Abner (M)
Abraham (M)
Absalom (M)
Adah (F)
Adam (M)
Adelbert (M)
Adrian (M)
Agatha (F)
Agnes (F)
Aidan (M)

Ailbe (M)
Akiba (M)
Alban (M)
Albert (M)
Albrecht (M)
Aldred (M)
Aldwyn (M)
Alessandro (M)
Alexander (M)
Alexandre (M)
Alexis (F)
Alfonso (M)
Alfreda (F)
Alma (F)
Alonzo (M)
Aloysius (M)
Amand (M)
Ambrose (M)
Amnon (M)
Amos (M)
Ananda (F)
Anastasia (F)
Andreas (M)
Andrew (M)
Angela (F)
Angelo (M)
Annas (M)
Anne (F)
Anselm (M)
Anta (F)
Antony (M)
Aquila (M)
Archibald (M)
Arius (M)
Arnold (M)
Asher (M)
Augusta (F)
Augustine (M)
Avram (M)
Azariah (M)
Barbara (F)
Barnabas (M)
Barry (M)
Bartholomew (M)
Bartolomé (M)
Barton (M)
Baruch (M)
Basil (M)
Bathsheba (F)
Beatrice (F)
Bede (M)
Benedict (M)
Benito (M)
Benjamin (M)
Bernadette (F)
Bernard (M)
Bernardino (M)
Bernarr (M)
Bithia (F)
Blaise (M)
Blane (M)
Boniface (M)
Boris (M)
Brendan (M)
Bridget (F)
Brigham (M)
Brigid (F)
Brigit (F)
Brooke (F)
Bruno (M)
Caius (M)
Camille (F)
Camillus (M)
Caradog (M)
Carlo (M)
Casimir (M)
Caspar (M)
Catherine (F)
Cecilia (F)
Chad (M)
Chaim (M)
Charles (M)
Christian (M)
Christina (F)
Christopher (M)
Clement (M)
Clotilda (F)
Colleen (F)
Columba (M)
Conan (M)
Constantine (M)
Cornelius (M)
Cosmo (M)
Crispin (M)
Crispina (F)
Cuthbert (M)
Cyprian (M)
Cyril (M)
Damian (M)
Damien (M)
Dan (M)
Daniel (M)
David (M)
Deborah (F)
Declan (M)
Delilah (F)
Denis (M)
Dermot (M)
Desire (F)
Dina (F)
Dionysius (M)
Dom (M)
Dominic (F)
Donatus (M)
Dorothy (F)
Dunstan (M)
Dympna (F)
Edith (F)
Edmond (M)
Edmund (M)
Edna (F)
Edward (M)
Edwin (M)
Egbert (M)
Eleazar (M)
Eli (M)
Elias (M)
Eliezer (M)
Elijah (M)
Elizabeth (F)
Ellen (F)
Elspeth (F)
Elwin (M)
Engelbert (M)
Enoch (M)
Ephraim (M)
Erasmus (M)
Esther (F)
Ethelbert (M)
Etheldreda (F)
Ethelwin (M)
Eulalia (F)
Eustace (M)
Eve (F)
Ezekiel (M)
Ezra (M)
Fabian (M)
Faith (F)
Felix (M)
Fenton (M)
Ferdinand (M)
Fidelis (M)
Flavian (M)
Flora (F)
Frances (F)
Francis (M)
Gabriel (M)
Gaius (M)
Garfield (M)
Gemma (F)
Genevieve (F)
Geoffrey (M)
George (M)
Gerald (M)
Gerard (M)
Germain (M)
Gershom (M)
Gertrude (F)
Gervase (M)
Giacomo (M)
Gidon (M)
Gil (M)
Gilbert (M)
Giles (M)
Goliath (M)
Gregorios (M)
Gregory (M)
Gwen (F)
Gwladys (F)
Hagar (F)
Ham (M)
Hari (M)
Hāshim (M)
Heber (M)
Hedda (F)
Hedwig (F)
Helen (F)
Héloïse (F)
Henry (M)
Herbert (M)
Hezekiah (M)
Hilda (F)
Hildegarde (F)
Hiram (M)
Howard (M)
Hubert (M)
Hugh (M)
Humbert (M)
Hung (M)
Hyacinth (F)
Ian (M)
Ibrāhīm (M)
Ignatius (M)
Irene (F)
Isaac (M)
Isaak (M)
Isaiah (M)
Isidore (M)

Occupation/Activity

Ismael (M)
Ives (M)
Jacob (M)
Jacques (M)
Ja'far (M)
James (M)
Japheth (M)
Jason (M)
Jasper (M)
Javan (M)
Jedidiah (M)
Jehu (M)
Jemima (F)
Jephtha (M)
Jeremy (M)
Jermey (M)
Jerome (M)
Jesse (M)
Jesús (M)
Jethro (M)
Jezebel (F)
Jim (M)
Joab (M)
Joan (F)
Joanna (F)
Job (M)
Jocelin (F)
Joel (M)
John (M)
Jonah (M)
Jonathan (M)
Joseph (M)
Joshua (M)
Josiah (M)
Josip (M)
Jotham (M)
Juan (M)
Juana (F)
Judah (M)
Judas (M)
Jude (M)
Judith (F)
Judson (M)
Julián (M)
Juliana (F)
Julitta (F)
Julius (M)
Justin (M)
Justina (F)
Justinus (M)
Justus (M)
Karol (M)
Katharina (F)
Kentigern (M)
Kerenhappuch (F)
Keturah (F)
Keverne (M)
Kevin (M)
Kezia (F)
Kilian (M)
Klemens (M)
Laban (M)
Lambert (M)
Lancelot (M)
Lars (M)
Laurence (M)
Leah (F)
Leander (M)
Leo (M)
Leonard (M)
Leonhard (M)
Levi (M)
Liliosa (F)
Linus (M)
Lois (F)
Lorenzo (M)
Lot (M)
Louis (M)
Louise (F)
Lucian (M)
Lucius (M)
Lucy (F)
Luisa (F)
Luke (M)
Luther (M)
Lyman (M)
Magnus (M)
Malachi (M)
Malachy (M)
Malcolm (M)
Manasseh (M)
Marcellus (M)
Marco (M)
Margaret (F)
Maria (F)
Marian (F)
Mariana (F)
Marina (F)
Mark (M)
Markos (M)
Martha (F)
Martin (M)
Mary (F)
Mason (M)
Matteo (M)
Matthaus (M)
Matthew (M)
Matthias (M)
Matyas (M)
Maurice (M)
Maximilian (M)
Mel (M)
Merab (F)
Meshach (M)
Michael (M)
Mihály (M)
Miki (M)
Mildred (F)
Mincho (M)
Miriam (F)
Moïse (M)
Monica (F)
Mordechai (M)
Morwenna (F)
Moses (M)
Moshe (M)
Mungo (M)
Naomi (F)
Napthali (M)
Narcissus (M)
Nathan (M)
Nathaniel (M)
Nehemiah (M)
Nicholas (M)
Nicodemus (M)
Nicolaas (M)
Nicole (F)
Nigel (M)
Nikita (M)
Nikolai (M)
Nimrod (M)
Noah (M)
Norbert (M)
Norman (M)
Obadiah (M)
Octavius (M)
Odo (M)
Olga (F)
Oliver (M)
Orange (F)
Orestes (M)
Orpah (F)
Oswald (M)
Ottone (M)
Paolo (M)
Patrick (M)
Paul (M)
Paula (F)
Peregrine (M)
Peter (M)
Petter (M)
Philander (M)
Philemon (M)
Philip (M)
Philipp (M)
Philomena (F)
Phineas (M)
Pinchas (M)
Piotr (M)
Piran (M)
Pninah (F)
Quentin (M)
Rachel (F)
Randall (M)
Raphael (M)
Raymond (M)
Rebecca (F)
Remy (M)
Reuben (M)
Rhys (M)
Richard (M)
Rita (F)
Robert (M)
Roger (M)
Ronan (M)
Rose (F)
Rufus (M)
Rupert (M)
Ruth (F)
Ruy (M)
Saba (F)
Sabina (F)
Salome (F)
Samson (M)
Samuel (M)
Samuil (M)
Sarah (F)
Saul (M)
Sebastian (M)
Selwyn (M)
Seraphina (F)
Serena (F)
Sergey (M)
Sergius (M)
Seth (M)
Shadrach (M)
Shaul (M)
Shelah (F)
Shem (M)
Sidney (M)
Sidwell (M)
Sigfrid (M)
Sigmund (M)
Silas (M)
Silva (F)
Simon (M)
Sita (F)
Solomon (M)
Stanislaus (M)
Stephen (M)

Sulwyn (M)
Susanna (F)
Susannah (F)
Sylvanus (M)
Sylvester (M)
Tabitha (F)
Tadeusz (M)
Tamar (F)
Teresa (F)
Thekla (F)
Theodoric (M)
Theodosia (F)
Therese (F)
Thomas (M)
Timothy (M)
Titus (M)
Tzipora (F)
Urban (M)
Uri (M)
Uriah (M)
Ursula (F)
Valentine (M)
Vasily (M)
Veronica (F)
Victor (M)
Victoria (F)
Vincent (M)
Virgil (M)
Vitalis (M)
Vitus (M)
Vladimir (M)
Walburga (F)
Wallace (M)
Walter (M)
Ward (M)
Washington (M)
Webster (M)
Wells (M)
Wilbur (M)
Wilford (M)
Wilfred (M)
William (M)
Winefride (F)
Wolfgang (M)
Xavier (M)
Yisrael (M)
Zachariah (M)
Zacharias (M)
Zachary (M)
Zebulon (M)
Zedekiah (M)
Zephaniah (M)
Zillah (F)
Zilpah (F)
Zimri (M)
Zita (F)

Business and Finance

Aaron (M)
Adolphus (M)
Alejandro (M)
Aleksey (F)
Alois (M)
Alvin (M)
Amadeo (M)
Amory (M)
Amos (M)
André (M)
Andrew (M)
Angela (F)
Archer (M)
Armand (M)
Asa (M)
Axel (M)
Barney (M)
Benedetto (M)
Caspar (M)
Charles (M)
Chester (M)
Claus (M)
Collis (M)
Conrad (M)
Cornelius (M)
Curt (M)
Donald (M)
Elbert (M)
Eli (M)
Elizabeth (F)
Elliot (M)
Elmer (M)
Ezra (M)
Frederick (M)
Gabriel (M)
Gail (F)
Geoffrey (M)
Gerard (M)
Giovanni (M)
Grover (M)
Gustave (M)
Haley (F)
Harry (M)
Hayward (M)
Henri (M)
Henrietta (F)
Henry (M)
Houston (M)
Howard (M)
Ibrāhīm (M)
Irvin (M)
Isaac (M)
Ivar (M)
Ivy (M)
Jacques (M)
Jay (M)
Jeanne (F)
Job (M)
Josiah (M)
Kenneth (M)
Kirk (M)
Leroy (M)
Levi (M)
Lorenzo (M)
Luke (M)
Lydia (F)
Maisie (F)
Marshall (M)
Matthaus (M)
Meyer (M)
Milton (M)
Nelson (M)
Oliver (M)
Orville (M)
Ray (M)
Richard (M)
Russell (M)
Salomon (M)
Samo (M)
Samuel (M)
Sandford (M)
Selina (F)

Seth (M)
Sophia (F)
Stafford (M)
Stephen (M)
Sylvia (F)
Titus (M)
Washington (M)
William (M)
Willis (M)
Yaakov (M)
Yegor (M)

Fiction and Literature

Abner (M)
Abraham (M)
Ada (F)
Adam (M)
Adelaide (F)
Adine (F)
Affery (F)
Agatha (F)
Albert (M)
Alberto (M)
Albin (M)
Aldous (M)
Alec (M)
Aleksey (F)
Alexandros (M)
Alfredo (M)
Algernon (M)
Alice (F)
Allegra (F)
Althea (F)
Amanda (F)
Amber (F)
Amelia (F)
Amory (M)
Amy (F)
Amyas (M)
András (M)
Andy (M)
Angel (F)
Angela (F)
Angus (M)
Anna (F)
Anne (F)
Anthony (M)
Antonia (F)
Aphra (F)
Arabella (F)
Archer (M)
Armando (M)
Arne (M)
Arthur (M)
Ashley (F)
Astra (F)
Astrid (F)
Athelstan (M)
Augusta (F)
Aurelia (F)
Aylmer (M)
Barnabe (M)
Barnaby (M)
Bartholomew (M)
Beatrice (F)
Beatrix (F)
Belle (F)
Benito (M)
Bernard (M)
Bertha (F)
Beryl (F)
Bess (F)
Beverly (F)
Booth (M)
Bram (M)
Brendan (M)
Brigid (F)
Budington (M)
Burt (M)
Camilla (F)
Carlo (M)
Caroline (F)
Carolyn (F)
Carson (M)
Charlotte (F)
Christian (M)
Christina (F)
Cinderella (F)
Ciro (M)
Clara (F)
Clarence (M)
Clement (M)
Cleveland (M)
Clifford (M)
Clive (M)
Colleen (F)
Constance (F)
Cora (F)
Coralie (F)
Cornelia (F)
Craig (M)
Cynthia (F)
Daisy (F)
Damon (M)
Daniele (M)
Danielle (F)
Daphne (F)
Dave (M)
Dawn (F)
Dennis (M)
Denton (M)
Dick (M)
Diego (M)
Dinah (F)
Dino (M)
Donald (M)
Dora (F)
Dorian (F)
Doris (F)
Dorothy (F)
Dulcinea (F)
Earl (M)
Ebenezer (M)
Eden (F)
Edith (F)
Edmondo (M)
Edna (F)
Elaine (F)
Eleanor (F)
Elisabeth (F)
Ellen (F)
Ellery (M)
Elliot (M)
Ellis (M)
Else (F)
Emilia (F)
Emilio (M)
Emily (F)
Emma (F)
Enid (F)
Enrique (M)
Eppie (F)
Eric (M)
Erica (F)
Erich (M)
Ernest (M)
Erskine (M)
Erwin (M)
Eudora (F)
Eva (F)
Evelyn (F)
Faith (F)
Fanny (F)
Felipe (M)
Felix (M)
Fern (F)
Finley (M)
Fiona (F)
Fleur (F)
Florence (F)
Forrest (M)
Frans (M)
Franz (M)
Freeman (M)
Gabrielle (F)
Garth (M)
Gavin (M)
George (M)
Georgette (F)
Gerard (M)
Gerda (F)
Gertrude (F)
Gilbert (M)
Glorvina (F)
Gordon (M)
Graham (M)
Grazia (F)
Gregorio (M)
Griselda (F)
Gustave (M)
Gustavo (M)
Guy (M)
Hall (M)
Hamilton (M)
Hamlin (M)
Hans (M)
Harald (M)
Harold (M)
Harper (M)
Harriet (F)
Harvey (M)
Hector (M)
Heidi (F)
Helene (F)
Henrik (M)
Henryk (M)
Herbert (M)
Herman (M)
Holly (F)
Horace (M)
Horatio (M)
Hugh (M)
Ian (M)
Ichabod (M)
Ilona (F)
India (F)
Iris (F)
Isabella (F)
Israel (M)
Ivan (M)
Ivo (M)
Jacinto (M)
Jackie (M)
Jacqueline (F)
James (M)
Jane (F)
Janice (F)
Jean (M)
Jens (M)
Jeremias (M)
Joaquim (M)
Joel (M)
Johanna (F)
John (M)
Jolyon (M)
Jonas (M)
Jonathan (M)
Jorge (M)
José (M)
Josephine (F)
Joyce (F)
Jude (M)
Jules (M)
Julia (F)
Juliette (F)
Jun (M)
Justin (M)
Justine (F)
Kálmán (M)
Karel (M)
Karolina (F)
Karoline (F)
Kasimir (M)
Kate (F)
Kathleen (F)
Kay (F)
Kerensa (F)
Kingsley (M)
Kizzy (F)
Knut (M)
Kristofer (M)
Lalage (F)
Langston (M)
Lanny (M)
Lara (F)
Larry (M)
Laurence (M)
Leo (M)
Leon (M)
Leonhard (M)
Leonid (M)
Lewis (M)
Lolly (F)
Lorna (F)
Louis (M)
Louisa (F)
Louise (F)
Lucie (F)
Lucinda (F)
Lucretia (F)
Lucy (F)
Lyle (M)
Lyman (M)
Mabel (F)
Maeve (F)
Maggie (F)
Magnolia (F)
Major (M)
Maksim (M)
Manfred (M)
Marcel (F)
Marcellus (M)
Margaret (F)
Marguerite (F)
Maria (F)
Marianne (F)
Mario (M)
Marius (M)
Marjorie (F)
Mark (M)
Martha (F)
Mary (F)
Massimo (M)
Mateo (M)
Matilda (F)
Matthew (M)
Maxwell (M)
Melanie (F)
Melville (M)
Mervyn (M)
Michael (M)
Mickey (M)
Mignon (F)
Mihail (M)
Mika (M)
Mikhail (M)
Minna (F)
Muriel (F)
Nadine (F)
Nancy (F)
Nathan (M)
Nathaniel (M)
Newman (M)
Nigel (M)
Nikos (M)
Nils (M)
Norman (M)
Ödön (M)
Olav (M)
Ole (M)
Olive (F)
Otto (M)
Ouida (F)
Pamela (F)
Pansy (F)
Pauline (F)
Pearl (F)
Pelham (M)
Perceval (M)
Peregrine (M)
Peter (M)
Phil (M)
Phyllis (F)
Pollyanna (F)
Poul (M)
Rafael (M)
Ramona (F)
Randall (M)
Rawdon (M)
Raymond (M)
Rebecca (F)
Rene (F)
Rex (M)
Rhett (M)
Rhoda (F)
Ricardo (M)
Roald (M)
Robert (M)
Robinson (M)
Roderich (M)
Roderick (M)
Rodney (M)
Rodolphe (M)
Rohan (M)
Rolf (M)
Rollo (M)
Romain (M)
Rosa (F)

Occupation/Activity

Rosalia (F)
Rosalind (F)
Rosetta (F)
Ross (M)
Roxana (F)
Rudolf (M)
Rupert (M)
Ruth (F)
Salvador (M)
Salvatore (M)
Sam (M)
Sarah (F)
Saul (M)
Scarlett (F)
Scott (M)
Sébastien (M)
Selma (F)
Sergey (M)
Seumas (M)
Shalom (M)
Shen (M)
Sheridan (M)
Sidney (M)
Sidonie (F)
Sigrid (F)
Sigurd (M)
Sinclair (M)
Sloan (M)
Sonia (F)
Sophie (F)
Sophronia (F)
Stanisław (M)
Steele (M)
Stella (F)
Storm (F)
Stuart (M)
Susannah (F)
Sybil (F)
Sydney (M)
Tabitha (F)
Tanis (F)
Tansy (F)
Tess (F)
Tessa (F)
Thelma (F)
Theodore (M)
Thomasin (F)
Thornton (M)
Topsy (F)
Tristram (M)
Upton (M)
Uriah (M)
Valery (F)
Vance (M)
Vanda (F)
Vanessa (F)
Vera (F)
Vicente (M)
Vicki (F)
Victor (M)
Vilhelm (M)
Violet (F)
Virginia (F)
Vivian (F)
Wade (M)
Walt (M)
Wanda (F)
Warwick (M)
Washington (M)
Wilfred (M)
Willa (F)
Willard (M)
Wilson (M)
Winifred (F)
Winthrop (M)
Xavier (M)
Zane (M)
Zenobia (F)
Zoe (F)
Zona (F)
Zora (F)

Folklore and Myth

Aeneas (M)
Alma (F)
Althea (F)
Arthur (M)
Atalanta (F)
Casey (M)
Diana (F)
Dione (M)
Flora (F)
Fortuna (F)
Freja (F)
Guinevere (F)
Hebe (F)
Hector (M)
Helen (F)
Hercules (M)
Hermione (F)
Hippolyta (F)
Icarus (M)
Ilia (F)
Jason (M)
Narcissus (M)
Orestes (M)
Penelope (F)
Pillan (M)
Rhea (F)
Sabra (F)
Selina (F)
Stepan (M)
Thetis (F)

History and Politics

Aaron (M)
Abdul (M)
Abdulaziz (M)
Abdullah (M)
Abel (M)
Abigail (F)
Abraham (M)
Absalon (M)
Adelaide (F)
Adlai (M)
Adolph (M)
Adolphus (M)
Adrian (M)
Adrien (M)
Aeneas (M)
Agamemnon (M)
Agnes (F)
Ahmed (M)
Alaric (M)
Albert (M)
Albrecht (M)
Aldo (M)
Alejandro (M)
Aleksander (M)
Aleksandr (M)
Aleksandŭr (M)
Aleksey (F)
Alexander (M)
Alexandre (M)
Alexandros (M)
Alexius (F)
Alfonso (M)
Alfred (M)
Alfredo (M)
Ali (F)
Alois (M)
Alonso (M)
Aloys (M)
Alphonse (M)
Alphonso (M)
Alvar (M)
Alvaro (M)
Alvin (M)
Amalia (F)
Amand (M)
Ambrose (M)
Amelia (F)
Ami (F)
Amin (M)
Amos (M)
Ana (F)
Anastasia (F)
Andrei (M)
Andrej (M)
Andrés (M)
Andrew (M)
Anibal (M)
Anson (M)
Anthony (M)
Antonia (F)
Antonín (M)
Antonio (M)
Anwar (M)
Archelaus (M)
Ariadne (F)
Armand (M)
Armando (M)
Artemas (M)
Arturo (M)
Arvid (M)
As'ad (M)
Asoka (F)
Aspasia (F)
Astrid (F)
Athelstan (M)
Audie (M)
Augusta (F)
Augustine (M)
Augustus (M)
Aurelian (M)
Austen (M)
Averell (M)
Axel (M)
Azariah (M)
'Azīz (M)
Bainbridge (M)
Bal (M)
Baldwin (M)
Barbara (F)
Barthelemy (M)
Bartholomew (M)
Bartolomé (M)
Basil (M)
Beatrice (F)
Beatrix (F)
Bella (F)
Ben (M)
Benito (M)
Berenice (F)
Bernal (M)
Bernardine (F)
Bernardino (M)
Bernardo (M)
Bertha (F)
Bianca (F)
Birch (M)
Blanche (F)
Bohdan (M)
Braxton (M)
Brent (M)
Brigham (M)
Brock (M)
Burke (M)
Burton (M)
Caesar (M)
Calvin (M)
Carla (F)
Carlo (M)
Carlos (M)
Carlota (F)
Caroline (F)
Carroll (M)
Carter (M)
Casimir (M)
Caspar (M)
Cecil (M)
Charles (M)
Charlotte (F)
Charmian (F)
Chester (M)
Christina (F)
Claire (F)
Clark (M)
Claude (M)
Claudius (M)
Claus (M)
Clayton (M)
Clemens (M)
Clement (M)
Clemente (M)
Cleopatra (F)
Clifford (M)
Clinton (M)
Clotilda (F)
Cola (M)
Coleman (M)
Colin (M)
Conn (M)
Connor (M)
Constantine (M)
Cordell (M)
Coretta (F)
Cornelia (F)
Cornelius (M)
Cort (M)
Corydon (M)
Creighton (M)
Crispus (M)
Cristóbal (M)
Curtis (M)
Cuthbert (M)
Cyrus (M)
Dafydd (M)
Dag (M)
Daniele (M)
Danilo (M)
Darius (M)
Davy (M)
Dean (M)
Deborah (F)
Decimus (M)
Demetrius (M)
Dermot (M)
Diane (F)
Dick (M)
Diego (M)
Dinh (M)
Dion (M)
Dionisio (M)
Dionysius (M)
Dixon (M)
Domingo (M)
Don (M)
Douglas (M)
Drusilla (F)
Duarte (M)
Dudley (M)

Dusan (M)
Dwight (M)
Ebenezer (M)
Ed (M)
Eden (F)
Edmund (M)
Edric (M)
Eduardo (M)
Edvard (M)
Egbert (M)
Eleanor (F)
Eleazar (M)
Elie (M)
Elihu (M)
Elisabeth (F)
Elisha (F)
Eliza (F)
Ella (F)
Elliot (M)
Eloy (M)
Emilio (M)
Emory (M)
Engelbert (M)
Enoch (M)
Enrique (M)
Eoghan (M)
Ephraim (M)
Ernesto (M)
Esme (M)
Ethan (M)
Étienne (M)
Eustace (M)
Eva (F)
Evan (M)
Evelyn (F)
Everett (M)
Ewen (M)
Ezra (M)
Faith (F)
Feargus (M)
Ferdinand (M)
Fernando (M)
Fidel (M)
Filippo (M)
Filips (M)
Fitzroy (M)
Fletcher (M)
Flora (F)
Florence (F)
Florian (M)
Frances (F)
Francis (M)
Francisco (M)
Franklin (M)
Fred (M)

Freeman (M)
Gábor (M)
Gabriel (M)
Gabriele (M)
Galina (F)
Garnet (M)
Garret (M)
Gaspar (M)
Gaspard (M)
Gautier (M)
Gavril (M)
George (M)
Georgi (M)
Georgiana (F)
Georgios (M)
Georgy (M)
Gerald (M)
Geraldine (F)
Gian (M)
Gideon (M)
Gil (M)
Giles (M)
Gilles (M)
Gino (M)
Gisela (F)
Godfrey (M)
Godwin (M)
Golda (F)
Grace (F)
Granville (M)
Gregory (M)
Griffin (M)
Grover (M)
Guadalupe (M)
Gunnar (M)
Gustaf (M)
Gustav (M)
Gustavo (M)
Guy (M)
Gwynfor (M)
Haakon (M)
Hadrian (M)
Ham (M)
Hamilton (M)
Hannes (M)
Hannibal (M)
Harold (M)
Harrison (M)
Harry (M)
Harun (M)
Hāshim (M)
Hattie (F)
Hazael (M)
Hector (M)
Henri (M)
Henrique (M)
Henry (M)
Henryk (M)
Herbert (M)
Herman (M)
Hippolyte (M)
Hiram (M)
Ho (M)
Holland (M)
Homer (M)
Horatio (M)
Howell (M)
Hubert (M)
Hudson (M)
Huey (M)
Hugo (M)
Humberto (M)
Humphrey (M)
Hung (M)
Huntly (M)
Hyman (M)
Ian (M)
Ida (F)
Inés (F)
Ingeborg (F)
Ioannis (M)
Iosif (M)
Ira (M)
Irene (F)
Irvin (M)
Isabeau (F)
Iskandar (M)
Ismael (M)
Israel (M)
István (M)
Jaan (M)
Jacobo (M)
Ja'far (M)
Jan (M)
János (M)
Jean-François (M)
Jedediah (M)
Jefferson (M)

Jeffrey (M)
Jesse (M)
Jimmy (M)
João (M)
Joaquim (M)
Joaquín (M)
Johan (M)
John (M)
Jonas (M)
Jorge (M)
José (M)
Josephus (M)
Joshua (M)
Josip (M)
Jovan (M)
Juan (M)
Juanita (F)
Jubal (M)
Judah (M)
Judson (M)
Juho (M)
Jules (M)
Julián (M)
Juliana (F)
Julie (F)
Julien (M)
Julio (M)
Julius (M)
Jürgen (M)
Justin (M)
Justo (M)
Kálmán (M)
Kāmil (M)
Karl (M)
Karlis (M)
Karoline (F)
Károly (M)
Kasimir (M)
Kaspar (M)
Kató (F)
Kei (F)
Keith (M)
Kenelm (M)
Kenneth (M)
Khālid (M)
Khalīl (M)
Kingsley (M)
Kit (M)
Klemens (M)
Klement (M)
Kliment (M)
Knud (M)
Knut (M)
Konni (M)
Kurt (M)
Lachlan (M)
Lafayette (M)
Lal (M)
Lala (F)
Lars (M)
Laurent (M)
Lavr (M)
Lázaro (M)
Leif (M)
Leon (M)
Leonhard (M)
Leonid (M)
Leonidas (M)
Leopold (M)
Leslie (F)
Lester (M)
Lev (M)
Levi (M)
Lewis (M)
Li (F)
Lilia (F)
Liliha (F)
Lincoln (M)
Lola (F)
Lucas (M)
Lucien (M)
Lucius (M)
Lucretia (F)
Lucrezia (F)
Lucy (F)
Luigi (M)
Luis (M)
Luke (M)
Luther (M)
Lyman (M)
Lyndon (M)
Mackenzie (M)
Maeve (F)
Magda (F)
Magnus (M)
Maḥmūd (M)
Maksim (M)
Malcolm (M)
Malik (M)
Malin (F)
Manco (M)
Manfred (M)
Manius (M)
Mansa (M)
Manuel (M)
Marcel (F)
Marco (M)
Marcos (M)
Marcus (M)
Marguerite (F)
Mariya (F)
Mark (M)
Marko (M)
Markos (M)
Marlin (M)
Marshall (M)
Martin (M)
Massimiliano (M)
Massimo (M)
Mathieu (M)
Matías (M)
Matteo (M)
Matthew (M)
Matyas (M)
Maurice (M)
Maxime (M)
Maximilian (M)
Maximiliano (M)
Máximo (M)
Melvin (M)
Mena (F)
Menachem (M)
Miguel (M)
Mihail (M)
Mihály (M)
Mikhail (M)
Miles (M)
Millard (M)
Molly (F)
Morgan (M)
Moses (M)
Moshe (M)
Mungo (M)
Myron (M)
Napoleon (M)
Natalya (F)
Nathan (M)
Nathaniel (M)
Necho (F)
Ned (M)
Nehemiah (M)
Neil (M)
Nellie (F)
Nelson (M)
Nero (M)
Neville (M)
Newton (M)
Nicholas (M)
Nicola (F)
Nicolás (M)
Niels (M)
Nikita (M)
Nikolai (M)
Nils (M)
Ninian (M)
Numa (M)
Nuri (M)
Octavia (F)
Octavius (M)
Odette (F)
Ogden (M)
Olafur (M)
Olav (M)
Olivier (M)
Omar (M)
Orestes (M)
Orla (F)
Orville (M)
Oscar (M)
Osyth (F)
Otis (M)
Pál (M)
Pancho (M)
Pascual (M)
Patrice (M)
Patricia (F)
Paul (M)
Paulo (M)
Pavel (M)
Peder (M)
Pedro (M)
Pepi (M)
Pepin (M)
Per (M)
Peregrine (M)
Pero (M)
Peyton (M)
Philander (M)
Philippa (F)
Phillips (M)
Pierre (M)
Piers (M)
Poul (M)
Priscilla (F)
Pyotr (M)
Quincy (M)
Quintin (M)
Rafael (M)
Raimundo (M)
Ralph (M)
Ramsay (M)
Ranald (M)
Raoul (M)
Raphael (M)
Raymond (M)
Rayner (M)
Redvers (M)
Reed (M)
Rene (M)
Renée (F)
Ricardo (M)
Rinaldo (M)
Roald (M)
Roberto (M)
Robin (M)
Roderick (M)
Rodolfo (M)
Rodrigo (M)
Rogers (M)
Ronald (M)
Rory (M)
Rosa (F)
Rosamond (F)
Rose (F)
Roy (M)
Royal (M)
Rüdiger (M)
Rudolf (M)
Ruggerio (M)
Rupert (M)
Rurik (M)
Russell (M)
Rutger (M)
Ruth (F)
Rutherford (M)
Ruy (M)
Ryszard (M)
Saba (F)
Sa'īd (M)
Sāliḥ (M)
Sally (F)
Salome (F)
Salvador (M)
Sándor (M)
Santiago (M)
Saul (M)
Schuyler (M)
Sean (M)
Sebastian (M)
Selim (M)
Septimus (M)
Sergio (M)
Sergius (M)

Occupation/Activity

Seth (M)
Shaka (M)
Sheridan (M)
Sherman (M)
Shirley (F)
Shu (F)
Sidonio (M)
Sigurd (M)
Sinclair (M)
Smith (M)
Sonny (M)
Sophia (F)
Spencer (M)
Stafford (M)
Stanislas (M)
Stanisław (M)
Stanley (M)
Stefan (M)
Stepan (M)
Stephan (M)
Stéphanie (F)
Stephanus (M)
Sterling (M)
Sylvanus (M)
Tadeusz (M)
Tamara (F)
Theodor (M)
Theodore (M)
Theodoric (M)
Theophilus (M)
Thor (M)
Thorvald (M)
Thurlow (M)
Timofey (M)
Tobias (M)
Todor (M)
Tomas (M)
Tome (M)
Tristan (M)
Tudor (M)
Tung (M)
Ulrich (M)
Ulysses (M)
Urbano (M)
Uriah (M)
Uzziah (M)
Vaino (M)
Vannevar (M)
Vasil (M)
Vasile (M)
Vera (F)
Vernon (M)
Vicente (M)
Victor (M)
Viktor (M)
Vilhelm (M)
Vincent (M)
Vincente (M)
Vittorio (M)
Vitus (M)
Vladimir (M)
Wade (M)
Warren (M)
Washington (M)
Watkin (M)
Wendell (M)
Werner (M)
Wesley (M)
Wilbur (M)
Willard (M)
Willis (M)
Wilson (M)
Winfield (M)
Winston (M)
Winthrop (M)
Woodrow (M)
Wright (M)
Xerxes (M)
Yaakov (M)
Yazid (M)
Yegor (M)
Yekaterina (F)
Yelizaveta (F)
Yitzchak (M)
Yves (M)
Yvon (M)
Zachary (M)
Zebulon (M)
Zedekiah (M)
Zenobia (F)
Zigfrids (M)
Zoltán (M)

Journalism and Publishing

Adolph (M)
Aleksey (F)
Algernon (M)
Allen (M)
Alpheus (M)
Alvin (M)
Ambrose (M)
Anne (F)
Art (M)
Bennett (M)
Bert (M)
Bob (M)
Brendan (M)
Clay (M)
Clifton (M)
Cyril (M)
Damon (M)
Dan (M)
Desire (F)
Donn (M)
Drew (M)
Ed (M)
Edgar (M)
Eduardo (M)
Ella (F)
Eppie (F)
Ernesto (M)
Eustace (M)
Finley (M)
Franklin (M)
Gabriele (M)
Goeffrey (M)
Hamilton (M)
Harold (M)
Hedda (F)
Hezekiah (M)
Hodding (M)
Hugh (M)
Ida (F)
Ioan (M)
Irvin (M)
Isaiah (M)
Janet (F)
Jaroslav (M)
Jay (U)
Jennie (F)
Jens (M)
Joaquín (M)
Joel (M)
Jovan (M)
Jude (M)
Károly (M)
Kitty (F)
Leonard (M)
Lincoln (M)
Louella (F)
Maxime (M)
Melville (M)
Miles (M)
Milton (M)
Nathan (M)
Nehemiah (M)
Nellie (F)
Ogden (M)
Otto (M)
Pauline (F)
Pierce (M)
Ramón (M)
Raoul (M)
Rebecca (F)
Rollo (M)
Ronald (M)
Rudi (M)
Rupert (M)
Seumas (M)
Sheldon (M)
Sylvanus (M)
Valentine (M)
Waldo (M)
Walter (M)
Westbrook (M)
Whittaker (M)
Wolf (M)

Law

Abe (M)
Ada (F)
Alton (M)
Anthony (M)
Barnabas (M)
Bartolo (M)
Benedikt (M)
Byron (M)
Chauncey (M)
Clarence (M)
Clement (M)
Cosmo (M)
David (M)
Dionisio (M)
Earl (M)
Erskine (M)
Étienne (M)
Gabriel (M)
Gaius (M)
Gil (M)
Harlan (M)
Hartley (M)
Horace (M)
Howell (M)
Hugo (M)
Hunter (M)
John (M)
Josiah (M)
Justus (M)
Laurence (M)
Levi (M)
Lucius (M)
Manley (M)
Mathieu (M)
Melville (M)
Morrison (M)
Moses (M)
Nathan (M)
Newton (M)
Nikolaos (M)
Noah (M)
Owen (M)
Pierce (M)
Redmond (M)

Rufus (M)
Samuel (M)
Sandra (F)
Sheldon (M)
Sherman (M)
Silas (M)
Smith (M)
Stafford (M)
Stephen (M)
Wallace (M)
Ward (M)
Warren (M)
Wayne (M)
Wiley (M)
Willis (M)
Wyatt (M)

Medicine

Alexis (F)
Alfonso (M)
Anders (M)
Antoni (M)
Armand (M)
Bailey (M)
Bela (M)
Benjamin (M)
Berkeley (M)
Bertrand (M)
Carl (M)
Carlo (M)
Clara (F)
Crawford (M)
Denton (M)
Dominique (M)
Elie (M)
Elijah (M)
Engelbert (M)
Ephraim (M)
Eugen (M)
Filippo (M)
Florence (F)
François (M)
Friedrich (M)
Galen (M)
Grantly (M)
Havelock (M)
Herman (M)
Homer (M)
Horace (M)
Ivan (M)
Julien (M)
Kiyoshi (M)
Leone (M)
Lewis (M)
Lillian (F)
Logan (M)
Marcello (M)
Margaret (F)
Marshall (M)
Matthew (M)
Max (M)
Michele (M)
Morton (M)
Niels (M)
Ole (M)
Olof (M)
Osborne (M)
Paolo (M)
Patrick (M)
Paul (M)
Rodney (M)
Rufus (M)
Silas (M)
Siôn (M)
Sophia (F)
Theodor (M)
Tobias (M)
Virginia (F)
Walter (M)
Wendell (M)
Werner (M)
Wilfred (M)
Wolf (M)

Movies

Abby (F)
Abel (M)
Adela (F)
Adolph (M)
Al (M)
Alain (M)
Alastair (M)
Alec (M)
Alexandra (F)
Alfred (M)
Ali (F)
Aline (F)
Almira (F)
Amy (F)
Andrey (M)
Andy (M)
Angela (F)
Anita (F)
Anna (F)
Annabella (F)
Annette (F)
Anthony (M)
Arlene (F)
Arnold (M)
Åsta (F)
Audrey (F)
Ava (F)
Barbi (F)
Barbra (F)
Barnabas (M)
Barry (M)
Barton (M)
Basil (M)
Beatrice (F)
Beau (M)
Bela (M)
Ben (M)
Bernadette (F)
Bernard (M)
Bernardo (M)
Bess (F)
Bessie (F)
Beth (F)
Betsy (F)
Betty (F)
Beverly (F)
Bill (M)

Billie (F)
Billy (M)
Blake (M)
Blythe (F)
Bo (M)
Bob (M)
Bonnie (F)
Bradford (M)
Brandon (M)
Brenda (F)
Brent (M)
Brian (M)
Brigitte (F)
Brock (M)
Bronson (M)
Brooke (F)
Bruce (M)
Bruno (M)
Burt (M)
Buster (M)
Camelia (F)
Carmen (F)
Carol (F)
Carole (F)
Carrie (F)
Cary (M)
Catherine (F)
Cecil (M)
Cedric (M)
Celeste (F)
Celia (F)
Charlie (M)
Charlton (M)
Charo (F)
Cher (F)
Cherilyn (F)
Cheryl (F)
Chester (M)
Chevy (M)
Chico (M)
Chuck (M)
Chynna (F)
Cicely (F)
Claire (F)
Clara (F)
Clark (M)
Claudette (F)
Claudia (F)
Cliff (M)
Clifton (M)
Clint (M)
Clive (M)
Colin (M)
Colleen (F)
Conan (M)
Connie (F)
Conrad (M)
Constance (F)
Corey (M)
Corinne (F)
Cosmo (M)
Craig (M)
Dale (M)
Damien (M)
Dan (M)
Dana (F)
Daniel (M)
Danielle (F)
Danny (M)
Darryl (M)
Daryl (M)
Dawn (F)
Dean (M)
Deanna (F)
Debbie (F)
Deborah (F)
Debra (F)
Dee (F)
Delbert (M)
Delmar (M)
Denholm (M)
Dennis (M)
Derek (M)
Desmond (M)
Diana (F)
Diane (F)
Dick (M)
Dimitri (M)
Dina (F)
Dinah (F)
Dirk (M)
Dixie (F)
Dolly (F)
Dolores (F)
Dom (M)
Don (M)
Donald (M)
Donna (F)
Donny (M)
Doris (F)
Douglas (M)
Drew (M)
Dudley (M)
Duncan (M)
Dustin (M)
Ed (M)
Eddie (M)
Edie (F)
Edna (F)
Edward (M)

Edwin (M)
Effie (F)
Eileen (F)
Elaine (F)
Eleanor (F)
Eli (M)
Elia (M)
Elisabeth (F)
Elizabeth (F)
Elke (F)
Ella (F)
Elsa (F)
Emma (F)
Ernest (M)
Errol (M)
Erwin (M)
Estelle (F)
Ethel (F)
Eva (F)
Everett (M)
Fanny (F)
Farley (M)
Fay (F)
Felicia (F)
Felicity (F)
Fidelma (F)
Ford (M)
Forrest (M)
Francis (M)
Franco (M)
François (M)
Frank (M)
Franklin (M)
Fred (M)
Freddie (F)
Friedrich (M)
Fritz (M)
Gary (M)
Gemma (F)
Gena (F)
Gene (M)
Geraldine (F)
Gig (M)
Gilda (F)
Gina (F)
Ginger (F)
Gladys (F)
Glenda (F)
Glenn (M)
Gloria (F)
Goldie (F)
Grace (F)
Gracie (F)
Greer (F)
Greta (F)
Haidee (F)
Hal (M)
Hannah (F)
Hardy (M)
Harrison (M)
Hattie (F)
Hayley (F)
Heather (F)
Hedy (F)
Helen (F)
Helena (F)
Hezekiah (M)
Holly (F)
Hope (F)
Howard (M)
Humphrey (M)
Ida (F)
Ilona (F)
Ingrid (F)
Ione (F)
Irene (F)
Irma (F)
Isabella (F)
Jack (M)
Jackie (M)
Jacqueline (F)
Jane (F)
Janet (F)
Janis (F)
Jason (M)
Jeanette (F)
Jeremy (M)
Jesse (M)
Jessica (F)
Jill (F)
Jim (M)
Jimmy (M)
Joan (F)
Joanne (F)
Jodie (F)
Joe (M)
Joel (M)
Joey (M)
Johnny (M)
Josef (M)
Judith (F)
Judy (F)
Jules (M)
Julia (F)
Julie (F)
Justine (F)
Karen (F)
Karl (M)
Kate (F)
Kathleen (F)
Kathy (F)
Keir (M)
Kevin (M)
King (M)
Kirk (M)
Kristi (F)
Kurt (M)
Lana (F)
Laura (F)
Lauren (F)
Lee (F)
Lena (F)
Leslie (F)
Lex (M)
Libby (F)
Lillian (F)
Lily (F)
Linda (F)
Lindsay (F)
Lionel (M)
Liza (F)
Lizabeth (F)
Lloyd (M)
Lon (M)
Loretta (F)
Lorraine (F)
Louise (F)
Mabel (F)
Macaulay (M)
Madeleine (F)
Madeline (F)
Mae (F)
Maggie (F)
Mamie (F)
Marcus (M)
Mare (F)
Margarita (F)
Margaux (F)
Marianne (F)
Mariel (F)
Marilyn (F)
Marlee (F)
Marlene (F)
Marlon (M)
Martin (M)
Mary (F)
Matt (M)
Maureen (F)
Maximilian (M)
Maxine (F)
May (F)
Mel (M)
Melanie (F)
Melina (F)
Melvyn (M)
Mercedes (F)
Meryl (F)
Mia (F)
Michael (M)
Michelle (F)
Mickey (M)
Mike (M)
Millicent (F)
Mimi (F)
Minnie (F)
Mitzi (F)
Moira (F)
Molly (F)
Muriel (F)
Myrna (F)
Nanette (F)
Natalie (F)
Nerys (F)
Neville (M)
Nick (M)
Nicole (F)
Nigel (M)
Nina (F)
Noah (M)
Norma (F)
Nova (F)
Odile (F)
Oliver (M)
Olivia (F)
Omar (M)
Orson (M)
Otis (M)
Otto (M)
Paddy (M)
Patricia (F)
Patrick (M)
Paula (F)
Paulette (F)
Pearl (F)
Peggy (F)
Penny (F)
Petula (F)
Phil (M)
Preston (M)
Priscilla (F)
Raoul (M)
Raquel (F)
Raúl (M)
Ray (M)
Rebecca (F)
Reginald (M)
Rex (M)
Rhonda (F)
Ricky (M)
Rip (M)
Rita (F)
Rob (M)
Robby (M)
Robert (M)
Roberto (M)
Rock (M)
Rocky (M)
Rod (M)
Roddy (M)
Roger (M)
Romy (F)
Ronald (M)
Rory (M)
Rosalind (F)
Rosanna (F)
Ross (M)
Rudolph (M)
Ryan (M)
Sada (F)
Sally (F)
Sally-Ann (F)
Sam (M)
Samantha (F)
Sandra (F)
Sandy (F)
Sarah (F)
Scott (M)
Sean (M)
Sergei (M)
Seymour (M)
Shari (F)

Occupation/Activity

Shawn (M)
Sheila (F)
Shelley (F)
Sherman (M)
Shirley (F)
Sid (M)
Sidney (M)
Signe (F)
Sigourney (F)
Simone (F)
Sinead (F)
Siobhan (F)
Sissy (F)
Sophia (F)
Spencer (M)
Stacy (F)
Stan (M)
Stanley (M)
Stella (F)
Stephanie (F)
Sterling (M)
Steve (M)
Stockard (F)
Susan (F)
Susanna (F)
Susannah (F)
Suzanne (F)
Swoosie (F)
Sylvester (M)
Sylvia (F)
Tab (M)
Tad (M)
Talia (F)
Tallulah (F)
Tatum (F)
Thelma (F)
Thora (F)
Tim (M)
Timothy (M)
Tom (M)
Tony (M)
Tracey (F)
Trevor (M)
Trish (F)
Troy (M)
Tuesday (F)
Tula (F)
Tyrone (M)
Una (F)
Ursula (F)
Valerie (F)
Van (M)
Vanessa (F)
Velma (F)
Verna (F)
Veronica (F)
Vic (M)
Vicki (F)
Victor (M)
Vilmos (M)
Vince (M)
Vincente (M)
Viola (F)
Vittorio (M)
Vivien (F)
Wade (M)
Walt (M)
Wanda (F)
Ward (M)
Warren (M)
Wendell (M)
Wendy (F)
Wes (M)
Wesley (M)
Whoopi (F)
Will (M)
Wilson (M)
Windsor (M)
Winona (F)
Woody (M)
Yahoo (M)
Yul (M)
Yvette (F)
Yvonne (F)

Music

Aaron (M)
Ace (M)
Adelina (F)
Adeline (F)
Adina (F)
Adrian (M)
Adriano (M)
Al (M)
Alan (M)
Alban (M)
Alberta (F)
Alessandro (M)
Alexander (M)
Alma (F)
Alois (M)
Alvin (M)
Amadeo (M)
Amy (F)
André (M)
Andreas (M)
Andres (M)
Andrew (M)
Anita (F)
Annie (F)
Antoine (M)
Anton (M)
Antonín (M)
Antonio (M)
Arabella (F)
Aretha (F)
Ariadne (F)
Arlo (M)
Arne (M)
Art (M)
Arthur (M)
Arturo (M)
Arvid (M)
August (M)
Augustus (M)
Barbra (F)
Barry (M)
Basia (F)
Bedřich (M)
Bela (M)
Belinda (F)
Benedetto (M)
Beniamino (M)
Benjamin (M)
Benny (M)
Bernard (M)
Bernhard (M)
Bessie (F)
Bette (F)
Beverly (F)
Billie (F)
Billy (M)
Bing (M)
Birgit (F)
Blanche (F)
Bob (M)
Bobby (M)
Bonnie (F)
Boyd (M)
Brenda (F)
Brent (M)
Brian (M)
Brooke (F)
Bruce (M)
Bruno (M)
Buck (M)
Burt (M)
Burton (M)
Camille (F)
Candy (F)
Carl (M)
Carlos (M)
Carly (F)
Carmen (F)
Carole (F)
Carolina (F)
Cecil (M)
Chad (M)
Charlie (M)
Chauncey (M)
Cher (F)
Cherilyn (F)
Chet (M)
Chick (M)
Chrissie (F)
Christoph (M)
Chuck (M)
Chynna (F)
Claude (M)
Claudio (M)
Clemens (M)
Clementina (F)
Clementine (F)
Cleo (F)
Cliff (M)
Clifford (M)
Clifton (M)
Cole (M)
Coleman (M)
Connie (F)
Conrad (M)
Constant (M)
Conway (M)
Corey (M)
Cornell (M)
Cristóbal (M)
Crystal (F)
Curt (M)
Curtis (M)
Cy (M)
Cyril (M)
Daniel (M)
Darius (M)
Daryl (M)
Dave (M)
David (M)
Dean (M)
Deanna (F)
Debbie (F)
Del (M)
Delbert (M)
Della (F)
Dennis (M)
Desire (F)
Dexter (M)
Dimitri (M)
Dinah (F)
Dion (M)
Dionne (F)
Dolly (F)
Domenico (M)
Don (M)
Donna (F)
Donny (M)
Donovan (M)
Doris (F)
Dorothy (F)
Dottie (F)
Douglas (M)
Duane (M)
Duff (M)
Duke (M)
Dusty (M)
Earl (M)
Earlene (F)
Eartha (F)
Eben (M)
Ebenezer (M)
Edgar (M)
Edgard (M)
Edie (F)
Effie (F)
Eileen (F)
Elena (F)
Elias (M)
Elisabeth (F)
Eliza (F)
Ella (F)
Ellen (F)
Elsie (F)
Elton (M)
Elvis (M)
Emmanuel (M)
Emmy (F)
Engelbert (M)
Enrico (M)
Eric (M)
Erich (M)
Erik (M)
Ernestine (F)
Errol (M)
Ethel (F)
Ethelbert (M)
Étienne (M)
Etta (F)
Eugene (M)
Eugenia (F)
Eugenio (M)
Fabian (M)
Feliks (M)
Felipe (M)
Felix (M)
Ferdinand (M)
Fernando (M)
Filippo (M)
Fletcher (M)
Frances (F)
Francesco (M)
Franco (M)
Frank (M)
Frankie (M)
Franz (M)
Frederica (F)
Frederick (M)
Friedrich (M)
Fritz (M)
Garth (M)
Gary (M)
Gene (M)
Geoffrey (M)
Georg (M)
Geraint (M)
Gerald (M)
Geraldine (F)
Gertrude (F)
Giacomo (M)
Gian (M)
Giles (M)
Gilles (M)
Giovanni (M)
Giuseppe (M)
Gladys (F)
Glenn (M)
Gloria (F)
Gordon (M)
Graham (M)
Granville (M)
Gregor (M)
Guido (M)
Guillaume (M)
Gunnar (M)
Gustav (M)
Gustave (M)
Hall (M)
Hank (M)
Harry (M)
Hector (M)
Henryk (M)
Horatio (M)
Howard (M)
Humphrey (M)
Ignace (M)
Ira (M)
Irving (M)
Isaac (M)
Ivan (M)
Jack (M)
Jackson (M)
James (M)
Janet (F)
Jay (M)
Jeanette (F)
Jenny (F)
Jerome (M)
Jezebel (F)
Jimmy (M)
Jo (M)
Joan (F)
Joaquín (M)
Johan (M)
Johann (M)
Johanna (F)
Johnnie (M)
Johnny (M)
Joni (F)
Jordan (M)
José (M)
Josef (M)
Jude (M)
Judith (F)
Judson (M)
Judy (F)
Julián (M)
Julio (M)
Karol (M)
Kate (F)
Katharina (F)
Kathleen (F)
Keith (M)

Kenny (M)
Kirsten (F)
Kitty (F)
Kris (M)
Kylie (F)
Lady (F)
Latoya (F)
Lena (F)
Lenny (M)
Leo (M)
Leon (M)
Leonard (M)
Leonardo (M)
Leopold (M)
Leos (M)
Les (M)
Liam (M)
Lillian (F)
Lily (F)
Linda (F)
Lisa (F)
Lonnie (M)
Loretta (F)
Lotte (F)
Lou (M)
Louis (M)
Lowell (M)
Luca (M)
Lucia (F)
Lucrezia (F)
Ludovic (M)
Ludwig (M)
Luis (M)
Luisa (F)
Luka (M)
Mabel (F)
Mahalia (F)
Manfred (M)
Marc (M)
Marcos (M)
Marie (F)
Marni (F)
Marvin (M)
Mary (F)
Matthias (M)
Maureen (F)
Maurice (M)
Meade (M)
Mel (M)
Melissa (F)
Merle (M)
Michael (M)
Michal (M)
Michelle (F)
Mick (M)
Mignon (F)
Miles (M)
Millicent (F)
Milton (M)
Minnie (F)
Mitch (M)
Myra (F)
Naomi (F)
Nat (M)
Natalie (F)
Neil (M)
Nellie (F)
Nelson (M)
Nicholas (M)
Nicola (F)
Nicolaus (M)
Ola (F)
Olin (M)
Olivia (F)
Orlando (M)
Oscar (M)
Otis (M)
Ozzy (M)
Pablo (M)
Pascal (M)

Patience (F)
Patrice (M)
Patti (F)
Paul (M)
Paula (F)
Pearl (F)
Pelham (M)
Percy (M)
Perry (M)
Pete (M)
Petula (F)
Phil (M)
Phyllis (F)
Pietro (M)
Prince (M)
Randy (M)
Ravi (M)
Ray (M)
Reba (F)
Regina (F)
Regine (F)
Renata (F)
Renātus (M)
Rickie (M)
Ricky (M)
Rikard (M)
Riley (M)
Ringo (M)
Rita (F)
Roberta (F)
Rod (M)
Rodolfo (M)
Rodolphe (M)
Roger (M)
Roi (M)
Rosamond (F)
Rosemary (F)
Rosina (F)
Roy (M)
Rudi (M)
Rudolph (M)
Rudy (M)
Salomon (M)
Salomone (M)
Salvatore (M)
Samson (M)
Sándor (M)
Sarah (F)
Saverio (M)
Scott (M)
Sean (M)
Selim (M)
Septimus (M)
Serge (M)
Sergei (M)
Seth (M)
Sheldon (M)
Shulamit (F)
Sid (M)
Siegfried (M)
Sigfrid (M)
Sigmund (M)
Silas (M)
Sinead (F)
Solomon (M)
Sonny (M)
Stanisław (M)
Sterling (M)
Steve (M)
Stevie (M)
Sting (M)
Stormy (F)
Sylvester (M)
Tessa (F)
Tessie (F)
Tex (M)
Tiffany (F)
Timothy (M)
Tina (F)
Tito (M)
Todd (M)
Tom (M)
Tommy (M)
Toni (F)
Tony (M)
Tracey (F)
Trevor (M)
Tristan (M)
Val (F)
Valery (F)
Van (M)
Vasily (M)
Vaughn (M)
Vic (M)
Victor (M)
Vincent (M)
Vincenzo (M)
Violetta (F)
Virgil (M)
Vladimir (M)
Waldo (M)
Wanda (F)
Waylon (M)
Wayne (M)
Webster (M)
Whitney (F)
Will (M)
Wolfgang (M)
Woody (M)
Xavier (M)
Yehudi (M)
Yoko (F)
Yvette (F)
Zachary (M)
Zoltán (M)

Poetry

Abram (M)
Ada (F)
Adelaide (F)
Alan (M)
Albin (M)
Aleksander (M)
Alessandro (M)
Alexander (M)
Alexis (F)
Alfred (M)
Alfredo (M)
Algernon (M)
Ali (F)
Alicia (F)
Alma (F)
Alonso (M)
Althea (F)
Alun (M)
Amado (M)
Ambrose (M)
Amir (M)
Amy (F)
Aneirin (M)
Angelica (F)
Angelo (M)
Anna (F)
Anne (F)
Annette (F)
Antoni (M)
Antonín (M)
Antonio (M)
Arabella (F)
Archibald (M)
Ariel (F)
Arno (M)
Ate (M)
Aubrey (M)
Aurelius (M)
Aurora (F)
Barnabe (M)
Benedetto (M)
Bernat (M)
Bernhard (M)
Bertel (M)
Bertrand (M)
Cecil (M)
Chaim (M)
Charlotte (F)
Christina (F)
Christine (F)
Christoph (M)
Christopher (M)
Clement (M)
Conrad (M)
Corinna (F)
Cristóbal (M)
Cyprian (M)
Dafydd (M)
Dante (M)
Decimus (M)
Desire (F)
Duncan (M)
Dylan (M)
Eben (M)
Ebenezer (M)
Edgar (M)
Edna (F)
Ella (F)
Emily (F)
Emma (F)
Endre (M)
Estéban (M)
Étienne (M)
Eugene (M)
Eugenio (M)
Eunice (F)
Evan (M)
Evangeline (F)
Ezra (M)
Felicia (F)
Fernando (M)
Florimel (F)
Francesca (F)
Franco (M)
François (M)
Frederik (M)
Gabriela (F)
Gabriello (M)
Gaius (M)
Gareth (M)
Gaspar (M)
Gautier (M)
Genevieve (F)
Gerald (M)
Gian (M)
Gilbert (M)
Giles (M)
Giorgos (M)
Gottfried (M)
Gregorio (M)
Guillaume (M)
Gunnar (M)
Gutierre (M)
Haidee (F)
Hannes (M)
Ḥassan (M)
Heinrich (M)
Hendrik (M)
Henriette (F)
Henrik (M)
Henry (M)
Herman (M)
Hervey (M)
Hilda (F)
Homer (M)
Humbert (M)
Huw (M)
Immanuel (M)
Isa (F)
Isabella (F)
Isidore (M)
István (M)
Ivan (M)
Iwan (M)
Jami (F)
János (M)
Jaroslav (M)
Jean (M)
Jean-François (M)
Jens (M)
João (M)
Johann (M)
Jonas (M)
Jorgen (M)
Josephine (F)
Joyce (F)
Juana (F)
Julia (F)
Karel (M)
Katherine (F)
Keith (M)
Kenneth (M)
Klaus (M)
Knud (M)
Kostas (M)
Langston (M)
Larisa (F)
Lars (M)
Leigh (F)
Leone (M)
Lesya (F)
Louise (F)
Lucian (M)
Lucila (F)
Lucius (M)
Luigi (M)
Lydia (F)
Madeline (F)
Magnus (M)
Mairi (F)

Occupation/Activity

Marceline (F)
Marcellus (M)
Marcin (M)
Marco (M)
Marianne (F)
Marina (F)
Mario (M)
Marja (F)
Marko (M)
Matteo (M)
Matthew (M)
Matthias (M)
Max (M)
Maxwell (M)
Medora (F)
Mihály (M)
Moshe (M)
Myra (F)
Nicolaas (M)
Nicolau (M)
Ogden (M)
Ola (F)
Olav (M)
Olindo (M)
Olivier (M)
Olof (M)
Omar (M)
Pablo (M)
Padraic (M)
Paolo (M)
Patience (F)
Pauline (F)
Per (M)
Percy (M)
Petar (M)
Petr (M)
Peyo (M)
Philander (M)
Philip (M)
Phoebe (F)
Priscilla (F)
Ralph (M)
Remy (M)
Renée (F)
Rhys (M)
Robert (M)
Robinson (M)
Rodrigo (M)
Rosalind (F)
Rudolf (M)
Rufus (M)
Rupert (M)
Ryszard (M)
Sabrina (F)
Salomon (M)
Salvatore (M)
Sándor (M)
Saul (M)
Sergey (M)
Seumas (M)
Sidney (M)
Solomon (M)
Stacy (F)
Stanislas (M)
Stanislav (M)
Stella (F)
Stephan (M)
Stéphane (M)
Stephen (M)
Stevie (M)
Stuart (M)
Sydney (M)
Sylvia (F)
Taliesin (M)
Tam (M)
Tamara (F)
Tara (F)
Titus (M)
Tristan (M)
Tristram (M)
Tula (F)
Tulsidas (M)
Valdemar (M)
Valery (F)
Vasily (M)
Vernon (M)
Vicente (M)
Victoria (F)
Vilhelm (M)
Vincenzo (M)
Violet (F)
Vittorio (M)
Wallace (M)
Walt (M)
Wenonah (F)
Wilfred (M)
Zacharias (M)
Zona (F)

Science

Adam (M)
Addison (M)
Adelbert (M)
Adolph (M)
Adriano (M)
Albert (M)
Alberto (M)
Albrecht (M)
Alessandro (M)
Alexander (M)

Alexis (F)
Alfred (M)
Alonso (M)
Alpheus (M)
Alphonse (M)
Alvan (M)
Ami (F)
An (M)
Anders (M)
Andreas (M)
Andrei (M)
Andrew (M)
Andrey (M)
Annie (F)
Antonio (M)
Arie (M)
Arne (M)
Arnold (M)
Asa (M)
Augustus (M)
Axel (M)
Bailey (M)
Baron (M)
Barthelemy (M)
Benjamin (M)
Beno (M)
Benoît (M)
Bernhard (M)
Bertha (F)
Berthold (M)
Bjorn (M)
Blaise (M)
Boris (M)
Bradley (M)
Brook (M)
Bruno (M)
Burt (M)
Calvin (M)
Carl (M)
Caspar (M)
Cato (M)
Charles (M)
Christa (F)
Christen (F)
Christian (M)
Christoph (M)
Christopher (M)
Claudius (M)
Clemens (M)
Cleveland (M)
Clinton (M)
Cyprian (M)
Daniel (M)
Denis (M)
Dirk (M)
Dugald (M)
Edmond (M)
Édouard (M)
Edwin (M)
Ejnar (M)
Elias (M)
Elihu (M)
Elisha (F)
Elliot (M)
Elmer (M)
Elwin (M)
Emile (M)
Enrico (M)
Ephraim (M)
Erasmus (M)
Ernest (M)
Erwin (M)
Euclid (M)
Eugen (M)
Felix (M)
Feodor (M)
Florence (F)
Florian (M)
Floyd (M)
Francesco (M)
François (M)
Friedrich (M)
Fritz (M)
Gail (F)
Gaspard (M)
Geoffrey (M)
Georg (M)
Georgy (M)
Gerald (M)
Germain (M)
Gerty (F)
Gideon (M)
Gifford (M)
Gilbert (M)
Gilles (M)
Giuseppe (M)
Glenn (M)
Gottfried (M)
Gregor (M)
Gregorio (M)
Guillaume (M)
Gustav (M)
Halford (M)
Hannibal (M)
Hans (M)
Harald (M)
Hardy (M)
Harold (M)
Harry (M)
Harvey (M)
Hayward (M)
Heber (M)
Heinrich (M)
Hendrik (M)
Henri (M)
Henrietta (F)
Henrik (M)
Hippolyte (M)
Hiram (M)
Horatio (M)
Hubert (M)
Hugo (M)
Ibrāhīm (M)
Ieuan (M)
Ira (M)
Isaac (M)
Israel (M)
James (M)
Jan (M)
Jaroslav (M)
Jeremias (M)
Jethro (M)
Josef (M)
Joseph (M)
Joshua (M)
Jules (M)
Julián (M)
Julius (M)
Justus (M)
Karl (M)
Kasimir (M)
Kelvin (M)
King (M)
Kirk (M)
La Verne (F)
Lambert (M)
Lancelot (M)
Lars (M)
Laurens (M)
Leonardo (M)
Leonhard (M)
Leonor (F)
Lewis (M)
Linus (M)
Lise (F)
Louis (M)
Luca (M)
Luigi (M)
Luther (M)
Magnus (M)
Manasseh (M)
Marcel (F)
Marguerite (F)
Maria (F)
Marie (F)
Marja (F)
Marston (M)
Mathieu (M)
Matthias (M)
Matthieu (M)
Max (M)
Maximilian (M)
Maxwell (M)
Melville (M)
Merle (M)
Michael (M)
Mungo (M)
Nathaniel (M)
Nehemiah (M)
Neil (M)
Newton (M)
Nicolás (M)
Nicolaus (M)
Niels (M)
Nils (M)
Obed (M)
Ogden (M)
Ole (M)
Olive (F)
Oliver (M)
Olli (F)
Orville (M)
Osborne (M)
Oswald (M)
Otis (M)
Owen (M)
Paolo (M)
Patrick (M)
Percival (M)
Percy (M)
Philipp (M)
Ransom (M)
Raphael (M)
Reg (M)
Reginald (M)
Rene (M)
Rhea (F)
Richard (M)
Rob (M)
Robert (M)
Roderick (M)
Roger (M)
Roland (M)
Ronald (M)
Rosalind (F)
Ross (M)
Royal (M)
Rudolf (M)
Rudolph (M)
Rufus (M)
Russell (M)
Sally (F)
Sébastien (M)
Sergie (M)
Seth (M)
Shen (M)
Sherburne (M)
Shiro (M)
Sidney (M)
Siegfried (M)
Silvanus (M)
Smith (M)
Spencer (M)
Squire (M)
Stanislao (M)
Stanislas (M)
Stefan (M)
Stephan (M)
Suzuki (F)
Svetlana (F)
Sylvester (M)
Theodor (M)
Thomas (M)
Valdemar (M)
Valentina (F)
Vasily (M)
Viktor (M)
Vilhelm (M)
Vincenzo (M)
Virgil (M)
Vito (M)

Waldemar (M)
Wallace (M)
Walter (M)
Walther (M)
Warren (M)
Werner (M)
Wilbur (M)
Wiley (M)
Wilhelm (M)
Willard (M)
William (M)
Willis (M)
Wolfgang (M)
Yves (M)
Zachariah (M)
Zacharias (M)

Show Biz

Annie (F)
Benjamin (M)
Betty (F)
Bill (M)
Billy (M)
Bob (M)
Bud (M)
Byron (M)
Carmen (F)
Carol (F)
Chevy (M)
Claire (F)
Clyde (M)
Danny (M)
Dean (M)
Derek (M)
Dom (M)
Don (M)
Eddie (M)
Edgar (M)
Elsie (F)
Emmett (M)
Fanny (F)
Gilda (F)
Gracie (F)
Gunther (M)
Harry (M)
Imogene (F)
Isaiah (M)
Jeannie (F)
Jerry (M)
Jim (M)
Jimmy (M)
Joan (F)
Josephine (F)
Kathryn (F)
Lenny (M)
Leslie (F)
Libby (F)
Lillian (F)
Lily (F)
Lou (M)
Milton (M)
Minnie (F)
Morton (M)
Nora (F)
Oliver (M)
Phineas (M)
Precious (F)
Rich (M)
Rodney (M)
Roy (M)
Ruby (F)
Sally (F)
Sam (M)
Sammy (M)
Shari (F)
Shelley (F)
Sid (M)
Sophie (F)
Thelma (F)
Vesta (F)
Wayne (M)
Will (M)
Yaakov (M)

Social Science

Ahmed (M)
Alberto (M)
Albion (M)
Aleksandr (M)
Aleš (M)
Alexius (F)
Alfredo (M)
Alvin (M)
Amado (M)
Anders (M)
Anton (M)
Archibald (M)
Ari (M)
Arni (F)
Arnold (M)
Augustin (M)
Aurel (M)
Austen (M)
Bedřich (M)
Bernal (M)
Berthold (M)
Bertram (M)
Bogdan (M)
Brooks (M)
Carlo (M)
Carlos (M)
Carter (M)
Chester (M)
Clark (M)
Claudius (M)
Clyde (M)
Constantine (M)
Cornelius (M)
Cosmo (M)
Desmond (M)
Diego (M)
Dino (M)
Dion (M)
Edward (M)
Elsie (F)
Emile (M)
Erich (M)
Eugen (M)
Flavio (M)
Florian (M)
Frans (M)
Franz (M)
Georg (M)
Gerard (M)
Giovanni (M)
Giuseppe (M)
Gordon (M)
Graham (M)
Gustave (M)
Hannah (F)
Hector (M)
Heinrich (M)
Horace (M)
Hugo (M)
Jared (M)
Jens (M)
Josiah (M)
Joyce (F)
Judd (M)
Karel (M)
Karen (F)
Knut (M)
Laurel (F)
Leonid (M)
Lev (M)
Loren (F)
Lucien (M)
Lyman (M)
Marcin (M)
Margaret (F)
Matías (M)
Melanie (F)
Melville (M)
Michal (M)
Milton (M)
Numa (M)
Paolo (M)
Pietro (M)
Ragnar (M)
Ramón (M)
Ravi (M)
Reynold (M)
Richard (M)
Sakari (M)
Samuel (M)
Sándor (M)
Sheldon (M)
Siegfried (M)
Sigmund (M)
Stanisław (M)
Sven (M)
Svend (M)
Sylvain (M)
Thomas (M)
Tyler (M)
Vilhelm (M)
Vladimir (M)
Wallis (M)
Walt (M)
Wesley (M)
Wilhelm (M)
Wilson (M)
Zelia (F)

Sports and Games

Abner (M)
Abraham (M)
Ace (M)
Akeem (M)
Al (M)
Alain (M)
Alberto (M)
Alphonse (M)
Amos (M)
André (M)
Angel (F)
Angelo (M)
Archie (M)
Armando (M)
Arnold (M)
Artis (F)
Asa (M)
Ashley (F)
August (M)
Avery (M)
Barry (M)
Bart (M)
Benny (M)
Bertrand (M)
Beryl (F)
Billie Jean (F)
Billy (M)
Birgit (F)
Bjorn (M)
Bo (M)
Bobby (M)
Boris (M)
Bowie (M)
Brian (M)
Bruce (M)
Buck (M)
Bud (M)
Byron (M)
Carl (M)
Carlos (M)
Carlton (M)
Carol (F)
Cary (M)
Casey (M)
Cecelia (F)
Cedric (M)
Chantal (F)
Charlotte (F)
Chet (M)
Chris (M)
Christa (F)
Christian (M)
Clarence (M)
Clark (M)
Clarke (M)
Clem (M)
Clint (M)
Clinton (M)
Clyde (M)
Connie (F)
Cornelius (M)
Cornell (M)
Cory (M)
Curt (M)
Curtis (M)
Cy (M)
Daley (M)
Dallas (M)
Dana (F)
Daniela (F)
Daniele (M)
Danny (M)
Dano (M)
Dante (M)
Darryl (M)
Daryl (M)
Dave (M)
Dawn (F)
Delbert (M)
Denis (M)
Denny (M)
Denton (M)
Dexter (M)
Dixie (F)
Dominic (F)
Dominique (M)
Donal (M)
Donny (M)
Dorothy (F)
Doug (M)
Douglas (M)
Doyle (M)
Duane (M)
Duke (M)
Duncan (M)
Dusty (M)
Dwight (M)
Eamonn (M)
Elena (F)
Elmer (M)
Elroy (M)
Elston (M)
Elvin (M)
Ely (M)
Emanuel (M)
Emerson (M)
Emlen (F)
Enos (M)
Eric (M)
Erna (F)
Ernest (M)
Errol (M)
Ervin (M)
Esther (F)
Eugene (M)
Evonne (F)
Ezekiel (M)
Florence (F)
Floyd (M)
Forrest (M)
Franco (M)
Frederick (M)
Gareth (M)
Garfield (M)
Gene (M)
Gilberto (M)
Gino (M)
Glenn (M)
Greg (M)
Grete (F)
Grover (M)
Gustavo (M)
Guy (M)
Hana (F)
Hank (M)
Harald (M)
Harold (M)
Hazel (F)
Herman (M)
Ian (M)
Igor (M)
Ina (F)
Inés (F)
Ingemar (M)
Ingrid (F)
Iolanda (F)
Irena (F)
Ivan (M)
Jack (M)
Jackie (M)
Jackson (M)
Jay (M)
Jerry (M)
Jess (F)
Jesse (M)
Jill (F)
Joaquín (M)
Joe (M)
John (M)
Johnny (M)
Joie (F)
Jorge (M)

Josephus (M)
Jules (M)
Julie (F)
Jürgen (M)
Just (M)
Kareem (M)
Katarina (F)
Katrin (F)
Keith (M)
Kennedy (M)
Kevin (M)
Kiki (M)
Kitty (F)
Klaus (M)
Knute (M)
Kornelia (F)
Kristo (M)
Lamar (M)
Lance (M)
Len (M)
Lennox (M)
Lester (M)
Madge (F)
Magda (F)
Manfred (M)
Marcus (M)
Marina (F)
Mario (M)
Marita (F)
Marjorie (F)
Mark (M)
Martina (F)
Matti (F)
Maureen (F)
Mavis (F)
Melvin (M)
Merlin (M)
Mickey (M)
Midori (F)
Mike (M)
Mikko (M)
Mildred (F)
Milo (M)
Murray (M)
Myer (M)
Nadia (F)
Natalia (F)
Natalya (F)
Nigel (M)
Noëlle (F)
Nolan (M)
Nona (F)
Norval (M)
Olga (F)
Olivier (M)
Otto (M)
Parry (M)
Pearl (F)
Pedro (M)
Pete (M)
Petra (F)
Pietro (M)
Piotr (M)
Precious (F)
Ralph (M)
Ray (M)
Renaldo (M)
Rene (F)
Rick (M)
Rocky (M)
Roderick (M)
Roger (M)
Rogers (M)
Romy (F)
Ruby (F)
Ruth (F)
Ryne (M)
Samantha (F)
Samīr (M)
Scott (M)
Sebastian (M)
Sergey (M)
Sheena (F)
Shirley (F)
Sigrid (F)
Sonja (F)
Stan (M)
Stanley (M)
Steffi (F)
Stefka (F)
Stéphane (M)
Stirling (M)
Suzanne (F)
Sylvain (M)
Terry (M)
Tiffany (F)
Tim (M)
Todd (M)
Tom (M)
Tomas (M)
Tommy (M)
Tony (M)
Trevor (M)
Tristram (M)
Troy (M)
Ty (M)
Tyrone (M)
Ulrich (M)
Urban (M)
Valentina (F)
Vasili (M)
Vera (F)
Vern (M)
Vida (M)
Viktor (M)
Vin (M)
Vince (M)
Vladimir (M)
Wade (M)
Wah[illegible] (M)
Wally (M)
Wayne (M)
Wes (M)
Westbrook (M)
Wilbur (M)
Wilfredo (M)
Wilma (F)
Wilt (M)
Woody (M)
Yale (M)
Yvonne (F)
Zane (M)
Zola (F)

Theater

Abby (F)
Abigail (F)
Absalom (M)
Ada (F)
Adah (F)
Adam (M)
Adelaide (F)
Adeline (F)
Adrian (M)
Adriana (F)
Adrienne (F)
Agatha (F)
Agnes (F)
Al (M)
Alastair (M)
Alec (M)
Aleksandr (M)
Alfred (M)
Aline (F)
Almira (F)
Amanda (F)
Amintor (M)
Angel (F)
Angela (F)
Angelina (F)
Angelo (M)
Annie (F)
Antoine (M)
Anton (M)
Ariel (F)
Arlene (F)
Arthur (M)
Ashley (F)
Aspasia (F)
August (M)
Augustin (M)
Augustus (M)
Ava (F)
Avery (M)
Barry (M)
Barton (M)
Basil (M)
Beatrice (F)
Bela (M)
Ben (M)
Benito (M)
Bernadette (F)
Bette (F)
Blythe (F)
Boris (M)
Brendan (M)
Buster (M)
Carole (F)
Cary (M)
Cedric (M)
Celeste (F)
Celia (F)
Charlton (M)
Charmian (F)
Cheryl (F)
Christopher (M)
Cissie (F)
Clara (F)
Clemence (F)
Clemens (M)
Cliff (M)
Clifford (M)
Colley (M)
Constance (F)
Cora (F)
Cordelia (F)
Cornelia (F)
Craig (M)
Cyd (M)
Cyril (M)
Danny (M)
David (M)
Delia (F)
Desdemona (F)
Diana (F)
Dinah (F)
Dion (M)
Edith (F)
Edmond (M)
Edvard (M)
Edward (M)
Elmer (M)
Else (F)
Erwin (M)
Eugene (M)
Ferdinand (M)
Fernando (M)
Forrest (M)
Francesco (M)
Francisco (M)
Friederike (M)
Gaspar (M)
Gemma (F)
Geraldine (F)
Gertrude (F)
Gil (M)
Gladys (F)
Glenda (F)
Gloria (F)
Gordon (M)
Greer (F)
Gregorio (M)
Hamlet (M)
Hannah (F)
Harley (M)
Hedda (F)
Helena (F)
Hermione (F)
Hezekiah (M)
Hildegarde (F)
Holmes (M)
Hope (F)
Howard (M)
Hubert (M)
Hugh (M)
Hung (M)
Hypatia (F)
Iago (M)
Ian (M)
Ibrāhīm (M)
Ida (F)
Imogen (F)
Ivor (M)
Iwan (M)
Jacinta (F)
Jacob (M)
Jacques (M)
Jason (M)
Jasper (M)
Jeanne (F)
Jerome (M)
Jerry (M)
Jessica (F)
Jo (M)
Joanna (F)
Joel (M)
Joey (M)
Johan (M)
Johanna (F)
José (M)
Judah (M)
Judith (F)
Judy (F)
Juliet (F)
Justine (F)
Karl (M)
Kay (F)
Keir (M)
Kenneth (M)
Kitty (F)
Konstantin (F)
Laurette (F)
Lee (F)
Lena (F)
Lennox (M)
Libby (F)
Lillian (F)
Lionel (M)
Lloyd (M)
Lorenzo (M)
Lorraine (F)
Lotta (F)
Lotte (F)
Louisa (F)
Lucia (F)
Lucian (M)
Lucrece (F)
Lydia (F)
Madge (F)
Magda (F)
Maggie (F)
Mamie (F)
Marcel (F)
Mariana (F)
Marius (M)
Marlon (M)
Massimo (M)
Maud (F)
Maximilian (M)
Maxine (F)
Maxwell (M)
May (F)
Melantha (F)
Mercedes (F)
Micheal (M)
Mikhail (M)
Millicent (F)
Minnie (F)
Miranda (F)
Mitzi (F)
Moira (F)
Moss (M)
Nanette (F)
Nehemiah (M)
Neil (M)
Nerys (F)
Nils (M)
Nora (F)
Norval (M)
Odile (F)
Ödön (M)
Olivia (F)
Ophelia (F)
Orson (M)
Osborne (M)
Oscar (M)
Otis (M)
Padraic (M)
Paulina (F)
Pauline (F)
Peggy (F)
Perdita (F)
Rachel (F)
Ralph (M)
Raúl (M)
Regan (M)
Reginald (M)
Rex (M)
Rhonda (F)

Richard (M)
Ricky (M)
Rip (M)
Rita (F)
Roberto (M)
Romeo (M)
Rory (M)
Rosalind (F)
Rosetta (F)
Roxane (F)
Sabrina (F)
Sada (F)
Sally (F)
Sally-Ann (F)
Salome (F)
Samson (M)
Sarah (F)
Sean (M)
Sebastian (M)
Sem (M)
Seymour (M)
Shawn (M)
Sheila (F)
Shelagh (F)
Sheldon (M)
Shelley (F)
Sid (M)
Signe (F)
Sigourney (F)
Simone (F)
Sinead (F)
Siobhan (F)
Sophia (F)
Sorrel (M)
Stanley (M)
Stella (F)
Stéphanie (F)
Stephen (M)
Sterling (M)
Steve (M)
Stockard (F)
Susan (F)
Susanna (F)
Susannah (F)
Suzanne (F)
Sybil (F)
Sylvia (F)
Talbert (M)
Tallulah (F)
Tennessee (M)
Terence (M)
Thora (F)
Thornton (M)
Timothy (M)
Titus (M)
Tony (M)
Tracey (F)
Trevor (M)
Trish (F)
Tristan (M)
Troy (M)
Tuesday (F)
Tula (F)
Tyrone (M)
Una (F)
Ursula (F)
Valentine (M)
Valerie (F)
Valery (F)
Van (M)
Vanessa (F)
Velma (F)
Vera (F)
Verna (F)
Veronica (F)
Vic (M)
Vicki (F)
Vince (M)
Vincent (M)
Viola (F)
Wanda (F)
Ward (M)
Wendell (M)
Wendy (F)
Whoopi (F)
Will (M)
William (M)
Wilson (M)
Windsor (M)
Winifred (F)
Winthrop (M)
Wolf (M)
Yahoo (M)
Yul (M)
Yvette (F)
Zacharias (M)
Zara (F)

TV *and* Radio

Aaron (M)
Abby (F)
Abe (M)
Alan (M)
Alistair (M)
Alvar (M)
Andy (M)
Angie (F)
Art (M)
Audrey (F)
Barbara (F)
Barton (M)
Bea (F)
Becca (F)
Bennett (M)
Benson (M)
Bernice (F)
Beverly (F)
Bill (M)
Billie (F)
Blair (F)
Blake (M)
Blanche (F)
Bob (M)
Bobby (M)
Bonnie (F)
Brandon (M)
Brent (M)
Brittany (F)
Bronson (M)
Buck (M)
Bud (M)
Byron (M)
Candace (F)
Carl (M)
Carla (F)
Carroll (M)
Casey (M)
Chad (M)
Charlene (F)
Chase (M)
Chet (M)
Chuck (M)
Cindy (F)
Claire (F)
Clara (F)
Clayton (M)
Cliff (M)
Clifton (M)
Clint (M)
Connie (F)
Corbin (M)
Courtney (F)
Curt (M)
Daisy (F)
Dale (M)
Dan (M)
Dana (F)
Danny (M)
Darlene (F)
Darren (M)
Dave (M)
David (M)
Deidre (F)
Della (F)
Delta (F)
Denise (F)
Dennis (M)
Denver (M)
Diane (F)
Dick (M)
Didi (F)
Dimitri (M)
Dirk (M)
Dixie (F)
Dominic (F)
Don (M)
Donna (F)
Dorian (F)
Doug (M)
Douglas (M)
Duke (M)
Duncan (M)
Dusty (M)
Ed (M)
Edna (F)
Elaine (F)
Eliot (M)
Ellie (F)
Elvira (F)
Elyse (F)
Emma (F)
Enos (M)
Erica (F)
Erik (M)
Erin (F)
Estelle (F)
Esther (F)
Ethel (F)
Eva (F)
Eve (F)
Fanny (F)
Farrah (F)
Fay (F)
Fred (M)
Gail (F)
Geraldo (M)
Gerry (F)
Hal (M)
Harriet (F)
Honor (F)
Hughie (M)
Isla (F)
Jaclyn (F)
Jane (F)
Jay (M)
Jill (F)
Jim (M)
Joan (F)
Joanna (F)
Jodie (F)
Johnny (M)
Jonathon (M)
Joyce (F)
Judd (M)
June (F)
Karen (F)
Kathleen (F)
Kay (F)
Keenan (M)
Ken (M)
Kenneth (M)
Kent (M)
Kirk (M)
Kirstie (F)
Kyle (M)
Lara (F)
Leon (M)
Linda (F)
Lindsay (F)
Loni (F)
Loretta (F)
Lorne (M)
Lou (M)
Lucille (F)
Mariette (F)
Marlo (F)
Maureen (F)
Mel (M)
Melissa (F)
Meredith (F)
Meshach (M)
Mike (M)
Morgan (M)
Nell (F)
Nora (F)
Noreen (F)
Oprah (F)
Pam (F)
Parker (M)
Pat (M)
Paula (F)
Peggy (F)
Penny (F)
Perry (M)
Peter (M)
Phil (M)
Pierce (M)
Polly (F)
Raymond (M)
Remington (M)
Rhea (F)
Ricardo (M)
Robyn (F)
Rod (M)
Rosie (F)
Samantha (F)
Sandy (F)
Sanford (M)
Sherilyn (F)
Sorrell (M)
Spangler (M)
Steve (M)
Suzanne (F)
Tabitha (F)
Tara (F)
Thurston (M)
Tim (M)
Tina (F)
Tom (M)
Trixie (F)
Una (F)
Valentine (M)
Valerie (F)
Vanna (F)
Veronica (F)
Vic (M)
Vicki (F)
Vin (M)
Vince (M)
Vivian (F)
Wally (M)
Warren (M)
Will (M)
Woody (M)
Yvonne (F)

What's in a Name?

Names are defined here in one of two forms: main (root) names and derivative names (those based on root names).

For main names, the following information, in the following order, appears in each entry:

Name
Current language or ethnicity
Original language or ethnicity. Experts sometimes disagree about the origin of a name. Where there is no clearly preferable explanation, the entry will list more than one original language and give the meaning in both languages.
Meaning
Biblical citation, if any. If a name appears in the Bible, a chapter and verse in which it is mentioned are given.
Namesakes. Last names of famous people who have had this name are given, along with brief descriptions of them. Where no nationality is listed, the namesake is usually American or someone who spent most of his or her working life in America. Where no century is given, in most cases the namesake lived most of his or her life in the present century. A male namesake may sometimes appear in an entry for a name most commonly given as a female name, and vice versa.
Current popularity. Names are described as extremely popular, very popular, popular, less popular, or unusual. The rankings "extremely popular," "very popular," and "popular" are based on detailed birth records from seven states. The rankings "less popular" and "unusual" are subjective.
Nicknames, if any. A "+" after a nickname indicates that the nickname can end with a *y, ie,* or other common spelling variation.
Alternative spellings. Spellings that do not create a different pronunciation, and for which there are no namesakes, are usually listed at the end of the main entry.

For derivative names, the following information, in the following order, will appear in each entry:

Name
Current language or ethnicity
Root name
Meaning (if derivative name is more than a few pages from its root name)
Biblical citation
Namesakes
Current popularity
Nicknames

Names sometimes given to both girls and boys will be listed in both sections, with the complete definition given under the gender for which the name is more common. Notable namesakes are listed without regard to gender.

A typical entry will look something like this:

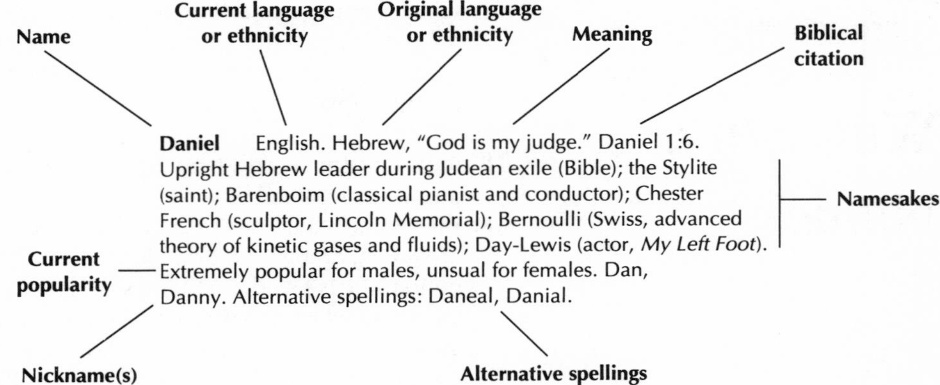

GIRLS' *Names*

Aaron See under Boys' Names.
Aba African. Ghanaian, "Born on Thursday." Unusual.
Abagail English. From Abigail. Less popular. Abby+.
Abagil English. From Abigail. Unusual.
Abana African. From Abina, Ghanaian, "Born on Thursday." Unusual.
Abby English. From Abigail. Dalton (actress); Kelley Foster (advocated woman suffrage); Ewing (character in "Knot's Landing"); Perkins (character in "L.A. Law"). Less popular. Alternative spellings: Abbe, Abbey, Abbi, Abbie.
Abebi Nigerian. Nigerian, "We asked for her and she came to us." Unusual.
Abena African. From Abina, Ghanaian, "Born on Thursday." Unusual.
Abeni Nigerian. From Abebi, Nigerian, "We asked for her and she came to us." Unusual.
Abigail English. Hebrew (Abigal), "My father rejoices." 1 Samuel 25:24. Wife of Nabal, and later of King David; character in Beaumont and Fletcher's "The Scornful Lady"; Smith Adams (wife of President John, mother of President John Quincy); Powers Fillmore (wife of President Millard); Hill Masham, Lady (British courtier). Less popular. Abby+. Alternative spellings: Abbigale, Abbygale, Abigale.
Abigal English and Hebrew/Israeli, from Abigail. Unusual. Abby+. Alternative spelling: Abigall.
Abigel English. From Abigail. Unusual.
Abigil English. From Abigail. Unusual.
Abijah See under Boys' Names.
Abina African. Ghanaian, "Born on Thursday." Unusual.
Abiona Nigerian. Nigerian, "Born during a journey." Unusual for males, unusual for females.
Abira Hebrew/Israeli. Hebrew, "Strong." Unusual.
Abishag Hebrew/Israeli. Hebrew, "Father of error." 1 Kings 1:15. Ministered to aged King David. Unusual.
Abital Hebrew/Israeli. Hebrew, "My father is dew." Unusual for males, unusual for females.
Abmaba African. Ghanaian, "Born on Tuesday." Unusual.
Abrial French. From April, Latin, "To open up." Unusual.
Acadia Created. Created, meaning unknown. Unusual.
Ada Czech. From Adelaide, Old German (Adelheidis), "Nobility." Kepley (first woman to graduate from law school, 1870); Negri (Italian poet); Rehan (comedic actress); Bayly (real name of Edna Lyall) British novelist, *Won by Waiting*; Howard (educator, first president of Wellesley College, 1875–1881). Unusual.
Adah Hebrew/Israeli. Hebrew, "Ornament." Genesis 4:19, 36:2. One of Lamech's wives; one of Esau's wives; Menken (actress). Unusual.
Adalheid English. From Adelaide, Old German (Adelheidis), "Nobility." Unusual.
Adaline English. From Adelaide, Old German (Adelheidis), "Nobility." Less popular.
Adamina English. From Adam, Hebrew, "Redness" or "man." Genesis 2:19. Unusual.
Adamma Nigerian. Nigerian, "Beautiful child." Unusual.
Adara Greek. Greek, "Beauty." Unusual.
Adda English. From Adelaide. Unusual.
Addie English. From Adelaide. Less popular. Alternative spelling: Addi.
Adeana Hebrew/Israeli. From Adina, Hebrew, "Gentle" or "desire" (?). 1 Chronicles 11:42. Unusual.
Adela Czech. From Adelaide. Daughter of William the Conqueror; Rogers St. John (screenplay writer). Less popular.
Adelaida Polish. From Adelaide. Unusual.
Adelaide English. Old German (Adelheidis), "Nobility." "Good queen," wife of British King William IV; Ristori (Italian actress, especially in tragedies); Procter (real name of Mary Berwick) (poet and author, *The Lost Chord*). Less popular. Ada. Alternative spellings: Adalaide, Adalaid.
Adele French (Adèle), Italian. From Adelaide. Unusual.
Adelia English. From Adelaide. Unusual.
Adelicia German. From Adelaide. Unusual.
Adelina Italian. From Adelaide. Patti (operatic soprano). Unusual.
Adeline English. From Adelaide. Genée, Dame (Danish ballerina); subject of barbershop-quartet song "Sweet Adeline";

character in George Gordon Byron's "Don Juan." Less popular.

Adelita Hispanic. From Adelaide. Unusual.

Adeliya Russian. From Adelaide. Unusual.

Adeliza English. English, combination of Adela (Adelaide, Old German, "Nobility") + Liza (Elizabeth, Hebrew [Elisheva], "Oath of God" or "God is my oath"). Unusual.

Adelka Czech. From Adelaide. Unusual.

Adella English. From Adelaide. "Nobility." Unusual. Ada.

Adelle English. From Adelaide. Davis (author on nutrition). Less popular. Ada. Alternative spelling: Adell.

Aderes Hebrew/Israeli. Hebrew, "Outer garment" or "cape." Unusual.

Aderet Hebrew/Israeli. From Aderes. Unusual.

Adesina Nigerian. Nigerian, "The arrival of this child has given us opportunity for more children." Used when a child has been long awaited. Unusual.

Adia African. African, "Gift" or "present." Implies child is gift from God. Unusual.

Adie Hebrew/Israeli. From Adah, Hebrew, "Ornament." Genesis 4:19, 36:2. Unusual.

Adiella Hebrew/Israeli. From Adah, Hebrew, "Ornament." Genesis 4:19, 36:2. Unusual.

Adina Hebrew/Israeli. Hebrew, "Gentle" or "desire" (?). 1 Chronicles 11:42. Character in Gaetano Donizetti's opera "L'Elisir d'amore." Less popular.

Adine Hebrew/Israeli. From Adina. Character in Ouida's novel "Moths." Unusual.

Adira Hebrew/Israeli. From Abira, Hebrew, "Strong." Unusual.

Aditi Indo-Pakistani. Hindi, "Unbounded." Aditi is the mother of Hindu gods. She blesses children and cattle, bestows forgiveness, and offers protection. Unusual.

Adoette Native American. Native American, "Big tree." Given to a baby born under a tree. The child may be seen as related to a tree spirit. Unusual.

Adria English. From Adrian, Latin (Hadrianus), "Black earth" or "of Adria," a city in northern Italy. Less popular.

Adrian See under Boys' Names.

Adriana Italian. From Adrian, Latin (Hadrianus), "Black earth" or "of Adria," a city in northern Italy. Character in Shakespeare's "Comedy of Errors"; Martínez (her 67-year engagement, to Octavio Guillen, is the longest on record). Unusual.

Adriane German. From Adrian, Latin (Hadrianus), "Black earth" or "of Adria," a city in northern Italy. Unusual.

Adrianna English. From Adrian, Latin (Hadrianus), "Black earth" or "of Adria," a city in northern Italy. Less popular.

Adrianne English. From Adrian, Latin (Hadrianus), "Black earth" or "of Adria," a city in northern Italy. Less popular.

Adrie English. From Adrian, Latin (Hadrianus), "Black earth" or "of Adria," a city in northern Italy. Unusual.

Adrien See Adriene under Boys' Names.

Adriena English. From Adrian, Latin (Hadrianus), "Black earth" or "of Adria," a city in northern Italy. Unusual.

Adrienne French. From Adrian, Latin (Hadrianus), "Black earth" or "of Adria," a city in northern Italy. Lecouvreur (French stage actress). Less popular.

Adya Indo-Pakistani. Hindi, "Sunday." Given to a girl born on Sunday. Unusual.

Aenea Scottish. From Aeneas, Greek, "Praiseworthy." Unusual.

Aesha American. From Aisha, Arabic, "Woman" or "life." Unusual.

Aethelthryth English. Old English, "Noble strength." Unusual.

'Afa'f Arabic. Arabic, "Chastity." Unusual.

Affery English. From Aphra, Hebrew, "Dust." Possibly a misunderstanding of Micah 1:10, which refers to "the house of Aphra." Some thought Aphra to be a personal name. Flintwich (character in Charles Dickens' "Little Dorrit"). Unusual.

Afra English. From Aphra, Hebrew, "Dust." Possibly a misunderstanding of Micah 1:10, which refers to "the house of Aphra"; some thought Aphra to be a personal name. Unusual.

Afton English. Old English, "One from Afton." Less popular.

Ag English. From Agatha. Unusual.

Aga Polish. From Agatha. Unusual.

Agafia Russian. From Agatha. Unusual.

Agasha Russian. From Agatha. Unusual.

Agata English. From Agatha. Unusual.

Agate English. English, the name of a stone once believed to have magical powers. Supposedly gave victory over enemies if worn around neck. Unusual.

Agatha English. Greek, "agathos" ("good"). Patron saint of fire fighters; Miller Christie, Dame (British mystery writer and playwright, "The Mousetrap"). Less popular. Aggie+.

Agathe French. From Agatha. Unusual.

Agathi Greek. From Agatha. Unusual.

Agatka Polish. From Agatha. Unusual.

Aggie English. From Agatha. Less popular. Alternative spellings: Aggi, Aggy.

Agi Hungarian. From Agatha. Unusual.

Agna Scandinavian. From Agnes. Unusual.

Agne Italian. From Agnes. Unusual.

Agnella Italian. From Agnes. Unusual.

Agnes English. Greek, "agnos" "Pure" or "chaste". Saint; de Mille (choreographer); Moorehead (actress); MacPhail (Canadian politician, first woman elected to legislature); Repplier (essayist, "Points of View"); Robertson Arber (British botanist); Strickland (British biographer, novelist, and poet). Less popular. Aggie+. Alternative spelling: Agness.

Agnesa Czech. From Agnes. Unusual.

Agnesca Italian. From Agnes. Unusual.

Agnese Italian. From Agnes. Unusual.

Agnesina Italian. From Agatha. Unusual.

Agneska Czech. From Agnes. Unusual.

Agnessa Bulgarian. From Agnes. Unusual.

Agneta Scandinavian. From Agnes. Unusual.

Agneti English. From Agnes. Unusual.

Agnetta Scandinavian. From Agnes. Unusual.

Agnies French. From Agnes. Unusual.

Agnieszka Polish. From Agnes. Unusual.

Agniya Lithuanian. From Agnes. Unusual.

Agnola Italian. From Agnes. Unusual.

Ágota Hungarian. From Agatha. Unusual.

Agotha Hungarian. From Agatha. Unusual.

Agueda Portuguese. From Agatha. Unusual.

Agusta English. From Augustus, Latin, "Venerable" or "majestic." Unusual.

Agustus English. From Augustus, Latin, "Venerable" or "majestic." Unusual.

Ah Kum Chinese. Chinese, "Orchid-like" or "good as gold." Unusual.

Ah Lam Chinese. Chinese, "Like an orchid." Unusual.

Ahava Hebrew/Israeli. Hebrew, "Beloved." Unusual.

Ahouva Hebrew/Israeli. From Ahava. Unusual. Alternative spelling: Ahuva.

Ahuda Hebrew/Israeli. From Ahava. Unusual.

Ahulani Hawaiian. Hawaiian, "Heavenly shrine." Unusual.

Aibhlin Irish. From Helen, Greek, "Bright one" or "shining one." Unusual.

Aiesha American. From Aisha, Arabic, "Woman" or "life." Unusual. Alternative spellings: Ayeisha, Ieasha, Ieesha.

Aila Finnish. From Helen, Greek, "Bright one" or "shining one." Unusual.

Aileen English. From Helen, Greek, "Bright one" or "shining one." Unusual. Alternative spellings: Ailean, Ailene.

Aili Finnish. From Helen, Greek, "Bright one" or "shining one." Unusual.

Ailie English. From Helen, Greek, "Bright one" or "shining one." Unusual. Alternative spelling: Ailey.

Ailinn Portuguese. From Helen, Greek, "Bright one" or "shining one." Unusual.

Ailis Irish. From Adelaide, Old German (Adelheidis), "Nobility." Unusual.

Ailsa Scottish. Scottish, from "Ailsa Craig," an island-rock at the mouth of the Forth of Firth. Unusual.

Aimee French. From Amy, Old French, "Loved." Semple McPherson (Pentecostal preacher). Unusual. Alternative spelling: Aime.

Aimil English. From Amelia, Latin, "Industrious" or "striving." Unusual.

Aingeal Irish. From Angel, Greek, "angelos" ("messenger"). Unusual.

Ainsley See under Boys' Names.

Ainslie See under Boys' Names.

Aisha American. Arabic, "Woman" or "life." Unusual. Alternative spelling: Ayesha.

Aisia American. From Aisha. Unusual.

Aisling Irish. Irish, "Vision" or "dream." Unusual.

Aislinn Irish. From Aisling. Unusual.

Aithne Irish. From Ethne, Irish, "Little fire." Unusual.

Aiyana Native American. Native American, "Everlasting bloom." Unusual.

Aja Indo-Pakistani. Hindu, "Goat." Unusual.

Ajua African. Ghanaian, "Born on Monday." Unusual.

Ajuji African. African, "Refuse-heap child." Given to a child when the mother's previous children have died. To fool demons, baby is taken to the refuse heap (juji) by grandparents, where the mother then reclaims it. Unusual.

Akako Japanese. Japanese, "Red." The name has been thought to have magical powers to cure blood diseases. Unusual.

Akanke Nigerian. Nigerian, "To know her is to pet her." Unusual.

Akela Hawaiian. From Adelaide, Old German (Adelheidis), "Nobility." Unusual.

Aki Japanese. Japanese, "Born in autumn." Unusual.

Akilah Arabic. Arabic, "Logical" or "intelligent." Unusual.

Akisatan Nigerian. Nigerian, "Burial rags are unfinished." Tribal belief holds that evil spirits are incarnated in some children. The name was meant to prevent the child's early death if its spirit left the world. Unusual.

Akosua African. Ghanaian, "Born on Sunday." Unusual.

Ala Polish. From Alexander, Greek, "Defender of men" or "warding off men." Mark 16:21; Acts 4:6, 19:33. Unusual.

Alaina English. From Alan, Gaelic, meaning uncertain, but may include "rock," "noble," "handsome," "harmony," and/or "cheerful." Unusual. Alternative spelling: Alayna.

Alaine English. From Alan, Gaelic, meaning uncertain, but may include "rock," "noble," "handsome," "harmony," and/or "cheerful." Unusual. Alternative spellings: Alayne, Aleine.

Alais Created. Created, meaning unknown. Unusual.

Alake Nigerian. Nigerian, "She will be petted if she survives." Usually given to unhealthy infant. Unusual.

Alala Greek. Greek, "Sister of Mars" or "goddess of war." Unusual.

Alamea Hawaiian. Hawaiian, "Ripe" or "precious." Unusual.

Alameda Native American. Native American, "Cottonwood grove." Unusual.

Alani Hawaiian. Hawaiian, "Orange" or "orange tree." Refers to the oahu tree, which has perfumed leaves used to scent fabric. Unusual for males, unusual for females.

Alanna English. From Alan, Gaelic, meaning uncertain, but may include "rock," "noble," "handsome," "harmony," and/or "cheerful." Unusual. Alternative spellings: Alana, Allana.

Alaqua Native American. Native American, "Sweet gum tree." Unusual.

Alathea English. From Alethea, Greek, "Truth." Unusual.

Alauda Unknown. Old French, "Lark." Unusual.

Alaula Hawaiian. Hawaiian, "Early dawn's light" or "sunset glow." Unusual for males, unusual for females.

Alba English. From Alban, Latin, "Of Alba," a town on a white hill. Alba was capital of the first Roman kings, as well as an ancient name for the Scottish highlands. Unusual.

Alberta English. From Albert, Old English (Aethelbeorht), "Noble-bright." Hunter (blues singer). Unusual.

Albertina English. From Albert, Old English (Aethelbeorht), "Noble-bright." Rasch (ballerina and choreographer). Unusual.

Albertine French. From Albert, Old English (Aethelbeorht), "Noble-bright." Unusual.

Albertyna Polish. From Albert, Old English (Aethelbeorht), "Noble-bright." Unusual.

Albina English. From Albin, Latin, "White." Unusual.

Albinia English. From Albin, Latin, "White." Unusual.

Albinka Polish. From Albin, Latin, "White." Unusual.

Albreda English. Old German, "Elf counsel." Unusual.

Alda Italian. From Aldous, Old German, "Old." Unusual.

Aldreda English. From Aldred, Old English, "Old counsel." Unusual.

Ale Lithuanian. From Helen, Greek, "Bright one" or "shining one." Unusual.

Alea Arabic. Arabic, "High" or "exalted." Less popular.

Aleah Arabic. From Alea. Unusual.

Alecia English. From Adelaide, Old German (Adelheidis), "Nobility." Less popular.

Aleeka Nigerian. From Alike, Nigerian, "Girl who drives out beautiful women." Given to a pretty child. Unusual.

Aleela African. From Alile, African, "She cries." Given when a baby is born into adverse circumstances. Unusual.

Aleen Dutch. From Helen, Greek, "Bright one" or "shining one." Unusual.

Aleena English. From Helen, Greek, "Bright one" or "shining one." Unusual.

Aleene English. From Helen, Greek, "Bright one" or "shining one." Unusual. Alternative spelling: Aleine.

Aleesha English. From Adelaide, Old German (Adelheidis), "Nobility." Less popular. Alternative spellings: Aleisha, Alešha.

Aleeza Hebrew/Israeli. From Aliza, Hebrew, "Joy" or "joyful." Unusual.

Alejandra Hispanic. From Alexander, Greek, "Defender of men" or "warding off men." Mark 16:21; Acts 4:6, 19:33. Unusual.

Alejandrina Hispanic. From Alexander, Greek, "Defender of men" or "warding off men." Mark 16:21; Acts 4:6, 19:33. Unusual.

Aleka Greek. From Alexander, Greek, "Defender of men" or "warding off men." Mark 16:21; Acts 4:6, 19:33. Unusual.

Aleks Russian. From Alexander, Greek, "Defender of men" or "warding off men." Mark 16:21; Acts 4:6, 19:33. Unusual.

Aleksasha Russian. From Alexander, Greek, "Defender of men" or "warding off men." Mark 16:21; Acts 4:6, 19:33. Unusual.

Aleksey Russian. From Alexander, Greek, "Defender of men" or "warding off men." Mark 16:21; Acts 4:6, 19:33. Peshkov (Russian novelist, developed socialist realism); Suvorin (Russian journalist, established daily newspaper); Arakcheyev, Count (Russian political adviser to Alexander I, 1801–25); Stakhanov (Russian coal miner, improved production speed). Unusual.

Aleksi Bulgarian. From Alexander, Greek, "Defender of men" or "warding off men." Mark 16:21; Acts 4:6, 19:33. Unusual.

Alena Russian. From Helen, Greek, "Bright one" or "shining one." Unusual.

Alene Dutch. From Helen, Greek, "Bright one" or "shining one." Unusual.

Alenka Russian. From Helen, Greek, "Bright one" or "shining one." Unusual.

Aleska Polish. From Alexander, Greek, "Defender of men" or "warding off men." Mark 16:21; Acts 4:6, 19:33. Unusual.

Alessandra Italian. From Alexander, Greek, "Defender of men" or "warding off men." Mark 16:21; Acts 4:6, 19:33. Less popular.

Alessio Italian. From Alexander, Greek, "Defender of men" or "warding off men." Mark 16:21; Acts 4:6, 19:33. Unusual.

Aleta English, Hispanic. From Alethea, Greek, "Truth." Unusual.

Aletea Hispanic. From Aletea, Hispanic, "Truth." Unusual.

Aletha English. From Alethea; or from Adelaide, Old German (Adelheidis), "Nobility." Unusual.

Alethea English. From Alethea, Greek, "Truth." Unusual. Alternative spelling: Alethia.

Aletta French. From Alette. Unusual.

Alette French. From Alette, Latin, "Wing." Unusual.

Alex See under Boys' Names.

Alexa English, Hungarian. From Alexander, Greek, "Defender of men" or "warding off men." Mark 16:21; Acts 4:6, 19:33. Less popular.

Alexanderia English. From Alexander, Greek, "Defender of men" or "warding off men." Mark 16:21; Acts 4:6, 19:33. Less popular. Alex.

Alexanderina English. From Alexander, Greek, "Defender of men" or "warding off men." Mark 16:21; Acts 4:6, 19:33. Less popular. Alex.

Alexanderine French. From Alexander, Greek, "Defender of men" or "warding off men." Mark 16:21; Acts 4:6, 19:33. Less popular. Alex.

Alexandra English. From Alexander, Greek, "Defender of men" or "warding off men." Mark 16:21; Acts 4:6, 19:33. Danish princess, married Edward VII of England when he was prince of Wales; Zuck (real name of actress Sandra Dee). Popular. Alex.

Alexandraeana English. From Alexander, Greek, "Defender of men" or "warding off men." Mark 16:21; Acts 4:6, 19:33. Unusual. Alex.

Alexandrea English. From Alexander, Greek, "Defender of men" or "warding off men." Mark 16:21; Acts 4:6, 19:33. Less popular. Alex. Alternative spelling: Alexandria.

Alexandrena English. From Alexander, Greek, "Defender of men" or "warding off men." Mark 16:21; Acts 4:6, 19:33. Less popular. Alex. Alternative spelling: Alexandrina.

Alexandrene English. From Alexander, Greek, "Defender of men" or "warding off men." Mark 16:21; Acts 4:6, 19:33. Less popular. Alex.

Alexandrie French. From Alexander, Greek, "Defender of men" or "warding off men." Mark 16:21; Acts 4:6, 19:33. Unusual.

Alexandrine English. From Alexander, Greek, "Defender of men" or "warding off men." Mark 16:21; Acts 4:6, 19:33. Less popular. Alex.

Alexena English. From Alexander, Greek, "Defender of men" or "warding off men." Mark 16:21; Acts 4:6, 19:33. Less popular. Alex.

Alexene English. From Alexander, Greek, "Defender of men" or "warding off men." Mark 16:21; Acts 4:6, 19:33. Less popular. Alex. Alternative spelling: Alexine.

Alexi English. From Alexander, Greek, "Defender of men" or "warding off men." Mark 16:21; Acts 4:6, 19:33. Less popular. Alex.

Alexia English, German. From Alexander, Greek, "Defender of men" or "warding off men." Mark 16:21; Acts 4:6, 19:33. Unusual. Alternative spelling: Alexea.

Alexie German. From Alexander, Greek, "Defender of men" or "warding off men." Mark 16:21; Acts 4:6, 19:33. Unusual.

Alexina English. From Alexander, Greek, "Defender of men" or "warding off men." Mark 16:21; Acts 4:6, 19:33. Less popular.

Alexiou Greek. From Alexander, Greek, "Defender of men" or "warding off men." Mark 16:21; Acts 4:6, 19:33. Unusual.

Alexis English. From Alexander, Greek, "Defender of men" or "warding off men." Mark 16:21; Acts 4:6, 19:33. Saint; 4th-century Greek poet, wrote 245 comedies; Smith (actress); Littre (French physician, type of hernia named after him); Millardet (French botanist, developed Bordeaux mixture of grapevines, 1885); Bouvard (French astronomer, discovered eight comets). Less popular for males, less popular for females. Alex.

Alexius French, German. From Alexander, Greek, "Defender of men" or "warding off men." Mark 16:21; Acts 4:6, 19:33. Byzantine emperor (I, 1081-V, 1204); Meinong (Austrian philosopher and psychologist, established first psychological institute in Austria, 1894). Unusual.

Aley Scottish. From Adelaide, Old German (Adelheidis), "Nobility." Unusual.

Alfreda English. From Alfred, Old English, "Elf-counsel." Saint. Less popular.

Algoma Native American. Native American, "Valley of flowers." Unusual.

Alhena Arabic. Arabic, "Ring." Refers to a star in the constellation Gemini. Unusual.

Ali English. Arabic, "Highest" or "greatest." MacGraw (actress, "Love Story"); Sastroamidjojo (Indonesian prime minister, 1953–57); Neuva'i (Turkish poet and scholar); Mubarak (Egyptian minister of education, 1888–91, modernized school system); Mahir Pasha (Egyptian prime minister, 1930s-50s). Less popular for males, less popular for females. Alternative spellings: Alie, Allie, Ally.

Alia English. From Ali, Arabic, "Highest" or "greatest." Unusual.

Alica Czech. From Adelaide, Old German (Adelheidis), "Nobility." Unusual.

Alice English. From Adelaide, Old German (Adelheidis), "Nobility." Hathaway Lee Roosevelt (wife of President Theodore); Wykeham-Martin Pollock (British, oldest author: at age 102, "Portrait of My Victorian Youth"); Paul (suffragette); Salomon (German feminist, established school of social work); Walker (novelist). Less popular. Alternative spellings: Alis, Allice, Alles, Allyce.

Alicia English, Hispanic, Swedish. From Adelaide, Old German (Adelheidis), "Nobility." Rutherford Cockburn (Scottish poet, "Flowers of the Forest"); Alonso (ballerina); Markova, Dame (British ballerina). Very popular. Alternative spellings: Alesha, Alesia, Alicea, Alisha, Alysha, Alysia, Alyshia, Alycia.

Alida English, Hispanic. From Alette, Latin, "Wing." Unusual.

Alika Nigerian, from Alike; or Hawaiian, from Adelaide, Old German (Adelheidis), "Nobility." Unusual.

Alike Nigerian. Nigerian, "Girl who drives out beautiful women," given to a pretty child; or from Adelaide, Old German (Adelheidis), "Nobility." Unusual.

Alila African. From Alile. Unusual.

Alile African. African, "She cries." Given when a baby is born into adverse circumstances. Unusual.

Alima Arabic. Arabic, "Sea maiden" or "skilled in dancing and making music." Unusual.

Alina Russian. From Adelaide, Old German (Adelheidis), "Nobility." Unusual.

Aline English. From Adelaide, Old German (Adelheidis), "Nobility." MacMahon (British actress). Less popular.

Alisa Bulgarian, English, Russian. From Adelaide, Old German (Adelheidis), "Nobility." Unusual.

Alisanne English. From Adelaide, Old German (Adelheidis), "Nobility." Less popular.

Alise English. From Adelaide, Old German (Adelheidis), "Nobility." Unusual. Alternative spellings: Alyce, Alyse, Alysse.

Alisha English. From Adelaide, Old German (Adelheidis), "Nobility." Less popular.

Alisia Polish. From Adelaide, Old German (Adelheidis), "Nobility." Less popular.

Alissa English. From Adelaide, Old German (Adelheidis), "Nobility." Less popular. Alternative spellings: Alysa, Alyssa.

Alita Hispanic. From Adelaide, Old German (Adelheidis), "Nobility." Unusual.

Alithea English. From Alethea, Greek, "Truth." Unusual. Alternative spelling: Alithia.

Alitza Hebrew/Israeli. From Aliza, Hebrew, "Joy" or "joyful." Unusual. Alternative spelling: Alitzah.

Aliute Lithuanian. From Helen, Greek, "Bright one" or "shining one." Unusual.

Alix English, from Alexander, Greek, "Defender of men" or "warding off men," Mark 16:21, Acts 4:6, 19:33; and French, from Adelaide, Old German (Adelheidis), "Nobility." Unusual.

Aliya Hebrew/Israeli. Hebrew, "To go up." Unusual.

Aliz Hungarian. From Adelaide, Old German (Adelheidis), "Nobility." Unusual.

Aliza Hebrew/Israeli. Hebrew, "Joy" or "joyful." Unusual. Alternative spelling: Alizah.

Alizka Hungarian. From Adelaide, Old German (Adelheidis), "Nobility." Unusual.

Aljexi English. From Alexander, Greek, "Defender of men" or "warding off men." Mark 16:21; Acts 4:6, 19:33. Unusual.

Alka Polish. From Alexander, Greek, "Defender of men" or "warding off men." Mark 16:21; Acts 4:6, 19:33. Unusual.

Alkas Native American. Native American, "She is afraid." Unusual.

Alleen Dutch. Dutch, "Alone." Unusual.

Allegra English. Italian, "Lively," "joyful," or "merry." Musical term used as first name. Kent (ballerina); character in Elizabeth Taylor's novel "A View of the Harbour." Unusual.

Allena English. From Alan, Gaelic, meaning uncertain, but may include "rock," "noble," "handsome," "harmony," and/or "cheerful." Unusual.

Allene English. From Alan, Gaelic, meaning uncertain, but may include "rock," "noble," "handsome," "harmony," and/or "cheerful." Unusual. Alternative spelling: Alleyne.

Alli English. From Alexander, Greek, "Defender of men" or "warding off men." Mark 16:21; Acts 4:6, 19:33. Unusual.

Allina English. From Alan, Gaelic, meaning uncertain, but may include "rock," "noble," "handsome," "harmony," and/or "cheerful." Less popular.

Allison English. From Adelaide, Old German (Adelheidis), "Nobility." Popular. Alternative spellings: Alison, Allyson, Alyson.

Allsun Irish. From Adelaide, Old German (Adelheidis), "Nobility." Unusual.

Alltrinna Created. Created, African-American. Unusual.

Allys English. From Adelaide, Old German (Adelheidis), "Nobility." Unusual.

Alma English, from Alma, Latin, "Nurturing," "loving," or "kind"; and Hebrew/Israeli, from Alumit, Hebrew, "Girl" or "secret." Roman goddess; character in Spenser's poem "The Faerie Queene" (published 1589–96); Gluck (opera singer); Bridwell White (clergyman, established Methodist Pentecostal Union church, 1901). Less popular.

Almena English. From William, Old German, "Will" + "helmet." Unusual. Alternative spellings: Almeina, Almina.

Almira Arabic. Arabic, "Princess." Sessions (character actress). Unusual.

Almond English. Greek, "amygdale"; a plant name used as first name. Unusual.

Alnaba Native American. Native American, "Wars passed each other." Indicates two battles that were waged in opposite directions. Unusual.

Aloha Hawaiian. Hawaiian, expresses greeting and farewell. Connotes love, kindness, charity, and mercy. Unusual.

Alohi Hawaiian. Hawaiian, "Brilliant" or "shining." Unusual for males, unusual for females.

Alohilani Hawaiian. Hawaiian, "Bright sky." Unusual.

Aloisa German. From Louis, Old German (Hlutwig), "Famous warrior." Unusual.

Aloisia Hispanic. From Louis, Old German (Hlutwig), "Famous warrior." Unusual.

Alona Hebrew/Israeli. From Alon, Hebrew, "Oak tree." Unusual.

Alonza English. From Alphonso, Old German (Hildefuns), "Ready for battle." Unusual.

Aloyse English. From Louis, Old German (Hlutwig), "Famous warrior." Unusual.

Aloysia Dutch. From Louis, Old German (Hlutwig), "Famous warrior." Unusual.

Alpha English. Greek, the first letter of the alphabet. Symbolizes "the beginning," particularly in relation to God. Unusual.

Alphonsine French, Italian. From Alphonso, Old German (Hildefuns), "Ready for battle." Unusual.

Althea English. Greek, "Healing." Refers to a bush known for its healing powers. Subject of Richard Lovelace's poem "To Althea from Prison"; character in "The Iliad." Unusual.

Altsoba Native American. Native American, "All are at war." Unusual.

Aludra Greek. Greek, "Virgin." Related to the astrological sign Virgo. Unusual.

Aluma Hebrew/Israeli. From Alumit. Unusual.

Alumice Hebrew/Israeli. From Alumit. Unusual.

Alumit Hebrew/Israeli. Hebrew, "Girl" or "secret." Unusual.

Alva English. Hebrew, "Brightness" (?). Genesis 36:40. Reimer Myrdal (Swedish social reformer, won Nobel Peace Prize, 1982); Smith Belmont (socialite and suffragist); Lee Davis (professor, Illinois Institute of Technology). Unusual for males, unusual for females. Alternative spelling: Alvah.

Alvedine English. From Alfred, Old English, "Elf-counsel." Unusual.

Alvena English. From Alvin, Old English, "Elf-friend," "noble friend," "everyone's friend," or "old friend." Unusual. Alternative spelling: Alvina.

Alverdine English. From Alfred, Old English, "Elf-counsel." Unusual.

Alverta Greek. From Albert, Old English (Aethelbeorht), "Noble-bright." Unusual.

Alvie English. From Alvin, Old English, "Elf-friend," "noble friend," "everyone's friend," or "old friend." Less popular for males, less popular for females.

Alvine English. From Alvin, Old English, "Elf-friend," "noble friend," "everyone's friend," or "old friend." Unusual.

Alvinia English. From Albin, Latin, "White." Unusual.

Alwyna English. From Alvin, Old English, "Elf-friend," "noble friend," "everyone's friend," or "old friend." Unusual.

Alwynne English. From Alvin, Old English, "Elf-friend," "noble friend," "everyone's friend," or "old friend." Unusual. Alternative spellings: Alwine, Alwyne.

Alya Russian. From Alexander, Greek, "Defender of men" or "warding off men." Mark 16:21; Acts 4:6, 19:33. Unusual.

Alys Welsh. From Adelaide, Old German (Adelheidis), "Nobility." Unusual.

Alysanne English. From Adelaide, Old German (Adelheidis), "Nobility." Unusual.

Alyse English. From Adelaide, Old German (Adelheidis), "Nobility." Unusual.

Alysoun English. From Adelaide, Old German (Adelheidis), "Nobility." Unusual. Alternative spelling: Alisoun.

Alžběta Czech. From Elizabeth, Hebrew (Elisheva), "Oath of God" or "God is my oath." Exodus 6:23. Unusual.

Alzubra Arabic. Arabic, the name of a small star in the constellation Leo. Unusual.

Am Vietnamese. Vietnamese, "Lunar" or "female principle." The latter is tied to the Oriental concept of creation, which is that the world was born from two sources of energy, male and female. Unusual.

Ama African. Ghanaian, "Born on Saturday." Unusual.

Amabel English. Latin, "Lovable." Unusual.

Amada Hispanic. From Amy, Old French, "Loved." Unusual.

Amadea Italian. From Amado, Latin, "Loving deity" or "lover of the divine." Unusual.

Amadika African. Rhodesian, "To be beloved." A mother gives herself this name if her life is tragic. It implies that her husband once loved her but no longer does. Unusual.

Amali English. From Amelia, Latin, "Industrious" or "striving." Unusual.

Amalia English, German, Hispanic, Hungarian, Italian, Polish, Romanian, Slavic. From Amelia, Latin, "Industrious" or "striving." 18th-century Duchess of Saxe-Weimar, patroness of art and literature. Unusual. Alternative spelling: Amalea.

Amalie French. From Amelia, Latin, "Industrious" or "striving." Heiter (Duchess of Saxony and playwright, "Die Furstenbraut"). Unusual.

Amaliya Russian. From Amelia, Latin, "Industrious" or "striving." Unusual.

Amanda English. Latin, "Fit to be loved." Douglas (author of children's books); Prynne (character in Noël Coward's "Private Lives"); character in Sir John Vanbrugh's "Relapse"; character in Colley Cibber's "Love's Last Shift"; character in novels "Tristram Shandy" and "Peregrine Pickle." Extremely popular. Mandy+.

Amanda-Jane English. English, combination of Amanda (English, "Fit to be loved") + Jane (John, Hebrew (Yochanan), "Jehovah has been gracious"). Less popular. Mandy+.

Amandeep See under Boys' Names.

Amandine French. From Amanda, Latin, "Fit to be loved." Unusual.

Amara Esperanto. From Miriam, Hebrew (Miryam), "Bitterness," "rebellion," "wished-for child," or "sea" (?). Exodus 15:20. Unusual.

Amaris Hebrew/Israeli. From Amariah, Hebrew, "Whom God has promised." Unusual.

Amata Hispanic. From Amy, Old French, "Loved." Unusual.

Amaui Hawaiian. Hawaiian, "Thrush." A songbird with olive-brown color. Unusual.
Amayeta Native American. Native American, "Big manzanita berries." Unusual.
Ambarish Indo-Pakistani. Hindi, "Saint" or "philosopher." Unusual.
Amber English. Arabic, "Ambergris." Character in Kathleen Winsor's novel "Forever Amber." Very popular.
Amberetta English. From Amber. Unusual.
Amberly English. From Amber. Unusual.
Ambika Indo-Pakistani. Hindi, "The mother." One of 1,000 names for Sakti, the Hindu goddess of power and destruction. Unusual.
Ambrosina English. From Ambrose, Greek, "Immortal." Unusual.
Ambrosine English. From Ambrose, Greek, "Immortal." Unusual. Alternative spelling: Ambrozine.
Amelcia Polish. From Amelia. Unusual.
Ameldy English. From Amelia. Unusual.
Amelia English. Latin, "Industrious" or "striving." Earhart (aviator, first woman to cross Atlantic solo, 1932); Adelaide (British queen of William IV); Sedley (character in Thackeray's "Vanity Fair"); Jenks Bloomer (suffragette, wore trousers later called "bloomers"); Barr (novelist, "Cluny McPherson"). Less popular.
Amélie French. From Amelia. Unusual.
Amelina English. From Amelia. Unusual.
Amelita English. From Amelia. Unusual.
Amella English. From Amelia. Unusual.
Ami English. From Amy. Perrin (16th-century Swiss politician, led anti-Calvinist Libertine movement); Boué (Austrian geologist, helped establish Société Geologique de France, 1830). Less popular.
Amia English. From Amy. Unusual.
Amias See under Boys' Names.
Amica Italian. From Amicus, Latin, "Beloved friend." Unusual.
Amice French. From Amicus, Latin, "Beloved friend." Unusual.
Amie French. From Amy. Unusual.
Amilia English. From Amelia. Unusual.
Amilie English. From Amelia. Unusual.
Amina Arabic. Arabic, "Peace" or "security." Unusual. Alternative spelling: Aminah.
Amineh Arabic. Arabic, "Faithful." Unusual.
Aminta Italian. From Amyntas, Greek, meaning unknown. Unusual.
Amira Hebrew/Israeli. Hebrew, "Speech" or "utterance." Unusual.
Amissa Hebrew/Israeli. Hebrew, "Truth" or "friend." Unusual. Alternative spelling: Amisa.
Amma Indo-Pakistani. Hindi, "Mother goddess." Unusual.
Amoke Nigerian. Nigerian, "To know her is to pet her." Unusual.
Amplias Unknown. Meaning and origin unknown. Unusual.
Amy English. Old French, "Loved." Lowell (Pulitzer Prize-winning poet, 1926, "Lilacs"); character in Alcott's "Little Women"; Johnson (British aviator, first woman to fly solo from London to Australia, 1930); Cheney Beach (pianist and composer, "Festival Jubilate"); Irving (actress). Popular. Alternative spellings: Aimy, Ame, Amey.
Amyntas Greek. Greek, meaning unknown. Unusual.
An See under Boys' Names.
Ana English. From Hannah, Hebrew (Chanah), "Grace [of God]" or "favor." 1 Samuel 1:2. Mendoza de la Cerda (16th-century Spanish princess). Less popular.
Anaba Native American. Native American, "She returns from battle." Unusual.
Anabela Hawaiian. From Amabel, Latin, "Lovable." Unusual.
Anabella English. From Amabel, Latin, "Lovable." Less popular. Anna, Belle.
Anaca American. From Anika, African-American, "Sweetness of face." Unusual.
Anais Hebrew/Israeli. Hebrew, "One of grace" or "gracious." Unusual.
Anaka American. From Anika, African-American, "Sweetness of face." Unusual.
Anala Indo-Pakistani. Hindi, "Fire." Another name for Agni, the Hindu god of fire. Unusual for males, unusual for females.
Ananda Indo-Pakistani. From Anand, Hindi, "Bliss." Disciple of Buddha; Coomaraswamy (Indian scholar, led cultural revival). Unusual.
Anastace English. From Anastasia. Unusual.
Anastacia English. From Anastasia. Unusual.
Anastacie German. From Anastasia. Unusual.
Anastasia English. Greek, "anastasis" ("resurrection"). Saint; Russian princess, daughter of Czar Nicholas II. Unusual.
Anastasie French. From Anastasia. Unusual.
Anastatia English. From Anastasia. Unusual.
Anastazia Czech. From Anastasia. Unusual.
Anastice English. From Anastasia. Unusual. Alternative spelling: Anastyce.
Anci Hungarian. From Hannah, Hebrew (Chanah), "Grace [of God]" or "favor." 1 Samuel 1:2. Unusual.
Anda Hispanic. Hispanic, "Going." Unusual.
Anděla Czech. From Angel, Greek, "angelos" ("messenger"). Unusual.
Andera English. From Andrew, Greek, "Manly." Unusual.
Anders Scottish. From Andrew, Greek, "Manly." Unusual.
Andra Scottish. From Andrew, Greek, "Manly." Unusual.
Andrea English. From Andrew, Greek, "Manly." Sansovino (Italian Renaissance sculptor, "Baptism of Christ"); Mantegna (Italian Renaissance fresco artist, "Triumph of Caesar"); Palladio (Italian architect, designed palaces on Venice's Grand Canal); Solari (Italian painter, "Flight into Egypt"); Alciati (Italian jurist). Less popular for males, popular for females. Andy+. Alternative spellings: Andria, Andreea.
Andrean English. From Andrew, Greek, "Manly." Unusual.
Andreana English. From Andrew, Greek, "Manly." Unusual.
Andree English. From Andrew, Greek, "Manly." Unusual.
Andrene English. From Andrew, Greek, "Manly." Unusual. Alternative spelling: Andrine.
Andrette English. From Andrew, Greek, "Manly." Unusual.
Andrewina English. From Andrew, Greek, "Manly." Unusual.
Andriana English. From Andrew, Greek, "Manly." Unusual. Alternative spelling: Andrianna.
Andrienne English. From Andrew, Greek, "Manly." Unusual.

Andrietta English. From Andrew, Greek, "Manly." Unusual.

Andrina English. From Andrew, Greek, "Manly." Unusual. Alternative spelling: Andreena.

Andula Czech. From Hannah, Hebrew (Chanah), "Grace [of God]" or "favor." 1 Samuel 1:2. Unusual.

Andulka Czech. From Hannah, Hebrew (Chanah), "Grace [of God]" or "favor." 1 Samuel 1:2. Unusual.

Ane Hawaiian. From Hannah, Hebrew (Chanah), "Grace [of God]" or "favor." 1 Samuel 1:2. Unusual.

Anecky American. From Anika, African-American, "Sweetness of face." Unusual.

Anela Hawaiian. From Anela, Hawaiian, "Angel." Unusual.

Aneska Czech. From Agnes, Greek, "agnos" ("pure" or "chaste"). Unusual.

Anesse English. From Agnes, Greek, "agnos" ("pure" or "chaste"). Unusual.

Anetta English. From Hannah, Hebrew (Chanah), "Grace [of God]" or "favor." 1 Samuel 1:2. Unusual.

Anette English. From Hannah, Hebrew (Chanah), "Grace [of God]" or "favor." 1 Samuel 1:2. Unusual.

Anevay Native American. Native American, "Superior." Unusual.

Anežka Czech. From Hannah, Hebrew (Chanah), "Grace [of God]" or "favor." 1 Samuel 1:2. Unusual.

Angel English. Greek, "angelos" ("messenger"). Nieto (Spanish, world champion in 125 cc motorcycle race a record seven times); Ganivet (Spanishnovelist); Guimera (Catalan playwright, "Mar i Cel"); Clare (character in Thomas Hardy's "Tess of the D'Urbervilles"). Less popular for males, unusual for females. Alternative spelling: Angelle.

Angela English. From Angel. Merici (saint); Lansbury (actress, "Murder She Wrote"); Burdett-Coutts, Baroness (British philanthropist, raised Turkish relief fund, 1877–78); Mackail Thirkell (British novelist, "Coronation Summer"). Very popular. Angie+.

Angèle French. From Angel. Unusual.

Angelene French. From Angel. Less popular.

Angelia English. From Angel. Unusual.

Angelic English. From Angel. Unusual.

Angelica Greek. From Angel. Kauffmann (Swiss neoclassical painter); character in John Milton's poem "Paradise Regained." Unusual.

Angelika German. From Angel. Unusual.

Angeliki Greek. From Angel. Unusual.

Angelina Russian. From Angel. Character in Gilbert and Sullivan's "Trial by Jury." Unusual.

Angeline French. From Angel.

Angélique French. From Angel. Unusual.

Angelita Hispanic. From Angel. Unusual.

Angeni Native American. Native American, "Spirit angel." Unusual.

Angharad Welsh. Welsh, "Much loved." Unusual.

Angie English. From Angel. Dickinson (actress). Less popular. Alternative spellings: Angi, Angy.

Angusina Scottish. From Angus, Gaelic, "Unique choice." Also a Scottish place name, now called Forfarshire. Unusual.

Anh See under Boys' Names.

Anhelina Russian. From Angel. Unusual.

Ani Hawaiian. From Kanani, Hawaiian, "The beauty." Unusual.

Ania Polish. From Hannah, Hebrew (Chanah), "Grace [of God]" or "favor." 1 Samuel 1:2. Unusual.

Anica Hispanic. From Hannah, Hebrew (Chanah), "Grace [of God]" or "favor." 1 Samuel 1:2. Unusual.

Anice English. From Agnes, Greek, "agnos" ("pure" or "chaste"). Unusual.

Anicka Czech. From Hannah, Hebrew (Chanah), "Grace [of God]" or "favor." 1 Samuel 1:2. Unusual.

Anicuta Romanian. From Hannah, Hebrew (Chanah), "Grace [of God]" or "favor." 1 Samuel 1:2. Unusual.

Anika American. African-American, "Sweetness of face." Unusual.

Anikee American. From Anika. Unusual.

Anikke Lithuanian. From Hannah, Hebrew (Chanah), "Grace [of God]" or "favor." 1 Samuel 1:2. Unusual.

Anikó Hungarian. From Hannah, Hebrew (Chanah), "Grace [of God]" or "favor." 1 Samuel 1:2. Unusual.

Anila Indo-Pakistani. Hindi, "Wind god." Forty-nine offspring of the wind are associated with this Hindu god. Unusual for males, unusual for females.

Anis English. From Agnes, Greek, "agnos" ("pure" or "chaste"). Unusual.

Anise English. From Agnes, Greek, "agnos" ("pure" or "chaste"). Unusual.

Anisha English. From Annice, Greek, "Fulfillment" or "completion." Unusual.

Anissa English. From Annice, Greek, "Fulfillment" or "completion." Unusual.

Anita English, Hispanic. From Hannah, Hebrew (Chanah), "Grace [of God]" or "favor." 1 Samuel 1:2. Ekberg (Swedish actress, "La Dolce Vita"); Loos (movie writer, "I Married an Angel"); Bryant (singer); Baker (singer, "Giving You The Best That I Got"). Less popular. Nita. Alternative spellings: Annita, Annitta.

Anitte German. From Hannah, Hebrew (Chanah), "Grace [of God]" or "favor." 1 Samuel 1:2. Unusual.

Aniweta Nigerian. Nigerian, "Ani brought it." Ani is a spirit in Ibo culture. Unusual for males, unusual for females.

Anja Russian. From Hannah, Hebrew (Chanah), "Grace [of God]" or "favor." 1 Samuel 1:2. Unusual.

Anjelica English. From Angel, Greek, "angelos" ("messenger"). Huston (actress, "Prizzi's Honor"). Less popular. Angie+.

Anka Polish. From Hannah, Hebrew (Chanah), "Grace [of God]" or "favor." 1 Samuel 1:2. Unusual.

Anna English. From Hannah, Hebrew (Chanah), "Grace [of God]" or "favor." 1 Samuel 1:2. Green (developed detective fiction, "Leavenworth Case"); character in Tolstoy's "Anna Karenina"; Sewell (British author, "Black Beauty"); Pavlova (Russian ballerina); Gorenko (Russian neoclassical poet); Magnani (Italian actress, "Rose Tattoo"). Popular. Annie+. Alternative spelling: Annah.

Anna Mary English. English, combination of Anna (Hannah, Hebrew (Chanah), "Grace") + Mary (Miriam, Hebrew (Miryam), "Bitterness"). Robertson (primitivist painter) (real name of Grandma Moses). Less popular.

Annabelle English. From Amabel, Latin, "Lovable." Less popular. Alternative spellings: Anabel, Anabele, Anabell, Anabelle, Annabel, Annabell.

Annaka American. From Anika, African-American, "Sweetness of face." Unusual.

Annalie English. From Hannah, Hebrew (Chanah), "Grace [of God]" or "favor." 1 Samuel 1:2. Unusual.

Annalisa English. English, combination of Anna (Hannah, Hebrew (Chanah),

"Grace") + Lisa (Elizabeth, Hebrew (Elisheva), "Oath of God" or "God is my oath"). Unusual. Alternative splling: Annaleisa.

Annamarie English. English, combination of Anna (Hannah, Hebrew (Chanah), "Grace") + Marie (Miriam, Hebrew (Miryam), "Bitterness"). Less popular.

Annaple English. From Amabel, Latin, "Lovable." Unusual.

Annchen German. From Hannah, Hebrew (Chanah), "Grace [of God]" or "favor." 1 Samuel 1:2. Unusual.

Anne English. From Hannah, Hebrew (Chanah), "Grace [of God]" or "favor." 1 Samuel 1:2. Saint; Harvey Sexton (won Pulitzer Prize for poetry, 1966, "Live or Die"); O'Hare McCormick (first woman to win Pulitzer Prize for journalism, 1937); Sullivan Macy (educator, companion of Helen Keller); character in Montgomery's "Anne of Green Gables." Less popular. Annie+. Alternative spellings: Ann, Ayn.

Anne-Marie English. English, combination of Anne (Hannah, Hebrew (Chanah), "Grace") + Marie (Miriam, Hebrew (Miryam), "Bitterness"). Less popular.

Anneka Swedish. From Hannah, Hebrew (Chanah), "Grace [of God]" or "favor." 1 Samuel 1:2. Unusual.

Anneli German. From Hannah, Hebrew (Chanah), "Grace [of God]" or "favor." 1 Samuel 1:2. Unusual.

Annelie English. From Hannah, Hebrew (Chanah), "Grace [of God]" or "favor." 1 Samuel 1:2. Unusual.

Anneliese English. English, combination of Anne (Hannah, Hebrew (Chanah), "Grace") + Liese (Elizabeth, Hebrew (Elisheva), "Oath of God" or "God is my oath"). Unusual. Alternative spelling: Annelise.

Annelisa English. English, combination of Anne (Hannah, Hebrew (Chanah), "Grace") + Lisa (Elizabeth, Hebrew (Elisheva), "Oath of God" or "God is my oath"). Unusual.

Annelise English. English, combination of Anne (Hannah, Hebrew (Chanah), "Grace") + Liese (Elizabeth, Hebrew (Elisheva), "Oath of God" or "God is my oath"). Unusual.

Annes English. From Agnes, Greek, "agnos" ("pure" or "chaste"). Unusual. Alternative spelling: Anness.

Anneth English. From Hannah, Hebrew (Chanah), "Grace [of God]" or "favor." 1 Samuel 1:2. Unusual.

Annett English. From Hannah, Hebrew (Chanah), "Grace [of God]" or "favor." 1 Samuel 1:2. Unusual. Alternative spelling: Annet.

Annetta Italian. From Hannah, Hebrew (Chanah), "Grace [of God]" or "favor." 1 Samuel 1:2. Unusual.

Annette French. From Hannah, Hebrew (Chanah), "Grace [of God]" or "favor." 1 Samuel 1:2. Funicello (actress, "Beach Blanket Bingo"); von Droste-Hülshoff (German poet, "Gedichte"). Less popular.

Annice English. Greek, "Fulfillment" or "completion." Unusual.

Annie English. From Hannah, Hebrew (Chanah), "Grace [of God]" or "favor." 1 Samuel 1:2. Oakley (sharpshooter in Buffalo Bill's Wild West Show); Smith Peck (mountain climber); Horniman (British, managed Gaiety Theater, 1908–21, and established repertory company); Cannon (astronomer, discovered 300 stars); Little Orphan (cartoon character); Lennox (British pop singer). Less popular. Alternative spellings: Anni, Anny.

Annik American. From Anika, African-American, "Sweetness of face." Unusual.

Annika Swedish. From Hannah, Hebrew (Chanah), "Grace [of God]" or "favor." 1 Samuel 1:2. Unusual.

Annikki Finnish. From Hannah, Hebrew (Chanah), "Grace [of God]" or "favor." 1 Samuel 1:2. Unusual.

Annina Italian. From Hannah, Hebrew (Chanah), "Grace [of God]" or "favor." 1 Samuel 1:2. Unusual.

Anninka Russian. From Hannah, Hebrew (Chanah), "Grace [of God]" or "favor." 1 Samuel 1:2. Unusual.

Annis English. From Annice, Greek, "Fulfillment" or "completion." Unusual.

Annmaria English. English, combination of Ann (Hannah, Hebrew (Chanah), "Grace") + Maria (Miriam, Hebrew (Miryam), "Bitterness"). Less popular. Ann, Annie+.

Annmarie English. English, combination of Ann (Hannah, Hebrew (Chanah), "Grace") + Marie (Miriam, Hebrew (Miryam), "Bitterness"). Less popular. Ann, Annie+.

Annora English. From Honoria, Latin, "Honorable woman." Unusual.

Annthea English. From Anthea, Greek, "Flower" or "flowery." An "anth"ology is literally a collection of flowers. Unusual.

Anntoinette English. From Anthony, Latin, a Roman clan name used as a first name. Unusual. Toni. Alternative spellings: Antionette, Antoinet.

Annus Hungarian. From Hannah, Hebrew (Chanah), "Grace [of God]" or "favor." 1 Samuel 1:2. Unusual.

Annuska Hungarian, Russian. From Hannah, Hebrew (Chanah), "Grace [of God]" or "favor." 1 Samuel 1:2. Unusual.

Annze Lithuanian. From Hannah, Hebrew (Chanah), "Grace [of God]" or "favor." 1 Samuel 1:2. Unusual.

Anona English. Latin, "Pineapple." May also refer to the Roman goddess of provisions. Unusual.

Anouska Russian. From Hannah, Hebrew (Chanah), "Grace [of God]" or "favor." 1 Samuel 1:2. Unusual.

Anselma English. From Anselm, Old German, "Divine" + "helmet." Unusual.

Ansley See under Boys' Names.

Anstice English. From Anastasia, Greek, "anastasis" ("resurrection"). Unusual.

Anta Polish. From Anthony, Latin, a Roman clan name used as a first name. Saint. Unusual.

Anthea English. Greek, "Flower" or "flowery." An "anth"ology is literally a collection of flowers. Unusual.

Antoinette French. From Anthony, Latin, a Roman clan name used as a first name. Perry (actress and director, established American Theater Wing, 1941; Tony award named for her); Brown Blackwell (first woman pastor, 1852); Bourignon (Flemish religious figure, spread Bourignianism through Scotland and Holland). Less popular.

Antonella English. From Anthony, Latin, a Roman clan name used as a first name. Unusual. Toni.

Antonetta Slavic, Swedish. From Anthony, Latin, a Roman clan name used as a first name. Unusual.

Antonette Russian. From Anthony, Latin, a Roman clan name used as a first name. Unusual.

Antonia Italian. From Anthony, Latin, a

Roman clan name used as a first name. Major (Roman noblewoman, grandmother of Nero); Minor (Roman noblewoman, mother of Emperor Claudius); Merce (Argentine, developed neoclassical style of Spanish dance); character in Willa Cather's "My Antonia." Unusual.

Antonie French. From Anthony, Latin, a Roman clan name used as a first name. Unusual.

Antonieta Italian. From Anthony, Latin, a Roman clan name used as a first name. Unusual.

Antonina Hispanic, Polish, Russian. From Anthony, Latin, a Roman clan name used as a first name. Unusual.

Antuca Hispanic. From Anthony, Latin, a Roman clan name used as a first name. Unusual.

Anuška Czech. From Hannah, Hebrew (Chanah), "Grace [of God]" or "favor." 1 Samuel 1:2. Unusual.

Anwen Welsh. Welsh, "Very beautiful" or "very fair." Unusual.

Anwyn Welsh. From Anwen. Unusual.

Anya Latvian, Russian. From Hannah, Hebrew (Chanah), "Grace [of God]" or "favor." 1 Samuel 1:2. Unusual.

Anyuta Latvian. From Hannah, Hebrew (Chanah), "Grace [of God]" or "favor." 1 Samuel 1:2. Unusual.

Anzu Japanese. Japanese, "Apricot." Unusual.

Aolani Hawaiian. Hawaiian, "Heavenly cloud." Unusual.

Apangela African. African, "One who doesn't intend to complete her journey." A name taken from a proverb, it implies that the child may not live. Unusual.

Apara Nigerian. Nigerian, "One who comes and goes." Tribal belief holds that evil spirits are incarnated in some children. The name was concocted to prevent the child's early death if its spirit leaves the world. Unusual.

Aphra English. Hebrew, "Dust." Possibly a misunderstanding of Micah 1:10, which refers to "the house of Aphra." Some thought Aphra to be a personal name. Behn (17th-century British, first woman professional writer, "False Count" and other coarse comedies). Unusual.

Aponi Native American. Native American, "Butterfly." Unusual.

April English. Latin, "To open up." Popular. Alternative spelling: Apryl.

Aquene Native American. Native American, "Peace." Unusual.

Arabella English. Latin, "Yielding to prayer." Churchill (British, mistress of James II); Allen (character in Dickens' "Pickwick Papers"); Fermor (character in Pope's 1712 poem "Rape of the Lock"); character in Strauss's opera "Arabella." Unusual. Alternative spelling: Arabela.

Araminta Created. Created by Sir John Vanbrugh in his 1705 comedy "The Confederacy." Unusual.

Arella Hebrew/Israeli. Hebrew, "Angel" or "messenger." Unusual. Alternative spelling: Arela.

Areta American. Greek, "Virtue." Unusual.

Arete Greek. From Grace, Latin, "Grace." Unusual.

Aretha American. From Areta. Franklin (singer, 14 million-selling singles from 1967–73). Less popular.

Arethi Greek. From Areta. Unusual.

Aretta American. From Areta. Unusual.

Arette French. From Areta. Unusual.

Ariadne Greek. Greek, "Very holy one." Daughter of King Minos of Crete; character in Strauss's opera "Ariadne auf Naxos." Unusual.

Ariane French. From Ariadne. Unusual.

Arianna English. From Ariadne. Unusual. Alternative spelling: Ariana.

Arianne English. From Ariadne. Unusual.

Ariel Hebrew/Israeli. Hebrew, "Lion(ess) of God." Spirit in Shakespeare's "Tempest"; character (a sprite) in Pope's 1712 poem "Rape of the Lock"; title of biography of Shelley by Maurois. Less popular for males, less popular for females. Ari+.

Ariella Hebrew/Israeli. From Ariel, Hebrew, "Lion(ess) of God." Less popular. Ari+. Alternative spelling: Ariela.

Arielle Hebrew/Israeli. From Ariel, Hebrew, "Lion(ess) of God." Less popular. Ari+.

Arina Russian. From Irene, Greek (Eirene), "Peace." Unusual.

Arinka Russian. From Irene, Greek (Eirene), "Peace." Unusual.

Arista English. Latin, "Harvest." Unusual.

Ariza Hebrew/Israeli. Hebrew, "Cedar panels." Unusual.

Arlena English. From Charles, Old English, "ceorl" ("man" or "husbandman"). Unusual. Alternative spelling: Arlina.

Arlene English. From Charles, Old English, "ceorl" ("man" or "husbandman"). Dahl (actress); Francis (actress). Less popular. Alternative spellings: Arleen, Arline.

Arletta English. From Charles, Old English, "ceorl" ("man" or "husbandman"). Unusual.

Arlette English. From Charles, Old English, "ceorl" ("man" or "husbandman"). Less popular.

Arlyne English. From Charles, Old English, "ceorl" ("man" or "husbandman"). Unusual.

Armina English. From Herman, Old German, "Army" + "man." Unusual.

Armine French. From Herman, Old German, "Army" + "man." Unusual.

Arna Hebrew/Israeli. Hebrew, "Cedar tree." Bontemps (author, "Story of the Negro"). Unusual.

Árni Icelandic. From Arne, Old German, "Eagle." Magnusson (Icelandic philologist, established collection of early manuscripts). Unusual.

Arnice Hebrew/Israeli. From Arna. Unusual.

Arnina Hebrew/Israeli. Hebrew, "Mountain," "to shine," "singer," or "messenger." Unusual.

Arnit Hebrew/Israeli. From Arna. Unusual.

Arriet Swedish. From Henry, Old German (Heimerich), "Home ruler." Unusual.

Artemesia English. From Artemas, Greek, "Belonging to Artemis," also known as Diana, goddess of the hunt. Titus 3:12. Unusual.

Artemisia English. From Artemas, Greek, "Belonging to Artemis," also known as Diana, goddess of the hunt. Titus 3:12. Queen of Halicarnassus, 5th-century B.C.; queen of Caria, 4th-century B.C., erected mausoleum that was one of the seven Wonders of the World. Unusual.

Artha Indo-Pakistani. Hindi, "Wealth" or "prosperity." Unusual.

Artheia English. From Arthur, Gaelic, "Rock," "noble," or "lofty hill." Unusual.

Arthelia English. From Arthur, Gaelic, "Rock," "noble," or "lofty hill." Unusual.

Arthene English. From Arthur, Gaelic, "Rock," "noble," or "lofty hill." Unusual.

Arthuretta English. From Arthur, Gaelic, "Rock," "noble," or "lofty hill." Unusual.
Arthurina From Arthur, Gaelic, "Rock," "noble," or "lofty hill." Unusual.
Arthurine English. From Arthur, Gaelic, "Rock," "noble," or "lofty hill." Unusual.
Artina English. From Arthur, Gaelic, "Rock," "noble," or "lofty hill." Unusual.
Artis English. From Arthur, Gaelic, "Rock," "noble," or "lofty hill." Gilmore (basketball great, has highest lifetime field goal percentage in NBA: .599). Unusual.
Artlette English. From Arthur, Gaelic, "Rock," "noble," or "lofty hill." Unusual.
Artrice English. From Arthur, Gaelic, "Rock," "noble," or "lofty hill." Unusual. Artie+.
Arza Hebrew/Israeli. From Ariza, Hebrew, "Cedar panels." Unusual.
Arzice Hebrew/Israeli. From Ariza, Hebrew, "Cedar panels." Unusual.
Arzit Hebrew/Israeli. From Ariza, Hebrew, "Cedar panels." Unusual.
Asabi Nigerian. Nigerian, "Child of select birth." Unusual.
Asela Hispanic. Hispanic, "Slender ash tree." Unusual.
Asenka Latvian, Russian. From Hannah, Hebrew (Chanah), "Grace [of God]" or "favor." 1 Samuel 1:2. Unusual.
Asha Arabic. From Ayasha, Arabic, "Life." Unusual.
Ashanta American. From Ashanti. Unusual.
Ashante American. From Ashanti. Unusual.
Ashanti American. African, the name of a tribe. Unusual.
Ashaunta American. From Ashanti. Unusual.
Ashia Arabic. From Ayasha, Arabic, "Life." Unusual.
Ashlea English. From Ashley. Less popular for males, less popular for females.
Ashley English. Old English, "Ash wood" or "ash-tree meadow." Wilkes (character in Mitchell's "Gone With the Wind"); Dukes (British playwright, "Matchmaker's Arms"); Thorndike (educator and authority on Elizabethan drama, wrote "Shakespeare's Theatre"); Brophy (Australian high-wire walker). Less popular for males, extremely popular for females. Alternative spellings: Ashely, Ashlee, Ashlei, Ashleigh, Ashli, Ashlie, Ashly.
Ashling Irish. From Aisling, Irish, "Vision" or "dream." Unusual.
Ashlyn Irish. From Aisling, Irish, "Vision" or "dream." Unusual. Alternative spelling: Ashlynn.
Ashtin English. From Ashton, English, "Ash-tree farm." Surname and place name used as a first name. Unusual.
Ashton See under Boys' Names.
Ashuntae American. From Ashanti. Unusual.
Asia English. "Eastern sunrise," origin unknown; the word used as a first name. Unusual.
Asisa Hebrew/Israeli. From Asisa, Hebrew, "Ripe" or "juicy." Unusual.
Asiza African. African, "Forest spirit." Unusual.
Aska Latvian. From Hannah, Hebrew (Chanah), "Grace [of God]" or "favor." 1 Samuel 1:2. Unusual.
Asoka Indo-Pakistani. Hindi, "Non-sorrow flower," which is said to bloom crimson or orange when touched by a sweet girl's foot. King of India, 3rd-century B.C.; made Buddhism the state religion. Unusual.
Aspasia English. Greek, "Welcome." Fifth-century B.C. Greek consort of Pericles; character in Beaumont and Fletcher's "Maid's Tragedy." Unusual.
Aspen English. Latvian, "apsa"; a tree name used as a first name. Unusual.
Assa Scandinavian. From Astrid. Unusual.
Assi Scandinavian. From Astrid. Unusual.
Åsta Norwegian. From Astrid. Nielsen (Danish silent-film actress). Unusual.
Astera Hebrew/Israeli. Hebrew, "Aster flower." Unusual.
Asteria Hebrew/Israeli. From Astera. Unusual.
Astra English, from Astra, Latin, "Of the stars"; and Hebrew/Israeli, from Astera, Hebrew, "Aster flower." Character in Grace Livingston Hill's "Astra." Unusual.
Astri Scandinavian. From Astrid. Unusual.
Astrid Scandinavian. Old Norse, "Divine beauty" or "divine strength." Queen of Belgium; Ehrencron-Kidde (Danish novelist). Unusual.
Astrud Scandinavian. From Astrid. Unusual.
Astyr Scandinavian. From Astrid. Unusual.
Asya Latvian, Russian. Hebrew (Chanah), "Grace [of God]" or "favor." 1 Samuel 1:2. Unusual.
Atalanta English. Greek, "Unswaying." Greek mythological maiden who agreed to marry whoever could overcome her in a foot race. Unusual.
Atara Hebrew/Israeli. Hebrew, "Crown." Unusual.
Ataret Hebrew/Israeli. From Atara. Unusual.
Athena Greek. From Athene, Greek. Unusual.
Athene Greek. Greek, the name of the goddess of wisdom. Unusual.
Atida Hebrew/Israeli. Hebrew, "The future." Unusual.
Atira Hebrew/Israeli. Hebrew, "A prayer." Unusual.
Atka Polish. From Agatha, Greek, "agathos" ("good"). Unusual.
Atrice English. From Arthur, Gaelic, "Rock," "noble," or "lofty hill." Unusual.
Atti Scandinavian. From Astrid. Unusual.
Aubree English. From Aubrey, Old German, "Elf-counsel." Unusual. Alternative spelling: Aubrie.
Aubrey See under Boys' Names.
Aud Norwegian. Norwegian, "Empty" or "deserted." Unusual.
Audey English. From Etheldreda, Old English (Aethelthryth), "Noble strength." Unusual. Alternative spelling: Audi.
Audra English. From Etheldreda, Old English (Aethelthryth), "Noble strength." Unusual.
Audreen English. From Etheldreda, Old English (Aethelthryth), "Noble strength." Unusual.
Audrey English. From Etheldreda, Old English (Aethelthryth), "Noble strength." Hepburn (actress, "Roman Holiday," won 1953 Oscar); Meadows (actress, "Honeymooners"). Less popular. Alternative spellings: Audree, Audri, Audrie, Audry.
Audria English. From Etheldreda, Old English (Aethelthryth), "Noble strength." Unusual.
Augusta English. From Augustus, Latin, "Venerable" or "majestic." Queen consort of Prussia, 1861–88; Simmons Stet-

son (Christian Science clergyman); Maywood (prima ballerina); character in P.G. Wodehouse's stories of Bertie Wooster. Unusual.

Augustia English. From Augustus, Latin, "Venerable" or "majestic." Unusual.

Augustina English. From Augustus, Latin, "Venerable" or "majestic." Unusual.

Aulii Hawaiian. Hawaiian, "Dainty." Unusual.

Aurea English. From Aurora. Unusual.

Aurelia English. Latin, "Golden." Unusual. Alternative spelling: Auralia.

Auriol English. From Auriel. Unusual.

Aurora English. Latin, the Roman goddess of dawn. Raby (character in Lord Byron's 19th-century epic satire "Don Juan"); character in E.B. Browning's 1856 romantic poem "Aurora Leigh." Unusual.

Aurore French. From Aurora. Unusual.

Austin See under Boys' Names.

Autumn American. Latin, "autumnus"; the word used as a first name. Unusual.

Ava English. From Eve, Hebrew (Chava), "Life." Genesis 3:20. Gardner (actress). Less popular.

Aveen English. From Eve, Hebrew (Chava), "Life." Genesis 3:20. Unusual.

Averhilda English. From Averil. May also be related to the month of April. Unusual.

Averil English. Old English, "Boar" + "battle." May also be related to the month of April. Unusual. Alternative spellings: Avaril, Averill, Averyl.

Averilda English. From Averil. Unusual.

Averilla English. From Averil. Unusual.

Avery See under Boys' Names.

Avice English. Latin, a family name found in the early Roman empire. Unusual. Alternative spelling: Avis.

Avital See under Boys' Names.

Aviva Hebrew/Israeli. Hebrew, "Spring." Suggests freshness and youth. Unusual. Alternative spelling: Avivah.

Avivi Hebrew/Israeli. Hebrew, "Like Spring." Unusual.

Avivice Hebrew/Israeli. From Avivi. Unusual.

Avril English. From April, Latin, "To open up." Unusual. Alternative spellings: Avrill, Avrille, Avryl.

Avrit Hebrew/Israeli. From Avivi. Unusual.

Awanata Native American. Native American, "Turtle." Unusual.

Awanta Native American. Native American, "Turtle." Unusual.

Awendela Native American. Native American, "Early day." Given to a baby born at dawn. Unusual.

Awenita Native American. Native American, "Fawn." Unusual.

Ayame Japanese. Japanese, "Iris." Unusual.

Ayania Created. From Ayanna. Unusual.

Ayanna Created. From Ayanna, Created, African-American. Unusual. Alternative spelling: Ayana.

Ayasha Arabic. Arabic, "Life." Unusual.

Ayelet Hebrew/Israeli. Hebrew, "Deer" or "gazelle." Unusual.

Ayita Native American. Native American, "Worker." Unusual.

Ayla Hebrew/Israeli. Hebrew, "Oak tree." Unusual.

Ayleen English. From Helen, Greek, "Bright one" or "shining one." Unusual.

Ayoka Nigerian. Nigerian, "She brings joy to all." Unusual.

Ayondela African. African, "A sapling bending." A name taken from a proverb. Unusual.

Ayshea American. From Aisha, Arabic, "Woman" or "life." Unusual.

Azami Japanese. Japanese, "Thistle flower," symbolic of defiance. Unusual.

Azaria Hebrew/Israeli. From Azariah, Hebrew, "Whom Jehovah helps." Unusual.

Aziza African. Swahili, "Precious." Unusual.

Azize Turkish. Turkish, "Precious" or "rare." Unusual.

Azuba Unknown. Meaning and origin unknown. 1 Kings 22:42. Unusual.

Bab English. From Barbara. Unusual.

Babara Hawaiian. From Barbara. Unusual.

Babb English. From Barbara. Unusual.

Babe English. From Barbara. Unusual.

Babette English, German. From Barbara. Less popular.

Babica English. From Barbara. Unusual.

Babita English. From Barbara. Unusual.

Babs English. From Barbara. Less popular.

Bailey See under Boys' Names.

Baka Indo-Pakistani. Hindi, "Crane." The crane is a symbol of longevity. Unusual.

Bakula Indo-Pakistani. Hindi, "The bakula flower." According to myth, a beautiful girl would sprinkle the bakula with wine from her mouth and it would burst into bloom. Unusual.

Balala African. African, "You must eat a lot to grow." Given to a frail child. Unusual.

Balaniki Hawaiian. From Blanche, French, "White." Unusual.

Bandi Czech. From Andrew, Greek, "Manly." Unusual.

Banjoko African. Nigerian, "Sit down and stay with me." "Reverse psychology" intended to drive away evil spirits. Unusual.

Bao See under Boys' Names.

Bára Czech. From Barbara. Unusual.

Barba English. From Barbara. Unusual.

Barbara English. Greek, "Strange" or "foreign." Patron saint of architects, gunners, miners, and the dying; Pierce Bush (wife of President George); Eden (actress); Cartland (romantic novelist, longest entry in British "Who's Who": 143 lines); Villiers (Countess of Castlemaine). Less popular. Babs, Barbie+, Bobbie.

Barbary English. From Barbara. Unusual.

Barbe French. From Barbara. Unusual.

Barbette English. From Barbara. Unusual.

Barbi English. From Barbara. Benton (actress and former Playboy bunny). Less popular. Alternative spellings: Barbie, Barby.

Barbora Czech. From Barbara. Unusual.

Barborka Czech. From Barbara. Unusual.

Barbra English. From Barbara. Streisand (actress and singer, highest-paid actress for "Nuts": $5 million). Less popular. Babs, Barbie+, Bobbie.

Barbro Swedish. From Barbara. Unusual.

Barika Arabic. Arabic, "Bloom" or "be successful." Unusual.

Barrie English. Old English, surname and place name used as a first name; derived from places in Scotland, Wales, or Normandy. Unusual for males, unusual for females. Alternative spelling: Barri.

Barrie Anne English. English, combination of Barrie (Old English, first name based on a surname) + Anne (Hannah, Hebrew (Chanah), "Grace"). Unusual.

Barrie Jane English. English, combination of Barrie (Old English, first name based on a surname) + Jane (John, Hebrew (Yochanan), "God has been gracious"). Unusual.

Barta English. From Bertha, Old German (Berahta), "Bright." Unusual.

Bartha English. From Bertha, Old German (Berahta), "Bright." Unusual.

Baruška Czech. From Barbara. Unusual.

Basia Hebrew/Israeli. From Bithia, Hebrew, "Daughter of God." Trzetrzelewska (popular singer, 1990s; known as "Basia"). Unusual. Alternative spelling: Basya.

Basilia English. From Basil, Greek, "Kingly." Unusual.

Basilie English. From Basil, Greek, "Kingly." Unusual.

Basimah Arabic. Arabic, "Smiling." Unusual.

Bathia Hebrew/Israeli. From Bithia, Hebrew, "Daughter of God." Unusual.

Bathsheba English. Hebrew (Batsheva), "Daughter of an oath to God." 2 Samuel 11:3. Wife of David, mother of Solomon. Unusual.

Bathshua English. From Bathsheba. Unusual.

Batia Hebrew/Israeli. From Bithia, Hebrew, "Daughter of God." Unusual. Alternative spelling: Batya.

Batini African. Swahili, "Innermost thoughts." Unusual.

Batsheva Hebrew/Israeli. Hebrew, "Daughter of an oath to God." 2 Samuel 11:3. Unusual.

Baubie Scottish. From Barbara, Greek, "Strange" or "foreign." Unusual.

Bea English. From Beatrice, Latin, "She who makes happy." Arthur (actress, "The Golden Girls"). Unusual. Alternative spelling: Bee.

Beata English. Latin, "Blessed." Unusual.

Beathag Irish. Gaelic, "Servant of God." Unusual.

Beatrice English, Italian. Latin, "She who makes happy." Saint and martyr; Lillie (actress); Portinari (Florentine noblewoman); Harraden (British novelist, "Rachel"); Grimshaw (British traveler and writer); character in Shakespeare's "Much Ado About Nothing." Unusual. Bea, Trissie+, Trixie+.

Beatriks Russian. From Beatrice. Unusual.

Beatrisa Russian. From Beatrice. Unusual.

Beatrise Latvian. From Beatrice. Unusual.

Beatrix French, German. From Beatrice. Twelfth-century French noblewoman; Potter (British writer and illustrator of children's books) (real name: Helen Beatrix Potter). Unusual.

Beatriz Hispanic, Portuguese. From Beatrice. Unusual.

Beattie English. From Beatrice. Unusual. Alternative spelling: Beatty.

Bebe Hispanic. From Beatrice. Shopp (Miss America, 1948). Unusual.

Becca English. From Rebecca, Hebrew (Rivka), "Noose" or "yoke." Genesis 24:15. Thatcher (character in TV's "Life Goes On"). Unusual. Alternative spellings: Becka, Bekka.

Becky English. From Rebecca, Hebrew (Rivka), "Noose" or "yoke." Genesis 24:15. Less popular. Alternative spellings: Becki, Beckie, Bekki, Bekkie.

Bedelia Irish. From Bridget, Irish, "Strength." Unusual.

Bedřiška Czech. From Frederick, Old German, "Peaceful ruler." Unusual.

Behira Hebrew/Israeli. From Behira, Hebrew, "Light," "clear," or "brilliant." Unusual.

Bel Indo-Pakistani. From Bel, Hindi, "Wood apple tree." A sacred tree. Unusual.

Bela See under Boys' Names.

Belia Hispanic. From Elizabeth, Hebrew (Elisheva), "Oath of God" or "God is my oath." Exodus 6:23. Unusual.

Belica Hispanic. From Elizabeth, Hebrew (Elisheva), "Oath of God" or "God is my oath." Exodus 6:23. Unusual.

Belicia Hispanic. From Elizabeth, Hebrew (Elisheva), "Oath of God" or "God is my oath." Exodus 6:23. Unusual.

Belinda English. From Belinda, German, "Dragon" (?). Carlisle (pop singer). Unusual.

Belita Hispanic. From Elizabeth, Hebrew (Elisheva), "Oath of God" or "God is my oath." Exodus 6:23. Unusual.

Bell See under Boys' Names.

Bella English. From Elizabeth, Hebrew (Elisheva), "Oath of God" or "God is my oath." Exodus 6:23. Abzug (former Congresswoman from New York, famous for her choice of hats). Unusual.

Belle English. From Belle, French, "Beautiful." Sherwin (suffragist); Watling (character in "Gone With the Wind"). Unusual.

Belloma English. Latin, "Warlike" or "war goddess." Unusual.

Belynda English. From Belinda. Unusual.

Bena Native American, from Bena, Native American, "Pheasant"; and English, from Benedict, Latin, "Blessed." Unusual.

Bene African. African, "Born on Fenibene." Refers to one of the eight days in the African Kalabariljaw market week. Unusual.

Benedetta Italian. From Benedict, Latin, "Blessed." Unusual.

Benedicta Hispanic. From Benedict, Latin, "Blessed." Unusual.

Bengta Scandinavian. From Benedict, Latin, "Blessed." Unusual.

Benicia Hispanic. From Benedict, Latin, "Blessed." Unusual.

Benita Hispanic. From Benedict, Latin, "Blessed." Unusual.

Benna English. From Benjamin, Hebrew (Benyamin), "Son of my right hand." Genesis 35:18. Unusual.

Benni English. From Benedict, Latin, "Blessed." Unusual.

Bennie See Benny under Boys' Names.

Benoîte French. From Benedict, Latin, "Blessed." Unusual.

Berek Greek. From Bridget, Irish, "Strength." Unusual.

Berenice English. Greek, "Bringing victory." Egyptian princesses (I-IV); name of two Jewish Idumean princesses. Unusual. Barrie+, Bernie, Bunny.

Berenike Greek. From Berenice. Unusual.

Berget English. From Bridget, Irish, "Strength." Unusual.

Bergette French. From Bridget, Irish, "Strength." Unusual.

Bergit English. From Bridget, Irish, "Strength." Unusual.

Berna English. From Bernard, Old German, "Bear-brave." Unusual.

Bernadett English. From Bernard, Old German, "Bear-brave." Unusual.

Bernadette French. From Bernard, Old German, "Bear-brave." of Lourdes (patron saint of shepherds); Peters (actress). Unusual.

Bernadina English. From Bernard, Old German, "Bear-brave." Unusual.

Bernadine English. From Bernard, Old German, "Bear-brave." Unusual. Alternative spelling: Bernadene.

Bernarda Polish. From Bernard, Old German, "Bear-brave." Unusual.

Bernardette English. From Bernard, Old German, "Bear-brave." Unusual.

Bernardina Hispanic, Italian, Portuguese. From Bernard, Old German, "Bear-brave." Unusual.

Bernardine English. From Bernard, Old German, "Bear-brave." Desiree (Queen of Sweden, 1818–44). Unusual.

Bernetta English. From Bernard, Old German, "Bear-brave." Unusual. Alternative spelling: Berneta.

Bernette English. From Bernard, Old German, "Bear-brave." Unusual.

Bernice English. From Berenice, Greek, "Bringing victory." Fish (character in TV's "Barney Miller"). Unusual. Barrie+, Bernie, Bunny. Alternative spelling: Bernyce.

Bernie English. From Bernard, Old German, "Bear-brave." Unusual. Alternative spellings: Berni, Berny.

Bernita English. From Bernard, Old German, "Bear-brave." Unusual.

Berry See under Boys' Names.

Bersaba English. From Bathsheba, Hebrew (Batsheva), "Daughter of an oath to God." 2 Samuel 11:3. Unusual.

Berta German. From Bertha. Unusual.

Bertha English. Old German (Berahta), "Bright." Carolingian queen, mother of Charlemagne; Skram (Norwegian novelist and naturalist); Suttner (Austrian novelist, founded Austrian Society of Friends of Peace, 1895; won Nobel Peace Prize, 1905). Less popular. Bertie+. Alternative spelling: Birtha.

Bertina English. From Albert, Old English (Aethelbeorht), "Noble-bright." Unusual.

Bertine English. From Albert, Old English (Aethelbeorht), "Noble-bright." Unusual.

Beryl English. Sanskrit, place name used as a first name. Burton (most world titles for cycling: seven); Markham (author, "West With the Night"). Unusual.

Bess English. From Elizabeth, Hebrew (Elisheva), "Oath of God" or "God is my oath." Exodus 6:23. Truman (wife of President Harry); Myerson (Miss America, 1945, and consumer advocate); Aldrich (novelist, "Song of Years"); Armstrong (actress, "High Road to China"). Less popular.

Bessie English. From Elizabeth, Hebrew (Elisheva), "Oath of God" or "God is my oath." Exodus 6:23. Smith (blues singer, "Back Water Blues"); Rue (actress, "Tobacco Road"). Unusual. Alternative spellings: Bessey, Bessi, Bessy.

Běta Czech. From Elizabeth, Hebrew (Elisheva), "Oath of God" or "God is my oath." Exodus 6:23. Unusual.

Beth English. From Elizabeth, Hebrew (Elisheva), "Oath of God" or "God is my oath." Exodus 6:23. Henley (model and actress); March (character in Louisa May Alcott's "Little Women"). Less popular.

Beth Ann English. English, combination of Beth (Elizabeth, Hebrew (Elisheva), "Oath of God" or "God is my oath") + Ann (Hannah, Hebrew (Chanah), "Grace"). Less popular. Alternative spellings: Beth Anne, Bethanne.

Bethan English. From Bethany. Unusual.

Bethanie English. From Bethany. Unusual. Beth. Alternative spelling: Bethany.

Bethel See under Boys' Names.

Bethell See Bethel under Boys' Names.

Bethia Hebrew/Israeli. From Bithia, Hebrew, "Daughter of God." Unusual.

Bethsabee English. From Bathsheba, Hebrew (Batsheva), "Daughter of an oath to God." 2 Samuel 11:3. Unusual.

Bethsheba English. From Bathsheba, Hebrew (Batsheva), "Daughter of an oath to God." 2 Samuel 11:3. Unusual.

Beti Gypsy. From Beti, English Gypsy, "Little" or "small." Unusual.

Betina Hispanic. From Elizabeth, Hebrew (Elisheva), "Oath of God" or "God is my oath." Exodus 6:23. Unusual.

Bětka Czech. From Elizabeth, Hebrew (Elisheva), "Oath of God" or "God is my oath." Exodus 6:23. Unusual.

Betsy English. From Elizabeth, Hebrew (Elisheva), "Oath of God" or "God is my oath." Exodus 6:23. Ross (designed first American flag); Palmer (actress, "Marty"). Less popular. Alternative spellings: Betsi, Betsey.

Bett English. From Elizabeth, Hebrew (Elisheva), "Oath of God" or "God is my oath." Exodus 6:23. Unusual.

Betta English, Italian. From Elizabeth, Hebrew (Elisheva), "Oath of God" or "God is my oath." Exodus 6:23. Unusual.

Bette French. From Elizabeth, Hebrew (Elisheva), "Oath of God" or "God is my oath." Exodus 6:23. Cooper (Miss America, 1937); Davis (actress); Midler (singer). Unusual.

Betti Estonian, German, Russian. From Elizabeth, Hebrew (Elisheva), "Oath of God" or "God is my oath." Exodus 6:23. Unusual.

Bettina German, Italian. From Elizabeth, Hebrew (Elisheva), "Oath of God" or "God is my oath." Exodus 6:23. Arnim (19th-century German romantic writer). Unusual.

Bettine English. From Elizabeth, Hebrew (Elisheva), "Oath of God" or "God is my oath." Exodus 6:23. Unusual.

Betty English. From Elizabeth, Hebrew (Elisheva), "Oath of God" or "God is my oath." Exodus 6:23. Taylor (performer in the longest-running revue: 47,250 shows over 31 years, Disneyland); Comden (screen writer); Grable (actress and "pin-up girl"); Bloomer Warren Ford (wife of President Gerald) (real name: Elizabeth); Friedan (feminist author). Less popular. Alternative spelling: Bettie.

Betty Ann English. English, combination of Betty (Elizabeth, Hebrew (Elisheva), "Oath of God" or "God is my oath") + Ann (Hannah, Hebrew (Chavah), "Grace"). Less popular.

Betty Jo English. English, combination of Betty (Elizabeth, Hebrew (Elisheva), "Oath of God" or "God is my oath") + Jo (Joseph, Hebrew, "God will add"). Less popular.

Betty Lou English. English, combination of Betty (Elizabeth, Hebrew (Elisheva), "Oath of God" or "God is my oath") + Lou (Louis, Old German, "Famous warrior"). Less popular.

Betty Mae English. English, combination of Betty (Elizabeth, Hebrew (Elisheva), "Oath of God" or "God is my oath") + Mae (Matthew, Hebrew, "Gift of the Lord"). Less popular.

Betty Sue English. English, combination

of Betty (Elizabeth, Hebrew (Elisheva), "Oath of God" or "God is my oath") + Sue (Susannah, Hebrew (Shoshanah), "Lily"). Less popular.

Betula Hebrew/Israeli. Hebrew, "Girl" or "maiden." Unusual.

Betuška Czech. From Elizabeth, Hebrew (Elisheva), "Oath of God" or "God is my oath." Exodus 6:23. Unusual.

Beulah English. Hebrew, "Married." Isaiah 62:4. Unusual.

Beverly English. From Beverley, English, "Beaver stream." Russell (3 feet, 11 inches tall, she married a man of 6 feet, 7 inches); Sills (opera singer); Cleary (author of children's stories); Garland (actress, "My Three Sons"); D'Angelo (actress, "Coal Miner's Daughter"). Less popular. Bev. Alternative spelling: Beverley.

Bian Vietnamese. Vietnamese, "To be hidden" or "secretive." Unusual.

Bianca English. Italian, "White." Capello (16th-century Italian noblewoman and adventuress); Jagger (ex-wife of rock star Mick). Unusual.

Bibi Arabic. Arabic, "Lady." A Swahili term of politeness. Unusual.

Biddie Irish. From Bridget, Irish, "Strength." Unusual.

Biddy English. From Elizabeth, Hebrew (Elisheva), "Oath of God" or "God is my oath." Exodus 6:23. Unusual.

Bidelia Irish. From Bridget, Irish, "Strength." Unusual.

Billie English. From William, Old German, "Will" + "helmet." Holiday (blues singer); Burke (actress, "Wizard of Oz"); Newman (character in "Lou Grant"); Jo Bradley (character in "Petticoat Junction"). Unusual. Alternative spelling: Billi.

Billie Jean English. English, combination of Billie (William, Old German, "Will" + "helmet") + Jean (John, Hebrew (Yochanan), "Jehovah has been gracious"). King (record six-time tennis singles champion). Unusual.

Bina Hebrew/Israeli. Hebrew, "Understanding" or "intelligence." Unusual.

Binnie English. From Benedict, Latin, "Blessed." Unusual.

Binti African. African, "Daughter." Unusual.

Birdie English. "Bird," origin unknown. Unusual.

Birgit Norwegian. From Bridget, Irish, "Strength." Meineke (world record in 4 x 100 meter swimming medley relay: 4 minutes, 3.69 seconds, 1984); Nilsson (soprano). Unusual. Alternative spelling: Birget.

Birgitta Swedish. From Bridget, Irish, "Strength." Unusual.

Bithia Hebrew/Israeli. Hebrew, "Daughter of God." Daughter of Pharaoh who found and saved Moses. Unusual.

Bitki Turkish. Turkish, "Plant." Unusual.

Bittan Swedish. From Bridget, Irish, "Strength." Unusual.

Blair English. Scottish, surname used as first name. Warner (character in TV's "The Facts of Life"); Brown (actress, "The Days and Nights of Molly Dodd"). Less popular for males, less popular for females. Alternative spelling: Blaire.

Blanca Hispanic. From Blanche, French, "White." Unusual.

Blanch English. From Blanche. Unusual.

Blanche English. French, "White." of Castile (13th-century queen of France); Thebom (mezzo-soprano); Bruce (senator, first minority-group member to serve full term); Devereaux (character in "The Golden Girls"); Ames (suffragist and artist). Unusual. Alternative spelling: Blanch.

Blanchefleur Welsh. From Blodwen, Welsh, "Flower." Unusual.

Blanka Czech, Swedish. From Blanche. Unusual.

Blanshe English. From Blanche. Unusual.

Blaza Czech. From Beatrice, Latin, "She who makes happy." Unusual.

Blazena Czech. From Beatrice, Latin, "She who makes happy." Unusual.

Blenda Swedish. From Blanche. Unusual.

Blodwen Welsh. Welsh, "Flower." Unusual.

Blodwyn Welsh. From Blodwen. Unusual.

Blodyn Welsh. From Blodwen. Unusual.

Blom African. African, "Flower." Unusual.

Blossom English. Old English, "Flower." Unusual.

Bluebell English. English, the name of a flower. Unusual. Alternative spelling: Bluebelle.

Blum Yiddish. Yiddish, "Flower." Unusual.

Bluma Yiddish. From Blum. Unusual.

Bly See under Boys' Names.

Blythe English. Adaptation of "blithe" now used as a first name; origin unknown. Danner (actress). Less popular.

Bo See under Boys' Names.

Boadicea English. English, meaning unknown. Unusual.

Bobbette English. From Robert, Old English (Hreodbeorht), "Fame-bright." Unusual. Alternative spelling: Bobbet.

Bobbie English. From Robert, Old English (Hreodbeorht), "Fame-bright." Gentry (singer); Jo Bradley (character in TV's "Petticoat Junction"). Less popular for males, unusual for females. Alternative spelling: Bobbi.

Bobbi-Jo English. English, combination of Bobbi (Robert, Old English, "Bright-fame") + Jo (Joseph, Hebrew (Yosef), "God will add"). Less popular.

Bobby See under Boys' Names.

Bobina Czech. From Robert, Old English (Hreodbeorht), "Fame-bright." Unusual.

Bona Hebrew/Israeli. Hebrew, "A builder." Unusual.

Bonita English. Spanish, "Pretty." Unusual.

Bonnie English. French, "bonne" ("good"). Raitt (blues singer); Franklin (actress, TV's "One Day at a Time"); Bedelia (actress, "Die Hard"); Tyler (rock singer). Less popular. Alternative spellings: Boni, Bonie, Bonni, Bonny.

Boske Hungarian. From Lily, Latin, "lilium"; a flower name used as a first name. Unusual.

Boski Hungarian. From Elizabeth, Hebrew (Elisheva), "Oath of God" or "God is my oath." Exodus 6:23. Unusual.

Bözsi Hungarian. From Elizabeth, Hebrew (Elisheva), "Oath of God" or "God is my oath." Exodus 6:23. Unusual.

Bracha Hebrew/Israeli. From Baruch, Hebrew, "Blessed." Unusual.

Branca Portuguese. From Blanche, French, "White." Unusual.

Brandy English. Middle Dutch, "brantwijn" ("distilled wine"). Less popular. Alternative spellings: Brandee, Brandi, Brandie.

Breana English. From Brian, Celtic, "Strong," "virtuous," "honorable." Unusual. Alternative spellings: Breanna, Briana, Brianna, Bryanna.

Breann English. From Brian, Celtic, "Strong," "virtuous," "honorable." Unusual. Alternative spellings: Breanne, Briane, Briann, Brianne, Bryanne.

Bree English. From Bree, Latin, "From England." Unusual.

Brenda English. Old Norse, "Sword." Vaccaro (actress); Lee (singer). Less popular.

Brenna English. From Brennan, Irish, "Raven." Unusual.

Brett See Bret under Boys' Names.

Briar English. From Briar, French, "Heather." Unusual.

Bride Unknown. From Bridget. Unusual.

Bridget English. Irish, "Strength." of Sweden (saint, founder of the Bridgettine order). Less popular. Alternative spellings: Bridgett.

Bridgette German. From Bridget. Less popular.

Bridie English. From Bridget. Unusual.

Brie English. From Brian, Celtic, "Strong," "virtuous," "honorable." Unusual.

Brielle Created. Created, meaning unknown. Unusual.

Brienne English. From Brian, Celtic, "Strong," "virtuous," "honorable." Unusual.

Brietta English. From Bridget. Unusual.

Brigada Italian. From Bridget. Unusual.

Brigette German. From Bridget. Less popular.

Brigid Irish. From Bridget. Of Ireland (patron saint of poets, blacksmiths, and healers); Brophy (Irish author). Unusual. Alternative spelling: Brighid.

Brigida Hispanic, Italian. From Bridget. Unusual.

Brigide French. From Bridget. Unusual.

Brigit Irish. From Bridget. Of Kildare (pious 6th-century Irishwoman, established four monasteries). Unusual.

Brigita Latvian. From Bridget. Unusual.

Brigitta French, German. From Bridget. Unusual.

Brigitte French. From Bridget. Bardot (actress); Nielsen (actress, "Red Sonya"). Unusual.

Brita Swedish. From Bridget, Irish, "Strength." Unusual.

Britannia English. Latin, the feminine personification of Blitain on coins, etc. Unusual. Alternative spellings: Britania, Brittannia.

Britt Swedish. From Bridget, Irish, "Strength." Unusual for males, unusual for females.

Britta Swedish. From Bridget. Unusual.

Brittan English. From Britannia. Unusual.

Brittany English. From Britannia. Weston (character in TV's "thirtysomething"). Extremely popular. Alternative spellings: Britany, Brittaney, Brittani, Brittanie, Britteny.

Brittnay English. From Britannia. Unusual.

Brittney English. From Britannia. Popular. Alternative spellings: Britney, Britni, Brittnee, Brittni, Brittnie, Brittny.

Broňa Czech. From Berenice, Greek, "Bringing victory." Unusual.

Bronwyn Welsh. From Bronwen, Welsh, "White breast." Unusual.

Brooke English. From Brook, Old English, "Dweller by the brook." Shields (model and actress, "Pretty Baby"); Adams (actress, "Days of Heaven"); Hayward (ex-wife of Dennis Hopper); Westcott (bishop of Durham, 1890–1901); Benton (singer). Popular.

Brookie English. From Brook, Old English, "Dweller by the brook." Unusual.

Brucine English. From Bruce, Scottish, surname used as a first name. Unusual.

Brunetta English. From Bruno, Old German, "Of dark complexion" or "brown." Unusual.

Brydie English. From Bridget, Irish, "Strength." Unusual.

Bryga Polish. From Bridget, Irish, "Strength." Unusual.

Brygida Polish. From Bridget, Irish, "Strength." Unusual.

Brygitka Polish. From Bridget, Irish, "Strength." Unusual.

Bryn Welsh. Welsh, "Hill" or "mound." Unusual. Alternative spelling: Brynn.

Bryony English. Botanical name used as a first name; origin unknown. Unusual. Alternative spelling: Briony.

Bua Vietnamese. Vietnamese, "Hammer." Unusual.

Buffa English. From Elizabeth, Hebrew (Elisheva), "Oath of God" or "God is my oath." Exodus 6:23. Unusual.

Bunny English. From Bonnie, French, "bonne" ("good"). Berrigan (jazz musician). Less popular. Alternative spelling: Bunni.

Cäcilia German. From Cecil, Latin, "Blind." Unusual.

Cai Vietnamese. Vietnamese, "Female." Unusual.

Cailin Scottish. From Nicholas, Greek, "Victorious people." Unusual.

Caimile African. African, "A tree bears fruit, which falls to the ground; a family has children, and they all die." A name taken from a proverb. Unusual.

Caitlin Irish. From Katherine, Greek, "katharos" ("pure"). Popular. Alternative spelling: Caitlyn.

Caitlon English. From Katherine, Greek, "katharos" ("pure"). Unusual. Cate+, Catie+.

Caitria Irish. From Katherine, Greek, "katharos" ("pure"). Unusual.

Caitrin English. From Katherine, Greek, "katharos" ("pure"). Unusual. Cait+, Catie+, Cathy+.

Caitriona Irish. From Katherine, Greek, "katharos" ("pure"). Unusual.

Cakusola African. African, "If you loved, you followed the messenger." A name taken from a proverb. Unusual.

Calandra English. Greek, "Lark." Unusual.

Calida Hispanic. Spanish, "Loving." Unusual.

Callie English. From Caltha. Unusual. Alternative spellings: Caleigh, Caley, Cali, Calli.

Calliope Greek. Greek, "Beautiful face." Unusual. Alternative spelling: Kalliope.

Caltha English. Latin, "Marigold" or "yellow flower." Unusual. Alternative spelling: Kaltha.

Cam English. From Camillus, Latin, an attendant at religious services. Unusual.

Camelia English. "Flower"; origin unknown. Kath (actress). Unusual. Cam, Cammie+. Alternative spelling: Camellia.

Cameron See under Boys' Names.

Camila Hispanic. From Camillus, Latin,

an attendant at religious services. Unusual.

Camilla English, Italian. From Camillus, Latin, an attendant at religious services. Collett (19th-century Norwegian novelist, leader of feminist movement). Less popular.

Camille French. From Camillus, Latin, an attendant at religious services. Saint; Saint-Saëns (French organist, pianist, and composer). Unusual.

Cammi English. From Camillus, Latin, an attendant at religious services. Unusual. Alternative spellings: Cami, Cammie, Cammy.

Candace English. African, a dynastic title used by the queens of Ethiopia. Cameron (actress, "Full House"); Wheeler (textile designer). Popular. Candy+. Alternative spellings: Candice, Candis, Candyce, Kandace, Kandice, Kandis.

Candida English. Latin, "White." Unusual. Candy+.

Candra English. "Moon"; origin unknown. Unusual.

Candy English. From Candace. Clark (actress). Less popular. Alternative spellings: Candee, Candi, Candie, Kandi, Kandie.

Caprice Italian. Italian, "Fanciful one." Unusual.

Cara English. Latin, "Dear." Unusual. Alternative spelling: Carra, Karah.

Caren English. From Katherine, Greek, "katharos" ("pure"). Unusual. Alternative spellings: Carin, Carran, Carren, Carrin, Caryn, Karan, Karenne, Karon, Karran, Karren.

Carey See under Boys' Names.

Cari Turkish, "Flowing like water"; and English, from Charles, Old English, "ceorl" ("man" or "husbandman"). Hayer (youngest international log-rolling champion: 7 years old, 1984). Unusual.

Caridad English. Meaning and origin unknown. Unusual.

Carina Italian. From Katherine, Greek, "katharos" ("pure"). Unusual.

Carissa Unknown. From Charis, Greek, "Grace." Unusual.

Carita Italian. Latin, "Charity." Unusual.

Carla English, Italian. From Charles, Old English, "ceorl" ("man" or "husbandman"). Hills (secretary of housing and urban development under Ford); Lebec (character in TV's "Cheers"). Less popular.

Carleen English. From Charles, Old English, "ceorl" ("man" or "husbandman"). Unusual. Alternative spellings: Carlene, Karleen, Karline.

Carletta English. From Charles, Old English, "ceorl" ("man" or "husbandman"). Unusual.

Carlina English. From Charles, Old English, "ceorl" ("man" or "husbandman"). Unusual. Carli+.

Carline English. From Charles, Old English, "ceorl" ("man" or "husbandman"). Unusual. Carli+.

Carlota Hispanic, Portuguese. From Charles, Old English, "ceorl" ("man" or "husbandman"). Empress of Mexico, 1864–67. Unusual.

Carlotta Italian. From Charles, Old English, "ceorl" ("man" or "husbandman"). Grisi (19th-century Italian dancer, created title role in "Giselle" at Paris opera). Less popular.

Carly English. From Charles, Old English, "ceorl" ("man" or "husbandman"). Simon (singer and songwriter). Less popular. Alternative spellings: Carlee, Carley, Carli, Carlie, Karlee, Karley, Karli, Karlie, Karly.

Carlyn English. From Charles, Old English, "ceorl" ("man" or "husbandman"). Unusual. Carli+. Alternative spelling: Carlynn.

Carma English. From Carmel, Hebrew, "Garden." Unusual.

Carmela Hebrew/Israeli, Italian. From Carmel, Hebrew, "Garden." Unusual.

Carmeli English, Hebrew/Israeli. From Carmel, Hebrew, "Garden." Unusual.

Carmelina English. From Carmel, Hebrew, "Garden." Unusual.

Carmelita English. From Carmel, Hebrew, "Garden." Unusual.

Carmella English. From Carmel, Hebrew, "Garden." Unusual.

Carmelle English. From Carmel, Hebrew, "Garden." Unusual.

Carmen Hispanic. From Carmel, Hebrew, "Garden." Cavallaro (band leader); Miranda (actress); McRae (entertainer). Less popular.

Carmencita Hispanic. From Carmel, Hebrew, "Garden." Unusual.

Carmi English, Hebrew/Israeli. From Carmel, Hebrew, "Garden." Unusual.

Carmia English, Hebrew/Israeli. From Carmel, Hebrew, "Garden." Unusual.

Carmiel English, Hebrew/Israeli. From Carmel, Hebrew, "Garden." Unusual.

Carmilla Italian. From Carmel, Hebrew, "Garden." Unusual.

Carmina English. From Carmel, Hebrew, "Garden." Unusual. Alternative spelling: Karmina.

Carmita English. From Carmel, Hebrew, "Garden." Unusual.

Carna Hebrew/Israeli. Hebrew, "Horn." Unusual.

Carniella Hebrew/Israeli. From Carna. Unusual. Alternative spelling: Karniella.

Carnit Hebrew/Israeli. From Carna. Unusual. Alternative spelling: Karnit.

Carol English. From Charles, Old English, "ceorl" ("man" or "husbandman"). Burnett (comedian); Channing (actress, "Hello, Dolly"); Heiss (skater). Unusual for males, less popular for females.

Carol Ann English. English, combination of Carol (Charles, Old English, "Man" or "husbandman") + Ann (Hannah, Hebrew (Chanah), "Grace"). Less popular. Alternative spelling: Carol Anne.

Carol Lee English. English, combination of Carol (Charles, Old English, "Man" or "husbandman") + Lee (English, "Wood," "clearing," or "meadow"). Less popular.

Carol Sue English. English, combination of Carol (Charles, Old English, "Man" or "husbandman") + Sue (Susannah, Hebrew (Shoshanah), "Lily"). Less popular.

Carola Latin. From Charles, Old English, "ceorl" ("man" or "husbandman"). Unusual.

Carole French. From Charles, Old English, "ceorl" ("man" or "husbandman"). King (most successful American female songwriter: eight number-one hits); Lombard (actress). Less popular.

Carolee English. From Charles, Old English, "ceorl" ("man" or "husbandman"). Unusual.

Caroleen English. From Charles, Old English, "ceorl" ("man" or "husbandman"). Unusual.

Carolenia English. From Charles, Old English, "ceorl" ("man" or "husbandman"). Unusual.

Carolina English. From Charles, Old English, "ceorl" ("man" or "husbandman"). Nairne (19th-century Scottish songwriter, especially of humorous ballads and political songs). Unusual.

Carolinda English. From Charles, Old English, "ceorl" ("man" or "husbandman"). Unusual.

Caroline English. From Charles, Old English, "ceorl" ("man" or "husbandman"). Norton (19th-century British author, crusader for reform of marriage and infant custody laws); Spurgeon (British educator, first woman to hold professorship in England); Yale (educator, especially of the deaf); Kennedy (daughter of John F.); of Monaco (princess). Less popular. Alternative spelling: Caraline.

Caroll English. From Charles, Old English, "ceorl" ("man" or "husbandman"). Less popular.

Carolyn English. From Charles, Old English, "ceorl" ("man" or "husbandman"). Wells (author, "The Killer"). Less popular. Alternative spellings: Caralyn, Caralyne, Carolin, Carolyne, Carolynn, Carolynne, Karolyn.

Caron Welsh. Welsh, "To love." Unusual. Alternative spelling: Carron.

Carrie English. From Charles, Old English, "ceorl" ("man" or "husbandman"). Fisher (actress, "Star Wars"); White (oldest living person as of June 1991: born Nov. 18, 1874); Chapman Catt (feminist and reformer, led campaign leading to 19th amendment—women's vote); Nation (temperance crusader). Less popular. Alternative spellings: Carie, Carri, Karee, Karey, Kari, Karie, Karri, Karrie, Karry, Kary.

Carrie Ann English. English, combination of Carrie (Charles, Old English, "Man" or "husbandman") + Ann (Hannah, Hebrew (Chanah), "Grace"). Less popular. Alternative spelling: Carrie Anne.

Carrone Welsh. From Caron. Unusual.

Caryl English. From Charles, Old English, "ceorl" ("man" or "husbandman"). Unusual. Alternative spellings: Caryle, Caryll, Carylle.

Carys Welsh. Welsh, "To love." Unusual.

Cassandra English. From Alexander, Greek, "Defender of men" or "warding off men." Mark 16:21; Acts 4:6, 19:33. Popular. Cass, Cassie+, Sandy+. Alternative spellings: Casandera, Casandra, Kassandra.

Casandrey English. From Alexander, Greek, "Defender of men" or "warding off men." Mark 16:21; Acts 4:6, 19:33. Unusual. Cass, Cassie+, Sandy+.

Casey See under Boys' Names.

Casie English. From Alexander, Greek, "Defender of men" or "warding off men." Mark 16:21; Acts 4:6, 19:33. Unusual.

Cass See under Boys' Names.

Cassi English. From Katherine, Greek, "katharos" ("pure"). Unusual. Alternative spellings: Cassie, Cassy.

Cassidy English. Gaelic, "Clever." Unusual for males, unusual for females. Alternative spelling: Kassidy.

Casson English. From Alexander, Greek, "Defender of men" or "warding off men." Mark 16:21; Acts 4:6, 19:33. Unusual.

Cassondra English. From Alexander, Greek, "Defender of men" or "warding off men." Mark 16:21; Acts 4:6, 19:33. Unusual. Cass, Cassie+, Sandy+.

Catalina Hispanic. From Katherine, Greek, "katharos" ("pure"). Unusual.

Catant French. From Katherine, Greek, "katharos" ("pure"). Unusual.

Catarina English, Portuguese. From Katherine, Greek, "katharos" ("pure"). Unusual.

Catarine English. From Katherine, Greek, "katharos" ("pure"). Unusual.

Catava African. African, "It consented to sleep; it protested pain." A name taken from a proverb. Unusual.

Cateline French. From Katherine, Greek, "katharos" ("pure"). Unusual.

Caterina English, Italian. From Katherine, Greek, "katharos" ("pure"). Unusual.

Catharina English. From Katherine, Greek, "katharos" ("pure"). Unusual. Cathy+.

Cathe Italian. From Katherine, Greek, "katharos" ("pure"). Unusual.

Cathelina English. From Katherine, Greek, "katharos" ("pure"). Unusual. Cathy+.

Catherina English. From Katherine, Greek, "katharos" ("pure"). Less popular. Cathy+.

Catherine English. From Katherine, Greek, "katharos" ("pure"). Of Alexandria (patron saint of philosophers, students, young girls, and craftsmen); of Sienna (saint); Greenaway (British painter and illustrator, "Mother Goose"); Deneuve (French actress); Traill (19th-century Canadian writer on frontier life). Popular. Cathy+. Alternative spellings: Catharin, Catharine, Catherin, Catheryn, Catherene, Cathrene, Cathrine, Cathryn, Katharin, Katharine, Katharyn, Katherin, Katherine, Katheryn, Katheryne, Kathren, Kathrine, Kathryn, Kathryne, Kathyrine.

Cathy English. From Katherine, Greek, "katharos" ("pure"). Less popular. Alternative spellings: Cathi, Cathie, Kathe, Kathi, Kathie, Kathy.

Catrin Welsh. From Katherine, Greek, "katharos" ("pure"). Unusual.

Catrina English. From Katherine, Greek, "katharos" ("pure"). Unusual.

Catrine English. From Katherine, Greek, "katharos" ("pure"). Unusual.

Catriona Welsh. From Katherine, Greek, "katharos" ("pure"). Unusual.

Cayla English. From Katherine, Greek, "katharos" ("pure"). Unusual. Alternative spelling: Kayla.

Caylee English. From Katherine, Greek, "katharos" ("pure"). Unusual.

Cecelia English. From Cecil, Latin, "Blind." Colledge (British figure skater, first woman to achieve two turns in the air, mid-1920s). Unusual. Sissy+.

Cecely English. From Cecil, Latin, "Blind." Unusual. Sissy+.

Cecile English, French. From Cecil, Latin, "Blind." Less popular. Alternative spellings: Cecyl, Cecyle.

Cecilia English. From Cecil, Latin, "Blind." Patron saint of musicians and singers. Less popular. Sissy+.

Cecilie Czech, French. From Cecil, Latin, "Blind." Unusual.

Ceciliia Bulgarian. From Cecil, Latin, "Blind." Unusual.

Cecilija Latvian. From Cecil, Latin, "Blind." Unusual.

Cecilla Hispanic. From Cecil, Latin, "Blind." Unusual.

Cecylia Polish. From Cecil, Latin, "Blind." Unusual.

Ceinwen Welsh. Welsh, "Jewels" + "beautiful." Unusual.

Cela Polish, Russian. From Celestin, Latin, "Heavenly." Unusual.

Cele English. From Cecil, Latin, "Blind." Unusual.

Celek Polish. From Celestin, Latin, "Heavenly." Unusual.

Celena English. From Selina, Greek, "Moon," after the Greek goddess of the moon, Selene; or "parsley sprig." Unusual.

Celene English. From Selina, Greek, "Moon," after the Greek goddess of the moon, Selene; or "parsley sprig." Unusual.

Celesta English. From Celestin, Latin, "Heavenly." Unusual.

Celeste English, French (Céleste). From Celestin, Latin, "Heavenly." Holm (actress). Less popular.

Celestina English, Hispanic, Italian, Portuguese. From Celestin, Latin, "Heavenly." Unusual.

Celestine English, French. From Celestin, Latin, "Heavenly." Unusual.

Celestyn Russian. From Celestin, Latin, "Heavenly." Unusual.

Celestyna Czech, Russian. From Celestin, Latin, "Heavenly." Unusual.

Celia English, Swedish. From Cecil, Latin, "Blind." Johnson (actress). Less popular. Alternative spellings: Seelia, Selia.

Celie English, French (Célie). From Cecil, Latin, "Blind." Unusual.

Celina English. From Selina, Greek, "Moon," after the Greek goddess of the moon, Selene; or "parsley sprig." Unusual.

Celinda English. From Selina, Greek, "Moon," after the Greek goddess of the moon, Selene; or "parsley sprig." Unusual.

Céline French. From Selina, Greek, "Moon," after the Greek goddess of the moon, Selene; or "parsley sprig." Unusual.

Celinka Polish. From Celestin, Latin, "Heavenly." Unusual.

Celka Polish. From Celestin, Latin, "Heavenly." Unusual.

Cella Italian. From Francis, Latin, "Frenchman." Unusual.

Cellina English. From Selina, Greek, "Moon," after the Greek goddess of the moon, Selene; or "parsley sprig." Unusual.

Cerelia English. From Cerella, "Of the spring"; origin unknown. Unusual.

Cerella English. From Cerella, "Of the spring"; origin unknown. Unusual.

Ceri Welsh. Welsh, "To love." Unusual for males, unusual for females. Alternative spellings: Cerri, Cerrie.

Ceridwen Welsh. Welsh, "Poetry." Unusual.

Ceris Welsh. From Cerys. Unusual. Alternative spelling: Cerris.

Cerise French. French, "Cherry." Unusual.

Cerys Welsh. Welsh, "To love." Unusual. Alternative spelling: Ceries.

Cesia Polish, Russian. From Cecil, Latin, "Blind." Unusual.

Chabela Hispanic. From Elizabeth, Hebrew (Elisheva), "Oath of God" or "God is my oath." Exodus 6:23. Unusual.

Chabi Hispanic. From Elizabeth, Hebrew (Elisheva), "Oath of God" or "God is my oath." Exodus 6:23. Unusual.

Chalina Hispanic. From Rose, Latin, "rosa," a flower name used as a first name. Unusual.

Chana Indo-Pakistani. From Channa. Unusual.

Chanah Hebrew/Israeli. Hebrew, "Grace [of God]" or "favor." 1 Samuel 1:2. Unusual.

Chanda Indo-Pakistani. Punjabi, "Moon." Unusual.

Chandi Indo-Pakistani. Hindi, "Angry" or "fierce." Unusual.

Chandra Indo-Pakistani. Hindi, "Moon." Unusual.

Chanel American. Name of a French perfume used as a first name in the 1980s; origin unknown. Unusual. Alternative spellings: Chanell, Chanelle, Channel.

Channa Indo-Pakistani. Hindi, "Chickpea." In Hindu mythology, herbs, plants, and trees (including the chickpea) were "fathered by heaven, mothered by earth, and rooted in the primeval ocean." Unusual.

Channing See under Boys' Names.

Chantal American. French, "Stony place"; a place name used as a first name. Langlace (French, ran women's best 100-kilometer race on a roadway: 27 minutes, 22 seconds, 1980). Unusual. Alternative spelling: Chantalle.

Chantale American. From Chantal. Unusual. Alternative spelling: Shantale.

Chante American. From Chantal. Unusual.

Chantel American. From Chantal. Unusual. Alternative spellings: Chantele, Chantell, Chantelle, Shantel, Shantele, Shantell, Shantelle.

Chaoxing Chinese. Chinese, "Morning star." Unusual.

Chara Hispanic. From Rose, Latin, "rosa," a flower name used as a first name. Unusual.

Chardae Arabic. Arabic, "Runaway." Unusual. Alternative spellings: Sade, Shardae, Sharday.

Charde Arabic. From Chardae. Unusual. Alternative spelling: Sharde.

Charis Greek. Greek, "Grace." Unusual.

Charissa Greek. From Charis. Unusual.

Charisse Greek. From Charis. Unusual.

Charita Hispanic. From Sarah, Hebrew, "Princess." Genesis 17:15. Unusual.

Charity English. Latin, "carus" ("dear"); one of the Puritan "virtue" names. Caughlin (one of longest-lived triplets, with sisters Faith and Hope: born March 27, 1868). Unusual.

Charla English. From Charles, Old English, "ceorl" ("man" or "husbandman"). Unusual.

Charlaine English. From Charles, Old English, "ceorl" ("man" or "husbandman"). Unusual.

Charlena English. From Charles, Old English, "ceorl" ("man" or "husbandman"). Unusual.

Charlene English. From Charles, Old English, "ceorl" ("man" or "husbandman"). Tilton (actress in TV's "Dallas"); Frazier (character in TV's "Designing Women"). Unusual. Alternative spellings: Charleen, Charline, Sharleen, Sharlene, Sharline.

Charlesena English. From Charles, Old English, "ceorl" ("man" or "husbandman"). Unusual. Alternative spelling: Charlesina.

Charletta English. From Charles, Old English, "ceorl" ("man" or "husbandman"). Unusual.

Charlie See under Boys' Names.

Charlinna English. From Charles, Old English, "ceorl" ("man" or "husbandman"). Unusual.

Charlisa English. From Charles, Old English, "ceorl" ("man" or "husbandman"). Unusual.

Charlita English. From Charles, Old English, "ceorl" ("man" or "husbandman"). Unusual.

Charlotta English. From Charles, Old English, "ceorl" ("man" or "husbandman"). Unusual. Charlie+.

Charlotte English, French, German. From Charles, Old English, "ceorl" ("man" or "husbandman"). Sophia (18th-century British queen); Brontë (19th-century British author, "Jane Eyre"); Dod (British, most versatile athlete: champion at tennis, golf, archery; excelled at skating, tobogganing); Lennox (18th-century British novelist and poet, "The Sister"); von Stein (18th-century German writer). Less popular. Charlie+, Lottie+, Totty+. Alternative spelling: Charlot.

Charlotty French. From Charles, Old English, "ceorl" ("man" or "husbandman"). Unusual.

Charlzina English. From Charles, Old English, "ceorl" ("man" or "husbandman"). Unusual.

Charmaine American. Latin (Carminea), a Roman clan name used as a first name. Less popular. Alternative spelling: Charmain.

Charmian Greek. Greek, "Joy." Cleopatra's faithful attendant in "Antony and Cleopatra." Unusual.

Charo Hispanic. From Rose, Latin, "rosa," a flower name used as a first name. Actress (real name: María Rosario Pilar Martínez). Unusual.

Chasity English. From Chastity. Unusual.

Chassidy English. From Chastity. Unusual.

Chastity English. Latin, "Purity." Bono (daughter of Cher and Sonny Bono). Unusual.

Chatty English. From Charles, Old English, "ceorl" ("man" or "husbandman"). Unusual.

Chava Hebrew/Israeli. Hebrew, "Life." Unusual.

Chavon English. From John, Hebrew (Yochanan), "God has been gracious." Unusual. Alternative spelling: Chavonne.

Chaya Hebrew/Israeli. From Chaim, Hebrew, "Life." Unusual.

Chela Hispanic. From Cecil, Latin, "Blind." Unusual.

Chelsea English. Old English, "Ship's port." Very popular.

Chelsey English. From Chelsea. Unusual. Alternative spellings: Chelsi, Chelsie, Chelsy.

Chenoa Native American. Native American, "White dove"; connotes peace in nature. Unusual.

Cher English. From Chérie. Singer and actress (real name: Cherilyn LaPiere). Unusual.

Chereen English. From Chérie. Unusual. Cher.

Cherelle English. From Charity. Unusual. Cher. Alternative spelling: Cherrelle.

Chérie French. French, "Dear one" or "sweetheart." Unusual. Alternative spelling: Cheri.

Cherilyn English. From Charity. LaPiere (real name of singer and actress Cher). Unusual. Cher. Alternative spellings: Cheralyn, Cherilynn, Cherralyn, Cherrilyn, Cherrylin, Cherylyn, Sherolyn, Sheralyn, Sherilyn, Sherralyn, Sherralynn, Sherryllyn, Sherrylyn.

Cherise French. From Cerise, French, "Cherry." Unusual.

Cherish English. From Chérie. Unusual.

Cherry English. From Charity. Unusual. Cher. Alternative spelling: Cherrie.

Cheryl English. From Charity. Crawford (actress); Tiegs (model and actress); Prewitt (Miss America, 1980); Ladd (actress) (real name: Cheryl Stoppelmoor); Crawford (stage producer). Less popular. Cher. Alternative spellings: Cherill, Cherril, Cherrill, Cherryl, Cherryle, Cherryll, Cheryle, Cheryll, Sheral, Sherell, Sheril, Sherill, Sherrell, Sherryll.

Cherylene English. From Charity. Unusual. Cher. Alternative spellings: Cherrylene, Cherryline, Cheryline.

Chevon English. From John, Hebrew (Yochanan), "God has been gracious." Unusual. Alternative spellings: Chevonne, Shevon, Shevonne.

Cheyenne Native American. Native American, the name of a tribe. Brando (daughter of actor Marlon). Unusual.

Chhaya Indo-Pakistani. Hindi, "Shadow." Unusual.

Chiara Italian. From Clara, Latin, "clarus" ("clear"). Unusual.

Chica Hispanic. From Francis, Latin, "Frenchman." Unusual.

Chidori Japanese. Japanese, "Sanderling" (a bird). Unusual.

Chika Japanese. Japanese, "Near" (?). Unusual.

Chikako Japanese. From Chika. Unusual.

Chila Hispanic. From Cecil, Latin, "Blind." Unusual.

Chilali Native American. Native American, "Snowbird." Unusual.

Chimalis Native American. Native American, "Bluebird." Unusual.

Chimene French. From Xenia, Greek, "Hospitable." Unusual.

Chiquita Hispanic. Spanish, "Little one." Unusual.

Chiriga African. African, "Girl of poor parents." Unusual.

Chitsa Native American. Native American, "Fair one." Unusual.

Chizu Japanese. Japanese, "Thousand storks." In Japan, the stork is traditionally considered a symbol of longevity. Unusual.

Chizuko Japanese. From Chizu. Unusual.

Chloe English. From Chloe, Greek, "Young grass." Less popular.

Cho Korean. Korean, "Beautiful." Unusual.

Chofa Hispanic. From Sophia, Greek, "Wisdom." Unusual.

Chofi Hispanic. From Sophia, Greek, "Wisdom." Unusual.

Cholena Native American. Native American, "Bird." Unusual.

Choomia Gypsy. English Gypsy, "A kiss." Unusual.

Chrisanda English. From Christian, Greek, "christos" ("anointed"). Unusual. Chris, Sandy+.

Chrissie English. From Christian, Greek, "christos" ("anointed"). Hynde (singer in group The Pretenders). Less popular. Alternative spellings: Chrissy, Crissey, Crissie, Crissy, Krissi, Krissie, Krissy.

Christa German. From Christian, Greek, "christos" ("anointed"). Rothenburger (German, won Olympic gold medal, 1988, 1000-meter speed-skating: 1 minute, 17.65 seconds); McAuliffe (Challenger astronaut and teacher). Unusual. Alternative spellings: Crista.

Christabel English. Created, meaning unknown. Unusual. Chris, Christy+. Alternative spellings: Christabelle, Christobel, Chrystabel.

Christabella English. From Christabel. Unusual. Chris, Christy+.

Christeen English. From Christian, Greek, "christos" ("anointed"). Unusual. Chris, Christy+. Alternative spelling: Christene.

Christella English. From Christabel. Unusual. Chris, Christy+.

Christen English. From Christian, Greek, "christos" ("anointed"). Raunkiaer

(Danish botanist, developed classification system for plants). Less popular. Chris, Christy+. Alternative spellings: Christin, Cristen, Cristin, Kristen, Kristyn, Krysten, Krystin.

Christian See under Boys' Names.

Christiana Hispanic. From Christian, Greek, "christos" ("anointed"). Unusual.

Christiane German. From Christian, Greek, "christos" ("anointed"). Unusual.

Christiann English. From Christian, Greek, "christos" ("anointed"). Unusual. Chris, Christy+. Alternative spelling: Christien.

Christianna English. From Christian, Greek, "christos" ("anointed"). Unusual. Chris, Christy+.

Christina English, Greek. From Christian, Greek, "christos" ("anointed"). Of Markyate (saint); Rossetti (19th-century British poet, sister of Dante Gabriel); Stead (Australian novelist, "The Man Who Loved Children"); 17thcentury queen of Sweden. Very popular. Chris, Christy+, Tina. Alternative spelling: Cristina.

Christine English, French. From Christian, Greek, "christos" ("anointed"). De Pisan (14th-century French poet, wrote especially of courtly love). Very popular. Chris, Christy+. Alternative spelling: Cristine.

Christmas See under Boys' Names.

Christy English. From Christopher, Greek, "One who carries Christ in his heart." Less popular. Alternative spellings: Christi, Christie, Christy, Kristie, Kristy, Krysti.

Chrys English. From Christopher, Greek, "One who carries Christ in his heart." Unusual.

Chrystel German. From Christopher, Greek, "One who carries Christ in his heart." Unusual. Alternative spelling: Christel.

Chu Hua Chinese. Chinese, "Chrysanthemum," which in China is the flower of autumn. Unusual.

Chumana Native American. From Shumana, Native American, "Rattlesnake girl." Unusual.

Chumina Hispanic. From Dominic, Latin, "Lord." Unusual.

Chun Chinese. Chinese, "Spring." Unusual.

Chynna English. Meaning and origin unknown. Phillips (actress and singer). Unusual.

Ciara Irish. Irish, "Black." Unusual. Alternative spelling: Ciarra.

Cicelia English. From Cecil, Latin, "Blind." Unusual. Cissie+.

Cicely English. From Cecil, Latin, "Blind." Tyson (actress). Unusual. Cissie+. Alternative spellings: Ciceley, Cicily, Cicley.

Ciera Irish. From Ciara. Unusual. Alternative spelling: Cierra.

Cile Czech. From Cecil, Latin, "Blind." Unusual.

Cilehe African. African, "Just let it stink, let it be." A name taken from a proverb. Unusual.

Cilka Czech. From Cecil, Latin, "Blind." Unusual.

Cilla English. From Priscilla, Latin, "Old," "primitive." Acts 18:26. Unusual.

Cilli German. From Cecil, Latin, "Blind." Unusual. Alternative spelling: Cilly.

Cilly German. From Cecil, Latin, "Blind." Unusual.

Cilombo See under Boys' Names.

Cinderella English. French, "Little cinder girl." Fairy tale heroine. Unusual.

Cindy English. From Cynthia, Greek name for the goddess of the moon, also known as Artemis. Williams (actress, TV's "Laverne and Shirley"); Crawford (model). Less popular. Alternative spellings: Cindi, Cindie, Cyndi, Cyndie, Sindy.

Cinofila African. African, "A thing you die for only if you eat it." A name taken from a proverb. Unusual.

Cipriana Greek. Greek, "From the island of Cyprus." Unusual.

Cissie English. From Cecil, Latin, "Blind." Loftus (Scottish actress). Unusual. Alternative spellings: Cissi, Cissy, Sisie, Sissey, Sissi, Sissie, Sissy.

Ciyeva African. African, "You hear it, but you don't do it." A name taken from a proverb. Unusual.

Claire English. From Clara. Bloom (British actress); Luce (actress in Ziegfeld Follies); Trevor (actress); Chennault (aviator, formed "Flying Tigers" flying group to aid China); Huxtable (character in TV's "The Cosby Show"). Less popular. Alternative spellings: Clair, Clare.

Clairette French. From Clara. Unusual. Alternative spelling: Clarette.

Clairine English. From Clara, Latin, "clarus" ("clear"). Unusual. Alternative spellings: Clarine.

Clara English. Latin, "clarus" ("clear"). Barton (established American Red Cross); Bow (1920s actress); Morris (actress, "Camille"); Dutton Noyes (nurse, Florence Nightingale medal recipient); Reeve (18th-century British gothic novelist); Peller (TV commercial splash with phrase "Where's the beef?"). Less popular.

Clareta Hispanic. From Clara. Unusual.

Clarey English. From Clara. Unusual. Alternative spellings: Clari, Clarie, Clarrie, Clarry.

Claribel English. From Clara. Unusual. Clare.

Clarice Italian. From Clara. Unusual.

Clarina English. From Clara. Unusual. Clare.

Clarinda English. From Clara. Unusual. Clare.

Claris English. From Clara. Unusual. Clare.

Clarisa Hispanic. From Clara. Unusual.

Clarissa English, German, Italian. From Clara. Less popular. Alternative spelling: Klarissa.

Clarisse French. From Clara. Less popular.

Clarita English, Hispanic. From Clara. Unusual. Clare.

Claudeen English. From Claudius, Latin, "Lame." Unusual.

Claudelle French. From Claudius, Latin, "Lame." Unusual.

Claudette French. From Claudius, Latin, "Lame." Colbert (actress, won Oscar, 1934, for "It Happened One Night") (real name: Lily Chauchoin). Unusual.

Claudia English, Italian. From Claudius, Latin, "Lame." Alta Taylor Johnson (wife of President Lyndon, known as "Lady Bird"); Cardinale (actress). Less popular.

Claudina English. From Claudius, Latin, "Lame." Unusual.

Claudine French. From Claudius, Latin, "Lame." Unusual.

Clemence English. From Clement, Latin, "Mild," "merciful." Dane (novelist and playwright "A Bill of Divorcement" and "Will Shakespeare") (real name: Winifred Ashton). Unusual. Clem.

Clemency English. From Clement, Latin, "Mild," "merciful." Unusual.

Clementia English. From Clement, Latin, "Mild," "merciful." Unusual.

Clementina English. From Clement, Latin, "Mild," "merciful." Campbell (British jazz singer) (real name of Cleo Laine). Unusual.

Clementine English. From Clement, Latin, "Mild," "merciful." Character in song "My Darling Clementine." Unusual.

Clemenza Italian. From Clement, Latin, "Mild," "merciful." Unusual.

Cleo English. From Cleopatra. Laine (British jazz singer) (real name: Clementina Campbell). Unusual.

Cleopatra English. Greek, "Fame of her father's." Name of several queens of Egypt, circa 200–50 B.C.; Cleopatra VII (69–30 B.C.) relinquished government to her brother, became Julius Caesar's mistress, had two children by Mark Antony, killed herself with poison. Unusual. Cleo.

Clio Greek. Greek, the name of the muse of history. Unusual.

Clodagh Irish. Irish, the name of a river. Unusual.

Clotilda French. Old German, "Loud battle." Sixth-century French saint; first-century Frankish queen, daughter of Chilperic, king of the Burgundians. Unusual.

Cocheta Native American. Native American, "The unknown." Unusual.

Codi English. From Cody, Old English, "A cushion." Less popular.

Cody See under Boys' Names.

Cohila African. African, "It is silent on the part of the young; at heart it hurts." A name taken from a proverb. Unusual.

Colby English. Old English, "From the black farm." Less popular for males, unusual for females.

Coleen English. From Colleen. Kay Hutchins (Miss America, 1952). Unusual. Alternative spellings: Colene, Coline.

Colena English. From Nicholas, Greek, "Victorious people." Unusual.

Coletta French. From Nicholas, Greek, "Victorious people." Unusual.

Colina English. From Nicholas, Greek, "Victorious people." Unusual.

Colleen English. Gaelic, "cailin" ("girl"). Saint; Dewhurst (actress); McCullough (novelist, "The Thorn Birds"); Gray (actress); Moore (actress). Popular.

Collett English. From Nicholas, Greek, "Victorious people." Unusual. Alternative spellings: Collet, Collete.

Colletta French. From Nicholas, Greek, "Victorious people." Unusual.

Collette French. From Nicholas, Greek, "Victorious people." Unusual. Alternative spelling: Colette.

Columbina Irish. From Columba, Latin, "Dove." Unusual.

Comfort English. From Comfort, Latin, "Strengthen." Unusual.

Concetta American. Italian, a reference to the Immaculate Conception. Unusual.

Concettina Italian. From Constance. Unusual.

Connie English. From Constance. Francis (singer) (real name: Concetta Franconero); Chung (TV journalist); Mack (baseball player and manager); Stevens (singer); Sellecca (actress, "Hotel"). Less popular.

Constancia Hispanic. From Constance. Unusual.

Constance English. Latin, "constans" ("constant" or "unwavering"). Bennett (actress who wore most expensive costume: $50,000 sable coat, in "Madam X"); Collier (British actress); Lindsay Skinner (poet, "Songs of the Coast Dwellers"); Fenimore Woolson (author, novel "Dorothy" and sketches of the Northeast and South). Unusual for males, less popular for females. Connie.

Constancy English. From Constance. Unusual.

Constanta English. From Constance. Unusual.

Constantia English, Italian. From Constance. Unusual.

Constanz German. From Constance. Unusual.

Constanza Hispanic, Italian. From Constance. Unusual.

Consuela Hispanic. Spanish, "Consolation." Unusual.

Cora English. Greek, "Maiden." Munroe (heroine in James Fenimore Cooper's 1826 novel "The Last of the Mohicans"); Baird (puppeteer, led U.S. revival of puppet theater). Less popular. Alternative spelling: Kora.

Coral English. English, the word used as a name. Unusual.

Coralee English. From Cora. Unusual.

Coralena English. From Coral. Unusual. Alternative spelling: Coralina.

Coralie French. From Cora. Brack (character in William Makepeace Thackeray's novel "The History of Pendennis," published serially, 1848–50). Unusual.

Coraline English. From Coral. Unusual.

Coralyn English. From Coral. Unusual.

Corbetta English. From Corbet, surname used as a first name; origin unknown. Indicates an ancestor with raven-black hair. Unusual.

Cordelia English. Latin, "Heart." Youngest daughter of King Lear in Shakespeare's "King Lear." Unusual.

Cordula German. From Cordelia. Unusual.

Corella English. From Cora. Unusual.

Coretta English. From Cora. King (civil rights leader, widow of Martin Luther King, Jr.). Unusual.

Corette English. From Cora. Unusual.

Corey See under Boys' Names.

Cori English. From Corey, Irish, "From the hollow." Less popular. Alternative spellings: Corie, Corrie, Corry, Correy, Correye, Corri, Corrie, Corry.

Corin English. From Cora. Unusual. Alternative spellings: Corinn, Corrin, Corrinne.

Corina English. From Cora. Unusual.

Corinna English. From Cora. Greek poet, 6th-century B.C. Unusual.

Corinne French. From Cora. Calvet (actress). Unusual.

Corissa English. From Cora. Unusual.

Cornalia English. From Cornelius, Latin, "A horn." Acts 10:1. Unusual.

Cornelia English. From Cornelius, Latin, "A horn." Acts 10:1. Influential mother of the Gracchi brothers, Roman democrats, 2nd-century B.C.; Otis Skinner (actress, humorous author); Oschkenat (German, holds indoor 50-meter hurdling record: 6.58 seconds, 1989); Augusta Connelly (19th-century, founded Catholic schools, U.S. and abroad). Unusual.

Cornelie English. From Cornelius, Latin, "A horn." Acts 10:1. Unusual.

Cornella English. From Cornelius, Latin, "A horn." Acts 10:1. Unusual. Alternative spelling: Cornela.

Cornelle English. From Cornelius, Latin, "A horn." Acts 10:1. Unusual.

Cornie English. From Cornelius, Latin, "A horn." Acts 10:1. Unusual.

Cornilear English. From Cornelius, Latin, "A horn." Acts 10:1. Unusual.

Corona Created. Created, inspired by the "corona"tion of Edward VII in 1902. Unusual.

Coronar Created. From Corona. Unusual.

Coronetta Created. From Corona. Unusual.

Correen English. From Cora. Unusual. Alternative spelling: Corene, Corine, Correne, Corrine.

Corrienne English. From Cora. Unusual.

Corrina English. From Cora. Unusual.

Corrinna English. From Cora. Unusual.

Cory See Corey under Boys' Names.

Cory Anne English. English, combination of Cory (Gaelic, "From the hollow") + Anne (Hannah, Hebrew (Chanah), "Grace"). Less popular.

Cory Lee English. English, combination of Cory (Gaelic "From the hollow") + Lee (English, "Wood," "clearing," or "meadow"). Less popular.

Cosette English. From Nicholas, Greek, "Victorious people." Unusual.

Courtenay English. From Courtney, Old French, "One who lives at the court or on the farm." Less popular.

Courtney English. Old French, "One who lives at the court or on the farm." Gibbs (Miss U.S.A., 1988); Cox (actress, "Family Ties"). Less popular for males, very popular for females. Alternative spellings: Cortney, Courtnie.

Cressida English. Greek, "Gold." Unusual.

Crestienne French. From Christian, Greek, "christos" ("anointed"). Unusual.

Crispina Latin. From Crispin, Latin, "crispus" ("curly"). Of Tagora (saint). Unusual.

Cristin Irish. From Christian, Greek, "christos" ("anointed"). Unusual.

Cristiona Irish. From Christian, Greek, "christos" ("anointed"). Unusual.

Cristy Hispanic. From Christian, Greek, "christos" ("anointed"). Less popular.

Crystal English. From Christopher, Greek, "One who carries Christ in his heart." Gayle (country singer) (real name: Brenda Gayle Webb). Popular. Cris, Cristy+. Alternative spellings: Christal, Chrystal, Cristal, Cristel, Crystle, Kristel, Kristal, Krystal, Krystel, Krystl.

Crystina Czech. From Christian, Greek, "christos" ("anointed"). Unusual.

Crystol English. From Christopher, Greek, "One who carries Christ in his heart." Less popular. Cris, Cristy+. Alternative spellings: Cristol, Kristol.

Custance See under Boys' Names.

Cyd See Sid under Boys' Names.

Cylvia English. From Silva, Latin, "Woods." Unusual.

Cynthia English. From Cynthia, Greek name for the goddess of the moon, also known as Artemis. Gregory (ballerina); Freeman (novelist). Less popular. Cindy+.

Dacey See under Boys' Names.

Daci English. From Dacey, Gaelic, "A southerner." Unusual. Alternative spellings: Dacie, Dasey, Dasi, Dasie, Dasy.

Daga Polish. From Dragomira, Slavic, "Glory of the day." Unusual.

Dagan Hebrew/Israeli. Hebrew, "Corn" or "grain." Unusual.

Dagana Hebrew/Israeli. From Dagan. Unusual.

Dagania Hebrew/Israeli. From Dagan. Unusual. Alternative spelling: Deganya.

Daggi Estonian. From Dragomira, Slavic, "Glory of the day." Unusual. Alternative spelling: Dagi.

Dagmar Scandinavian. From Dragomira, Slavic, "Glory of the day." Unusual.

Dagmara Czech. From Dragomira, Slavic, "Glory of the day." Unusual.

Dagny Norwegian. Old Norse, "Day." Unusual. Alternative spelling: Dagney.

Dahlia English. After Anders Dahl, 18th-century Swiss botanist; a flower name used as a first name. Less popular.

Dai Japanese. Japanese, "Great." Unusual.

Dain English. From Dane, Old English, "Trickling stream." Unusual.

Daisy English. Old English, "Day's eye"; a flower name used as a first name. Buchanan (character in F. Scott Fitzgerald's novel "The Great Gatsby"); Duke (character in TV's "The Dukes of Hazzard"). Less popular. Alternative spellings: Daisey, Daisie.

Dakota See under Boys' Names.

Dalice Hebrew/Israeli. From Dalit. Unusual.

Dalilah Hebrew/Israeli. Hebrew, "Delicate," "languishing," or "amorous." Unusual.

Dalit Hebrew/Israeli. Hebrew, "To draw water" or "tree branch." Unusual.

Dallas See under Boys' Names.

Dalya Hebrew/Israeli. Hebrew, name of a flowering branch (not a dahlia, which is a different plant). Unusual. Alternative spelling: Dalia.

Damaris Latin. Latin, "Calf." Unusual. Alternative spelling: Dameris, Damiris, Dameress, Dammeris.

Damita Hispanic. Spanish, "A little noble lady." Unusual.

Dampris English. From Damaris. Unusual.

Damris Latin. From Damaris. Unusual.

Dana English. Celtic, "From Denmark." Andrews (actor) (real name: Carver Daniel Andrews); Wynter (actress); Dover (took longest merry-go-round ride: 312 hours, 43 minutes, 1976); Zatopkova (oldest female Olympic medalist (javelin): 37 years, 248 days, 1960); Delaney (actress, "China Beach"). Less popular for males, popular for females. Alternative spelling: Daina.

Danae English. From Daniel, Hebrew, "God is my judge." Daniel 1:6. Unusual.

Daneen English. From Daniel, Hebrew, "God is my judge." Daniel 1:6. Unusual.

Danella English. From Daniel, Hebrew, "God is my judge." Daniel 1:6. Unusual. Alternative spelling: Danela.

Danelle English. From Daniel, Hebrew, "God is my judge." Daniel 1:6. Unusual.

Danetta American. From Daniel, Hebrew, "God is my judge." Daniel 1:6. Unusual.

Danette American. From Daniel, Hebrew, "God is my judge." Daniel 1:6. Unusual. Alternative spelling: Danett.

Dani English, Hebrew/Israeli, Hungarian, Slavic. From Daniel, Hebrew, "God is my judge." Daniel 1:6. Unusual for males, less popular for females.

Dania Hebrew/Israeli. From Daniel, Hebrew, "God is my judge." Daniel 1:6. Unusual.

Danica American. From Daniel, Hebrew, "God is my judge." Daniel 1:6. Unusual.

Danice American. From Daniel, Hebrew, "God is my judge." Daniel 1:6. Unusual.

Danie English. From Daniel, Hebrew, "God is my judge." Daniel 1:6. Unusual.

Daniel See under Boys' Names.

Daniela English, Italian, Russian. From Daniel, Hebrew, "God is my judge." Daniel 1:6. Silivas (Romanian, Olympic medalist for uneven bars, 1988). Unusual. Dani+. Alternative spelling: Daniella.

Danielka Polish. From Daniel, Hebrew, "God is my judge." Daniel 1:6. Unusual.

Daniell French. From Daniel, Hebrew, "God is my judge." Daniel 1:6. Unusual.

Danielle English. From Daniel, Hebrew, "God is my judge." Daniel 1:6. Darrieux (French actress); Steel (novelist, "Heartbeat," mid-1991; had at least one book on best-seller list for record 393 consecutive weeks, 1981–88). Very popular. Dani+. Alternative spellings: Dannielle, Danyel.

Danika English. From Daniel, Hebrew, "God is my judge." Daniel 1:6. Unusual.

Danikla Russian. From Daniel, Hebrew, "God is my judge." Daniel 1:6. Unusual.

Danila Russian. From Daniel. Unusual for males, unusual for females.

Danilka Russian. From Daniel. Unusual for males, unusual for females.

Danilla English. From Daniel, Hebrew, "God is my judge." Daniel 1:6. Unusual.

Danille English. From Daniel, Hebrew, "God is my judge." Daniel 1:6. Unusual.

Danise English. From Daniel, Hebrew, "God is my judge." Daniel 1:6. Unusual.

Danit Hebrew/Israeli. From Daniel, Hebrew, "God is my judge." Daniel 1:6. Unusual.

Danita English. From Daniel, Hebrew, "God is my judge." Daniel 1:6. Unusual.

Danka Polish. From Daniel, Hebrew, "God is my judge." Daniel 1:6. Unusual.

Danna English. From Dana, Celtic, "From Denmark." Unusual.

Danne English. From Daniel, Hebrew, "God is my judge." Daniel 1:6. Unusual.

Danya Hebrew/Israeli. From Daniel, Hebrew, "God is my judge." Daniel 1:6. Unusual.

Danyele English. From Daniel. Unusual for males, unusual for females. Dani+.

Danyelle American. From Daniel, Hebrew, "God is my judge." Daniel 1:6. Unusual. Dani+.

Daphne English. From Daphne, Greek, "Laurel." Du Maurier (British writer, "Rebecca"). Less popular. Alternative spellings: Daphney, Daphny.

Dara English. From Dar, Hebrew, "Pearl" or "mother-of-pearl." Unusual for males, unusual for females.

Darcey See Darcy under Boys' Names.

Darci English. From Darcy, Irish, "Dark man." Unusual. Alternative spellings: Darcee, Darcie, Darsi, Darsie.

Darcy See under Boys' Names.

Darda Hungarian. Hebrew, "Pearl of wisdom." Unusual.

Daria English. From Darren, Gaelic, "Small great one." Unusual.

Darla English. From Darlene. Unusual.

Darlene English. Old English, "Darling." Merriman (character in TV's "Head of the Class"); Conner (character in TV's "Roseanne"). Less popular. Alternative spelling: Darleen.

Darrellyn English. From Darryl, surname used as a first name; origin unknown. Unusual. Alternative spelling: Daryllyn.

Daru Indo-Pakistani. Hindu, "Divine daru," a species of pine or cedar tree. Unusual.

Daryl See Darryl under Boys' Names.

Dasa Czech. From Dragomira, Slavic, "Glory of the day." Unusual.

Dasha Russian. From Dorothy, Greek (Dorothea), "Gift from God." Unusual.

Daveen Scottish. From David, Hebrew, "Beloved," "friend," or "darling." 1 Samuel 16:19. Unusual. Alternative spelling: Davene.

Davida Italian, Scottish. From David, Hebrew, "Beloved," "friend," or "darling." 1 Samuel 16:19. Unusual.

Davine Scottish. From David, Hebrew, "Beloved," "friend," or "darling." 1 Samuel 16:19. Unusual.

Dawn English. Old English, "To become day." Addams (actress); Fraser (Australian, Olympic gold medalist, 100-meter freestyle swim, 1956, '60, '64; average time: 1 minute); Steel (actress); Powell (novelist, "The Golden Spur"). Less popular. Alternative spellings: Dawne, Dawnn.

Dawna English. From Dawn. Unusual.

Dawnetta English. From Dawn. Unusual. Dawn.

Dawnielle English. From Dawn. Unusual. Dawn.

Dawnysia English. From Dawn. Unusual. Dawn.

Dayana Arabic. From Diana, Latin, "Divine." Unusual.

Dayle See Dale under Boys' Names.

Dayna English. From Dana, Celtic, "From Denmark." Unusual.

Deana English. From Dean, Old English, "Valley." Unusual. Dee.

Deandra Created. From Deandre, Created, African-American. Unusual.

Deane English. From Dean, Old English, "Valley." Unusual. Dee.

Deanna English. From Diana, Latin, "Divine." Durbin (singer and actress) (real name: Edna Mae Durbin). Unusual. Dee. Alternative spelling: Deeanna.

Deanne English. From Diana, Latin, "Divine." Unusual. Dee. Alternative spelling: Deann.

Deb English. From Deborah. Less popular.

Debbie English. From Deborah. Reynolds (actress) (real name: Marie Frances Reynolds); Allen (dancer, choreographer, and actress, "Fame"); Boone (singer, "You Light Up My Life"); Gibson (singer). Less popular. Alternative spellings: Debbi, Debby, Debi.

Deberah English. From Deborah. Unusual. Deb, Debbie+.

Deborah English. Hebrew (Devorah), "Bee." Genesis 35:8; Judges 4:4. Rebecca's faithful nurse (Bible); prophetess and judge, ancient Israel; Harry (singer with group Blondie); Kerr (British actress); Bryant (Miss America, 1966). Less popular. Deb, Debbie+. Alternative spellings: Debbora, Debora.

Deboran German. From Deborah. Unusual.

Deborha American. From Deborah. Deb, Debbie+. Alternative spelling: Deborrah.

Debra English. From Deborah. Winger (actress, "Terms of Endearment"); Barnes (Miss America, 1968); Maffett (Miss America, 1983). Less popular. Deb, Debbie+. Alternative spellings: Debbra, Debbrah, Debrah.

Decima Latin. From Decimus, Latin, "Tenth." Unusual.

Decla Irish. From Declan, Irish, meaning unknown. Unusual.

Dede African. African, "First-born daughter." Unusual.

Dee English. English, nickname based on any first name beginning with "D." Wallace (actress, "E.T.—The Extraterrestrial"). Unusual for males, less popular for females.

Deidre English. From Deirdre. Hall (actress, "Our House"). Unusual. Dee. Alternative spellings: Dedra, Deidra, Diedre.

Dela Czech. From Adelaide, Old German (Adelheidis), "Nobility." Unusual.

Delia English. Greek, "Visible." Salter Bacon (19th-century writer, headed attempt to prove that group headed by Francis Bacon wrote plays attributed to Shakespeare). Less popular. Del.

Delice English. From Delicia. Unusual. Alternative spellings: Delise, Delys, Delyse.

Delicia English. Latin, "Delight." Unusual. Alternative spelling: Delesha.

Delilah English. Hebrew (Dahlilah), "Delicate," "languishing," or "amorous." Samson's mistress and betrayer (Bible). Less popular. Della.

Delisa English. From Delicia. Unusual.

Delisha English. From Delicia. Unusual.

Delisiah English. From Delicia. Unusual.

Dell See under Boys' Names.

Della English. From Adelaide, Old German (Adelheidis), "Nobility." Reese (singer) (real name: Deloreese Patricia Early); Street (character in TV's "Perry Mason"). Less popular.

Delle English. From Adelaide, Old German (Adelheidis), "Nobility." Unusual.

Delma English. From Fidelma, Irish, combination of Fidel (Faithful, Latin, the word used as a name) + Mary (Miriam, Hebrew (Miryam), "Bitterness"). Unusual.

Delora English. From Dolores. Unusual.

Delore English. From Dolores. Unusual. Del.

Delores English. Spanish, "Sorrow." Less popular. Del, Dolly+, Dotty.

Deloris English. From Dolores. Unusual. Del, Dolly+, Dotty.

Delorita English. From Dolores. Unusual.

Delpha English. From Philadelphia, Greek, "Brotherly love." Revelations 3:7. Unusual.

Delphe English. From Philadelphia, Greek, "Brotherly love." Revelations 3:7. Unusual.

Delphi English. From Delphine. Unusual.

Delphia English. From Philadelphia, Greek, "Brotherly love." Revelations 3:7. Unusual.

Delphine French. Greek, "A dolphin." Unusual.

Delsie English. From Elizabeth, Hebrew (Elisheva), "Oath of God" or "God is my oath." Exodus 6:23. Unusual.

Delta English. Greek, fourth letter of Greek alphabet used as a first name. Burke (actress, "Designing Women"). Unusual.

Delu African. African, "First girl born after three boys." Unusual.

Delwyn Welsh. Welsh, "Pretty and fair." Unusual.

Delya English. From Delia, Greek, "Visible." Unusual.

Delys English. From Delicia. Unusual. Alternative spelling: Delyse.

Delysia English. From Delicia. Unusual.

Delyth Welsh. Welsh, "Pretty" or "neat." Unusual.

Demaras English. From Damaris. Unusual.

Demelza English. Cornish, place name used as a first name. Unusual.

Demetria English. From Demetrius, Greek, "Lover of the earth" or "from Demeter," the earth mother. Unusual.

Dena Native American. Native American, "Valley." Unusual.

Denae Hebrew/Israeli. Hebrew, "Vindicated." Unusual.

Denise English. From Dennis, Greek, "Of Dionysos," the Greek name for the god of wine. Huxtable (character in TV's "The Cosby Show"). Less popular. Dennie+. Alternative spellings: Deneice, Denice, Deniece, Dennice.

Denisha English. From Dennis, Greek, "Of Dionysos," the Greek name for the god of wine. Unusual.

Dennie English. From Dennis, Greek, "Of Dionysos," the Greek name for the god of wine. Less popular.

Dennise English. From Dennis, Greek, "Of Dionysos," the Greek name for the god of wine. Unusual. Dennie+. Alternative spellings: Denese, Denize.

Denva English. From Denver, English, "Dane's crossing-place." Unusual.

Denyce American. From Dennis, Greek, "Of Dionysos," the Greek name for the god of wine. Unusual. Dennie+. Alternative spelling: Denyse.

Derenda Created. Created, meaning unknown. Unusual.

Derinda Created. From Derenda. Unusual.

Deroit Hebrew/Israeli. From Deror, Hebrew, "Freedom," "free-flowing brook," or "swallow." Unusual.

Deron See under Boys' Names.

Derora Hebrew/Israeli. From Deror, Hebrew, "Freedom," "free-flowing brook," or "swallow." Unusual.

Derorice Hebrew/Israeli. From Deror, Hebrew, "Freedom," "free-flowing brook," or "swallow." Unusual.

Derren Welsh. From Deryn. Unusual. Alternative spellings: Derron, Deryn.

Derrie See under Boys' Names.

Derrin See Deron under Boys' Names.

Derrine Welsh. From Deryn. Unusual.

Desdemona English. Greek, "Misery." Tragic heroine in Shakespeare's "Othello." Unusual.

Desdemonia English. From Desdemona. Unusual.

Desire English. French, "To crave." Nisard (19th-century French journalist and literary critic); Defauw (Belgian violinist and conductor, founded Orchestre National de Belgique, 1937); Joseph Mercier (Belgian prelate and philosopher, spiritual leader during German occupation, WWI). Unusual for males, unusual for females. Alternative spelling: Desyre.

Desirée English. From Desire, French,

"To crave." Less popular. Alternative spelling: Desirae.

Desna Created. Created, meaning unknown. Unusual.

Desne Created. Created, meaning unknown. Unusual.

Desney Created. From Desne. Unusual.

Destiny English. Old French, the word used as a first name. Unusual.

Detta Italian. From Benedict, Latin, "Blessed." Unusual.

Deva Indo-Pakistani. Hindi, "Divine." A Hindu name for the moon goddess. Unusual.

Devaki Indo-Pakistani. Hindi, "Black." A Hindu name for the mother of the powerful god Krishna. Unusual.

Devan See Devon under Boys' Names.

Devene Scottish. From David, Hebrew, "Beloved," "friend," or "darling." 1 Samuel 16:19. Unusual. Alternative spellings: Devean, Deveen.

Devi Indo-Pakistani. Hindi, "Goddess." One of many names for the Hindu goddess of power and destruction. Unusual.

Devin See Devon under Boys' Names.

Devon See under Boys' Names.

Devona English. From Devon, English, place name used as a first name. Unusual.

Devora Bulgarian. From Deborah, Hebrew (Devorah), "Bee." Genesis 35:8; Judges 4:4. Unusual.

Devorah Hebrew/Israeli. Hebrew, "Bee." Genesis 35:8; Judges 4:4. Unusual.

Devra English. From Deborah, Hebrew (Devorah), "Bee." Genesis 35:8; Judges 4:4. Unusual.

Dezba Native American. Native American, "Going to war." Unusual.

Di English. From Diana. Unusual.

Diamond English. English, the name of the jewel used as a first name. Unusual.

Diana English. Latin, "Divine." Roman goddess of the chase and of childbirth, identified with the moon; character in Shakespeare's "All's Well That Ends Well"; Barrymore (actress); Rigg (actress, "The Avengers"); Ross (singer and actress, "Lady Sings the Blues"); wife of Prince Charles. Less popular. Di. Alternative spellings: Dianna, Dyana.

Diane English. From Diana. de France (16th-century French noblewoman noted for beauty, culture); Ladd (actress); Sawyer (TV journalist); von Furstenberg (fashion designer) (real name: Diane Halfin); Keaton (actress, "Baby Boom"); Witt (world's longest hair: 10 feet, 9 inches, 1989). Less popular. Di. Alternative spellings: Diahann, Dian, Dianne, Dyan, Dyane, Dyanne.

Diani Portuguese. From Diana. Unusual.

Dickla Hebrew/Israeli. Hebrew, "Palm tree" or "date tree." Unusual. Alternative spelling: Dikla.

Didi Hebrew/Israeli. From Deedee, Hebrew, "Beloved." Conn (actress, "Benson"). Unusual for males, unusual for females.

Diedre English. From Deirdre, Irish, "Fear" or "one who rages." Unusual. Dee.

Dierdre English. From Deirdre, Irish, "Fear" or "one who rages." Less popular. Dee. Alternative spelling: Deirdre.

Dierdrie English. From Deirdre, Irish, "Fear" or "one who rages." Unusual. Dee. Alternative spelling: Deirdrie.

Diklice Hebrew/Israeli. From Dickla. Unusual.

Diklit Hebrew/Israeli. From Dickla. Unusual.

Dina Hebrew/Israeli. Hebrew, "God has judged" or "God has vindicated." Genesis 30:21. Jacob's only daughter, with Leah; Merrill (actress). Less popular. Alternative spelling: Deena.

Dinah English. From Dina. Shore (actress and singer); Mulock Craik (19th-century British novelist and author of children's stories); Washington (singer); Manoff (actress, "Empty Nest"). Less popular.

Dinka African. African, "People." Unusual.

Dionna English. From Dennis, Greek, "Of Dionysos," the Greek name for the god of wine. Unusual. Di.

Dionne English. From Dennis, Greek, "Of Dionysos," the Greek name for the god of wine. Warwick (singer, "Walk On By"). Unusual. Di.

Dionysia Greek. From Dennis, Greek, "Of Dionysos," the Greek name for the god of wine. Unusual.

Disa English. Old Norse, "Active spite." Unusual.

Dita Czech. From Edith, Old English, "Valuable gift" or a combination of "rich" + "war." Unusual.

Ditka Czech. From Edith, Old English, "Valuable gift" or a combination of "rich" + "war." Unusual.

Ditzah Hebrew/Israeli. From Diza. Unusual. Alternative spelling: Ditza.

Divina English. From David, Hebrew, "Beloved," "friend," or "darling." 1 Samuel 16:19. Unusual.

Divinia English. From David, Hebrew, "Beloved," "friend," or "darling." 1 Samuel 16:19. Unusual.

Dixie English. English, surname used as a first name. Carter (actress, "Designing Women"); Dean (British soccer player); Watley (film critic). Unusual. Alternative spelling: Dixee.

Diza Hebrew/Israeli. Hebrew, "Joy." Unusual.

Doba Native American. Native American, "There was no war." Unusual.

Doda English. From Dodie. Unusual.

Dode English. From Dorothy, Greek (Dorothea), "Gift from God." Unusual.

Dodie Hebrew/Israeli. Hebrew, "Beloved." Unusual. Alternative spelling: Dodi.

Dol Romanian. From Dorothy, Greek (Dorothea), "Gift from God." Unusual.

Doll English. From Dorothy, Greek (Dorothea), "Gift from God." Unusual.

Dolly English. From Dorothy, Greek (Dorothea), "Gift from God." Parton (highest-paid entertainer, singer, and actress: earns up to $400,000 for a performance). Unusual. Alternative spellings: Dolley, Dolli, Dollie.

Dolorcitas Hispanic. From Dolores. Unusual.

Dolores English. Spanish, "Sorrow." Costello (actress); Del Rio (actress); Gray (actress, "Kismet"). Less popular. Del, Dolly+, Dotty+.

Doloritas Hispanic. From Dolores. Unusual.

Dolphin English. The word used as a first name; origin unknown. Unusual.

Doma Czech. From Dominic, Latin, "Lord." Unusual.

Domek See under Boys' Names.

Dominga Hispanic. From Dominic. Unusual.

Domini English. From Dominic. Unusual.

Dominic English. Latin, "Lord." Patron saint of astronomers; Santini (character in TV's "Airwolf"); DiMaggio (baseball player, brother of Joe). Unusual.

Dominica English. From Dominic. Unusual.

Dominik See under Boys' Names.

Dominika Russian. From Dominic. Unusual.
Domka Russian. From Dominic. Unusual.
Domonique French. From Dominic. Unusual.
Dona English. From Donald, Gaelic (Domhnall), "Mighty in the world." Unusual.
Donalda English. From Donald, Gaelic (Domhnall), "Mighty in the world." Unusual.
Donaldina English. From Donald, Gaelic (Domhnall), "Mighty in the world." Unusual.
Donaleen English. From Donald, Gaelic (Domhnall), "Mighty in the world." Unusual.
Donelda English. From Donald, Gaelic (Domhnall), "Mighty in the world." Unusual.
Donellia English. From Donald, Gaelic (Domhnall), "Mighty in the world." Unusual.
Donette English. From Donald, Gaelic (Domhnall), "Mighty in the world." Unusual.
Doni English. From Donald, Gaelic (Domhnall), "Mighty in the world." Unusual. Alternative spelling: Donie.
Donita English. From Donald, Gaelic (Domhnall), "Mighty in the world." Unusual.
Donna English. Latin, "Mistress of the house." Mills (actress, "Knots Landing"); Axum (Miss America, 1964); Douglas (actress, "The Beverly Hillbillies"); Reed (actress, "It's a Wonderful Life"); Summers (singer, "Bad Girls"). Less popular.
Donna Maria English. English, combination of Donna (Latin, "Mistress of the house") + Maria (Miriam, Hebrew (Miryam), "Bitterness"). Less popular.
Donna Marie English. English, combination of Donna (Latin, "Mistress of the house") + Marie (Miriam, Hebrew (Miryam), "Bitterness"). Less popular.
Donna Michelle English. English, combination of Donna (Latin, "Mistress of the house") + Michelle (Michael, Hebrew, "Who is like the Lord?"). Less popular.
Donnella English. From Donald, Gaelic (Domhnall), "Mighty in the world." Unusual. Alternative spelling: Donella.
Donnelle English. From Donald, Gaelic (Domhnall), "Mighty in the world." Unusual.
Dooriya Irish. English Gypsy, "The deep sea." Unusual.
Dooya Irish. From Dooriya. Unusual.
Dora Czech, English. From Dorothy. Character in Dickens' "David Copperfield." Less popular.
Dorah English. From Dorothy. Unusual.
Doralice French. From Dorothy. Unusual.
Dorcas English. From Tabitha, Aramaic, "Gazelle." Acts 9:36. Unusual.
Dorchen German. From Dorothy. Unusual.
Dore German. From Dorothy. Unusual.
Doreen English. Gaelic, "Sullen," "gloomy." Less popular. Alternative spelling: Dorene.
Doretha English. From Dorothy. Unusual. Alternative spelling: Doritha.
Dorette French. From Dorothy. Unusual.
Dori English. From Doris. Unusual.
Doria English. From Doris. Unusual.
Dorian English. Greek, place name used as a first name. Gray (character in Oscar Wilde's novel "The Picture of Dorian Gray"); Lord (character in TV's "One Life to Live"). Unusual for males, unusual for females. Alternative spelling: Dorien.
Doriana English. From Dorian, Greek, place name used as a first name. Unusual. Dori+.
Dorianne English. From Dorian, Greek, place name used as a first name. Unusual. Dori+.
Dorice English. From Doris. Unusual. Dori+.
Dorinda English. From Dorothy. Unusual.
Doris English. Greek, "One from the ocean." Day (singer and actress); Humphrey (dancer and choreographer); Lessing (novelist). Less popular. Dori+. Alternative spelling: Dorris.
Dorisa Hawaiian. From Doris. Unusual.
Dorit Hebrew/Israeli. Hebrew, "Generation." Unusual.
Dorita English. From Doris. Unusual.
Doritt English. From Dorothy. Unusual. Alternative spelling: Dorrit.
Dorka Czech, Polish, Russian. From Dorothy. Unusual.
Dorle German. From Dorothy. Unusual.
Dorlisa German. From Dorothy. Unusual.
Dorolice French. From Dorothy. Unusual.
Dorosia Polish. From Dorothy. Unusual.
Dorota Czech, Polish. From Dorothy. Unusual.
Dorotea Hispanic. From Dorothy. Unusual.
Doroteya Russian. From Dorothy. Unusual.
Dorothea English, Greek. From Dorothy. Lange (photographer known especially for photos of indigents during Depression); Beale (19th-century British educator, founded two colleges for female teachers). Less popular. Dolly+, Dot, Dotty+, Dori+, Thea. Alternative spellings: Dorothia, Dorthea, Dorethea.
Dorothee French. From Dorothy. Unusual.
Dorothy English. Greek (Dorothea), "Gift from God." Patron saint of florists; Collins (Canadian singer); Benham (Miss America, 1977); character in "The Wizard of Oz"; Hamill (ice skater); Lamour (actress). Less popular. Dolly+, Dot, Dotty+, Dori+. Alternative spelling: Dorthy.
Dorotthea Romanian. From Dorothy. Unusual.
Dorte Norwegian. From Dorothy. Unusual.
Dory English. French, "Golden-haired." Unusual for males, unusual for females. Alternative spellings: Dorri, Dorrie, Dorry.
Dosi English. From Dorothy. Unusual.
Dosya Russian. From Dorothy. Unusual.
Dot English. From Dorothy. Less popular.
Dottie English. From Dorothy. West (country-western singer). Unusual. Alternative spellings: Dotti, Dotty.
Douglasina Scottish. From Douglas, Gaelic, "Dark blue or black water." Unusual.
Dowsabel English. From Dulcibella, Latin, "Sweetly beautiful." Unusual.
Dragomira Slavic. Slavic, "Glory of the day." Unusual.
Drina English. From Alexander, Greek, "Defender of men" or "warding off men." Mark 16:21; Acts 4:6, 19:33. Unusual. Alternative spellings: Dreena, Drena.
Drisana English. Sanskrit, "Daughter of the sun." Unusual.
Drucella English. From Drusilla. Unusual.
Drusilla English. Latin (Drusus), meaning unknown. Judean princess, daughter of Herod. Unusual. Alternative spellings: Drewsila, Drucilla, Druscilla.
Duci Hungarian. From Edith, Old En-

glish, "Valuable gift" or a combination of "rich" + "war." Unusual.

Dudee Gypsy. English Gypsy, "Star" or "light." Unusual.

Dulcibel Latin. From Dulcibella. Unusual.

Dulcibella Latin. Latin, "Sweetly beautiful." Unusual.

Dulcie English. Latin, "Sweet." Unusual. Alternative spellings: Dulce, Dulsie.

Dulcinea English. Spanish, "Mild" or "sweet." del Toboso (Don Quixote's lady love). Unusual.

Dumin See under Boys' Names.

Durosimi African. Nigerian, "Wait and bury me." An African born-to-die name given to drive away evil spirits. Unusual.

Durosomo African. Nigerian, "Stay and play with the child." An African born-to-die name given to drive away evil spirits. Unusual.

Durva Indo-Pakistani. Hindi, a name for Hindu holy grass used in worship. Unusual.

Duscha Russian. Russian, "Soul" or "sweetheart." Unusual.

Dustine English. From Dustin, Old English, "Dusty place." Unusual.

Dusty See under Boys' Names.

Dusya Russian. From Nadia, Russian, "Hope." Unusual.

Dwora Greek, Russian, Yiddish. From Deborah, Hebrew (Devorah), "Bee." Genesis 35:8; Judges 4:4. Unusual.

Dyani Native American. Native American, "Deer." Unusual.

Dyllis English. From Dilys, Welsh, "Certain," "genuine," or "sincere." Unusual. Alternative spellings: Dilys, Dylis, Dylys.

Dymphna Irish. From Dympna. Unusual.

Dympna Irish. Irish, meaning unknown. Patron saint of the mentally ill. Unusual.

Earlene English. From Earl, English, title of nobility and surname used as a first name. Mandrell (musician and singer, sister of Barbara). Unusual. Alternative spellings: Earlean, Earleen, Earline.

Earlina English. From Earl, English, title of nobility and surname used as a first name. Unusual. Alternative spelling: Earlena.

Earlinda English. From Earl, English, title of nobility and surname used as a first name. Unusual.

Eartha English. From Eartha, OldEnglish, "Earth." Kitt (singer). Unusual.

Easter English. Old German, "eastre," from the name of a pagan Spring festival. Unusual.

Ebba English. From Eve, Hebrew (Chava), "Life." Genesis 3:20. Unusual. Alternative spelling: Eba.

Ebony American. The word used as a first name; origin unknown. Ebony is a very dark, almost black wood. Less popular. Alternative spellings: Ebbony, Eboney, Eboni, Ebonie, Ebonyi.

Echo English. Greek, "Repeated sound." Unusual.

Eda English. From Edith. Unusual.

Edda Polish. From Edith. Unusual.

Eddye English. From Edward, Old English, "Property guardian." Unusual.

Edeline English. From Adelaide, Old German (Adelheidis), "Nobility." Unusual.

Eden English. Hebrew, "Pleasantness." Phillpotts (British novelist and playwright; some work describes Devonshire); Gómez (Nicaraguan rebel leader). Unusual for males, less popular for females.

Edena Hawaiian. From Edna. Unusual.

Edetta Italian. From Edith. Unusual.

Edi Hawaiian. From Edith. Unusual.

Edie English. From Edith. Adams (singer); Sedgwick (artist, protégé of Andy Warhol); Hart (character in TV's "Peter Gunn"). Unusual. Alternative spellings: Ede, Edye.

Edit Hungarian. From Edith. Unusual.

Edita Czech, Italian. From Edith. Unusual.

Edite Latvian. From Edith. Unusual.

Edith English. Old English, "Valuable gift" or a combination of "rich" + "war." Saint; Head (most individual awards for costume design: eight); Marsh (New Zealand playwright and author, "Final Curtain"); Wharton (novelist, "Ethan Frome"). Less popular. Edie+. Alternative spellings: Edithe, Edyth, Edythe.

Editha English, German. From Edith. Unusual. Alternative spelling: Edytha.

Ediva English. From Edith. Unusual.

Edka Polish. From Edith. Unusual.

Edmee English. From Edmund, Old English, "Rich protector." Unusual.

Edna English. Hebrew, "Pleasure and delight." Wife of Enoch (Bible); Bayly (British novelist, "In the Golden Days"); St. Vincent Millay (poet, "Second April"); Mae Oliver (actress); Garrett (character in TV's "Facts of Life"). Less popular. Ed, Edi+. Alternative spelling: Ednah.

Edrice English. From Edric, Old English, "Powerful with property." Unusual.

Edwina English. From Edwin, Old English, "Friend" or "prosperity." Unusual. Alternative spellings: Edweena, Edwena.

Edwyna English. From Edwin, Old English, "Friend" or "prosperity." Unusual.

Edyta Polish. From Edith. Unusual.

Effam English. From Euphemia, Greek (Euphmia), "Spoken well of." Unusual.

Effie English. From Euphemia, Greek (Euphmia), "Spoken well of." Carlton (actress and author, wrote lullaby "Rock-a-Bye Baby," 1887). Unusual. Alternative spelling: Ephie.

Efua African. Ghanaian, "Born on Friday." Unusual.

Ega Nigerian. Nigerian, "Palm bird." Unusual.

Egidia Scottish. From Egidius, Scottish, from the Greek "aigidion" ("young goat"). Unusual.

Eibhlin Irish. From Helen, Greek, "Bright one" or "shining one." Unusual.

Eifiona Welsh. From Eifion, English, place name used as a first name. Unusual.

Eileen English. From Helen, Greek, "Bright one" or "shining one." Farrell (opera soprano); Heckart (actress); Brennan (actress, "Private Benjamin"); Ford (modelingagency owner). Less popular. Alternative spellings: Eilean, Eilleen.

Eiley English. From Helen, Greek, "Bright one" or "shining one." Unusual.

Eilidh Scottish. From Helen, Greek, "Bright one" or "shining one." Unusual.

Eilis Irish. From Elizabeth, Hebrew (Elisheva), "Oath of God" or "God is my oath." Exodus 6:23. Unusual.

Eiluned Welsh. From Eluned, Welsh, "Idol." Unusual.
Eilwen Welsh. Welsh, "Fair brow" or "white brow." Unusual.
Eily English. From Helen, Greek, "Bright one" or "shining one." Unusual.
Eimile Irish. From Emile, Latin, a clan name probably meaning "eager." Unusual.
Eira Welsh. Welsh, "Snow." Unusual.
Eiralys Welsh. From Eirlys, Welsh, "Snow-drop." Unusual.
Eirena English. From Irene, Greek (Eirene), "Peace." Unusual.
Eirene Scottish. Old Norse, "Peace." Unusual.
Eirian Welsh. Welsh, "Silver." Unusual.
Eirini Greek. From Irene, Greek (Eirene), "Peace." Unusual.
Eirlys Welsh. Welsh, "Snow-drop." Unusual.
Eirwen Welsh. Welsh, "Golden-fair." Unusual. Alternative spelling: Eirwyn.
Eithne Irish. From Ethne, Irish, "Little fire." Unusual.
Ekua African. Ghanaian, "Born on Wednesday." Unusual.
Ela Polish. From Adelaide, Old German (Adelheidis), "Nobility." Unusual.
Elaina English. From Helen, Greek, "Bright one" or "shining one." Unusual. Alternative spelling: Eleana.
Elaine English, French. From Helen, Greek, "Bright one" or "shining one." May (actress and author); Lefkowitz (character in TV's "Soap"). Less popular. Alternative spellings: Elane, Elayn, Elayne, Ellaine
Elamma Indo-Pakistani. Hindi, "Mother goddess." Unusual.
Elanit Hebrew/Israeli. From Ilana, Hebrew, "Tree." Unusual.
Elberta American. From Albert, Old English (Aethelbeorht), "Noble-bright." Unusual.
Elbertina American. From Albert, Old English (Aethelbeorht), "Noble-bright." Unusual.
Elbertine American. From Albert, Old English (Aethelbeorht), "Noble-bright." Unusual.
Elbie American. From Albert, Old English (Aethelbeorht), "Noble-bright." Unusual. Alternative spellings: Elbi, Elby.
Eldreda English. From Eldred, Old English, "Elderly counsel." Unusual.
Eleanor English. From Helen, Greek, "Bright one" or "shining one." Roosevelt (wife of President Franklin Delano) (real name: Anna Eleanor); Trent (character in Dickens' "The Old Curiosity Shop"); Powell (actress); Parker (actress). Less popular. Ella, Elli+, Nellie+, Nora. Alternative spellings: Elanor, Elanore, Eleanore, Elenore, Eleonore, Elinor, Ellenor, Ellinor.
Elena Bulgarian, Czech, English, Greek, Russian. From Helen, Greek, "Bright one" or "shining one." Chevtchenko (Russian Olympic champion gymnastics team member, 1988); Shushunova (same; also best all-around gymnast); Gerhardt (German lieder singer and educator). Unusual.
Elene English. From Helen, Greek, "Bright one" or "shining one." Unusual. Alternative spelling: Eleen.
Eleni Greek. From Helen, Greek, "Bright one" or "shining one." Unusual.
Elenitsa Greek. From Helen, Greek, "Bright one" or "shining one." Unusual.
Elenka Czech. From Helen, Greek, "Bright one" or "shining one." Unusual.
Elenora English. From Helen, Greek, "Bright one" or "shining one." Unusual. Ella, Elli+, Nellie+, Nora. Alternative spellings: Elenorah, Eleonora, Ellenora, Ellenorah.
Eleonor Hispanic. From Helen, Greek, "Bright one" or "shining one." Unusual. Alternative spelling: Elenor.
Eleora Hebrew/Israeli. From Eliora, Hebrew, "The Lord is my light." Unusual. Alternative spelling: Eliora.
Elese Hawaiian. From Adelaide, Old German (Adelheidis), "Nobility." Unusual.
Elfrida English. Old English, "Elf" + "strength." Unusual. Alternative spelling: Elfreda.
Elfride English. From Elfrida. Unusual.
Elga English. From Helga, Old Norse, "Holy." Unusual.
Eliana Hebrew/Israeli. Hebrew, "God has answered me." Unusual.
Elica Romanian. From Adelaide, Old German (Adelheidis), "Nobility." Unusual.
Elicia English. From Adelaide, Old German (Adelheidis), "Nobility." Unusual.
Elida Created. Created, meaning unknown. Unusual.
Elidi English. "Sun's gift"; origin unknown. Unusual.
Elin Welsh. Welsh, "Angel" or "nymph." Unusual.
Elina English. From Helen, Greek, "Bright one" or "shining one." Unusual.
Elinda Created. Created, meaning unknown. Unusual.
Elined Welsh. From Eluned, Welsh, "Idol." Unusual.
Elis German. From Elizabeth. Unusual.
Elisa English, French, Hispanic, Italian. From Elizabeth. Unusual.
Elisabet Estonian, German. From Elizabeth. Unusual.
Elisabeta Romanian. From Elizabeth. Unusual.
Elisabeth English. From Elizabeth. Schumann (opera singer known especially for Mozart and lieder); Wolff-Bekker (18th-century Dutch, co-authored first Dutch novels); Shue (actress); queen of the Belgians, 1909–34. Less popular.
Elisabetta Italian. From Elizabeth. Unusual.
Elisavet German. From Elizabeth. Unusual.
Elisavetta Russian. From Elizabeth. Unusual.
Élise French. From Elizabeth. Unusual.
Elisha Hebrew/Israeli. Hebrew, "God is salvation." Otis (inventor, patented steam elevator, 1861); Allen (19th-century politician, minister of finance under king of Hawaii, 1856–57); Kane (19th-century explorer, headed expedition into uncharted Arctic areas, 1853–55). Unusual for males, unusual for females.
Elisheba Hebrew/Israeli. From Elizabeth. Unusual.
Elisheva Hebrew/Israeli. Hebrew, "Oath of God" or "God is my oath." Exodus 6:23. Unusual.
Elisie English. From Elizabeth. Unusual.
Eliska Czech. From Adelaide, Old German (Adelheidis), "Nobility." Unusual.
Elisveta English. From Elizabeth. Unusual. Elli+, Liz.
Elita English. Latin, "Chosen." Unusual.
Eliza English, Polish. From Elizabeth. McCardle Johnson (wife of President Andrew); Doolittle (character in "My Fair Lady"); Orzeszkowa (19th-century Polish author, advocated better treatment for the downtrodden); Farnham (reformer and author, matron of Sing Sing prison,

1844–48). Less popular. Elli+, Liz. Alternative spelling: Elizah.

Elizabete Latvian. From Elizabeth. Unusual.

Elizabeth English. Hebrew (Elisheva), "Oath of God" or "God is my oath." Exodus 6:23. Seton (first U.S.-born saint); of Hungary (patron saint of bakers, charitable organizations, nurses); Arden (established cosmetics empire); Stanton (suffrage pioneer); Taylor (actress, most costume changes in a movie: 65, in "Cleopatra," 1963; cost $130,000). Very popular. Beth, Betsy, Betty, Liz.

Elka Polish. From Elizabeth. Unusual.

Elke German. From Adelaide, Old German (Adelheidis), "Nobility." Sommers (actress). Unusual.

Ella English. Old German, "All." Fitzgerald (singer); Wilcox (journalist and poet, wrote daily syndicated poem for many years); Raines (actress); Grasso (former governor of Connecticut). Less popular.

Ellama Indo-Pakistani. Hindi, "Mother goddess." Unusual.

Ellen English. From Helen, Greek, "Bright one" or "shining one." Beach Yaw (hit highest note ever sung: e‴," 1896); Futter (youngest college president: age 31, Barnard, 1981); Pendleton (president, Wellesley College, 1911–36); White (Adventist preacher); Glasgow (novelist, won Pulitzer Prize, 1941, "In This Our Life"). Less popular. Alternative spellings: Elen, Ellan, Ellin, Ellon, Ellyn, Ellynn, Elyn.

Elli Estonian, German. From Helen, Greek, "Bright one" or "shining one." Unusual.

Ellice English. From Adelaide, Old German (Adelheidis), "Nobility." Unusual for males, unusual for females. Alternative spelling: Elice.

Ellie English, from Helen, Greek, "Bright one" or "shining one"; or from Adelaide, Old German (Adelheidis), "Nobility." Ewing (character in TV's "Dallas" known as Miss Ellie). Less popular. Alternative spelling: Elly.

Elliner English. From Helen, Greek, "Bright one" or "shining one." Unusual. Ella, Elli+, Nellie+, Nora.

Elma Turkish. Turkish, "Apple." Unusual.

Elmena English. From William, Old German, "Will" + "helmet." Unusual. Alternative spelling: Elmina.

Elnora English. From Helen, Greek, "Bright one" or "shining one." Unusual. Ella, Elli+, Nellie+, Nora.

Eloisa Italian. From Aloysius, Old German, "Very wise." Unusual.

Eloise English. From Aloysius, Old German, "Very wise." Less popular.

Eloisia English. From Aloysius, Old German, "Very wise." Unusual.

Elon English. From Helen, Greek, "Bright one" or "shining one." Unusual.

Elsa Hispanic, Scottish, Swedish. From Adelaide, Old German (Adelheidis), "Nobility." Schiaparelli (French dress designer, designed padded shoulder, 1932); Lanchester (actress, "The Bride of Frankenstein"). Less popular.

Elsbet Frisian. From Elizabeth. Unusual.

Elsbeth German. From Elizabeth. Unusual.

Elsbietka Polish. From Elizabeth. Unusual.

Elschen German. From Elizabeth. Unusual.

Else German. From Adelaide, Old German (Adelheidis), "Nobility." Lasker-Schüler (German author, novelist, and playwright). Unusual.

Elsi English. From Elizabeth. Unusual. Alternative spelling: Elsey.

Elsie English. From Adelaide, Old German (Adelheidis), "Nobility." Parsons (anthropologist, studied the family and American Indians); Fogerty (British voice teacher, taught John Gielgud and Laurence Olivier); Janis (impressionist and vaudeville actress); DeWolf (interior decorator). Less popular.

Elspet Scottish. From Elizabeth. Unusual.

Elspeth Scottish. From Elizabeth. Buchan (18th-century Scottish founder of fanatical religious sect). Unusual.

Elspie Scottish. From Elizabeth. Unusual.

Elts Estonian. From Elizabeth. Unusual.

Eluned Welsh. Welsh, "Idol." Unusual.

Elva English. From Olive, Greek, "elaia," the name of a fruit. Unusual.

Elvera English. From Elvira, Spanish, place name used as a first name. Unusual.

Elvie English. From Alvin, Old English, "Elf-friend," "noble friend," "everyone's friend," or "old friend." Unusual.

Elvina English. From Alvin, Old English, "Elf-friend," "noble friend," "everyone's friend," or "old friend." Unusual.

Elvira Hispanic. From Elvira, Spanish, place name used as a first name. Character in TV's "Mistress of the Dark." Less popular.

Elvire German. From Elvira. Unusual.

Elvy Welsh. From Alvin, Old English, "Elf-friend," "noble friend," "everyone's friend," or "old friend." Unusual.

Elwina Welsh. From Alvin, Old English, "Elf-friend," "noble friend," "everyone's friend," or "old friend." Unusual.

Elyse English. From Elizabeth, Hebrew (Elisheva), "Oath of God" or "God is my oath." Exodus 6:23. Keaton (character in TV's "Family Ties"). Unusual.

Elysia English. "The home of the blessed"; origin unknown. Unusual.

Elyssa English. From Elizabeth, Hebrew (Elisheva), "Oath of God" or "God is my oath." Exodus 6:23. Unusual. Alternative spelling: Elissa.

Elza Hebrew/Israeli. Hebrew, "My joy is God"; and Slavic, from Adelaide, Old German (Adelheidis), "Nobility." Unusual.

Elzbieta Lithuanian, Polish (Elżbieta). From Elizabeth, Hebrew (Elisheva), "Oath of God" or "God is my oath." Exodus 6:23. Unusual.

Elzunia Polish. From Elizabeth, Hebrew (Elisheva), "Oath of God" or "God is my oath." Exodus 6:23. Unusual.

Em English. From Amelia, Latin, "Industrious" or "striving." Unusual.

Ema Romanian. From Amy, Old French, "Loved." Unusual.

Emalia Gypsy. From Amelia, Latin, "Industrious" or "striving." Unusual.

Emanuela English. From Emanuel, Hebrew, "God is with us," referring to a child about to be born. Isaiah 7:14. Unusual.

Emblem Unknown. From Emeline, Old French, meaning unknown. Unusual.

Emblyn English. From Emeline, Old French, meaning unknown. Unusual.

Emele Hawaiian. From Amelia, Latin, "Industrious" or "striving." Unusual.

Emelen English. From Emeline. Unusual.

Emelia English. From Amelia, Latin, "Industrious" or "striving." Unusual. Em, Emmie+.

Emelina English. From Amelia, Latin, "Industrious" or "striving." Unusual.

Emeline English. From Emeline, Old French, meaning unknown. Unusual. Alternative spellings: Emaline, Emiline, Emmaline, Emmeline, Emmiline.

Emelita English. From Amelia, Latin, "Industrious" or "striving." Unusual.

Emelyn English. From Emeline. Unusual. Alternative spellings: Emylin, Emylynn.

Emera English. From Amelia, Latin, "Industrious" or "striving." Unusual.
Emerald English. From Emerald, Spanish, the name of a jewel. Unusual.
Emila English. From Amelia, Latin, "Industrious" or "striving." Unusual.
Emilia Bulgarian, Italian. From Amelia, Latin, "Industrious" or "striving." Pardo Bazán (Spanish naturalist novelist and critic). Unusual.
Emilie Czech, English, French (Émilie). From Amelia, Latin, "Industrious" or "striving." Unusual. Em, Emmie+.
Emilka Czech. From Amelia, Latin, "Industrious" or "striving." Unusual.
Emillia English. From Amelia, Latin, "Industrious" or "striving." Unusual.
Emily English. From Amelia, Latin, "Industrious" or "striving." Carr (Canadian painter, especially of western landscapes and Indians); Dickinson (reclusive, great 19th-century poet); Post (etiquette expert); Brontë (author, "Wuthering Heights"); Kaye-Smith (British novelist, especially of stories set in Sussex). Very popular. Em, Emmie+. Alternative spellings: Emelie, Emely, Emilee, Emilie, Emiley.
Emlen English. From Emeline. Tunnell (football player, New York Giants, Green Bay Packers, 1948–61). Unusual.
Emlyn English. Welsh, place name used as a first name. Unusual for males, unusual for females. Alternative spelling: Emlynne.
Emma English. Old German, "All-embracing." Lazarus (poet and essayist, especially known for "The New Colossus," inscribed on the base of Statue of Liberty); Southworth (novelist, "Hidden Hand"); Samms (actress, "Dynasty"); Peel (character in TV's "The Avengers"); title character in Jane Austen's 1816 novel. Less popular.
Emmalene English. From Emeline. Unusual.
Emmali Arabic. From Amelia, Latin, "Industrious" or "striving." Unusual.
Emmet See Emmett under Boys' Names.
Emmett See under Boys' Names.
Emmot See Emmett under Boys' Names.
Emmy English. From Amelia, Latin, "Industrious" or "striving." Noether (German professor of mathematics, creative abstract algebraist); Destinn (operatic soprano, sang title role in London premiere of "Madame Butterfly," 1905). Less popular. Alternative spellings: Emi, Emie, Emmi, Emmie.
Emuna Hebrew/Israeli. Hebrew, "Faithful." Unusual.
Ena Irish. From Helen, Greek, "Bright one" or "shining one." Unusual.
Engracia Hispanic. From Grace, Latin, "Grace." Unusual.
Enid English. Welsh, "Soul of life." Bagnold (British novelist, "National Velvet"). Unusual.
Enola Native American. Native American. Meaning unknown, but the name is "alone" spelled backwards. Unusual.
Enrieta English. From Henry, Old German (Heimerich), "Home ruler." Unusual.
Enriqueta Hispanic. From Henry, Old German (Heimerich), "Home ruler." Unusual.
Eolanda English. From Yolande, Greek, "ion" ("violet") + "anthos" ("flower"). Unusual.
Eolande English. From Yolande, Greek, "ion" ("violet") + "anthos" ("flower"). Unusual.
Eppie English. From Euphemia, Greek (Euphmia), "Spoken well of." Character in George Eliot's 1861 novel "Silas Marner"; Lederer (real name of advice columnist Ann Landers). Unusual.
Erene English. From Erin, Gaelic, place name used as a first name. The name Erin commonly refers to Ireland. Unusual.
Ereni English. From Erin, Gaelic, place name used as a first name. The name Erin commonly refers to Ireland. Unusual.
Eri English. From Erin, Gaelic, place name used as a first name. The name Erin commonly refers to Ireland. Unusual.
Erica English. From Eric, Old Norse, "Ruler of all" or "always ruler." Jong (poet and novelist, "Fear of Flying"); character in TV's "All My Children." Popular. Alternative spelling: Ericka, Erika.
Erin English. Gaelic, place name used as a first name. The name Erin commonly refers to Ireland. Everly (married rock star Axl Rose); Moran (actress, "Happy Days"); Gray (actress, "Silver Spoons"). Less popular for males, popular for females. Alternative spelling: Eryn.
Erina English. From Erin, Gaelic, place name used as a first name. The name Erin commonly refers to Ireland. Unusual. Alternative spellings: Erena, Erinna.
Erinn Hungarian. From Erin, Gaelic, place name used as a first name. The name Erin commonly refers to Ireland. Unusual.
Erna English. From Ernest, English, "Vigor" or "earnestness." Ross (oldest woman to score a hole-in-one: 95 years, 257 days old, 1986). Unusual.
Ernestina English. From Ernest, English, "Vigor" or "earnestness." Unusual.
Ernestine English. From Ernest, English, "Vigor" or "earnestness." Schumann-Heink (contralto opera singer). Less popular.
Errolyn English. From Errol, place name used as a first name; origin unknown. Unusual.
Eryl Welsh. Welsh, "Watcher." Unusual for males, unusual for females.
Esma English. From Esme, Latin, "Esteem." Unusual.
Esmarelda Hispanic. From Emerald, Spanish, the name of a jewel. Unusual. Alternative spellings: Esmerelda, Esmiralda.
Esme See under Boys' Names. Alternative spelling: Esmee.
Esmerilda Hispanic. From Emerald, Spanish, the name of a jewel. Unusual.
Esperance English. From Hope, Old English, "hopian"; the word used as a name. Unusual.
Esperanza English. From Hope, Old English, "hopian"; the word used as a name. Unusual.
Essie English. From Esther, Persian, "Star." Book of Esther. Unusual. Alternative spellings: Essey, Essy.
Esta English. From Esther. Unusual.
Estanislao Hispanic. From Stanislaus, Latin, "Camp glory" (?). Unusual.
Estella English. Latin, "Star." Unusual.
Estelle English. From Estella, Latin, "Star." Parsons (actress, "Bonnie and Clyde); Getty (actress, "The Golden Girls"). Less popular.
Esther English. Persian, "Star." Book of Esther. Biblical queen and heroine; Williams (actress and Olympic gold medalist swimmer); Rolle (actress, "Good Times"). Less popular. Alternative spelling: Ester.
Estrella English. "Child of the stars"; origin unknown. Unusual.

Estrid English. From Astrid, Old Norse, "Divine beauty" or "divine strength." Unusual.

Etenia Native American. Native American, "Wealthy." Unusual.

Ethel English. Old English, "Noble." Merman (singer and actress); Mertz (character in TV's "I Love Lucy"); Waters (actress, "The Member of the Wedding"); Barrymore (actress); Kennedy (widow of Robert Kennedy); Smith, Dame (British composer and suffragist, wrote battle song of suffragettes). Less popular. Alternative spellings: Ethelle, Ethyl.

Ethelberta Unknown. From Ethelbert, Old English, "Noble-bright." Unusual.

Etheldreda English. Old English (Aethelthryth), "Noble strength." Saint. Unusual.

Ethelena English. From Ethelinda. Unusual. Alternative spelling: Ethelina.

Ethelind English. From Ethelinda. Unusual. Alternative spelling: Ethelende.

Etheline English. From Ethelinda. Unusual. Alternative spelling: Etheleen.

Ethelwin See Ethelwyn under Boys' Names.

Ethelwyne See Ethelwyn under Boys' Names.

Ethelwynne See Ethelwyn under Boys' Names.

Ethna Irish. From Ethne. Unusual.

Ethne Irish. Irish, "Little fire." Unusual. Alternative spelling: Ethnee.

Ethnea Irish. From Ethne. Unusual.

Ethylinda English. From Ethelinda. Unusual. Alternative spellings: Ethelenda, Ethelinda, Etholinda.

Etta English. English, meaning unknown. James (blues singer). Unusual.

Ettie English. From Henry, Old German (Heimerich), "Home ruler." Unusual.

Etty Estonian. From Elizabeth, Hebrew (Elisheva), "Oath of God" or "God is my oath." Exodus 6:23. Unusual. Alternative spelling: Etti.

Etumu Native American. Native American, "Bear warming itself in the sunlight." Unusual.

Etumuye Native American. Native American, "Bear climbing a hill." Unusual.

Eudora English. Greek, "Good gift." Welty (novelist). Unusual.

Eugenia English. From Eugene, Greek, "Well born." Zuckerman (musician). Unusual.

Eugénie French. From Eugene, Greek, "Well born." Unusual.

Eula English. From Eulalia. Unusual.

Eulalia English. Greek, "Sweetly speaking." Saint. Unusual.

Eulalie French. From Eulalia. Unusual.

Eun Korean. Korean, "Silver." Unusual.

Eunice English. Greek, "Victorious." Tietjens (author of texts on Japan and China, poet); Shriver (John F. Kennedy's sister). Less popular.

Euphan English. From Euphemia. Unusual.

Euphemia English. Greek (Euphmia), "Spoken well of." Unusual.

Eustacia English. From Eustace, Greek, "Fruitful." Unusual.

Eva English. From Eve. Gabor (actress, "Green Acres"); Peron (Argentine leader); Bartók (Hungarian actress); Marie Saint (actress); character in Harriet Beecher Stowe's 1852 novel "Uncle Tom's Cabin." Less popular.

Evadne Greek. Greek, "Good fortune." Unusual. Alternative spelling: Evadnie.

Evaine French. From Eve. Unusual.

Evan See under Boys' Names.

Evangelia English. From Eve. Unusual.

Evangelina English. From Eve. Unusual.

Evangeline English. Greek, "euangelion" ("good news"). Tragic Acadian lover, and title character, in Longfellow's 1847 narrative poem. Unusual.

Evathia Greek. From Eve. Unusual.

Evchen German. From Eve. Unusual.

Eve English. Hebrew (Chava), "Life." Genesis 3:20. First woman, wife of Adam; Arden (actress, "Our Miss Brooks"); Plumb (actress, "The Brady Bunch"). Less popular.

Eveleen Irish. From Evelina. Unusual.

Evelina English. Old French, "Hazelnut." Unusual.

Eveline English. From Evelina. Unusual. Alternative spelling: Evaline.

Evelyn English. From Evelina, Old French, "Hazelnut." Ay (Miss America, 1954); Strachey (British socialist and politician); Ruggles-Brise (British penologist, reformed treatment of juveniles); Waugh (British satirical author, "Brideshead Revisited," 1945). Unusual for males, less popular for females. Eve, Evie+. Alternative spellings: Evalyn, Evelyne, Evelynn, Evlyn.

Everelda English. From Averil, Old English, "Boar" + "battle." May also be related to the month of April. Unusual.

Everelder English. From Averil, Old English, "Boar" + "battle." May also be related to the month of April. Unusual.

Everell English. From Averil, Old English, "Boar" + "battle." May also be related to the month of April. Unusual.

Everil English. From Averil, Old English, "Boar" + "battle." May also be related to the month of April. Unusual.

Everilda English. From Averil, Old English, "Boar" + "battle." May also be related to the month of April. Unusual. Alternative spelling: Everhilda.

Evette English. From Ivo, Teutonic, "Yew wood" or "archer." Yew wood was used to make bows. Unusual.

Evi Hungarian. From Eve. Unusual.

Evička Czech. From Eve. Unusual.

Evie English. From Eve. Unusual.

Evike Hungarian. From Eve. Unusual.

Evita Hispanic. From Eve. Unusual.

Evka Czech. From Eve. Unusual.

Evonne English. From Ivo, Teutonic, "Yew wood" or "archer." Yew wood was used to make bows. Goolagong (Australian tennis player). Unusual. Alternative spelling: Evon.

Evuška Czech. From Eve. Unusual.

Evy German. From Eve. Unusual.

Ewa Polish. From Eve. Unusual.

Eyota See under Boys' Names.

Ezraella Hebrew/Israeli. From Ezrela. Unusual. Alternative spelling: Ezraela.

Ezrela Hebrew/Israeli. Hebrew, "God is my strength." Unusual.

Fabiana English. From Fabian, Latin, "Bean-grower." Unusual.

Faith English. Latin, "fides"; the word used as a first name. Patron saint of soldiers, prisoners, and pilgrims; Baldwin (novelist); Ringgold (artist); Popcorn (futurist); Caughlin (one of the longest-lived triplets: past 93 years old). Less popular. Alternative spelling: Fayth.

Faithful English. From Faith, Latin, "fides"; the word used as a first name. Unusual for males, unusual for females.

Faizah Arabic. Arabic, "Victorious." Unusual.

Falda Icelandic. Icelandic, "Folded wings." Unusual.

Falon Irish. Irish, "Grandchild of the ruler." Unusual. Alternative spelling: Fallon.

Fan English. From Francis, Latin, "Frenchman." Unusual.

Fancy English. From Fiance, French, "Betrothed." Unusual.

Fanny English. From Francis, Latin, "Frenchman." Burney (British novelist, won European fame for "Evelina," 1778); Brice (star of Ziegfeld Follies, character "Baby Snooks" on radio) (real name: Fannie Borach); Lewald (19th-century German novelist, "Clementine"); Flagg (actress); Hurst (author). Unusual. Alternative spellings: Fani, Fanney, Fanni, Fannie.

Fanya Russian. From Francis, Latin, "Frenchman." Unusual.

Farewell English. English, "Beautiful spring." Unusual for males, unusual for females.

Farrah English. From Farah. Fawcett (actress, "Charlie's Angels"). Unusual. Alternative spelling: Farah.

Farren English. From Faron, English, surname used as a first name. Unusual. Alternative spelling: Faren.

Faron See under Boys' Names.

Fāṭima Arabic. Arabic, meaning unknown. Unusual. Alternative spellings: Fāṭimah, Fāṭima.

Fatma Arabic. From Fāṭima.

Faustina Latin. From Faustina, Latin, "Lucky" or "fortunate." Unusual.

Fawn English. Old French, "Young deer." Less popular.

Fay English. From Faith. Wray (actress, "King Kong"); Lamphier (Miss America, 1925); Furillo (character in TV's "Hill Street Blues"). Less popular. Alternative spelling: Faye.

Fayina Russian, Ukrainian. From Francis, Latin, "Frenchman." Unusual.

Fayola Nigerian. From Fayola, Nigerian, "Good luck" or "with honor she walks." Unusual.

Fedora English. From Theodore, Greek, "theodoros" ("God's gift"). Unusual.

Fela Czech, Polish. From Felix, Latin, "Happy," "fortunate," or "lucky." Unusual.

Felcia Polish. From Felix, Latin, "Happy," "fortunate," or "lucky." Unusual.

Felda English. Old German, "From the field." Unusual.

Felica English. From Felix, Latin, "Happy," "fortunate," or "lucky." Unusual.

Felice English. From Felix, Latin, "Happy," "fortunate," or "lucky." Less popular.

Felicia English. From Felix, Latin, "Happy," "fortunate," or "lucky." Hemans (19th-century British light romantic poet); Farr (actress). Popular. Alternative spellings: Felecia, Felisha, Phylicia.

Felicity English. From Felix, Latin, "Happy," "fortunate," or "lucky." Kendal (British actress). Unusual.

Felka Polish. From Felix, Latin, "Happy," "fortunate," or "lucky." Unusual.

Femi Nigerian. Nigerian, "Love me." Unusual.

Fenella English. Gaelic (Fionnghal), "White shoulder." Unusual.

Feodora Russian. From Theodore, Greek, "theodoros" ("God's gift"). Unusual.

Ferike Hungarian. From Francis, Latin, "Frenchman." Unusual.

Fern English. Sanskrit, "wing," "leaf"; a plant name used as a first name. Arable (character in White's "Charlotte's Web"). Less popular. Alternative spelling: Ferne.

Fernley English. English, "Clearing with ferns." Unusual for males, unusual for females. Alternative spelling: Fernleigh.

Fidelia English. From Faith. Unusual.

Fidelma Irish. Irish, combination of Fidel (Faithful, Latin, the word used as a name) + Mary (Miriam, Hebrew (Miryam), "Bitterness"). Murphy (Irish actress). Unusual.

Fifi English. From Joseph, Hebrew (Yosef), "God will add." Unusual.

Fiipote French. From Philip, Greek, "philippos" ("lover of horses"). Matthew 10:3. Unusual.

Filipa Polish. From Philip, Greek, "philippos" ("lover of horses"). Matthew 10:3. Unusual.

Filippa Italian. From Philip, Greek, "philippos" ("lover of horses"). Matthew 10:3. Unusual.

Filippina Italian. From Philip, Greek, "philippos" ("lover of horses"). Matthew 10:3. Unusual.

Filomena Italian. From Philomena, Greek, "Beloved." Unusual.

Filpina Polish. From Philip, Greek, "philippos" ("lover of horses"). Matthew 10:3. Unusual.

Finella Irish. From Fenella, Gaelic (Fionnghal), "White shoulder." Unusual.

Finola Irish. From Fenella, Gaelic (Fionnghal), "White shoulder." Unusual.

Fiona English. Gaelic, "Fair" or "white." Macleod (18th-century Scottish author, wrote mystical stories about early Celtic world) (real name: William Sharp). Unusual.

Flavere French. From Flavia. Unusual.

Flavia English. Latin, "Yellow," signifying blond hair. Unusual.

Flavie French. From Flavia. Unusual.

Flavien See Flavian under Boys' Names.

Flavio Hispanic. From Flavia. Unusual.

Fleur English. French, "Flower." Character in John Galsworthy's "Forsyte Saga" (written 1906–28). Unusual.

Flo English. From Florence. Unusual for males, less popular for females.

Flora English. Latin, "Flower." Roman goddess of flowers and spring; 9th-century martyr; Macdonald (18th-century Scottish heroine, helped Prince Charles Edward escape after battle of Culloden Moor, 1746). Unusual. Flo, Florie+, Floss, Flossie+.

Florann English. English, combination of Flora (Latin, "Flower") + Ann (Hannah, Hebrew (Chanah), "Grace"). Unusual. Alternative spelling: Floranne.

Flore French. From Flora. Unusual.

Florella English. From Flora. Unusual.

Florelle English. From Flora. Unusual.

Florence English. Latin, "Flourishing" or "blooming." Nightingale (British nurse in Crimean War); Dombey (character in Dickens' "Dombey & Son"); Griffith Joyner (1988 Olympic gold medalist, track); DeWolfe Harding (wife of President Warren); Merriam Bailey (ornithologist, wrote on birds of western U.S.). Unusual for males, less popular for females. Flo, Florie+, Floss, Flossie+. Alternative spelling: Florance.

Floretta English. French, "Little flower." Unusual.
Florette English. From Floretta. Unusual.
Florida English. Spanish, "Flowery." Unusual.
Florimel English. Latin, "Flower" + "honey." Character in Edmund Spenser's "The Faerie Queene" (printed 1589–96). Unusual.
Florina English. From Florence, Latin, "Flourishing" or "blooming." Unusual.
Florinda English. From Flora. Unusual.
Florine English. From Florence, Latin, "Flourishing" or "blooming." Unusual.
Floris English. From Flora, Latin, "Flower." Unusual for males, unusual for females.
Florry English. From Flora, Latin, "Flower." Unusual for males, unusual for females. Alternative spellings: Flori, Florie, Florri, Florrie, Flory.
Floss English. From Florence, Latin, "Flourishing" or "blooming." Unusual.
Flossie English. From Florence, Latin, "Flourishing" or "blooming." Unusual. Alternative spelling: Flossy.
Flow English. From Florence, Latin, "Flourishing" or "blooming." Unusual.
Flower English. Latin, "flora"; the word used as a name. Unusual.
Floy American. From Florence, Latin, "Flourishing" or "blooming." Unusual.
Fortuna English. From Fortunatus, Latin, "Fortune." Roman goddess of prosperity. Unusual.
Fortune English. From Fortunatus, Latin, "Fortune." Unusual.
Fotina Greek. From Francis, Latin, "Frenchman." Unusual.
Fraka Polish. From Francis, Latin, "Frenchman." Unusual.
Fran English. From Francis. Less popular for males, less popular for females.
Franca Czech. From Francis, Latin, "Frenchman." Unusual.
Francena English. From Francis, Latin, "Frenchman." Unusual.
Frances English. From Francis, Latin, "Frenchman." of Rome (patron saint of motorists); Folsom Cleveland (wife of President Grover); Perkins (first female cabinet member: secretary of labor, 1933); Willard (educator, reformer; first president, National Council of Women, 1888–90); Alda (operatic soprano). Less popular. Fran, Francie+, Frannie+.
Francesca Italian. From Francis, Latin, "Frenchman." Malatesta (Italian adulteress slain by husband, 1289; immortalized as Francesca da Rimini in Dante's "Inferno"); Cerrito (lively 19th-century Italian dancer and choreographer, "Alma"). Less popular.
Francetta English. From Francis, Latin, "Frenchman." Unusual.
Francette French. From Francis, Latin, "Frenchman." Unusual.
Franchesca French. From Francis, Latin, "Frenchman." Unusual.
Franci English, Hungarian. From Francis, Latin, "Frenchman." Less popular. Alternative spelling: Francie.
Francina English. From Francis, Latin, "Frenchman." Unusual.
Francine English. From Francis, Latin, "Frenchman." Less popular. Fran, Francie+, Frannie+. Alternative spellings: Francene, Francyne.
Francis See under Boys' Names.
Francisca Hispanic. From Francis, Latin, "Frenchman." Unusual.
Francise Romanian. From Francis, Latin, "Frenchman." Unusual.
Franciszka Polish. From Francis, Latin, "Frenchman." Unusual.
Francka Czech. From Francis, Latin, "Frenchman." Unusual.
Françoise French. From Francis, Latin, "Frenchman." de la Valliere (18th-century French duchess, mistress of Louis XIV). Less popular.
Frania Polish. From Francis, Latin, "Frenchman." Unusual.
Frankey See Frankie under Boys' Names.
Frankie See under Boys' Names.
Franklyn See Franklin under Boys' Names.
Frannie English. From Francis, Latin, "Frenchman." Less popular. Alternative spelling: Franni.
Franz See under Boys' Names.
Franze German. From Francis, Latin, "Frenchman." Unusual.
Franzetta English. From Francis, Latin, "Frenchman." Unusual.
Franziska German. From Francis, Latin, "Frenchman." Unusual.
Fredalena English. From Frederick, Old German, "Peaceful ruler." Unusual.
Fredaline English. From Frederick, Old German, "Peaceful ruler." Unusual.
Freddie English. From Frederick, Old German, "Peaceful ruler." Bartholomew (child actor). Less popular for males, unusual for females. Alternative spelling: Fredie.
Frederica English. From Frederick, Old German, "Peaceful ruler." Von Stade (mezzo-soprano). Unusual. Alternative spellings: Fredericka, Frederika.
Frederickina English. From Frederick, Old German, "Peaceful ruler." Unusual.
Frederika English. From Frederick, Old German, "Peaceful ruler." Unusual.
Frederine English. From Frederick, Old German, "Peaceful ruler." Unusual.
Frédérique French. From Frederick, Old German, "Peaceful ruler." Unusual.
Fredi German. From Frederick, Old German, "Peaceful ruler." Unusual.
Fredith English. From Frederick, Old German, "Peaceful ruler." Unusual.
Fredora English. From Frederick, Old German, "Peaceful ruler." Unusual.
Fredrica English. From Frederick, Old German, "Peaceful ruler." Unusual.
Fredricia English. From Frederick, Old German, "Peaceful ruler." Unusual.
Fredrika Norwegian. From Frederick, Old German, "Peaceful ruler." Bremer (19th-century Swedish novelist; also wrote impressions of America). Unusual.
Freeda English. From Frederick, Old German, "Peaceful ruler." Unusual. Alternative spellings: Freada, Freda, Freida, Frida.
Freja Swedish. Swedish, "Noble lady." Norse goddess of love and fertility. Unusual.
Freya English. From Freja. Unusual.
Frici Hungarian. From Frederick, Old German, "Peaceful ruler." Unusual.
Frieda German. From Frederick, Old German, "Peaceful ruler." Unusual.
Friederike See Friedrich under Boys' Names.
Fritze German. From Frederick, Old German, "Peaceful ruler." Unusual.
Fritzinn German. From Frederick, Old German, "Peaceful ruler." Unusual.
Fryda Polish. From Frederick, Old German, "Peaceful ruler." Unusual.
Fryderyka Polish. From Frederick, Old German, "Peaceful ruler." Unusual.
Fulleretta English. From Fuller, English, "One who shrinks and thickens cloth." An occupational surname used as a first name. Unusual.

Gabi See under Boys' Names.
Gabriel See under Boys' Names.
Gabriela English, Italian. From Gabriel, Hebrew (Gavriel), "Hero of God" or "man of God." Daniel 8:16. Mistral (Chilean poet, won 1945 Nobel Prize for literature) (real name: Lucila Godoy Alcayaga). Unusual. Gabi+.
Gabriella English. From Gabriel, Hebrew (Gavriel), "Hero of God" or "man of God." Daniel 8:16. Unusual. Gabi+.
Gabrielle English. From Gabriel, Hebrew (Gavriel), "Hero of God" or "man of God." Daniel 8:16. Campbell Long (prolific British novelist, historian especially concerned with the Renaissance) (real name of Marjorie Bowen, George Runnell Preedy, and Joseph Shearing). Less popular. Gabi+. Alternative spelling: Gabriell.
Gaby English. From Gabriel, Hebrew (Gavriel), "Hero of God" or "man of God." Daniel 8:16. Unusual.
Gada Hebrew/Israeli. Hebrew, "Happy" or "lucky." Unusual.
Gaenor Welsh. From Guinevere, Welsh (Gwenhwyfar), "Fair," "white" + "smooth," "yielding." Unusual.
Gafna Hebrew/Israeli. Hebrew, "Vine." Unusual.
Gaila English. From Abigail, Hebrew (Abigal), "My father rejoices." 1 Samuel 25:24. Unusual.
Gail English. From Abigail, Hebrew (Abigal), "My father rejoices." 1 Samuel 25: 24. Borden (19thcentury, invented condensed milk, 1856; established company that bears his name); Hamilton (19th-century, wrote on women's worth, among other things) (real name: Mary Abigail Dodge); Patrick (TV producer, "Perry Mason" series) (real name: Margaret Fitzpatrick). Unusual for males, less popular for females. Alternative spellings: Gael, Gale, Gaile, Gayle.
Gal Hebrew/Israeli. From Gali. Unusual.
Gala Scandinavian. Old Norse, "Singer." Unusual.
Galena English. From Galen, Greek, "Healer" or "calm." Unusual.
Gali Hebrew/Israeli. Hebrew, "Hill," "mound," "fountain," or "spring." Unusual.
Galice Hebrew/Israeli. From Gali. Unusual.
Galina Russian. From Helen, Greek, "Bright one" or "shining one." Aleksandrovna Lastovskaya (Russian, one of the first three women to reach the North Pole, 1977); Ulanova (Russian ballerina). Unusual.
Galinka Russian. From Helen, Greek, "Bright one" or "shining one." Unusual.
Galka Russian. From Helen, Greek, "Bright one" or "shining one." Unusual.
Galya Russian. From Helen, Greek, "Bright one" or "shining one." Unusual.
Gamma English. From Gamma, Greek, the third letter of the alphabet. Most often given to third child. Unusual.
Gana Hebrew/Israeli. From Ganit. Unusual.
Ganesa Indo-Pakistani. Hindi, the name of the god of wisdom and good luck. Unusual.
Ganice Hebrew/Israeli. From Ganit. Unusual.
Ganit Hebrew/Israeli. Hebrew, "Garden." Unusual.
Ganya Hebrew/Israeli. Hebrew, "Garden of God." Unusual.
Gari See Gary under Boys' Names.
Garnet See under Boys' Names.
Garnett See Garnet under Boys' Names.
Garnetta English. From Garnet, English, "Shelter," "protection." Also a jewel name. Unusual.
Gasha Russian. From Agatha, Greek, "agathos" ("good"). Unusual.
Gashka Russian. From Agatha, Greek, "agathos" ("good"). Unusual.
Gauri Indo-Pakistani. Hindi, "Yellow" or "fair." Another name for Hindu goddess Sakti. Yellow refers to color of the harvest or the gauri buffalo, both of which are associated with the goddess. Unusual.
Gavrilla Hebrew/Israeli. Hebrew, "Heroine" or "strong." Unusual.
Gay English. Old French, "Joyful." Less popular. Alternative spelling: Gaye.
Gayna English. From Guinevere, Welsh (Gwenhwyfar), "Fair," "white" + "smooth," "yielding." Unusual. Alternative spelling: Gaynah.
Gaynor English. From Guinevere, Welsh (Gwenhwyfar), "Fair," "white" + "smooth," "yielding." Unusual. Alternative spelling: Gayner.
Gazit. Hebrew/Israeli. From Gisa, Hebrew, "Hewn stone." Unusual.
Geela Hebrew/Israeli. Hebrew, "Joy." Unusual.
Gelsi English. From Gilsey, a variety of jasmine; origin unknown. Unusual. Alternative spelling: Gelsy.
Gelya Russian. From Angel, Greek, "angelos" ("messenger"). Unusual.
Gem English. Latin, "gemma" ("bud"); the word used as a first name. Unusual.
Gemelle English. From Gemelle, Latin, "Twin." Unusual.
Gemina English. From Gemini. Unusual.
Gemini English. Greek, "Twin." Unusual.
Geminine English. From Gemini. Unusual.
Gemma English. From Gem. Galgani (Italian 19th-century saint); Jones (actress); Craven (actress). Unusual.
Gena English. From Eugene, Greek, "Well born." Rowlands (actress). Unusual.
Gene See under Boys' Names.
Geneva English. From Genevieve. Unusual.
Genève French. From Genevieve. Unusual.
Genevieve English. Celtic, "White" or "magic sighs." Patron saint of Paris; Boullongne (17th-century French still-life painter); Taggard (poet and critic). Less popular. Genny+.
Genevra English. From Guinevere, Welsh (Gwenhwyfar), "Fair," "white" + "smooth," "yielding." Unusual.
Genn English. From Guinevere, Welsh (Gwenhwyfar), "Fair," "white" + "smooth," "yielding." Unusual. Alternative spelling: Jenn.
Genna Arabic. Arabic, "Small bird." Unusual.
Gennifer English. From Guinevere, Welsh (Gwenhwyfar), "Fair," "white" + "smooth," "yielding." Unusual. Alternative spellings: Jenefer, Jenifer, Jeniffer, Jennafer, Jennifer.
Genny English. From Guinevere, Welsh

(Gwenhwyfar), "Fair," "white" + "smooth," "yielding." Unusual. Alternative spellings: Jenney, Jenni, Jennie, Jenny, Jeny.

Genoveva Hispanic. From Genevieve. Unusual.

Geoffroie French. From Geoffrey, Old German (Gottfried), "peace" (?). Unusual.

Geogana English. From George, Greek, "Husbandman," "farmer," or "earth-worker." Unusual. Alternative spelling: Geoganna.

Georgana English. From George, Greek, "Husbandman," "farmer," or "earth-worker." Unusual. Alternative spelling: Georganna.

George See under Boys' Names.

Georgeina English. From George, Greek, "Husbandman," "farmer," or "earth-worker." Unusual. Georgie+. Alternative spellings: Georgiena, Georgena.

Georgene English. From George, Greek, "Husbandman," "farmer," or "earth-worker." Unusual. Georgie+.

Georgenia English. From George, Greek, "Husbandman," "farmer," or "earth-worker." Unusual. Georgie+.

Georgetta English. From George, Greek, "Husbandman," "farmer," or "earth-worker." Unusual. Georgie+.

Georgette French. From George, Greek, "Husbandman," "farmer," or "earth-worker." Heyer (British novelist, "Black Moth"). Unusual.

Georgia English. From George, Greek, "Husbandman," "farmer," or "earth-worker." O'Keeffe (painter of abstract floral and desert scenes). Less popular.

Georgiana English. From George, Greek, "Husbandman," "farmer," or "earth-worker." Cavendish (British Duchess of Devonshire, 18th-century). Unusual. Georgie+. Alternative spellings: Georgeana, Georgeanna, Georgianna.

Georgie English. From George. Unusual for males, unusual for females.

Georgienne French. From George, Greek, "Husbandman," "farmer," or "earth-worker." Unusual.

Georgina German, Hispanic, Russian. From George, Greek, "Husbandman," "farmer," or "earth-worker." Unusual.

Georgine German. From George, Greek, "Husbandman," "farmer," or "earth-worker." Unusual.

Geralda English. From Gerald, Old German, "Spear" + "ruler." Unusual.

Geraldine English. From Gerald, Old German, "Spear" + "ruler." Ferraro (first female candidate for vice-president, Democratic party, 1984); Chaplin (actress); Page (actress); Farrar (opera singer). Less popular. Gerry+. Alternative spelling: Geraldene.

Geralyn English. From Gerald, Old German, "Spear" + "ruler." Unusual. Gerry+. Alternative spellings: Geralynn, Gerilyn, Gerrilyn.

Gerda Latvian, from George, Greek, "Husbandman," "farmer," or "earth-worker"; and Scandinavian, from Gerda, Norse, "Protection." Character in Hans Christian Andersen's "Snow Queen." Unusual.

Germain See under Boys' Names.

Germaine See under Boys' Names.

Germana English. From Germain, Latin, "A German." Unusual.

Gerry English. From Gerald, Old German, "Spear" + "ruler." Wilmot (Canadian ice hockey commentator, fastest broadcaster: spoke at over 300 understandable words per minute). Less popular for males, unusual for females. Alternative spelling: Geri.

Gertina English. From Gertrude. Unusual.

Gertrude English. Old German, "Spear-strength." Saint; character, Shakespeare's "Hamlet"; Lawrence (British stage, musical actress); Ederle (youngest to break a nonmechanical record: 12 years, 298 days (880-yard freestyle swim in 13 minutes, 19 seconds, 1919)); Stein (experimental American author, led Paris salon). Less popular. Gert, Gertie+, Trudy+.

Gerty English. From Gertrude. Radnitz Cori (biochemist, studied carbohydrate metabolism; shared Nobel Prize with her husband, 1947). Unusual. Alternative spelling: Gertie.

Gervaise French. From Gervase, Latin, meaning unknown. Unusual.

Gessica Italian. From Jessica, Hebrew, "He beholds" or "wealthy." Unusual.

Geva Hebrew/Israeli. Hebrew, "Hill." Unusual.

Ghādah Arabic. Arabic, "Young," "fresh," or "tender." Unusual.

Ghislaine English. Old German, "Pledge" (?). Unusual.

Gia Italian. From Regina, Latin, "Queen." Unusual.

Gianetta English. From John, Hebrew (Yochanan), "God has been gracious." Unusual.

Gianina Hispanic. From John, Hebrew (Yochanan), "God has been gracious." Unusual.

Gianna Italian. From John, Hebrew (Yochanan), "God has been gracious." Unusual.

Gidita Hispanic. From Bridget, Irish, "Strength." Unusual.

Gilada Hebrew/Israeli. Hebrew, "My joy is everlasting" or "my hill is a witness." Unusual.

Gilberta English. From Gilbert, Old German, "Pledge" + "bright." Unusual.

Gilda English. Anglo-Saxon, "The golden." Radner (comedian, "Saturday Night Live"); Gray (actress). Unusual.

Giles See under Boys' Names.

Gill English. From Julius, Latin, a Roman clan name meaning "downy" or "bearded." Unusual.

Gillianne English. From Julius, Latin, a Roman clan name meaning "downy" or "bearded." Unusual. Gill+, Gillie+. Alternative spellings: Gilian, Gillian, Gillyanne.

Gilly English. From Julius, Latin, a Roman clan name meaning "downy" or "bearded." Unusual. Alternative spellings: Gilli, Gillie.

Gilsey English. A variety of jasmine; origin unknown. Unusual.

Gina English, Hispanic, Russian, from George, Greek, "Husbandman," "farmer," or "earth-worker"; and Japanese, Japanese, "Silvery." Lollobrigida (Italian actress). Popular.

Ginata Hispanic. From Virgil, Latin, "Vergilius"; a Roman clan name. Unusual.

Ginetta English. From Genevieve, Celtic, "White" or "magic sighs." Unusual.

Ginette English. From Genevieve, Celtic, "White" or "magic sighs." Spanier (French haute couturiere, first woman to appear live on a transatlantic satellite transmission, 1962). Unusual.

Ginevra Italian. From Guinevere, Welsh (Gwenhwyfar), "Fair," "white" + "smooth," "yielding." Unusual.

Ginger English. From Virgil, Latin, "Vergilius"; a Roman clan name. Rogers (dancer and actress) (real name: Virginia McMath). Less popular.

Ginia Hispanic. From Virgil, Latin, "Vergilius"; a Roman clan name. Unusual.

Ginnette English. From Genevieve, Celtic, "White" or "magic sighs." Unusual.

Ginnifer English. From Guinevere, Welsh (Gwenhwyfar), "Fair," "white" + "smooth," "yielding." Unusual.

Ginny English. From Virgil, Latin, "Vergilius"; a Roman clan name. Less popular. Alternative spellings: Ginney, Ginni, Ginnie.

Giovanna Italian. From John, Hebrew (Yochanan), "God has been gracious." Unusual.

Girisa Indo-Pakistani. Hindi, "Mountain lord." Another name for the god Siva. Unusual for males, unusual for females.

Gisa Hebrew/Israeli. Hebrew, "Hewn stone." Unusual. Alternative spellings: Giza, Gizza.

Gisela English, Hispanic, Italian, Yiddish. From Giselle. Eleventh-century Holy Roman empress. Unusual. Alternative spelling: Gisella.

Giselle English. Old German, "Pledge" or "hostage." Title character in Gautier's ballet. Unusual. Alternative spelling: Gisele.

Gissa Hebrew/Israeli. From Gisa, Hebrew, "Hewn stone." Unusual.

Gita Polish, from Margaret, Greek, "margaron" ("pearl"); and Yiddish, from Gita, Yiddish, "Good." Unusual.

Gitana Hispanic. Spanish, "Gypsy girl." Unusual.

Gitka Czech. From Margaret, Greek, "margaron" ("pearl"). Unusual.

Gitta Hungarian. From Margaret, Greek, "margaron" ("pearl"). Unusual.

Gituska Czech. From Margaret, Greek, "margaron" ("pearl"). Unusual.

Giulia Italian. From Judith, Hebrew (Yehudit), "Of Judah," "praised one," or "praise to the Lord." Judith 8:1. Unusual.

Gizela Czech, Latvian. From Giselle. Unusual.

Gizi Hungarian. From Giselle. Unusual.

Gizike Hungarian. From Giselle. Unusual.

Gizus Hungarian. From Giselle. Unusual.

Gladi Hawaiian. From Claudius, Latin, "Lame." Unusual.

Gladness English. From Claudius, Latin, "Lame." Unusual.

Gladwys English. From Claudius, Latin, "Lame." Unusual.

Gladys English. From Claudius, Latin, "Lame." Knight (singer); Swarthout (soprano); Cooper, Dame (British actress); Smith (real name of Canadian actress Mary Pickford). Less popular. Alternative spelling: Gladis.

Gleda Icelandic. Icelandic, "Make happy." Unusual.

Glenda English. Welsh, "Holy" or "fair" + "good." Farrell (British actress); Jackson (British actress, won 1970 Oscar for "Women in Love"). Less popular.

Glenna English. From Glen, Celtic, "Valley." Unusual.

Glenwys English. From Glenys. Unusual.

Glenys English. Welsh, "Holy" or "fair." Unusual. Alternative spellings: Glenice, Glenis, Glenise, Glennis, Glennys, Glenyss, Glenise, Glenyse.

Gloria English. Latin, "Glory." Character in George Bernard Shaw's play "You Never Can Tell"; Swanson (actress, "Sunset Boulevard"); Estefan (lead singer, Miami Sound Machine); Steinem (feminist); Vanderbilt (fashion designer); DeHaven (actress). Less popular.

Gloris English. From Gloria. Unusual.

Glorvina Created. Created by Irish author Lady Morgan for a character in her 1806 novel "Wild Irish Girl." Character in William Makepeace Thackeray's "Vanity Fair" (published serially, 1847–48). Unusual.

Glory English. From Gloria. Unusual. Alternative spellings: Glori, Glorie

Glynis Welsh. From Glyn, Welsh, "Small valley." Johns (British actress). Unusual.

Glynnis English. From Glyn, Welsh, "Small valley." Unusual. Alternative spellings: Glynes, Glinys, Glinnis.

Golda English. From Golden. Meir (Israeli prime minister, 1969–74) (birth name: Goldie Meyerson). Unusual.

Golden English. Old English, "Golden-haired." Unusual.

Goldie English. From Golden. Hawn (actress, "Foul Play"). Less popular. Alternative spellings: Goldi, Goldy.

Goldina English. From Golden. Unusual.

Graca Portuguese. From Grace. Unusual.

Grace English. Latin, "Grace." Goodhue Coolidge (wife of President Calvin); Kelly (actress, won 1954 Oscar, "Country Girl"); Abbott (social worker, organized Immigrants' Protective League); Darling (British; with father, rescued five shipwreck victims at lighthouse he kept, 1838). Less popular.

Gracia Hispanic, Hungarian. From Grace. Unusual.

Graciana Hispanic. From Grace. Unusual.

Gracie English. From Grace. Allen (actress and comedian) (real name: Grace Ethel Cecile Rosalie Allen); Fields (British comedian) (real name: Grace Stansfield). Less popular. Alternative spellings: Gracey, Graci.

Grainne Irish. From Grania. Unusual.

Grainnia Irish. From Grania. Unusual.

Grania Irish. Irish, "Love." Unusual.

Gratia German. From Grace. Unusual.

Gray See under Boys' Names.

Grazia Italian. From Grace. Deledda (Italian novelist, especially known for writings on Sardinia; won 1926 Nobel Prize for literature). Unusual.

Grazielle French. From Grace. Unusual.

Graziosa Italian. From Grace. Unusual.

Greer English. From Gregory, Greek, "Watchful." Garson (Irish actress). Unusual.

Greeta German. From Margaret, Greek, "margaron" ("pearl"). Unusual.

Gressa Norwegian. Norwegian, "Grass." Unusual.

Greta English. From Margaret, Greek, "margaron" ("pearl"). Garbo (solitude-seeking actress, "Grand Hotel"). Less popular. Alternative spelling: Gretta.

Gretal German. From Margaret, Greek, "margaron" ("pearl"). Unusual. Alternative spelling: Greatel.

Gretchen German. From Margaret, Greek, "margaron" ("pearl"). Carlson (Miss America, 1989). Less popular.

Grete German. From Margaret, Greek, "margaron" ("pearl"). Waitz (Norwegian, won women's marathon title a record ninth time, 1988). Unusual.

Grethal German. From Margaret, Greek, "margaron" ("pearl"). Unusual. Alternative spelling: Grethel.

Gretna English. Scottish, name of a village to which English couples have frequently eloped. Unusual.

Grieta Latvian. From Margaret, Greek, "margaron" ("pearl"). Unusual.

Griselda English. German, "Grey battle-maid." Character in Chaucer's 1387 "Canterbury Tales." Unusual.

Gruzia Hungarian. From George, Greek, "Husbandman," "farmer," or "earth-worker." Unusual.

Guadalupe See under Boys' Names.

Guilette French. From William, Old German, "Will" + "helmet." Unusual.

Guilla Hispanic. From William, Old German, "Will" + "helmet." Unusual.

Guillerma Hispanic. From William, Old German, "Will" + "helmet." Unusual.

Guinevere English. Welsh (Gwenhwyfar), "Fair," "white" + "smooth," "yielding." Wife of King Arthur in the Arthurian legend. Unusual.

Gunda Norwegian. Norwegian, "Warrior" or "battle maiden." Unusual.

Gurice Hebrew/Israeli. From Gur, Hebrew, "Lion cub." Unusual.

Gurit Hebrew/Israeli. From Gur, Hebrew, "Lion cub." Unusual.

Gurpreet See under Boys' Names.

Gusta German. From Augustus, Latin, "Venerable" or "majestic." Unusual.

Gwen English. From Gwendolen. Saint; Matthewman (British, most prolific hand-knitter: knitted 915 garments, using 11,012 ounces of wool, in 1979). Less popular.

Gwenda Welsh. Welsh, "Fair" + "good." Unusual.

Gwendolen English. Welsh, "Fair," "blessed" + "ring," "bow." Less popular. Gwen. Alternative spellings: Gwendolin, Gwendolyn, Gwendolyne, Gwendolynn, Gwendolynne.

Gwendolene English. From Gwendolen. Unusual. Gwen.

Gwendoline English. From Gwendolen. Unusual. Gwen.

Gwenllian Welsh. Welsh, "White," "fair" + "flaxen." Unusual.

Gwennie English. From Gwendolen. Unusual. Alternative spelling: Gwenny.

Gwenyth English. From Gwyneth. Unusual. Alternative spellings: Gwenith, Gwennyth.

Gwladys Welsh. From Claudius, Latin, "Lame." Saint. Unusual.

Gwynedd Welsh. From Gwyneth. Unusual.

Gwyneth English. Welsh, "Happiness," "felicity." Unusual. Alternative spellings: Gweneth, Gwenneth, Gwenneth.

Gwynfa Welsh. From Gwynfor, Welsh, "Fair," "good" + "lord." Unusual.

Gwynne Welsh. From Gwyn, Welsh, "Fair," "blessed." Unusual.

Gyorci Hungarian. From George, Greek, "Husbandman," "farmer," or "earth-worker." Unusual.

Ha Vietnamese. Vietnamese, "River." Unusual.

Ḥabībah Arabic. From Ḥabīb, Arabic, "Beloved." Unusual.

Hadassah Hebrew/Israeli. Hebrew, "Myrtle." Original name of Esther. Esther 2:7. Unusual.

Hadiya African. Swahili, "Gift." Unusual.

Hagar English. Hebrew, "Forsaken." Genesis 16:1. Sarah's handmaiden, mother of Ishmael. Unusual.

Haggar English. From Hagar. Unusual.

Hagia Hebrew/Israeli. Hebrew, "Joyful" or "festive." Unusual.

Hagice Hebrew/Israeli. From Hagia. Unusual.

Hagit Hebrew/Israeli. From Hagia. Unusual.

Haidee English. Greek, "Modest." Character in Lord Byron's epic satire "Don Juan," published 1819–24; Wright (actress). Unusual.

Halcyon English. Greek, "Mythical bird" or "calm," "peaceful." Unusual.

Halina Russian. From Helen, Greek, "Bright one" or "shining one." Unusual.

Hallie English. From Hayley. Unusual. Alternative spellings: Halley, Halli, Hally.

Halona Native American. Native American, "Happy fortune." Unusual.

Hama Japanese. Japanese, "Shore." Unusual.

Hana Czech, English, Polish, from Hannah, Hebrew (Chanah), "Grace [of God]" or "favor," 1 Samuel 1:2; and Japanese, from Hana, Japanese, "Flower" or "blossom." Mandlikova (Czech tennis player). Unusual.

Hania Hebrew/Israeli. Hebrew, "Resting place." Unusual. Alternative spelling: Haniya.

Hanicka Czech. From Hannah, Hebrew (Chanah), "Grace [of God]" or "favor." 1 Samuel 1:2. Unusual.

Hanka Czech, Polish. From Hannah. Unusual.

Hannah English, German. Hebrew (Chanah), "Grace [of God]" or "favor." 1 Samuel 1:2. Mother of prophet Samuel, wife of Elkanah; Arendt (historian, "Origins of Totalitarianism," 1951); Hoes Van Buren (wife of President Martin); Vaughan Pritchard (British actress); Parkhouse Cowley (18th-century British playwright, "The Belle's Strategem," 1782). Popular. Alternative spelling: Hanna.

Hanne German. From Hannah. Unusual.

Hannele German. From Hannah. Unusual.

Hanni Finnish, German. From Hannah. Unusual.

Happy English. Middle English, "hap"; the word used as a first name. Unusual for males, unusual for females.

Hara Indo-Pakistani. From Hari, Hindi, "Tawny." Another name for the Hindu god Vishnu. Unusual.

Haralda English. From Harold, Old English, "Army power." Unusual.

Harmony English. Latin, "Harmony." Unusual.

Haroldene English. From Harold, Old English, "Army power." Unusual.

Harper See under Boys' Names.

Harpreet See under Boys' Names.

Harriet English. From Henry, Old German (Heimerich), "Home ruler." Beecher Stowe (abolitionist and author, "Uncle Tom's Cabin"); Tubman (abolitionist, helped 300+ slaves escape to North via Underground Railroad); Nelson (actress) (real name: Peggy Lou Snyder); Stone Lothrop (author of juvenile books). Less popular. Hattie+. Alternative spellings: Harriett, Harriette.

Harrietta English. From Henry, Old German (Heimerich), "Home ruler." Unusual. Hattie+.

Harriot English. From Henry, Old German (Heimerich), "Home ruler." Stanton Blatch (suffragette, established Equality League of Self-Supporting Women,

1907). Unusual. Alternative spelling: Harriott.

Haru Japanese. Japanese, "Spring." Unusual.

Hasana Nigerian. Nigerian, "First-born female twin." Unusual.

Hasina African. Swahili, "Good." Unusual.

Hateya Native American. Native American, "To press with the foot." Unusual.

Hattie English. From Henry, Old German (Heimerich), "Home ruler." Wyatt Caraway (first woman elected to senate, 1932); McDaniel (first black actress to win Oscar, "Gone With the Wind," 1939). Unusual. Alternative spelling: Hatty.

Hausu Native American. Native American, "Bear yawning as it wakes." Unusual.

Haven English. Dutch, "Harbor." Unusual for males, unusual for females.

Haviva Hebrew/Israeli. Hebrew, "Beloved." Unusual.

Hayley English. English, "Hay-meadow." Surname used as a first name. Mills (British actress, "Pollyanna"). Unusual. Alternative spellings: Hailee, Hailey, Haley, Hali, Halie, Haylee.

Hazael See under Boys' Names.

Hazel English. English, name of a tree. Hotchkiss Wightman (tennis player, won 45 national titles). Less popular. Alternative spellings: Hazal, Hazell, Hazelle.

Hazelgrove English. From Hazel. Unusual.

Hazeline English. From Hazel. Unusual.

Heather English. Middle English, "hather"; the name of a flowering shrub. Locklear (actress, "Return of the Swamp Thing"); O'Roarke (actress, "Poltergeist"). Very popular.

Heaven English. Old English, "heofon"; the word used as a name. Unusual.

Hebe English. Greek, "Youth." Greek goddess of youth. Unusual.

Hedda English. From Hedwig. Saint; Gabler (title character in Ibsen's play); Hopper (syndicated gossip columnist, 1938–66) (real name: Elda Furry). Less popular. Alternative spelling: Heda.

Hede German. From Hedwig. Unusual.

Hedia Hebrew/Israeli. Hebrew, "Voice of God" or "echo of God." Unusual.

Hedvick Czech. From Hedwig. Unusual.

Hedvika Czech. From Hedwig. Unusual.

Hedwig English. German, "Struggle" or "strife." Saint. Unusual.

Hedy English. From Hedwig. Lamarr (Austrian actress) (real name: Hedwig Kiesler). Unusual. Alternative spellings: Heddi, Heddie, Heddy, Hedi.

Heidi English. From Adelaide, Old German (Adelheidis), "Nobility." Title character in Johanna Spyri's novel; Brandt (designed Christmas seals, 1956 and 1961). Less popular. Alternative spelling: Heide.

Hela Czech. From Helen. Unusual.

Hele Estonian. From Helen. Unusual.

Helen English. Greek, "Bright one" or "shining one." Saint; of Troy (character in Homer's "Iliad"); Herron Taft (wife of President William); Keller (blind, deaf, and mute author and lecturer, wrote "The World I Live In"); Hayes (actress, won 1932 Oscar for "Sin of Madelon Claudet"). Less popular. Alternative spelling: Hellen.

Helena English. From Helen. Hahn (theosophist, established society and journal; real name of Elena Blavatsky); Modjeska (actress); character in Shakespeare's "All's Well That Ends Well" and "A Midsummer Night's Dream." Less popular.

Helene English. From Helen. Böhlau (German novelist). Less popular.

Helenka Czech. From Helen. Unusual.

Helenor English. From Helenor, English, combination of Helen + Eleanor (Helen). Unusual. Alternative spelling: Hellenor.

Helga Scandinavian. Old Norse, "Holy." Unusual.

Helki Native American. Native American, "To touch." Unusual.

Helli Finnish. From Helen. Unusual.

Helma English. From William, Old German, "Will" + "helmet." Unusual.

Helmi English. From William, Old German, "Will" + "helmet." Unusual. Alternative spelling: Helmy.

Helmine German. From William, Old German, "Will" + "helmet." Unusual.

Héloïse French. From Aloysius, Old German, "Very wise." 12th-century niece of Fulbert, abbess of Le Paraclet. Less popular.

Heltu Native American. Native American, "Bear reaching out toward people." Unusual.

Heluska Czech. From Helen. Unusual.

Heneretta English. From Henry, Old German (Heimerich), "Home ruler." Unusual.

Henia Polish. From Henry, Old German (Heimerich), "Home ruler." Unusual.

Henka Polish. From Henry, Old German (Heimerich), "Home ruler." Unusual.

Henrieta Polish. From Henry, Old German (Heimerich), "Home ruler." Unusual.

Henriete English. From Henry, Old German (Heimerich), "Home ruler." Unusual.

Henrietta English. From Henry, Old German (Heimerich), "Home ruler." Leaver (Miss America, 1935); Leavitt (astronomer, discovered four novas); Szold (Zionist leader, first woman elected to World Zionist Organization); Green (reputed to be biggest miser in America: died with estate worth $95 million). Less popular. Etta, Henny+, Hetty+. Alternative spelling: Henryetta.

Henriette French, Latvian. From Henry, Old German (Heimerich), "Home ruler." Roland Holst-Van der Schalk (Dutch socialist poet). Unusual.

Henrika English. From Henry, Old German (Heimerich), "Home ruler." Unusual.

Hephzabah Hebrew/Israeli. From Hephzibah. Unusual.

Hephzibah Hebrew/Israeli. Hebrew, "My delight is in her." 2 Kings 21:1. Unusual. Alternative spellings: Hephsibah, Hepzibah.

Hephzibeth English. From Hephzibah. Unusual.

Hepsie English. From Hephzibah. Unusual. Alternative spellings: Hepsey, Hepsy.

Hepzabah Hebrew/Israeli. From Hephzibah. Unusual.

Hericlea Greek. From Henry, Old German (Heimerich), "Home ruler." Unusual.

Herma Czech. From Hermes, Greek, name of the Greek mythological messenger of the gods, meaning unknown. Szabo-Planck (set Olympic Winter Games figure skating record, 1924). Unusual.

Hermia English. From Hermes, Greek, name of the Greek mythological messenger of the gods, meaning unknown. Unusual.

Hermina Czech. From Hermes, Greek, name of the Greek mythological messenger of the gods, meaning unknown. Unusual.

Hermione English. From Hermes, Greek, name of the Greek mythological messenger of the gods, meaning unknown. Greek, mythological daughter of Helen of Troy; queen in Shakespeare's "The Winter's Tale." Unusual.

Hertha English. "Child of the earth"; origin unknown. Unusual.

Hester English. From Esther, Persian, "Star." Book of Esther. Piozzi (British writer); Bateman (18th-century British silversmith); Chapone (18th-century British essayist on "improving the mind"). Unusual.

Heta Native American. Native American, "Race after a rabbit hunt." Unusual.

Hetta German. From Hedwig, German, "Struggle" or "strife." Unusual.

Hettie English. From Henry, Old German (Heimerich), "Home ruler." Unusual. Alternative spellings: Hetti, Hetty.

Heulwen Welsh. Welsh, "Sunshine." Unusual.

Hiedi German. From Adelaide, Old German (Adelheidis), "Nobility." Unusual.

Hilda English. Old German, "Battle." Saint; Doolittle (imagist poet). Less popular. Alternative spelling: Hylda.

Hildegarde English. Old German, "War stronghold." Saint; Knef (German actress) (real name: Loretta Sell). Unusual. Hilda. Alternative spellings: Hildagard, Hildagarde.

Hildie English. From Hilda. Unusual. Alternative spellings: Hilde, Hildi, Hildy.

Hildred English. Old English, "Battle-counsel." Unusual.

Hillary English. From Hilary, Latin (Hilarius), "Cheerful." Rodham Clinton (wife of President William). Unusual for males, less popular for females. Alternative spellings: Hilary, Hilery, Hillarie, Hillery.

Hilma English. From William, Old German, "Will" + "helmet." Unusual.

Hinda Yiddish. Yiddish, "Female deer." Unusual.

Hippolyta Greek. Greek, "Horses." Greek, mythological Queen of the Amazons. Unusual.

Hisa Japanese. Japanese, "Long lasting." Unusual.

Hisae Japanese. From Hisa. Unusual.

Hisako Japanese. From Hisa. Unusual.

Hisayo Japanese. From Hisa. Unusual.

Hiti Eskimo. Eskimo, "Hyena." Unusual.

Hoa Vietnamese. Vietnamese, "Flower" or "peace." Unusual.

Hoku See under Boys' Names.

Hokulani Hawaiian. Hawaiian, "Star in the sky." Unusual.

Hola Native American. Native American, "Seed-filled club." Unusual.

Holly English. Old English, "hullis"; a plant name used as a first name. Character in John Galsworthy's "Forsyte Saga"; Hunter (actress, "Broadcast News"). Popular. Alternative spellings: Holley, Holli, Hollie.

Hong Vietnamese. Vietnamese, "Pink." Unusual.

Honor English. From Honoria. Blackman (British actress, "The Avengers"). Unusual. Alternative spellings: Honner, Honnor, Honnour, Honour, Honoure.

Honora English. From Honoria. Unusual. Alternative spelling: Honorah.

Honoria Latin. Latin, "Honorable woman." Unusual.

Honorine French. From Honoria, Latin, "Honorable woman." Unusual.

Hope English. Old English, "hopian"; the word used as a name. Lange (actress); Daniels (one of the longest-lived triplets, died at age 93). Less popular.

Horatia English. From Horatio, Latin, a Roman clan name. Unusual.

Hortensia English. Latin, a Roman clan name or flower name. Unusual.

Hoshi Japanese. Japanese, "Star." Unusual. Alternative spelling: Hoshie.

Hoshiko Japanese. From Hoshi. Unusual.

Hoshiyo Japanese. From Hoshi. Unusual.

Hrisoula Greek. From Hrisoula, Greek, "Golden." Unusual.

Hrodohaidis German. Old German, "Fame-kind." Unusual.

Hua Chinese. Chinese, "Flower." Unusual.

Huata Native American. Native American, "Carrying a basket of seeds." Unusual.

Hughina Scottish. From Hugh, Old German, "Mind" or "thought." Unusual.

Hulda Scandinavian. From Huldah. Unusual.

Huldah Hebrew/Israeli. Hebrew, "Weasel" or "mole." 2 Kings 22:14. Unusual.

Huong Vietnamese. Vietnamese, "Flower." Unusual.

Hyacinth English. Greek, "hyacinthus"; the name of a flower and a precious stone. Saint. Unusual for males, unusual for females.

Hye Korean. Korean, "Gracefulness." Unusual.

Hypatia Greek. Greek, "Highest." Greek philosopher renowned for learning, eloquence, and beauty; character in Shaw's "Misalliance." Unusual.

Iantha English. From Ianthe. Unusual.

Ianthe English. Greek, "Violet flower." Unusual.

Ida English. German, "Youthful" or "labor." Lupino (British actress and director); Saxton McKinley (wife of President William); Tarbell (author, "Life of Abraham Lincoln"); Wells (journalist, established Negro Fellowship League, 1910); Kaminska (Polish actress and theater producer). Less popular.

Idalia English. From Ida. Unusual.

Idalina English. From Ida. Unusual.

Idaline English. From Ida. Unusual. Alternative spellings: Idaleene, Idalene.

Ide French. From Ida. Unusual.

Idella English. From Ida. Unusual.

Idelle English. From Ida. Unusual.

Idette German. From Ida. Unusual.

Iduska Czech. From Ida. Unusual.

Ieasha American. From Aisha, Arabic, "Woman" or "life." Unusual. Alternative spellings: Aiesha, Ayeisha, Ieesha.

Ieashia American. From Aisha, Arabic, "Woman" or "life." Unusual. Alternative spelling: Ieeshia.

Iesha American. From Aisha, Arabic, "Woman" or "life." Unusual.

Iestin Welsh. From Justin, Latin, "Just." Unusual.

Ikia Unknown. From Isaiah, Hebrew, "God is my help and salvation." Book of Isaiah. Unusual.

Ila Hungarian. From Helen, Greek, "Bright one" or "shining one." Unusual.

Ilana Hebrew/Israeli. Hebrew, "Tree." Less popular.

Ilanit Hebrew/Israeli. From Ilana. Unusual.

Ileana Hungarian. From Helen, Greek, "Bright one" or "shining one." Unusual.

Ilena English. From Helen, Greek, "Bright one" or "shining one." Unusual.

Ilene English. From Helen, Greek, "Bright one" or "shining one." Less popular. Alternative spellings: Ileane, Ileen, Ileene.

Ilia English. Latin, "From Ilium [Troy]." Mother of Romulus and Remus in Roman mythology. Unusual.

Iliana English. From Helen, Greek, "Bright one" or "shining one." Unusual.

Ilka Hungarian. From Helen, Greek, "Bright one" or "shining one." Unusual.

Ilma English. From William, Old German, "Will" + "helmet." Unusual.

Ilona Hungarian. From Helen, Greek, "Bright one" or "shining one." Massey (actress) (real name: Ilona Hajmassy); title character in novel by Hans Habe. Unusual.

Ilonka Hungarian. From Helen, Greek, "Bright one" or "shining one." Unusual.

Ilse German. From Elizabeth, Hebrew (Elisheva), "Oath of God" or "God is my oath." Exodus 6:23. Unusual.

Iluska Hungarian. From Helen, Greek, "Bright one" or "shining one." Unusual.

Ima English. From Amelia, Latin, "Industrious" or "striving." Unusual.

Imala Native American. Native American, "Disciplinarian." Unusual.

Imalda English. From Imelda. Unusual.

Imān Arabic. Arabic, "Faith" or "belief." Unusual.

Imelda Italian, Swiss. German (Irmhild), "All-embracing battle." Unusual.

Imma Acadian. Acadian (Mesopotamian), "Water bearer." Unusual.

Imogen English. Latin, "Last born" or "innocent." Heroine of Shakespeare's "Cymbeline"; Cunningham (photographer, "Two Callas"). Unusual.

Imogene English. From Imogen. Coca (comedian). Unusual.

In Korean. Korean, "Humanity." Unusual.

Ina Irish. From Agnes, Greek, "agnos" ("pure" or "chaste"). Kleber (German, set 1984 world record for 200-meter backstroke: 1 minute, 0.59 seconds). Unusual.

India English. Country's name used as a first name; origin unknown. Wilkes (character in Mitchell's "Gone With the Wind"). Unusual.

Inés Hispanic, Italian. From Agnes, Greek, "agnos" ("pure" or "chaste"). Geissler (German swimmer; her team set 1984 world record in medley relay: 4 minutes, 3.69 seconds); de Castro (14th-century Spanish noblewoman). Unusual. Inez.

Inésita Hispanic. From Agnes, Greek, "agnos" ("pure" or "chaste"). Unusual.

Inessa Russian. From Agnes, Greek, "agnos" ("pure" or "chaste"). Unusual.

Inga Scandinavian. From Ingeborg. Unusual.

Inge Scandinavian. From Ingeborg. Unusual.

Ingeberg Scandinavian. From Ingeborg. Unusual.

Ingeborg Scandinavian. Old Norse, "Ing's protection." Ing is the Norse god of peace, prosperity, and fertility. 13th-century queen of France. Unusual.

Ingrid Scandinavian. Old Norse, "Ing" + "beautiful." Ing is the Norse god of peace, prosperity, and fertility. Bergman (Swedish actress, won 1944 Oscar for "Gaslight"); Kristiansen (Norwegian, set 1985 record for women's marathon: 2 hours, 21 minutes, 6 seconds). Less popular.

Inka Polish, Russian. From Celestin, Latin, "Heavenly." Unusual.

Innes See under Boys' Names.

Innis See under Boys' Names.

Inoa Hawaiian. Hawaiian, "Name" or "name chant." Unusual.

Inok Polish. From Celestin, Latin, "Heavenly." Unusual.

Ioanna Greek, Russian. From John, Hebrew (Yochanan), "God has been gracious." Unusual.

Iola Welsh. From Iorwerth, Welsh, "Lord" + "worth." Unusual.

Iolanda English. From Yolande, Greek, "ion" ("violet") + "anthos" ("flower"). Balas (Romanian, won Olympic gold medals for running high jump, 1960–64). Unusual.

Iolande English. From Yolande, Greek, "ion" ("violet") + "anthos" ("flower"). Unusual.

Iolanthe English. From Yolande, Greek, "ion" ("violet") + "anthos" ("flower"). Unusual.

Iona Scottish. Gaelic, name of an island in the Hebrides. Unusual.

Ione English. Greek, "Violet." Skye (actress, daughter of pop singer Donovan). Unusual.

Ioudith Greek. From Judith, Hebrew (Yehudit), "Of Judah," "praised one," or "praise to the Lord." Judith 8:1. Unusual.

Iren English, Hungarian. From Irene. Unusual.

Irena English, Russian. From Irene. Szewinska (Polish, won record seven Olympic medals in track and field; only woman to win medals in track in four successive Olympic games). Unusual. Alternative spelling: Irina.

Irene English. From Irene, Greek (Eirene), "Peace." Saint; name of three rulers of the Eastern Roman Empire; Dunne (actress). Less popular. Alternative spellings: Ireen, Irine.

Irenea Hispanic. From Irene. Unusual.

Irenka Czech, Hungarian. From Irene. Unusual.

Irin English. From Irene. Unusual.

Irini Romanian. From Irene. Unusual.

Iris English. Greek name for the goddess of the rainbow. Also a plant name. Murdoch (British novelist). Less popular.

Irisa Russian. From Iris. Unusual.

Irisha Russian. From Irene. Unusual.

Irka Czech, Latvian. From Irene. Unusual.

Irma German. Old German, "Whole," "universal." la Douce (title character in film starring Shirley Maclaine). Unusual.

Irusya Latvian. From Irene. Unusual.

Iryna Russian. From Irene. Unusual.

Isa English. From Elizabeth, Hebrew (Elisheva), "Oath of God" or "God is my oath." Exodus 6:23. Necati (Turkish poet). Unusual.

Isabeau French. From Elizabeth, Hebrew (Elisheva), "Oath of God" or "God is my oath." Exodus 6:23. of Bavaria (15th-century consort of Charles VI of France). Unusual.

Isabel Hispanic. From Elizabeth, Hebrew (Elisheva), "Oath of God" or "God is my oath." Exodus 6:23. Less popular.

Isabelita Hispanic. From Elizabeth, Hebrew (Elisheva), "Oath of God" or "God is my oath." Exodus 6:23. Unusual.

Isabella Italian. From Elizabeth, Hebrew (Elisheva), "Oath of God" or "God is my oath." Exodus 6:23. Rossellini (Italian actress, "Cousins"); Banks (British novelist); Bishop (British traveler, lecturer, and writer; first woman fellow of Royal Geographical Society, 1892); Crawford (19th-century Canadian poet); Gardner (art collector). Unusual.

Isabelle English. From Elizabeth, Hebrew (Elisheva), "Oath of God" or "God is my oath." Exodus 6:23. Less popular.

Isadora English. From Isidore, Greek (Isidoros), "Gift of Isis." Duncan (dancer). Unusual.

Ishbel Scottish. From Elizabeth, Hebrew (Elisheva), "Oath of God" or "God is my oath." Exodus 6:23. Unusual.

Ishi Japanese. Japanese, "Stone." Unusual. Alternative spelling: Ishie.

Ishiko Japanese. From Ishi. Unusual.

Ishiyo Japanese. From Ishi. Unusual.

Isidora English. From Isidore, Greek (Isidoros), "Gift of Isis." Unusual.

Isla Scottish. From Isla, Scottish, the name of a river. St. Clair (Scottish TV personality). Unusual.

Ismay English. Surname used as a first name; origin unknown. Unusual.

Isobel English. From Elizabeth, Hebrew (Elisheva), "Oath of God" or "God is my oath." Exodus 6:23. Unusual.

Isolda English. From Isolde. Unusual.

Isolde Unknown. Meaning and origin unknown. Unusual.

Issi English. From Elizabeth, Hebrew (Elisheva), "Oath of God" or "God is my oath." Exodus 6:23. Unusual. Alternative spelling: Issie.

Istas Native American. Native American, "Snow." Unusual.

Ita Irish, from Ita, Old Irish, "Thirst"; and Yiddish, from Ida, German, "Youthful" or "labor." Unusual.

Itka Polish. From Ida, German, "Youthful" or "labor." Unusual.

Ituha Native American. Native American, "Sturdy oak tree." Unusual.

Iuana Native American. Native American, "Blown backwards over the rippling brook." Unusual for males, unusual for females.

Iulia Romanian. From Julius, Latin, a Roman clan name meaning "downy" or "bearded." Unusual.

Iva Slavic. From John, Hebrew (Yochanan), "God has been gracious." Unusual.

Ivah English. Biblical place name; origin unknown. 2 Kings 18:34. Unusual.

Ivanka Slavic. From John, Hebrew (Yochanan), "God has been gracious." Unusual.

Ivanna Russian. From John, Hebrew (Yochanan), "God has been gracious." Unusual.

Iverna English. Celtic, meaning unknown. Unusual.

Ivette French. From Ivo, Teutonic, "Yew wood" or "archer." Yew wood was used to make bows. Unusual.

Ivie English. From Ivy, Old English, "ifig"; a plant name used as a first name. Unusual.

Ivona Russian. From Ivo, Teutonic, "Yew wood" or "archer." Yew wood was used to make bows. Unusual.

Ivone Portuguese. From Ivo, Teutonic, "Yew wood" or "archer." Yew wood was used to make bows. Unusual.

Ivorine English. From Ivor, Old Norse, the name of a god. Unusual.

Ivory American. Latin, "ebur"; the word used as a first name. Unusual for males, unusual for females.

Ivria Hebrew/Israeli. Hebrew, "From the other side of the Euphrates River" or "from Abraham's land." Unusual. Alternative spelling: Ivriah.

Ivrit Hebrew/Israeli. From Ivria. Unusual.

Ivy See under Boys' Names.

Iwalani Hawaiian. Hawaiian, "Heavenly sea bird." Unusual.

Iwilla Created. African-American, "I will rise again." Unusual.

Iwona Polish. From Ivo, Teutonic, "Yew wood" or "archer." Yew wood was used to make bows. Unusual.

Iwonka Polish. From Ivo, Teutonic, "Yew wood" or "archer." Yew wood was used to make bows. Unusual.

Iza Polish. From Elizabeth, Hebrew (Elisheva), "Oath of God" or "God is my oath," Exodus 6:23; or from Louis, Old German (Hlutwig), "Famous warrior." Unusual.

Izabel Polish. From Elizabeth, Hebrew (Elisheva), "Oath of God" or "God is my oath." Exodus 6:23. Unusual.

Izabele Russian. From Elizabeth, Hebrew (Elisheva), "Oath of God" or "God is my oath." Exodus 6:23. Unusual.

Izabella Czech, Polish, Russian. From Elizabeth, Hebrew (Elisheva), "Oath of God" or "God is my oath." Exodus 6:23. Unusual.

Izusa Native American. Native American, "White stone." Unusual.

Jacalyn English. From Jacob, Hebrew (Yaakov), "Supplanter" or "heel." Genesis 25:26. Unusual.

Jacey Created. From Jace, Created, possibly from initials "J" and "C." Unusual.

Jacinda Hispanic. From Jacinto, Spanish, "Hyacinth." Unusual.

Jacinta Hispanic. From Jacinto, Spanish, "Hyacinth." Benavente y Martínez (Spanish playwright, won Nobel Prize for literature, 1922). Unusual.

Jackie See under Boys' Names. Alternative spellings: Jacki, Jacky.

Jacklyn English. From Jacob, Hebrew (Yaakov), "Supplanter" or "heel." Genesis 25:26. Unusual. Jackie+. Alternative spellings: Jaclyn, Jaclynn.

Jacobina Scottish. From Jacob, Hebrew (Yaakov), "Supplanter" or "heel." Genesis 25:26. Unusual.

Jacqueline English. From Jacob, Hebrew (Yaakov), "Supplanter" or "heel." Genesis 25:26. Bisset (actress, "Under the Volcano"); Suzanne (author, "Valley of the Dolls"). Popular. Jackie+. Alternative spellings: Jackqueline, Jacquelin, Jacquelyn, Jacquelynn, Jacquline, Jaqueline.

Jacquely English. From Jacob, Hebrew (Yaakov), "Supplanter" or "heel." Genesis 25:26. Unusual. Jackie+. Alternative spelling: Jacqueli.

Jacquelyn English. From Jacob, Hebrew (Yaakov), "Supplanter" or "heel." Genesis 25:26. Mayer (Miss America, 1963). Less popular. Jackie+.

Jacqueta English. From Jacob, Hebrew (Yaakov), "Supplanter" or "heel." Genesis 25:26. Unusual. Alternative spelling: Jacquetta.

Jada Hispanic. From Jade, Spanish, the name of a precious stone. Unusual.

Jade English. Spanish, the name of a precious stone. Unusual for males, unusual for females. Alternative spelling: Jayde.

Jaffa Hebrew/Israeli. From Yaffa, Hebrew, "Beautiful" or "lovely." Unusual.

Jaffice Hebrew/Israeli. From Yaffa, Hebrew, "Beautiful" or "lovely." Unusual.

Jafit Hebrew/Israeli. From Yaffa, Hebrew, "Beautiful" or "lovely." Unusual.

Jaga Polish. From Agnes, Greek, "agnos" ("pure" or "chaste"). Unusual.

Jaime See under Boys' Names.

Jalīla Arabic. Arabic, "Great." Unusual.

Jamelia Arabic. From Jamīl, Arabic, "Handsome." Unusual.

Jamell Arabic. From Jamīl, Arabic, "Handsome." Unusual.

Jamesina English. From Jacob, Hebrew (Yaakov), "Supplanter" or "heel." Genesis 25:26. Unusual.

Jametta Hebrew/Israeli. From Jacob, Hebrew (Yaakov), "Supplanter" or "heel." Genesis 25:26. Unusual.

Jamie English. From Jacob, Hebrew (Yaakov), "Supplanter" or "heel." Genesis 25:26. Less popular for males, very popular for females. Alternative spellings: Jaimee, Jaimi, Jaime, Jaimy, Jamee, Jami, Jammie, Jaymee, Jaymi, Jaymie.

Jamie-Lee English. English, combination of Jamie (Jacob, Hebrew (Yaakov), "Supplanter") + Lee (Old English, "Meadow"). Less popular.

Jamie-Lynn English. English, combination of Jamie (Jacob, Hebrew (Yaakov), "Supplanter") + Linda (Spanish, "Pretty one"). Less popular.

Jamila Arabic. From Jamīl, Arabic, "Handsome." Unusual. Alternative spellings: Jamilah, Jamillah.

Jamille American. From Jacob, Hebrew (Yaakov), "Supplanter" or "heel." Genesis 25:26. Unusual.

Jamillia Arabic. From Jamīl, Arabic, "Handsome." Unusual.

Jan See under Boys' Names.

Jana Czech, English, Latvian, Polish. From John, Hebrew (Yochanan), "God has been gracious." Unusual.

Janae English. From John, Hebrew (Yochanan), "God has been gracious." Unusual. Alternative spellings: Janay, Jenae.

Jandina Hispanic. From Alexander, Greek, "Defender of men" or "warding off men." Mark 16:21; Acts 4:6, 19:33. Unusual.

Jane English. From John, Hebrew (Yochanan), "God has been gracious." Wyman (actress) (real name: Sarah Fulks); Fonda (actress, won 1971 Oscar, "Klute"); Pauley (TV host, "Real Life With Jane Pauley"); Harrison (British scholar); Austen (British novelist, "Pride and Prejudice"). Less popular. Janie+. Alternative spellings: Jaine, Jayne.

Janean English. From John, Hebrew (Yochanan), "God has been gracious." Unusual.

Janella English. From John, Hebrew (Yochanan), "God has been gracious." Unusual. Alternative spelling: Janela.

Janelle English. From John, Hebrew (Yochanan), "God has been gracious." Unusual. Alternative spellings: Janel, Janell, Jannelle.

Janene English. From John, Hebrew (Yochanan), "God has been gracious." Unusual.

Janeska English. From John, Hebrew (Yochanan), "God has been gracious." Unusual.

Janessa English. From John, Hebrew (Yochanan), "God has been gracious." Unusual.

Janet English. From John, Hebrew (Yochanan), "God has been gracious." Jackson (pop singer, sister of Michael); Flanner (journalist, wrote biweekly "Letter from Paris" in "New Yorker" magazine, 1925–75); Leigh (actress); Gaynor (actress, won first "Best Actress" Oscar, 1929, for her roles in three films). Less popular. Jan. Alternative spellings: Jannet, Janyte.

Janeta English. From John, Hebrew (Yochanan), "God has been gracious." Unusual. Alternative spelling: Jenetta.

Janica Czech. From John, Hebrew (Yochanan), "God has been gracious." Unusual.

Janice English. From John, Hebrew (Yochanan), "God has been gracious." Character in Paul Leicester Ford's novel "Janice Meredith." Less popular. Jan. Alternative spellings: Janis, Janise, Jannice.

Janie English. From John, Hebrew (Yochanan), "God has been gracious." Less popular. Alternative spellings: Jaine, Janey, Jany, Jaynie.

Janina English, Latvian, Lithuanian. From John, Hebrew (Yochanan), "God has been gracious." Unusual.

Janine English. From John, Hebrew (Yochanan), "God has been gracious." Aiello (set women's world record for stair-climbing: 1,575 steps of Empire State Building in 13 minutes, 14 seconds, 1985). Unusual.

Janita English. From John, Hebrew (Yochanan), "God has been gracious." Unusual.

Janka Czech. From John, Hebrew (Yochanan), "God has been gracious." Unusual.

Janna English. From John, Hebrew (Yochanan), "God has been gracious." Unusual.

Jannetta English. From John, Hebrew (Yochanan), "God has been gracious." Unusual.

Jannine English. From John, Hebrew (Yochanan), "God has been gracious." Unusual.

Jardena Hebrew/Israeli. From Jordan, Hebrew (Yarden), "To descend." Also the name of a river. Unusual.

Jarita Arabic. Arabic, "Earthen water jug." Unusual.

Jasia Polish. From John, Hebrew (Yochanan), "God has been gracious." Unusual.

Jasmeen English. From Jasmine. Unusual.

Jasmine English. Persian, "yasamin"; a flower name used as a first name. Popular. Alternative spellings: Jasmin, Jazmin, Jazmine.

Jaspreet Indo-Pakistani. From Jaspal, Punjabi, "Virtuous." Unusual.

Jave See under Boys' Names.

Jay See under Boys' Names.

Jaylene English. From Jay, Old French, "Blue jay." Unusual.

Jayme See under Boys' Names.

Jayna English. From John, Hebrew (Yochanan), "God has been gracious." Unusual.

Jaynell English. From John, Hebrew (Yochanan), "God has been gracious." Unusual.

Jean See under Boys' Names.

Jeane English. From John, Hebrew (Yochanan), "God has been gracious." Dixon (self-proclaimed psychic). Unusual.

Jeanetta English. From John, Hebrew (Yochanan), "God has been gracious." Unusual. Alternative spelling: Jeannetta, Jenetta, Jennetta.

Jeanette English. From John, Hebrew (Yochanan), "God has been gracious." La Biancia (youngest opera singer: debuted at age 15 years, 361 days); MacDonald (actress and soprano). Less popular. Alternative spellings: Janette, Jeannette, Jenet, Jennet, Jenette, Jennette.

Jeanna English. From John, Hebrew (Yochanan), "God has been gracious." Unusual. Alternative spelling: Jeana.

Jeanne French. From John, Hebrew (Yochanan), "God has been gracious." Crain (actress); Mance (17th-century French philanthropist). Unusual.

Jeannie English. From John, Hebrew (Yochanan), "God has been gracious." Carson (British actress and entertainer) (real name: Jean Shufflebottom). Unusual. Alternative spellings: Jeani, Jeanie.

Jeannine English. From John, Hebrew (Yochanan), "God has been gracious." Unusual. Alternative spellings: Jeanine, Jennine, Jenine.

Jeays See under Boys' Names.

Jelena Russian. From Helen, Greek, "Bright one" or "shining one." Unusual.

Jem English. From Jacob, Hebrew (Yaakov), "Supplanter" or "heel." Genesis 25:26. Unusual for males, unusual for females.

Jemima English. Hebrew, "Dove." Job 42:14. Daughter of Job; Wilkinson (19th-century religious leader, established colony near Seneca Lake, New York). Unusual.

Jemma English. From Gem, Latin, "gemma" ("bud"); the word used as a first name. Unusual.

Jemmi English. From Jemima. Unusual. Alternative spelling: Jemi.

Jenelle English. From Guinevere, Welsh (Gwenhwyfar), "Fair," "white" + "smooth," "yielding." Unusual.

Jenica Romanian. From John, Hebrew (Yochanan), "God has been gracious." Unusual.

Jenilee English. English, combination of Jennifer (Guinevere, Welsh, "Fair," "white" + "yielding," "smooth") + Lee (Old English, "Meadow"). Unusual.

Jenka Czech. From John, Hebrew (Yochanan), "God has been gracious." Unusual.

Jenn English. From Guinevere, Welsh (Gwenhwyfar), "Fair," "white" + "smooth," "yielding." Unusual. Alternative spelling: Genn.

Jenna English. From Guinevere, Welsh (Gwenhwyfar), "Fair," "white" + "smooth," "yielding." Very popular.

Jennica English. From John, Hebrew (Yochanan), "God has been gracious." Unusual.

Jennifer English. From Guinevere, Welsh (Gwenhwyfar), "Fair," "white" + "smooth," "yielding." Grey (actress, "Dirty Dancing"); O'Neill (actress); Jones (actress) (real name: Phyllis Isley); Cavilleri (character in novel and film "Love Story"). Extremely popular. Jenny+. Alternative spellings: Gennifer, Jenefer, Jenifer, Jeniffer, Jennafer.

Jenny English. From Guinevere, Welsh (Gwenhwyfar), "Fair," "white" + "smooth," "yielding." Lind (Swedish soprano) (real name: Johanna Maria Lind). Less popular. Alternative spellings: Genny, Jenney, Jenni, Jennie, Jeny.

Jensine Danish. From John, Hebrew (Yochanan), "God has been gracious." Unusual.

Jeraldine English. From Gerald, Old German, "Spear" + "ruler." Unusual. Jeri+.

Jereni Russian. From Irene, Greek (Eirene), "Peace." Unusual.

Jerica English. Meaning and origin unknown. Unusual. Alternative spelling: Jerrica.

Jerilyn English. From Gerald, Old German, "Spear" + "ruler." Unusual.

Jermain See Jermane under Boys' Names.

Jermaine See Jermane under Boys' Names.

Jermayne See Jermane under Boys' Names.

Jerri English. From Gerald, Old German, "Spear" + "ruler." Unusual. Alternative spelling: Jeri.

Jerry See under Boys' Names.

Jess English. From Jesse. Willard (heavyweight boxing champion, 1915). Less popular for males, unusual for females.

Jessalyn English. From Jessica. Unusual.

Jessamine English. From Jasmine. Unusual. Alternative spellings: Jessemine, Jessimine.

Jessamy English. From Jasmine. Unusual.

Jessamyn English. From Jasmine. Unusual.

Jesse See under Boys' Names.

Jessenia Arabic. Arabic, "Flower." Unusual.

Jessey See Jesse under Boys' Names.

Jessi English. From Jessica. Less popular.

Jessica English. Hebrew, "He beholds" or "wealthy." Tandy (actress, won Oscar, 1989, for "Driving Miss Daisy"); Lange (actress, won Oscar, 1982, for "Tootsie"); character in Shakespeare's "Merchant of Venice." Extremely popular. Jessie+. Alternative spellings: Jesica, Jesseca, Jessika.

Jessie Scottish. From John, Hebrew (Yochanan), "God has been gracious." Less popular.

Jestina Welsh. From Justin, Latin, "Just." Unusual.

Jesusa Hispanic. From Joshua, Hebrew (Yehoshua), "God is my salvation." Exodus 17:9. Unusual.

Jewel English. Latin, "jocus" ("game"); the word used as a first name. Unusual. Alternative spellings: Jewell, Jewelle.

Jeyes See Jeays under Boys' Names.

Jezebel Hebrew/Israeli. Hebrew, "Chaste," "unmarried." Phoenician princess, wife of Israel's King Ahab; subject of a song by Frankie Laine. Unusual.

Jibon Indo-Pakistani. Hindi, "Life." Unusual.

Jill English. From Julius, Latin, a Roman clan name meaning "downy" or "bearded." Ireland (actress); St. John (actress); Trenary (figure skating world champion, 1990); Eikenberry (actress, "L.A. Law"); Clayburgh (actress). Less popular.

Jillian English. From Julius, Latin, a Roman clan name meaning "downy" or "bearded." Less popular. Jill.

Jilliana English. From Julius, Latin, a Roman clan name meaning "downy" or "bearded." Unusual. Jill.

Jillie English. From Julius, Latin, a Roman clan name meaning "downy" or "bearded." Unusual. Alternative spelling: Jilly.

Jina African. Swahili, "Name." Unusual.

Jindraska Czech. From Henry, Old German (Heimerich), "Home ruler." Unusual.

Jinni English. From John, Hebrew (Yochanan), "God has been gracious." Unusual. Alternative spelling: Jinny.

Jirca Czech. From George, Greek, "Husbandman," "farmer," or "earth-worker." Unusual. Alternative spelling: Jirka.

Jiřina Czech. From George, Greek, "Husbandman," "farmer," or "earth-worker." Unusual.

Jitka Czech. From Judith, Hebrew (Yehudit), "Of Judah," "praised one," or "praise to the Lord." Judith 8:1. Unusual.

Jo See under Boys' Names.

Joan English. From John, Hebrew (Yochanan), "God has been gracious." of Arc (patron saint of France); Collins (actress, "Dynasty"); Crawford (actress, "Possessed"); Rivers (comedian); Baez (folk singer). Less popular. Jo. Alternative spelling: Joann.

Joani English. From John, Hebrew (Yochanan), "God has been gracious." Less popular.

Joanka Polish. From John, Hebrew (Yochanan), "God has been gracious." Unusual.

Joanna English. From John, Hebrew (Yochanan), "God has been gracious." Kerns (actress, "Growing Pains"); Southcott (19th-century British religious fanatic, wrote "Book of Wonders"); Bailli (19th-century British dramatist and poet). Less popular. Jo. Alternative spellings: Jo Anna, Joana, Joannah.

Joanne English. From John, Hebrew (Yochanan), "God has been gracious." Woodward (actress, won 1957 Oscar for "Three Faces of Eve"). Less popular. Jo. Alternative spellings: Joeann, Joeanne.

Joasia Polish. From John, Hebrew (Yochanan), "God has been gracious." Unusual.

Jobi English. From Job, Hebrew, possibly "afflicted" or "persecuted." Book of Job. Unusual.

Jobie See Joby under Boys' Names.

Joby See under Boys' Names.

Jocelyn English. Old German, meaning unknown. Unusual for males, less popular for females. Alternative spellings: Joceline, Jocelyne, Joscelin, Joscelyn, Joselyn, Joselyne.

Joclyn English. From Jocelyn, Old German, meaning unknown. Unusual. Alternative spellings: Josline, Joslyn, Josslyn.

Jodie English. From Judith, Hebrew (Yehudit), "Of Judah," "praised one," or "praise to the Lord." Judith 8:1. Foster (actress, won 1988 Oscar for "The Accused"); Sweetin (actress, "Full House"). Unusual for males, less popular for females. Alternative spellings: Jodi, Jody.

Joel See under Boys' Names.

Joela English. From Joellen, English, combination of Jo (Joseph, Hebrew (Yosef), "Jehovah adds") + Ellen (Helen, Greek, "Bright, shining one"). Unusual for males, unusual for females. Alternative spelling: Joella.

Joëlle French. From Joel, Hebrew, "Jehovah is the Lord." Book of Joel. Unusual.

Joellen English. English, combination of Jo (Joseph, Hebrew (Yosef), "Jehovah adds") + Ellen (Helen, Greek, "Bright, shining one"). Less popular. Jo. Alternative spelling: Joellyn.

Johan See under Boys' Names.

Johana English. From John, Hebrew (Yochanan), "God has been gracious." Unusual for males, unusual for females.

Johanka Czech. From John, Hebrew (Yochanan), "God has been gracious." Unusual.

Johanna Czech, English, German, Hungarian. From John, Hebrew (Yochanan), "God has been gracious." Lind (Swedish soprano) (real name of Jenny Lind); Muzakova (Czech novelist); Ammers Kuler (Dutch author of plays and children's books). Less popular.

Johnie See Johnny under Boys' Names.

Johnna English. From John, Hebrew (Yochanan), "God has been gracious." Unusual.

Johnnie See Johnny under Boys' Names.

Johnny See under Boys' Names.

Joi American. From Joy, Latin, "Joy." Unusual.

Joie French. From Joy, Latin, "Joy." Chitwood (performer in thrill show with motorcycle stunts). Unusual.

Jola Polish. From Yolande, Greek, "ion" ("violet") + "anthos" ("flower"). Unusual.

Jolán Hungarian. From Yolande, Greek, "ion" ("violet") + "anthos" ("flower"). Unusual.

Jolanka Hungarian. From Yolande, Greek, "ion" ("violet") + "anthos" ("flower"). Unusual.

Jolánta Polish. From Yolande, Greek, "ion" ("violet") + "anthos" ("flower"). Unusual.

Jolean English. From Joseph, Hebrew (Yosef), "God will add"; or from Julius, Latin, a Roman clan name meaning "downy" or "bearded." Unusual. Alternative spellings: Jolene, Joleen.

Joli Hungarian. From Yolande, Greek, "ion" ("violet") + "anthos" ("flower"). Unusual.

Jolie English. French, "Pretty." Unusual. Alternative spelling: Joley.

Jolinda English. From Joseph, Hebrew (Yosef), "God will add." Unusual.

Jolly English. From Jolie, French, "Pretty." Unusual for males, unusual for females.

Jolyn English. From Joseph, Hebrew (Yosef), "God will add." Unusual. Alternative spelling: Jolynne.

Jona Hebrew/Israeli. From Jonina. Unusual.

Jonati Hebrew/Israeli. From Jonina. Unusual.

Jonella English. English, combination of John (Hebrew (Yochanan), "God has been gracious") + Ella (Old German, "All" or "entirely"). Unusual.

Jonelle American. From Jonella. Unusual.

Joni English. From John, Hebrew (Yochanan), "God has been gracious." Mitchell (singer and songwriter); Eareckson Tada (quadriplegic artist, author, inspirational speaker). Less popular. Alternative spellings: Jonie, Jony.

Jonina Hebrew/Israeli. Hebrew, "Dove." Unusual.

Jonit Hebrew/Israeli. From Jonina. Unusual.

Jonna English. From John, Hebrew (Yochanan), "God has been gracious." Unusual. Alternative spelling: Johnna.

Jonnie See Johnny under Boys' Names.

Jonny See Johnny under Boys' Names.

Jonquil English. Latin, "juniperus"; a flower name used as a first name. Unusual.

Jora Hebrew/Israeli. Hebrew, "Autumn rain." Unusual. Alternative spelling: Jorah.

Jordan English. Hebrew (Yarden), "To descend." Also the name of a river. Knight (singer, New Kids on the Block). Popular for males, popular for females. Alternative spellings: Jorden, Jordon, Jordyn.

Jordana English. From Jordan, Hebrew (Yarden), "To descend." Also the name of a river. Unusual. Alternative spelling: Jordanna.

Jorgina Hispanic. From George, Greek, "Husbandman," "farmer," or "earthworker." Unusual.

Josalene English. From Jocelyn, Old German, meaning unknown. Unusual. Alternative spellings: Joseline, Josiline.

Josée Hispanic. From Joseph, Hebrew (Yosef), "God will add." Unusual.

Josepha English. From Joseph, Hebrew (Yosef), "God will add." Unusual.

Josephina English. From Joseph, Hebrew (Yosef), "God will add." Unusual. Josie+.

Josephine English. From Joseph, Hebrew (Yosef), "God will add." Tey (British author of detective novels, "Singing Sands") (real name: Elizabeth Mackintosh); Peabody (poet and playwright); Baker (jazz singer and dancer) (real name: Freda Josephine McDonald). Less popular. Josie+. Alternative spelling: Joséphene.

Josette French. From Joseph, Hebrew (Yosef), "God will add." Unusual.

Josie English. From Joseph, Hebrew (Yosef), "God will add." Less popular.

Joy English. Latin, "Joy." Gessner Adamson (British naturalist and writer, "Born Free"). Less popular.

Joya English. From Joy. Unusual.

Joyce English. From Joy, Latin, "Joy." Brothers (psychologist, author, radio and TV personality); DeWitt (actress, "Three's Company"); Cary (British novelist) (real name: Arthur Joyce Lunel); Kilmer (poet, "Trees") (real name: Alfred Joyce Kilmer). Unusual for males, less popular for females.

Joycelyn English. From Joy. Unusual.

Joyita Hispanic. Spanish, "An little jewel." Unusual.

Juana Hispanic. From John, Hebrew (Yochanan), "God has been gracious." Inés de la Cruz (Mexican nun and poet). Unusual.

Juanita Hispanic. From John, Hebrew (Yochanan), "God has been gracious." Kreps (secretary of commerce under Carter). Less popular.

Juci Hungarian. From Judith. Unusual.

Jucika Hungarian. From Judith. Unusual.

Judit Hungarian, Scandinavian. From Judith. Unusual.

Judita Bulgarian. From Judith. Unusual.

Judite Latvian, Portuguese. From Judith. Unusual.

Judith English. Hebrew (Yehudit), "Of Judah," "praised one," or "praise to the Lord." Judith 8:1. Biblical heroine; saint; Anderson (actress); Blegen (opera singer); Anne Ford (Miss America, 1969). Less popular. Judy.

Judithe French. From Judith. Unusual.

Judy English. From Judith. Collins (singer); Garland (actress and singer). Less popular. Alternative spellings: Judi, Judie.

Jula Czech, Polish, Serbian. From Julius, Latin, a Roman clan name meaning "downy" or "bearded." Unusual.

Julca Czech. From Julius, Latin, a Roman clan name meaning "downy" or "bearded." Unusual.

Julcia Polish. From Julius, Latin, a Roman clan name meaning "downy" or "bearded." Unusual.

Julia English. From Julius, Latin, a Roman clan name meaning "downy" or "bearded." Roberts (actress, "Steel Magnolias"); Childs (gourmet cook); Lathrop (socialservice worker); Moore (poet); Peterkin (won Pulitzer Prize for fiction, 1928, "Scarlet Sister Mary"). Popular.

Juliana Czech, English, Hispanic, Serbian. From Julius, Latin, a Roman clan name meaning "downy" or "bearded." Saint, 4th-century martyr, established the Servite nuns; Barnes (15th-century British religious author); queen of the Netherlands. Less popular.

Julianna Hungarian. From Julius, Latin, a Roman clan name meaning "downy" or "bearded." Less popular.

Julianne English. From Julius, Latin, a Roman clan name meaning "downy" or "bearded." Less popular. Alternative spellings: Juliane, Juliann, Julieann, Julieanne.

Julie English. From Julius, Latin, a Roman clan name meaning "downy" or "bearded." Krone (female jockey); Andrews (actress and singer, "Sound of Music") (real name: Julia Wells); Christie (actress, won 1965 Oscar for "Darling"); de Lespinasse (18th-century French hostess of Parisian salons). Popular. Alternative spelling: Juli.

Julienne French. From Julius, Latin, a Roman clan name meaning "downy" or "bearded." Unusual.

Juliet English. From Julius, Latin, a Roman clan name meaning "downy" or "bearded." Capulet (character in Shakespeare's "Romeo and Juliet"); character in Shakespeare's "Measure for Measure"; Prowse (dancer and actress); Corson (educator, established New York Cooking School). Less popular.

Julieta Hispanic. From Julius, Latin, a Roman clan name meaning "downy" or "bearded." Unusual.

Julietta English. From Julius, Latin, a Roman clan name meaning "downy" or "bearded." Unusual.

Juliette French. From Julius, Latin, a Roman clan name meaning "downy" or "bearded." Low (established Girl Scouts, 1912); Adam (French novelist). Unusual.

Julina English. From Julius, Latin, a Roman clan name meaning "downy" or "bearded." Unusual.

Juline English. From Julius, Latin, a Roman clan name meaning "downy" or "bearded." Unusual.

Julinka Hungarian. From Julius, Latin, a Roman clan name meaning "downy" or "bearded." Unusual.

Juliska Czech, Hungarian. From Julius, Latin, a Roman clan name meaning "downy" or "bearded." Unusual.

Julissa English. From Julius, Latin, a Roman clan name meaning "downy" or "bearded." Unusual.

Julita Hispanic. From Julius, Latin, a Roman clan name meaning "downy" or "bearded." Unusual.

Julitta English. From Julius, Latin, a Roman clan name meaning "downy" or "bearded." Saint. Unusual.

Julka Czech. From Julius, Latin, a Roman clan name meaning "downy" or "bearded." Unusual.

July English. From Julius, Latin, a Roman clan name meaning "downy" or "bearded." Unusual.

Jun See under Boys' Names.

June English. Latin, "junius"; the name of a summer month. Lockhart (actress). Less popular.

Junella English. English, combination of June + Ellen (Helen, Greek, "Bright, shining one"). Unusual.

Junita Hispanic. From John, Hebrew (Yochanan), "God has been gracious." Less popular.

Justina English. From Justin, Latin, "Just." Saint. Less popular.

Justine French. From Justin, Latin, "Just."

Title character in Lawrence Durrell's novel, part of his "Alexandria Quartet"; McCarthy (British actress) (real name of Kay Kendall). Less popular.

Jutka Hungarian. From Judith, Hebrew (Yehudit), "Of Judah," "praised one," or "praise to the Lord." Judith 8:1. Unusual.

Jutta German. From John, Hebrew (Yochanan), "God has been gracious." Unusual.

Jyoti Indo-Pakistani. Hindi, "Light." Unusual.

Kaarina Finnish. From Katherine, Greek, "katharos" ("pure"). Unusual.

Kacey See under Boys' Names.

Kachina Native American. Native American, "Sacred dancer." Unusual.

Kaci English. From Casimir, Old Slavic, "He announces [or "commands"] peace." Unusual. Alternative spellings: Kacie, Kacy.

Kady English. From Katherine, Greek, "katharos" ("pure"). Unusual.

Kaela Arabic. From Kalila. Unusual. Alternative spelling: Kaila.

Kaelyn Arabic. From Kalila. Unusual.

Kagami Japanese. Japanese, "Mirror." Unusual.

Kahsha Native American. From Kasa, Native American, "Fur-robe dress." Unusual.

Kai See under Boys' Names.

Kaija Hebrew/Israeli. From Chaim, Hebrew, "Life." Unusual.

Kailey Arabic. From Kalila. Unusual. Alternative spellings: Kaile, Kailee.

Kaitlin English. From Katherine, Greek, "katharos" ("pure"). Unusual. Kate, Katie+. Alternative spellings: Kaitlynn, Katelin, Katelyn, Katelynn.

Kajsa Swedish. From Katherine, Greek, "katharos" ("pure"). Unusual.

Kakaulani Hawaiian. Hawaiian, "Placed in the sky." Unusual.

Kal English. From Caltha, Latin, "Marigold" or "yellow flower." Unusual.

Kalama Hawaiian. Hawaiian, "Flaming torch." Wife of 19th-century Hawaiian King Kamehameha. Unusual.

Kalanit Hebrew/Israeli. Hebrew; a flower name used as a first name. Unusual.

Kalee Arabic. From Kalila. Unusual.

Kaleela Arabic. From Kalila. Unusual.

Kaleena Unknown. Meaning and origin unknown. Unusual.

Kaleenda Indo-Pakistani. From Kalinda, Hindi, "The sun." Also a mythical mountain range. Unusual.

Kaleigh Unknown. From Caltha, Latin, "Marigold" or "yellow flower." Unusual. Alternative spelling: Kaley.

Kalere African. African, "Short woman." Unusual.

Kali Indo-Pakistani. Hindi, "Black goddess" or "time, the destroyer." Another name for the Hindu mother goddess Sakti. Unusual.

Kalica Greek. From Kalyca. Unusual.

Kalie Greek. From Kalyca. Unusual.

Kalila Arabic. Arabic, "Girlfriend" or "sweetheart." Unusual. Alternative spelling: Kalilla.

Kalinda Indo-Pakistani. Hindi, "The sun." Also a mythical mountain range. Unusual.

Kalindi Indo-Pakistani. Hindi, an ancient name for the sacred Jumna River. Unusual.

Kaliska Native American. Native American, "Coyote chasing deer." Unusual.

Kallie English. From Calandra, Greek, "Lark." Unusual. Alternative spellings: Kalli, Kally.

Kalliope Greek. From Calliope, Greek, "Beautiful face." Unusual. Alternative spelling: Calliope.

Kalpana Indo-Pakistani. Hindi, "Imagination." Unusual.

Kaltha English. From Caltha, Latin, "Marigold" or "yellow flower." Unusual. Alternative spelling: Caltha.

Kaluwa African. African, "Forgotten one." The name is given to deter demons from finding the child and doing evil. Unusual.

Kaly English. From Kalyca. Unusual.

Kalyca Greek. Greek, "Rosebud." Unusual.

Kalyn Arabic. From Kalila. Unusual.

Kama Hawaiian, from Thelma, created by novelist Marie Corelli; may be based on Greek, "thelema" ("will"); and Indo-Pakistani, from Kama, Hindi, "Love." The name of a god. Unusual.

Kamali African. Rhodesian, the name of a spirit that protects newborns from sickness. Unusual.

Kamaria African. Swahili, "Like the moon." Unusual.

Kamata Native American. Native American, "Tossing gambling bones." Unusual.

Kameke African. African, "Blind person." This name is given to a child with squinted eyes. Unusual.

Kameko Japanese. Japanese, "Tortoise child." Indicates hope for longevity. Unusual.

Kami Japanese. Japanese, "Divine power" or "aura." Unusual.

Kamila Hungarian, Latvian, Polish. From Camillus, Latin, an attendant at religious services; and Arabic, from Kamāl, Arabic, "Perfect." Unusual.

Kamilka Polish. From Camillus, Latin, an attendant at religious services. Unusual.

Kamillah Arabic. From Kāmil, Arabic, "Perfect." Unusual.

Kanani Hawaiian. Hawaiian, "The beauty." Unusual.

Kanda Native American. From Wakanda, Native American, "Magical power." Unusual.

Kandace English. From Candace, African, a dynastic title used by the queens of Ethiopia. Unusual. Kandi+. Alternative spellings: Candace, Candice, Candis, Candyce, Kandice, Kandis.

Kandi English. From Candace, African, a dynastic title used by the queens of Ethiopia. Unusual. Alternative spelling: Kandy.

Kanene African. African, "A little thing in the eye is big." From a proverb. Unusual.

Kanika African. Kenyan, "Black cloth." Unusual.

Kanoa Hawaiian. Hawaiian, "Free one." Unusual for males, unusual for females.

Kanya Indo-Pakistani. Hindi, "Virgin." Another name for the Hindu goddess Sakti. Unusual.

Kapua Hawaiian. Hawaiian, "Blossom." Unusual.

Kapuki African. African, "First-born daughter." Unusual.

Kara English. From Katherine, Greek, "katharos" ("pure"). Unusual.

Karah Unknown. From Cara, Latin, "Dear." Unusual. Alternative spellings: Cara, Carra.

Karen Danish, English. From Katherine, Greek, "katharos" ("pure"). Valentine (actress); Silkwood (found contamination of radioactive material at workplace); Dinesen (Danish author, "Out of Africa") (real name of Isak Dinesen); Horney (psychoanalyst and teacher); Black (actress). Popular.

Karena Norwegian. From Katherine, Greek, "katharos" ("pure"). Unusual.

Karenza English. From Kerensa, Cornish, "Love," "affection." Unusual.

Karida Arabic. From Karida, Arabic, "Untouched" or "virginal." Unusual.

Kari English. From Charles, Old English, "ceorl" ("man" or "husbandman"). Unusual. Alternative spellings: Carie, Carri, Carrie, Karee, Karey, Karie, Karri, Karrie, Karry, Kary.

Karin Scandinavian. From Katherine, Greek, "katharos" ("pure"). Kania (German, won record five world overall speed-skating titles); Michaelis (Danish novelist); Boye (Swedish poet). Unusual.

Karina English, Latvian, Russian. From Katherine, Greek, "katharos" ("pure"). Unusual.

Karine Russian. From Katherine, Greek, "katharos" ("pure"). Unusual.

Karissa English. Meaning and origin unknown. Unusual.

Karla Czech, English, German. From Charles, Old English, "ceorl" ("man" or "husbandman"). Less popular.

Karlene Latvian. From Charles, Old English, "ceorl" ("man" or "husbandman"). Unusual.

Karli English. From Charles, Old English, "ceorl" ("man" or "husbandman"). Unusual. Alternative spellings: Carlee, Carley, Carli, Carlie, Carly, Karlee, Karley, Karlie, Karly.

Karlicka Czech. From Charles, Old English, "ceorl" ("man" or "husbandman"). Unusual.

Karlinka Czech. From Charles, Old English, "ceorl" ("man" or "husbandman"). Unusual.

Karlotta Greek. From Charles, Old English, "ceorl" ("man" or "husbandman"). Unusual.

Karma Indo-Pakistani. Hindi, "Action," "fate," or "destiny." Unusual.

Karmen English. From Carmel, Hebrew, "Garden." Unusual.

Karmina English. From Carmel, Hebrew, "Garden." Unusual. Alternative spelling: Carmina.

Karmine English. From Carmel, Hebrew, "Garden." Unusual.

Karmita English. From Carmel, Hebrew, "Garden." Unusual.

Karniella Hebrew/Israeli. From Carna, Hebrew, "Horn." Unusual. Alternative spellings: Carniella, Karniela.

Karnis Hebrew/Israeli. From Carna, Hebrew, "Horn." Unusual. Alternative spelling: Carnis.

Karnit Hebrew/Israeli. From Carna, Hebrew, "Horn." Unusual. Alternative spelling: Carnit.

Karola Czech. From Charles, Old English, "ceorl" ("man" or "husbandman"). Unusual.

Karolina Czech, Polish. From Charles, Old English, "ceorl" ("man" or "husbandman"). Muzakova (Czech novelist). Unusual.

Karoline German. From Charles, Old English, "ceorl" ("man" or "husbandman"). Mikkelsen (first woman to set foot in Antarctica, 1935); Pichler (Austrian novelist); Wolzogen (German novelist, published anonymously). Unusual.

Karolinka Polish. From Charles, Old English, "ceorl" ("man" or "husbandman"). Unusual.

Karolyn English. From Charles, Old English, "ceorl" ("man" or "husbandman"). Unusual. Alternative spellings: Carolyn, Carolin, Carolynn, Carolynne.

Karuna Indo-Pakistani. Hindi, "Compassion." Unusual.

Karyna Russian. From Katherine. Unusual.

Kasa Native American. Native American, "Fur-robe dress." Unusual.

Kasandra English. From Alexander, Greek, "Defender of men" or "warding off men." Mark 16:21; Acts 4:6, 19:33. Unusual.

Kasey See Kacey under Boys' Names.

Kasha Native American. From Kasa. Unusual.

Kasi Indo-Pakistani. Hindi, "From the holy city." Unusual.

Kasia Polish. From Katherine. Unusual.

Kasie English. From Casimir, Old Slavic, "He announces [or "commands"] peace." Unusual.

Kasienka Polish. From Katherine. Unusual.

Kasin Polish. From Katherine. Unusual.

Kasinda African. African, "Burrowing animal in front of blocked passage." Used for a child born after twins. Unusual.

Kaska Polish. From Katherine. Unusual.

Kassandra Greek. From Alexander, Greek, "Defender of men" or "warding off men." Mark 16:21; Acts 4:6, 19:33. Unusual. Alternative spellings: Casandra, Casandera, Cassandra.

Kassia Polish. From Katherine. Unusual.

Kassidy English. From Cassidy, Gaelic, "Clever." Unusual. Alternative spellings: Cassidy.

Kassie English. From Alexander, Greek, "Defender of men" or "warding off men." Mark 16:21; Acts 4:6, 19:33. Unusual. Alternative spellings: Cassey, Kassi.

Kata Czech, Hungarian. From Katherine. Unusual.

Katarina Czech. From Katherine. Witt (German, won Olympic gold medal for figure skating, 1988). Unusual.

Katchen German. From Katherine. Unusual.

Kate English. From Katherine. Capshaw (actress); Wiggin (novelist. Less popular.

Kateke African. African, "We used to eat from dishes; now we eat from wooden bowls." A name from a proverb that refers to someone who has worn out his welcome. Unusual.

Katenka Russian. From Katherine. Unusual.

Kateřina Czech. From Katherine. Unusual.

Katerini Greek. From Katherine. Unusual.

Katerinka Russian. From Katherine. Unusual.

Katharaine English. From Katherine. Unusual. Kate, Katie+, Kathy+.

Katharina Estonian, German. From Katherine. von Bora (German Cistercian nun, married Martin Luther, 1525); Klafsky (19th-century principal star of Hamburg Opera). Unusual.

Kathereen English. From Katherine. Unusual. Kate, Katie+, Kathy+.

Katherina English. From Katherine. Unusual. Kate, Katie+, Kathy+.

Katherine English. Greek, "katharos" ("pure"). Mansfield (British novelist) (real name: Kathleen Beauchamp); Philips (British poet); Ann Porter (author, "Ship of Fools"); Blodgett (physicist and chemist, invented non-reflecting glass); Chopin (author on Creole and Cajun life). Very popular. Kate, Katie+, Kathy+. Alternative spellings: Catharin, Catharine, Catherin, Catherine, Catheryn, Cathrene, Cathrine, Cathryn, Katharin, Katharine, Katharyn, Katherin, Katheryn, Katheryne, Kathren, Kathrine, Kathryn, Kathryne, Kathyrine.

Kathleen English. From Katherine. Battle (coloratura soprano); Turner (actress, "Body Heat"); Sullivan (TV news reporter); Norris (novelist, "Through a Glass Darkly"); Ferrier (British contralto opera singer); Beauchamp (British author) (real name of Katherine Mansfield). Popular. Kate, Katie+, Kathy+. Alternative spellings: Cathleen, Cathaleen, Katheleen, Kathelene, Kathileen.

Kathlyn English. From Katherine, Greek, "katharos" ("pure"). Unusual. Kate, Katie+, Kathy+. Alternative spelling: Kathlynn.

Kathy English. From Katherine. Bates (actress, won 1990 Oscar for "Misery"). Less popular. Alternative spellings: Cathi, Cathie, Cathy, Kathe, Kathi, Kathie.

Kati English, Estonian. From Katherine. Unusual.

Katia English. From Katherine. Unusual.

Katica Czech. From Katherine. Unusual.

Katie English. From Katherine. Very popular. Alternative spellings: Katey, Katy.

Katina Greek. From Katherine. Unusual.

Katinka Hungarian, Russian. From Katherine. Unusual.

Katka Russian. From Katherine. Unusual.

Katla Norwegian. From Katherine. Unusual.

Katleen English. From Katherine. Unusual. Kate, Katie+.

Katlin English. From Katherine. Unusual. Kate, Katie+. Alternative spelling: Katlyn.

Kató Hungarian. From Katherine. Komei (Japanese ambassador to London, 1894–99). Unusual.

Katoka Hungarian. From Katherine. Unusual.

Katrin Icelandic. From Katherine. Meissner (German swimmer, won 1988 Olympic gold medal in the 400-meter freestyle). Unusual.

Katrina German. From Katherine. Less popular.

Katrine English. From Katherine. Unusual. Kate, Katie+.

Katriona English. From Katherine, Greek, "katharos" ("pure"). Unusual.

Katryna Russian. From Katherine. Unusual.

Kattrina English. From Katherine. Unusual. Kate, Katie+. Alternative spelling: Katrena.

Katura African. Rhodesian, "I feel relieved." Unusual.

Katus Hungarian. From Katherine. Unusual.

Katuska Czech. From Katherine. Unusual.

Katya Russian. From Katherine. Unusual.

Kaula Hawaiian. Hawaiian, "Prophet." Unusual.

Kaulana Hawaiian. Hawaiian, "Famous one." Unusual.

Kaveri Indo-Pakistani. Hindi, the name of a sacred river. Unusual.

Kavindra Indo-Pakistani. Hindi, "Mighty poet." Unusual.

Kay English. From Katherine, Greek, "katharos" ("pure"). Kendall (British actress) (real name: Justine McCarthy); Boyle (novelist and short-story writer). Less popular. Alternative spelling: Kaye.

Kaya Native American. Native American, "My older little sister." Implies that the child is wise. Unusual.

Kaycee English. From Casimir, Old Slavic, "He announces [or "commands"] peace." Unusual.

Kayla English. From Katherine, Greek, "katharos" ("pure"). Very popular. Alternative spelling: Cayla.

Kayle Yiddish. From Kalila, Arabic, "Girlfriend" or "sweetheart." Unusual for males, unusual for females.

Kayleen Arabic. From Kalila, Arabic, "Girlfriend" or "sweetheart." Unusual. Alternative spelling: Kaylene.

Kaylene Arabic. From Kalila, Arabic, "Girlfriend" or "sweetheart." Unusual. Alternative spelling: Kayleen.

Kayley Arabic. From Kalila, Arabic, "Girlfriend" or "sweetheart." Unusual. Alternative spellings: Kaylee, Kayleigh, Kaylie.

Kaylil Arabic. From Kalila, Arabic, "Girlfriend" or "sweetheart." Unusual.

Kaylin Arabic. From Kalila, Arabic, "Girlfriend" or "sweetheart." Unusual. Alternative spelling: Kaylyn.

Kealey English. From Kelly, Gaelic (Ceallach), "A warrior." Surname used as a first name. Unusual. Alternative spellings: Kealy, Keeley, Keelie, Keellie, Keely, Keighley, Keiley, Keilly, Keily.

Keahi See under Boys' Names.

Keara Irish. From Kieran, Irish (Ciaran), "Dark" or "black." Unusual. Alternative spellings: Keira, Kiara, Kiera, Kierra.

Keena Unknown. Meaning and origin unknown. Unusual.

Keesha Created. From Lakeisha, Created, African-American. Unusual. Alternative spellings: Kecia, Keisha, Keshia, Keysha, Kiesha.

Kei Japanese. Japanese, "Rapture" or "reverence." Hara (Japanese prime minister, 1918–21). Unusual.

Keita English. From Keith, Scottish, "Wood" or "enclosed place." A Scottish place name and clan name. Unusual.

Kekona Hawaiian. Hawaiian, "Second-born child." Unusual.

Kelci English. From Kelsey, English, surname and place name used as a first name. Original meaning is possibly "Ceol's island." Unusual. Alternative spelling: Kelcie.

Kelda English, Scandinavian. Old Norse, "Fountain" or "spring." Unusual.

Kelday English. An Orkney Islands surname; origin unknown. Unusual.

Kelia English. From Kelly, Gaelic (Ceallach), "A warrior." Surname used as a first name. Unusual.

Kelila Arabic. From Kalila, Arabic, "Girlfriend" or "sweetheart." Unusual. Alternative spelling: Kelilah.

Kellia English. From Kelly, Gaelic (Ceallach), "A warrior." Surname used as a first name. Unusual.

Kellina English. From Kelly, Gaelic (Ceallach), "A warrior." Surname used as a first name. Unusual.

Kellisa English. From Kelly, Gaelic (Ceallach), "A warrior." Surname used as a first name. Unusual.

Kelly English. Gaelic (Ceallach), "A warrior." Surname used as a first name. Less popular for males, popular for females.

Alternative spellings: Keli, Kelie, Kelley, Kelli, Kellie, Kellye.

Kelly-Ann English. English, combination of Kelly (Gaelic, "A warrior") + Ann (Hannah, Hebrew (Chanah), "Grace" or "favor"). Unusual.

Kellyn English. English, combination of Kelly (Gaelic, "A warrior") + Lynn (Linda, Spanish, "Pretty one"). Unusual.

Kelsa English. From Kelsey, English, surname and place name used as a first name. Original meaning is possibly "Ceol's island." Unusual.

Kelsea English. From Kelsey, English, surname and place name used as a first name. Original meaning is possibly "Ceol's island." Unusual.

Kelsey English. English, surname and place name used as a first name. Original meaning is possibly "Ceol's island." Less popular for males, popular for females. Alternative spellings: Kelsi, Kelsie, Kelsy.

Kelula Yiddish. From Kalila, Arabic, "Girlfriend" or "sweetheart." Unusual.

Kenda American. "From the clear, cool water," origin unknown; and Native American, from Wakanda, Native American, "Magical power." Unusual.

Kendal See Kendall under Boys' Names.

Kendall See under Boys' Names.

Kendi English. From Kenda. Unusual. Alternative spellings: Kendie, Kendy, Kenndi, Kenndie, Kenndy.

Kendra English. English, combination of Kenneth (Gaelic, "Fair one" + "fire-sprung") and Sandra (Alexander, Greek, "Defender of men"). Popular.

Kenenza English. From Kenneth, Gaelic, "Fair one" + "fire-sprung." Unusual.

Kenia English. From Kenneth, Gaelic, "Fair one" + "fire-sprung." Unusual.

Kenna English. From Kenneth, Gaelic, "Fair one" + "fire-sprung." Unusual. Alternative spelling: Kena.

Kennda English. From Kenda. Unusual.

Kennice English. From Kenneth, Gaelic, "Fair one" + "fire-sprung." Unusual.

Kennie See Kenny under Boys' Names.

Kenya Hebrew/Israeli. Hebrew, "Animal horn." Unusual.

Kenza English. From Kenneth, Gaelic, "Fair one" + "fire-sprung." Unusual.

Kenzie English. From Mackenzie, Gaelic, "Son of the wise leader." Surname used as a first name. Unusual.

Kera Indo-Pakistani. From Kerani. Unusual.

Kerani Indo-Pakistani. Sanskrit, "Sacred bells." Unusual.

Keren English. From Kerenhappuch. Unusual.

Kerenhappuch Hebrew/Israeli. Hebrew, "Horn of antimony." In Biblical times, antimony was used as an eyelash dye to beautify the wearer. Job 42:14. Third daughter of Job. Unusual.

Kerensa English. Cornish, "Love," "affection." Character in Victoria Holt's "Legend of the Seventh Virgin." Unusual.

Keri English. From Kerry, Irish, "The place of Ciar's people"; also the name of a county. Unusual. Alternative spellings: Keree, Kerrey, Kerri, Kerrie, Kerry.

Kerri-Ann English. From Kerry-Ann, English, combination of Kerry (Irish, "The place of Ciar's people") + Ann (Hannah, Hebrew (Chanah), "Grace" or "favor"). Unusual. Alternative spellings: Karrianne, Kerry-Ann.

Kerry-Anne Irish. From Kerry-Ann. Unusual.

Kersten Swedish. From Christian, Greek, "christos" ("anointed"). Unusual.

Kery Indo-Pakistani. From Kerani, Sanskrit, "Sacred bells." Unusual. Alternative spelling: Kerie.

Kesava Indo-Pakistani. Hindi, "Abundance of fine hair." Another name for the Hindu god Vishnu. Unusual.

Kesi African. From Kesi, Swahili, "She was born when her father was in trouble." Unusual.

Kessie African. From Kesse, Ghanaian, "Born fat." Unusual.

Keturah Hebrew/Israeli. Hebrew, "Incense." Genesis 25:1. Second wife of Abraham. Unusual.

Ketzi Hebrew/Israeli. From Ketzia. Unusual.

Ketzia Hebrew/Israeli. Hebrew, "Cinnamon-like bark." Unusual.

Keva English. From Kevin, Irish, "Handsome." Unusual.

Kezi Hebrew/Israeli. From Ketzia. Unusual.

Kezia Hebrew/Israeli. From Ketzia. Daughter of Job. Unusual.

Keziah Hebrew/Israeli. From Ketzia. Wesley (sister of 18th-century religious leader John). Unusual.

Khadījah Arabic. Arabic, "Trustworthy." First wife of the prophet Muhammed. Unusual.

Khristina Russian. From Christian, Greek, "christos" ("anointed"). Unusual.

Khristya Russian. From Christian, Greek, "christos" ("anointed"). Unusual.

Kia American. From Hannah, Hebrew (Chanah), "Grace [of God]" or "favor." 1 Samuel 1:2. Unusual.

Kiana American. From Hannah, Hebrew (Chanah), "Grace [of God]" or "favor." 1 Samuel 1:2. Unusual.

Kichi Japanese. Japanese, "Fortunate." Unusual.

Kiele Hawaiian. Hawaiian, "Gardenia" or "fragrant blossom." Unusual. Alternative spellings: Kieley, Kieli.

Kiersten English. From Christian, Greek, "christos" ("anointed"). Unusual. Alternative spelling: Keirstan.

Kika Hispanic. From Henry, Old German (Heimerich), "Home ruler." Unusual.

Kikilia Hawaiian. From Cecil, Latin, "Blind." Unusual.

Kiku Japanese. Japanese, "Chrysanthemum." Unusual.

Kim English. From Kimberley, Old English, "From the royal-fortress meadow." Title character in Rudyard Kipling's novel; Novak (actress, "Vertigo"); Basinger (actress, "Batman"). Less popular for males, less popular for females.

Kim Marie English. English, combination of Kim (Kimberley, Old English, "From the royal-fortress meadow") + Marie (Miriam, Hebrew (Miryam), "Bitterness," "rebellion," "wished-for child," or "sea" (?)). Unusual.

Kimama Native American. Native American, "Butterfly." Unusual.

Kimarie English. From Kim Marie. Unusual.

Kimba English. From Kimberley, Old English, "From the royal-fortress meadow." Unusual.

Kimba Lee English. From Kimberley, Old English, "From the royal-fortress meadow." Unusual.

Kimbely English. From Kimberley, Old English, "From the royal-fortress meadow." Unusual.

Kimber English. From Kimberley, Old English, "From the royal-fortress meadow." Unusual.

Kimberlea English. From Kimberley, Old English, "From the royal-fortress meadow." Unusual. Kim.

Kimberly English. From Kimberley, Old English, "From the royal-fortress meadow." Unusual for males, unusual for females. Kim. Alternative spellings: Kimbereley, Kimberely, Kimberlee, Kimberlei, Kimberli, Kimberlie, Kimberley, Kymberly.
Kimberlyn English. From Kimberley, Old English, "From the royal-fortress meadow." Unusual. Kim.
Kimbley English. From Kimberley, Old English, "From the royal-fortress meadow." Unusual.
Kimette English. From Kimberley, Old English, "From the royal-fortress meadow." Unusual.
Kimi Japanese. Japanese, "Peerless" or "sovereign." Unusual. Alternative spelling: Kimie.
Kimiko Japanese. From Kimi. Unusual.
Kimiyo Japanese. From Kimi. Unusual.
Kimmi English. From Kimberley, Old English, "From the royal-fortress meadow." Unusual. Alternative spellings: Kimmie, Kimmy.
Kindra English. From Kendra, English, combination of Kenneth (Gaelic, "Fair one" + "fire-sprung") and Sandra (Alexander, Greek, "Defender of men"). Unusual.
Kini Hawaiian. From John, Hebrew (Yochanan), "God has been gracious." Unusual.
Kinsey English. From Kinsey, Old English, "Offspring" or "relative." Unusual.
Kira Bulgarian. From Cyrus, Latin, "Throne." Unusual.
Kiran Irish. From Kieran, Irish (Ciaran), "Dark" or "black." Unusual.
Kirby See under Boys' Names.
Kirima Eskimo. Eskimo, "Hill." Unusual.
Kirsi Indo-Pakistani. Hindi, "Flowering amaranth." Unusual.
Kirsta English. From Christian, Greek, "christos" ("anointed"). Unusual.
Kirsten Scandinavian. From Christian, Greek, "christos" ("anointed"). Flagstad (Norwegian operatic soprano). Less popular.
Kirstie English. From Christian, Greek, "christos" ("anointed"). Alley (actress, "Cheers"). Less popular. Alternative spellings: Kersti, Kerstie, Kirsti, Kirsty, Kyrsty.
Kirstin English. From Christian, Greek, "christos" ("anointed"). Less popular. Alternative spellings: Kirstien, Kirston, Kirstyn.
Kirstine English. From Christian, Greek, "christos" ("anointed"). Less popular. Alternative spellings: Kerstine, Kirsteen.
Kisa Russian. Russian, "Kitten." Unusual.
Kisha Created. From Lakeisha, Created, African-American. Unusual.
Kishanda Created. From Lakeisha, Created, African-American. Unusual.
Kishi Japanese. Japanese, "Beach." Implies longevity. Unusual.
Kiska Russian. From Katherine, Greek, "katharos" ("pure"). Unusual.
Kismet American. "Fate" or "destiny"; origin unknown. Unusual.
Kissa African. Ugandan, "Born after twins." Unusual.
Kissie Hebrew/Israeli. From Ketzia, Hebrew, "Cinnamon-like bark." Unusual.
Kita Japanese. Japanese, "North." Unusual.
Kitteen English. From Katherine, Greek, "katharos" ("pure"). Unusual.
Kitty English. From Katherine, Greek, "katharos" ("pure"). O'Neil (dived a record 180 feet from a helicopter onto an air cushion, 1979); Carruthers (pairs figure skater); Carlisle (singer and actress); Bowe Hearty (magazine photo essayist). Less popular. Alternative spellings: Kitti, Kittie.
Kiwa Japanese. Japanese, "Born on a border." Unusual.
Kizzy American. From Ketzia, Hebrew, "Cinnamon-like bark." Character in Alex Haley's "Roots." Unusual. Alternative spelling: Kizzie.
Klara Bulgarian, Czech, Polish, Russian, Swedish. From Clara, Latin, "clarus" ("clear"). Unusual.
Klarika Hungarian. From Clara, Latin, "clarus" ("clear"). Unusual.
Klarissa German. From Clara, Latin, "clarus" ("clear"). Unusual. Alternative spelling: Clarissa.
Koffi African. African, "Born on Friday." Unusual.
Kofryna Lithuanian. From Katherine, Greek, "katharos" ("pure"). Unusual.
Koko Japanese. Japanese, "Stork." Unusual.
Kolenya Native American. Native American, "To cough." Unusual.
Kolina Swedish. From Katherine, Greek, "katharos" ("pure"). Unusual.
Kona Indo-Pakistani. Hindi, "Angular." Another name for the Hindu god Saturn. Unusual.
Konstantin Russian. From Constance, Latin, "constans" ("constant" or "unwavering"). Stanislavsky (actor, cofounder and director of Moscow Art Theater). Unusual.
Konstanze German. From Constance, Latin, "constans" ("constant" or "unwavering"). Unusual.
Kora English. From Cora, Greek, "Maiden." Unusual. Alternative spelling: Cora.
Koreen English. From Cora, Greek, "Maiden." Unusual.
Koren English. From Cora, Greek, "Maiden." Unusual.
Kori English. From Cora, Greek, "Maiden." Unusual. Alternative spellings: Korie, Korri, Korrie, Korry, Kory.
Korina English. From Cora, Greek, "Maiden." Unusual. Alternative spelling: Korrina.
Kornelia German. From Cornelius, Latin, "A horn." Acts 10:1. Ender (German, won record 10 medals in world swimming championships, 1973–75). Unusual.
Kornelis Swedish. From Cornelius, Latin, "A horn." Acts 10:1. Unusual.
Kosoko African. Nigerian, "There is no hoe to dig a grave." An African born-to-die name given to drive away evil spirits. Unusual.
Kosta Greek. From Constance, Latin, "constans" ("constant" or "unwavering"). Unusual.
Kostatina Greek. From Constance, Latin, "constans" ("constant" or "unwavering"). Unusual.
Kostenka Russian. From Constance, Latin, "constans" ("constant" or "unwavering"). Unusual.
Kostya Russian. From Constance, Latin, "constans" ("constant" or "unwavering"). Unusual.
Kostyusha Russian. From Constance, Latin, "constans" ("constant" or "unwavering"). Unusual.
Kotik Russian. From Constance, Latin, "constans" ("constant" or "unwavering"). Unusual.
Kotinka Russian. From Katherine, Greek, "katharos" ("pure"). Unusual.
Koto Japanese. Japanese, "Harp." Unusual.

Kourtney English. From Courtney, Old French, "One who lives at the court or on the farm." Unusual. Alternative spellings: Courteney, Courtnie, Courtney, Kortney.

Kris See under Boys' Names.

Kriska Hungarian. From Christian, Greek, "christos" ("anointed"). Unusual.

Krissi English. From Christian, Greek, "christos" ("anointed"). Unusual. Alternative spellings: Chrissie, Chrissy, Crissey, Crissie, Crissy, Krissie, Krissy.

Krista Czech, English, Estonian, Latvian. From Christian, Greek, "christos" ("anointed"). Popular.

Kristan Danish. From Christian, Greek, "christos" ("anointed"). Unusual.

Kristen English. From Christian, Greek, "christos" ("anointed"). Kold (19th-century Danish educator, established basic pattern for the residential high school). Popular. Kris+, Krissy+. Alternative spellings: Christen, Christin, Cristen, Kristyn, Krysten, Krystin.

Kristi English. From Christian, Greek, "christos" ("anointed"). Zea (movie production designer). Less popular. Alternative spellings: Christi, Christie, Christy, Kristie, Kristy, Krysti.

Kristia Finnish. From Christian, Greek, "christos" ("anointed"). Unusual.

Kristin Scandinavian. From Christian, Greek, "christos" ("anointed"). Popular.

Kristina Swedish. From Christian, Greek, "christos" ("anointed"). Popular.

Kristine Latvian, Norwegian. From Christian, Greek, "christos" ("anointed"). Less popular.

Kristinka Czech. From Christian, Greek, "christos" ("anointed"). Unusual.

Krysia Polish. From Christian, Greek, "christos" ("anointed"). Unusual.

Krysta Polish. From Christian, Greek, "christos" ("anointed"). Unusual.

Krystal English. From Christopher, Greek, "One who carries Christ in his heart." Popular. Kris+, Krissy+. Alternative spellings: Christal, Chrystal, Cristal, Cristel, Crystal, Crystle, Kristel, Kristal, Krystel, Krystle.

Krystina Czech. From Christian, Greek, "christos" ("anointed"). Unusual.

Krystka Polish. From Christian, Greek, "christos" ("anointed"). Unusual.

Krystyna Polish. From Christian, Greek, "christos" ("anointed"). Unusual.

Krystynka Polish. From Christian, Greek, "christos" ("anointed"). Unusual.

Kuai Hua Chinese. Chinese, "Mallow blossom." Unusual.

Kubik Czech. From Jacob, Hebrew (Yaakov), "Supplanter" or "heel." Genesis 25:26. Unusual.

Kudio African. African, "Born on Monday." Unusual.

Kulya Native American. Native American, "Burnt sugar-pine nuts." Unusual.

Kuma Japanese. Japanese, "Bear." Unusual.

Kumi Japanese. Japanese, "Braid." Unusual.

Kumuda Indo-Pakistani. Sanskrit, "Lotus." Unusual.

Kuni Japanese. Japanese, "Born in the country." Unusual.

Kuniko Japanese. From Kuni. Unusual.

Kuri Japanese. Japanese, "Chestnut." Unusual.

Kusa Indo-Pakistani. Hindi, a sacred grass believed to provide protection against evil and purification for sins. Unusual.

Kutattoa Native American. Native American, "Bear scattering garbage." Unusual.

Kutcuyak Native American. Native American, "Bear with good hair." Unusual.

Květa Czech. From Flora, Latin, "Flower." Unusual.

Květka Czech. From Flora, Latin, "Flower." Unusual.

Kwabina African. African, "Born on Tuesday." Unusual.

Kwako See under Boys' Names.

Kwaku See under Boys' Names.

Kwamin See under Boys' Names.

Kwanita Native American. From John, Hebrew (Yochanan), "God has been gracious." Unusual.

Kwashi African. African, "Born on Sunday." Unusual.

Kwau African. African, "Born on Thursday." Unusual.

Kye Australian. From Kylie. Unusual.

Kyla Yiddish. From Kalila, Arabic, "Girlfriend" or "sweetheart." Unusual.

Kyle See under Boys' Names.

Kylene Australian. From Kylie. Baker (Miss America, 1979). Unusual.

Kylie Australian. Australian Aboriginal, "Curled stick" or "boomerang." Minogue (pop music singer). Unusual. Alternative spellings: Kylee, Kyleigh.

Kym English. From Kimberley, Old English, "From the royal-fortress meadow." Coberly (set hula-hoop record: 72 hours without a drop). Unusual. Alternative spelling: Kim.

Kyra English. From Cyril, Greek, "Lord" or "ruler." Unusual.

Kyrie Irish. From Kieran, Irish (Ciaran), "Dark" or "black." Unusual.

La Verne English. From Laverne, French, "Like spring." Noyes (invented the wire dictionary holder). Unusual.

Labrenda Created. From Labrenda, Created, African-American. Unusual.

Lacara Created. Created, African-American. Unusual.

Lacey English. French, surname and place name used as a first name. Unusual. Alternative spellings: Lacee, Laci, Lacie, Lacy.

Lachana Created. Created, African-American. Unusual.

Lachelle Created. Created, African-American. Unusual.

Lachina Created. Created, African-American. Unusual.

Lachlanina Scottish. From Lachlann, Gaelic, "Fjord-land." Unusual.

Lachonda Created. Created, African-American. Unusual.

Lachresa Created. Created, African-American. Unusual.

Lacole Created. Created, African-American. Unusual.

Lacrecia Created. Created, African-American. Unusual.

Lacyndora Created. Created, African-American. Unusual.

Ladaisha Created. Created, African-American. Unusual.

Ladawn Created. Created, African-American. Unusual.

Ladiva Created. Created, African-American. Unusual.
Ladonna Created. Created, African-American. Less popular.
Ladonne Created. From Ladonna. Unusual. Alternative spelling: Ladon.
Ladonya Created. From Ladonna. Unusual.
Lady English. Old English, "hloefdige" ("kneader of bread"); a title used as a first name. Kier (pop singer). Unusual.
Laetitia English. From Letitia, Latin, "Gladness." Unusual.
Lafondra Created. Created, African-American. Unusual.
Lahela Hawaiian. From Rachel, Hebrew, "Ewe" or "lamb." Genesis 29:16. Unusual.
Laine English. From Helen, Greek, "Bright one" or "shining one." Unusual. Alternative spelling: Lane.
Lajessica Created. Created, African-American. Unusual.
Lajoia Created. Created, African-American. Unusual.
Lajuliette Created. Created, African-American. Unusual.
Laka Hawaiian. Hawaiian, "Attract" or "tame." Unusual.
Lakaiya Created. Created, African-American. Unusual.
Lakea Created. Created, African-American. Unusual. Alternative spelling: Lakia.
Lakedia Created. Created, African-American. Unusual.
Lakeesh Created. From Lakeisha. Unusual.
Lakeisha Created. Created, African-American. Unusual. Alternative spellings: Lakecia, Lakesha, Lakesia, Lakeysha, Lakiesha.
Laken Created. Created, African-American. Unusual.
Lakendra Created. Created, African-American. Unusual.
Lakendria Created. Created, African-American. Unusual.
Lakenya Created. Created, African-American. Unusual.
Lakeshia Created. From Lakeisha. Unusual. Alternative spelling: Lakeyshia.
Lakila Created. Created, African-American. Unusual.
Lakisha Created. From Lakeisha. Unusual.
Lakita Created. Created, African-American. Unusual.
Lakiya Created. Created, African-American. Unusual.
Lakresha Created. Created, African-American. Unusual. Alternative spelling: Lakrisha.
Lakshana Created. Created, African-American. Unusual.
Lakya Indo-Pakistani. Hindu, "Born on Thursday." Unusual.
Lala Slavic. Slavic, "Tulip." Lajpat Rai (Indian writer and politician, leader of the Hindu supremacy movement). Unusual.
Lalage English. Greek, "To babble" or "to prattle." Character in John Fowles' novel "The French Lieutenant's Woman." Unusual.
Lalisa Created. Created, African-American. Unusual.
Lalita Indo-Pakistani. Hindi, "Charming." Another name for the Hindu goddess Sakti. Unusual.
Lallie English. From Lalage, Greek, "To babble" or "to prattle." Unusual. Alternative spelling: Lally.
Lameeka Created. Created, African-American. Unusual.
Lamonica Created. Created, African-American. Unusual.
Lana English. From Alan, Gaelic, meaning uncertain, but may include "rock," "noble," "handsome," "harmony," and/or "cheerful." Turner (actress). Unusual.
Lanata Created. Created, African-American. Unusual.
Laneetra Created. Created, African-American. Unusual.
Laneisha Created. Created, African-American. Unusual. Alternative spelling: Lanecia.
Lanetta Created. Created, African-American. Unusual.
Lanette Created. Created, African-American. Unusual.
Lani See under Boys' Names.
Laniece Created. Created, African-American. Unusual.
Lanisha Created. Created, African-American. Unusual.
Lanora Created. Created, African-American. Unusual.
Lapaula Created. Created, African-American. Unusual.
Laqualia Created. Created, African-American. Unusual.
Laquanda Created. Created, African-American. Unusual.
Laquarius Created. Created, African-American. Unusual.
Laqueena Created. Created, African-American. Unusual.
Laqueisha Created. From Lakeisha, Created, African-American. Unusual. Alternative spelling: Laquesha.
Laquela Created. From Laquela, Created, African-American. Unusual.
Laquilla Created. Created, African-American. Unusual.
Laquinda Created. Created, African-American. Unusual.
Laquisha Created. From Lakeisha, Created, African-American. Unusual.
Laquita Created. Created, African-American. Unusual. Alternative spelling: Laqueta.
Lara English. From Larissa. Character in Boris Pasternak's "Doctor Zhivago"; Flynn Boyle (actress, "Twin Peaks"). Less popular.
Laraine English. From Lorraine, French, the name of a province. Unusual. Alternative spelling: Larraine.
Larena Created. Created, African-American. Unusual.
Laresa Created. Created, African-American. Unusual.
Laresha Created. Created, African-American. Unusual.
Larette English. From Laura, Latin, "Bay" or "laurel." Unusual. Alternative spelling: Laret.
Lari English. From Laura, Latin, "Bay" or "laurel." Unusual.
Larilia English. From Laura, Latin, "Bay" or "laurel." Unusual.
Larinda Created. Created, African-American. Unusual.
Larine Created. Created, African-American. Unusual.
Larissa English. Latin, "Cheerful" or "laughing." Unusual.
Larita Created. Created, African-American. Unusual.
Lark English. Old German, "lerihha"; the name of a bird. Unusual.
Larochka Russian. From Larissa. Unusual.
Lashanda Created. Created, African-American. Unusual.

Lashanna Created. Created, African-American. Unusual. Alternative spelling: Lashana.
Lashannon Created. Created, African-American. Unusual.
Lashanta Created. Created, African-American. Unusual.
Lasharon Created. Created, African-American. Unusual.
Lashaun Created. Created, African-American. Unusual.
Lashauna Created. Created, African-American. Unusual. Alternative spellings: Laseana, Lashawna.
Lashaunda Created. Created, African-American. Unusual. Alternative spelling: Lashawnda.
Lashaunia Created. Created, African-American. Unusual.
Lashaunta Created. Created, African-American. Unusual.
Lashea Created. Created, African-American. Unusual.
Lasheba Created. Created, African-American. Unusual.
Lasheele Created. Created, African-American. Unusual.
Lashell Created. Created, African-American. Unusual. Alternative spelling: Lashelle.
Lashenia Created. Created, African-American. Unusual.
Lasherri Created. Created, African-American. Unusual.
Lashona Created. Created, African-American. Unusual.
Lashonda Created. Created, African-American. Unusual.
Lashunda Created. Created, African-American. Unusual.
Lashundra Created. Created, African-American. Unusual.
Lasonda Created. Created, African-American. Unusual.
Lasonia Created. Created, African-American. Unusual. Alternative spelling: Lasonya.
Lastarr Created. Created, African-American. Unusual.
Lataisha Created. Created, African-American. Unusual. Alternative spelling: Lateisha.
Latania Created. Created, African-American. Unusual. Alternative spelling: Latanya.
Latarisha Created. Created, African-American. Unusual.
Latarra Created. Created, African-American. Unusual. Alternative spelling: Latara.
Latasha Created. Created, African-American. Unusual.
Latashia Created. Created, African-American. Unusual.
Latavia Arabic. Arabic, "Pleasant." Unusual.
Latavis Created. Created, African-American. Unusual.
Latenna Created. Created, African-American. Unusual.
Latesha Created. Created, African-American. Unusual.
Latia Created. Created, African-American. Unusual.
Laticia American. From Letitia, Latin, "Gladness." Unusual. Alternative spelling: Latisha.
Latina Created. Created, African-American. Unusual.
Lativia Created. Created, African-American. Unusual.
Latoia Created. Created, African-American. Unusual.
Latona Created. Created, African-American. Unusual.
Latonia Created. Created, African-American. Unusual. Alternative spelling: Latonya.
Latora Created. Created, African-American. Unusual.
Latoria Created. Created, African-American. Unusual.
Latosha Created. Created, African-American. Unusual.
Latoshia Created. Created, African-American. Unusual.
Latoya Created. Created, African-American. Jackson (pop singer, sister of Michael and Janet). Unusual. Alternative spelling: Latoyia.
Latrecia Created. Created, African-American. Unusual.
Latrice Created. Created, African-American. Unusual.
Latricia Created. Created, African-American. Unusual. Alternative spellings: Latrica, Latrisha.
Latrina Created. Created, African-American. Unusual.
Laura English. Latin, "Bay" or "laurel." Dern (actress, "Wild at Heart"); Dean (minimalist choreographer). Very popular. Laurie+. Alternative spelling: Lora.
Laure French. From Laura. Permon Junot (French writer). Unusual.
Laureana Hispanic. From Laura. Unusual.
Laurel English. From Laura, Latin, "Bay" or "laurel." Ulrich (won Pulitzer Prize for history, "A Midwife's Tale," 1991). Unusual for males, less popular for females. Alternative spelling: Laural.
Lauren English. From Laura, Latin, "Bay" or "laurel." Bacall (actress, "Big Sleep") (real name: Betty Joan Perske); Hutton (actress and model). Unusual for males, extremely popular for females. Alternative spellings: Laurin, Lauryn, Loren, Lorin, Lorrin, Loryn, Lorynn, Lorynne.
Laurena English. From Laurence, Latin, "Crowned with laurel." Unusual. Alternative spelling: Lorena.
Laurene English. From Laura. Unusual. Alternative spelling: Laureen.
Laurentia English. From Laurence, Latin, "Crowned with laurel." Unusual.
Laurette French. From Laura. Taylor (actress, performed record 604 times on Broadway, in "Peg o' My Heart"). Unusual.
Lauriane French. From Laura. Unusual.
Laurice English. From Laurence, Latin, "Crowned with laurel." Unusual.
Lauricia English. From Laurence, Latin, "Crowned with laurel." Unusual.
Laurie English. From Laurence, Latin, "Crowned with laurel." Lea Schaefer (Miss America, 1972). Unusual for males, less popular for females. Alternative spellings: Lauri, Loree, Lorey, Lori, Lorie, Lorrie, Lorry, Lory.
Laurina English. From Laurence, Latin, "Crowned with laurel." Unusual. Alternative spellings: Laurena, Lorena, Lorina.
Laurka Polish. From Laura. Unusual.
Lavanna Created. Created, African-American. Unusual.
Laveda Created. Created, African-American. Unusual.
Lavenia English. From Lavinia. Unusual.
Laverna English. From Laverne. Unusual.
Laverne English. French, "Like spring." Less popular. Alternative spelling: Lavern.
Lavetta Created. Created, African-American. Unusual.

Lavina English. From Lavinia. Unusual. Alternative spellings: Lavena, Levina.
Laviner English. From Lavinia. Unusual.
Lavinia English. Latin, "Purified." Unusual. Alternative spellings: Levinia, Livinia.
Lavinie English. From Lavinia. Unusual.
Lavon American. Created, meaning unknown. Originally used by the Mormons. Unusual for males, unusual for females. Alternative spelling: Lavonne.
Lavra Russian. From Laura. Unusual.
Lawanda Created. Created, African-American. Unusual.
Lawanna Created. Created, African-American. Unusual.
Lawanza Created. Created, African-American. Unusual.
Lea English. From Leah. Less popular. Alternative spellings: Leia, Leigha, Lia, Liah.
Leah Hebrew/Israeli. Hebrew, "Weary" or "wild cow." Genesis 29:16, 23. First wife of Jacob, older sister of Rachel. Popular.
Leanda English. From Leander, Greek, "Lion man." Unusual.
Leander See under Boys' Names.
Leandra English. From Leander, Greek, "Lion man." Unusual.
Leanna English. From Liana, French, the name of a flowering tropical vine. Also a pet form of Juliana (Julius, Latin, Roman clan name meaning "downy" or "bearded"). Unusual. Alternative spellings: Leana, Liana, Lianna.
Leanne English. From Liana, French, the name of a flowering tropical vine. Also a pet form of Juliana (Julius, Latin, Roman clan name meaning "downy" or "bearded"). Less popular. Alternative spellings: Lean, Leane, Leann, Lee Ann, Lee Anne, Leeann, Leigh Ann, Leighann, Leighanne, Liane, Lianne.
Leanora English. From Helen, Greek, "Bright one" or "shining one." Less popular.
Leanore English. From Helen, Greek, "Bright one" or "shining one." Less popular.
Leda English. From Letitia, Latin, "Gladness." Unusual.
Ledah English. From Letitia, Latin, "Gladness." Unusual.
Lee English. Old English, "Meadow." Marvin (actor); Remick (actress); Meriwether (actress, Miss America, 1955); Strasberg (theatrical director, taught system of method acting) (real name: Israel Strassbert). Less popular for males, less popular for females. Alternative spelling: Leigh.
Leeanda English. From Leander, Greek, "Lion man." Unusual.
Leeba Hebrew/Israeli. Hebrew, "Heart." Unusual.
Leena Estonian. From Helen, Greek, "Bright one" or "shining one." Unusual.
Leeta English. From Letitia, Latin, "Gladness." Unusual.
Lehua Hawaiian. Hawaiian, "Sacred to the gods." Also the name of a Hawaiian flower. Unusual.
Leila English. Arabic, "Dark as night" or "born at night." Unusual. Alternative spellings: Laila, Layla, Leilah.
Leilani Hawaiian. Hawaiian, "Heavenly flower." Unusual.
Leilia English. From Leila. Unusual.
Leka Russian. From Helen, Greek, "Bright one" or "shining one." Unusual.
Leksi Hungarian. From Alexander, Greek, "Defender of men" or "warding off men." Mark 16:21; Acts 4:6, 19:33. Unusual.
Lela English. From Leila. Unusual.
Lelia Latin. Latin, from the Roman family name "Laelius." Unusual.
Lelya Russian. From Helen, Greek, "Bright one" or "shining one." Unusual.
Lena English. From Helen, Greek, "Bright one" or "shining one." Ashwell (British actress, organized entertainment for WWI troops) (real name: Lena Pocock); Horne (singer); Olin (actress, "Havana"). Less popular. Alternative spellings: Lenah, Lina, Linah.
Lenci Hungarian. From Helen, Greek, "Bright one" or "shining one." Unusual.
Lenda English. From Leonard, Old German (Leonhard), "Strong as a lion." Unusual.
Lene German. From Helen, Greek, "Bright one" or "shining one." Unusual. Alternative spellings: Leni, Line.
Leneen English. From Leonard, Old German (Leonhard), "Strong as a lion." Unusual.
Lenette English. From Leonard, Old German (Leonhard), "Strong as a lion." Unusual.
Lenia English. From Leonard, Old German (Leonhard), "Strong as a lion." Unusual.
Lenka Czech, Russian. From Helen, Greek, "Bright one" or "shining one." Unusual.
Lenna English. From Leonard, Old German (Leonhard), "Strong as a lion." Unusual. Alternative spelling: Lennah.
Lenni Estonian. From Helen, Greek, "Bright one" or "shining one." Unusual.
Lennox See under Boys' Names.
Lenor English. From Helen, Greek, "Bright one" or "shining one." Unusual.
Lenora Russian. From Helen, Greek, "Bright one" or "shining one." Unusual.
Lenorah English. From Helen, Greek, "Bright one" or "shining one." Unusual.
Lenore German. From Helen, Greek, "Bright one" or "shining one." Less popular.
Leodora English. From Leander, Greek, "Lion man." Unusual.
Leoline English. From Leander, Greek, "Lion man." Unusual.
Leonanie English. From Leander, Greek, "Lion man." Unusual.
Leone See under Boys' Names.
Leonelle English. From Leander, Greek, "Lion man." Unusual.
Leonette English. From Leander, Greek, "Lion man." Unusual.
Leonia English. From Leo, Latin, "Lion." Unusual. Alternative spelling: Leona.
Leonice English. From Leander, Greek, "Lion man." Unusual.
Leonicia English. From Leo, Latin, "Lion." Unusual.
Leonie English. From Leo, Latin, "Lion." Unusual.
Leonine English. From Leo, Latin, "Lion." Unusual.
Leonissa English. From Leander, Greek, "Lion man." Unusual.
Leonor Hispanic. From Helen, Greek, "Bright one" or "shining one." Michaelis (chemist, helped formulate Michaelis-Menten hypothesis on enzyme-catalyzed reactions). Unusual.
Leonora English. From Helen, Greek, "Bright one" or "shining one." Kearney Barry (labor leader) (real name of Mother Lake). Less popular.
Leonore English. From Helen, Greek, "Bright one" or "shining one." Less popular.
Leontine English. From Leo, Latin, "Lion." Unusual.

Leora English. From Helen, Greek, "Bright one" or "shining one." Unusual. Alternative spelling: Liora.

Leotie Native American. Native American, "Prairie flower." Unusual.

Lera Russian. From Valerie, Latin, "To be strong"; a Roman clan name. Unusual.

Lerka Russian. From Valerie, Latin, "To be strong"; a Roman clan name. Unusual.

Leska Czech. From Alexander, Greek, "Defender of men" or "warding off men." Mark 16:21; Acts 4:6, 19:33. Unusual.

Leslie English. Scottish, "Low meadow." Also a Scottish clan name. Howard (British actor, "Gone With the Wind"); Caron (French actress, "Gigi"); Hope (comedian) (real name of Bob Hope); Stephen, Sir (British biographer, "English Men of Letters" series); Groves (army general, commanded atomic bomb project, 1942–47). Less popular for males, popular for females. Les. Alternative spellings: Leslee, Lesley, Lesli, Lesly, Leslye, Lesslie, Lezli, Lezlie, Lezly.

Lesya Russian. From Alexander, Greek, "Defender of men" or "warding off men." Mark 16:21; Acts 4:6, 19:33. Ukrainka (Ukrainian poet) (real name: Laryssa Kosach-Kvitka). Unusual.

Leta English. Latin, "Glad." Unusual.

Letitia English. Latin, "Gladness." Unusual. Alternative spellings: Leticia, Letisha, Lettitia.

Letizia Italian. From Letitia. Unusual.

Lettice English. From Letitia. Unusual.

Letty English. From Letitia. Unusual. Alternative spellings: Letti, Lettie.

Letycia Polish. From Letitia. Unusual.

Leva English. From Levana. Unusual.

Levana Hebrew/Israeli. Hebrew, "Moon" or "white." Nehemiah 7:48. Unusual.

Levener English. From Lavinia, Latin, "Purified." Unusual.

Levenia English. From Lavinia, Latin, "Purified." Unusual.

Levia Hebrew/Israeli. From Levi, Hebrew, "Joined to" or "attached." Genesis 29:34. Unusual.

Levona Hebrew/Israeli. From Livona, Hebrew, "Spice" or "incense." Unusual.

Lexa Czech. From Alexander, Greek, "Defender of men" or "warding off men." Mark 16:21; Acts 4:6, 19:33. Unusual.

Lexi English. From Alexander, Greek, "Defender of men" or "warding off men." Mark 16:21; Acts 4:6, 19:33. Unusual. Alternative spellings: Lexie, Lexy.

Lexine English. From Alexander, Greek, "Defender of men" or "warding off men." Mark 16:21; Acts 4:6, 19:33. Unusual.

Leya Hispanic. Spanish, "Loyal to the law." Unusual.

Li Chinese. Chinese, "Pretty." Emperors of Chinese T'ang dynasty, 618–907. Unusual for males, unusual for females.

Li Hua Chinese. Chinese, "Pear blossom." Unusual.

Lian English, from Julius, Latin, a Roman clan name meaning "downy" or "bearded"; and Chinese, from Lian, Chinese, "Graceful willow." Unusual.

Libby English. From Elizabeth, Hebrew (Elisheva), "Oath of God" or "God is my oath." Exodus 6:23. Holman (actress); Morris (comedian). Unusual. Alternative spelling: Libbie.

Liberty English. Latin, "libertas" ("free"); the word used as a first name. Unusual for males, unusual for females.

Licha Hispanic. From Adelaide, Old German (Adelheidis), "Nobility." Unusual.

Lici Hispanic. From Adelaide, Old German (Adelheidis), "Nobility." Unusual.

Lida Polish, Russian. From Lydia, Greek, "Woman from Lydia," an ancient country in Asia Minor. Unusual.

Lidah English. From Lydia, Greek, "Woman from Lydia," an ancient country in Asia Minor. Unusual.

Lidi Hungarian. From Lydia, Greek, "Woman from Lydia," an ancient country in Asia Minor. Unusual.

Lidiya Russian. From Lydia, Greek, "Woman from Lydia," an ancient country in Asia Minor. Unusual.

Lidka Polish, Russian. From Lydia, Greek, "Woman from Lydia," an ancient country in Asia Minor. Unusual.

Lidochka Russian. From Lydia, Greek, "Woman from Lydia," an ancient country in Asia Minor. Unusual.

Lien Chinese. Chinese, "Lotus." Unusual.

Lien Hua Chinese. From Lien. Unusual.

Liene Latvian. From Helen, Greek, "Bright one" or "shining one." Unusual.

Liesa German. From Elizabeth, Hebrew (Elisheva), "Oath of God" or "God is my oath." Exodus 6:23. Unusual.

Lieschen German. From Elizabeth, Hebrew (Elisheva), "Oath of God" or "God is my oath." Exodus 6:23. Unusual.

Liesel German. From Elizabeth, Hebrew (Elisheva), "Oath of God" or "God is my oath." Exodus 6:23. Unusual. Alternative spellings: Liesl, Lisel.

Liisa Estonian. From Elizabeth, Hebrew (Elisheva), "Oath of God" or "God is my oath." Exodus 6:23. Unusual.

Liisi Estonian. From Elizabeth, Hebrew (Elisheva), "Oath of God" or "God is my oath." Exodus 6:23. Unusual.

Lil English. From Lily, Latin, "lilium"; a flower name used as a first name. Less popular.

Lila English. From Leila, Arabic, "Dark as night" or "born at night." Unusual. Alternative spellings: Lilah, Lyla.

Lilac English. From Lilac, Sanskrit, "nila" ("dark blue"); a plant name used as a first name. Unusual.

Lileana Hawaiian. From Lily. Unusual.

Lili German, Russian. From Helen, Greek, "Bright one" or "shining one"; and English, from Lily, Latin, "lilium"; a flower name used as a first name. Unusual. Alternative spelling: Lilli.

Lilia English, Hispanic. From Lily. Vladislavovna Minina (reached North Pole in 1977 via Russian atomic icebreaker). Unusual. Alternative spelling: Lillia.

Liliana Italian. From Lily. Unusual.

Lilias Scottish. From Lily. Unusual.

Liliha Hawaiian. Hawaiian, "Disgust." 19th-century governor of the Hawaiian island of Oahu. Unusual.

Lilika Greek. From Lily. Unusual.

Lilike Hungarian. From Lily. Unusual.

Liliosa Hispanic. From Lily. 9th-century martyr. Unusual.

Lilith Arabic. Arabic, "Of the night." Name of a female demon said to have been Adam's first wife. Isaiah 34:14. Unusual.

Lilium English. From Lily. Unusual.

Liljana Serbian. From Lily. Unusual.

Lilka Polish. From Louis, Old German (Hlutwig), "Famous warrior." Unusual.

Lillian English. From Lily. Gish (actress); Hellman (playwright, "Little Foxes"); Leitzel (circus aerialist) (real name: Leopoldina Alitza Pelikan); Nordica (soprano, first U.S. opera singer to achieve fame in Europe); Wald (established a public-health nursing service, 1893).

Less popular. Lill, Lilly+. Alternative spellings: Lilian, Liliane.

Liluye Native American. Native American, "Singing chicken hawk." Unusual.

Lily English. Latin, "lilium"; a flower name used as a first name. Pons (operatic singer); Tomlin (actress and comedian). Less popular. Alternative spellings: Lille, Lilley, Lillie, Lilly.

Linchen German. From Charles, Old English, "ceorl" ("man" or "husbandman"). Unusual.

Linda English. Spanish, "Pretty one." Also an abbreviated form of names like Belinda, Melinda, and Rosalinda (in which Linda is Germanic for "serpent," a symbol of wisdom). Darnell (actress) (real name: Manetta Eloisa Darnell); Christian (actress) (real name: Blanca Rosa Welter); Evans (actress, "Dynasty"); Ronstadt (pop singer); Ellerbee (news anchor, columnist, and author, "And So It Goes"). Less popular. Alternative spellings: Lynda, Lynnda.

Linden See Lyndon under Boys' Names.

Lindsay English. Old English, "Linden-tree island [or "hedge"]." Anderson (British film director); Wagner (actress, "Bionic Woman"). Less popular for males, very popular for females. Alternative spellings: Lindsaye, Lindsi, Lindsey, Lindsie, Lindsy, Lindzi, Lindzy, Linsay, Linsey, Linzey, Linzi, Linzie, Lyndsay, Lyndsey, Lynsie, Lyndsy, Lynsay, Lynsey, Lynsie.

Linka Hungarian. From Charles, Old English, "ceorl" ("man" or "husbandman"). Unusual.

Linnea English. From Linda. Unusual.

Linnette English. From Eluned, Welsh, "Idol." Unusual. Alternative spellings: Linet, Linette, Lynnet, Lynnette.

Linnie English. From Linda. Unusual.

Liolya Russian. From Helen, Greek, "Bright one" or "shining one." Unusual.

Liona Hawaiian. From Leo, Latin, "Lion." Unusual.

Lirit Hebrew/Israeli. Hebrew, "Lyrical," "musical," or "poetic." Unusual.

Lisa English. From Elizabeth, Hebrew (Elisheva), "Oath of God" or "God is my oath." Exodus 6:23. del Giocondo (subject of Leonardo da Vinci's "Mona Lisa"); Stansfield (rock singer); Marie Presley (daughter of Elvis). Very popular. Alternative spellings: Leesa, Leisa.

Lisa-Jane English. English, combination of Lisa (Elizabeth, Hebrew (Elisheva), "Oath of God" or "God is my oath") + Jane (John, Hebrew (Yochanan), "God has been gracious"). Less popular.

Lisa-Marie English. English, combination of Lisa (Elizabeth, Hebrew (Elisheva), "Oath of God" or "God is my oath") + Marie (Miriam, Hebrew (Miryam), "Bitterness," "rebellion," "wished-for child," or "sea" (?)). Less popular.

Lisanne English. From Elizabeth, Hebrew (Elisheva), "Oath of God" or "God is my oath." Exodus 6:23. Unusual.

Lisbete Latvian. From Elizabeth, Hebrew (Elisheva), "Oath of God" or "God is my oath." Exodus 6:23. Unusual.

Lise German. From Elizabeth, Hebrew (Elisheva), "Oath of God" or "God is my oath." Exodus 6:23. Meitner (Austrian physicist, discovered protactinium and helped accomplish fission of uranium). Unusual. Alternative spelling: Liese.

Liseli Native American. Native American, meaning unknown. Unusual.

Lisenka Russian. From Elizabeth, Hebrew (Elisheva), "Oath of God" or "God is my oath." Exodus 6:23. Unusual.

Liseta Hispanic. From Elizabeth, Hebrew (Elisheva), "Oath of God" or "God is my oath." Exodus 6:23. Unusual.

Lisettina Italian. From Elizabeth, Hebrew (Elisheva), "Oath of God" or "God is my oath." Exodus 6:23. Unusual.

Lissa English. From Elizabeth, Hebrew (Elisheva), "Oath of God" or "God is my oath." Exodus 6:23. Unusual.

Lissette French. From Elizabeth, Hebrew (Elisheva), "Oath of God" or "God is my oath." Exodus 6:23. Unusual. Alternative spelling: Lisette.

Lissie French. From Elizabeth, Hebrew (Elisheva), "Oath of God" or "God is my oath." Exodus 6:23. Unusual. Alternative spelling: Lissy.

Lissilma Native American. Native American, "Be there." Unusual.

Liszka Hungarian. From Elizabeth, Hebrew (Elisheva), "Oath of God" or "God is my oath." Exodus 6:23. Unusual.

Lita English. Abbreviated form of names ending in "-lita," like Lolita. Unusual.

Litonya Native American. Native American, "Hummingbird darting down." Unusual.

Litsa Greek. From Eve, Hebrew (Chava), "Life." Genesis 3:20. Unusual.

Liva English. From Levana, Hebrew, "Moon" or "white." Nehemiah 7:48. Unusual.

Livana Hebrew/Israeli. From Levana, Hebrew, "Moon" or "white." Nehemiah 7:48. Unusual.

Livanga African. African, "Think before you eat." A name from a proverb. Unusual.

Livia Hebrew/Israeli. From Liviya. Unusual. Alternative spelling: Liviya.

Livona Hebrew/Israeli. Hebrew, "Spice" or "incense." Unusual.

Liz English. From Elizabeth, Hebrew (Elisheva), "Oath of God" or "God is my oath." Exodus 6:23. Less popular. Lizzie+.

Liza English. From Elizabeth, Hebrew (Elisheva), "Oath of God" or "God is my oath." Exodus 6:23. Minnelli (actress and singer, daughter of film director Vincente Minnelli and actress Judy Garland). Less popular.

Lizabeth English. From Elizabeth, Hebrew (Elisheva), "Oath of God" or "God is my oath." Exodus 6:23. Scott (actress, appeared with Bogart in "Dead Reckoning"). Unusual. Beth, Betsy, Betty, Liz.

Lizanka Russian. From Elizabeth, Hebrew (Elisheva), "Oath of God" or "God is my oath." Exodus 6:23. Unusual.

Lizanne English. From Elizabeth, Hebrew (Elisheva), "Oath of God" or "God is my oath." Exodus 6:23. Unusual.

Lizbeth English. From Elizabeth, Hebrew (Elisheva), "Oath of God" or "God is my oath." Exodus 6:23. Unusual. Beth, Betsy, Betty, Liz. Alternative spelling: Lisbeth.

Lizina Latvian. From Elizabeth, Hebrew (Elisheva), "Oath of God" or "God is my oath." Exodus 6:23. Unusual.

Lizka Russian. From Elizabeth, Hebrew (Elisheva), "Oath of God" or "God is my oath." Exodus 6:23. Unusual.

Lizzy English. From Elizabeth, Hebrew (Elisheva), "Oath of God" or "God is my oath." Exodus 6:23. Less popular. Liz. Alternative spellings: Lizey, Lizzey, Lizzie.

Llinos Welsh. Welsh, "Linnet," a type of finch. Unusual.

Lodoiska Polish. From Louis, Old German (Hlutwig), "Famous warrior." Unusual.

Loena English. From Leander, Greek, "Lion man." Unusual.

Logan See under Boys' Names.

Lois English. Greek, meaning unknown. 2 Timothy 1:5. Timothy's grandmother (Bible). Less popular.

Loiyetu Native American. Native American, "Blooming farewell-to-spring." Farewell-to-spring is a plant. Unusual.

Lokelani Hawaiian. Hawaiian, "Heavenly rose." Unusual.

Lola English, from Dolores, Spanish, "Sorrow"; and Hawaiian, from Laura, Latin, "Bay" or "laurel." Montez (dancer, adventuress, mistress of Louis I of Bavaria) (real name: Marie Dolores Eliza Rosanna Gilbert). Less popular.

Loletta English. From Charles, Old English, "ceorl" ("man" or "husbandman"). Unusual. Alternative spelling: Loleta.

Lolita English, Hispanic. From Dolores, Spanish, "Sorrow." Unusual.

Lolly English. From Laura, Latin, "Bay" or "laurel." Character in Sylvia Townsend Warner's "Lolly Willowes." Unusual.

Lolotea Native American. From Dorothy, Greek (Dorothea), "Gift from God." Unusual.

Lolotte French. From Charles, Old English, "ceorl" ("man" or "husbandman"). Unusual.

Loma Unknown. Meaning and origin unknown. Unusual.

Lomasi Native American. Native American, "Pretty flower." Unusual.

Lona English. From Leo, Latin, "Lion." Unusual.

Loni English. From Alphonso, Old German (Hildefuns), "Ready for battle." Anderson (actress, "WKRP in Cincinnati"). Unusual.

Lopa Polish. From Penelope, Greek, "Bobbin" or "weaver." Unusual.

Lor English. From Laura, Latin, "Bay" or "laurel." Unusual.

Lorane English. From Laura, Latin, "Bay" or "laurel." Unusual. Alternative spelling: Lorrane.

Loreen English. From Laura, Latin, "Bay" or "laurel." Unusual. Alternative spellings: Laurine, Lorene.

Lorenza Hispanic, Italian. From Laurence, Latin, "Crowned with laurel." Unusual.

Loretta English. From Laura, Latin, "Bay" or "laurel." Swit (actress, "M*A*S*H"); Young (actress, won 1947 Oscar for "Farmer's Daughter") (real name: Gretchen Young); Lynn (country singer). Less popular. Alternative spellings: Lauretta, Laureta, Loreta.

Lorette English. From Laura, Latin, "Bay" or "laurel." Unusual. Alternative spellings: Lauret, Loret, Lorrette.

Lori Ann English. English, combination of Lori (Laura, Latin, "Bay" or "laurel") + Ann (Hannah, Hebrew (Chanah), "Grace" or "favor"). Unusual. Alternative spellings: Laurianne, Lori Anne.

Lorinda English. From Laura, Latin, "Bay" or "laurel." Unusual. Alternative spellings: Laurinda.

Loris English. From Laurence, Latin, "Crowned with laurel." Unusual.

Lorita English. From Laura, Latin, "Bay" or "laurel." Unusual.

Lorka Russian. From Flora, Latin, "Flower." Unusual.

Lorn See Lorne under Boys' Names.

Lorna Scottish. Scottish, place name (Lorn) used as a first name. Doone (title character in Blackmore's novel). Less popular.

Lorne See under Boys' Names.

Lorraine English. French, the name of a province. Hansberry (playwright, "Raisin in the Sun"); Bracco (actress). Less popular. Alternative spellings: Lauraine, Laurraine, Loraine, Lorayne, Lorrayne.

Lota Indo-Pakistani. Hindi, "Portable drinking cup." Hindus believe that God is present in household objects. When calling the child's name, they are also calling on God and working toward salvation. Unusual.

Lotta Swedish. From Charles, Old English, "ceorl" ("man" or "husbandman"). Crabtree (burlesque actress). Unusual.

Lottchen German. From Charles, Old English, "ceorl" ("man" or "husbandman"). Unusual.

Lotte German. From Charles, Old English, "ceorl" ("man" or "husbandman"). Lehmann (lyric-dramatic soprano); Lenya (Austrian actress and singer, "Eternal Road") (real name: Karoline Wilhelmine Blamauer). Unusual.

Lotti German. From Charles, Old English, "ceorl" ("man" or "husbandman"). Unusual.

Lottie English. From Charles, Old English, "ceorl" ("man" or "husbandman"). Less popular. Alternative spellings: Lottey, Lotty.

Lou See under Boys' Names.

Louann English. English, combination of Lou (Louis, Old German, "Famous warrior") + Ann (Hannah, Hebrew (Chanah), "Grace" or "favor"). Less popular. Alternative spelling: Louanne.

Louella English. English, combination of Lou (Louis, Old German, "Famous warrior") + Ella (Old German, "All"). Oettinger Parsons (wrote first movie gossip column, syndicated in 400+ newspapers). Unusual. Alternative spelling: Luella.

Louisa English. From Louis, Old German (Hlutwig), "Famous warrior." May Alcott (author, "Little Women"); Nisbett (19th-century British actress, "Love's Chase"); Costello (Irish miniature-painter). Less popular. Lou+. Alternative spelling: Louiza.

Louise English. From Louis, Old German (Hlutwig), "Famous warrior." de Marillac (saint); Brooks (actress, "Pandora's Box"); Michel (19th-century French anarchist); Bogan (poet, "Dark Summer"); Revoil Colet (French author of novels and verse); Guiney (poet and essayist, "Goose Quill Papers"); Beatty Homer (opera singer). Less popular. Lou+.

Louisetta English. From Louis, Old German (Hlutwig), "Famous warrior." Unusual. Lou+.

Lourdes French. French, place name used as a first name. Unusual.

Love English. Surname used as a first name; origin unknown. Unusual for males, unusual for females.

Loveday English. Surname used as a first name; origin unknown. Unusual for males, unusual for females.

Lovenah English. From Lavinia, Latin, "Purified." Unusual.

Loveviner English. From Lavinia, Latin, "Purified." Unusual.

Lovey English. From Love. Unusual for males, unusual for females. Alternative spelling: Lovie.

Lovina English. From Lavinia, Latin, "Purified." Unusual.

Lovinia English. From Lavinia, Latin, "Purified." Unusual.

Low English. From Laura, Latin, "Bay" or "laurel." Unusual.
Lu English. From Louis, Old German (Hlutwig), "Famous warrior." Unusual.
Luann English. From Louann. Less popular. Lu+. Alternative spellings: Luane, Luanne.
Luca Italian. From Luke, Greek (Loukas), "From Lucania," a district in Southern Italy. Book of Luke. Unusual.
Luce English. From Lucius, Latin, "lux" ("light"). A Roman clan name. Unusual.
Lucetta English. From Lucius, Latin, "lux" ("light"). A Roman clan name. Unusual.
Lucette French. From Lucius, Latin, "lux" ("light"). A Roman clan name. Unusual.
Lucia Italian. From Lucius, Latin, "lux" ("light"). A Roman clan name. Character in Donizetti's opera "Lucia di Lammermoor"; Chase (ballet dancer, co-director of American Ballet Theatre, 1945–80); Bartolozzi Vestris (19th-century British actress and singer). Unusual.
Luciana English. From Lucius, Latin, "lux" ("light"). A Roman clan name. Unusual.
Lucida English. From Lucius, Latin, "lux" ("light"). A Roman clan name. Unusual.
Lucie French. From Lucius, Latin, "lux" ("light"). A Roman clan name. Manette (character in Dickens' "Tale of Two Cities"); Austin Duff-Gordon (19th-century British author, "Letters from Egypt"). Unusual.
Lucienne English. From Lucius, Latin, "lux" ("light"). A Roman clan name. Unusual. Alternative spelling: Luciane.
Lucija Latvian. From Lucius, Latin, "lux" ("light"). A Roman clan name. Unusual.
Lucika Slavic. From Lucius, Latin, "lux" ("light"). A Roman clan name. Unusual.
Lucila Hispanic. From Lucius, Latin, "lux" ("light"). A Roman clan name. Godoy de Alcayaga (Chilean poet, awarded 1945 Nobel Prize for literature) (real name of Gabriela Mistral). Unusual.
Lucilla English. From Lucius, Latin, "lux" ("light"). A Roman clan name. Unusual. Lucy+.
Lucille English. From Lucius, Latin, "lux" ("light"). A Roman clan name. Ball (actress, "I Love Lucy"). Less popular. Lucy+. Alternative spelling: Lucile.
Lucina English. From Lucius, Latin, "lux" ("light"). A Roman clan name. Unusual. Alternative spelling: Lucinna.
Lucinda English. From Lucius, Latin, "lux" ("light"). A Roman clan name. Wierenga (organized creation of longest sand sculpture: 10,760 feet); character in Cervantes' "Don Quixote." Unusual.
Lucine Bulgarian. From Lucius, Latin, "lux" ("light"). A Roman clan name. Unusual.
Lucita Hispanic. From Lucius, Latin, "lux" ("light"). A Roman clan name. Unusual.
Lucka Slavic. From Lucius, Latin, "lux" ("light"). A Roman clan name. Unusual.
Lucky English. From Felix, Latin, "Happy," "fortunate," or "lucky." Unusual. Alternative spelling: Luckie.
Lucrece French. From Lucretia. Character in Shakespeare's "Rape of Lucrece." Unusual.
Lucretia Latin. Latin, from the Roman clan name "Lucretius." Rudolph Garfield (wife of President James); Coffin Mott (reformer, established American Equal Rights Association, 1866); Hale (writer of children's books, "Peterkin Papers"). Unusual.
Lucrezia Italian. From Lucretia. Agujari (18th-century Italian operatic soprano); Borgia (16th-century Duchess of Ferrara, married three times for political reasons). Unusual.
Lucrisha English. From Lucretia. Unusual.
Lucy English. From Lucius, Latin, "lux" ("light"). A Roman clan name. Patron saint of the blind; Maud Montgomery (Canadian novelist, "Anne of Green Gables"); Stone (suffragist, helped established American Woman Suffrage Association, 1869); Walter (British, mistress of Charles II); Hay (17th-century British courtier). Less popular.
Lucya Polish. From Lucius, Latin, "lux" ("light"). A Roman clan name. Unusual.
Ludka Polish. From Louis, Old German (Hlutwig), "Famous warrior." Unusual.
Ludmila Slavic. Slavic, "Loved by the people." Unusual.
Ludwika Polish. From Louis, Old German (Hlutwig), "Famous warrior." Unusual.
Lugia Italian. From Lucius, Latin, "lux" ("light"). A Roman clan name. Unusual.
Luisa Hispanic. From Louis, Old German (Hlutwig), "Famous warrior." Tetrazzini (Italian operatic soprano, Chicken Tetrazzini named in her honor); de Carvajal y Mendoza (17th-century Spanish missionary to English Catholics). Less popular.
Luiza Russian. From Louis, Old German (Hlutwig), "Famous warrior." Unusual.
Lula English. From Louis, Old German (Hlutwig), "Famous warrior." Unusual.
Lulani See under Boys' Names.
Lulie English. From Louis, Old German (Hlutwig), "Famous warrior." Unusual.
Lulu English. From Louis, Old German (Hlutwig), "Famous warrior." Unusual.
Luna Native American. Spanish, "Moon" or "satellite." Unusual.
Luned Welsh. From Eluned, Welsh, "Idol." Unusual.
Lupetu Native American. Native American, "Bear climbing over a man hiding between rocks." Unusual.
Lusa Finnish. From Elizabeth, Hebrew (Elisheva), "Oath of God" or "God is my oath." Exodus 6:23. Unusual.
Lusela Native American. Native American, "Bear licking its foot." Unusual.
Lusita Native American. From Lucius, Latin, "lux" ("light"). A Roman clan name. Unusual.
Luyiza Russian. From Louis, Old German (Hlutwig), "Famous warrior." Unusual.
Luz Hispanic. Spanish, "Light." The name is an abbreviated form of "María de la Luz" ("Mary of the Light"). Unusual.
Luzi German. From Lucius, Latin, "lux" ("light"). A Roman clan name. Unusual. Alternative spelling: Luzie.
Luzija Russian. From Lucius, Latin, "lux" ("light"). A Roman clan name. Unusual.
Lydia English. Greek, "Woman from Lydia," an ancient country in Asia Minor. Languish (character in Sheridan's play "The Rivals"); Litvak (Russian fighter pilot, scored record 12 aces in Eastern Front campaign, 1941–43); Estes Pinkham (manufactured widely advertised herbal patent medicine); Huntley Sigourney (poet). Less popular. Alternative spelling: Lidia.
Lydie English, French. From Lydia. Unusual.
Lyndel English. From Linda, Spanish, "Pretty one." Also an abbreviated form of names like Belinda, Melinda, and Rosalinda (in which Linda is Germanic

for "serpent," a symbol of wisdom). Unusual. Alternative spellings: Lyndell, Lyndelle.

Lyndi English. From Linda, Spanish, "Pretty one." Also an abbreviated form of names like Belinda, Melinda, and Rosalinda (in which Linda is Germanic for "serpent," a symbol of wisdom). Unusual. Alternative spellings: Lindey, Lindi, Lindie, Lindy, Lyndy.

Lynelle English. From Linda, Spanish, "Pretty one." Also an abbreviated form of names like Belinda, Melinda, and Rosalinda (in which Linda is Germanic for "serpent," a symbol of wisdom). Unusual. Alternative spellings: Linel, Linell, Linnell, Lynell.

Lynetta English. From Eluned, Welsh, "Idol." Unusual. Alternative spelling: Linetta.

Lynette French. From Eluned, Welsh, "Idol." Unusual.

Lynna English. From Linda, Spanish, "Pretty one." Also an abbreviated form of names like Belinda, Melinda, and Rosalinda (in which Linda is Germanic for "serpent," a symbol of wisdom). Unusual.

Lynne English. From Linda, Spanish, "Pretty one." Also an abbreviated form of names like Belinda, Melinda, and Rosalinda (in which Linda is Germanic for "serpent," a symbol of wisdom). Less popular. Lin, Linn, Lyn, Lynn.

Lynwen Welsh. Welsh, "Fair image." Unusual. Alternative spelling: Lynwyn.

Lyra English. Greek, "Lyre." Unusual.

Lyris English. From Lyra. Unusual.

Mab Irish. Gaelic, "Joy." Queen Mab is a legendary Irish fairy queen. Unusual.

Mabel English. From Amabel, Latin, "Lovable." Normand (silent-film actress, "Mabel's Strange Predicament"); Dodge Luhan (author, "Lorenzo in Taos"); Mercer (cabaret singer). Less popular. Alternative spellings: Mabelle, Mable.

Mabyn Irish. From Maeve, Irish, meaning unknown. Unusual.

Machi Japanese. Japanese, "Ten thousand." In Japanese lore, round numbers are thought to bring good luck. Unusual.

Macia Polish. From Miriam, Hebrew (Miryam), "Bitterness," "rebellion," "wished-for child," or "sea" (?). Exodus 15:20. Unusual.

Mackenzie See under Boys' Names.

Mada English. From Magdalen. Unusual.

Maddalena Italian. From Magdalen. Unusual. Alternative spelling: Maddelina.

Madalaina English. From Magdalen. Unusual. Maddie+.

Maddi English. From Magdalen. Unusual. Alternative spellings: Maddie, Maddy, Mady.

Madelaine English. From Magdalen. Unusual. Maddie+. Alternative spelling: Madelain.

Madeleine French. From Magdalen. Boullongne (17th-century French still-life painter); Carroll (British actress) (real name: Marie Madeleine Bernadette O'Carroll). Unusual.

Madelina English, Russian. From Magdalen. Unusual. Maddie+. Alternative spellings: Madalena, Maddelena, Madelena.

Madeline English. From Magdalen. Kahn (actress, "Young Frankenstein"); character in Keats' "Eve of St. Agnes." Less popular. Maddie+. Alternative spellings: Madaliene, Madaline, Madalyn, Madalyne, Maddaline, Madelene, Madelin, Madeilen, Madelyn, Madelyne, Madelynne, Madilyn, Madoline, Madylon.

Madge English. From Magdalen. Syers (British, won Olympic gold medal for figure skating, 1908); Kendal, Dame (British Shakespearean actress) (real name: Margaret Shafto Robertson). Less popular.

Madlyn English. From Magdalen. Unusual. Maddie+. Alternative spellings: Madlen, Madlin.

Mae English. From May, meaning and origin unknown. Possibly an early feminine form of Mayhew (Matthew, Hebrew, "Gift of the Lord") or a later nickname for M- names such as Mary. Murray (silent-film actress); West (actress, "She Done Him Wrong"). Unusual.

Maeve Irish. Irish, meaning unknown. First-century Irish queen; Binchy (wrote 1991 novel, "Circle of Friends," a best-seller). Unusual.

Mag English. From Margaret, Greek, "margaron" ("pearl"). Less popular.

Magaly Hispanic. From Magdalen. Unusual.

Magara African. Rhodesian, "To sit" or "to stay." Given to a child who needs much cuddling. Unusual.

Magda Czech, English, Hispanic, Polish, Russian. From Magdalen. Julin (Swedish, won Olympic gold medal for figure skating, 1920); Lupescu (Romanian adventuress) (real name of Princess Elena); character in Hauptmann's "Sunken Bell" and Sudermann's "Magda." Unusual.

Magdalen English. Greek, "From Magdala," an ancient city on the Sea of Galilee. The city was named in honor of its tower (Hebrew, "migdal"). Unusual. Alternative spellings: Magdalene, Magdaline, Magdelene.

Magdalena English. From Magdalen. Unusual. Maggie+. Alternative spelling: Magdelina.

Magdalina Russian. From Magdalen. Unusual.

Magdelana English. From Magdalen. Unusual. Maggie+.

Magdelena Czech. From Magdalen. Unusual.

Magdlen English. From Magdalen. Unusual. Maggie+.

Magdolna Hungarian. From Magdalen. Unusual.

Magena Native American. Native American, "Coming moon." Unusual.

Maggie English. From Margaret, Greek, "margaron" ("pearl"). Wylie (character in Barrie's "What Every Woman Knows"); Tulliver (character in George Eliot's "Mill on the Floss"); Smith, Dame (British actress, won 1969 Oscar for "The Prime of Miss Jean Brodie"). Less popular. Alternative spellings: Maggi, Maggy.

Magia Polish. From Magdalen. Unusual.

Magnolia English. English, after Pierre Magnol, an 18th-century French botanist; the name of a flowering tree. Character in Edna Ferber's "Showboat." Unusual.

Magola Hispanic. From Magdalen. Unusual.
Mahala English. Hebrew, "Tenderness." Unusual. Alternative spelling: Mahalah.
Mahalar English. From Mahala. Unusual.
Mahalia English. From Mahala. Jackson (gospel singer, "Move On Up a Little Higher"). Unusual.
Mahaut French. From Matilda, Old German (Mahthildis), "Battle maiden." Unusual.
Mahda Russian. From Magdalen. Unusual.
Maheesa English. From Mahesa. Another name for the Hindu god Siva. Unusual for males, unusual for females. Alternative spelling: Mahisa.
Mahela English. From Mahala. Unusual. Alternative spelling: Mahila.
Mahelea English. From Mahala. Unusual. Alternative spellings: Mahelia, Mahilia.
Mahesa See under Boys' Names.
Mahina Hawaiian. Hawaiian, "Moon." Unusual.
Mahira Hebrew/Israeli. From Mahir, Hebrew, "Expert," "industrious," or "quick." Unusual.
Mahlah Hebrew/Israeli. From Mahala. Unusual.
Maidie English. English, "Little maid." Unusual.
Maija Finnish. From Miriam, Hebrew (Miryam), "Bitterness," "rebellion," "wished-for child," or "sea" (?). Exodus 15:20. Unusual.
Maijii Finnish. From Miriam, Hebrew (Miryam), "Bitterness," "rebellion," "wished-for child," or "sea" (?). Exodus 15:20. Unusual.
Maikki Finnish. From Miriam, Hebrew (Miryam), "Bitterness," "rebellion," "wished-for child," or "sea" (?). Exodus 15:20. Unusual.
Mair Welsh. From Miriam, Hebrew (Miryam), "Bitterness," "rebellion," "wished-for child," or "sea" (?). Exodus 15:20. Unusual.
Maire Irish. From Miriam, Hebrew (Miryam), "Bitterness," "rebellion," "wished-for child," or "sea" (?). Exodus 15:20. Unusual.
Mairi Scottish. From Miriam, Hebrew (Miryam), "Bitterness," "rebellion," "wished-for child," or "sea" (?). Exodus 15:20. Macleod (17th-century Scottish poet). Unusual.
Maironа Irish. From Miriam, Hebrew (Miryam), "Bitterness," "rebellion," "wished-for child," or "sea" (?). Exodus 15:20. Unusual.
Mairwen Welsh. From Miriam, Hebrew (Miryam), "Bitterness," "rebellion," "wished-for child," or "sea" (?). Exodus 15:20. Unusual.
Maisie Scottish. From Margaret, Greek, "margaron" ("pearl"). Ward (with husband Frank Sheed, established publishing company Sheed & Ward for Catholic books). Unusual. Alternative spellings: Maisey, Maisy, Maizie.
Maita Hispanic. From Martha, Aramaic, "Lady" or "mistress of the house." Luke 10:38. Unusual.
Majorie English. From Margaret, Greek, "margaron" ("pearl"). Unusual.
Makadisa African. African, "Always selfish." Unusual.
Makana Hawaiian. From Makana, Hawaiian, "Gift" or "present." Unusual.
Makani See under Boys' Names.
Mal See under Boys' Names.
Mala English. From Magdalen, Greek, "From Magdala," an ancient city on the Sea of Galilee. The city was named in honor of its tower (Hebrew, "migdal"). Unusual.
Malcsi Hungarian. From Amelia, Latin, "Industrious" or "striving." Unusual.
Malena Danish. From Magdalen, Greek, "From Magdala," an ancient city on the Sea of Galilee. The city was named in honor of its tower (Hebrew, "migdal"). Unusual.
Máli Hungarian. From Amelia, Latin, "Industrious" or "striving." Unusual.
Malia Hawaiian. From Miriam, Hebrew (Miryam), "Bitterness," "rebellion," "wished-for child," or "sea" (?). Exodus 15:20. Unusual.
Malika Hungarian. From Amelia, Latin, "Industrious" or "striving." Unusual.
Malila Native American. Native American, "Salmon swimming upstream." Unusual.
Malin Swedish. From Magdalen, Greek, "From Magdala," an ancient city on the Sea of Galilee. The city was named in honor of its tower (Hebrew, "migdal"). Craig (army chief of staff, 1935–39). Unusual.
Malina English. From Magdalen, Greek, "From Magdala," an ancient city on the Sea of Galilee. The city was named in honor of its tower (Hebrew, "migdal"). Unusual.
Malinde English. From Melinda, Latin, "Honey" + a diminutive ending. Unusual.
Malka Hebrew/Israeli. Hebrew, "Queen." Unusual.
Malkin German. From Matilda, Old German (Mahthildis), "Battle maiden." Unusual.
Malkuyu Native American. Native American, "Drying farewell-to-spring flowers." The farewell-to-spring is a plant. Unusual.
Mallory English. French, "Unlucky" or "unfortunate." Unusual for males, popular for females. Alternative spellings: Mallorey, Mallorie, Malori, Malorie, Malory.
Mally English. From Miriam, Hebrew (Miryam), "Bitterness," "rebellion," "wished-for child," or "sea" (?). Exodus 15:20. Unusual. Alternative spelling: Mallie.
Malomo African. Nigerian, "Don't return to the spirit world." Per superstition, evil spirits are incarnated in some children. A name like this is given to prevent a child's death if its spirit leaves the world. Unusual.
Malonza English. Place name used as a first name; origin unknown. Unusual.
Malulani Hawaiian. Hawaiian, "Under heavenly protection." Unusual.
Malva English. From Melba, adaptation of a place name (Melbourne, Australia); origin unknown. Unusual.
Malvina Created. Created by James Macpherson in his Ossianic poems. Hoffman (sculptor, made bronzes of 110 racial types for Chicago Field Museum). Unusual.
Mame English. From Miriam, Hebrew (Miryam), "Bitterness," "rebellion," "wished-for child," or "sea" (?). Exodus 15:20. Unusual.
Mamie English. From Miriam, Hebrew (Miryam), "Bitterness," "rebellion," "wished-for child," or "sea" (?). Exodus 15:20. Doud Eisenhower (wife of President Dwight); Van Doren (actress). Unusual. Alternative spelling: Mamy.
Mamo Hawaiian. Hawaiian, "Saffron flower" or "yellow bird." Unusual for males, unusual for females.

Mamta Indo-Pakistani. Hindi, "Affection." Unusual.

Mana Hawaiian. Hawaiian, "Supernatural power." Unusual.

Manaba Native American. Native American, "War returned with her coming." Unusual.

Mancey English. From Mansi. Unusual. Alternative spellings: Manci, Mancie, Mansey, Mansie, Mansy.

Manda English. From Amanda, Latin, "Fit to be loved." Unusual.

Mandaline English. From Amanda, Latin, "Fit to be loved." Unusual. Mandy+.

Mandara Indo-Pakistani. Hindi, the name of a mythical tree. In Hindu lore, all worries are forgotten under the shade of this tree. Unusual.

Mandisa African. South African, "Sweet." Unusual.

Mandy English. From Amanda, Latin, "Fit to be loved." Less popular. Alternative spellings: Mande, Mandi, Mandie.

Manette French. From Miriam, Hebrew (Miryam), "Bitterness," "rebellion," "wished-for child," or "sea" (?). Exodus 15:20. Unusual.

Mangena Hebrew/Israeli. Hebrew, "Song" or "melody." Unusual. Alternative spelling: Mangina.

Mani Chinese. Chinese, from the Tibetan Buddhist prayer "om mani padme hum." Repeating these words is said to be a charm that conquers evil and imparts understanding. The meaning of the words is unknown. Unusual.

Manka Polish, Russian. From Miriam, Hebrew (Miryam), "Bitterness," "rebellion," "wished-for child," or "sea" (?). Exodus 15:20. Unusual.

Manon French. From Miriam, Hebrew (Miryam), "Bitterness," "rebellion," "wished-for child," or "sea" (?). Exodus 15:20. Unusual.

Mansi Native American. Native American, "Plucked flower." Unusual.

Manuela Hispanic. From Emanuel, Hebrew, "God is with us," referring to a child about to be born. Isaiah 7:14. Sáenz (mistress of South American soldier and statesman Simón Bolívar). Unusual.

Manya Russian. From Miriam, Hebrew (Miryam), "Bitterness," "rebellion," "wished-for child," or "sea" (?). Exodus 15:20. Unusual.

Mara English, Hungarian, Russian, Serbian. From Miriam, Hebrew (Miryam), "Bitterness," "rebellion," "wished-for child," or "sea" (?). Exodus 15:20. Unusual.

Marabel English. From Mariabella, Latin, "Beautiful Mary." Unusual. Alternative spelling: Marable.

Marah English. From Mara. Unusual.

Maranda English. From Miranda, Latin, "Fit to be admired." Unusual.

Marbella English. From Mariabella, Latin, "Beautiful Mary." Unusual.

Marca Czech. From Miriam, Hebrew (Miryam), "Bitterness," "rebellion," "wished-for child," or "sea" (?). Exodus 15:20. Unusual.

Marcalla English. From Mizela, meaning and origin unknown. May be a phonetic variant or misunderstanding of existing names like Marcus (Latin, "War-like one"). Unusual.

Marce French. From Marcus, Latin, "Warlike one." Derived from Mars, the Roman god of war. Unusual.

Marcel French. From Marcus, Latin, "Warlike one." Derived from Mars, the Roman god of war. Treich-LaPlene (19th-century French explorer in Africa); Ayme (French novelist); Depréz (French engineer and pioneer electrician, transmitted electric power 35 miles over telegraph wires); Proust (French novelist); Pagnol (French playwright). Less popular for males, unusual for females. Alternative spelling: Marcelle.

Marcelia English. From Marcus, Latin, "Warlike one." Derived from Mars, the Roman god of war. Unusual.

Marceline English. From Marcus, Latin, "Warlike one." Derived from Mars, the Roman god of war. Desborough (19th-century French poet). Unusual. Alternative spellings: Marcellin, Marcelyn.

Marcella English. From Marcus, Latin, "Warlike one." Derived from Mars, the Roman god of war. Unusual. Alternative spellings: Marcela, Marsella.

Marcena English. From Marcus, Latin, "Warlike one." Derived from Mars, the Roman god of war. Unusual. Alternative spelling: Marcina.

Marcene English. From Marcus, Latin, "Warlike one." Derived from Mars, the Roman god of war. Unusual. Alternative spelling: Marcine.

Marci English. From Marcus, Latin, "Warlike one." Derived from Mars, the Roman god of war. Unusual. Alternative spellings: Marcie, Marcy, Marsi, Marsie, Marsy.

Marcia English, from Marcus, Latin, "Warlike one," derived from Mars, the Roman god of war; and Polish, from Martha, Aramaic, "Lady" or "mistress of the house." Luke 10:38. Less popular. Alternative spellings: Marsha, Marshia.

Marciann English. From Marcus, Latin, "Warlike one." Derived from Mars, the Roman god of war. Unusual.

Marcianna English. From Marcus, Latin, "Warlike one." Derived from Mars, the Roman god of war. Unusual.

Marcille English. From Marcus, Latin, "Warlike one." Derived from Mars, the Roman god of war. Unusual.

Marcilyn English. From Marcus, Latin, "Warlike one." Derived from Mars, the Roman god of war. Unusual.

Marcsa Hungarian. From Miriam, Hebrew (Miryam), "Bitterness," "rebellion," "wished-for child," or "sea" (?). Exodus 15:20. Unusual.

Mardi English. French, "Tuesday." Unusual.

Mare Latvian. From Miriam, Hebrew (Miryam), "Bitterness," "rebellion," "wished-for child," or "sea" (?). Exodus 15:20. Winningham (actress). Unusual.

Marella English. English, combination of Mary (Miriam, Hebrew (Miryam), "Bitterness," "rebellion," "wished-for child," or "sea" (?)) + Ella (Old German, "All"). Unusual.

Marelle English. From Marella. Unusual.

Maren English. From Miriam, Hebrew (Miryam), "Bitterness," "rebellion," "wished-for child," or "sea" (?). Exodus 15:20. Unusual.

Marena English. From Marina, Latin, "Of the sea." Also may be derived from a Roman clan name. Unusual. Alternative spelling: Marrina.

Marenka Czech. From Miriam, Hebrew (Miryam), "Bitterness," "rebellion," "wished-for child," or "sea" (?). Exodus 15:20. Unusual.

Maretta English. From Miriam, Hebrew (Miryam), "Bitterness," "rebellion," "wished-for child," or "sea" (?). Exodus 15:20. Unusual.

Marette English. From Miriam, Hebrew

(Miryam), "Bitterness," "rebellion," "wished-for child," or "sea" (?). Exodus 15:20. Unusual.

Marga Estonian. From Margaret. Unusual.

Margalit Hebrew/Israeli. From Margaret. Unusual.

Marganit Hebrew/Israeli. Hebrew, the name of an Israeli flower. Unusual.

Margara Hispanic. From Margaret. Unusual.

Margaret English. Greek, "margaron" ("pearl"). Saint; Barnes (won Pulitzer Prize for fiction, 1931, "Years of Grace"); Mitchell (novelist, "Gone With the Wind"); Mead (cultural anthropologist); Sanger (birth control pioneer); Thatcher (first female British prime minister, 1974–91); Gorman (Miss America, 1921). Popular. Madge, Maggie, Peg, Peggy. Alternative spellings: Margarett, Margarette, Margeret, Margrett, Marguerette.

Margarete Finnish. From Margaret. Unusual.

Margaretha English. From Margaret. Unusual. Madge, Maggie, Peg, Peggy.

Margarid Armenian. From Margaret. Unusual.

Margarida Portuguese. From Margaret. Unusual.

Margarita English, Hispanic, Italian, Lithuanian. From Margaret. Cansino (real name of Rita Hayworth). Unusual. Madge, Maggie, Peg, Peggy. Alternative spellings: Margareta, Margharita, Marguarita, Marguerita, Margurita.

Margarite Hispanic. From Margaret. Unusual.

Margaritis Greek. From Margaret. Unusual.

Margaro Greek. From Margaret. Unusual.

Margaux English. French, the name of a champagne. Hemingway (actress). Less popular. Alternative spellings: Margo, Margot.

Marge English. From Margaret. Less popular.

Margeretta English. From Margaret. Unusual. Madge, Maggie, Peg, Peggy. Alternative spellings: Margarethe, Margaretta, Marguaretta.

Margerite English. From Margaret. Unusual. Madge, Maggie, Peg, Peggy. Alternative spellings: Marguarite, Margurite.

Marget English. From Margaret. Unusual. Madge, Maggie, Peg, Peggy.

Margherita Italian. From Margaret. Unusual.

Margie English. From Margaret. Less popular. Alternative spelling: Margy.

Margisia Polish. From Margaret. Unusual.

Margit Hungarian. From Margaret. Unusual.

Margita Czech, Laotian, Polish. From Margaret. Unusual.

Margret German. From Margaret. Unusual.

Margreta Scandinavian. From Margaret. Unusual.

Margrete Scandinavian. From Margaret. Unusual.

Margrett English. From Margaret. Unusual. Madge, Maggie, Peg, Peggy.

Margretta English. From Margaret. Unusual. Madge, Maggie, Peg, Peggy.

Margrieta Latvian. From Margaret. Unusual.

Margrita English. From Margaret. Unusual. Madge, Maggie, Peg, Peggy.

Marguerite French. From Margaret. Steen (British novelist, "Gilt Cape"); Gardiner (19th-century Irish author, "Grace Cassidy"); Perey (French physicist, first woman member of French Academy of Science, 1962); Gaudet (18th-century French politician). Unusual.

Mari English, Estonian, Hispanic. From Miriam, Hebrew (Miryam), "Bitterness," "rebellion," "wished-for child," or "sea" (?), Exodus 15:20, and from Margaret, Greek, "margaron" ("pearl"). Unusual.

Maria English, Hispanic (María), Italian, Russian. From Miriam, Hebrew (Miryam), "Bitterness," "rebellion," "wished-for child," or "sea" (?). Exodus 15:20. Saint; Mayer (won 1963 Nobel Prize for physics); Fletcher (Miss America, 1962); Zayas (17th-century Spanish novelist). Popular. Alternative spelling: Marea.

Mariabella Latin. Latin, "Beautiful Mary." Unusual.

Mariae English. From Miriam, Hebrew (Miryam), "Bitterness," "rebellion," "wished-for child," or "sea" (?). Exodus 15:20. Unusual.

Mariah English. From Miriam, Hebrew (Miryam), "Bitterness," "rebellion," "wished-for child," or "sea" (?). Exodus 15:20. Less popular.

Mariam English. From Miriam, Hebrew (Miryam), "Bitterness," "rebellion," "wished-for child," or "sea" (?). Exodus 15:20. Unusual.

Mariana English. From Miriam, Hebrew (Miryam), "Bitterness," "rebellion," "wished-for child," or "sea" (?). Exodus 15:20. van Rensselaer (art critic); Alcoforado (18th-century Portuguese nun); character in Shakespeare's "Measure for Measure." Unusual. Alternative spelling: Marianna.

Marianne English, French. From Mary-Ann, English, combination of Mary (Miriam, Hebrew (Miryam), "Bitterness," "rebellion," "wished-for child," or "sea" (?)) + Ann (Hannah, Hebrew (Chanah), "Grace" or "favor"). Moore (won Pulitzer Prize for poetry, 1951); von Willemer (19th-century German dancer, actress); Faithfull (British actress); Dashwood (character in Jane Austen's "Sense and Sensibility"). Unusual. Alternative spellings: Mariane, Mariann, Marrianne.

Maribelle English. From Mariabella, Latin, "Beautiful Mary." Unusual.

Maricara Romanian. From Miriam, Hebrew (Miryam), "Bitterness," "rebellion," "wished-for child," or "sea" (?). Exodus 15:20. Unusual.

Marice English. From Miriam, Hebrew (Miryam), "Bitterness," "rebellion," "wished-for child," or "sea" (?). Exodus 15:20. Unusual. Alternative spelling: Marise.

Maridel English. From Miriam, Hebrew (Miryam), "Bitterness," "rebellion," "wished-for child," or "sea" (?). Exodus 15:20. Unusual.

Marie English, French. From Miriam, Hebrew (Miryam), "Bitterness," "rebellion," "wished-for child," or "sea" (?). Exodus 15:20. Osmond (country singer); Tussaud (Swiss wax modeler, established "Madame's Tussaud's Exhibition" in London); Curie (French, discovered radium) (real name: Marja Skłodowska); Salle (18th-century French dancer and choreographer); de Sévigné (17th-century French writer). Popular. Alternative spelling: Maree.

Mariel English. From Miriam, Hebrew (Miryam), "Bitterness," "rebellion," "wished-for child," or "sea" (?). Exodus 15:20. Hemingway (actress). Unusual.

Mariela English. From Miriam, Hebrew (Miryam), "Bitterness," "rebellion," "wished-for child," or "sea" (?). Exodus 15:20. Unusual.

Mariella Italian. From Miriam, Hebrew (Miryam), "Bitterness," "rebellion," "wished-for child," or "sea" (?). Exodus 15:20. Unusual.

Marielle Dutch, French. From Miriam, Hebrew (Miryam), "Bitterness," "rebellion," "wished-for child," or "sea" (?). Exodus 15:20. Unusual.

Marienka Czech. From Miriam, Hebrew (Miryam), "Bitterness," "rebellion," "wished-for child," or "sea" (?). Exodus 15:20. Unusual.

Marietta English. From Miriam, Hebrew (Miryam), "Bitterness," "rebellion," "wished-for child," or "sea" (?). Exodus 15:20. Holley (humorist and author). Unusual. Alternative spelling: Marrietta.

Mariette English. From Miriam, Hebrew (Miryam), "Bitterness," "rebellion," "wished-for child," or "sea" (?). Exodus 15:20. Hartley (actress). Unusual.

Marigold English. English, a flower name. Derived from Mary (Miriam, Hebrew, "Bitterness," "rebellion," "wished-for child," or "sea" (?)) + gold. Unusual.

Marija Lithuanian. From Miriam, Hebrew (Miryam), "Bitterness," "rebellion," "wished-for child," or "sea" (?). Exodus 15:20. Unusual.

Marika Greek. From Miriam, Hebrew (Miryam), "Bitterness," "rebellion," "wished-for child," or "sea" (?). Exodus 15:20. Unusual.

Marilee English. From Miriam, Hebrew (Miryam), "Bitterness," "rebellion," "wished-for child," or "sea" (?). Exodus 15:20. Unusual.

Marilyn English. From Miriam, Hebrew (Miryam), "Bitterness," "rebellion," "wished-for child," or "sea" (?). Exodus 15:20. Monroe (actress); Meseke (Miss America, 1938); Buferd (Miss America, 1946); Van Derbur (Miss America, 1958); Horne (actress). Less popular. Alternative spellings: Maralin, Maralyn, Maralyne, Maralynn, Maralynne, Marilin, Marillyn, Marilynn, Marilynne, Marolyn, Marrilyn, Marrilynn, Marrilynne, Marylin, Marylinn, Marylyn.

Marina Greek, Russian. Latin, "Of the sea." Also may be derived from a Roman clan name. Saint; Lobatch (Russian, rhythmic gymnastics world champion, 1988); Tsvetayeva (Russian poet). Unusual.

Marinda English. From Miriam, Hebrew (Miryam), "Bitterness," "rebellion," "wished-for child," or "sea" (?). Exodus 15:20. Unusual.

Marini African. Swahili, "Fresh," "healthy," or "pretty." Unusual.

Marinka Russian. From Miriam, Hebrew (Miryam), "Bitterness," "rebellion," "wished-for child," or "sea" (?). Exodus 15:20. Unusual.

Marion English. From Miriam, Hebrew (Miryam), "Bitterness," "rebellion," "wished-for child," or "sea" (?). Exodus 15:20. Folsom (secretary of Health, Education, and Welfare under Eisenhower); Bergeron (Miss America, 1933); Delorme (17th-century French courtesan); Dorset (chemist). Unusual for males, less popular for females. Alternative spellings: Marian, Marrian, Marrion.

Mariquita Hispanic. From Miriam, Hebrew (Miryam), "Bitterness," "rebellion," "wished-for child," or "sea" (?). Exodus 15:20. Unusual.

Maris English. Latin, "Star of the sea." A title for the Virgin Mary. Unusual.

Marisha English, from Maris; or from Miriam, Hebrew (Miryam), "Bitterness," "rebellion," "wished-for child," or "sea" (?). Exodus 15:20. Unusual.

Mariska Hungarian, from Miriam, Hebrew (Miryam), "Bitterness," "rebellion," "wished-for child," or "sea" (?), Exodus 15:20. Unusual.

Marissa English. From Miriam, Hebrew (Miryam), "Bitterness," "rebellion," "wished-for child," or "sea" (?), Exodus 15:20; or from Maris, Latin, "Star of the sea," a title for the Virgin Mary. Less popular. Alternative spelling: Marisa.

Marita English, Hispanic. From Miriam, Hebrew (Miryam), "Bitterness," "rebellion," "wished-for child," or "sea" (?). Exodus 15:20. Koch (German, set 1985 world record for 400-meter run: 47.6 seconds). Unusual.

Mariya Russian. From Miriam, Hebrew (Miryam), "Bitterness," "rebellion," "wished-for child," or "sea" (?). Exodus 15:20. Miloslavskaya (17th-century Russian czarina, first wife of Czar Alexis). Unusual.

Mariyah Arabic. From Miriam, Hebrew (Miryam), "Bitterness," "rebellion," "wished-for child," or "sea" (?). Exodus 15:20. Unusual.

Marja Finnish. From Miriam, Hebrew (Miryam), "Bitterness," "rebellion," "wished-for child," or "sea" (?). Exodus 15:20. Skłodowska (discovered radium, awarded 1903 Nobel Prize for physics) (real name of Marie Curie); Konopnicka (Polish poet). Unusual.

Marjatta Finnish. From Margaret, Greek, "margaron" ("pearl"). Unusual.

Marjorie English. From Margaret, Greek, "margaron" ("pearl"). Gestring (youngest woman to win Olympic gold medal: 13 years, 9 months, in 1936, for women's springboard dive); Rawlings (Pulitzer Prize for fiction, 1938, "The Yearling"); Bowen (British novelist) (real name: Gabrielle Long). Less popular. Marge, Margie. Alternative spellings: Margerie, Margery, Margorie, Margory, Marjery, Marjori, Marjory.

Marka Czech. From Margaret, Greek, "margaron" ("pearl"). Unusual.

Marketa Bulgarian, Czech (Markéta). From Margaret, Greek, "margaron" ("pearl"). Unusual.

Marla English. From Marlene. Less popular.

Marlaina English. From Marlene. Unusual. Alternative spelling: Marlena.

Marlaine English. From Marlene. Unusual. Alternative spelling: Marlane.

Marlee English. From Marlene. Matlin (deaf actress, "Children of a Lesser God"). Unusual. Alternative spellings: Marlea, Marley, Marlie.

Marlene English. English, combination of Maria (Miriam, Hebrew (Miryam), "Bitterness," "rebellion," "wished-for child," or "sea" (?)) + Magdalene (Magdalen, Greek, "From Magdala," an ancient city on the Sea of Galilee). Dietrich (German actress) (real name: Maria Magdalena von Losch). Less popular. Alternative spellings: Marleen, Marline.

Marlin See under Boys' Names.

Marlo English. From Marlowe, surname used as a first name; origin unknown. Thomas (actress). Unusual. Alternative spelling: Marlow.

Marlyn English. From Marlene. Unusual. Alternative spelling: Marlyne.

Marna Scandinavian. From Marina,

Latin, "Of the sea." Also may be derived from a Roman clan name. Unusual.

Marni English, from Marina, Latin, "Of the sea"; also may be derived from a Roman clan name; or Hebrew/Israeli, from Marni, Hebrew, "To rejoice." Nixon (singer). Unusual. Alternative spellings: Marne, Marney.

Maroula Greek. From Miriam, Hebrew (Miryam), "Bitterness," "rebellion," "wished-for child," or "sea" (?). Exodus 15:20. Unusual.

Marquita English. From Marcus, Latin, "Warlike one." Derived from Mars, the Roman god of war. Unusual.

Marsail Scottish. From Margaret, Greek, "margaron" ("pearl"). Unusual.

Marta Italian. From Martha. Less popular.

Martha English. Aramaic, "Lady" or "mistress of the house." Luke 10:38. Patron saint of housewives; Dandridge Washington (wife of President George); Ostenso (novelist); Thomas (educator and author); Berry (educator, established Berry schools for underprivileged children). Less popular.

Marthe French. From Martha. Unusual.

Marthena English. From Martha. Unusual.

Marti English. From Martha. Unusual.

Marticka Czech. From Martha. Unusual.

Martie English. From Martha. Unusual.

Martina Hispanic, from Martha. Navratilova (Czech tennis great). Unusual.

Martine French. From Martin, Latin, "Warlike." Derived from Mars, the Roman god of war. Unusual.

Martus Hungarian. From Martha. Unusual.

Martuska Hungarian. From Martha. Unusual.

Maruca Hispanic. From Miriam, Hebrew (Miryam), "Bitterness," "rebellion," "wished-for child," or "sea" (?). Exodus 15:20. Unusual.

Maruja Hispanic. From Miriam, Hebrew (Miryam), "Bitterness," "rebellion," "wished-for child," or "sea" (?). Exodus 15:20. Unusual.

Maruska Russian. From Miriam, Hebrew (Miryam), "Bitterness," "rebellion," "wished-for child," or "sea" (?). Exodus 15:20. Unusual.

Mary English. From Miriam, Hebrew (Miryam), "Bitterness," "rebellion," "wished-for child," or "sea" (?). Exodus 15:20. Saint; Cassatt (impressionist painter, "Women Bathing"); Wells (musician, "My Guy"); Baker Eddy (established Christian Science religion); Shelley (British author, "Frankenstein"); Pickford (Canadian actress) (real name: Gladys Smith). Popular.

Mary-Ann English. English, combination of Mary (Miriam, Hebrew (Miryam), "Bitterness," "rebellion," "wished-for child," or "sea" (?)) + Ann (Hannah, Hebrew (Chanah), "Grace" or "favor"). Less popular. Alternative spellings: Mary-Anne, Maryann, Maryanne.

Marya English, Russian. From Miriam, Hebrew (Miryam), "Bitterness," "rebellion," "wished-for child," or "sea" (?). Exodus 15:20. Unusual.

Maryam Arabic. From Miriam, Hebrew (Miryam), "Bitterness," "rebellion," "wished-for child," or "sea" (?). Exodus 15:20. Unusual.

Maryanna English. From Mary-Ann. Unusual.

Marye Estonian. From Miriam, Hebrew (Miryam), "Bitterness," "rebellion," "wished-for child," or "sea" (?). Exodus 15:20. Unusual.

Maryla Polish. From Miriam, Hebrew (Miryam), "Bitterness," "rebellion," "wished-for child," or "sea" (?). Exodus 15:20. Unusual.

Maryna Polish. From Miriam, Hebrew (Miryam), "Bitterness," "rebellion," "wished-for child," or "sea" (?). Exodus 15:20. Unusual.

Maryse Dutch, French. From Miriam, Hebrew (Miryam), "Bitterness," "rebellion," "wished-for child," or "sea" (?). Exodus 15:20. Unusual.

Marzalie English. From Mizela, meaning and origin unknown. May be a phonetic variant or misunderstanding of existing names like Marcus (Latin, "War-like one"). Unusual.

Masago Japanese. Japanese, "Sand." Symbolizes longevity. Unusual.

Masella English. From Mizela, meaning and origin unknown. May be a phonetic variant or misunderstanding of existing names like Marcus (Latin, "War-like one"). Unusual.

Masha Russian. From Miriam, Hebrew (Miryam), "Bitterness," "rebellion," "wished-for child," or "sea" (?). Exodus 15:20. Unusual.

Mashenka Russian. From Miriam, Hebrew (Miryam), "Bitterness," "rebellion," "wished-for child," or "sea" (?). Exodus 15:20. Unusual.

Mashka Russian. From Miriam, Hebrew (Miryam), "Bitterness," "rebellion," "wished-for child," or "sea" (?). Exodus 15:20. Unusual.

Masia Polish. From Martha, Aramaic, "Lady" or "mistress of the house." Luke 10:38. Unusual.

Masika African. Swahili, "Born during the rainy season." Unusual.

Matana Hebrew/Israeli. Hebrew, "Gift." Unusual.

Matanmi African. Nigerian, "Do not deceive me." According to superstition, evil spirits are incarnated in some children. A name like this is given to prevent the child's death if its spirit should leave the world. Unusual.

Matelda Italian. From Matilda. Unusual.

Mathilde German. From Matilda. Kschessinskaya (Russian dancer). Unusual.

Matilda English. Old German (Mahthildis), "Battle maiden." Serao (Italian novelist). Unusual. Mat, Mattie+, Tillie+. Alternative spelling: Mathilda.

Matilde French, Hispanic. From Matilda. Unusual.

Matrika Indo-Pakistani. Hindi, "Mother." Another name for the Hindu goddess Sakti. Unusual.

Matsu Japanese. Japanese, "Pine." Unusual.

Matti English. From Matilda. Nykaenen (Finnish, won two gold medals for ski jump in 1988 Olympics). Unusual. Alternative spellings: Mattie, Matty.

Matusha Hispanic. From Matilda. Unusual.

Matuxa Hispanic. From Matilda. Unusual.

Matylda Czech. From Matilda. Unusual.

Maud English. From Matilda. Park (reformer, first president of National League of Woman Voters, 1920–24); Gonne (Irish actress and patriot). Unusual. Alternative spelling: Maude.

Maudie English. From Matilda. Unusual.

Maudlin English. From Magdalen, Greek, "From Magdala," an ancient city on the Sea of Galilee. The city was named in honor of its tower (Hebrew, "migdal"). Unusual.

Maura English, Irish. From Miriam, Hebrew (Miryam), "Bitterness," "rebellion," "wished-for child," or "sea" (?). Exodus 15:20. Less popular. Alternative spelling: Maure.

Maureen English, Irish. From Miriam, Hebrew (Miryam), "Bitterness," "rebellion," "wished-for child," or "sea" (?). Exodus 15:20. O'Sullivan (actress); Stapleton (actress); McGovern (singer); Connolly (tennis great, first woman to win "Grand Slam"). Less popular. Alternative spellings: Maurene, Maurine, Moreen, Morreen, Moureen.

Mausi Native American. Native American, "Plucking flowers." Unusual.

Mavies English. From Mavis. Unusual.

Mavin Irish. From Maeve, Irish, meaning unknown. Unusual. Alternative spelling: Mavon.

Mavine Irish. From Maeve, Irish, meaning unknown. Unusual.

Mavis English. French, "Thrush." Hutchinson (South African runner, set 1978 Trans-American race record: 69 days, 2 hours, 40 minutes). Unusual. Alternative spelling: Mayvis.

Maxima Latin. From Maximilian, Latin, "Greatest in excellence." Unusual.

Maxina English. From Maximilian, Latin, "Greatest in excellence." Unusual. Alternative spelling: Maxena.

Maxine English. From Maximilian, Latin, "Greatest in excellence." Elliott (actress) (real name: Jessie Dermot). Unusual. Alternative spellings: Maxeen, Maxene.

May English. Meaning and origin unknown. Possibly an early feminine form of Mayhew (Matthew, Hebrew, "Gift of the Lord") or a later nickname for M-names such as Mary. Robson (actress); Irwin (actress). Less popular.

Maya Indo-Pakistani. Hindi, "God's creative power." Chiburdanidze (Russian, youngest chess champion: age 17, 1978); Plisetskaya (Russian ballerina). Unusual.

Maybelle English. From Amabel, Latin, "Lovable." Unusual. Alternative spellings: Maybel, Maybell.

Mayberry English. From May. Unusual.

Maybeth English. From May. Unusual.

Maybull English. From Amabel, Latin, "Lovable." Unusual.

Mayday English. From May. Unusual.

Maydee English. From May. Unusual.

Mayelene English. From May. Unusual.

Mayella English. From May. Unusual.

Mayetta English. From May. Unusual.

Mayrene English. From May. Unusual.

Maysie English. From Margaret, Greek, "margaron" ("pearl"). Unusual.

Mayvoureen English. From May. Unusual.

Mazal Hebrew/Israeli. Hebrew, "Luck" or "destiny." Unusual.

Mazala English. From Mizela, meaning and origin unknown. May be a phonetic variant or misunderstanding of existing names like Marcus (Latin, "War-like one"). Unusual.

Mazella English. From Mizela, meaning and origin unknown. May be a phonetic variant or misunderstanding of existing names like Marcus (Latin, "War-like one"). Unusual.

Mazie Scottish. From Margaret, Greek, "margaron" ("pearl"). Unusual. Alternative spellings: Masie, Mazey.

Mazila English. From Mizela, meaning and origin unknown. May be a phonetic variant or misunderstanding of existing names like Marcus (Latin, "War-like one"). Unusual.

Meda Native American. Native American, "Prophet," "priestess," or "edible root." Unusual.

Medina Arabic. Arabic, "City"; place name used as a first name. Unusual.

Medora English. "Mother's gift"; origin unknown. Character in Byron's poem "Corsair." Unusual.

Meeri Estonian. From Margaret, Greek, "margaron" ("pearl"). Unusual.

Meg English. From Margaret, Greek, "margaron" ("pearl"). Less popular.

Mega Hispanic. Spanish, "Peaceful," "gentle," or "mild." Unusual.

Megan English, Irish, Welsh. From Margaret, Greek, "margaron" ("pearl"). Austin (had most living ascendants at birth in 1982: 19 grandparents, great-grandparents, or great-great-grandparents). Extremely popular. Meg. Alternative spellings: Meagan, Meaghan, Meaghen, Megen, Meghan, Meghann.

Meggie English. From Margaret, Greek, "margaron" ("pearl"). Unusual. Alternative spellings: Meggi, Meggy.

Mehala English. From Mahala, Hebrew, "Tenderness." Unusual. Alternative spelling: Mehalah.

Mehalia English. From Mahala, Hebrew, "Tenderness." Unusual.

Mehira Hebrew/Israeli. From Mahir, Hebrew, "Expert," "industrious," or "quick." Unusual. Alternative spelling: Meira.

Meirionfa Welsh. From Meirion, Welsh, place name. Unusual.

Meirionwen Welsh. From Meirion, Welsh, place name. Unusual.

Mel See under Boys' Names.

Mela Indo-Pakistani, from Mela, Hindi, "Religious gathering"; and Polish, from Melanie, Greek, "Black" or "dark-complected." Unusual.

Meladia English. From Melanie. Unusual.

Melaine English. From Melanie. Unusual. Alternative spelling: Melane.

Melana Russian. From Melanie. Unusual.

Melanie English. Greek, "Black" or "dark-complected." Hamilton (character in Mitchell's "Gone With the Wind"); Griffith (actress, "Working Girl"); Klein (British psychoanalyst). Popular. Mel. Alternative spellings: Melani, Melany, Mellanie, Melloney, Mellony, Meloni, Melonie, Melony.

Melaniya Russian. From Melanie. Unusual.

Melanka Russian. From Melanie. Unusual.

Melantha Greek. Greek, "Black flower." Character in Dryden's 1673 "Marriage à la Mode." Unusual.

Melanya Russian. From Melanie. Unusual.

Melashka Russian. From Melanie. Unusual.

Melasya Russian. From Melanie. Unusual.

Melba English. Adaptation of a place name (Melbourne, Australia); origin unknown. Unusual.

Melcia Polish. From Amelia, Latin, "Industrious" or "striving." Unusual.

Meleana English. From Melina. Unusual.

Melenia English. From Melanie. Unusual.

Melessa English. From Melissa. Unusual.

Meleta English. From Melita. Unusual.

Meli English. From Melissa. Unusual.

Melia English. From Amelia, Latin, "Industrious" or "striving." Unusual.

Melicent English. From Millicent, Old German (Amalswint), "Noble strength." Unusual. Alternative spelling: Meliscent.

Melina English. Greek, "Honey" + a diminutive ending. Mercouri (Greek actress). Unusual.

Melinda English. Latin, "Honey" + a diminutive ending. Unusual. Alternative spellings: Malinda, Mellinda, Melynda.

Melinder English. From Melinda. Unusual.

Meliora English. Latin, "Better." Unusual.

Melissa English. "Midnight Blue"); Gilbert (actress, "Little House on the Prairie"); Sue Anderson (actress, "Little House on the Prairie"). Very popular. Mel. Alternative spellings: Melisa, Melisse, Mellisa, Mellissa.

Melita English. Greek, "Honey." Unusual. Alternative spelling: Melitta.

Melka Polish. From Melanie. Unusual.

Mellear English. From Meliora. Unusual.

Melli English. From Melanie. Unusual. Alternative spellings: Melie, Mellie, Melly.

Mellicent English. From Millicent, Old German (Amalswint), "Noble strength." Unusual.

Mellisent English. From Millicent, Old German (Amalswint), "Noble strength." Unusual.

Melodia Latin. From Melody. Unusual.

Melody English. Greek, "Song." Less popular. Mel. Alternative spelling: Melodie.

Melosa Hispanic. Spanish, "Like honey" or "sweet." Unusual.

Melva English. From Malvina, Created by James Macpherson in his Ossianic poems. Unusual.

Melvina English. From Malvina, Created by James Macpherson in his Ossianic poems. Unusual. Mel.

Melyor English. From Meliora. Unusual.

Mema Hispanic. From Amelia, Latin, "Industrious" or "striving." Unusual.

Membta Native American. Native American, "To taste crushed farewell-to-spring seeds." Farewell-to-spring is a plant. Unusual.

Mena Dutch, German. German, "Strength." First king of unified Egypt, circa 3100 B.C. Unusual. Alternative spelling: Menna.

Menora Hebrew/Israeli. Hebrew, "Candelabrum." Unusual. Alternative spelling: Menorah.

Mentie English. From Araminta, Created by Sir John Vanbrugh in his 1705 comedy "The Confederacy." Unusual. Alternative spelling: Menty.

Merab Hebrew/Israeli. Hebrew, "Multiplication." Oldest daughter of Saul. Unusual.

Mercedes Hispanic. Spanish, "Grace" or "mercy." McCambridge (actress). Unusual.

Mercia English. Anglo-Saxon, the name of a kingdom. Harrison (wife of actor Rex Harrison). Unusual.

Mercy English. Latin, "merced" ("wages"); the word used as a first name. Warren (19th-century author of political satires). Less popular. Alternative spelling: Mercey.

Meredith English. Old Welsh, "Great chief." Baxter (actress, "Family Ties"). Less popular for males, less popular for females. Missy. Alternative spellings: Meridith, Meridath, Merideth, Merridith.

Meri English. From Miriam, Hebrew (Miryam), "Bitterness," "rebellion," "wished-for child," or "sea" (?). Exodus 15:20. Unusual.

Merial English. From Muriel, Irish, "Sea-bright." Unusual. Alternative spellings: Meriel, Meriol, Merrial, Merriel.

Merilyn English. From Muriel, Irish, "Sea-bright." Unusual. Alternative spellings: Merelyn, Merralyn, Merrilyn.

Merina English. From Marina, Latin, "Of the sea." Also may be derived from a Roman clan name. Unusual.

Meris English. From Maris, Latin, "Star of the sea." A title for the Virgin Mary. Unusual.

Merisa English. From Maris, Latin, "Star of the sea." A title for the Virgin Mary. Unusual. Alternative spelling: Merissa.

Meriwa Eskimo. Eskimo, "Thorn." Unusual.

Merlin See under Boys' Names.

Merlyn English. From Mervyn, Welsh, "Sea hill"; place name used as a first name. Unusual.

Merri English. From Meredith, Old Welsh, "Great chief." Unusual. Alternative spelling: Merrie.

Merrilee English. From Muriel, Irish, "Sea-bright." Unusual. Alternative spelling: Merrily.

Merry English. From Mercy, Latin, "merced" ("wages"); the word used as a first name. Unusual.

Meryem Turkish. From Miriam, Hebrew (Miryam), "Bitterness," "rebellion," "wished-for child," or "sea" (?). Exodus 15:20. Unusual.

Meryl English. From Muriel, Irish, "Sea-bright." Streep (actress, won 1982 Oscar for "Sophie's Choice"). Less popular. Alternative spellings: Merel, Meril, Merill, Merrall, Merrel, Merrell, Merril, Meryle, Meryll.

Mesella English. From Mizela, meaning and origin unknown. May be a phonetic variant or misunderstanding of existing names like Marcus (Latin, "War-like one"). Unusual. Alternative spelling: Messella.

Mesha Indo-Pakistani. Hindi, "Ram." Unusual.

Meta German. From Margaret, Greek, "margaron" ("pearl"). Unusual.

Mezillah English. From Mizela, meaning and origin unknown. May be a phonetic variant or misunderstanding of existing names like Marcus (Latin, "War-like one"). Unusual.

Mhairie Scottish. From Miriam, Hebrew (Miryam), "Bitterness," "rebellion," "wished-for child," or "sea" (?). Exodus 15:20. Unusual. Alternative spellings: Mhaire, Mhairi, Mhari, Mharie.

Mia English. From Miriam, Hebrew (Miryam), "Bitterness," "rebellion," "wished-for child," or "sea" (?). Exodus 15:20. Farrow (actress, "Hannah and Her Sisters"). Unusual.

Micaela English. From Michael, Hebrew, "Who is like God" Daniel 12:1. Unusual. Alternative spellings: Michaella, Michala, Mickala, Mycala, Myckala, Mykela.

Michael See under Boys' Names.

Michaela Scottish. From Michael, Hebrew, "Who is like God." Daniel 12:1. Unusual.

Michaelle Italian. From Michael, Hebrew, "Who is like God." Daniel 12:1. Unusual.

Michal English. From Michael, Hebrew, "Who is like God." Daniel 12:1. Unusual.

Michela English. From Michael, Hebrew, "Who is like God." Daniel 12:1. Unusual.

Michelle English, French. From Michael, Hebrew, "Who is like God." Daniel 12:1. Pfeiffer (actress, "Fabulous Baker Boys"); Phillips (singer). Very popular.

Alternative spellings: Michel, Michele, Michell.

Michi Japanese. Japanese, "Righteous way." Unusual.

Michiko Japanese. Japanese, "Beauty" + "wisdom." Unusual.

Micki English. From Michael, Hebrew, "Who is like God." Daniel 12:1. Unusual.

Mickie See Mickey under Boys' Names.

Micky See Mickey under Boys' Names.

Midori Japanese. Japanese, "Green." Ito (Japanese figure skater, first woman to complete triple axel in World Championships, 1989). Unusual.

Migina Native American. Native American, "Moon returning." Unusual.

Mignon English. French, "Cute." Eberhart (detective-story writer); Herione (title character in Ambroise Thomas's opera). Unusual.

Mignonette English. From Mignon. Unusual. Alternative spellings: Minnionette, Minnonette.

Mika Japanese, from Mika, Japanese, "New moon"; and Russian, from Dominic, Latin, "Lord." Unusual.

Miki Japanese. Japanese, "Stem." Unusual. Alternative spelling: Mikie.

Mikiyo Japanese. From Miki. Unusual.

Mila Slavic. From Ludmila, Slavic, "Loved by the people." Unusual.

Milada Czech. From Milada, Czech, "My love." Unusual.

Mildred English. Old English, "Mild strength." Saint; "Babe" Didrikson Zaharias (sports great, competed in basketball, track and field, and golf). Less popular. Milly+.

Milena Slavic. From Melanie, Greek, "Black" or "dark-complected." Unusual.

Milessa English. From Milo, Old German, "Generous" or "merciful." Unusual.

Mileta English. From Milo, Old German, "Generous" or "merciful." Unusual.

Milica Slavic. From Amelia, Latin, "Industrious" or "striving." Unusual.

Milka Czech. From Amelia, Latin, "Industrious" or "striving." Unusual.

Milla Polish. From Camillus, Latin, an attendant at religious services. Unusual.

Millie English. From Millicent. Less popular. Alternative spellings: Mili, Milley, Milli, Milly.

Millicent English. Old German (Amalswint), "Noble strength." Martin (British singer and actress). Unusual. Milly+. Alternative spelling: Millisent.

Milliestone English. From Millicent. Unusual.

Milya Russian. From Melanie, Greek, "Black" or "dark-complected." Unusual.

Mima English. From Jemima, Hebrew, "Dove." Job 42:14. Unusual.

Mimi English. From Miriam, Hebrew (Miryam), "Bitterness," "rebellion," "wished-for child," or "sea" (?). Exodus 15:20. Rogers (actress). Unusual. Alternative spelling: Mimie.

Min English. From William, Old German, "Will" + "helmet." Unusual.

Mina English. From William, Old German, "Will" + "helmet." Unusual.

Minal Native American. From Minal, Native American, "Fruit." Unusual.

Minda Indo-Pakistani. Hindi, "Knowledge" or "wisdom." Unusual.

Mindy English. From Melinda, Latin, "Honey" + a diminutive ending. Less popular. Alternative spellings: Mindi, Mindie.

Mineko Japanese. Japanese, "Peak." Unusual.

Minerva English. Latin, the name of the Roman goddess of wisdom. Unusual.

Minetta English. From William, Old German, "Will" + "helmet." Unusual.

Minette English. From William, Old German, "Will" + "helmet." Unusual.

Minivera English. From Minerva. Unusual.

Minka Polish. From William, Old German, "Will" + "helmet." Unusual.

Minna English. From William, Old German, "Will" + "helmet." Character in Sir Walter Scott's "Pirate." Unusual.

Minnehaha Created. "Laughing water," created by H.W. Longfellow in his 1855 poem "Hiawatha." Unusual.

Minnie English. From William, Old German, "Will" + "helmet." Fiske (actress) (real name: Marie Augusta); Hauk (opera singer, sang title roles in British and American premiers of "Carmen"); Pearl (comedian and country singer) (real name: Sarah Ophelia Colley Cannon). Unusual. Alternative spellings: Mini, Minie, Minni, Minny.

Minowa Native American. Native American, "Moving voice." Unusual.

Minty English. From Araminta, Created by Sir John Vanbrugh in his 1705 comedy "The Confederacy." Unusual.

Mio Japanese. Japanese, "Triple cord." Unusual.

Mira English. From Myra, Created, possibly based on Myron (Greek, "Sweet-smelling oil") or Mary (Miriam, Hebrew (Miryam), "Bitterness," "rebellion," "wished-for child," or "sea" (?)). Unusual.

Mirabel English. Latin, "Wonderful." Unusual. Alternative spellings: Mirabell, Mirabelle.

Mirabella English. From Mirabel. Unusual.

Miram English. From Miriam. Unusual. Alternative spelling: Mirham.

Miranda English. Latin, "Fit to be admired." Character in Shakespeare's "Tempest." Unusual.

Miri Gypsy, Hebrew/Israeli. From Miriam. Unusual.

Miriain English. From Miriam. Unusual. Alternative spelling: Miriaenne.

Miriam English. Hebrew (Miryam), "Bitterness," "rebellion," "wished-for child," or "sea" (?). Exodus 15:20. Sister of Moses and Aaron. Less popular. Alternative spellings: Mirriam, Myriam.

Miriama English. From Miriam. Unusual.

Mirjam Finnish. From Miriam. Unusual.

Mirra English. From Miriam. Unusual.

Mirrian English. From Miriam. Unusual. Alternative spelling: Mirian.

Miryam Hebrew/Israeli. From Miryam, Hebrew, "Bitterness," "rebellion," "wished-for child," or "sea" (?). Exodus 15:20. Unusual.

Mitchelle English. From Michael, Hebrew, "Who is like God." Daniel 12:1. Unusual.

Mituna Native American. Native American, "To roll up a salmon with leaves." Unusual.

Mitzi English. From Miriam. Gaynor (actress) (real name: Francesca Mitzi Marlene deChamey von Gerber). Less popular.

Miwa Japanese. Japanese, "Far-seeing." Unusual.

Miwako Japanese. From Miwa. Unusual.

Miya Japanese. Japanese, "Temple" or "Shinto." Unusual.

Miyo Japanese. Japanese, "Beautiful generations." Unusual.

Miyoko Japanese. From Miyo. Unusual.

Miyuki Japanese. Japanese, "Deep snow." Unusual.

Mizela English. Meaning and origin unknown. May be a phonetic variant or misunderstanding of existing names like Marcus (Latin, "War-like one"). Unusual. Alternative spelling: Mizella.

Mizelle English. From Mizela. Unusual.

Mizelli English. From Mizela. Unusual. Alternative spelling: Mizelly.

Mizzie English. From Mizela. Unusual.

Modesta Latin. From Modestus. Unusual.

Modestina English. From Modestus. Unusual.

Modestine English. From Modestus. Unusual.

Modestus Latin. Latin, "Modesty." Unusual.

Modesty English. From Modestus. Unusual.

Moemu Native American. Native American, "Bears meeting." Unusual.

Moira English, Irish, Scottish. From Miriam. Shearer (ballerina) (real name: Moira King); Lister (South African actress). Unusual. Alternative spelling: Moire.

Moll English. From Miriam. Unusual.

Molly English. From Miriam. Ringwald (actress, "Pretty in Pink"); Pitcher (American Revolution heroine, carried water to wounded soldiers) (real name: Mary McCauley). Less popular. Alternative spellings: Mollee, Molley, Molli, Mollie.

Mona English. Irish, "Noble." Less popular.

Monday English. Old English, "mona" ("moon") + "daeg" ("day"); the word used as a name. Unusual.

Monica English. Latin, "Adviser" or "nun." Patron saint of widows. Popular.

Monika German. From Monica. Less popular.

Monique French. From Monica. Less popular.

Mora Hispanic. Spanish, "Little blueberry." Unusual.

Morag Scottish. Gaelic, "Great." Unusual.

Moray Scottish. Scottish, surname and place name used as a first name. Unusual.

Morena Hispanic. From Miriam. Unusual.

Morfydd Welsh. Old Welsh, meaning unknown. Unusual. Alternative spelling: Morfudd.

Morgan Welsh. Welsh, "Great" + "bright." Fairchild (actress); Llwyd (17th-century Welsh writer); Russell (painter, established synchronist art movement); Smith (19th-century army officer). Less popular for males, popular for females.

Morganetta English. From Morgan, Welsh, "Great" + "bright." Unusual.

Morganne English. From Morgan, Welsh, "Great" + "bright." Unusual. Alternative spelling: Morgen.

Moria Hebrew/Israeli. From Moriah. Unusual. Alternative spelling: Moriah.

Morice English. From Maurice, Latin (Mauritius), "Moorish" (i.e., dark-skinned). Unusual.

Moriel Hebrew/Israeli. From Moriah. Unusual.

Morit Hebrew/Israeli. From Moriah. Unusual.

Morna Scottish. From Myrna, Gaelic, "Beloved," "gentle." Unusual.

Morwenna Welsh. Welsh, "Maiden." Saint. Unusual.

Moselle Hebrew/Israeli. From Moses, Hebrew (Moshe), "Drawn from the water." Exodus 2:10. Unusual.

Moya English. From Miriam, Hebrew (Miryam), "Bitterness," "rebellion," "wished-for child," or "sea" (?). Exodus 15:20. Unusual.

Moyna English. From Mona or Moyne. Unusual.

Moyne Irish. Irish, a place name referring to a small, flat area of land. Unusual.

Moyra English. From Miriam, Hebrew (Miryam), "Bitterness," "rebellion," "wished-for child," or "sea" (?). Exodus 15:20. Unusual.

Mozelle Hebrew/Israeli. From Moses, Hebrew (Moshe), "Drawn from the water." Exodus 2:10. Unusual.

Mu Lan Chinese. Chinese, "Magnolia blossom." Unusual.

Mu Tan Chinese. Chinese, "Tree-peony blossom." Unusual.

Muire Irish, Scottish. From Miriam, Hebrew (Miryam), "Bitterness," "rebellion," "wished-for child," or "sea" (?). Exodus 15:20. Unusual.

Muliya Native American. Native American, "To beat farewell-to-spring seeds." Farewell-to-spring is a plant. Unusual.

Mulya Native American. Native American, "To knock acorns off a tree." Unusual.

Muna Native American. Native American, "Freshet." Given to a child born during the rainy season when the streams swell. Unusual.

Mura Japanese. Japanese, "Village." Unusual.

Mureen English. From Miriam, Hebrew (Miryam), "Bitterness," "rebellion," "wished-for child," or "sea" (?). Exodus 15:20. Unusual.

Muriel English. Irish, "Sea-bright." Pavlov (British actress); Spark (Scottish novelist, "The Prime of Miss Jean Brodie"). Less popular. Alternative spellings: Murial, Muriell, Murielle.

Murnia Scottish. From Myrna. Unusual.

Myfannwy Welsh. From Myfanwy. Unusual. Alternative spelling: Myfanwy.

Mylie English. From Milo, Old German, "Generous" or "merciful." Unusual. Alternative spelling: Mylea.

Mylinda English. From Milo, Old German, "Generous" or "merciful." Unusual.

Myra English. Created, possibly based on Myron (Greek, "Sweet-smelling oil") or Mary (Miriam, Hebrew (Miryam), "Bitterness," "rebellion," "wished-for child," or "sea" (?)). Hess, Dame (British pianist, interpreter of Bach, Beethoven, Mozart, and Schumann); subject of Fulke Greville's 17th-century love poems. Less popular. Alternative spellings: Mira, Mirah, Mirra.

Myria English. From Miriam, Hebrew (Miryam), "Bitterness," "rebellion," "wished-for child," or "sea" (?). Exodus 15:20. Unusual.

Myrna Scottish. Gaelic, "Beloved," "gentle." Loy (actress, "Thin Man") (real name: Myrna Williams). Unusual. Alternative spelling: Muirna.

Myrtilla English. From Myrtle. Unusual.

Myrtle English. From Myrtle, Greek, "myrtos"; a plant name used as a first name. Less popular.

Mysie Scottish. From Margaret, Greek, "margaron" ("pearl"). Unusual.

Myzel English. From Mizela, meaning and origin unknown. May be a phonetic variant or misunderstanding of existing names like Marcus (Latin, "War-like one"). Unusual.

Nacia Polish. From Natalie, Latin, "Birthday of the Lord." Unusual.
Nada Russian. From Nadia. Unusual.
Nadena English. From Nadia. Unusual.
Nadenka Russian. From Nadia. Unusual.
Nadia Russian. Russian, "Hope." Comaneci (Romanian gymnast). Unusual. Alternative spellings: Nadiya, Nadja, Nadya.
Nadina Latvian, Russian. From Nadia. Unusual.
Nadine English, French. From Nadia. Gordimer (South African novelist, "My Son's Story"). Less popular. Alternative spellings: Nadeen, Nadene.
Nadka Russian. From Nadia. Unusual.
Nagida Hebrew/Israeli. Hebrew, "Wealthy" or "ruler." Unusual.
Naida English. Latin, "Water nymph." Unusual.
Nairne See under Boys' Names.
Nan English. From Hannah, Hebrew (Chanah), "Grace [of God]" or "favor." 1 Samuel 1:2. Less popular.
Nana Hispanic. From Hannah, Hebrew (Chanah), "Grace [of God]" or "favor." 1 Samuel 1:2. Unusual.
Nancy English. From Hannah, Hebrew (Chanah), "Grace [of God]" or "favor." 1 Samuel 1:2. Davis Reagan (wife of President Ronald); Fleming (Miss America, 1961); Mitford (British novelist, "Pursuit of Love"); Hanks (mother of Abraham Lincoln). Less popular. Alternative spellings: Nance, Nanci.
Nanette English. From Hannah, Hebrew (Chanah), "Grace [of God]" or "favor." 1 Samuel 1:2. Fabray (actress). Unusual.
Nani Hawaiian. Hawaiian, "Beautiful"; and Greek, from Hannah, Hebrew (Chanah), "Grace [of God]" or "favor," 1 Samuel 1:2. Unusual.
Nanna English. From Hannah, Hebrew (Chanah), "Grace [of God]" or "favor." 1 Samuel 1:2. Unusual.
Nanny English. From Hannah, Hebrew (Chanah), "Grace [of God]" or "favor." 1 Samuel 1:2. Unusual. Alternative spelling: Nannie.
Naomi English. Hebrew, "Pleasantness," "delight." Ruth 1:2. Mother-in-law of Ruth, returned from Moab with Ruth; Judd (country singer). Less popular. Alternative spelling: Naomie.
Naomia English. From Naomi. Unusual.
Nappy Irish. From Penelope, Greek, "Bobbin" or "weaver." Unusual.
Nara Japanese. Japanese, "Oak." Unusual.
Narelle Australian. Meaning and origin unknown. Possibly Australian Aboriginal, "Little." Unusual.
Nari Japanese. Japanese, "Thunderclap." Unusual.
Nariko Japanese. From Nari. Unusual.
Narilla Gypsy. English Gypsy, meaning unknown. Unusual.
Nashota Native American. Native American, "Twin." Unusual.
Nasnan Native American. Native American, "Surrounded by a song." Unusual.
Nastasya Latvian, Lithuanian, Russian. From Anastasia, Greek, "anastasis" ("resurrection"). Unusual.
Nastka Latvian, Lithuanian, Russian. From Anastasia, Greek, "anastasis" ("resurrection"). Unusual.
Nastusya Latvian, Lithuanian, Russian. From Anastasia, Greek, "anastasis" ("resurrection"). Unusual.
Nasya Hebrew/Israeli. Hebrew, "Miracle of God." Unusual. Alternative spelling: Nasia.
Nata Native American, from Nata, Native American, "Speaker" or "creator"; and Hispanic, "Hope"; and Polish, Russian, from Natalie, Latin, "Birthday of the Lord." Unusual.
Natacha Hispanic. From Natalie. Lachtchenova (Russian Olympic gymnast). Unusual.
Natalie English. Latin, "Birthday of the Lord." Cole (singer, daughter of Nat "King" Cole); Wood (actress) (real name: Natasha Gurdin). Popular. Alternative spellings: Natelie.
Natalina English. From Natalie. Unusual.
Nataline English. From Natalie. Unusual.
Natalka Russian. From Natalie. Unusual.
Natalya Russian. From Natalie. Beetemianova (Russian ice dancer, won 1988 Olympic gold medal); Naryshkina (17th-century consort of Czar Alexis). Unusual.
Natane Native American. From Nathan, Native American, "Daughter." Unusual.
Natasa Czech. From Natalie. Unusual.
Natasha Russian. From Natalie. Popular. Alternative spelling: Natashia.
Natesa Indo-Pakistani. Hindi, "Dance-lord." Another name for the Hindu god Siva. Unusual.
Nathalia English. From Natalie. Unusual.
Nathalie French. From Natalie. Unusual.
Natka Polish. From Natalie. Unusual.
Nattie English. From Natalie. Unusual. Alternative spellings: Nati, Natie, Natti.
Nava Hebrew/Israeli. From Navit. Unusual.
Navice Hebrew/Israeli. From Navit. Unusual.
Navit Hebrew/Israeli. Hebrew, "Beautiful" or "pleasant." Unusual.
Nealie English. From Neil, Irish, "Champion." Unusual. Alternative spellings: Nealy, Neeli, Neelie, Neely.
Necha Hispanic. From Agnes, Greek, "agnos" ("pure" or "chaste"). Unusual.
Nechama Hebrew/Israeli. Hebrew, "Comfort." Unusual.
Necho Hispanic. From Agnes, Greek, "agnos" ("pure" or "chaste"). I (Egyptian governor, 671–64 B.C.); II (Egyptian king, 610–595 B.C.). Unusual.
Neci Hungarian. Latin, "Intense," "fiery." Unusual.
Neda English, from Edward, Old English, "Property guardian"; and Slavic, from Natalie, Latin, "Birthday of the Lord." Unusual.
Nediva Hebrew/Israeli. Hebrew, "Noble" or "generous." Unusual.
Neema African. Swahili, "Born amidst prosperity." Unusual.
Neilla English. From Neil, Irish, "Champion." Unusual. Alternative spelling: Neila.
Neka Native American. Native American, "Wild goose." Unusual.
Nela Polish. From Peter, Greek, "Stone," "rock." John 1:42. Unusual.
Nele German. From Cornelius, Latin, "A horn." Acts 10:1. Unusual.
Nelia Hispanic. From Cornelius, Latin, "A horn." Acts 10:1. Unusual.
Nelka Polish. From Peter, Greek, "Stone," "rock." John 1:42. Unusual.
Nell English. From Helen, Greek, "Bright

one" or "shining one." Carter (actress). Unusual. Nellie+.

Nella English. From Helen, Greek, "Bright one" or "shining one." Unusual.

Nellie English. From Helen, Greek, "Bright one" or "shining one." Taylor-Ross (first woman elected governor of a state, Wyoming, 1925); Bly (journalist, wrote articles exposing insane asylums) (real name: Elizabeth Seaman); Melba, Dame (Australian operatic soprano) (real name: Helen Porter Mitchell). Less popular. Alternative spellings: Nelley, Nelli, Nelly.

Nelya Russian. From Helen, Greek, "Bright one" or "shining one." Unusual.

Neneca Hispanic. From Amelia, Latin, "Industrious" or "striving." Unusual.

Nenet Egyptian. Egyptian, the name of a goddess. Unusual.

Nepa Arabic. Arabic, "Walking backwards." Unusual.

Nerice English. From Nerida, Greek, "Sea nymph." Unusual.

Nerida English. Greek, "Sea nymph." Unusual.

Nerina English. From Nerida. Unusual.

Nerine English. From Nerida. Unusual.

Nerissa English. From Nerida. Unusual.

Nerisse English. From Nerida. Unusual.

Nerys Welsh. Welsh, "Lord." Hughes (Welsh actress). Unusual.

Nesa English. From Agnes, Greek, "agnos" ("pure" or "chaste"). Unusual.

Nesho Hispanic. From Agnes, Greek, "agnos" ("pure" or "chaste"). Unusual.

Ness English. From Agnes, Greek, "agnos" ("pure" or "chaste"). Unusual.

Nessa English. From Agnes, Greek, "agnos" ("pure" or "chaste"). Unusual.

Nessi English. From Agnes, Greek, "agnos" ("pure" or "chaste"). Unusual. Alternative spellings: Nesi, Nessy.

Nessia Russian. From Agnes, Greek, "agnos" ("pure" or "chaste"). Unusual.

Nessie Scottish. From Agnes, Greek, "agnos" ("pure" or "chaste"). Unusual.

Nest Welsh. From Agnes, Greek, "agnos" ("pure" or "chaste"). Unusual.

Nesta Welsh. From Agnes, Greek, "agnos" ("pure" or "chaste"). Unusual.

Neta Hebrew/Israeli. From Netia. Unusual.

Netia Hebrew/Israeli. Hebrew, "Plant" or "shrub." Unusual.

Netis See under Boys' Names.

Netta English. English, a nickname for names ending in "-nette" or "-netta," like Jeanette (John, Hebrew (Yochanan), "God has been gracious"). Unusual.

Nettchen German. From Hannah, Hebrew (Chanah), "Grace [of God]" or "favor." 1 Samuel 1:2. Unusual.

Nettie English. From Netta. Unusual. Alternative spellings: Netti, Netty, Nety.

Neva Hispanic. Spanish, "Snow." Langley (Miss America, 1953). Unusual.

Nevada English. Spanish, "Snowy." Unusual.

Neysa English. From Agnes, Greek, "agnos" ("pure" or "chaste"). Unusual.

Neza Slavic. From Agnes, Greek, "agnos" ("pure" or "chaste"). Unusual.

Ngu Vietnamese. Vietnamese, "Sleep." Unusual.

Niabi Native American. Native American, "Fawn." Unusual.

Nicholyn English. From Nicholas, Greek, "Victorious people." Unusual. Alternative spelling: Nicolyn.

Nicki English. From Nicholas, Greek, "Victorious people." Less popular. Alternative spellings: Nickie, Niki, Nikki.

Nicky See under Boys' Names.

Nicol See under Boys' Names.

Nicola English. From Nicholas, Greek, "Victorious people." Pašić (premier of Serbia and Yugoslavia, 1906–26); Pisano (14th-century Venetian admiral); Porpora (18th-century Italian composer and singing teacher); Sabbatini (17th-century Italian architect); Fabrizi (Garibaldi's chief of staff in war against Austria, 1866–67). Unusual. Nicki+. Alternative spellings: Nichola, Nickola, Nicolla, Nikola, Nykola.

Nicole English. From Nicholas, Greek, "Victorious people." Kidman (actress); d'Oresme (14th-century French prelate, advised Charles V on tax and coinage reforms). Very popular. Nicki+. Alternative spellings: Nichol, Nichole, Nicholle, Nickol, Nicolle.

Nicoletta Italian. From Nicholas, Greek, "Victorious people." Unusual.

Nicolette English, French. From Nicholas, Greek, "Victorious people." Unusual. Nicki+. Nicolette. Alternative spellings: Nicholette, Nikolette.

Nicoli English. From Nicholas, Greek, "Victorious people." Unusual. Nicki+.

Nicolina English. From Nicholas, Greek, "Victorious people." Unusual. Nicki+. Alternative spelling: Nicolena.

Nicoline English. From Nicholas, Greek, "Victorious people." Unusual. Nicki+. Alternative spellings: Nicoleen, Nicolene.

Nida Native American. Native American, the name of a mythical elf-like creature. Also a reference to bones of extinct animals. Unusual.

Nika Russian. From Dominic, Latin, "Lord." Unusual.

Nikita See under Boys' Names.

Nikky See under Boys' Names.

Nikolia English. From Nicholas, Greek, "Victorious people." Unusual. Nicki+.

Nili See under Boys' Names.

Nina English. From Hannah, Hebrew (Chanah), "Grace [of God]" or "favor." 1 Samuel 1:2. Foche (actress). Less popular.

Ninacska Hungarian. From Hannah, Hebrew (Chanah), "Grace [of God]" or "favor." 1 Samuel 1:2. Unusual.

Ninetta English. From Hannah, Hebrew (Chanah), "Grace [of God]" or "favor." 1 Samuel 1:2. Unusual. Alternative spelling: Ninnetta.

Ninette English. From Hannah, Hebrew (Chanah), "Grace [of God]" or "favor." 1 Samuel 1:2. Unusual. Alternative spelling: Ninnette.

Ninita Hispanic. Spanish, "Little girl." Unusual.

Nipa Indo-Pakistani. East Indian, "Stream." Unusual.

Nirel Hebrew/Israeli. Hebrew, "God's light" or "planted field." Unusual.

Nirveli Indo-Pakistani. East Indian, "Water" or "water child." Unusual.

Nishi Japanese. Japanese, "West." Unusual.

Nissa English. From Nisse. Unusual.

Nisse Scandinavian. Scandinavian, "Friendly elf or brownie." Unusual.

Nita Hispanic, from Hannah, Hebrew (Chanah), "Grace [of God]" or "favor," 1 Samuel 1:2; and Native American, from Nita, Native American, "Bear." Unusual.

Nitara Unknown. Sanskrit, "Deeply rooted." Unusual.

Nitsa Greek. From Helen, Greek, "Bright one" or "shining one." Unusual.

Nituna Native American. Native American, "My daughter." Unusual.

Nitza Hebrew/Israeli. From Nizana. Unusual.

Nitzana Hebrew/Israeli. From Nizana. Unusual.

Nizana Hebrew/Israeli. Hebrew, "Bud." Unusual.

Noela English. From Natalie, Latin, "Birthday of the Lord." Unusual. Alternative spelling: Noella.

Noeline English. From Natalie, Latin, "Birthday of the Lord." Unusual. Alternative spellings: Noeleen, Noelene.

Noelle English. From Natalie, Latin, "Birthday of the Lord." Van Lottum (holds record for longest game of junior tennis: 52 minutes). Unusual. Alternative spelling: Noël.

Noga Hebrew/Israeli. Hebrew, "Shining" or "morning light." Unusual for males, unusual for females.

Noksu Native American. Native American, "Smell of a chicken hawk's nest." Unusual.

Nola English. From Fenella, Gaelic (Fionnghal), "White shoulder." Unusual.

Nolcha Native American. Native American, "Sun." Unusual.

Noleen English. From Natalie, Latin, "Birthday of the Lord." Unusual.

Nollie English. From Magnolia, English, after Pierre Magnol, an 18th-century French botanist; the name of a flowering tree. Unusual.

Nona English. Latin, "Ninth." Given to the ninth-born child or to a child born on the ninth day or month. Gaprindashvili (held women's chess title, 1962–1978). Unusual.

Nora English. From Helen, Greek, "Bright one" or "shining one." Character in Ibsen's play "Doll's House"; Bayes (vaudeville actress and singer); Dunn (comedian, "Saturday Night Live"). Less popular. Alternative spelling: Norah.

Norazah Malaysian. Malaysian, "Light" + ?. Unusual.

Noreen English. From Helen, Greek, "Bright one" or "shining one." Cocheran (mousketeer, "Mickey Mouse Club"). Less popular. Alternative spellings: Norene, Norine.

Noreena English. From Helen, Greek, "Bright one" or "shining one." Unusual. Alternative spelling: Norina.

Norhaneza Malaysian. From Norazah. Unusual.

Nori Japanese. Japanese, "Precept" or "doctrine." Unusual.

Norlaili Malaysian. Malaysian, "Light" + ?. Unusual.

Norma English. Latin, "Pattern" or "model." Rae (title character in movie starring Sally Field); Smallwood (Miss America, 1926); Desmond (actress); Shearer (actress); Jean Baker (actress) (real name of Marilyn Monroe). Less popular.

Normah Malaysian. From Normah, Malaysian, "Light" + ?. Unusual.

Norna Scandinavian. Scandinavian, the name of one of the Fates. Unusual.

Notaku Native American. Native American, "Growling bear." Unusual.

Noula Greek. From Hannah, Hebrew (Chanah), "Grace [of God]" or "favor." 1 Samuel 1:2. Unusual.

Noura Arabic. Arabic, "Light." Unusual.

Nova English. Latin, "New." Pilbeam (British actress). Unusual.

Novella English. From Natalie, Latin, "Birthday of the Lord." Unusual.

Nuala English. From Fenella, Gaelic (Fionnghal), "White shoulder." Unusual.

Nuela Hispanic. From Amelia, Latin, "Industrious" or "striving." Unusual.

Numa See under Boys' Names.

Nuna Native American. Native American, "Land." Unusual.

Nuri See under Boys' Names.

Nuria Hebrew/Israeli. Hebrew, "Fire of the Lord." Unusual for males, unusual for females.

Nurice Hebrew/Israeli. From Nurit. Unusual.

Nuriel Hebrew/Israeli. From Nuria. Unusual for males, unusual for females.

Nurit Hebrew/Israeli. Hebrew, the name of a small yellow or red flower. Unusual.

Nurita Hebrew/Israeli. From Nurit. Unusual.

Nusi Hungarian. From Hannah, Hebrew (Chanah), "Grace [of God]" or "favor." 1 Samuel 1:2. Unusual.

Nutan Indo-Pakistani. Hindi, "New." Unusual.

Nydia English. Latin, "Nest." Unusual.

Nyree Australian. Maori, meaning unknown. Unusual.

Nyura Russian. From Hannah, Hebrew (Chanah), "Grace [of God]" or "favor." 1 Samuel 1:2. Unusual.

Nyusha Russian. From Agnes, Greek, "agnos" ("pure" or "chaste"). Unusual.

Oba Nigerian. Nigerian, the name of an ancient river goddess. Unusual.

Obelia Greek. Greek, "Needle." Unusual.

Ocean English. Greek, "okeanos"; the word used as a first name. Unusual for males, unusual for females.

Octavia Latin. From Octavius, Latin, "Eighth." Given to the eighth-born child or to a child born on the eighth day or month. Wife of Mark Antony, Roman empress 42–62, daughter of Claudius and wife of Nero. Unusual.

Odeda Hebrew/Israeli. Hebrew, "Strong." Unusual.

Odelette French. French, "Little song." Unusual.

Odelia Hebrew/Israeli. Hebrew, "I will praise God." Unusual.

Odella English. From Odell, Middle English, "Wood hill"; surname and place name used as a first name. Unusual.

Odelyn English. From Odell, Middle English, "Wood hill"; surname and place name used as a first name. Unusual.

Odera Hebrew/Israeli. Hebrew, "Plough." Unusual.

Odessa English. Greek, meaning unknown. The name of a Russian city. Unusual.

Odette French. From Otto, Old German, "Possessions." Brailly (French, supplied information to the Allies in WWII). Unusual.

Odile French. From Otto, Old German, "Possessions." Versois (French actress) (real name: Militza de Poliakoff-Baidarov). Unusual.

Ofira Hebrew/Israeli. Hebrew, "Gold." Unusual.

Ogin Native American. Native American, "Wild rose." Unusual.

Okalani Hawaiian. Hawaiian, "Of the heavens." Unusual.

Oki Japanese. Japanese, "In the middle of the ocean." Unusual.

Ola Polish. From Alexander, Greek, "Defender of men" or "warding off men." Mark 16:21; Acts 4:6, 19:33. Hansson (Swedish writer of lyrics and verse). Unusual.
Olathe Native American. Native American, "Beautiful." Unusual.
Oleda English. From Alida, Spanish, "Noble." Unusual.
Oleksa Russian. From Alexander, Greek, "Defender of men" or "warding off men." Mark 16:21; Acts 4:6, 19:33. Unusual.
Olena Russian. From Helen, Greek, "Bright one" or "shining one." Unusual.
Olenko Russian. From Helen, Greek, "Bright one" or "shining one." Unusual.
Olésia Polish. From Alexander, Greek, "Defender of men" or "warding off men." Mark 16:21; Acts 4:6, 19:33. Unusual.
Olésya Russian. From Alexander, Greek, "Defender of men" or "warding off men." Mark 16:21; Acts 4:6, 19:33. Unusual.
Oleta English. From Alida, Spanish, "Noble." Unusual.
Olga Russian. From Helga, Old Norse, "Holy." First Russian saint of the Orthodox church; Rukavishnikova (Russian, holds shortest reign for the pentathlon record: 0.4 seconds); Preobrajenska (Russian ballet dancer and teacher). Unusual.
Olia English. From Helga, Old Norse, "Holy." Unusual.
Oliana Hawaiian. Hawaiian, "Oleander," the name of a flowering evergreen. Unusual.
Oliff English. From Olive. Unusual. Alternative spelling: Oliffe.
Olina Czech. From Helga, Old Norse, "Holy." Unusual.
Olinda Italian. From Olindo, Italian, "From Olinthos," a Greek city. Unusual.
Olisa African. African, "God." Unusual.
Oliva English. From Olive. Unusual.
Olive English. Greek, "elaia," the name of a fruit. Miller (ornithologist and writer of children's books on birds); Schreiner (South African novelist and feminist). Unusual.
Olivette English. From Olive. Unusual. Alternative spelling: Olivet.
Olivia English. From Olive. Character in Shakespeare's "Twelfth Night"; de Havilland (actress, "Gone With the Wind"); Newton-John (pop singer and actress). Less popular.
Olka Russian. From Helga, Old Norse, "Holy." Unusual.
Olli Estonian. From Helga, Old Norse, "Holy." Lounasmaa (Finnish, attained lowest temperature: 3 x 10 (-8) degrees C, 1984). Unusual. Alternative spelling: Olly.
Ollie See under Boys' Names.
Olunka Czech. From Helga, Old Norse, "Holy." Unusual.
Oluska Czech. From Helga, Old Norse, "Holy." Unusual.
Olva English. From Helga, Old Norse, "Holy." Unusual.
Olwen Welsh. Welsh, "Footprint" + "white." Unusual. Alternative spellings: Olwin, Olwyn, Olwyne.
Olya Russian. From Helga, Old Norse, "Holy." Unusual.
Olyusha Russian. From Helga, Old Norse, "Holy." Unusual.
Oma English. From Omar, Hebrew, "Eloquent." Genesis 36:11. Unusual.
Omega Greek. English name for the last letter of the Greek alphabet. Most often given to last child parents intend to have. Unusual.
Omusa Native American. Native American, "To miss deer with arrows." Unusual.
Ona Lithuanian. From Hannah, Hebrew (Chanah), "Grace [of God]" or "favor." 1 Samuel 1:2. Unusual.
Onatah Native American. Native American, "Corn spirit," "daughter of the earth." Unusual.
Onawa Native American. Native American, "Wide-awake one." Unusual.
Onella Hungarian. From Helen, Greek, "Bright one" or "shining one." Unusual.
Oni Nigerian. Nigerian, "Born on holy ground," "desired." Unusual.
Onida Native American. Native American, "Looked-for one." Unusual.
Onita English. From Anthony, Latin, a Roman clan name used as a first name. Unusual.
Oona Irish. From Una, Native American, "Remember." Unusual.
Oonagh Irish. From Una, Native American, "Remember." Unusual.
Oonie Irish. From Una, Native American, "Remember." Unusual.
Opal English. Sanskrit, "upala" ("stone"); the name of a precious stone. Unusual.
Ophelia English. Greek, "Help" or "wisdom." Character in Shakespeare's "Hamlet." Unusual.
Ophira Hebrew/Israeli. From Ofira, Hebrew, "Gold." Unusual.
Oprah English, meaning and origin unknown, possibly created. Winfrey (TV personality). Less popular.
Orah Hebrew/Israeli. Hebrew, "Light." Unusual. Alternative spelling: Ora.
Oralee Hebrew/Israeli. From Orli. Unusual.
Oralia English. From Oriana. Unusual.
Orange English. Sanskrit, "naranga" ("orange tree"). Scott (clergyman and abolitionist, established the Wesleyan Methodist Church of America, 1843). Unusual.
Orangetta English. From Orange. Unusual.
Orelda English. From Oriana. Unusual.
Orelle English. From Oriana. Unusual.
Orenda Native American. Native American, "Magic powers." Unusual.
Ori Japanese. From Orino. Unusual.
Oriana Latin. Latin, "Dawn" or "sunrise." Unusual.
Oriel English. From Aurelia, Latin, "Golden." A Roman clan name used as a first name. Unusual.
Orina Russian. From Irene, Greek (Eirene), "Peace." Unusual.
Orinda English. From Orin, Created, possibly related to Orestes (Greek, "Mountain"). Unusual.
Orino Japanese. Japanese, "Weaver's field." Unusual.
Orinthia English. From Orin, Created, possibly related to Orestes (Greek, "Mountain"). Unusual.
Oriole English. From Aurelia, Latin, "Golden." A Roman clan name used as a first name. Unusual.
Orit Hebrew/Israeli. From Orah. Unusual.
Orla Irish. Irish, "Golden lady." Lehmann (Danish politician, headed National Liberal movement in Copenhagen, 1848) (real name: Peter Martin Orla Lehmann). Unusual.
Orlagh Irish. From Orla. Unusual.
Orlann English. From Oriana. Unusual.
Orlenda Russian. Russian, "Female eagle." Unusual.

Orlene English. From Oriana. Unusual.
Orli Hebrew/Israeli. Hebrew, "My light." Unusual. Alternative spelling: Orly.
Orlice Hebrew/Israeli. From Orli. Unusual.
Orna Hebrew/Israeli. From Ornice. Unusual.
Ornice Hebrew/Israeli. Hebrew, "Fir tree" or "cedar tree." Unusual.
Ornit Hebrew/Israeli. From Ornice. Unusual.
Orpah Hebrew/Israeli. Hebrew, meaning unknown. Ruth 1:44. Daughter-in-law of Naomi and Elimelech. Unusual.
Orpha Hebrew/Israeli. From Orpah. Unusual.
Orphy Hebrew/Israeli. From Orpah. Unusual.
Orsa English. From Ursula, Latin, "Little she-bear." Unusual.
Orsel English. From Ursula, Latin, "Little she-bear." Unusual.
Orsola English. From Ursula, Latin, "Little she-bear." Unusual.
Orya Russian. From Irene, Greek (Eirene), "Peace." Unusual.
Oryna Russian. From Irene, Greek (Eirene), "Peace." Unusual.
Osen Japanese. From Osen, Japanese, "Thousand." In Japanese lore, round numbers are thought to bring good luck. Unusual.
Osyth English. Old English, meaning unknown. Seventh-century Anglo-Saxon princess married to the king of the East Saxons. Unusual.
Ouida English. From Louis, Old German (Hlutwig), "Famous warrior." British novelist, "Strathmore" (real name: Marie Louise de la Ramée). Unusual.
Owena Welsh. From Owen, Greek, "Well-born." Unusual.
Oya Native American. Native American, "To name." Unusual.

Paca Hispanic. From Francis, Latin, "Frenchman." Unusual.
Padma Indo-Pakistani. Hindi, "Lotus." Unusual.
Paget See under Boys' Names.
Paige English. French, "Young attendant." Unusual for males, less popular for females. Alternative spelling: Page.
Paka African. Swahili, "Kitten." Unusual.
Palasha Russian. From Pasha, Greek, "pelagos" ("of the seas"). Unusual.
Palila Hawaiian. Hawaiian, "Bird." Unusual.
Paloma Hispanic. Spanish, "Dove." Unusual.
Pam English. From Pamela. Dawber (actress, "My Sister Sam"). Less popular.
Pamela English. Created, meaning uncertain. Possibly Greek, "All honey." Character in Sir Philip Sidney's "Arcadia"; Terry (one of tallest female twins: 6 feet); Johnson (British novelist, "This Bed Thy Centre"). Less popular. Pam. Alternative spellings: Pamella, Pamila, Pammala.
Pamelia English. From Pamela. Unusual. Alternative spelling: Pamilia.
Pamelina English. From Pamela. Unusual.
Pammy English. From Pamela. Unusual. Alternative spellings: Pammi, Pammie.
Pancha Hispanic. From Francis, Latin, "Frenchman." Unusual.
Panchita Hispanic. From Francis, Latin, "Frenchman." Unusual.
Pandita Indo-Pakistani. Hindi, "Scholar." Unusual.
Pansy English. French, "penser" ("to think"); a flower name used as a first name. Character in Henry James' "Portrait of a Lady." Unusual.
Panya Russian. From Stephen, Greek, "Crown" or "crowned." Acts 7:59. Unusual.
Paolina Italian. From Paul, Latin, "paulus" ("small"). Unusual.
Papina Native American. Native American, "Vine growing on an oak tree." Unusual.
Paquita Hispanic. From Francis, Latin, "Frenchman." Unusual.
Paris See under Boys' Names.
Parthenia English. Greek, "Virgin" or "maiden." Unusual. Alternative spelling: Parthania.
Parthina English. From Parthenia. Unusual. Alternative spelling: Parthena.
Parthine English. From Parthenia. Unusual.
Pascale French. From Pascal, French, "Easter child." Unusual.
Pasha English. Greek, "pelagos" ("of the seas"). Unusual.
Pat See under Boys' Names.
Pathania English. From Parthenia. Unusual. Alternative spelling: Pathenia.
Pathena English. From Parthenia. Unusual. Alternative spelling: Pathina.
Pathenia English. From Parthenia. Unusual.
Pathina English. From Parthenia. Unusual.
Pati Native American. Native American, "Twisting willows for carrying fish." Unusual.
Patia Gypsy. Spanish Gypsy, "Leaf." Unusual.
Patience English. Greek, "pema" ("suffering"); the word used as a first name. Lovell Wright (18th-century sculptor of wax models of well-known persons); Strong (poet) (real name: Winifred May); heroine of a Gilbert and Sullivan opera. Unusual.
Patient English. From Patience. Unusual.
Patrice See under Boys' Names.
Patricia English. From Patrick, Latin, "Noble man." Neal (actress); Terry (one of tallest twins: 6 feet); Harris (secretary of housing and urban development under Carter); Donnelly (Miss America, 1939). Popular. Pat, Patsy, Patty+.
Patrizia Italian. From Patrick, Latin, "Noble man." Unusual.
Patsy English. From Patrick, Latin, "Noble man." Unusual for males, less popular for females.
Patty English. From Patrick, Latin, "Noble man." Duke (actress) (real name: Anna Marie Duke); Smith Hill (educator, advocate of nursery school movement). Less popular. Alternative spellings: Pattey, Patti, Pattie.
Paula English. From Paul, Latin, "paulus" ("small"). Patron saint of widows; Prentiss (comedic actress); Abdul (pop musician and dancer); Zahn (TV hostess, "CBS This Morning"); Modersohn-Becker (German painter). Less popular. Alternative spelling: Paule.
Paulann English. English, combination of Paula (Paul, Latin, "Small") + Ann (Hannah, Hebrew (Chanah), "Grace" or "favor"). Unusual.
Pauletta English. From Paul, Latin, "paulus" ("small"). Unusual.

Paulette English. From Paul, Latin, "paulus" ("small"). Goddard (actress). Unusual.
Pauli English. From Paul, Latin, "paulus" ("small"). Unusual. Alternative spellings: Paulie, Pauly.
Paulina Bulgarian, English. From Paul, Latin, "paulus" ("small"). Character in Shakespeare's "Winter's Tale"; Porizkova (model and actress). Less popular.
Pauline English. From Paul, Latin, "paulus" ("small"). Phillips (advice columnist, "Dear Abby"); Trigere (French fashion designer); Smith (South African novelist, "Beadle"); Tarn (French poet) (real name of Renée Vivien); Déjazet (19th-century French actress). Less popular. Alternative spellings: Pauleen, Paulene.
Paulita English, Hispanic. From Paul, Latin, "paulus" ("small"). Unusual.
Paulyne English. From Paul, Latin, "paulus" ("small"). Unusual.
Pausha Indo-Pakistani. From Pausha, Hindi, the name of a Hindu lunar month. Unusual.
Pavla Czech, Russian. From Paul, Latin, "paulus" ("small"). Unusual.
Pavla Russian. From Paul, Latin, "paulus" ("small"). Unusual.
Pavlina Czech, Russian. From Paul, Latin, "paulus" ("small"). Unusual.
Pavlinka Russian. From Paul, Latin, "paulus" ("small"). Unusual.
Pawlina Polish. From Paul, Latin, "paulus" ("small"). Unusual.
Paz See under Boys' Names.
Paza Hebrew/Israeli. From Pazia. Unusual.
Pazia Hebrew/Israeli. Hebrew, "Golden." Unusual.
Pazice Hebrew/Israeli. From Pazia. Unusual.
Pazit Hebrew/Israeli. From Pazia. Unusual.
Peace English. Latin, "pax"; the word used as a first name. Unusual.
Pearl English. Latin, "perna" ("sea mussel"); the word used as a first name. Bailey (singer); Moore (scored a record 4,061 points in her college basketball career, 1975–79); S. Buck (won Pulitzer Prize for fiction 1931, "Good Earth"); White (actress, "Perils of Pauline"); Craigie (British novelist) (real name of John Oliver Hobbes). Less popular. Alternative spellings: Pearle, Perl.
Pearla English. From Pearl. Unusual. Alternative spelling: Perla.
Pearlena English. From Pearl. Unusual.
Pearline English. From Pearl. Unusual. Alternative spelling: Pearleen.
Pedzi African. African, "Finisher." Given to the last child in a family. Unusual.
Peg English. From Margaret, Greek, "margaron" ("pearl"). Less popular. Peggy+.
Peggotty English. Surname used as a first name; origin unknown. Often seen as an extended form of Peggy (Margaret, Greek, "Pearl"). Unusual. Alternative spelling: Peggetty.
Peggy English. From Margaret, Greek, "margaron" ("pearl"). Lipton (actress); Ashcroft, Dame (British actress, "Jewel in the Crown"). Less popular. Alternative spellings: Peggey, Peggi, Peggie.
Peke Hawaiian. From Bertha, Old German (Berahta), "Bright." Unusual.
Pela Polish. From Penelope. Unusual.
Pelageya Russian. From Pasha, Greek, "pelagos" ("of the seas"). Unusual.
Pelagia Greek. Greek, "From the sea." Unusual. Alternative spelling: Pelegia.
Pelcia Polish. From Penelope. Unusual.
Pelga English. From Pelagia. Unusual.
Pelgia Greek. From Pelagia. Unusual.
Pelipa Native American. From Philip, Greek, "philippos" ("lover of horses"). Matthew 10:3. Unusual.
Pemba African. African, the name of a force that directs affairs on earth and in the sky. Unusual.
Pen English. From Penelope. Unusual.
Penda African. Swahili, "Loved one." Unusual.
Penelopa Polish. From Penelope. Unusual.
Penelope English. Greek, "Bobbin" or "weaver." Wife of Odysseus in Homer's "Odyssey"; Devereux (daughter of the first Earl of Essex, object of Sir Philip Sidney's love sonnets). Less popular. Penny+. Alternative spelling: Pinelopi.
Peni Native American. Native American, "His mind." Unusual.
Penina English. From Penelope. Unusual.
Peninah Hebrew/Israeli. From Pninah, Hebrew, "Pearl" or "coral." Unusual.
Penine English. From Penelope. Unusual.
Peninit Hebrew/Israeli. From Pninah, Hebrew, "Pearl" or "coral." Unusual.
Penny English. From Penelope. Marshall (actress and director). Less popular. Alternative spellings: Penney, Penni, Pennie.
Pepita Hispanic. From Joseph, Hebrew (Yosef), "God will add." Unusual.
Perdita English. Latin, "To lose." Character in Shakespeare's "Winter's Tale." Unusual.
Perlie English. From Pearl, Latin, "perna" ("sea mussel"); the word used as a first name. Unusual. Alternative spellings: Pearley, Pearly, Perly.
Pernel English. From Petronella. Unusual.
Pernelle French. From Petronella. Unusual.
Peronel English. From Petronella. Unusual.
Peronelle French. From Petronella. Unusual.
Peta English. From Peter, Greek, "Stone," "rock." John 1:42. Unusual.
Petena English. From Peter, Greek, "Stone," "rock." John 1:42. Unusual.
Peterina English. From Peter, Greek, "Stone," "rock." John 1:42. Unusual.
Peternella English. From Peter, Greek, "Stone," "rock." John 1:42. Unusual.
Petra English. From Peter, Greek, "Stone," "rock." John 1:42. Schneider (set 1982 world record for individual 400-meter swimming medley: 4 minutes, 36.10 seconds). Unusual.
Petrice English. From Peter, Greek, "Stone," "rock." John 1:42. Unusual.
Petrina English. From Peter, Greek, "Stone," "rock." John 1:42. Unusual.
Petrona English. From Peter, Greek, "Stone," "rock." John 1:42. Unusual.
Petronella Latin. Latin, from the Roman clan name "Petronius." Unusual.
Petronilla Latin. From Petronella. Saint. Unusual.
Petula English. Possibly Latin, "Saucy," or from Peter (Greek, "Stone," "rock"). Clark (British actress and singer). Unusual.
Pheba English. From Phoebe. Unusual.
Phemie English. From Euphemia, Greek (Euphmia), "Spoken well of." Unusual.
Philadelphia English. Greek, "Brotherly love." Revelations 3:7. Unusual.
Philippa English. From Philip, Greek, "philippos" ("lover of horses"). Matthew 10:3. of Hainaut (14th-century queen of Edward III of England); of Lan-

caster (14th-century queen of John I of Portugal). Unusual. Alternative spellings: Philipa, Phillipa, Phillippa.

Philippe See under Boys' Names.

Philippine French. From Philip, Greek, "philippos" ("lover of horses"). Matthew 10:3. Unusual.

Phillida English. From Phyllis, Greek, "Green bough." Unusual.

Phillie English. From Philip, Greek, "philippos" ("lover of horses"). Matthew 10:3. Unusual. Alternative spelling: Philli.

Phillipina English. From Philip, Greek, "philippos" ("lover of horses"). Matthew 10:3. Unusual.

Philomena English. Greek, "Beloved." Saint. Unusual.

Philomene English. From Philomena. Unusual.

Philomina English. From Philomena. Unusual.

Phobe English. From Phoebe. Unusual.

Phoebe English. Greek, "phoibos" ("pure" or "bright"). Romans 16:1. Cary (poet and hymn writer, "Nearer Home"). Less popular. Alternative spellings: Pheabe, Pheaby, Phebe, Pheby, Pheobe, Pheoby.

Phoeboe English. From Phoebe. Unusual.

Phylicia English. From Felix, Latin, "Happy," "fortunate," or "lucky." Ayers-Allen Rashad (TV wife of Bill Cosby). Unusual. Alternative spellings: Felecia, Felicia, Felisha.

Phyllida English. From Phyllis. Unusual.

Phyllis English. Greek, "Green bough." Curtis (soprano); George (briefly Miss America, 1971); Bentley (British novelist, "Spinner of Years"); Bottome (British novelist, "London Pride"). Less popular. Alternative spellings: Philis, Phillis, Philliss, Phillys, Phylis, Phylliss.

Pilar See under Boys' Names.

Pililani Hawaiian. Hawaiian, "Close to heaven." Unusual.

Pilis Hawaiian. From Philip, Greek, "philippos" ("lover of horses"). Matthew 10:3. Unusual.

Pilisi Hawaiian. From Phyllis. Unusual.

Pinga Indo-Pakistani. Hindi, "Dark" or "tawny." Another name for the Hindu goddess Sakti. Unusual.

Pipitsa Greek. From Penelope, Greek, "Bobbin" or "weaver." Unusual.

Pippa English, Italian. From Philip, Greek, "philippos" ("lover of horses"). Matthew 10:3. Unusual.

Pippy English. From Philip, Greek, "philippos" ("lover of horses"). Matthew 10:3. Unusual.

Pita African. African, "Fourth-born daughter." Unusual.

Pixie English. Meaning and origin unknown; the word used as a first name. Unusual.

Pleasance English. English, "Pleasure," "delight." Unusual. Alternative spellings: Pleasants, Pleasence.

Pleasant English. From Pleasance. Unusual.

Pninah Hebrew/Israeli. Hebrew, "Pearl" or "coral." Wife of Elkanah (Bible). Unusual.

Pola Polish. From Paul, Latin, "paulus" ("small"). Negri (girlfriend of Rudolph Valentino). Unusual.

Polcia Polish. From Paul, Latin, "paulus" ("small"). Unusual.

Poll English. From Miriam, Hebrew (Miryam), "Bitterness," "rebellion," "wished-for child," or "sea" (?). Exodus 15:20. Unusual.

Polly English. From Miriam, Hebrew (Miryam), "Bitterness," "rebellion," "wished-for child," or "sea" (?). Exodus 15:20. Bergen (actress). Less popular. Alternative spellings: Polley, Polli, Pollie.

Pollyam Indo-Pakistani. Hindi, a goddess of the plague. Unusual for males, unusual for females.

Pollyann English. From Pollyanna, English, combination of Polly (Miriam, Hebrew (Miryam), "Bitterness," "rebellion," "wished-for child," or "sea" (?)) + Anna (Hannah, Hebrew (Chanah), "Grace" or "favor"). Unusual.

Pollyanna English. From Pollyanna, English, combination of Polly (Miriam, Hebrew (Miryam), "Bitterness," "rebellion," "wished-for child," or "sea" (?)) + Anna (Hannah, Hebrew (Chanah), "Grace" or "favor"). Heroine and title character of Eleanor H. Porter's novel. Unusual.

Poni African. African, "Second-born daughter." Unusual.

Popi Greek. From Penelope, Greek, "Bobbin" or "weaver." Unusual.

Poppy English. Latin, "papaver"; a flower name used as a first name. Unusual.

Portia English. Latin, a Roman clan name. Unusual.

Posala Native American. Native American, "Pounding farewell-to-spring seed." Farewell-to-spring is a plant. Unusual.

Precious English. Latin, "premium" ("price"); the word used as a name. Mackenzie (British weight-lifter); Wilson (British singer and dancer). Unusual for males, unusual for females.

Primrose English. Middle English, a flower name used as a first name. Unusual.

Primula English. Latin, "First"; also a flower name used as a first name. Unusual.

Prin English. From Prince, Latin, "princeps" ("one who takes the first part"); the royal title used as a first name. Unusual.

Princess English. From Prince, Latin, "princeps" ("one who takes the first part"); the royal title used as a first name. Unusual.

Priscilla English. Latin, "Old," "primitive." Acts 18:26. Presley (actress, "Naked Gun"); Mullens ("Mayflower" colonist, subject of Longfellow's "Courtship of Miles Standish"). Less popular. Priss, Prissy. Alternative spellings: Precilla, Prescilla, Pricilla, Prissilla.

Priss English. From Priscilla. Unusual.

Prissy English. From Priscilla. Unusual.

Pru English. From Prudence. Unusual.

Prudence English. Latin, "prudens"; the word used as a first name. Crandall (19th-century school teacher, opened girls' school and aroused controversy by admitting a black pupil). Unusual.

Prue English. From Prudence. Unusual.

Prunella English. Latin, "Little plum." Unusual.

Pualani Hawaiian. Hawaiian, "Heavenly flower." Unusual.

Puni Hawaiian. From Pualani, Hawaiian, "Heavenly flower." Unusual.

Purly English. From Pearl, Latin, "perna" ("sea mussel"); the word used as a first name. Unusual.

Putepu Unknown. Meaning and origin unknown. Unusual.

Qiturah Arabic. Arabic, "Fragrance." Unusual.
Queen English. Old English, "qwen" ("woman"); the royal title used as a first name. Unusual.
Queena English. From Queen. Unusual.
Queenation English. From Queen. Unusual.
Queeneste English. From Queen. Unusual.
Queenette English. From Queen. Unusual.
Queenie English. From Queen. Unusual. Alternative spelling: Queeny.
Querida Hispanic. Spanish, "Beloved." Unusual.
Questa French. French, "Searcher." Unusual.
Queta Hispanic. From Henry, Old German (Heimerich), "Home ruler." Unusual.
Quiana American. From Hannah, Hebrew (Chanah), "Grace [of God]" or "favor." 1 Samuel 1:2. Unusual. Alternative spelling: Quianna.
Quin See Quinn under Boys' Names.
Quinci English. From Quincy, Old French, "From the fifth son's estate." Unusual. Alternative spelling: Quincie.
Quincy See under Boys' Names.
Quinella English. From Quintin, Latin, "Fifth." Usually given to the fifth-born child or to a child born on the fifth day or month. Unusual.
Quinetta English. From Quintin, Latin, "Fifth." Usually given to the fifth-born child or to a child born on the fifth day or month. Unusual.
Quinette English. From Quintin, Latin, "Fifth." Usually given to the fifth-born child or to a child born on the fifth day or month. Unusual.
Quintana English. From Quintin, Latin, "Fifth." Usually given to the fifth-born child or to a child born on the fifth day or month. Unusual.
Quintessa English. From Quintin, Latin, "Fifth." Usually given to the fifth-born child or to a child born on the fifth day or month. Unusual.
Quintina English. From Quintin, Latin, "Fifth." Usually given to the fifth-born child or to a child born on the fifth day or month. Unusual.
Quintona English. From Quintin, Latin, "Fifth." Usually given to the fifth-born child or to a child born on the fifth day or month. Unusual.
Quintonice English. From Quintin, Latin, "Fifth." Usually given to the fifth-born child or to a child born on the fifth day or month. Unusual.
Quiterie French. Latin, "Tranquil." Unusual.

Rabi See under Boys' Names.
Rabiah Arabic. From Rabi, Arabic, "Breeze." Unusual.
Rachel English. Hebrew, "Ewe" or "lamb." Genesis 29:16. Second wife of Jacob; Marete (created tallest hairdo, a freestanding 8-foot high "flagpole"); Robards Jackson (wife of President Andrew); Ruysch (18th-century Dutch court painter); Crothers (playwright, "The Three of Us"); Carson (biologist and author). Very popular. Rae. Alternative spellings: Rachael, Racheal, Rachele, Rachell, Rachelle.
Rachele Italian. From Rachel. Unusual.
Radinka Slavic. Slavic, "Energetic" or "active." Unusual.
Radmilla Slavic. Slavic, "Works for the people." Unusual.
Rae English. From Rachel. Unusual.
Rae Ann English. From Rae Ann, English, combination of Rae (Rachel, Hebrew, "Ewe") + Ann (Hannah, Hebrew (Chanah), "Grace" or "favor"). Unusual. Alternative spelling: Rayann.
Rae Louise English. From Rae Louise, English, combination of Rae (Rachel, Hebrew, "Ewe") + Louise (Louis, Old German, "Famous in battle"). Unusual.
Rae Lynn English. From Rae Lynn, English, combination of Rae (Rachel, Hebrew, "Ewe") + Lynn (Linda, Spanish, "Pretty one"). Unusual.
Rafaela Hispanic. From Raphael, Hebrew, "God heals" or "God cures." Job 4:17. Unusual.
Rahel German. From Rachel. Unusual.
Rahela Hawaiian. From Rachel. Unusual.
Rahil Bulgarian. From Rachel. Unusual.
Raimunde German. From Raymond, Old German, "Counsel-protection." Unusual.
Raina English, Russian. From Regina, Latin, "Queen." Unusual. Alternative spellings: Raenah, Rana, Reyna.
Rainbow English. Old English, "regn" + "bugan"; the word used as a first name. Unusual.
Raine English. From Regina, Latin, "Queen." Unusual.
Rainell Created. Created, "rain" (Old English, "regn") + a feminine ending. Unusual. Alternative spelling: Rainelle.
Rainy English. From Rainy, Old English, "regn"; the word used as a first name. Unusual.
Raizel Yiddish. Yiddish, "Rose flower." Unusual.
Rakel Scandinavian. From Rachel. Unusual.
Rakhil Russian. From Rachel. Unusual.
Rakhila Russian. From Rachel. Unusual.
Raku Japanese. Japanese, "Pleasure." Unusual.
Ralphina English. From Ralph, Anglo-Saxon, "Wolf-counsel." Unusual.
Ralphine English. From Ralph, Anglo-Saxon, "Wolf-counsel." Unusual.
Ramla African. From Ramla, Swahili, "Teller of fortunes." Unusual.
Ramona English. From Raymond, Old German, "Counsel-protection." Character in Helen Hunt Jackson's "Ramona." Less popular.
Randee English. From Randolph, Old English (Randwulf), "Shield-wolf." Unusual.
Randey See Randy under Boys' Names.
Randi See Randy under Boys' Names.
Randie See Randy under Boys' Names.
Randy See under Boys' Names.
Rane Norwegian. From Regina, Latin, "Queen." Unusual.
Rani Indo-Pakistani. Hindi, "Queen." Unusual.
Ranice Hebrew/Israeli. From Ranita. Unusual.
Ranit Hebrew/Israeli. From Ranita. Unusual.
Ranita Hebrew/Israeli. Hebrew, "Song" or "joy." Unusual.
Raoule French. From Ralph, Anglo-Saxon, "Wolf-counsel." Unusual.

Raphaela English. From Raphael, Hebrew, "God heals" or "God cures." Job 4:17. Unusual.

Raquel Hispanic, Portuguese. From Rachel, Hebrew, "Ewe" or "lamb." Genesis 29:16. Welch (actress). Less popular.

Rasheda American. From Rashid, Turkish, "Rightly guided." Unusual. Alternative spellings: Rasheeda, Rasheedah, Rasheida.

Rashel Russian. From Rachel, Hebrew, "Ewe" or "lamb." Genesis 29:16. Unusual.

Rashida American. From Rashid, Turkish, "Rightly guided." Unusual.

Rasia Greek. Greek, "Rose." Unusual.

Ratri Indo-Pakistani. Hindi, "Night." Another a name for the Hindu goddess Sakti. Unusual.

Raven English. Old German, "hraban"; the name of a bird used as a first name. Unusual.

Rawnie Gypsy. English Gypsy, "Lady." Unusual.

Raycene English. From Rachel, Hebrew, "Ewe" or "lamb." Genesis 29:16. Unusual.

Raye English. From Rachel, Hebrew, "Ewe" or "lamb." Genesis 29:16. Unusual.

Rayetta English. From Rachel, Hebrew, "Ewe" or "lamb." Genesis 29:16. Unusual.

Raylena English. From Rachel, Hebrew, "Ewe" or "lamb." Genesis 29:16. Unusual.

Raylene English. From Rachel, Hebrew, "Ewe" or "lamb." Genesis 29:16. Unusual. Alternative spellings: Raelene, Rayleen.

Rayma English. From Rachel, Hebrew, "Ewe" or "lamb." Genesis 29:16. Unusual.

Raymonde French. From Raymond, Old German, "Counsel-protection." Unusual.

Rayna English. From Rachel, Hebrew, "Ewe" or "lamb." Genesis 29:16. Unusual.

Raynelle English. From Rachel, Hebrew, "Ewe" or "lamb." Genesis 29:16. Unusual.

Raynette English. From Rachel, Hebrew, "Ewe" or "lamb." Genesis 29:16. Unusual.

Rayona English. From Rachel, Hebrew, "Ewe" or "lamb." Genesis 29:16. Unusual.

Rayzil Yiddish. From Raizel. Unusual. Alternative spelling: Razil.

Razilee Hebrew/Israeli. From Razi, Aramaic, "My secret." Unusual. Alternative spelling: Razili.

Rea English. From Andrew, Greek, "Manly." Unusual.

Reba English. From Rebecca. McIntyre (country singer). Unusual.

Rebbie English. From Rebecca. Unusual.

Rebecca English. Hebrew (Rivka), "Noose" or "yoke." Genesis 24:15. Wife of Isaac, mother of Jacob and Esau; King (Miss America, 1974); Latimer Felton (first woman appointed to the senate, 1922); West, Dame (British journalist, novelist, and suffragette) (real name: Cicily Isabel Fairfield); de Mornay (actress). Very popular. Becca, Becky+. Alternative spellings: Rebbecca, Rebeca, Rebeccah, Rebecka, Rebeckah.

Rebeka Czech. Genesis 24:15. Unusual. Becca, Becky+.

Rebekah Yiddish. From Rebecca. Unusual.

Rebekka German. From Rebecca. Unusual. Alternative spelling: Rebekke.

Rebeque French. From Rebecca. Unusual.

Rebi English. From Rebecca. Unusual. Alternative spelling: Reby.

Reenie English. From Irene, Greek (Eirene), "Peace." Less popular.

Reet Estonian. From Margaret, Greek, "margaron" ("pearl"). Unusual.

Regan See under Boys' Names.

Reggie English. From Regina. Unusual. Alternative spellings: Reggi, Reggy, Regi, Regie.

Regina English. Latin, "Queen." Resnik (mezzo-soprano opera singer). Less popular. Reggie+. Alternative spellings: Regena, Regiena.

Regine English. From Regina, Latin, "Queen." Crespin (French operatic soprano). Unusual. Reggie+.

Reginia English. From Regina. Unusual. Reggie+.

Reginna English. From Regina. Unusual. Reggie+.

Reina Hispanic. From Regina, Latin, "Queen." Unusual.

Reine French. From Regina. Unusual.

Reinette French. From Regina. Unusual.

Rekha Indo-Pakistani. Hindi, "Line." Unusual.

Ren Japanese. Japanese, "Lotus." Unusual.

Rena Greek. From Irene, Greek (Eirene), "Peace." Unusual.

Renata English. Latin, "Reborn." Tebaldi (Italian lyric soprano); Scotto (Italian operatic soprano). Less popular.

Rene English. From Irene, Greek (Eirene), "Peace." Richards (tennis player); Tardivaux (French novelist, "Mademoiselle Cloque") (real name of René Boylesve). Less popular. Alternative spelling: Renay.

Renée French. From Renata. of France (daughter of Louis XII, 16th-century); Vivien (French poet) (real name: Pauline Tarn). Less popular.

Renelle English. From Renata. Unusual.

Renia Polish. From Regina. Unusual.

Renita English. From Renata. Unusual. Alternative spelling: Reneeta.

Rennie English. From Renata. Unusual. Alternative spellings: Reney, Reni, Renie, Renni, Renny.

Reseda English. Latin, "Fragrant mignonette blossom." Unusual.

Resel German. From Teresa, Greek, "Therasia," the name of two islands, or "theros" ("summer"). Unusual.

Resi German. From Teresa, Greek, "Therasia," the name of two islands, or "theros" ("summer"). Unusual.

Reta English. From Margaret, Greek, "margaron" ("pearl"). Unusual.

Reubena English. From Reuben, Hebrew (Reuven), "Behold a son." Genesis 29:32. Unusual.

Reubina English. From Reuben, Hebrew (Reuven), "Behold a son." Genesis 29:32. Unusual.

Reva Indo-Pakistani. Hindi, "The sacred Narmada River." Unusual.

Reveca Romanian. From Rebecca, Hebrew (Rivka), "Noose" or "yoke." Genesis 24:15. Unusual.

Reveka Bulgarian, Greek. From Rebecca, Hebrew (Rivka), "Noose" or "yoke." Genesis 24:15. Unusual.

Revekka Russian. From Rebecca, Hebrew (Rivka), "Noose" or "yoke." Genesis 24:15. Unusual.

Rez See under Boys' Names.

Reza Czech. From Teresa, Greek, "Therasia," the name of two islands, or "theros" ("summer"). Abbasi (17th-century Persian painter). Unusual.

Rezi Hungarian. From Teresa, Greek, "Therasia," the name of two islands, or "theros" ("summer"). Unusual.

Rezka Czech. From Teresa, Greek, "Therasia," the name of two islands, or "theros" ("summer"). Unusual.

Rhea English. Greek, "Flowing river." In Greek mythology, mother of Zeus; in Roman mythology, mother of Romulus and Remus; Perlman (actress, "Cheers"); Seddon (space shuttle astronaut). Unusual.

Rhian Welsh. Welsh, "Maiden." Unusual. Alternative spelling: Rian.

Rhiannon Welsh. Welsh, "Nymph," "goddess." Unusual. Alternative spelling: Rhianon.

Rhoda English. Latin, "Woman from Rhodas" (the "island of roses"). Acts 12:13. Broughton (British novelist, "Cometh Up As a Flower"). Less popular. Alternative spelling: Roda.

Rhona English. Old Norse, "Rough isle." Less popular. Alternative spelling: Rona.

Rhonda English. Welsh, "Grand"; place name used as a first name. Fleming (actress) (real name: Marilyn Louis). Less popular.

Rhonwen Welsh. Welsh, "Slender" + "fair." Unusual.

Ría Hispanic. Spanish, "River's mouth." van der Honing (completed a crocheted chain a record 38.83 miles long, 1986). Unusual.

Richarda English. From Richard, Old German, "Strong ruler." Unusual.

Richenda English. From Richard, Old German, "Strong ruler." Unusual.

Richenza English. From Richard, Old German, "Strong ruler." Unusual.

Richmal English. German, "Ruler" + ?. Unusual.

Ricki See Ricky under Boys' Names.

Rickie See Ricky under Boys' Names.

Ricquie English. From Richard, Old German, "Strong ruler." Unusual.

Riḍa Arabic. Arabic, "In God's favor." Unusual for males, unusual for females.

Rifka Yiddish. From Rebecca, Hebrew (Rivka), "Noose" or "yoke." Genesis 24:15. Unusual.

Rihana Arabic. "Sweet basil"; origin unknown. Unusual.

Rika Swedish. From Eric, Old Norse, "Ruler of all" or "always ruler." Márkus (Austrian bridge player, first woman World Grand Master, 1974). Unusual. Alternative spelling: Rica.

Rikki English. From Richard, Old German, "Strong ruler." Less popular. Alternative spellings: Ricquie, Rikky.

Rimona Hebrew/Israeli. From Rimon, Hebrew, "Pomegranate." Unusual.

Rin Japanese. Japanese, "Park"; place name used as a first name. Unusual.

Rina English. Created, a nickname for names ending in "-rina," like Katrina and Sabrina. Unusual.

Risa English. Latin, "Laughter." Unusual.

Risha Indo-Pakistani. Hindi, "Born in the month of Vrishabna." Unusual.

Rissa English. From Nerida, Greek, "Sea nymph." Unusual.

Rita English, Hispanic, Polish. From Margaret, Greek, "margaron" ("pearl"). Of Cascia (patron saint of desperate cases); Moreno (actress, has won Oscar, Emmy, Tony, and Grammy awards); Coolidge (singer); Hayworth (actress) (real name: Margarita Cansino). Less popular.

Ritsa Greek. From Alexander, Greek, "Defender of men" or "warding off men." Mark 16:21; Acts 4:6, 19:33. Unusual.

Rivka Hebrew/Israeli. Hebrew, "Noose" or "yoke." Genesis 24:15. Unusual.

Riza Hungarian. From Teresa, Greek, "Therasia," the name of two islands, or "theros" ("summer"). Unusual.

Rizus Hungarian. From Teresa, Greek, "Therasia," the name of two islands, or "theros" ("summer"). Unusual.

Roba Czech. From Robert, Old English (Hreodbeorht), "Fame-bright." Unusual.

Robbi See Robby under Boys' Names.

Robbie English. From Robert, Old English (Hreodbeorht), "Fame-bright." Less popular for males, unusual for females.

Robby See under Boys' Names.

Roberta English. From Robert, Old English (Hreodbeorht), "Fame-bright." Flack (singer); character in Jerome Kern's light opera "Roberta." Less popular. Bobbie, Robbie.

Robertina Scottish. From Robert, Old English (Hreodbeorht), "Fame-bright." Unusual. Alternative spelling: Robertena.

Robin See under Boys' Names.

Robina English. From Robert, Old English (Hreodbeorht), "Fame-bright." Unusual. Alternative spelling: Robena.

Robinette English. From Robert, Old English (Hreodbeorht), "Fame-bright." Unusual.

Robinia English. From Robert, Old English (Hreodbeorht), "Fame-bright." Unusual.

Robyn English. From Robert, Old English (Hreodbeorht), "Fame-bright." Mattson (soap opera actress). Unusual. Alternative spellings: Robbin, Robine.

Rochelle English. French, "Little rock." Less popular. Shelley+. Alternative spellings: Rochele, Roshele, Roshelle.

Rohana Indo-Pakistani. Hindi, "Sandalwood." Unusual.

Rolande French. From Roland, Old German (Hrodland), "Famous land." Unusual.

Rollie See under Boys' Names.

Roma English. Italian, the name of the city of Rome. Unusual.

Romaine French. From Romain, French, "Roman." Unusual. Alternative spelling: Romayne.

Romany Gypsy. Gypsy, "Man" or "husband." Also the name of the Gypsy language. Unusual.

Romy English. From Rosemary, Latin, "Dew of the sea." Schneider (Austrian actress) (real name: Rosemarie Albach-Retty); Müller (German track star; her team set world record for 4 x 200-meter relay: 1 minute, 28.15 seconds). Unusual. Alternative spelling: Romi.

Ronella English. From Rhona, Old Norse, "Rough isle." Unusual.

Ronelle English. From Rhona, Old Norse, "Rough isle." Unusual.

Roni See under Boys' Names.

Ronia Hebrew/Israeli. From Roni, Hebrew, "Joy is mine." Unusual.

Ronice Hebrew/Israeli. From Roni, Hebrew, "Joy is mine." Unusual.

Ronit Hebrew/Israeli. From Roni, Hebrew, "Joy is mine." Unusual.

Ronli Hebrew/Israeli. From Roni. Unusual for males, unusual for females.

Ronna English. From Reynold, Old English (Regenweald), "Counsel" + "power." Less popular. Alternative spelling: Ronne.

Ronnette English. From Reynold, Old English (Regenweald), "Counsel" + "power." Unusual.

Ronni See Ronney under Boys' Names.

Ronnie See Ronney under Boys' Names.

Ronny See Ronney under Boys' Names.
Ronwen Welsh. From Rhonwen, Welsh, "Slender" + "fair." Unusual.
Rosa English. From Rose, Latin, "rosa," a flower name used as a first name. Parks (started bus boycott in Alabama); Luxemburg (German Socialist, helped establish Polish Social Democratic Party); Bonheur (French painter, first woman to receive Grand Cross of Lègion d'Honneur); Dartle (character in Dickens' "David Copperfield"). Less popular. Rosie+.
Rosabella English. English, "Beautiful rose." Unusual.
Rosabelle English. From Rosabella. Unusual. Alternative spellings: Rosabel, Rosabell.
Rosaleen Irish. From Rose, Latin, "rosa," a flower name used as a first name. Unusual. Alternative spelling: Rosalene.
Rosalia English. Latin, "Rose." The name of an Italian ceremony during which garlands of roses are draped on tombs and mausoleums. de Castro (19th-century Spanish novelist). Unusual.
Rosalie English, French. From Rosalia. Unusual. Alternative spellings: Rosalea, Rosalee.
Rosalina English. From Rosalind. Unusual.
Rosalind English. From Rosalind, Created by poet Edmund Spenser as an anagram for Rosa Daniel. Also associated with Spanish "rosa linda" ("pretty rose"). Franklin (British biophysicist, contributed to discovery of DNA molecular structure); Russell (actress); character in Shakespeare's "As You Like It"; character in Thackeray's novel "Newcomes"; character in Spenser's 1579 poem "The Shepheards Calender." Less popular. Alternative spellings: Rosalynd, Rosalynde, Roselind.
Rosalinda English. From Rosalind. Unusual.
Rosalinde German. From Rosalind. Unusual.
Rosalyn English. From Rosalind. Less popular. Alternative spellings: Rosalin, Rosaline, Rosalyne, Rosalynn, Rosalynne, Roselin, Roseline, Roselyn, Rosilyn.
Rosamond English. From Rosamund. Clifford (British, mistress of Henry II, 12th-century); title character in Addison's 1707 opera. Unusual. Alternative spelling: Rosamund.
Rosan English. From Rosanne. Unusual.
Rosanna English. From Rosanne. Arquette (actress, "Desperately Seeking Susan"). Unusual. Alternative spellings: Rosana, Rosannah, Roseana, Roseanna, Roseannah, Rosehanah, Rosehannah.
Rosanne English. English, combination of Rose (Latin, "rosa," a flower name used as a first name) + Anne (Hannah, Hebrew (Chanah), "Grace" or "favor"). Unusual. Alternative spellings: Rosan, Rosann, Rose Ann, Rose Anne, Roseanne.
Rose English. Latin, "rosa," a flower name used as a first name. Saint; O'Neill Wilson (illustrator, designed kewpies); Duchesne (French missionary to America); Greenhow (Confederate spy); Coyle (Miss America, 1936); Hartwick Thorpe (poet, "Curfew Must Not Ring Tonight"). Less popular. Rosie+.
Roselani Hawaiian. Hawaiian, "Heavenly rose." Unusual.
Roselia English. From Rosalia. Unusual.
Rosella English. From Rose. Unusual.
Roselle English. From Rose. Unusual.
Rosemaria English. From Rosemary. Unusual.
Rosemarie English. From Rosemary, Latin, "Dew of the sea." Less popular.
Rosemary English. Latin, "Dew of the sea." Clooney (singer); LaPlanche (Miss America, 1941). Less popular.
Rosena English. From Rose. Unusual. Alternative spelling: Rosenah.
Rosetta Italian. From Rose. Character in Bickerstaff's "Love in a Village"; character in Moore's "Foundling." Unusual.
Rosette English. From Rose. Unusual.
Rosheen English. From Rose. Unusual.
Rosie English. From Rose. O'Neill (TV lawyer played by Sharon Gless). Unusual. Alternative spellings: Rosey, Rosi, Rosy
Rosina Italian. From Rose. Character in Rossini's opera "Barber of Seville"; Lhévinne (Russian pianist and teacher). Unusual.
Rosita Hispanic. From Rose. Unusual.
Roslynn English. From Rosalind. Unusual. Alternative spellings: Roslin, Roslyn, Roslyne, Rozlyn.
Rossalyn Scottish. From Ross, Gaelic, "Cape" or "promontory"; surname and place name used as a first name. Unusual. Alternative spelling: Rosselyn.
Rosslyn Scottish. From Ross, Gaelic, "Cape" or "promontory"; surname and place name used as a first name. Unusual. Alternative spelling: Rosslynn.
Roula Greek. From Miriam, Hebrew (Miryam), "Bitterness," "rebellion," "wished-for child," or "sea" (?). Exodus 15:20. Unusual.
Rowena English. From Rhonwen, Welsh, "Slender" + "fair." Jackson (Australian ballerina who achieved record 121 spins). Unusual.
Roxana Latin. Persian, "Dawn." Wife of Alexander the Great; character in Daniel Defoe's novel "Roxana." Unusual.
Roxane Greek. From Roxana. Character in Edmond Rostand's "Cyrano de Bergerac." Unusual.
Roxann English. From Roxana. Rose (hula-hooped for record 90 hours). Unusual. Alternative spelling: Roxanne.
Roxanna English. From Roxana. Unusual.
Roxianne English. From Roxana. Unusual.
Roxy English. From Roxana. Unusual. Alternative spelling: Roxie.
Royalene English. From Royal, French, "Like a king." Unusual.
Royalyn English. From Royal, French, "Like a king." Unusual.
Roza Hungarian. From Rose, Latin, "rosa," a flower name used as a first name. Unusual.
Rozalia Hungarian. From Rose, Latin, "rosa," a flower name used as a first name. Unusual.
Rozalyn English. From Rose, Latin, "rosa," a flower name used as a first name. Unusual. Roz.
Rozanna English. From Rosanne, English, combination of Rose (Latin, "rosa," a flower name used as a first name) + Anne (Hannah, Hebrew (Chanah), "Grace" or "favor"). Unusual. Roz.
Roze Lithuanian. From Rose, Latin, "rosa," a flower name used as a first name. Unusual.
Rozele Lithuanian. From Rose, Latin, "rosa," a flower name used as a first name. Unusual.
Rozena English. From Rose, Latin, "rosa," a flower name used as a first name. Unusual. Roz.
Rozene Native American. From Rose,

Latin, "rosa," a flower name used as a first name. Unusual.

Rozsi Hungarian. From Rose, Latin, "rosa," a flower name used as a first name. Unusual.

Rozy English. From Rose, Latin, "rosa," a flower name used as a first name. Unusual. Rose.

Rozyte Lithuanian. From Rose, Latin, "rosa," a flower name used as a first name. Unusual.

Ruana Indo-Pakistani. From Ruana, Hindi, a musical instrument much like a violin. Unusual.

Rubena English. From Reuben, Hebrew (Reuven), "Behold a son." Genesis 29:32. Unusual.

Rubenia English. From Reuben, Hebrew (Reuven), "Behold a son." Genesis 29:32. Unusual.

Rubin See under Boys' Names.

Rubina English. From Ruby, Latin, "Red." The most precious gem. Unusual. Alternative spelling: Rubyna.

Rubine English. From Reuben, Hebrew (Reuven), "Behold a son." Genesis 29:32. Unusual.

Ruby English. Latin, "Red." The most precious gem. Goldstein (boxing referee, collapsed during a title fight, had to be replaced); Keeler (singer and dancer) (real name: Ethel Keeler). Unusual for males, unusual for females. Alternative spellings: Rubey, Rubie, Rubye.

Ruchel Yiddish. From Rachel, Hebrew, "Ewe" or "lamb." Genesis 29:16. Unusual.

Ruchi Indo-Pakistani. Hindi, "A love that becomes a wish to please the beloved." Unusual.

Rudra Indo-Pakistani. Hindi, "Rudraksha-plant child." Hindus use the berries of this sacred plant to make rosaries. Unusual.

Ruperta Hispanic. From Robert, Old English (Hreodbeorht), "Fame-bright." Unusual.

Ruri Japanese. Japanese, "Emerald." Unusual.

Rusalka Czech. Czech, "Wood nymph." Unusual.

Ruth English. From Ruth, Hebrew, "Companion." Book of Ruth 1:14. Character in Bible; Malcolmson (Miss America, 1924); Fuchs (German, won Olympic gold medal, javelin throw, 1972, 1976); McKenney (author of humorous sketches); Rohde (first American woman diplomat); Gordon (actress, 1968 Oscar, "Rosemary's Baby"). Less popular. Ruthy+.

Ruthalma English. From Ruth. Unusual.

Ruthanne English. From Ruthann, English, combination of Ruth (Hebrew, "Companion") + Ann (Hannah, Hebrew (Chanah), "Grace"). Less popular. Alternative spelling: Ruthann.

Ruthella English. From Ruth. Unusual.

Ruthetta English. From Ruth. Unusual.

Ruthie English. From Ruth. Less popular.

Ruthina English. From Ruth. Unusual.

Ruthine English. From Ruth. Unusual.

Ruthven Scottish. Scottish, aristocratic family name based on Ruth (Hebrew, "Companion"). Unusual.

Ruza Czech. From Rose, Latin, "rosa," a flower name used as a first name. Unusual.

Růžena Czech. From Rose, Latin, "rosa," a flower name used as a first name. Unusual.

Ruzenka Czech. From Rose, Latin, "rosa," a flower name used as a first name. Unusual.

Ruzha Russian. From Rose, Latin, "rosa," a flower name used as a first name. Unusual.

Ruzsa Hungarian. From Rose, Latin, "rosa," a flower name used as a first name. Unusual.

Ryan See under Boys' Names.

Ryba Czech. Czech, "Fish." Unusual.

Saba English. From Bathsheba, Hebrew (Batsheva), "Daughter of an oath to God." 2 Samuel 11:3. Saint; another name for the Queen of Sheba. Unusual.

Sabina English. Latin, "A Sabine," a person from central Italy. Saint (Roman). Unusual. Alternative spelling: Sebina.

Sabra Hebrew/Israeli. Hebrew, "Cactus." Daughter of Ptolemy, king of Egypt, in 13th-century "Golden Legend"; Starr (danced the Charleston for record 110 hours, 58 minutes, 1979). Unusual. Alternative spelling: Sabrah.

Sabre English. From Sabrina. Unusual.

Sabrina English. Latin, after the English Severn River; the name is attributed to the legendary daughter of King Locrine by his mistress. Sabrina and her mother were thrown into the river by Queen Guendolen. Character in Fletcher's play "Faithful Shepherdess"; character in Milton's poem "Comus"; character in Samuel Taylor's play "Sabrina Fair." Less popular.

Sachi Japanese. Japanese, "Bliss." Unusual.

Sada Japanese. Japanese, "Chaste." Thompson (actress). Unusual.

Sadella English. From Sarah, Hebrew, "Princess." Genesis 17:15. Unusual.

Sadhana Indo-Pakistani. Hindi, "Devotion." Unusual.

Sadie English. From Sarah, Hebrew, "Princess." Genesis 17:15. Unusual. Alternative spellings: Sadye, Saidee.

Sadira Persian. Persian, "Lotus tree." Unusual.

Sadzi Native American. Native American, "Sun heart." Unusual.

Saffron English. English, name of a flower. Unusual.

Sagara Indo-Pakistani. Hindi, "Ocean." Unusual.

Saida English. From Sarah, Hebrew, "Princess." Genesis 17:15. Unusual.

Saint English. Latin, "sanctus" ("sacred"); the word used as a first name. Unusual.

Sakari Indo-Pakistani. Hindi, "Sweet one." Unusual.

Saki Japanese. Japanese, "Cape." Unusual.

Sakti Indo-Pakistani. Hindi, "Energy." The name of a principal Hindu goddess who represents both innocence and destruction. Unusual.

Sakuna Native American. Hindi, "Bird." Unusual.

Sakura Japanese. Japanese, "Cherry blossom." Unusual.

Sal English. From Solomon, Hebrew, "Peace." Schillizzi (opened a safe in 9 minutes, 40 seconds, for 1986 record). Unusual.

Sala Indo-Pakistani. Hindi, the name of a sacred tree. Unusual.

Salama Arabic. From Solomon, Hebrew, "Peace." Unusual.

Salcia Polish. From Sarah, Hebrew, "Princess." Genesis 17:15. Unusual.

Salena English. From Selina, Greek, "Moon," after the Greek goddess of the moon, Selene; or "parsley sprig." Unusual. Alternative spellings: Salina, Salinah.

Sally English. From Sarah, Hebrew, "Princess." Genesis 17:15. Field (actress, 1984 Oscar, "Places in the Heart"); Ride (astronaut); Tompkins (19th-century hospital administrator; only woman commissioned in Confederate army); Rand (acrobatic carnival dancer) (real name: Helen Gould Beck); Kellerman (actress). Less popular. Sal. Alternative spellings: Salley, Sallie.

Sally-Ann English. From Sally-Ann, English, combination of Sally (Sarah, Hebrew, "Princess") + Ann (Hannah, Hebrew (Chanah), "Grace"). Struthers (actress). Less popular. Alternative spellings: Sallian, Sallianne, Sally-Anne, Sallyann, Sallyanne.

Saloma English. From Solomon, Hebrew, "Peace." Unusual.

Salome English. From Solomon, Hebrew, "Peace." Saint; biblical woman who ministered to Jesus; Alexandra (Queen of Judea, 76–67 B.C.); 1st-century Judean princess, daughter of Herodius—asked King Herod for John the Baptist's head; title character in Oscar Wilde's play. Unusual. Alternative spelling: Salomi.

Samantha English. From Samuel, Hebrew (Shmuel), "His name is God" or "God has heard." 1 Samuel 1:20. Druce (youngest female to swim English Channel: 12 years old, 1983); Eggar (British actress); Stevens (witch on TV series "Bewitched," played by Elizabeth Montgomery). Extremely popular. Sam. Alternative spellings: Samanntha, Symantha.

Samara English. Hebrew, "Guardian" or "guarded by God." Unusual.

Samaria American. From Samuel, Hebrew (Shmuel), "His name is God" or "God has heard." 1 Samuel 1:20. Unusual.

Samarie American. From Samuel, Hebrew (Shmuel), "His name is God" or "God has heard." 1 Samuel 1:20. Unusual.

Samarthur American. From Samuel, Hebrew (Shmuel), "His name is God" or "God has heard." 1 Samuel 1:20. Unusual.

Sameh Arabic. From Sameh, Arabic, "One who forgives." A quality of God listed in the Koran. Unusual.

Samella American. From Samuel, Hebrew (Shmuel), "His name is God" or "God has heard." 1 Samuel 1:20. Unusual.

Samentha American. From Samuel, Hebrew (Shmuel), "His name is God" or "God has heard." 1 Samuel 1:20. Unusual.

Sammi English. From Samuel, Hebrew (Shmuel), "His name is God" or "God has heard." 1 Samuel 1:20. Unusual. Sam.

Sammie See Sammy under Boys' Names.

Sammy See under Boys' Names.

Samuela American. From Samuel, Hebrew (Shmuel), "His name is God" or "God has heard." 1 Samuel 1:20. Unusual.

Samuella English. From Samuel, Hebrew (Shmuel), "His name is God" or "God has heard." 1 Samuel 1:20. Unusual.

Sanā Arabic. From Sanā, Arabic, "Radiance" or "splendor." Unusual.

Sancha Hispanic. From Sanchia. Unusual.

Sanchia Hispanic. Latin, "Holy." Unusual. Alternative spelling: Sancia.

Sandeep African. Punjabi, "Enlightened being." Unusual for males, unusual for females.

Sandra English. From Alexander, Greek, "Defender of men" or "warding off men." Mark 16:21; Acts 4:6, 19:33. Day O'Connor (first woman Supreme Court Justice); Dee (actress) (real name: Alexandra Zuck). Less popular. Sandi+.

Sandrea English. From Alexander, Greek, "Defender of men" or "warding off men." Mark 16:21; Acts 4:6, 19:33. Unusual. Alternative spelling: Sandria.

Sandrell English. From Alexander, Greek, "Defender of men" or "warding off men." Mark 16:21; Acts 4:6, 19:33. Unusual.

Sandrina English. From Alexander, Greek, "Defender of men" or "warding off men." Mark 16:21; Acts 4:6, 19:33. Unusual.

Sandy English. From Alexander, Greek, "Defender of men" or "warding off men." Mark 16:21; Acts 4:6, 19:33. Duncan (TV actress, "Hogan Family"); Allen (tallest American woman: 7 feet, 7.25 inches); Dennis (actress). Less popular for males, less popular for females. Alternative spellings: Sandi, Sandie.

Santana Hispanic. Spanish, "Saint." Unusual.

Sanura African. Swahili, "Kitten-like." Unusual.

Sanuye Native American. Native American, "Red cloud at sundown." Unusual.

Sanya Indo-Pakistani. Hindi, "Born on Saturday." Unusual.

Sapata Native American. Native American, "Bear dancing around a tree." Unusual.

Sapphire English. Hebrew, "Lapis lazuli," a gemstone. Unusual.

Sarah English. Hebrew, "Princess." Genesis 17:15. Wife of Abraham; Bernhardt (French actress) (real name: Henriette-Rosine Bernard); Flower Adams (British hymn writer, "Nearer My God to Thee"); Woolsey (writer of juvenile books, "Just Sixteen") (real name of Susan Coolidge); Miles (British actress). Extremely popular. Sadie, Sally. Alternative spellings: Sara, Sarra.

Sarah-Jane English. English, combination of Sarah (Hebrew, "Princess") + Jane (John, Hebrew (Yochanan), "God has been gracious"). Less popular. Alternative spellings: Sara-jane, Sarah-jayne.

Sarai English. From Sarah. Unusual.

Sarann English. From Sarann, Hebrew, combination of Sarah (Hebrew, "Princess") + Ann (Hannah, Hebrew (Chanah), "Grace"). Unusual.

Sarauniya Nigerian. Nigerian, "Queen." Unusual.

Sarena English. From Sarah. Unusual. Alternative spelling: Sarina.

Sarene English. From Sarah. Unusual. Alternative spellings: Sareen, Sarine.

Saretta English. From Sarah. Unusual.

Sarette English. From Sarah. Unusual.

Sari English. From Sarah. Unusual.

Sarika Hungarian. From Sarah. Unusual.

Saril Turkish. Turkish, "Sound of running water." Unusual.

Sarita Hispanic. From Sarah. Unusual.

Saritia Hispanic. From Sarah. Unusual.

Sarka Russian. From Sarah. Unusual.

Sarlote Latvian. From Charles, Old English, "ceorl" ("man" or "husbandman"). Unusual.
Sarolta Hungarian. From Sarah. Unusual.
Sarotte French. From Sarah. Unusual.
Sasa Russian, from Alexander, Greek, "Defender of men" or "warding off men," Mark 16:21, Acts 4:6, 19:33; and Hungarian, from Sarah, Hebrew, "Princess." Genesis 17:15. Unusual.
Sascha See under Boys' Names.
Sasha Russian. From Alexander, Greek, "Defender of men" or "warding off men." Mark 16:21; Acts 4:6, 19:33. Unusual.
Saskia Dutch. Meaning and origin unknown. Possibly related to "Saxon." Van Uijlenburgh (wife of Rembrandt and subject of many of his portraits). Unusual.
Satinka Native American. Native American, "Magic dancer." Unusual.
Sato Japanese. Japanese, "Sugar." Unusual.
Saundra American. From Alexander, Greek, "Defender of men" or "warding off men." Mark 16:21; Acts 4:6, 19:33. Less popular. Sandi+.
Saura Indo-Pakistani. Hindi, "Sun worshiper." Unusual.
Savanna English. Spanish, "Treeless plain." Unusual. Alternative spellings: Savana, Savanah, Savannah.
Savina Italian. From Sabina, Latin, "A Sabine," a person from central Italy. Unusual.
Sawa Japanese. Japanese, "Marsh." Unusual.
Sayo Japanese. Japanese, "Born at night." Unusual.
Scarlett English. English, occupational surname indicating someone who wore or worked with scarlet fabric. O'Hara (character in Margaret Mitchell's novel "Gone With the Wind"). Unusual. Alternative spelling: Scarlet.
Sebastienne French. From Sebastian, Latin, "Man from Sebastia," a city in Asia Minor. Unusual.
Sebra English. From Sabra, Hebrew, "Cactus." Unusual.
Seda Armenian. Armenian, "An echo in the forest." Unusual.
Sedna Eskimo. Eskimo, the name of the goddess of food. Unusual.
Seelia English. From Cecil, Latin, "Blind." Unusual. Alternative spellings: Celia, Selia.
Seki Japanese. Japanese, "Great," "stone," or "barrier." Unusual.
Sela English. From Selina, Greek, "Moon," after the Greek goddess of the moon, Selene; or "parsley sprig." Unusual.
Selah See under Boys' Names.
Selby-Ann English. English, combination of Selby (English, "Willow farm") + Ann (Hannah, Hebrew (Chanah), "Grace"). Unusual.
Selima Hebrew/Israeli. From Solomon, Hebrew, "Peace." Unusual.
Selina English. Greek, "Moon," after the Greek goddess of the moon, Selene; or "parsley sprig." Greek moon goddess; countess of Huntington (donated fortune to the Methodists). Unusual. Alternative spelling: Selena.
Selinda English. From Selina. Unusual.
Seline English. From Selina. Unusual. Alternative spelling: Selene.
Selinka Russian. From Celestin, Latin, "Heavenly." Unusual.
Selma English. From Anselm, Old German, "Divine" + "helmet." Lagerlöf (Swedish novelist, won Nobel Prize for literature, 1909, "The Wonderful Adventures of Nils"). Unusual.
Sema Greek. Greek, "Sign from above." Unusual.
Sen See under Boys' Names.
Sena English. From Selina. Unusual.
Senga Scottish. Scottish, reversal of Agnes (Greek, "Pure," "chaste"). Unusual.
Seonaid Scottish. From John, Hebrew (Yochanan), "God has been gracious." Unusual.
September English. English, the name of the month used as a first name. Unusual.
Septima Latin. From Septimus, Latin, "Seventh." Unusual.
Seraphina English. Hebrew, "Angel" or "ardent." Saint (13th-century). Unusual.
Seraphine English. From Seraphina. Unusual.
Serena English. Latin, "Calm." Saint. Unusual. Alternative spellings: Sereena, Serenah, Serina.
Serenna English. From Serena. Unusual.
Serofina English. From Seraphina. Unusual.
Sesiliia English. From Cecil, Latin, "Blind." Unusual.
Sevilla Hispanic. From Sibyl, Latin, the name of the mythical priestess who spoke the messages of the gods at the oracles. Unusual.
Seville Hispanic. From Sibyl, Latin, the name of the mythical priestess who spoke the messages of the gods at the oracles. Unusual.
Shaaron American. From Sharon, Hebrew, "A plain." Most likely a reference to the fertile plain between Jaffa and Mt. Carmel, Israel. Unusual.
Shaba Hispanic. From Rose, Latin, "rosa," a flower name used as a first name. Unusual.
Shada Native American. Native American, "Pelican." Unusual.
Shae English. From Shea, Hebrew, "Asked-for." Unusual.
Shafaye Created. Created, African-American. Unusual.
Shahar Arabic. Arabic, "By the moon." Unusual.
Shaina Yiddish. From Shayna, Yiddish, "Pretty." Unusual. Alternative spelling: Shayna.
Shaita Created. Created, African-American. Unusual.
Shajuan Created. Created, African-American. Unusual.
Shajuana Created. Created, African-American. Unusual.
Shaka See under Boys' Names.
Shakeena Created. Created, African-American. Unusual. Alternative spelling: Shakina.
Shakela Created. Created, African-American. Unusual.
Shakera Created. Created, African-American. Unusual.
Shaketa Created. Created, African-American. Unusual.
Shakia Created. Created, African-American. Unusual. Alternative spelling: Shakeya.
Shakilah Created. Created, African-American. Unusual.
Shakira Created. Created, African-American. Unusual. Alternative spellings: Shakirah, Shakirra.
Shakita Created. Created, African-American. Unusual.
Shalanda Created. Created, African-American. Unusual.
Shalane Created. Created, African-American. Unusual.

Shalaun Created. Created, African-American. Unusual.
Shalay Created. Created, African-American. Unusual.
Shalaya Created. Created, African-American. Unusual.
Shalena Created. Created, African-American. Unusual.
Shaleta Created. Created, African-American. Unusual.
Shaletta Created. Created, African-American. Unusual.
Shalika Created. Created, African-American. Unusual.
Shalinda Created. Created, African-American. Unusual.
Shalisa Created. Created, African-American. Unusual.
Shalonda Created. Created, African-American. Unusual.
Shalonde Created. Created, African-American. Unusual.
Shalyn Created. Created, African-American. Unusual.
Shameka Created. Created, African-American. Unusual.
Shamica Created. Created, African-American. Unusual. Alternative spelling: Shamika.
Shamira Hebrew/Israeli. From Shamir, Hebrew, a hard, precious stone possibly used in building Solomon's temple. Unusual.
Shamita Created. Created, African-American. Unusual.
Shammara Arabic. Arabic, "Prepare for battle." Unusual.
Shan American. From John, Hebrew (Yochanan), "God has been gracious." Unusual.
Shana English. From John, Hebrew (Yochanan), "God has been gracious." Unusual.
Shanae English. From John, Hebrew (Yochanan), "God has been gracious." Unusual. Alternative spelling: Shanay.
Shanda Created. Created, African-American. Unusual.
Shandi English. From John, Hebrew (Yochanan), "God has been gracious." Unusual.
Shandra English. From John, Hebrew (Yochanan), "God has been gracious." Unusual.
Shane See Shaine under Boys' Names.
Shanea Created. Created, African-American. Unusual. Alternative spelling: Shania.
Shaneen Created. Created, African-American. Unusual.
Shaneka Created. Created, African-American. Unusual.
Shanekia Created. Created, African-American. Unusual.
Shanelle Created. Created, African-American. Unusual. Alternative spellings: Shanel, Shanell, Shannel.
Shanequa Created. Created, African-American. Unusual.
Shanetha Created. Created, African-American. Unusual.
Shanethis Created. Created, African-American. Unusual.
Shanetta Created. Created, African-American. Unusual.
Shanette Created. Created, African-American. Unusual.
Shani African, from Shani, Swahili, "Marvelous"; and English, from Susannah, Hebrew (Shoshanah), "Lily," Luke 8:3. Unusual.
Shanida Created. Created, African-American. Unusual.
Shanika Created. Created, African-American. Unusual. Alternative spellings: Shanicka, Shenika.
Shanisha Created. Created, African-American. Unusual.
Shanita Created. Created, African-American. Unusual.
Shanitha Created. Created, African-American. Unusual.
Shanitra Created. Created, African-American. Unusual.
Shann English. From Shannon, Celtic, "Old one," "wise one," or "small one." Refers to an ancient divinity. Unusual.
Shannah English. From Shannon, Celtic, "Old one," "wise one," or "small one." Refers to an ancient divinity. Unusual. Alternative spelling: Shanna.
Shannie English. From Shannon, Celtic, "Old one," "wise one," or "small one." Refers to an ancient divinity. Unusual.
Shannon English. Celtic, "Old one," "wise one," or "small one." Refers to an ancient divinity. Less popular for males, very popular for females. Alternative spellings: Shanan, Shannan, Shannen, Shanon.
Shanta American. From Chantal, French, "Stony place"; a place name used as a first name. Unusual.
Shantae American. From Chantal, French, "Stony place"; a place name used as a first name. Unusual.
Shante Created. Created, African-American. Unusual.
Shanteka Created. Created, African-American. Unusual.
Shantelle American. From Chantal, French, "Stony place"; a place name used as a first name. Unusual. Alternative spellings: Chantal, Chantale, Chantalle, Chantel, Chantel, Chantele, Chantelle, Shantale, Shantel, Shantele, Shantell.
Shantia Created. Created, African-American. Unusual.
Shantilli Created. Created, African-American. Unusual.
Shantina Created. Created, African-American. Unusual.
Shantrice Created. Created, African-American. Unusual.
Shappa Native American. Native American, "Red thunder." Unusual.
Shaquita Created. Created, African-American. Unusual.
Shara English. From Sharon, Hebrew, "A plain." Most likely a reference to the fertile plain between Jaffa and Mt. Carmel, Israel. Unusual.
Sharai Hebrew/Israeli. Hebrew, "Princess." Unusual.
Sharayah Created. Created, African-American. Unusual.
Sharda English. From Chardae, Arabic, "Runaway." Unusual.
Sharday English. From Chardae, Arabic, "Runaway." Unusual. Alternative spellings: Chardae, Sade, Shardae, Sharde.
Sharde English. From Chardae, Arabic, "Runway." Unusual. Alternative spelling: Charde.
Sharee English. From Sharon. Unusual. Alternative spelling: Sheree.
Sharene American. From Sharon. Unusual.
Shari American. From Sharon. Lewis (puppeteer); Headley (film actress). Unusual. Alternative spelling: Sharie.
Sharine American. From Sharon. Unusual.
Sharissa American. From Sharon. Unusual.
Sharita Created. From Sharita. Unusual.
Sharla Created. From Sharla. Unusual.
Sharlene English. From Charles, Old En-

glish, "ceorl" ("man" or "husbandman"), Wells (Miss America, 1985). Unusual. Alternative spellings: Charleen, Charlene, Charline, Sharleen, Sharline.

Sharma American. Combination of Sharon (Hebrew, "A plain") + Mary (Hebrew (Miryam), "Bitterness," "rebellion," "wished-for child," or "sea (?)"). Unusual.

Sharmaine English. From Charmaine, Latin (Carminea), a Roman clan name used as a first name. Unusual. Alternative spellings: Sharmain, Sharmane.

Sharman English. From Charmaine, Latin (Carminea), a Roman clan name used as a first name. Unusual.

Sharmine American. From Sharma. Unusual.

Sharon English. Hebrew, "A plain." Most likely a reference to the fertile plain between Jaffa and Mt. Carmel, Israel. Ritchie (Miss America, 1956); Tate (film actress); Falconer (character in Sinclair Lewis's novel "Elmer Gantry"); Stone (actress). Less popular. Alternative spellings: Sharan, Sharen, Sharin, Sharron, Sharran, Sharyn, Sheren, Sheron, Sherryn.

Sharona American. From Sharon. Unusual.

Sharonda American. From Sharon. Unusual.

Sharone American. From Sharon. Unusual.

Sharran American. From Sharon. Unusual. Alternative spellings: Sharone, Sharren, Sharronne.

Sharronda American. From Sharon. Unusual.

Shasta Native American. Native American, meaning unknown. Unusual.

Shatara Arabic. Arabic, "Good" or "industrious." Unusual.

Shaun See under Boys' Names.

Shauna English. From John, Hebrew (Yochanan), "God has been gracious." Less popular. Alternative spellings: Shaune, Shaunna, Shawna, Shawnna.

Shaunda English. From John, Hebrew (Yochanan), "God has been gracious." Unusual. Alternative spelling: Shawnda.

Shauneen English. From John, Hebrew (Yochanan), "God has been gracious." Unusual.

Shaunette English. From John, Hebrew (Yochanan), "God has been gracious." Unusual.

Shavonne American. From John, Hebrew (Yochanan), "God has been gracious." Unusual. Alternative spellings: Shavon, Shavone.

Shawn See under Boys' Names.

Shawnee American. From John, Hebrew (Yochanan), "God has been gracious." Unusual.

Shawni English. From Shannon, Celtic, "Old one," "wise one," or "small one." Refers to an ancient divinity. Unusual.

Shay English. From Shea, Hebrew, "Asked-for." Unusual.

Shayla American. From Cecil, Latin, "Blind." Unusual.

Shaylee Created. created, meaning unknown. Unusual.

Shea See under Boys' Names.

Sheba English. From Bathsheba, Hebrew (Batsheva), "Daughter of an oath to God." 2 Samuel 11:3. Unusual.

Sheena Scottish. From John, Hebrew (Yochanan), "God has been gracious." Thompson (pool-playing endurance record: 363 hours, 9 minutes). Unusual. Alternative spellings: Sheenagh, Sheenah, Shena.

Sheila English. From Cecil, Latin, "Blind." Guyse (actress). Less popular. Alternative spellings: Sheelagh, Sheelah, Sheilah, Sheilagh, Shelah, Shelia, Shiela.

Shelby English. English, "From the ledge estate." Less popular for males, popular for females.

Shelley English. English, "Meadow on a ledge or slope"; surname and place name used as a first name. Berman (comedian); Fabares (film actress); Winters (film actress) (real name: Shirley Schrift); Hack (film actress); Duvall (film actress). Unusual for males, less popular for females. Alternative spellings: Shelli, Shellie, Shelly.

Sheona Scottish. From John, Hebrew (Yochanan), "God has been gracious." Unusual.

Shera Aramaic. Aramaic, "Light." Unusual.

Shereen English. From Chérie, French, "Dear one" or "sweetheart." Unusual. Alternative spelling: Sherene.

Shereena English. From Chérie, French, "Dear one" or "sweetheart." Unusual. Alternative spellings: Sherena, Sherina.

Sheri American. From Chérie, French, "Dear one" or "sweetheart." Unusual. Alternative spellings: Sherri, Sherrie.

Sherice American. From Sharon, Hebrew, "A plain." Most likely a reference to the fertile plain between Jaffa and Mt. Carmel, Israel. Unusual. Alternative spelling: Sharice.

Shericia English. From Chérie, French, "Dear one" or "sweetheart." Unusual.

Sherida English. From Sheridan, Irish, surname used as a first name. Unusual.

Sheridawn English. From Sheridan, Irish, surname used as a first name. Unusual.

Sherika Arabic. Arabic, "Easterner." Unusual.

Sherilyn English. From Charity, Latin, "carus" ("dear"); one of the Puritan "virtue" names. Fenn (TV actress). Unusual. Alternative spellings: Cheralyn, Cherilyn, Cherilynn, Cherrilyn, Cherrylin, Cherylyn, Sharolyn, Sheralyn, Sherralyn, Sherralynn, Sherryllyn, Sherrylyn.

Sherissa American. From Sharon, Hebrew, "A plain." Most likely a reference to the fertile plain between Jaffa and Mt. Carmel, Israel. Unusual.

Sherita English. From Chérie, French, "Dear one" or "sweetheart." Unusual. Alternative spelling: Sherrita.

Sherleen English. From Shirley. Unusual. Alternative spellings: Sherlean, Sherline.

Sherry English. From Chérie, French, "Dear one" or "sweetheart." Less popular.

Sherryll English. From Charity, Latin, "carus" ("dear"); one of the Puritan "virtue" names. Unusual. Alternative spellings: Cherill, Cherril, Cherrill, Cherryl, Cherryle, Cherryll, Cheryl, Cheryle, Cheryll, Sheral, Sherell, Sheril, Sherrell, Sherill.

Sherryllyn English. From Charity, Latin, "carus" ("dear"); one of the Puritan "virtue" names. Unusual.

Sherrylyn English. From Charity, Latin, "carus" ("dear"); one of the Puritan "virtue" names. Unusual.

Sherryn English. From Sharon, Hebrew, "A plain." Most likely a reference to the fertile plain between Jaffa and Mt. Carmel, Israel. Unusual.

Shervan American. From John, Hebrew (Yochanan), "God has been gracious." Unusual.

Sheryl English. From Chérie, French, "Dear one" or "sweetheart." Unusual.

Shevon English. From John, Hebrew (Yochanan), "God has been gracious." Unusual. Alternative spellings: Chevon, Chevonne, Shevonne.

Shika Japanese. Japanese, "Deer." Unusual.

Shilo Hebrew/Israeli. Hebrew, a biblical site, near Jerusalem. Unusual.

Shina Japanese. Japanese, "Possessions" or "virtue." Unusual.

Shino Japanese. Japanese, "Thin bamboo." A symbol of fidelity. Unusual.

Shiona Scottish. From John, Hebrew (Yochanan), "God has been gracious." Unusual.

Shira Hebrew/Israeli. From Shiri. Unusual. Alternative spelling: Shirah.

Shiri Hebrew/Israeli. Hebrew, "My song." Unusual.

Shirleen English. From Shirley. Unusual. Alternative spelling: Shirlean.

Shirlene English. From Shirley. Unusual.

Shirley English. English, "Bright clearing"; also an aristocratic surname. Temple Black (film star, youngest to receive honorary Oscar); Hufstedler (secretary of education, 1979–81); de la Hunty (Australian, Olympic gold medal for 80-meter hurdles, 1952, 1956: 10.7 seconds); Cothran (Miss America, 1975); Maclaine (film actress). Less popular. Alternative spellings: Sherley, Sherlie, Shirlee, Sherlie, Shirly, Shurley, Shurly.

Shirlynn English. From Shirley. Unusual.

Shivohn American. From John, Hebrew (Yochanan), "God has been gracious." Unusual. Alternative spelling: Shivon.

Shizu Japanese. Japanese, "Quiet" or "clear." Unusual. Alternative spelling: Shizue.

Shizuka Japanese. From Shizu. Unusual.

Shizuko Japanese. From Shizu. Unusual.

Shona English. From John, Hebrew (Yochanan), "God has been gracious." Unusual.

Shonah Scottish. From John, Hebrew (Yochanan), "God has been gracious." Unusual. Alternative spelling: Shonagh.

Shone Scottish. From John, Hebrew (Yochanan), "God has been gracious." Unusual.

Shoshanah Hebrew/Israeli. Hebrew, "Lily." Luke 8:3. Unusual. Alternative spellings: Shoshanna, Shushanah.

Shoushan Armenian. From Susannah, Hebrew (Shoshanah), "Lily." Luke 8:3. Unusual.

Shu Chinese. From Shu, Chinese, "Kind and gentle." Name of two Chinese dynasties (earlier Shu, 907–25; later Shu, 934–65). Unusual.

Shulamit Hebrew/Israeli. Hebrew, "Peaceful." Song of Songs 6:23. Ran (conductor in residence, Chicago Symphony Orchestra, 1990s). Unusual.

Shuma Native American. From Shumana. Unusual.

Shumana Native American. Native American, "Rattlesnake girl." Unusual.

Shuna English. From John, Hebrew (Yochanan), "God has been gracious." Unusual.

Shura Russian. From Alexander, Greek, "Defender of men" or "warding off men." Mark 16:21; Acts 4:6, 19:33. Unusual.

Shuri Gypsy. English Gypsy, meaning unknown. Unusual.

Shurka Russian. From Alexander, Greek, "Defender of men" or "warding off men." Mark 16:21; Acts 4:6, 19:33. Unusual.

Shyla English. From Cecil, Latin, "Blind." Unusual.

Shyvonia American. From John, Hebrew (Yochanan), "God has been gracious." Unusual.

Siân Welsh. From John, Hebrew (Yochanan), "God has been gracious." Unusual.

Sibby English. From Sibyl. Unusual.

Sidney See Sydney under Boys' Names.

Sidonie French. From Sidonia. Gabrielle Colette (French writer of "Claudine" novels). Unusual.

Sidony English. From Sidonia. Unusual.

Sidra Latin. Latin, "Related to constellations," "related to the stars." Unusual.

Sierra English. English, place name used as a first name. Unusual. Alternative spelling: Siera.

Signe Norwegian. Old Norse, "Beautiful, victorious counselor." Hasso (Swedish actress). Unusual.

Sigourney English. Meaning and origin unknown. Weaver (film actress). Less popular.

Sigrid Norwegian. Old Norse, "Beautiful victory." Wolf (Austrian Olympic skier, Super Giant Slalom, gold medalist, 1988); Undset (Norwegian novelist, "Jenny"; Nobel Prize for literature, 1928). Unusual.

Sihu Native American. Native American, "Flower" or "bush." Unusual.

Siko African. African, "One who cries." Unusual.

Sile Irish. From Cecil, Latin, "Blind." Unusual.

Sileas English. From Julius, Latin, a Roman clan name meaning "downy" or "bearded." Unusual.

Silence English. Latin, "silens." Puritan name, emphasizing learning in silence. Unusual.

Silivia Hawaiian. From Silva. Unusual.

Sill See under Boys' Names.

Silva Latin. Latin, "Woods." Saint. Unusual.

Silvaine French. From Silva. Unusual.

Silvania Latin. From Silva. Unusual.

Simmina English. From Simon, Hebrew (Shimon), "God heard." Genesis 29:33. Unusual.

Simona American. From Simon, Hebrew (Shimon), "God heard." Genesis 29:33. Unusual.

Simone French. From Simon, Hebrew (Shimon), "God heard." Genesis 29:33. de Beauvoir (French writer and activist; "Second Sex," 1949); Martini (14th-century Italian painter); Weil (French philosopher and writer); Signoret (French actress). Unusual for males, less popular for females.

Simonia English. From Simon, Hebrew (Shimon), "God heard." Genesis 29:33. Unusual.

Simonne English. From Simon, Hebrew (Shimon), "God heard." Genesis 29:33. Unusual.

Sina Irish. From John, Hebrew (Yochanan), "God has been gracious." Unusual. Alternative spelling: Sinah.

Sindy English. From Cynthia, Greek name for the goddess of the moon, also known as Artemis. Unusual. Alternative spellings: Cindi, Cindie, Cindy, Cyndi, Cyndie.

Sinead Irish. From John, Hebrew (Yochanan), "God has been gracious." O'Connor (musician); Cusack (actress, "Revenge"; daughter of Cyril). Unusual for males, less popular for females.

Siobhan Irish. From John, Hebrew (Yochanan), "God has been gracious." McKenna (film actress, "Of Human Bondage"). Less popular. Alternative spellings: Sioban, Siobahn.

Siobhian Irish. From John, Hebrew (Yochanan), "God has been gracious." Unusual.

Sipeta Native American. Native American, "Pulling out" fish from under a rock. Unusual.

Sisika Native American. Native American, "Swallow" or "thrush." Unusual.

Sissy English. From Cecil, Latin, "Blind." Spacek (film actress, "Coal Miner's Daughter"). Less popular. Alternative spellings: Cissi, Cissie, Cissy, Sisie, Sissey, Sissi, Sissie.

Sita Indo-Pakistani. Hindi, "Furrow," a reference to Mother Earth. Hindu goddess of mother earth, wife of god Rama. Unusual.

Siti African. Swahili, "Lady." Unusual.

Siusan Scottish. From Susannah, Hebrew (Shoshanah), "Lily." Luke 8:3. Unusual. Alternative spelling: Suisan.

Skye English. From Schuyler, Dutch, "Scholar." Unusual.

Snowdrop English. From Snowdrop, English, name of a flower. Unusual.

Soffrona English. From Sophronia. Unusual.

Sofi Greek, Swedish. From Sophia. Unusual.

Sofia Hispanic. From Sophia. Unusual.

Soficita Hispanic. From Sophia. Unusual.

Sofka Russian. From Sophia. Unusual.

Sofronia Icelandic. From Sophronia. Unusual.

Sofya Russian. From Sophia, Greek, "Wisdom." Unusual.

Solana Hispanic. Spanish, "Sunshine." Unusual.

Solenne English. From Solana. Unusual.

Solina English. From Solana. Unusual.

Soline English. From Solana. Unusual.

Soma Indo-Pakistani. Hindi, "Moon." Refers to a child born under sign of Cancer, ruled by moon. Unusual.

Sommer English. From Summer, Sanskrit, "sama" ("year"); the word used as a first name. Unusual. Alternative spelling: Summer.

Sondra English. From Alexander, Greek, "Defender of men" or "warding off men." Mark 16:21; Acts 4:6, 19:33. Less popular.

Sonel English. From Susannah, Hebrew (Shoshanah), "Lily." Luke 8:3. Unusual.

Sonja Russian. From Sophia. Henie (Norwegian Olympic figure skater; gold medalist 1928, 1932, 1936; holds women's record for 10 individual titles); Morgenstern (German figure skater, performed first triple Salchow jump). Unusual. Alternative spellings: Sonia, Sonya.

Sook Korean. Korean, "Purity." Unusual.

Sophia Greek. Greek, "Wisdom." Loren (Italian actress); Smith (philanthropist, funded Smith College); Jex-Blake (British physician, established London School of Medicine for Women, 1874); Byzantine empress, wife of Justin II; Alekseyevna (Regent of Russia, daughter of Czar Alexis). Unusual.

Sophie French. From Sophia. La Roche (wrote first German novel by a woman, 1771); Rostopchin (noble French author of children's books); Tucker ("last of the red hot mamas," vaudeville/burlesque performer); character in William Styron's novel "Sophie's Choice." Unusual.

Sophoon Greek. From Sophia. Unusual.

Sophronia Greek. Greek, "Self-disciplined," "judicious." Jobson (character in Charles Dickens' "Bound for the Great Salt Lake"); Akershem (character in Dickens' "Our Mutual Friend"); Sphynx (character in Dickens' "The Old Curiosity Shop"). Unusual.

Sophy English. From Sophia. Unusual.

Sora Native American. Native American, "Warbling songbird." Unusual.

Soraya Persian. Persian, meaning unknown. Wife of the former Shah of Iran. Unusual.

Sorcha Irish. Old Irish, "Bright." Unusual.

Sorrel See under Boys' Names.

Sorrell See Sorrel under Boys' Names.

Sorrelle See Sorrel under Boys' Names.

Sosanna Irish. From Susannah, Hebrew (Shoshanah), "Lily." Luke 8:3. Unusual.

Soso Native American. Native American, "Tree squirrel gnawing a pine nut." Unusual.

Souline French. From Solana. Unusual.

Soulle French. From Solana. Unusual.

Stacia English. From Anastasia, Greek, "anastasis" ("resurrection"). Unusual. Alternative spelling: Stasia.

Stacy English. From Anastasia, Greek, "anastasis" ("resurrection"). Keach (TV and film star, "The Heart Is a Lonely Hunter"). Popular. Alternative spellings: Staci, Stacie, Stacey.

Stamatios Greek. From Stephen, Greek, "Crown" or "crowned." Acts 7:59. Unusual.

Stanisława Polish. From Stanislaus, Latin, "Camp glory" (?). Unusual.

Star English. Middle English, "Star." Unusual. Alternative spelling: Starr.

Starla English. From Star. Less popular.

Starling English. Diminutive form of Robert (Old English, "Bright fame"), or name of bird. Unusual.

Stasa Czech. From Anastasia, Greek, "anastasis" ("resurrection"). Unusual.

Staska Czech. From Anastasia, Greek, "anastasis" ("resurrection"). Unusual.

Stasya Latvian, Lithuanian, Russian. From Anastasia, Greek, "anastasis" ("resurrection"). Unusual.

Stefa Polish. From Stephen, Greek, "Crown" or "crowned." Acts 7:59. Unusual.

Stefania Czech, Polish, Russian. From Stephen, Greek, "Crown" or "crowned." Acts 7:59. Unusual.

Stefanie English. From Stephen, Greek, "Crown" or "crowned." Acts 7:59. Less popular. Alternative spellings: Stefani, Stefany, Stephani, Stephannie, Stephany.

Stefcia Polish. From Stephen, Greek, "Crown" or "crowned." Acts 7:59. Unusual.

Steffi English. From Stephen, Greek, "Crown" or "crowned." Acts 7:59. Graf (German tennis champion, Grand Slam and Olympic medalist, 1988). Unusual. Alternative spelling: Steffie.

Stefka Czech, Polish. From Stephen, Greek, "Crown" or "crowned." Acts 7:59. Kosadinova (Bulgarian track and field champion; world record high-jumper: 6 feet, 10.25 inches, 1987). Unusual.

Stella American. Latin, "Star." Stevens (actress); characters in Sir Philip Sidney's sonnet, "Astrophel to Stella," 1580s, and in Jonathan Swift's 18th-century "Journal to Stella"; Adler (actress and teacher). Less popular.

Stepa Russian. From Stephen, Greek, "Crown" or "crowned." Acts 7:59. Unusual.

Stepania English. From Stephen, Greek, "Crown" or "crowned." Acts 7:59. Unusual.

Stepanida Russian. From Stephen, Greek, "Crown" or "crowned." Acts 7:59. Unusual.

Stepanie English. From Stephen, Greek, "Crown" or "crowned." Acts 7:59. Unusual.

Stepanyda Russian. From Stephen, Greek, "Crown" or "crowned." Acts 7: 59. Unusual.

Stepha English. From Stephen, Greek, "Crown" or "crowned." Acts 7:59. Unusual.

Stephana English. From Stephen, Greek, "Crown" or "crowned." Acts 7:59. Unusual. Alternative spelling: Stephena.

Stephanie English, French (Stéphanie). From Stephen, Greek, "Crown" or "crowned." Acts 7:59. Princess of Monaco; Powers (actress); Zimbalist (actress). Extremely popular. Alternative spelling: Stephenie.

Stephanine German. From Stephen, Greek, "Crown" or "crowned." Acts 7: 59. Unusual.

Stephene English. From Stephen, Greek, "Crown" or "crowned." Acts 7:59. Unusual.

Stephney English. From Stephen, Greek, "Crown" or "crowned." Acts 7:59. Unusual. Alternative spelling: Stephne.

Stesha Russian. From Stephen, Greek, "Crown" or "crowned." Acts 7:59. Unusual.

Steshka Russian. From Stephen, Greek, "Crown" or "crowned." Acts 7:59. Unusual.

Stevena English. From Stephen, Greek, "Crown" or "crowned." Acts 7:59. Unusual.

Stevi American. From Stephen, Greek, "Crown" or "crowned." Acts 7:59. Unusual.

Stevie See under Boys' Names.

Stina German. From Christian, Greek, "christos" ("anointed"). Unusual.

Stine English. From Christian, Greek, "christos" ("anointed"). Unusual.

Stockard English. Meaning and origin unknown. Channing (movie actress) (real name: Susan). Unusual.

Storm English. Middle English, "Storm." Jameson (British novelist). Unusual.

Stormy English. From Storm. Character in 1968 pop song by the Classics IV. Unusual.

Sue English. From Susannah. Less popular.

Sue Ellen English. From Sue Ellen, Combination of Sue (Hebrew, Susannah (Shoshanah), "Lily") + Ellen (Greek, Helen, "Bright one"). Less popular.

Suela Hispanic. From Consuela, Spanish, "Consolation." Unusual.

Suelita Hispanic. From Consuela, Spanish, "Consolation." Unusual.

Sugi Japanese. Japanese, "Cedar tree." Unusual.

Suka English. From Susannah. Unusual.

Suke Hawaiian. From Susannah. Unusual.

Suki English, from Susannah; and Japanese, "Beloved." Unusual. Alternative spellings: Sukee, Sukey, Sukie, Suky.

Sukoji African. African, "First-born daughter following a son." Unusual.

Sula Icelandic. Icelandic, "Gannett," a large sea bird. Unusual.

Suletu Native American. Native American, "To fly like a bird." Unusual.

Sulwen Welsh. From Sulwyn, Welsh, "Fair as the sun." Unusual.

Sumati Indo-Pakistani. Hindi, "Unity." Unusual.

Sumi Japanese. Japanese, "Clear" or "refined." Unusual.

Suni Native American. Native American, "A Zuni Indian." Unusual.

Sunki Native American. Native American, "Overtaker"; refers to one who overtakes an enemy or wild game. Unusual.

Sunny English. Latin, "sol" ("sun"); or variation on Sonny, affectionate social title for a young man. Unusual for males, unusual for females.

Sunshine English. Latin, "sol" ("sun"); the word used as a first name. Unusual.

Sunya English. From Sophia, Greek, "Wisdom." Unusual.

Surata Indo-Pakistani. Hindi, "Blessed joy." Unusual.

Suri Indo-Pakistani. Hindi, "Knife." Unusual.

Surya Indo-Pakistani. Hindi, the name of the sun god. Unusual.

Susan English. From Susannah. Anthony (reformer, active in temperance, abolitionist, and women's suffrage movements); Blow (educator, established first U.S. public kindergarten, 1873); Hayward (Oscar-winning actress, "I Want to Live," 1958); Akin (Miss America, 1986); Dey (film star). Less popular. Sue, Susie+. Alternative spellings: Suson, Suzan.

Susanka Russian. From Susannah. Unusual.

Susann German. From Susannah. Unusual.

Susannah English. Hebrew (Shoshanah), "Lily." Luke 8:3. Biblical heroine; York (British actress); Moodie (19th-century Canadian writer on life in the Canadian wilderness). Less popular. Sue, Susan, Susie+. Alternative spellings: Susana, Susanah, Susanna, Suzanna, Suzannah.

Suse Hawaiian. From Susannah. Unusual.

Susetta English. From Susannah. Unusual.

Susette French. From Susannah. La Flesche (reformer, daughter of Omaha Indian chief) (Indian name: Inshta Theumba, "Bright Eyes"). Unusual. Alternative spelling: Suzette.

Susie English. From Susannah. Less popular. Sue. Alternative spellings: Susey, Susi, Susy, Suze, Suzi, Suzie, Suzy.

Suszanne French. From Susannah. Unusual.

Sutki Native American. Native American, "A broken piece of clay." Unusual.

Suzamni Native American. Native American (originally French), combination of Susan (Susannah, Hebrew (Shoshanah), "Lily") + Annie (Hannah, Hebrew (Chanah), "Grace"). Unusual.

Suzana Bulgarian, English. Unusual. Sue, Susie+.

Suzanne English. From Susannah. Farrell (ballerina); Somers (TV actress, "Three's Company"); Pleshette (actress); Curchod (wife of 18th-century French financier and statesman Jacques Necker); Lenglen (French tennis player; won Wimbledon, French Open, and Olympics, 1920s). Less popular. Sue, Susie+. Alternative spellings: Susanne, Suzane, Suzann, Suzzann, Suzzanne.

Suzetta French. From Susannah. Unusual.

Suzu Japanese. Japanese, "Little bell." Unusual. Alternative spelling: Suzue.

Suzuki Japanese. From Suzuki, Japanese, "Bell tree." Harunobu (18th-century Japanese painter and printer, invented color printing in Japan; best known for paintings of mothers and children). Unusual.

Suzuko Japanese. From Suzu. Unusual.

Svetlana Russian. Meaning and origin unknown. Savitskaya (Russian aircraft pilot, achieved highest speed by a woman: 1,669.89 miles per hour, June 1975); Stalina (Stalin's daughter). Unusual.

Swoosie Created. Created, meaning unknown. Kurtz (film actress, "Dangerous Liaisons"). Unusual. Alternative spelling: Swoozy.

Sy French. From Sidney, Old French, "From Saint-Denis." A Norman surname derived from a village named for a saint. Unusual.

Sybella English. From Sibyl, Latin, the name of the mythical priestess who spoke the messages of the gods at the oracles. Unusual. Alternative spellings: Sibbella, Sibella.

Sybil English. From Sibyl, Latin, the name of the mythical priestess who spoke the messages of the gods at the oracles. Title character in Benjamin Disraeli's 1845 novel; Thorndike (British Shakespearean actress, created character of St. Joan in G.B. Shaw's play of same name). Less popular. Alternative spellings: Sibell, Sibbill, Sybel, Sybille.

Sybilla English. From Sibyl, Latin, the name of the mythical priestess who spoke the messages of the gods at the oracles. Unusual. Alternative spellings: Sibilla, Sibylla.

Sydney See under Boys' Names.

Sydonah English. From Sidonia, Latin, "Woman from Sidon." Unusual. Alternative spelling: Sidona.

Sydonia English. From Sidonia, Latin, "Woman from Sidon." Unusual.

Sylvana English. From Silva, Latin, "Woods." Unusual.

Sylvia American. From Silva, Latin, "Woods." Miles (British actress); Beach (book seller, published James Joyce's banned "Ulysses," 1922); Plath (poet, "The Bell Jar," 1963) (also known as Victoria Lucas); Warner (British novelist, poet, and biographer, "Kingdoms of Elfin," 1977). Less popular. Alternative spelling: Silvia.

Sylvie French. From Silva, Latin, "Woods." Unusual.

Syndonia English. From Sidonia, Latin, "Woman from Sidon." Unusual.

Syreeta Arabic. From Syreeta, Arabic, "Companion." Unusual.

Tabby English. From Tabitha. Unusual. Alternative spellings: Tabbi, Tabbie.

Tabia African. Swahili, "Talents." Unusual.

Tabitha English. Aramaic, "Gazelle." Acts 9:36. Character in Bible, Acts 9:36; character in TV series "Bewitched"; character in A. Colton's "Tabitha's Dancing of the Minuet." Less popular. Alternative spellings: Tabatha, Tabbitha, Tabetha, Tabotha.

Tace English. From Silence, Latin, "silens." Puritan name, emphasizing learning in silence. Unusual for males, unusual for females.

Tacey English. From Silence, Latin, "silens." Puritan name, emphasizing learning in silence. Unusual.

Taci Native American. Native American, "Washtub." Unusual.

Tadewi Native American. From Tadi, Native American, "Wind." Unusual.

Tadita Native American. Native American, "Runner." Unusual. Alternative spelling: Tadeta.

Tahnee English. From Tahnee, Old English, "Little one." Unusual.

Taima Native American. Native American, "Thunder's crash." Unusual.

Taipa Native American. Native American, "Quail flying." Unusual.

Taka Japanese. Japanese, "Honorable," "falcon," "tall," or "hawk." Unusual.

Takala Native American. Native American, "Corn tassel." Unusual.

Takara Japanese. Japanese, "Treasure." Unusual.

Takenya Native American. Native American, "Falcon swooping." Unusual.

Taki Japanese. Japanese, "Waterfall." Unusual.

Takia Arabic. Arabic, "Worshiper." Unusual.

Takuhi Armenian. Armenian, "Queen." Unusual. Alternative spelling: Takoohi.

Tal See under Boys' Names.

Tala Native American. Native American, "Wolf." Unusual.

Talasi Native American. Native American, "Corn-tassel flower." Unusual.

Talia Hebrew/Israeli. Hebrew, "Dew" or "rain." Shire (film actress). Unusual. Alternative spelling: Talya.

Talisha English. From Talitha. Unusual. Alternative spelling: Talicia.

Talita English. From Talitha. Unusual.

Talitha English. Aramaic, "Small girl child." Mark 5:41. Unusual. Alternative spelling: Taletha.

Talullah Native American. Native American, "Water running," referring to a river or waterfall. Bankhead (actress). Unusual. Alternative spelling: Talula.

Talor See under Boys' Names.

Talora English. From Talia. Unusual.

Tama Russian, from Tamar; and Japanese, Japanese, "Jewel." Unusual.

Tamah English. From Tamar. Unusual.

Tamaki Japanese. Japanese, "Bracelet." Unusual.

Tamako Japanese. From Tamaki. Unusual.

Tamar Hebrew/Israeli. Hebrew, "Date palm." 2 Samuel 13:1. Daughter of David. Unusual. Alternative spelling: Thamar.

Tamara Russian. From Tamar. Queen in Soviet Georgia, 12th century; character in poem by 19th-century Russian romantic poet Mikhail Lermontov. Unusual. Alternative spellings: Tamarra, Tammara, Tammera, Tamyra.

Tamaris. English. From Damaris, Latin, "Calf." Unusual.

Tamarka Scottish. From Tamar. Unusual.

Tamasin English. From Thomas, Aramaic, "Twin." Unusual.

Tamasine English. From Thomas, Aramaic, "Twin." Unusual.

Tamayo Japanese. From Tamaki. Unusual.

Tameka English. From Thomas, Aramaic, "Twin." Unusual.

Tamer English. From Tamar. Unusual.

Tamera English. From Tamar. Unusual.

Tamika Japanese. Japanese, "People child." Unusual. Alternative spelling: Tamike.

Tamiko Japanese. From Tamika. Unusual.

Tamiyo Japanese. From Tamika. Unusual.

Tammy Scottish. From Thomas, Aramaic, "Twin." Unusual for males, less popular

for females. Alternative spellings: Tami, Tamie, Tammi, Tammie.
Tamor English. From Tamar. Unusual. Alternative spelling: Tamour.
Tamra Russian. From Tamar. Unusual.
Tamsyn English. From Thomas, Aramaic, "Twin." Unusual. Alternative spellings: Tamsin, Tamzen, Tamzin.
Tana Russian. From Tatius, name of a Sabine king, Titus Tatius; origin unknown. Unusual.
Tanaka Japanese. Japanese, "Lives in or near a rice swamp." Unusual.
Taneshia American. From Tanisha. Unusual. Alternative spellings: Taneisha, Tanesha, Taneshea, Taniesha, Tenecia, Teneisha, Tenesha, Teniesha, Tenisha.
Tani Japanese. Japanese, "Valley." Unusual for males, unusual for females.
Tania Russian. From Tatius, name of a Sabine king, Titus Tatius; origin unknown. Unusual. Alternative spellings: Tanja, Tannia, Tanya.
Tanicha American. From Tanisha. Unusual.
Tanis English. From Tatius, name of a Sabine king, Titus Tatius; origin unknown. Judique (character in Sinclair Lewis's 1923 novel "Babbitt"). Unusual. Alternative spelling: Tannis.
Tanish American. From Tanisha. Unusual.
Tanita English. From Tanith. Unusual.
Tanith English. Phoenician, the name of a goddess of love. Unusual.
Tanitha English. From Tanith. Unusual.
Tanka Russian. From Tatius, name of a Sabine king, Titus Tatius; origin unknown. Unusual.
Tansy English. Greek, "athanasia" ("immortality"); a flower name used as a first name. Title character in Tickner Edwarde's 1921 novel; title character in novel by Maureen Peters. Unusual.
Tany English. From Tahnee, Old English, "Little one." Unusual.
Tanya Russian. From Tatius, name of a Sabine king, Titus Tatius; origin unknown. Unusual.
Tao Chinese. Chinese, "Peach," a symbol of longevity. Unusual.
Tara English. Irish, "Hill." Character in Thomas Moore's 1814 poem "Irish Melodies"; character in TV series "All My Children." Popular. Alternative spellings: Tarah, Tarra.
Tareena English. From Terence, Latin, "Terentius," the name of a Roman clan. Unusual. Alternative spelling: Tarena.
Tareva Meaning and origin unknown. Unusual.
Tarnia Russian. From Tatius, name of a Sabine king, Titus Tatius; origin unknown. Unusual. Alternative spelling: Tarnya.
Tarryn English. From Tara. Unusual. Alternative spellings: Taran, Tarin, Taryn.
Taryna English. From Tara. Unusual. Alternative spelling: Tarina.
Tasarla English. English Gypsy, "Dusk" or "dawn." Unusual.
Tasenka Latvian, Lithuanian, Russian. From Anastasia, Greek, "anastatis" ("resurrection"). Unusual.
Tasha Russian. From Natalie, Latin, "Birthday of the Lord." Unusual. Alternative spelling: Tasia.
Tashina Russian. From Natalie, Latin, "Birthday of the Lord." Unusual.
Tashka Russian. From Natalie, Latin, "Birthday of the Lord." Unusual.
Tasia From Anastasia, Greek, "anastasis" ("resurrection"). Unusual.
Tasida Native American. Native American, "A horse rider." Unusual for males, unusual for females.
Taska Latvian, Lithuania, Russian. From Anastasia, Greek, "anastasis" ("resurrection"). Unusual.
Tasmine English. From Thomas, Aramaic, "Twin." Unusual. Alternative spelling: Tasmin.
Tassos Greek. From Teresa, Greek, "Therasia," the name of two islands, or "theros" ("summer"). Unusual.
Tasya Latvian, Lithuania, Russian. From Anastasia, Greek, "anastasis" ("resurrection"). Unusual.
Tata Russian. From Tatius, name of a Sabine king, Titus Tatius; origin unknown.
Tatiana Scottish. From Tatius, name of a Sabine king, Titus Tatius; origin unknown. Unusual.
Tatsu Japanese. Japanese, "Dragon." Unusual.
Tatum English. Middle English, "Cheerful." O'Neal (film actress). Unusual.
Tawia African, African, "Born after twins"; and Polish, from Octavius, Latin, "Eighth," given to the eighth- born child or a child born on the eighth day or in the eighth month. Unusual.
Tawnie Gypsy. English Gypsy, "Little one." Unusual. Alternative spelling: Tawny.
Tawnya English. From Tatius, name of a Sabine king, Titus Tatius; origin unknown. Unusual.
Taylor See under Boys' Names.
Tayma English. From Tamar. Unusual.
Tazu Japanese. Japanese, "Rice field stork," a symbol of longevity. Unusual.
Teca Hungarian. From Teresa, Greek, "Therasia," the name of two islands, or "theros" ("summer"). Unusual.
Techa Hispanic. From Teresa, Greek, "Therasia," the name of two islands, or "theros" ("summer"). Unusual.
Tegan Welsh. Welsh, "Beautiful" or "fair." Unusual.
Tegwen Welsh. From Tegan. Unusual. Alternative spelling: Tegwyn.
Temira Hebrew/Israeli. Hebrew, "Tall." Unusual.
Temperance English. Latin, "temperare" ("to moderate"). Unusual.
Tempest English. Latin, "tempus" ("time"). Unusual. Alternative spelling: Tempestt.
Tennille French. French, surname used as a first name. Unusual. Alternative spelling: Tenille.
Teodora Czech. From Dorothy, Greek (Dorothea), "Gift from God." Unusual.
Tera English. From Tara, Irish, "Hill." Unusual. Alternative spelling: Terra.
Terasa English. From Teresa. Unusual.
Tercza Hungarian. From Teresa. Unusual.
Tere Hispanic. From Teresa. Unusual.
Terecena English. From Terence, Latin, "Terentius," the name of a Roman clan. Unusual.
Teree English. From Teresa. Unusual.
Terelyn English. From Terence, Latin, "Terentius," the name of a Roman clan. Unusual. Alternative spelling: Terilyn.
Terenia Polish. From Teresa. Unusual.
Terenne English. From Terence, Latin, "Terentius," the name of a Roman clan. Unusual.
Teresa English, Hungarian, Italian. "Therasia," the name of two islands, or "theros" ("summer"). Saint (16th century). Unusual. Alternative spellings: Teressa, Theresa, Theressa, Thereza.
Terese English, Norwegian. From Teresa. Unusual. Alternative spellings: Terise, Terrise.

Teresia English, German. From Teresa. Unusual. Alternative spellings: Terresia, Terricia, Theresia.
Teresina Italian. From Teresa. Unusual.
Teresita Hispanic. From Teresa. Unusual.
Tereska Polish. From Teresa. Unusual.
Tereson French. From Teresa. Unusual.
Terez Hungarian. From Teresa. Unusual.
Tereza Bulgarian, Portuguese. From Teresa. Unusual.
Terezia Czech, Hungarian. From Teresa. Unusual.
Terezie Czech. From Teresa. Unusual.
Terezilya Russian. From Teresa. Unusual.
Terezka Czech. From Teresa. Unusual.
Terike Hungarian. From Teresa. Unusual.
Terrall English. From Terence, Latin, "Terentius," the name of a Roman clan. Unusual. Alternative spellings: Teral, Terall.
Terrell See Terell under Boys' Names.
Terrene English. From Terence, Latin, "Terentius," the name of a Roman clan. Unusual.
Terri English. From Teresa. Less popular. Alternative spellings: Teri, Terie, Teree, Terrie, Tery.
Terri-Lynn English. Combination of Terri (from Teresa) and Lynn (Linda, Spanish, "Pretty one.") Unusual.
Terriel English. From Terence, Latin, "Terentius," the name of a Roman clan. Unusual. Alternative spellings: Terrylle, Teryl.
Terrina English. From Terence, Latin, "Terentius," the name of a Roman clan. Unusual. Alternative spelling: Terrena, Terina.
Terrosina English. From Terence, Latin, "Terentius," the name of a Roman clan. Unusual.
Terry See under Boys' Names.
Terryl See Terell under Boys' Names.
Tersa Italian. From Teresa. Unusual.
Tersia Italian. From Tertius, Latin, "Third." Given to the third-born child. Unusual. Alternative spelling: Tertia.
Tertia Italian. From Tertius, Latin, "Third." Given to the third-born child. Unusual.
Teruska Hungarian. From Teresa. Unusual.
Terza English. From Thirza, Hebrew, "Pleasant." Numbers 27:1. Unusual.
Tesa Polish. From Teresa. Unusual.
Tesia Polish. From Theophilus, "Loved by God." Unusual.
Tess English. From Teresa. Character in Thomas Hardy's 1891 novel "Tess of the D'Urbervilles, A Pure Woman." Less popular.
Tessa English. From Teresa. Character in George Eliot's 1862 novel "Romola" and in Gilbert and Sullivan's 1889 operetta "The Gondoliers." Unusual.
Tessie English. From Teresa. O'Shea (British singer). Unusual. Alternative spellings: Tessi, Tessy.
Teté Hispanic. From Teresa. Unusual.
Tetsu Japanese, "Iron." A number of oriental peoples ascribe protective power to metals. Unusual.
Tetty English. From Elizabeth, Hebrew, (Elisheva), "Oath of God" or "God is my oath." Exodus 6:23. Unusual.
Thalia Greek. Greek, "thalia" ("bloom" or "plenty"). One of the three Graces. Unusual.
Thama English. From Tamar, Hebrew, "Date palm." 2 Samuel 13:1. Unusual.
Thamer English. From Tamar, Hebrew, "Date palm." 2 Samuel 13:1. Unusual.
Thanh Vietnamese. Vietnamese, "Brilliant." Unusual.
Thao Vietnamese. Vietnamese, "Courtesy" or "respects parents." Unusual.
Thea From Dorothy, Greek (Dorothea), "Gift from God." Unusual.
Thekla English. Greek, "theocleia" ("God-famed"). Saint, first virgin martyr. Unusual.
Thelma Created. Created by novelist Marie Corelli; may be based on Greek, "thelema" ("will"). Title character in Corelli's 1887 novel; Ritter (film actress and comedian). Unusual.
Thema African. African, "Queen." Unusual.
Theodora English. From Theodore, Greek, "theodoros" ("God's gift"). Unusual. Theo. Alternative spelling: Theadora.
Theodosia Greek. Greek, "God's gift." Saint (4th century). Unusual.
Theophila Greek. Greek, from Theophilus, "Loved by God." Unusual.
Therese French, German. From Teresa. Of Lisieux (19th-century saint). Unusual.
Thersa English. From Teresa. Unusual. Alternative spellings: Therza, Thirsa, Thursa, Thurza.
Thersea English. From Thirza. Unusual.
Theta Greek. Greek, "theta," the name of a letter of the alphabet. Unusual.
Thetis Greek. Greek, "tithemi" ("to dispose"). Mother of Achilles. Unusual.
Thi Vietnamese. Vietnamese, "Poem." Unusual.
Thirza Hebrew/Israeli. Hebrew, "Pleasant." Numbers 27:1. Unusual. Alternative spellings: Thyrza, Tirza, Tirzah.
Thomasa English. From Thomas, Aramaic, "Twin." Unusual.
Thomasin English. From Thomas, Aramaic, "Twin." Character in Thomas Hardy's 1878 novel "Return of the Native." Unusual. Tommi+. Alternative spellings: Thomasine, Thomason, Thomazin, Thomazine.
Thomasina English. From Thomas, Aramaic, "Twin." Unusual. Tommi+. Alternative spelling: Thomasena.
Thora English. From Thyra, Old Norse, "Thor-battle." Hird (British actress). Unusual.
Thordis Norwegian. Old Norse, "Dedicated to Thor." Unusual.
Thuy Vietnamese. Vietnamese, "Gentle." Unusual.
Thyra Scandinavian. Old Norse, "Thor-battle." Unusual.
Tia Hispanic. Spanish, "Aunt." Unusual.
Tiana Hispanic. From Tia. Unusual. Alternative spelling: Tianna.
Tiara Hispanic. From Tiera. Unusual.
Ticha Hispanic. From Beatrice, Latin, "She who makes happy." Unusual.
Tiernan English. Gaelic, "Lord." Unusual.
Tierney English. From Tiernan. Unusual.
Tierra English. From Tiera. Unusual. Alternative spelling: Tiera.
Tiff English. From Tiffany. Unusual.
Tiffany English. Greek, "theophania" ("appearance of God"). Pop singer, "I Think We're Alone Now"; Chin (1985 figure skating champion). Very popular. Alternative spellings: Tifani, Tiffaney, Tiffani, Tiffanie, Tiffiney, Tiffini, Tiffney.
Tiffy English. From Tiffany. Unusual.
Tila Polish. From Matilda, Old German (Mathildis), "Battle maiden." Unusual.
Tilda English, Estonian. From Matilda, Old German (Mathildis), "Battle maiden." Unusual.
Tildy English. From Matilda, Old German (Mathildis), "Battle maiden." Unusual.
Tillie English. From Matilda, Old German (Mathildis), "Battle maiden." Unusual. Alternative spellings: Tilley, Tilli, Tilly.

Timaula American. From Timothy, Greek, "timotheos" ("honoring God"). Unusual.
Timmi English. From Timothy, Greek, "timotheos" ("honoring God"). Unusual. Alternative spellings: Timi, Timie.
Timmie See Timmy under Boys' Names.
Timora Hebrew/Israeli. From Temira, Hebrew, "Tall." Unusual.
Timothea English. From Timothy, Greek, "timotheos" ("honoring God"). Unusual.
Tina English. From Christian, Greek, "christos" ("anointed"). Louise (actress in TV's "Gilligan's Island"); Turner (rock singer). Less popular. Alternative spellings: Teena, Tena, Tinah.
Tine English. From Christian, Greek, "christos" ("anointed"). Unusual.
Tiponya Native American. "Great horned owl poking an egg." Unusual.
Tirtha Indo-Pakistani. Hindi, "Ford." Unusual.
Tisa African. Swahili, "Ninth-born." Unusual.
Tish English. From Letitia, Latin, "Gladness." Less popular.
Tisha English. From Letitia, Latin, "Gladness." Unusual.
Tita Hispanic. From Margaret, Greek, "margaron" ("pearl"). Unusual.
Tivona Hebrew/Israeli. From Tivon, Hebrew, "Naturalist" or "lover of nature." Unusual.
Tiwa Native American. Native American, "Onions." Unusual.
Tiwolu Native American. Native American, "Chicken Hawk helping its eggs hatch." Unusual.
Tobi English. From Tobias, Hebrew, "God is good." Less popular.
Tobie See Toby under Boys' Names.
Tobit Hebrew/Israeli. From Tovi, Hebrew, "My good." Unusual.
Toby See under Boys' Names.
Toinetta English. From Anthony, Latin, a Roman clan name used as a first name. Unusual.
Toinette English. From Anthony, Latin, a Roman clan name used as a first name. Unusual.
Toinon French. From Anthony, Latin, a Roman clan name used as a first name. Unusual.
Toki Japanese. Japanese, "Time of opportunity." Unusual.
Tokiwa Japanese. Japanese, "Eternally constant." Unusual.
Tola Polish. From Anthony, Latin, a Roman clan name used as a first name. Unusual.
Tolikna Native American. Native American, "Coyote's long ears flapping." Unusual.
Toloisi Native American. Native American, "Chicken Hawk tearing apart a snake." Unusual.
Tolsia Polish. From Anthony, Latin, a Roman clan name used as a first name. Unusual.
Tomasina English. From Thomas, Aramaic, "Twin." Unusual.
Tomasine English. From Thomas, Aramaic, "Twin." Unusual.
Tomina English. From Thomas, Aramaic, "Twin." Unusual. Alternative spelling: Tommina.
Tommie See Tommy under Boys' Names.
Tomo Japanese. Japanese, "Knowledge" or "intelligence." Unusual.
Tomochka Russian. From Tamar, Hebrew, "Date palm." 2 Samuel 13:1. Unusual.
Tona Hispanic. From Anthony, Latin, a Roman clan name used as a first name. Unusual.
Toni English. From Anthony, Latin, a Roman clan name used as a first name. Tenille (singer in duo "Captain and Tenille). Less popular. Alternative spellings: Toney, Tonie.
Tonia English. From Anthony, Latin, a Roman clan name used as a first name. Unusual.
Tonya English, Russian. From Anthony, Latin, a Roman clan name used as a first name. Mistal (hula-hoop champion: 88 hours without dropping hoop). Unusual. Alternative spellings: Tonja, Tonyia.
Topsy English. English, "Top sail" (?); a slave name, from the part of the ships on which slaves were transported. Character in Harriet Beecher Stowe's 1852 novel "Uncle Tom's Cabin." Unusual. Alternative spellings: Toppsy, Topsey, Topsie.
Tora Japanese, "Tiger"; and English, from Thordis, Old Norse, "Dedicated to Thor." Unusual.
Tori Japanese. Japanese, "Bird." Kuratsukuri (7th-century Japanese sculptor, created 16-foot-high Buddha). Unusual.
Tory English. From Terence, Latin, "Terentius," the name of a Roman clan. Unusual for males, unusual for females. Alternative spelling: Torrie.
Tosha Russian. From Anthony, Latin, a Roman clan name used as a first name. Unusual. Alternative spelling: Tosya.
Toshi See under Boys' Names.
Toshie Japanese. From Toshio, Japanese, "Year-boy." Unusual.
Toshiko Japanese. From Toshio, Japanese, "Year-boy." Unusual.
Toshiyo Japanese. From Toshio, Japanese, "Year-boy." Unusual.
Tosia Polish. From Anthony, Latin, a Roman clan name used as a first name. Unusual.
Toski Native American. Native American, "A squash bug." Unusual.
Tosky Russian. From Anthony, Latin, a Roman clan name used as a first name. Unusual.
Tota Slavic. From Charles, Old English, "ceorl" ("man" or "husbandman"). Unusual.
Totsi Native American. Native American, "Moccasins." Unusual.
Tottie English. From Charles, Old English, "ceorl" ("man" or "husbandman"). Unusual. Alternative spelling: Totty.
Tovah Hebew/Israeli. From Tovi, Hebrew, "My good." Unusual. Alternative spelling: Tova.
Tracy English. From Teresa, Greek, "Therasia," the name of two islands, or "theros" ("summer"). Chapman (rock singer, "Crossroads"); Caulkins (won six swimming medals in one championship, a women's record, 1978); Austin (youngest player to win a tennis title: 16 years old); Tupman (character in Dickens' "The Pickwick Papers"). Unusual for males, less popular for females. Alternative spellings: Trace, Tracee, Tracey, Traci, Tracie, Trasey.
Trava Czech. Czech, "Grass." Unusual.
Treacy English. From Teresa, Theresia, the name of two islands, or "theros" ("summer"). Unusual. Alternative spelling: Treesy.
Treaser English. From Teresa, "Therasia," the name of two islands, or "theros" ("summer"). Unusual.
Trella Hispanic. From Estrella, "Child of the stars"; origin unknown. Unusual.
Tresa German. From Teresa, "Therasia," the name of two islands, or "theros"

("summer"). Unusual. Alternative spellings: Tressa, Treza.
Trescha German. From Teresa, "Therasia," the name of two islands, or "theros" ("summer"). Unusual.
Treska German. From Teresa, "Therasia," the name of two islands, or "theros" ("summer"). Unusual.
Treva English. From Trevor, Old English, "Sea homestead." Unusual.
Trevina English. From Trevor, Old English, "Sea homestead." Unusual.
Tricia English. From Patrick, Latin, "Noble man." Nixon Cox (daughter of Richard Nixon). Less popular. Alternative spellings: Trichia, Trisha.
Trina English. From Katherine, Greek, "katharos" ("pure"); and Indo-Pakistani, Hindi, "Piercing," referring to the sacred Kusa grass. Unusual. Alternative spellings: Treena, Treina, Trena.
Trinchen German. From Katherine, Greek, "katharos" ("pure"). Unusual.
Trine German. From Katherine, Greek, "katharos" ("pure"). Unusual.
Trinita German. From Katherine, Greek, "katharos" ("pure"). Unusual.
Trinnette English. From Katherine, Greek, "katharos" ("pure"). Unusual. Alternative spelling: Trinette.
Triphena Greek. From Tryphena, Greek, "tryphaina" ("delicacy"). Romans 16:12. Unusual.
Tris English. From Beatrice, Latin, "She who makes happy." Unusual.
Trisa English. From Teresa, "Therasia," the name of two islands, or "theros" ("summer"). Unusual.
Trish English. From Patrick, Latin, "Noble man." Van Devere (actress, wife of George C. Scott). Less popular.
Trissie English. From Beatrice, Latin, "She who makes happy." Unusual.
Trissina English. From Beatrice, Latin, "She who makes happy." Unusual.
Trista French. From Tristan, French, "Sad." Unusual.
Tristen French. From Tristan, French, "Sad." Unusual.
Trixie English. From Beatrice, Latin, "She who makes happy." Norton (neighbor of the Kramdens in TV's "The Honeymooners"). Unusual. Alternative spellings: Trixi, Trixy.
Truc Vietnamese. Vietnamese, "Wish." Unusual.
Truda Polish. From Gertrude, Old German, "Spear-strength." Unusual.
Trudie English. From Gertrude, Old German, "Spear-strength." Styler (girlfriend of rock musician Sting, 1991). Unusual. Alternative spellings: Trude, Trudey, Trudi, Trudye.
Tryphana Greek. From Tryphena. Unusual.
Tryphena Greek. Greek, "tryphaina" ("delicacy"). Romans 16:12. Unusual. Alternative spellings: Triphena, Tryphina.
Tryphene Greek. From Tryphena. Unusual.
Tryphenia Greek. From Tryphena. Unusual.
Tuesday English. Old German, "ziostag"; day name used as a first name. Weld (actress) (real name: Susan). Unusual.
Tula Indo-Pakistani. Hindu, "Born under the sign of Libra." Finklea (real name of dancer and actress Cyd Charisse). Unusual.
Tulsi Indo-Pakistani. Hindi, name of a sacred plant (in English, basil). Unusual.
Tusa Native American. Native American, "Prairie dog." Unusual.
Tuska Russian. From Tatius, name of a Sabine king, Titus Tatius; origin unknown. Unusual.
Tusya Russian. From Tatius, name of a Sabine king, Titus Tatius; origin unknown. Unusual.
Tuwa Native American. Native American, "Earth." Unusual.
Tuyen Vietnamese. Vietnamese, "Angel." Unusual.
Tuyet Vietnamese. Vietnamese, "Snow." Unusual.
Twyla Created. Created, African-American, "Birth at twilight" (?). Tharp (dancer and choreographer). Unusual. Alternative spelling: Twila.
Tyesha American. Created, African-American. Unusual. Alternative spelling: Tyisha.
Tylda Czech. From Matilda, Old German (Mathildis), "Battle maiden." Unusual.
Tyler See under Boys' Names.
Tyna Czech. From Christian, Greek, "christos" ("anointed"). Unusual.
Tynka Slavic. From Celestin, Latin, "Heavenly." Unusual.
Tyra Scandinavian. From Thyra, Old Norse, "Thor-battle." Unusual.
Tzipora Hebrew/Israeli. Hebrew, "Bird." Genesis 2:21. Wife of Moses. Unusual.

Ula English. Celtic, "Jewel of the sea." Unusual.
Ulani Hawaiian. Hawaiian, "Cheerful." Unusual.
Ulla German. From Ursula. Unusual.
Ulli Estonian. From Usula. Unusual.
Uulrica English. From Ulric, Old German (Wulfric), "Ruler of all" or "wolf ruler." Unusual.
Uma Indo-Pakistani. Hindi, "Mother." One of the many names for the goddess Sakti. Thurman (wife of actor Gary Oldman). Unusual.
Umay Turkish. Turkish, "Hope." Unusual.
Ume Japanese. From Umeko. Unusual.
Umeko Japanese. Japanese, "Plum-blossom child." Unusual.
Umeyo Japanese. From Umeko. Unusual.
Una Native American. Native American, "Remember." Merkel (stage and TV actress); O'Connor (actress). Unusual.
Undine English. Latin, "Wave." Unusual.
Unice English. From Eunice, Greek, "Victorious." Unusual.
Unique English. Latin, "unus" ("one"); the word used as a first name. Unusual.
Unita English. From Unique. Unusual.
Unite English. From Unique. Unusual.
Unity English. From Unique. Unusual.
Urania Greek. Greek, "Heavenly." The Muse of astronomy. Unusual.
Urbana English. From Urban, Latin, "One from the city." Romans 16:9. Unusual. Alternative spelling: Urbanah.
Urena English. From Uriah, Hebrew, "My light is the Lord." 2 Samuel 11:3. Unusual. Alternative spelling: Urina.
Urmi Estonian. From Ursula. Unusual.
Ursa Latin. From Ursula. Unusual.
Ursel Latin. From Ursula. Unusual.
Ursella Latin. From Ursula. Unusual.
Ursie Latin. From Ursula. Unusual. Alternative spelling: Urse.
Ursley Latin. From Ursula. Unusual.
Ursula English. Latin, "Little she-bear."

Saint; Andress (Swedish actress); Benincasa (Italian religious leader, established Oblate Sisters of Immaculate Conception, 1583, and Contemplative Hermit Sisters, 1617); character in Shakespeare's "Much Ado About Nothing." Less popular. Alternative spelling: Ursola.

Ursule French, Romanian. From Ursula. Unusual.

Ursulina Hispanic. From Ursula. Unusual.

Ursleline English. From Ursula. Unusual.

Ursy English. From Ursula. Unusual.

Urszula Latvian. From Ursula. Unusual.

Ushi Chinese. Chinese, "The ox," a sign of the zodiac. Unusual.

Utina Native American. Native American, "Woman of my country." Unusual.

Val English. From Valentine, Latin, "To be strong." Doonican (British singer). Unusual for males, unusual for females.

Valaria English. From Valerie. Unusual.

Valda English. Old Norse, "Ruler" or "governor." Unusual.

Valence English. From Valentia. Unusual.

Valencia Italian. From Valentia. Unusual.

Valene English. From Valentia. Unusual.

Valentia English. Latin, "Strong" or "healthy." Unusual.

Valentina English. From Valentia. Visconti (Italian, grandmother of King Louis XII); Tereshkova (Russian, first woman to orbit Earth); Zakoretskaya (Russian, holds women's record for most parachute jumps: 8,000). Unusual. Val.

Valentine See under Boys' Names.

Valeria English. From Valerie. Unusual.

Valeriana Hispanic. From Valerie. Unusual.

Valerie English. Latin, "To be strong"; a Roman clan name. Harper (actress, "Last Married Couple in America"); Bertinelli (actress, "One Day at a Time"; wife of musician Eddie Van Halen). Popular. Val. Alternative spellings: Valaree, Valarie, Valerey, Valery, Valerye, Vallerie.

Valka Russian. From Valerie. Unusual.

Vallie English. From Valerie. Unusual. Alternative spellings: Valli, Vally.

Valya English. From Valerie. Unusual.

Van English. From Vanessa. Unusual.

Vanda Czech, English, Portuguese, Russian, Slavic. From Wanda, Old German, "Wanderer"; or Slavic name for the Vandals, a tribe. Character in Sir Walter Scott's 1825 novel "The Bethrothed." Unusual.

Vanecia English. From Venice, a place name used as a first name; origin unknown. Also a variation of Venus, the Roman goddess of beauty and love. Unusual. Alternative spellings: Venecia, Venetia.

Vanessa English. Greek, "Butterflies"; or created by author Jonathan Swift in his poem "Cadenus and Vanessa." Williams (briefly Miss America, 1984); Redgrave (actress, won Oscar for supporting role in "Julia"); Bell (wife of British critic Clive Bell; follower of Bloomsbury group); title character in Walpole's 1933 novel; Brown (actress) (real name: Smylla Brind). Very popular. Alternative spellings: Vanesa, Vannessa, Venesa, Venessa.

Vanesse English. From Vanessa. Unusual.

Vanetta English. Created, meaning unknown. Unusual.

Vania Russian. From Vanessa. Unusual.

Vanicia English. From Venice, a place name used as a first name; origin unknown. Also a variation of Venus, the Roman goddess of beauty and love. Unusual. Alternative spelling: Venitia.

Vanna English. From Vanessa. White (TV personality, "Wheel of Fortune"). Unusual. Alternative spelling: Vana.

Vanetta English. Created, meaning unknown. Unusual.

Vanni English. From Vanessa. Unusual. Alternative spellings: Vannie, Vanny.

Varda English. From Vardis. Unusual.

Vardia English. From Vardis. Unusual.

Vardice Hebrew/Israeli. From Vardis. Unusual. Alternative spelling: Vardis.

Vardina English. From Vardis. Unusual.

Vardit Hebrew. From Vardis. Unusual.

Varenka Russian. From Barbara, Greek, "Strange" or "foreign." Unusual.

Varina Slavic. From Barbara, Greek, "Strange" or "foreign." Unusual.

Varka Russian. From Barbara, Greek, "Strange" or "foreign." Unusual.

Varvara Russian. From Barbara, Greek, "Strange" or "foreign." Unusual.

Varya Russian. From Barbara, Greek, "Strange" or "foreign." Unusual.

Vashti Persian. Persian, "Beautiful." Esther 1:9. Unusual.

Vatusia African. African, "The dead leave us behind." Unusual.

Vava Russian. From Barbara, Greek, "Strange" or "foreign." Unusual.

Vavka Russian. From Barbara, Greek, "Strange" or "foreign." Unusual.

Veda English, from David, Hebrew. "Beloved," "friend," or "darling," 1 Samuel 16:19; Indo-Pakistani, Sanskrit, "Holy understanding." Unusual. Alternative spelling: Veeda.

Veenie Unknown. From Vina, meaning and origin unknown. Unusual.

Vegenia Hawaiian. From Virgil, Latin, "Vergilius"; a Roman clan name. Unusual.

Veina Unknown. From Vina, meaning and origin unknown. Unusual.

Velda English. From Valda, Old Norse, "Ruler" or "governor." Unusual.

Velia English. Greek, a place name. Unusual.

Velma Created. From Thelma, created by novelist Marie Corelli; may be based on Greek, "thelema" ("will"). Banky (actress in Valentino films). Unusual.

Venetia Latin. From Venice. Stanley (17th-century member of the British lower class, married Sir Kenelm Digby in celebrated inter-class match). Unusual. Alternative spelling: Venecia.

Venetta English. Created, meaning unknown. Unusual. Alternative spelling: Veneta.

Venezia Italian. From Venice. Unusual.

Venia Unknown. From Vina, meaning and origin unknown. Unusual.

Venice Latin. A place name used as a first name; origin unknown. Also a variation of Venus, the Roman goddess of beauty and love. Unusual.

Venise French. From Venice. Unusual.

Venita English. From Vanetta, created, meaning unknown. Unusual.

Vennice English. From Venice. Unusual.

Venus Latin. Latin, Roman goddess of

beauty and love. Ramey (Miss America, 1944). Unusual.
Vera Russian. Slavic, "Faith." Stevenson (Russian chess champion, 1927–44); Miles (actress); Brittain (British, wrote feminist and pacifist works, 1933–57); Figner (Russian revolutionary involved in assassination of Czar Alexander II); character in Ouida's 1860 novel "Moths." Unusual.
Verasha Russian. From Vera. Unusual.
Vere English. From Vera. Unusual.
Verene English. From Vera. Unusual. Alternative spelling: Verine.
Verenice French. From Veronica, Latin, "accurate image"; also a flower name used as a first name. Unusual.
Verina English. From Vera. Unusual. Alternative spelling: Verena.
Verinka Russian. From Vera. Unusual.
Verita Created. From Verity. Unusual.
Verity English. Latin, "veritas" ("truth"); the word used as a first name. Unusual.
Verka Czech (Věrka), Russian. From Vera. Unusual.
Verla English. From Vera. Unusual.
Verna Latin. Latin, "Spring." Felton (1950s actress). Unusual.
Vernetta English. From Verna. Unusual.
Vernice English. From Veronica. Unusual.
Vernie English. From Verna. Unusual.
Vernita English. From Verna. Unusual.
Veron English. From Veronica. Unusual.
Verona Czech, German. From Veronica. Unusual.
Verone French. From Veronica. Unusual.
Veronica English. Latin, "accurate image"; also a flower name used as a first name. Saint (Christ is said to have left image on cloth she used to wipe His face before crucifixion); Hamel (actor, "Hill Street Blues"); Lake (1940s actress). Less popular. Alternative spellings: Veronika.
Veronice English. From Veronica. Unusual.
Veronike German. From Veronica. Unusual.
Véronique French. From Veronica. Unusual.
Veronka Czech. From Veronica. Unusual.
Verusya Russian. From Vera. Unusual.
Vessy English. From Vesta. Unusual.
Vest English. From Vesta. Unusual.
Vesta Latin. Latin, the name of the goddess of the hearth. Tilley (British entertainer, male impersonator). Unusual.
Veta Slavic. From Elizabeth, Hebrew (Elisheva), "Oath of God" or "God is my oath." Exodus 6:23. Unusual.
Vica Hungarian. From Eve, Hebrew (Chava), "Life." Genesis 3:20. Unusual.
Vicki English. From Victoria. Lawrence (actress, "Carol Burnett Show"); Baum (novelist and playwright, "Grand Hotel"). Less popular. Alternative spellings: Viccy, Vickie, Vickki, Vicky, Viki, Vikie, Vikki, Viky.
Victoire French. From Victor, Latin, "Conqueror." Unusual.
Victoria English. Latin, "Victory." Saint; Sackville-West (British poet, novelist, and biographer); Woodhull (social reformer, first woman to run for president, 1872); Tennant (wife of comedian Steve Martin); Benedictsson (19th-century Swedish writer on Swedish folk life). Popular. Vicki+.
Victoriana Hispanic. From Victoria. Unusual.
Victorina Hispanic. From Victoria. Unusual.
Victorine French. From Victoria. Unusual.
Victory English. From Victoria. Unusual.
Vida See under Boys' Names.
Vidette English. From David, Hebrew, "Beloved," "friend," or "darling." 1 Samuel 16:19. Unusual.
Viera Czech. From Vera, Slavic, "Faith." Unusual.
Vika Russian, Serbian. From Victoria, Latin, "Victory." Unusual for males, unusual for females.
Viktoria Bulgarian, Russian, Scandinavian. From Victoria. Unusual.
Viktorie Czech. From Victoria. Unusual.
Viktorka Czech. From Victoria. Unusual.
Vilma Czech, English, Russian, Swedish. From William, Old German, "Will" + "helmet." Unusual.
Vina Unknown. Meaning and origin unknown. Unusual. Alternative spelling: Vena.
Vincentia English. From Vincent, Latin, "Vincentius," from "vincere" ("to conquer"). Unusual.
Vincetta English. From Vincent, Latin, "Vincentius," from "vincere" ("to conquer"). Unusual.
Vinia English. From Lavinia, Latin, "Purified." Unusual.
Vinnie English. From Lavinia, Latin, "Purified." Hoxie (sculptor, created full-length marble statue of Lincoln in Capitol rotunda). Unusual. Alternative spelling: Viney.
Viola Latin. Latin, "Violet." Allen (actress); sister of Sebastian in Shakespeare's "Twelfth Night." Unusual.
Violante Latin. From Yolande, Greek, "ion" ("violet") + "anthos" ("flower"). Unusual.
Violet English. From Viola. Martin (19th-century Irish novelist, described Irish life); Paget (British writer and art critic); Jacob (Scottish poet and novelist, "The Interloper," 1904); heroine of Lord Lytton's 1839 novel "The Sea-Captain." Less popular.
Violetta Italian. From Viola. Valery (character in Verdi's opera "La Traviata"). Unusual.
Violette French. From Viola. Unusual.
Virginia English. From Virgil, Latin, "Vergilius"; a Roman clan name. Woolf (British novelist, "Orlando"; central figure in the Bloomsbury group); Apgar (physician, developed test of newborns' development); Dare (first English child born in North America, 1587). Less popular.
Virginie French. From Virgil, Latin, "Vergilius"; a Roman clan name. Unusual.
Virgy English. From Virgil, Latin, "Vergilius"; a Roman clan name. Unusual. Alternative spelling: Vergie.
Virida Hispanic. Spanish, "Green." Unusual.
Virtue English. Latin, "virtus" ("strength"). Unusual.
Visolela African. African, "Reality is limited, but dreams and hopes know no bounds." Unusual.
Vitoria Hispanic, Portuguese. From Victoria. Unusual.
Vittoria Italian. From Victoria. Unusual.
Viv English. From Vivian, Latin, "Full of life." Unusual.
Viva English. From Vivian, Latin, "Full of life." Unusual.
Vivia English. From Vivian, Latin, "Full of life." Unusual.
Vivian English. Latin, "Full of life." Vance (actress, played Ethel on "I Love Lucy"); character in Benjamin Disraeli's

novel "Vivian Grey." Unusual for males, less popular for females. Alternative spellings: Viviane, Vivianne, Vivien.
Viviana Italian. From Vivian, Latin, "Full of life." Unusual.
Vivienne French. From Vivian, Latin, "Full of life." Unusual.
Vorsila Czech. From Ursula, Latin, "Little she-bear." Unusual.
Voska Greek. From Barbara, Greek, "Strange" or "foreign." Unusual.

Wahoo See under Boys' Names.
Wakanda Native American. Native American, "Magical power." Unusual.
Wakenda Native American. From Wakanda. Unusual.
Wala Polish. From Valerie, Latin, "To be strong"; a Roman clan name. Unusual.
Walburga English. Old German, "Power-protection." Saint. Unusual.
Waleria Polish. From Valerie, Latin, "To be strong"; a Roman clan name. Unusual.
Wallis See Wallace under Boys' Names.
Wanda English. Old German, "Wanderer"; or Slavic name for the Vandals, a tribe. Landowska (Polish harpsichordist); Hendrix (actress); title character in Ouida's 1883 novel. Less popular.
Wandi English. From Wanda. Unusual. Alternative spelling: Wandie.
Wandis English. From Wanda. Unusual.
Wandja Swedish. From Wanda. Unusual.
Wandzia Polish. From Wanda. Unusual.
Waneta Native American. Native American, "Charger." Unusual.
Washi Japanese. Japanese, "Eagle." Unusual.
Wattan Arabic. Arabic, "Homeland." Unusual.
Wenda English. From Wendy. Unusual.
Wendeline English. From Wanda. Unusual.
Wendelle English. From Wendell, Old German, "Wanderer." Unusual.
Wendy English. Created by the author of "Peter Pan," J.M. Barrie. Hiller (British actress); Craig (British actress); Barrie (British actress). Less popular. Alternative spellings: Wendi, Wendie.
Wenonah Native American. Native American, "First-born." Mother of Hiawatha in Longfellow's 1855 poem "Hiawatha." Unusual.
Wera Polish, Swedish. From Vera, Slavic, "Faith." Unusual.
Whitney English. Old English, "White island." Young, Jr. (civil rights leader); Houston (pop singer). Less popular for males, very popular for females. Alternative spellings: Whitnie, Whittney.
Whoopi English. Old French, "houpper," meaning unknown. Goldberg (actress). Unusual.
Wiera Polish. From Vera, Slavic, "Faith." Unusual.
Wiercia Polish. From Vera, Slavic, "Faith." Unusual.
Wierka Polish. From Vera, Slavic, "Faith." Unusual.
Wiletta English. From William, Old German, "Will" + "helmet." Unusual.
Wilette English. From William, Old German, "Will" + "helmet." Unusual.
Wilfreda English. From Wilfred, English, "Will-peace." Unusual.
Wilhelmina English. From William, Old German, "Will" + "helmet." Unusual. Alternative spellings: Willamina, Williamina.
Wilhelmine French. From William, Old German, "Will" + "helmet." Unusual.
Willa English. From William, Old German, "Will" + "helmet." Cather (novelist, won Pultitzer Prize for "One of Ours," 1922). Unusual.
Willi See Willie under Boys' Names.
Willie See under Boys' Names.
Willow English. Greek, "hilike" ("willow"); a tree name used as a first name. Unusual.
Willy See Willie under Boys' Names.
Wilma English. From William, Old German, "Will" + "helmet." Unusual. Alternative spelling: Wylma.
Wilmette English. From William, Old German, "Will" + "helmet." Unusual.
Wilmotina English. From William, Old German, "Will" + "helmet." Unusual.
Winda African. Swahili, "Hunt." Unusual.
Winefride English. From Winifred. Unusual. Alternative spellings: Winifrede, Winifride, Winifryde.
Winema Native American. Native American, "Woman chief." Unusual.
Winiefrida English. From Winifred. Unusual.
Winifred English. Welsh, "Blessed reconciliation." Ashton (British novelist and playwright); Holt (social worker, worked to help the blind). Unusual. Alternative spellings: Winefred, Winifrid, Winnafred, Winnefred, Winniefred, Winnifred, Winnifrid, Wynifred.
Winnie English. From Winifred. Mandela (South African, wife of political activist Nelson). Less popular.
Winona Native American. From Wenonah, Native American, "First-born." Ryder (actress, "Edward Scissorhands"). Unusual.
Winsome English. Old English, "Attractive" or "cheerful." Unusual.
Winter English. Old German, "wintar"; the name of a season used as a first name. Unusual.
Wira Polish. From Elvira, Spanish, place name used as a first name. Unusual.
Wirke Polish. From Elvira, Spanish, place name used as a first name. Unusual.
Wisdom English. Old English, "wis"; the word used as a first name. Unusual for males, unusual for females.
Wisia Polish. From Victoria, Latin, "Victory." Unusual.
Wyanet Native American. Native American, "Beautiful." Unusual.
Wyn English. From Wynn. Unusual. Alternative spelling: Winn.
Wynn Welsh. Welsh, "Pure" or "white." Unusual. Alternative spellings: Winne, Wynne.

Xanthe Greek. Greek, "Golden yellow," referring to hair color. Unusual.

Xanthippe Greek. From Xanthe. Socrates' wife. Unusual.
Xavier See under Boys' Names.
Xaviera English. From Xavier, Spanish, "New house." Unusual.
Xena English. From Xenia. Unusual. Alternative spellings: Zena, Zina.
Xenia Greek. Greek, "Hospitable." Unusual.
Xiang Chinese. Chinese, "Fragrant." Unusual.
Xiomara Meaning and origin unknown. Unusual.
Xylia Greek. Greek, "Wood." Unusual.
Xylina. Greek. From Xylia. Unusual.

Yachi Japanese. Japanese, "Eight thousand," suggesting good luck. Unusual.
Yachiko Japanese. From Yachi. Unusual.
Yachiyo Japanese. From Yachi. Unusual.
Yachne Hebrew/Israeli. Hebrew, "Gracious." Unusual.
Yael Hebrew/Israeli. Hebrew, "Strength of God." Unusual.
Yaella Arabic. Arabic, "Prominent." Unusual.
Yaffa Hebrew/Israeli. Hebrew, "Beautiful" or "lovely." Unusual.
Yahoo See under Boys' Names.
Yalinda English. From Yolande, Greek, "ion" ("violet") + "anthos" ("flower"). Unusual.
Yaluta Native American. Native American, "Women talking." Unusual.
Yamka Native American. Native American, "Flower budding." Unusual.
Yanaba Native American. Native American, "She meets the enemy." Unusual.
Yarina Russian. From Irene, Greek (Eirene), "Peace." Unusual.
Yarkona Hebrew/Israeli. Hebrew, "Green." Unusual.
Yarmilla Slavic. Slavic, "Trader at market." Unusual.
Yaryna Russian. From Irene, Greek (Eirene), "Peace." Unusual.
Yasiman Indo-Pakistani. Persian, "yasamin"; a flower name used as a first name. Unusual.
Yasmeen Arabic. Persian, "yasamin"; a flower name used as a first name. Unusual.
Yasmīn Arabic. Persian, "yasamin"; a flower name used as a first name. Unusual.
Yasmine Indo-Pakistani. Persian, "yasamin"; a flower name used as a first name. Unusual.
Yasu Japanese. Japanese, "Tranquil" or "peaceful." Unusual.
Yasuko Japanese. From Yasu. Unusual.
Yasuyo Japanese. From Yasu. Unusual.
Yehudit Hebrew/Israeli. Hebrew, "Of Judah," "praised one," or "praise to the Lord." Judith 8:1. Unusual.
Yekaterina Russian. From Katherine, Greek, "katharos" ("pure"). Dashkova (18th-century Russian princess); Geltzer (Russian dancer, Bolshoi Ballet, 1894–1935). Unusual.
Yelena Russian. From Helen, Greek, "Bright one" or "shining one." Unusual.
Yelisabeta Russian. From Elizabeth, Hebrew, (Elisheva), "Oath of God" or "God is my oath." Exodus 6:23. Unusual.
Yelizaveta Russian. From Elizabeth, Hebrew, (Elisheva), "Oath of God" or "God is my oath." Exodus 6:23. Tarakanova (18th-century Russian princess). Unusual.
Yemina Hebrew/Israeli. Hebrew, "Right hand," implying strength. Unusual.
Yenene Native American. Native American, "Wizard." Unusual.
Yepa Native American. Native American, "Snow maiden." Unusual.
Yesenia Arabic. Arabic, "Flower." Unusual.
Yetta English. From Henry, Old German (Heimerich), "Home ruler." Unusual.
Yette English. From Henry, Old German (Heimerich), "Home ruler." Unusual.
Yeva Russian. From Eve, Hebrew (Chava), "Life." Genesis 3:20. Unusual.
Yevka Russian. From Eve, Hebrew (Chava), "Life." Genesis 3:20. Unusual.
Yiesha Arabic. From Aisha, Arabic, "Woman" or "life." Unusual.
Yippee See under Boys' Names.
Ynesita Hispanic. From Agnes, Greek, "agnos" ("pure" or "chaste"). Unusual.
Ynez Hispanic. From Agnes, Greek, "agnos" ("pure" or "chaste"). Unusual. Alternative spelling: Ynes.
Yoi Japanese. Japanese, "Born in the evening." Unusual.
Yoki Native American. Native American, "Bluebird." Unusual.
Yoko Japanese. Japanese, "Ocean child." (Ono, pop singer and widow of John Lennon). Unusual.
Yola English. From Yolande. Unusual
Yolanda English. From Yolande. Unusual. Alternative spellings: Yalanda, Yalonda, Ylonda, Yolonda, Youlanda, Yulanda, Yulonda.
Yolande English. Greek, "ion" ("violet") + "anthos" ("flower"). Betbeze (Miss America, 1951); Polignac (French, wealthy close friend of Marie-Antoinette). Unusual. Alternative spelling: Yoland.
Yolane French. From Yolande. Unusual.
Yolette English. From Yolande. Unusual.
Yoli Hispanic. From Yolande. Unusual.
Yoluta Native American. Native American, the name of a seed commonly sown at the beginning of summer. Unusual.
Yon Burmese. Burmese, "Rabbit." Unusual.
Yonah See under Boys' Names.
Yonina Hebrew/Israeli. Hebrew (Yonah), "Dove." Book of Jonah. Unusual.
Yonit Hebrew/Israeli. Hebrew (Yonah), "Dove." Book of Jonah. Unusual.
Yonita Hebrew/Israeli. Hebrew (Yonah), "Dove." Book of Jonah. Unusual.
Yori Japanese. Japanese, "Trustworthy." Unusual.
Yoshie Japanese. From Kiyoshi, Japanese, "Quiet." Unusual.
Yoshiko Japanese. From Kiyoshi, Japanese, "Quiet." Unusual.
Yoshino Japanese. Japanese, "Good field." Unusual.
Yoshiyo Japanese. From Kiyoshi, Japanese, "Quiet." Unusual.
Yovela Hebrew/Israeli. Yovela, Hebrew, "Rejoicing." Unusual.
Ysabel Hispanic. From Elizabeth, Hebrew, (Elisheva), "Oath of God" or "God is my oath." Exodus 6:23. Unusual.
Ysanne English. Combination of Isabel (Elizabeth, Hebrew, (Elisheva), "Oath of God" or "God is my oath") + Ann

(Hannah, Hebrew (Chanah), "Grace"). Unusual.

Yudif Russian. From Judith, Hebrew (Yehudit), "Of Judah," "praised one," or "praise to the Lord." Judith 8:1. Unusual.

Yudita Russian. From Judith, Hebrew (Yehudit), "Of Judah," "praised one," or "praise to the Lord." Judith 8:1. Unusual.

Yuki Japanese. Japanese, "Snow." Unusual.

Yula Russian. From Julius, Latin, a Roman clan name meaning "downy" or "bearded." Unusual.

Yulinka Russian. From Julius, Latin, a Roman clan name meaning "downy" or "bearded." Unusual.

Yuliya Russian. From Julius, Latin, a Roman clan name meaning "downy" or "bearded." Unusual. Alternative spelling: Yulya.

Yulka Russian. From Julius, Latin, a Roman clan name meaning "downy" or "bearded." Unusual.

Yutkiye Native American. Native American, "Chicken Hawk hunting." Unusual.

Yuttciso Native American. Native American, "Lice on a hawk." Unusual.

Yvette French. From Ivo, Teutonic, "Yew wood" or "archer." Yew wood was used to make bows. Mimieux (actress); Guilbert (French, sang about lower-class Parisian life). Unusual.

Yvonne French. From Ivo, Teutonic, "Yew wood" or "archer." Yew wood was used to make bows. De Carlo (Canadian actress, "The Munsters," "Satan's Cheerleaders"); Van Gennip (Dutch, medalist in three Olympic skating events, 1988). Unusual. Alternative spelling: Yvone.

Zada Arabic. Arabic, "Lucky." Unusual. Alternative spelling: Zayda.

Zafina Arabic. Arabic, "Victorious." Unusual.

Zahava Hebrew/Israeli. Hebrew, "Golden." Unusual.

Zahira Arabic. Arabic, "Outstanding" or "luminous." Unusual.

Zahra Arabic. Arabic, "Blossom." Unusual.

Zahreh Persian. Persian, "Happiness." Unusual.

Zaida Arabic. From Zada. Unusual.

Zaidee French. From Sarah, Hebrew, "Princess." Genesis 17:15. Unusual.

Zaira Italian. From Sarah, Hebrew, "Princess." Genesis 17:15. Unusual.

Zakia Arabic. Arabic, "Bright" or "pure." Unusual.

Zaltana Native American. Native American, "High mountain." Unusual.

Zana English. From Susannah, Hebrew (Shoshanah), "Lily." Luke 8:3. Unusual.

Zandra English. From Alexander, Greek, "Defender of men" or "warding off men." Mark 16:21; Acts 4:6, 19:33. Unusual.

Zanna English, from Susannah, Hebrew (Shoshanah), "Lily." Luke 8:3; and Latvian, from John, Hebrew (Yochanan), "God has been gracious." Unusual.

Zannz Polish. From John, Hebrew (Yochanan), "God has been gracious." Unusual.

Zara Arabic, English. From Sarah, Hebrew, "Princess." Genesis 17:15. Character in Congreve's 1697 play "Mourning Bride." Unusual.

Zaria English. From Sarah, Hebrew, "Princess." Genesis 17:15. Unusual.

Zarifa Arabic. Arabic, "Graceful." Unusual.

Zarita Hispanic. From Sarah, Hebrew, "Princess." Genesis 17:15. Unusual.

Zawadi African. Swahili, "Gift." Unusual.

Zayit Hebrew/Israeli. Hebrew, "Olive." Unusual for males, unusual for females.

Zea Latin. Latin, "Grain." Unusual.

Zel Persian. Persian, "Cymbal." Unusual.

Zelda English. From Griselda, German, "Grey battle-maid." Less popular.

Zelene English. From Solana, Spanish, "Sunshine." Unusual. Alternative spelling: Zeline.

Zelenka Czech. Czech, "Little green one," meaning fresh. Unusual.

Zelia English. From Solana, Spanish, "Sunshine." Nuttall (archaeologist, expert on Mexico). Unusual.

Zélie English. From Solana, Spanish, "Sunshine." Unusual.

Zelina English. From Solana, Spanish, "Sunshine." Unusual.

Zella German. From Marcus, Latin, "Warlike one." Derived from Mars, the Roman god of war. Unusual.

Zelma English. From Anselm, Old German, "Divine" + "helmet." Unusual.

Zenobia Greek. Greek, "Zeus's strength." Ambitious 3rd-century queen of Palmyra, occupied Egypt, eventually defeated by Romans; character in Nathaniel Hawthorne's 1852 novel "Blithedale Romance." Unusual.

Zeppelina English. Slavic, meaning unknown. Taken from the name of the inventor of airships. Unusual.

Zera Hebrew/Israeli. Hebrew, "zera'im" ("seeds"). Unusual.

Zerdali Turkish. Turkish, "Wild apricot." Unusual.

Zerlinda English. Meaning and origin unknown. Unusual.

Zerren English. Turkish, "Narcissus," a flower name used as a first name. Unusual.

Zeta English. From Rose, Latin, "rosa," a flower name used as a first name. Unusual.

Zetta Portuguese. From Rose, Latin, "rosa," a flower name used as a first name. Unusual.

Zeynep Turkish. Turkish, "Ornament." Unusual.

Zhen Chinese. Chinese, "Chastity." Unusual.

Zigana Hungarian. Hungarian, "Gypsy girl." Unusual.

Zihna Native American. Native American, "Spinning," perhaps referring to a child's fondness for spinning tops. Unusual.

Zillah Hebrew/Israeli. Hebrew, "Shadow." Genesis 4:19. Wife of Lamech, mother of Tubal-Cain. Unusual. Alternative spellings: Zilah, Zilla, Zylla.

Zilpah Hebrew/Israeli. Hebrew, "Dropping" or "dignity." Genesis 30:9. Wife of Jacob. Unusual.

Zilya Russian. From Teresa, "Therasia," the name of two islands, or "theros" ("summer").

Zina English, from Xenia, Greek, "Hospitable"; and African, from Zina, African, "Name." Unusual. Alternative spellings: Xena, Zena.

Zinnia English. Flower named after Johann G. Zinn, German mineralogist. Unusual.

Zipporah English. Hebrew, "Bird." Exodus 2:21. Unusual. Alternative spelling: Ziporah.

Ziproh English. From Zipporah. Unusual.

Zita Hispanic. From Rose, Latin, "rosa," a flower name used as a first name, by way of Rosita. Saint, 13th-century; patron saint of domestic servants. Unusual.

Zizi Hungarian. From Elizabeth, Hebrew, (Elisheva), "Oath of God" or "God is my oath." Exodus 6:23. Unusual.

Zocha Polish. From Sophia, Greek, "Wisdom." Unusual.

Zoe Greek. Greek, "Life." Akins (author, won Pulitzer Prize for "The Old Maid," 1935); character in F. Marion Crawford's novel "Arethusa." Unusual. Alternative spellings: Zoë, Zoee, Zoey, Zoie.

Zofia Czech, Polish, Ukrainian. From Sophia, Greek, "Wisdom." Unusual.

Žofka Czech. From Sophia, Greek, "Wisdom." Unusual.

Zoheret Hebrew/Israeli. Hebrew, "She shines." Unusual.

Zola Italian. Italian, "Piece of earth." Budd (South African track star). Unusual.

Zona English. Meaning and origin unknown. Gale (poet and novelist, won Pulitzer Prize for "Miss Lulu Bett," 1921). Unusual.

Zonia English. Meaning and origin unknown. Unusual.

Zorah Hebrew/Israeli. Hebrew, Biblical place name mentioned in Joshua 19:41, meaning and origin unknown. Character in Gilbert and Sullivan's 1887 opera "Ruddigore." Unusual. Alternative spelling: Zora.

Zorana Slavic. From Zorina. Unusual.

Zorina Slavic. Slavic, "Golden." Unusual.

Zosha Polish. From Sophia, "Wisdom." Unusual. Alternative spelling: Zosia.

Zowie See under Boys' Names.

Zsa Zsa Hungarian. From Susannah, Hebrew (Shoshanah), "Lily." Luke 8:3. Unusual.

Zsanett Hungarian. From John, Hebrew (Yochanan), "God has been gracious." Unusual.

Zuba English. From Azubah, meaning and origin unknown. 1 Kings 22:42. Unusual.

Zudora Sanskrit. Sanskrit, "Laborer." Unusual.

Zuri African. Swahili, "Beautiful." Unusual.

Zusa Czech, Polish. From Susannah, Hebrew (Shoshanah), "Lily." Luke 8:3. Unusual. Alternative spelling: Zuza.

Zuzana Czech, Polish. From Susannah, Hebrew (Shoshanah), "Lily." Luke 8:3. Unusual.

Zuzanka Czech, Polish. From Susannah, Hebrew (Shoshanah), "Lily." Luke 8:3. Unusual.

Zuzia Polish. From Susannah, Hebrew (Shoshanah), "Lily." Luke 8:3. Unusual.

Zuzka Polish. From Susannah, Hebrew (Shoshanah), "Lily." Luke 8:3. Unusual.

Zylpha Hebrew/Israeli. From Zilpah, Hebrew, "Dropping" or "dignity." Genesis 30:9. Unusual. Alternative spelling: Zilpha.

Zytka Polish. From Rose, Latin, "rosa," a flower name used as a first name. Unusual.

BOYS' *Names*

Aaron English. Hebrew (Aharon). "Teaching" or "singing." Exodus 6:20. Older brother of Moses and Miriam, first high priest of Israel; Copland (composer, "Appalachian Spring"); Montgomery Ward (established first mail order company); Burr (vice-president under Jefferson, 1801–05); Spelling (TV producer). Popular for males, unusual for females. Alternative spellings: Aaran, Aaren, Aarron, Aeron, Aharon, Arin, Aron, Arran, Arron.

Abalard German. From Abelard. Unusual.

Abasi African. African, "Stern." One of God's 99 attributes listed in the Koran. Unusual.

Abbot English. Aramaic, "Father." Originally a surname given to one who worked for an abbot. Unusual.

Abdalla African. From Abdul. Unusual.

Abdel Arabic. From Abdul. Unusual.

Abdelgalil Arabic. Arabic, "Slave of God." Unusual.

Abdul Arabic. Arabic, "Servant of," suggesting the child is a servant of God. Muis (Indonesian leader of religious-nationalist organization); Rahman (Malaysian chief of state, 1957–60); Razak (Malaysian prime minister, defense minister, and foreign affairs minister, 1970–76). Unusual.

Abdulaziz Arabic. Arabic, "Slave of God." Oglu Maḥmūd II (Ottoman sultan, 1861–76). Unusual.

Abdullah Arabic. From Abdul. King of Jordan, 1946–51; bin Abdul Kadir (Malaysian author and translator). Unusual.

Abe English. From Abraham. Fortas (Supreme Court Justice, 1965–69); Vigoda (actor, "Barney Miller"). Less popular.

Abel English. Hebrew, "Breath." Genesis 4. Second son of Adam and Eve; King of Denmark, 1250–52; Tasman (Dutch, discovered Tasmania, New Zealand, and Fiji Islands); Gance (French director of silent films, "Napoleon"); Bonnard (French essayist and travel writer, "En Chine"). Less popular. Alternative spelling: Able.

Abelard German. Old German, "Resolute." Unusual.

Abi Turkish. Turkish, "Older brother." Unusual.

Abia Hebrew/Israeli. Hebrew, "My father is Jehovah." 1 Samuel 8:2. Unusual. Alternative spelling: Abiah.

Abiatha Hebrew/Israeli. From Abiathar. Unusual.

Abiathar Hebrew/Israeli. Hebrew, "Father of abundance." Unusual. Alternative spelling: Abiather.

Abie English. From Abraham. Unusual.

Abiel Hebrew/Israeli. Hebrew, "God is my father." 1 Samuel 9:1. Unusual.

Abijah Hebrew/Israeli. From Abia. Second king of Judah, circa 915–13 B.C. Unusual for males, unusual for females.

Abilard German. From Abelard. Unusual.

Abimelech Hebrew/Israeli. Hebrew, "My father is king." Name of three royal figures in the Old Testament. Unusual.

Abiona See under Girls' Names.

Abital See under Girls' Names.

Abna English. From Abner. Unusual.

Abner English. Hebrew, "Father of light." 1 Samuel 14:50. Commander of King Saul's army; character in Melville Davisson Post's "Uncle Abner, Master of Mysteries"; Doubleday (named and created sport of baseball). Less popular. Alternative spellings: Abnar, Abnor.

Abraham English. Hebrew (Avraham), "Exalted father" or "father of a multitude." Genesis 17:4,5. First Hebrew patriarch (original name was Avram); Kidunaia (saint); Lincoln (16th president); Mapu (Lithuanian, author of first Hebrew novel, "Ahavat Zion"); Mignon (Dutch Baroque painter); Hollandersky (boxer, fought 1,309 bouts, 1905–18). Less popular. Abe, Bram.

Abrahamo Italian. From Abraham. Unusual.

Abrahán Hispanic. From Abraham. Unusual.

Abram English. From Abraham. Ryan (poet, glorified the Confederate cause). Less popular. Abe, Bram.

Abramo Italian. From Abraham. Unusual.

Abrán Hispanic. From Abraham. Unusual.

Abrao Portuguese. From Abraham. Unusual.

Absalom Hebrew/Israeli. Hebrew, "My father is peace." 2 Samuel 3:3. Third son of King David, led rebellion; character in Dryden's "Absalom and Achitophel." Unusual.

Absalon French. From Absalom. Danish soldier, statesman, and archbishop of Lund, 1177-?; Beyer (Norman humanist, "Om Norgis rige"). Unusual.

ʿAbu Kamāl Arabic. Arabic, "Father of Kamāl." Unusual.
Acar Turkish. Turkish, "Bright." Unusual.
Ace English. Latin, "Unity." Frehley (musician with rock group Kiss); Ntsoelengoe (soccer player). Unusual.
Ackley English. Old English, "Meadow of oaks." Unusual.
Acton English. Old English, "Town with many oaks." Less popular.
Ad English. From Adam. Unusual.
Adair Scottish. From Edgar, Old English, "Prosperity" + "spear." Gellman (once held world record for youngest-ever female Life Master at bridge: 14 years, 6 months, 4 days, 1983). Unusual.
Adal German. German, "Noble." Unusual.
Adam English. Hebrew, "Redness" or "man." Genesis 2:19. First man; saint; Smith (author, "The Wealth of Nations"); Bede (character in George Eliot's "Adam Bede"); Clayton Powell (clergyman); Oehlenschläger (Danish dramatist and poet); Sedgwick (British geologist); van der Meulen (17th-century Flemish painter). Popular.
Adamec Czech. From Adam. Unusual. Alternative spellings: Adamek, Adamik, Adamok.
Adamka Russian. From Adam. Unusual.
Adamko Czech. From Adam. Unusual.
Adão Portuguese. From Adam. Unusual.
Adar Syrian. Syrian, "Ruler" or "prince." Unusual.
Adas Polish. From Adam. Unusual.
Addam English. From Adam. Less popular.
Addison English. Old English, "Adam's son"; a surname used as a first name. Mizner (architect); Verrill (zoologist). Less popular.
Addy English. From Adam. Unusual. Alternative spelling: Ade.
Adeben African. African, "12th-born son." Unusual.
Adél Hungarian. From Adelaide, Old German (Adelheidis), "Nobility." Unusual.
Adelbert English. From Albert, Old English (Aethelbeorht), "Noble-bright." Saint; Chamisso (German writer, editor, and botanist). Unusual.
Adem Turkish. From Adam. Unusual.
Adhamh Scottish. From Adam. Unusual.
Adi Yiddish. From Adam. Unusual.
ʿAdil Arabic. Arabic, "Equal." Unusual.
Adir Hebrew/Israeli. Hebrew, "Majestic" or "noble." Unusual.
Adiv Hebrew/Israeli. Hebrew, "Gentle" or "pleasant." Unusual.
Adlai English. Hebrew, "My ornament" or "justice of Jehovah." 1 Chronicles 27:29. Stevenson (vice-president under Cleveland, 1893–97); Stevenson, Jr. (ambassador to United Nations, 1961–65). Unusual.
Adler English. Old English, "Eagle." Unusual.
Adli Turkish. Turkish, "Just." Unusual.
Admiral English. Arabic, "amir" ("commander"); a title used as first name. Unusual.
Admon Hebrew/Israeli. Hebrew, "Red peony." A flower found in the upper Galilee. Unusual.
Adok Polish. From Adam. Unusual.
Adolph German. From Adolphus. Borie (secretary of navy under Grant); Zukor (movie producer); Loos (Austrian modernist architect); Ochs (newspaper publisher); Sutro (mining engineer, planned 20,000-foot tunnel into Mt. Davidson); von Menzel (German lithographer and illustrator). Unusual. Alternative spelling: Adolf.
Adolphe French. From Adolphus. Martens (Belgian avant-garde playwright); Pégoud (French aviator, performed first "loop the loop"); Yvon (French historical painter); Appia (Swiss stage designer, pioneered modern realistic settings and lighting); Blanqui (French economist). Unusual.
Adolphus German. Old German, "Noble wolf" or "hero." Frederick (British Duke of Cambridge, son of George III); Busch (president, Anheuser-Busch Brewing, 1879–1913); Greely (army officer, explored Arctic). Unusual.
Adom African. Ghanaian, "Help from God." Unusual.
Adomas Lithuanian. From Adam. Unusual.
Adorjan Hungarian. From Adrian, Latin (Hadrianus), "Black earth" or "of Adria," a city in northern Italy. Unusual.
Adri Indo-Pakistani. Hindi, "Rock." Adri is a minor Hindu god who acts as man's protector. He once saved the sun from being extinguished by evil spirits. Unusual.
Adrian English. Latin (Hadrianus), "Black earth" or "of Adria," a city in northern Italy. Of Canterbury (saint); of May (saint); pope (I, 772-VI, 1522); Boult, Sir (British orchestra conductor); von Bubenberg (Swiss army hero, 1476); character in Shakespeare's "Coriolanus." Less popular for males, less popular for females.
Adriano Italian. From Adrian, Latin (Hadrianus), "Black earth" or "of Adria," a city in northern Italy. Balbi (Italian geographer); Banchieri (Italian composer of church music). Unusual.
Adriel Hebrew/Israeli. Hebrew, "God's majesty" or "member of God's congregation." Unusual. Alternative spelling: Adrial.
Adriene French. From Adrian, Latin (Hadrianus), "Black earth" or "of Adria," a city in northern Italy. Unusual. Alternative spelling: Adrien.
Adrik Russian. From Adrian, Latin (Hadrianus), "Black earth" or "of Adria," a city in northern Italy. Unusual.
Aeneas Scottish. Greek, "Praiseworthy." Trojan hero. Unusual.
Afon Russian. From Tanek, Greek, "Immortal." Unusual.
Afonya Russian. From Tanek, Greek, "Immortal." Unusual.
Agamemnon Greek. Greek, "Resolute." King of Argos, led Greeks in Trojan War. Unusual.
Agni Indo-Pakistani. Hindi, the name of the fire god. Hindu lore depicts Agni riding in a chariot powered by the seven winds. He has three heads, four or seven arms, and seven tongues used to lap butter sacrifices. Unusual.
Agu Nigerian. Nigerian, "Leopard." Unusual.
Agustín Hispanic. From Augustus, Latin, "Venerable" or "majestic." Unusual.
Ahanu Native American. Native American, "He laughs." Unusual.
Ahdik Native American. Native American, "Caribou" or "reindeer." Unusual.
Ahe Hebrew/Israeli. From Abraham, Hebrew (Avraham), "Exalted father" or "father of a multitude." Genesis 17:4,5. Unusual.
Ahir Turkish. Turkish, "End" or "last." Given to last child mother intends to bear. Unusual.
Ahkeel Arabic. From Akil. Unusual.

Ahkeen Nigerian. From Akin. Unusual.

Ahmed Arabic. Arabic, "Most praised." One of Muḥammad's 500 names. Ottoman sultan (I, 1603-III, 1703); Bey Zogu (Zog I, King of Albania, 1928–39); Muneccimbasi (Turkish historian and author); Nedim (Turkish poet); Cevdet Pasa (Turkish politician and historian); Hasim (Turkish author). Unusual. Alternative spelling: Ahmad.

Ahmik Native American. Native American, "Beaver." In Indian folklore, the beaver represents skill. Unusual.

Ahren German. Old German, "Eagle." Unusual.

Aidan Irish. Gaelic, "Fire." Saint. Unusual. Alternative spellings: Aden, Adin, Aiden.

Ailan Irish. From Alan, Gaelic, meaning uncertain, but may include "rock," "noble," "handsome," "harmony," and/or "cheerful." Unusual. Alternative spelling: Ailin.

Ailbe Unknown. Meaning and origin unknown. Saint. Unusual.

Ailwyn English. From Alvin, Old English, "Elf-friend," "noble friend," "everyone's friend," or "old friend." Unusual.

Aindrea Irish. From Andrew, Greek, "Manly." Unusual.

Aindreas Scottish. From Andrew, Greek, "Manly." Unusual.

Ainsley English. From Ainslie. Unusual for males, less popular for females.

Ainslie Scottish. Surname and place name used as a first name; origin unknown. Unusual for males, unusual for females.

Aizik Yiddish. From Isaac, Hebrew (Yitzchak), "Laughter." Genesis 21:3. Unusual.

Ajay Indo-Pakistani. Punjabi, "Victorious." Unusual.

Akando Native American. Native American, "Ambush." The name may have commemorated the child's father's victory in battle. Unusual.

Akar Turkish. Turkish, "Running" or "flowing," referring to water. Unusual.

Akeel Arabic. From Akil. Unusual.

Akeem Hebrew/Israeli. Hebrew, "God will establish." Olajuwon (basketball player, blocked 1,577 shots). Unusual.

Akeen Nigerian. From Akin. Unusual.

Akiba Hebrew/Israeli. From Jacob, Hebrew (Yaakov), "Supplanter" or "heel." Genesis 25:26. Ben Joseph (Hebrew sage and martyr). Unusual.

Akil Arabic. Arabic, "Intelligent," "thoughtful," or "one who reasons." Unusual.

Akim Russian. From Joachim, Hebrew, "God will establish." Unusual.

Akin Nigerian. Nigerian, "Heroic" or "brave." Unusual.

Akio Japanese. Japanese, "Bright lad." Unusual.

Akira Japanese. From Akio. Unusual.

Akiva Hebrew/Israeli. From Jacob, Hebrew (Yaakov), "Supplanter" or "heel." Genesis 25:26. Unusual.

Akon African. From Akron. Unusual.

Akoni Hawaiian. From Anthony, Latin, a Roman clan name used as a first name. Unusual.

Akron African. African, "Ninth-born son." Unusual.

Akule Native American. Native American, "He looks up." Perhaps reflects a baby's first action after birth. Unusual.

Al English. From Alexander, Greek, "Defender of men" or "warding off men." Mark 16:21; Acts 4:6, 19:33. Oerter (Olympic gold medalist for discus throw, 1956–1968); Jolson (actor and singer, "The Jazz Singer"); Green (singer); Pacino (movie actor, "The Godfather"). Less popular.

ʿAlā Arabic. Arabic, "Glorious." Naite (Japanese; in 1937, juggled record 16 hoops simultaneously, using hands and feet). Unusual.

Alain French. From Alan. French philosopher and essayist (real name: Emile-Auguste Chartier); Locke (educator, first black Rhodes scholar, led "Harlem Renaissance"); Resnais (French film director); Prost (French, most Gran Prix victories: 35, in 140 races, 1980–89). Unusual. Alternative spelling: Allain.

Alaister Scottish. From Alexander, Greek, "Defender of men" or "warding off men." Mark 16:21; Acts 4:6, 19:33. Unusual. Alternative spellings: Alasdair, Alastaire, Alaster, Aleister, Alisdair, Alistaire, Alistar, Alister.

Alan English. Gaelic, meaning uncertain, but may include "rock," "noble," "handsome," "harmony," and/or "cheerful." Jay Lerner (librettist, lyricist, and screenplay writer, "An American in Paris"); Watts (philosopher, "The Spirit of Zen"); Seeger (poet); Milne (British poet, playwright, novelist, "Winnie-the-Pooh"); Bateman (Canadian geologist); Thicke (TV actor). Less popular. Al. Alternative spellings: Allan, Allen, Allin, Allon, Allyn, Alyn.

Aland English. From Alan. Unusual.

Alani See under Girls' Names.

Alano Hispanic. From Alan. Unusual.

Alao Portuguese. From Alan. Unusual.

Alaric German. Old German, "Noble ruler." King of the Visigoths (I, 395-II, 484). Unusual.

Alasid Arabic. From Asʿad, Arabic, "Lion." Unusual.

Alastor English. From Alexander, Greek, "Defender of men" or "warding off men." Mark 16:21; Acts 4:6, 19:33. Unusual.

Alaula See under Girls' Names.

Alban English. Latin, "Of Alba," a town on a white hill. Alba was capital of the first Roman kings, as well as an ancient name for the Scottish highlands. Saint; Berg (Austrian classical composer, "Wozzeck"); Butler (British hagiographer, "Lives of the Saints"). Unusual.

Albany English. From Alban. Alba was capital of the first Roman kings, as well as an ancient name for the Scottish highlands. Unusual.

Albek Polish. From Albin. Unusual.

Albert English. Old English (Aethelbeorht), "Noble-bright." Patron saint of scientists; Einstein (physicist, awarded Nobel Prize, 1921); Luthuli (Zulu chief, awarded Nobel Peace Prize, 1960); Camus (French novelist, playwright, and essayist, awarded Nobel Prize, 1957); Read (naval officer). Less popular. Al, Bert.

Albertik Czech. From Albert. Unusual.

Alberto Italian. From Albert. Lista y Aragon (Spanish educator, poet, and critic); Santos-Dumont (French, early aviator); Blest Gana (Chilean novelist); Ascari (Italian race-car driver, world champion, 1952–53); De Stefani (Italian economist). Less popular.

Alberts Latvian. From Albert. Unusual.

Albie English. From Albert. Unusual.

Albin English, Polish, Russian. Latin, "White"; and from Alvin, Old English, "Elf-friend," "noble friend," "everyone's friend," or "old friend." Zollinger (Swiss novelist and impressionist poet). Unusual. Alternative spelling: Alben.

Albinek Czech. From Albin. Unusual.

Albino Italian. From Albin. Unusual.

Albins Latvian. From Albin. Unusual.

Albion English. Celtic, "Rock" or "mountain." Small (sociologist, published first textbook on sociology). Unusual.

Albrecht German. From Albert. Dürer (16th-century German painter, engraver); Pfister (German printer); Penck (German geographer); Ritschl (German theologian, emphasized ethical-social concerns); Wallenstein (Austrian general, Prince of Sagan, 1627–34); Altdorfer (German painter, engraver). Unusual.

Alby English. From Albert. Unusual.

Alden English. From Alvin, Old English, "Elf-friend," "noble friend," "everyone's friend," or "old friend." Partridge (educator, established elementary and secondary grade military academies). Less popular.

Alder German. Old English, "From the alder tree." Unusual.

Aldo Italian. From Aldous. Mannucci (Italian scholar and printer, invented italic type); Moro (Italian prime minister, 1963–68, 1974–76); Leopold (forester, director of the Audubon Society, 1935–48). Unusual.

Aldous English. Old German, "Old." Huxley (novelist, "Brave New World"). Less popular.

Aldred English. Old English, "Old counsel." British, archbishop of York, 1060–69. Unusual.

Aldrich English. Old English, "Wise ruler." Unusual. Alternative spelling: Aldric.

Aldridge English. From Aldrich. Unusual.

Aldwyn English. Old English, "Old friend." Saint. Unusual. Alternative spelling: Aldwin.

Alec English. From Alexander, Greek, "Defender of men" or "warding off men." Mark 16:21; Acts 4:6, 19:33. Waugh (British author, "Island in the Sun"); Leamas (character in John Le Carre's novel and movie "The Spy Who Came in from the Cold"); Baldwin (actor); Guinness, Sir (British actor). Less popular. Al. Alternative spellings: Aleck, Alek, Alic, Alick, Alik.

Alein Yiddish. Yiddish, "Alone." Unusual.

Alejandro Hispanic. From Alexander. Aguado (Spanish financier, bequeathed costly paintings to the Louvre); Lerroux Garcia (Spanish politician, established Radical party, 1908). Unusual.

Alejo Hispanic. From Alexander. Unusual.

Alekko Bulgarian. From Alexander. Unusual.

Alekos Greek. From Alexander. Unusual.

Aleksander Estonian, Polish. From Alexander. Lenartowicz (Polish poet); Skrzynski, Count (Polish prime minister, 1925–26, helped organize the League of Nations); Wielopolski, Marquis (Polish politician, head of civil government, 1861–63). Unusual.

Aleksandr Russian. From Alexander. Menshikov (Russian general under Peter the Great, made prince, 1706); Archipenko (cubist and abstract sculptor); Turgenev (Russian historian); Tairov (Russian theatrical producer); Radishchev (Russian author, criticized autocracy and serfdom). Unusual.

Aleksandŭr Bulgarian. From Alexander. Stamboliski (Bulgarian premier, 1920–23, redistributed land to peasants); Tsankov (Bulgarian premier, 1923–26). Unusual.

Aleksei Russian. From Alexander. Unusual.

Aleš Czech. From Alexander. Hrdlička (anthropologist, curator of U.S. National Museum, 1910–42). Unusual.

Alešer Arabic. From Asʿad, Arabic, "Lion." Unusual.

Alessandro Italian. From Alexander. Scarlatti (Italian opera composer, credited with early thematic development and chromatic harmony); Albani (18th-century Italian cardinal, gathered famous art collection); Algardi (Italian sculptor); Volta, Count (Italian physicist); Poerio (Italian patriotic poet). Less popular.

Alex English. From Alexander. Less popular. Al. Alternative spelling: Aleks.

Alexander English. Greek, "Defender of men" or "warding off men." Mark 16:21; Acts 4:6, 19:33. Saint; pope (I, 105-VIII, 1689); Kilham (18th-century British clergyman; followers are Kilhamites); Mckenzie (Canadian explorer); Pope (British poet, "The Rape of the Lock"); Borodin (Russian composer, "Prince Igor"); Humboldt (German, originated ecology). Popular. Al, Alec+, Alex.

Alexandr Russian. From Alexander. Unusual.

Alexandre French. From Alexander. Millerand (French president, 1920–24); de Rhodes (French Jesuit missionary, brought Christianity to Vietnam); Serpa Pinto (Portuguese explorer of Africa); de Prouville Tracy, Marquis (French lieutenant-general of French territory in North America). Unusual.

Alexandros Greek. From Alexander. Zaïmis (Greek president, 1929–35); Papadiamadis (Greek short-story writer); Papagos (Greek premier, 1952–55). Unusual.

Alexio Portuguese. From Alexander. Unusual.

Alexis See under Girls' Names.

Alf English. From Alfred. Dean (Australian, holds record for largest fish ever caught on a rod: a Great White shark weighing 2,664 pounds and measuring 16 feet, 10 inches long, 1959). Less popular.

Alfie English. From Alfred. Turner (British, danced longest disco marathon on record: 462 hours, 30 minutes). Less popular. Alf.

Alfonso Hispanic. From Alphonso, Old German (Hildefuns), "Ready for battle." King of Aragon (I, 1104-V, 1416); Liguori (Italian bishop); Quiñónez Molina (president of El Salvador, 1923–27); Corti (19th-century Italian anatomist, discovered complex organization of the ear); López Pumarejo (Columbian president, 1934–38, 1942–45). Unusual.

Alfonsus English. From Alphonso, Old German (Hildefuns), "Ready for battle." Unusual. Al, Alf.

Alfred English. Old English, "Elf-counsel." "The Great," King of Wessex, 871–99; Nobel (Swedish inventor of dynamite, left funds to establish Nobel Prize); Tennyson, Lord (British poet, "Morte d'Arthur"); Hitchcock, Sir (British film director, "Rebecca"); Lunt (stage actor). Less popular. Al, Alf, Alfie, Fred.

Alfredo Hispanic, Italian. From Alfred. Niceforo (Italian sociologist, studied crime); Panzini (Italian novelist); Zayas y Alfonso (Cuban president, 1921–25); Baquerizo Moreno (Ecuadoran president, 1916–20); Oriani (Italian novelist, poet, and essayist). Less popular.

Alga English. From Algar. Unusual.
Algar English. Old English (Aelfgar), "Elf-spear." Unusual. Alternative spelling: Alger.
Algernon English. Old French, "With whiskers" or "with moustaches." Methuen, Sir (British publisher, compiled "An Anthology of English Verse"); Swinburne (British lyric poet, "Atalanta in Calydon"); Blackwood (British novelist, "Tales of the Uncanny and Supernatural"). Unusual. Algie+.
Algie English. From Algernon. Unusual. Alternative spelling: Algy.
Ali See under Girls' Names.
Alim Arabic. Arabic, "Learned" or "wise." Unusual. Alternative spellings: Alem, Aleem.
Alistair English. From Alexander. Cooke (TV narrator, host of PBS's "Masterpiece Theatre"). Unusual.
Almiron Indo-Pakistani. Hindi, "Clothes basket." Reflects the belief that God is manifested in every household object. Unusual.
Almon Hebrew/Israeli. Hebrew, "Forsaken" or "widower." Unusual.
Alohi See under Girls' Names.
Aloin French. From Alvin, Old English, "Elf-friend," "noble friend," "everyone's friend," or "old friend." Unusual.
Alois German. From Louis, Old German (Hlutwig), "Famous warrior." Wolfmuller (German, established first factory to make motorcycles in quantity); Rasin (Czech politician, helped lead Prague Revolution, 1918); Riehl (German neo-Kantian philosopher); Hába (Czech composer, noted for microtonal classical music). Unusual.
Aloisio Hispanic. From Louis, Old German (Hlutwig), "Famous warrior." Unusual.
Alon Hebrew/Israeli. Hebrew, "Oak tree." Unusual.
Alonso Italian. From Alphonso, Old German (Hildefuns), "Ready for battle." de Ojeda (15th-century Spanish explorer of Americas with Columbus and Vespucci); de Ledesma Buitrago (Spanish poet); Sánchez Coello (16th-century Spanish court painter); de Santa Cruz (Spanish cartographer); Cano (17th-century Spanish painter, sculptor, and architect). Unusual.
Alonzo Hispanic. From Alphonso, Old German (Hildefuns), "Ready for battle." Potter (Episcopal clergyman, established hospital, 1860, and divinity school, 1863); de Benavides (Spanish Franciscan missionary to Mexico 1603, established 10 missions and convents). Unusual.
Aloys Dutch. From Louis, Old German (Hlutwig), "Famous warrior." Reding (Swiss politician, headed Helvetian Republic, 1801–02); Senefelder (German, invented lithography, 1796, and color lithography, 1826). Unusual.
Aloysius English. From Louis, Old German (Hlutwig), "Famous warrior"; or Old German, "Very wise." Gonzaga (16th-century saint, patron saint of students). Unusual.
Alpheus Hebrew/Israeli. Hebrew, "Successor." Packard (19th-century entomologist, a founding editor of "American Naturalist," 1867–87); Hyatt (19th-century zoologist and paleontologist). Unusual. Alternative spellings: Alpheaus, Alphoeus.
Alphonse French, Italian. From Alphonso, Old German (Hildefuns), "Ready for battle." Jourdain (Count of Toulouse, 1112); Leemans (pro football Hall of Famer); Legros (British etcher and religious painter); Mucha (Czech Art Nouveau painter and illustrator, designed posters for Sarah Bernhardt); Renard (Belgian geologist). Less popular.
Alphonso English. From Alphonso, Old German (Hildefuns), "Ready for battle." Taft (attorney general under Grant, 1876–77). Unusual.
Alphonzus English. From Alphonso, Old German (Hildefuns), "Ready for battle." Unusual.
Alpin Scottish. From Albin, Latin, "White." Unusual.
Alpine Scottish. From Albin, Latin, "White." Unusual.
Alrik Swedish. Old German, "Ruler of all." Unusual.
Alroy Hispanic. Spanish, "King." Unusual.
Alsandair Irish. From Alexander, Greek, "Defender of men" or "warding off men." Mark 16:21; Acts 4:6, 19:33. Unusual.
Altair Arabic. Arabic, "Flying eagle." Also refers to a star in the constellation Lyra. Unusual.
Alton English. Old English, "Old town" or "high town." Place name used as a first name. Parker (chief justice, court of appeals, 1898–1904). Unusual. Alternative spellings: Alten, Altin.
Aluin French. From Alvin. Unusual.
Aluino Hispanic. From Alvin. Unusual.
Alun Welsh. From Alan, Gaelic, meaning uncertain, but may include "rock," "noble," "handsome," "harmony," and/or "cheerful." Lewis (Welsh poet, wrote of army experiences, "Raiders' Dawn"). Unusual.
Alured English. From Alfred, Old English, "Elf-counsel." Unusual.
Alva See under Girls' Names.
Alvah See Alva under Girls' Names.
Alvan Hebrew/Israeli. Hebrew, "Tall." Genesis 36:23. Clark (astronomer, made telescope lenses); Graham Clark (astronomer, discovered 16 double stars). Unusual.
Alvar English. Old English, "Elf-army." Aalto (Finnish architect noted for use of natural materials); Cabeza de Vaca (16th-century Spanish explorer of Florida and Brazil); Liddell (BBC news reader). Unusual.
Alvaro English. Latin, "Fair." de Mendaña de Neyra (Spanish explorer, discovered Solomon Islands, 1567); Obregón (president of Mexico, 1920–24, 1928); de Bazan (Spanish admiral, planned Armada); Fernandes (Portuguese explorer); Luna (Spanish constable of Castile, 1422). Unusual.
Alvertos Greek. From Albert, Old English (Aethelbeorht), "Noble-bright." Unusual.
Alvie See under Girls' Names.
Alvin English. Old English, "Elf-friend," "noble friend," "everyone's friend," or "old friend." York (WWI army sergeant, hero; won Medal of Honor); Adams (businessman, established Adams Express Company); Carter (Appalachian folk singer); Hansen (Keynesian economist); Johnson (economist, editor of "New Republic," 1917–23). Less popular. Alvie+. Alternative spellings: Alven, Alvyn.
Alvino Italian. From Alvin. Unusual.
Alvis Scandinavian. Scandinavian, "All-knowing." Unusual.
Alwin English, German, Portuguese. From Alvin. Unusual. Alternative spellings: Alwyn, Aylwin.

Amadeo Italian. From Amado. Vives (Spanish opera composer, "Balada de carnaval"); Giannini (banker, first to establish regional branch banks). Unusual.

Amado Hispanic. Latin, "Loving deity" or "lover of the divine." Alonso (Spanish linguist); Nervo (Mexican modernist poet, "Perlas negras"). Unusual.

Amāl Arabic. Arabic, "Hope." Unusual.

Amand French. From Amanda, Latin, "Fit to be loved." Saint; Bazard (French socialist, organized French Carbonari). Unusual.

Amandeep Indo-Pakistani. Punjabi, "Light" or "lamp of peace." Unusual for males, unusual for females.

Amando Hispanic. From Amado, Latin, "Loving deity" or "lover of the divine." Unusual.

Amar Indo-Pakistani. Hindi, "Immortal." Unusual.

Amariah Hebrew/Israeli. From Amariah, Hebrew, "Whom God has promised." Unusual.

Amato Hispanic. From Amy, Old French, "Loved." Unusual.

Ambrose English. Greek, "Immortal." Saint; Philips (British poet, "Pastorals"); Tomlinson (clergyman, established Tomlinson Church of God, 1923); Bierce (cynical journalist and author, "Devil's Dictionary"); Burnside (army general, type of side whiskers named after him—"burnsides"). Less popular.

Amias English. From Amyas, Latin, "Loved by God" or "to love God." Unusual for males, unusual for females.

Amico Italian. From Amicus. Unusual.

Amicus English. Latin, "Beloved friend." Unusual.

Amiel Hebrew/Israeli. Hebrew, "Lord of my people." Unusual.

Amin Indo-Pakistani. East Indian, "Faithful." al-Husayni (Arab, president of Supreme Muslim Council of Palestine, 1921–36). Unusual. Alternative spelling: Ameen.

Amintor Italian. From Amyntas, Greek, meaning unknown. Character in Beaumont and Fletcher's "Maid's Tragedy." Unusual.

Amir Arabic. From Ameer, Arabic, "Prince." Koshrow (Indian historical poet). Unusual. Alternative spelling: Ameer.

Amit Arabic. Arabic, "The most praised." Unusual.

Amitan Indo-Pakistani. From Amin. Unusual.

Amnon Hebrew/Israeli. Hebrew, "Faithful." 2 Samuel 3. First of David's sons; one of Saul's commanders. Unusual.

Amon Hebrew/Israeli. Hebrew, "Related to the sun." Unusual. Alternative spelling: Ammon.

Amor English. From Amory. Unusual.

Amorous English. Latin, "amare" ("to love"); the word used as a first name. Unusual.

Amory English. Old German, "Work ruler" or "always rich." Blaine (character in F. Scott Fitzgerald's "This Side of Paradise"); Houghton (industrialist, established Corning Glass Works, 1875). Unusual. Alternative spelling: Amery.

Amos English. Hebrew, "Borne" (by God), "bearer of a burden," or "burden." Amos 7:14, 15. Prophet; Stagg (football coach with longest career: 1889–1960; developed huddle and man-in-motion); Kendall (postmaster general, 1835–40); Lawrence (merchant, headed large mercantile company); Alcott (transcendental philosopher and teacher). Unusual.

Amyas English. Latin, "Loved by God" or "to love God." Leigh (character in Charles Kingsley's "Westward Ho!"). Unusual.

An Vietnamese. Vietnamese, "Peace," "security," or "safety." Wang (established Wang Laboratories, invented predecessor to microchip). Unusual for males, unusual for females.

Anala See under Girls' Names.

Anand Indo-Pakistani. Hindi, "Bliss." Unusual.

Anchor English. Greek, "ankyra"; the word used as a first name. Possibly a reference to Hebrews 6:19: "This hope we have as an anchor of the soul, a hope both sure and steadfast." Unusual.

Anders Scandinavian. From Andrew. Retzius (Swedish, invented cranial index, 1842); Vedel (Danish historian); Zorn (Swedish painter and sculptor); Ångström (Swedish physicist, angstrom unit of length named for him); Celsius (Swedish astronomer, developed centigrade thermometer). Unusual.

Andonios Greek. From Anthony, Latin, a Roman clan name used as a first name. Unusual.

Andonis Greek. From Anthony, Latin, a Roman clan name used as a first name. Unusual.

Andor Hungarian. From Andrew. Unusual.

András Hungarian. From Andrew. Dugonics (Hungarian novelist, "Etelka"). Unusual.

André French. From Andrew. Watts (concert pianist); Lenôtre (French landscape architect); Lhote (French painter of Fauvist, then cubist, style); Michelin (French, established company to manufacture rubber bicycle tires); Wallenberg (Swedish financier); Agassi (tennis champion). Less popular.

Andrea See under Girls' Names.

Andreas German, Greek. From Andrew. Busch (Danish, built early planetarium); Libau (German, discovered method to prepare hydrochloric acid); Marggraf (German, discovered the sugar in sugar beets); Osiander (German Lutheran theologian); Ruckers (Flemish harpsichord maker). Unusual.

Andrei Bulgarian (Andreĭ), Romanian. From Andrew. Gromyko (Russian diplomat); Sakharov (Russian, designed hydrogen bomb, won Nobel Peace Prize, 1975); Liapchev (Bulgarian prime minister, 1926–31). Unusual.

Andreian Russian. From Adrian, Latin (Hadrianus), "Black earth" or "of Adria," a city in northern Italy. Unusual. Alternative spellings: Andreyan, Andriyan.

Andrej Czech. From Andrew. Hlinka (Slovak patriot, established party to oppose unification with Bohemia). Unusual.

Andres Hispanic. From Andrew. Segovia (Spanish guitarist); Santa Cruz (president of Bolivia, 1829–39); Bello (established University of Chile); Bonifacio (Philippine nationalist, established Katipunan society, 1892); Cáceres (president of Peru, 1886–90, 1894–95). Unusual.

Andrew English. Greek, "Manly." Patron saint of fishermen; Kim (first Korean Catholic priest); Carnegie (established U.S. Steel); Jackson (7th president); Lloyd Webber (British composer); Meikle (Scottish, invented drum threshing machine); Marvell (British metaphysical poet). Extremely popular. Andy+, Drew.

Andrey Bulgarian, Russian. From Andrew. Markov (Russian mathematician, helped launch stochastic processes with his chains); Rublyov (Russian Byzantine painter, "Old Testament Trinity"); Tarkovsky (Russian film director, "Stalker"); Tupolev (Russian, designed 100 aircraft). Unusual.

Andreyan Russian. From Adrian, Latin (Hadrianus), "Black earth" or "of Adria," a city in northern Italy. Unusual.

Andreyka Russian. From Andrew. Unusual.

Andri Russian. From Adrian, Latin (Hadrianus), "Black earth" or "of Adria," a city in northern Italy. Unusual.

Andrik Russian. From Andrew. Unusual.

Andris Hungarian. From Andrew. Unusual.

Andrius Lithuanian. From Andrew. Unusual.

Andy English. From Andrew. Adams (wrote on cowboy life, "Cattle Brands"); Warhol (pop artist, Campbell soup can series); Rooney (TV personality, "60 Minutes"); Garcia (actor, "Godfather Part III"). Less popular. Alternative spellings: Andi, Andie.

Aneurin Welsh. Welsh, "Honor" or "gold." Bevan (British, Labor minister of health, 1945–51). Unusual. Alternative spelling: Aneirin.

Angel See under Girls' Names.

Angelo Italian. From Angel, Greek, "angelos" ("messenger"). Bertelli (Notre Dame football player, won 1943 Heisman trophy); Mai (Italian prelate, published old Cicero manuscript); Ambrogini (Italian poet); di Costanzo (Italian poet, "Rime"); Beolco (Italian playwright); Dundee (trained boxer Muhammad Ali). Unusual.

Angus Scottish. Gaelic, "Unique choice." Also a Scottish place name, now called Forfarshire. Og (character in James Stephens' "The Crock of Gold"); Wilson (British author, "Anglo-Saxon Attitudes"). Unusual.

Anh Vietnamese. Vietnamese, "Peace" or "safety." Unusual for males, unusual for females.

Anibal Unknown. Phoenician, "Grace of God." Pinto (president of Chile, 1876–81). Unusual.

Anila See under Girls' Names.

Aniol Polish. From Andrew. Unusual.

Aniweta See under Girls' Names.

Anka Turkish. Turkish, "Phoenix." Unusual.

Annan African. African, "Fourth-born son." Unusual.

Annas Greek. Greek, "Whom Jehovah graciously gave." Luke 3:2. Biblical high priest. Unusual.

Anndra Scottish. From Andrew. Unusual.

Anntoin Irish. From Anthony. Unusual.

Anoki Native American. Native American, "Actor." Unusual.

Ansel English. From Anselm. Adams (landscape photographer). Unusual. Alternative spellings: Ancel, Ancell, Ansell, Ansil, Ansill.

Anselm English. Old German, "Divine" + "helmet." Saint. Unusual.

Ansis Latvian. From John, Hebrew (Yochanan), "God has been gracious." Unusual.

Ansley English. From Ainslie, surname and place name used as a first name; origin unknown. Unusual for males, unusual for females.

Anson English. Old German, "John's son." Burlingame (minister to China, 1861–67); Jones (president of Texas, 1844–46). Unusual.

Antal Hungarian. From Anthony. Unusual.

Antavas Lithuanian. From Anthony. Unusual.

Antek Czech, Polish. From Anthony. Unusual.

Anthony English. Latin, a Roman clan name used as a first name. Eden, Sir (British prime minister, 1955–57); Quinn (actor); Kennedy (Supreme Court Justice, 1988-); Wayne (18th-century general); van Dyck (Flemish portraitist, "Portrait of Charles I Hunting"); Trollope (British novelist, "Barchester Towers"). Very popular. Tony.

Anti Hungarian. From Anthony. Unusual.

Antin Russian. From Anthony. Unusual.

Antinko Russian. From Anthony. Unusual.

Antjuan American. From Anthony. Unusual. Alternative spellings: Antajuan, Anthjuan, Antuan.

Antoine French. From Anthony. Domino (musician) (real name of Fats); Watteau (French rococo painter); Masson (French engraver, "Tablecloth"); de Montchrétien (French playwright, "Sophonisbe"); Pevsner (French constructivist sculptor, "Construction for an Airport"). Less popular.

Anton English. From Anthony. Chekhov (Russian playwright, "Cherry Orchard"); Makarenko (Russian social worker); Mengs (German neoclassical fresco artist, "Parnassus"); Reicha (Czech classical composer, "Natalie"); Schweigarrd (Norwegian, reformed economy to free enterprise). Less popular.

Antonello English. From Anthony. da Messina (15th-century Italian painter, "St. Jerome"). Unusual.

Antoni Polish. From Anthony. Lange (Polish lyric poet); van Leeuwenhoek (Dutch, first to describe red blood corpuscles, 1674); Malczewski (Polish narrative poet, "Marja"); Slonimski (Polish author of verse, novels, and essays). Unusual.

Antonín Czech, Polish. From Anthony. Dvořák (Bohemian composer, "New World" symphony); Mercie (French sculptor, tomb of Louis-Philippe); Raymond (modern architect); Sova (Czech poet); Švehla (Czech premier, 1922–29); Zapotocky (Czech president, 1953–57). Unusual.

Antonino Italian. From Anthony. Unusual.

Antonio Hispanic, Italian. From Anthony. Vivaldi (18th-century Italian classical composer, "Four Seasons"); Machado Ruiz (Spanish poet); Maura y Montaner (Spanish prime minister); Pacinotti (Italian physicist); Pisanello (Italian early-Renaissance fresco artist, "Annunciation"). Popular.

Antons Latvian. From Anthony. Unusual.

Antony English. From Anthony. Of Egypt (patron saint of basket makers); of Padua (patron saint of lost articles, the poor, and the starving); Claret (saint); Khrapovitshy (Russian archbishop, led Russian Orthodox church in exile, 1920–36). Less popular. Tony. Alternative spellings: Antione, Antoney.

Antos Polish. From Anthony. Unusual.

Antuwain Arabic. From Anthony. Unusual. Alternative spellings: Antwain, Antwaine.

Antwan Arabic. From Anthony. Unusual. Alternative spellings: Antwaun, Antwoin, Antwon, Antwone.

Anwar Arabic. Arabic, "Luminous." Sadat (president of Egypt, 1970–81, won

Nobel Peace Prize, 1978). Unusual.

Aquila Hispanic. Latin, "Eagle." Acts 18:2. Ponticus (2nd-century Jew, translated Old Testament from Hebrew into Greek). Unusual. Alternative spellings: Acquila, Acquilla, Aquilla.

Araldo Italian. From Harold, Old English, "Army power." Unusual.

Aralt French. From Harold, Old English, "Army power." Unusual.

Aranne Italian. From Aaron, Hebrew (Aharon), "Teaching" or "singing." Exodus 6:20. Unusual.

Arch English. From Archibald. Unusual.

Archaimbaud French. From Archibald. Unusual.

Archambault French. From Archibald. Unusual.

Archelaus Greek, "Ruler of the people." King of Macedonia, 413–399 B.C. Unusual.

Archer English. Latin, "Bowman" or "archer." Whiteoak (character in Mazo de la Roche's "Renny's Daughter"); Huntington (established and endowed Hispanic Society of America, 1904); Davidson (Australian, holds record for killing largest marine animal by hand harpoon: a 97-foot blue whale). Unusual.

Archibald English. Old German, "Noble" + "bold." MacLeish (won Pulitzer Prize for poetry, 1952, "Collected Poems"); Sayce (British philologist); Tait (British archbishop of Canterbury, Public Worship Regulation Act, 1874); Alison, Sir (Scottish historian); Willard (genre painter, "Yankee Doodle"). Unusual. Archie. Alternative spellings: Archabald, Archbald, Archbold.

Archibaldo Hispanic. From Archibald. Unusual.

Archie English. From Archibald. Moore (oldest light-heavyweight champion: 45–48 years old (birthdate uncertain)). Less popular.

Ardon Hebrew/Israeli. Hebrew, "Bronze." Unusual.

Areef Turkish. From Arif. Unusual.

Arek Polish. From Aaron, Hebrew (Aharon), "Teaching" or "singing." Exodus 6:20. Unusual.

Arel Hebrew/Israeli. Hebrew, "Lion of God." Unusual.

Areli Hebrew/Israeli. From Arel. Unusual.

Aren Scandinavian. Scandinavian, "Eagle" or "rule." Unusual.

Arfon Welsh. Welsh, "Opposite Anglesey"; a place name used as a first name. Unusual.

Ari Hebrew/Israeli. Hebrew, "Lion." Thorgilsson (Icelandic historian and author, wrote first vernacular history of Iceland, from settlement to 1120). Less popular. Alternative spellings: Arie, Arri.

Aric English. Old English, "Holy ruler." Unusual. Alternative spellings: Areck, Arick.

Ariel See under Girls' Names.

Arif Turkish. Turkish, "Wise" or "intelligent." Unusual.

Aristides Greek. Greek, "Son of the best." Second-century Greek statesman and rhetorician. Unusual.

Aristotle Greek. Greek, "Best" + "achieve." Fourth-century B.C. Greek philosopher especially concerned with logic, metaphysics, and natural science. Unusual.

Arius German. From Tanek, Greek, "Immortal." Greek ecclesiastic whose heretical teachings led emperor to call the Council of Nicaea. Unusual.

Arkin Norwegian. Norwegian, "Son of the eternal king." Unusual.

Arlen Irish. Gaelic, "A pledge." Unusual. Alternative spellings: Arlan, Arlin.

Arlend Irish. From Arlen. Unusual. Alternative spellings: Arland, Arlind.

Arley English. Old English, "Hunter" or "bowman." Also a place name and surname meaning "eagle-wood" or "from the rabbit meadow." Unusual.

Arlo Hispanic. Spanish, "Barberry." Guthrie (folk singer). Less popular.

Armand English. From Herman, Old German, "Army" + "man." Hammer (industrialist, paid $5 million for da Vinci illustrated manuscript); Quick (hematologist, expert on blood diseases); Călinescu (Romanian premier, 1939). Less popular. Alternative spellings: Arman, Armin, Armon.

Armando Hispanic, Italian. From Herman, Old German, "Army" + "man." Ramos (lightweight boxer); Palacio Valdés (Spanish novelist, "Maximina"); Díaz (Italian minister of war, 1922–24). Unusual.

Armands Latvian. From Herman, Old German, "Army" + "man." Unusual.

Armen Russian. From Herman, Old German, "Army" + "man." Unusual.

Armond French. From Herman, Old German, "Army" + "man." Unusual.

Armoni English, Hebrew/Israeli. From Armon. Unusual.

Armstrong English. Old English, "Man with a strong arm in battle." Unusual.

Arnaud French. From Arnold. Unusual.

Arne Scandinavian. Old German, "Eagle." Oldberg (composer, "Paolo and Francesca"); Tiselius (Swedish, won Nobel Prize for chemistry, 1948); Garborg (Norwegian novelist, wrote on peasant life); Aaaser (Norwegian, holds world record for autographs: 20,000 signatures in 16 hours, 2 minutes, 1982). Unusual. Alternative spellings: Arney, Arnie.

Arno Czech. From Ernest, English, "Vigor" or "earnestness." Holz (German poet, founder of naturalism). Unusual.

Arnold English. Old German (Arnwalt), "Eagle power" or "strong as an eagle." Of Brescia (12th-century Italian, fought corrupt clergy); Schwarzenegger (actor, "Total Recall"); Toynbee (British historian, divided history into 21 developed and five "arrested" civilizations); Lunn, Sir (British skier); Sommerfeld (German physicist). Less popular. Arnie+.

Arnon Hebrew/Israeli. Hebrew, "Rushing stream." Suggests that the child is full of energy. Unusual.

Aroldo Italian. From Harold, Old English, "Army power." Unusual.

Aronek Polish. From Aaron, Hebrew (Aharon), "Teaching" or "singing." Exodus 6:20. Unusual.

Aronne German. From Aaron, Hebrew (Aharon), "Teaching" or "singing." Exodus 6:20. Unusual.

Aronos Russian. From Aaron, Hebrew (Aharon), "Teaching" or "singing." Exodus 6:20. Unusual.

Arpiar Armenian. Armenian, "Sunny" or "of sunshine." Unusual.

Arram Swedish. From Abraham, Hebrew (Avraham), "Exalted father" or "father of a multitude." Genesis 17:4,5. Unusual.

Arrigo Italian. Italian, "Ruler of an estate." Unusual.

Arrio Hispanic. Hispanic, "Warlike." Unusual.

Arrow Hungarian. Latin, "arcus"

("bow"); the word used as a first name. Possibly a reference to Zechariah 9:14. Unusual.

Arry French. From Harold, Old English, "Army power." Unusual.

Arslan Turkish. Turkish, "Lion." Unusual.

Art English. From Arthur. Linkletter (radio and TV personality); Garfunkel (singer); Buchwald (columnist). Less popular.

Artair Scottish. From Arthur. Unusual.

Artek Polish. From Arthur. Unusual.

Artemas English. Greek, "Belonging to Artemis," also known as Diana, goddess of the hunt. Titus 3:12. Ward (American Revolution major general, second in command to Washington). Unusual. Art, Artie+. Alternative spellings: Artemise, Artemus, Artimas, Artimis.

Arthur English. Gaelic, "Rock," "noble," or "lofty hill." Legendary king of the Britons; Conan Doyle, Sir (British author, "Adventures of Sherlock Holmes"); Miller (won Pulitzer Prize for drama, 1949, "Death of a Salesman"); Sullivan, Sir (British composer, collaborated with Gilbert, "Pirates of Penzance"). Less popular. Art, Artie+. Alternative spelling: Arther.

Artie English. From Arthur. Less popular. Alternative spellings: Arte, Arty.

Artis Czech. From Arthur. Unusual.

Arto Finnish. From Arthur. Unusual.

Artur Bulgarian, Estonian, Hungarian, Irish, Norwegian, Polish, Romanian, Russian, Swedish. From Arthur. Unusual.

Arturo Italian, Hispanic. From Arthur. Toscanini (Italian conductor, National Broadcasting Company Symphony); Rawson (Argentine commander of cavalry, 1942); Alessandri Palma (president of Chile, 1920–25, 1932–38). Unusual.

Arve Norwegian. Norwegian, "Heir" or "inheritor of property." Unusual.

Arvid Swedish. Scandinavian, "Man of the people." Afzelius (Swedish, collected folk songs); Horn, Count (Swedish army general for Charles XII). Unusual.

Asa Hebrew/Israeli. Hebrew, "Physician." 1 Kings 15:11. Randolph (vice-president of AFL-CIO, 1955–79, organized largest civil rights demonstration in history, 1963); Whitney (invented cast-iron railroad car wheel); Hartford (British soccer player); Candler (bought Coca-Cola formula and built major business). Unusual.

Asʿad Arabic. Arabic, "Lion." Shirkuh (Kurdish general, commanded Syrian armies against Crusaders, 1163–69). Unusual.

Asadel Arabic. Arabic, "Most prosperous one." Unusual.

Ash English. From Ashley, Old English, "Ash wood" or "ash-tree meadow." Unusual.

Ashby English. English, "Farm by the ash trees." Originally a surname taken from a place name. Unusual.

Asher Hebrew/Israeli. Hebrew, "Happy" or "fortunate." Genesis 30:13. Eighth son of Jacob, the second with Zilpah; Durand (19th-century landscape painter, co-founder of Hudson River school); Benjamin (19th-century colonial-style architect, wrote "Practical House Carpenter," 1830). Unusual. Alternative spelling: Ashur.

Ashlea See under Girls' Names.

Ashlee See Ashley under Girls' Names.

Ashley See under Girls' Names.

Ashlin English. Old English, "From the pool amidst the ash trees." Unusual. Alternative spelling: Ashlen.

Ashon African. African, "Seventh-born son." Unusual.

Ashton English. English, "Ash-tree farm." Surname and place name used as a first name. Unusual for males, unusual for females.

ʿAsid Arabic. From Asʿad. Unusual. Alternative spelling: Assid.

Asiel Hebrew/Israeli. Hebrew, "Created by God." Unusual.

Asker Turkish. Turkish, "Soldier." Unusual.

Aston English. "Eastern settlement"; origin unknown. A surname and place name used as a first name. Webb, Sir (British architect, designed East facade of Buckingham Palace). Unusual.

Aswad Arabic. Arabic, "Black." Unusual.

Atanazy Polish. From Tanek, Greek, "Immortal." Unusual.

Ate Dutch. Meaning and origin unknown. De Jong (Dutch director, "Drop Dead Fred"). Unusual.

Atek Polish. From Tanek, Greek, "Immortal." Unusual.

Athanasios Greek. From Arthur, Gaelic, "Rock," "noble," or "lofty hill." Unusual.

Athelstan English. Old English, "Noblestone." Tenth-century king of Mercia, Wessex, and Northumbria, established rule over all England; character in Sir Walter Scott's "Ivanhoe." Unusual.

Athol Scottish. Scottish, meaning unknown; a place name used as a first name. Unusual.

Atlantic English. The name of the ocean; origin unknown. Often given to a child born at sea. Unusual.

Atlantis English. English, a legendary island that sank to the bottom of the sea. Unusual.

Atman Indo-Pakistani. Hindi, "Self." Unusual.

Atuanya Nigerian. Nigerian, "We throw the eyes." Implies that the parents expected a daughter instead of a son. Unusual.

Atur English. From Arthur, Gaelic, "Rock," "noble," or "lofty hill." Unusual.

Auberon English. Old German, "Noble bear-like." Unusual.

Aubert French. From Albert, Old English (Aethelbeorht), "Noble-bright." Unusual.

Aubery English. Old German, "Elf-counsel." Unusual. Alternative spellings: Aubary, Aubury.

Aubin French. From Albin, Latin, "White." Unusual.

Aubrey English. Old German, "Elf-counsel." Menen (British author, "Prevalence of Witches"); Beardsley (British illustrator, led 19th-century Aesthetic movement); De Vere (19th-century Irish poet, "Legends of St. Patrick"). Unusual for males, unusual for females.

Auburn English. Latin, "albus" ("white"); the word (describing a reddish-brown color) used as a first name. Unusual.

Audie English. From Edward, Old English, "Property guardian." Murphy (most decorated soldier in WWII). Unusual.

Audley English. English, surname and place name used as a first name. Unusual.

Audr Norwegian. From Otto, Old German, "Possessions." Unusual.

Audric French. From Aldrich, Old English, "Wise ruler." Unusual.

Audun Scandinavian. Scandinavian, "Deserted" or "desolate." Unusual.

August English. From Augustus. Wilson (won Pulitzer Prize for drama, 1980, "Piano Lesson"); Wilhelmj (German violinist); Macke (German expressionist painter, "Promenade"); Strindberg (Swedish naturalist playwright); Michalske (pro football guard, member of Hall of Fame). Unusual. Gus.

Augustin English. From Augustus. Le Prince (British photographer); Pajou (French sculptor, "Psyche"); de Rojas Villandrando (Spanish playwright); Thierry (French historian). Unusual. Gus.

Augustine English. From Augustus. Of Canterbury (saint); of Hippo (saint); Baker (Welsh, Benedictine author, "Holy Practices"); Birrell (British politician, established National University of Ireland). Unusual. Gus.

Augustus English. Latin, "Venerable" or "majestic." First Roman emperor; King of Poland (I, 1548-III, 1734); Saint-Gaudens (sculptor, "Lincoln"); Siebe (invented modern diving suit); Thomas (playwright, "Burglar"); Toplady (British hymn writer, "Rock of Ages"); Waller (British physiologist). Unusual. Gus.

Aulay Scottish. Gaelic, "Ancestor" or "forefather." Unusual.

Aurek Polish. Latin, "Golden-haired." Unusual.

Aurel Czech, Russian. From Aurek. Stein, Sir (British archaeologist, discovered Cave of the Thousand Buddhas). Unusual.

Aurèle French. From Aurek. Unusual.

Aureli Polish. From Aurek. Unusual.

Aurelian Romanian. From Aurek. Roman emperor, 270–75 B.C. Unusual.

Aurelio Italian. From Aurek. Unusual.

Aurelius German. From Aurek. Prudentius (Latin Christian poet, "Psychomachia"). Unusual.

Austin English. From Augustus, Latin, "Venerable" or "majestic." Palmer (educator, originated Palmer method of handwriting); Clarke (Irish poet); Dobson (British poet, "Vignettes in Rhyme"); Flint (physician, discovered heart murmur); Carr (Notre Dame basketball player, scored record 61 points in Division 1 tournament). Less popular for males, less popular for females. Alternative spellings: Austen, Austyn.

Avel Greek. Greek, "Breath." Unusual.

Averell English. From Averil, Old English, "Boar" + "battle." May also be related to the month of April. Harriman (secretary of commerce under Truman). Unusual. Alternative spellings: Averel, Avrel.

Avery English. From Alfred, Old English, "Elf-counsel." Hopwood (playwright, "Why Men Leave Home"); Brundage (president of International Olympic Committee, 1952–72). Less popular for males, unusual for females.

Avi Hebrew/Israeli. Hebrew, "My father" or "my God." Unusual.

Avidan Hebrew/Israeli. Hebrew, "God is just" or "Father of justice." Unusual.

Avidor Hebrew/Israeli. Hebrew, "Father of a generation." Refers to God. Unusual.

Aviel Hebrew/Israeli. Hebrew, "God is my Father." Unusual.

Avital Hebrew/Israeli. From Abital, Hebrew, "My father is dew." Unusual for males, unusual for females.

Aviv Hebrew/Israeli. Hebrew, "Youth," "spring," or "freshness." Unusual.

Avner Hebrew/Israeli. From Abner, Hebrew, "Father of light." 1 Samuel 14:50. Unusual.

Avniel Hebrew/Israeli. Hebrew, "My Father is my rock" or "My Father is my strength." Unusual.

Avraham Hebrew/Israeli. Hebrew, "Exalted father" or "father of a multitude." Genesis 17:4, 5. Unusual.

Avram Bulgarian, Hebrew/Israeli. From Abraham, Hebrew (Avraham), "Exalted father" or "father of a multitude." Genesis 17:4,5. Original name of Avraham, first Hebrew patriarch. Unusual.

Avreliy Russian. From Aurek. Unusual.

Avrum Yiddish. From Abraham, Hebrew (Avraham), "Exalted father" or "father of a multitude." Genesis 17:4,5. Unusual.

Awan Native American. Native American, "Somebody." Unusual.

Axel Scandinavian. From Absalom, Hebrew, "My father is peace." Samuel 3:3. Munthe (Swedish author); Oxenstierna, Count (Swedish statesman); Thue (Norwegian mathematician, expert in number theory); Wenner-Gren (Swedish industrialist, Electrolux Company); Brostrom (Swedish, largest shipping company in Scandinavia). Unusual. Alternative spelling: Axell.

Aylmer English. Old English, "Noble" + "famous." Maude (translator of Russian literature). Unusual.

Azad Turkish. Turkish, "Free." Unusual.

Azariah Hebrew/Israeli. Hebrew, "Whom Jehovah helps." King of Judah, 791–39 B.C. Unusual.

Azeem Arabic. From Azim, Arabic, "Defender." Unusual. Alternative spellings: Azim, Aseem, Asim.

Azi Nigerian. Nigerian, "Youth." Unusual.

ʿAzīz Arabic. Arabic, "Strong." Billah Nizar Abu Manṣūr (caliph of Fatimid dynasty, 975–90). Unusual.

Azriel Hebrew/Israeli. Hebrew, "God is my help." Unusual.

Baden English. Old English, surname used as a first name. Unusual.

Bail English. From Bailey, Old French, "Steward" or "bailiff." Unusual.

Bailey English. Old French, "Steward" or "bailiff." Willis (geologist known for studies of earthquakes, erosion, and mountain-building); Ashford (surgeon, discovered hookworms). Unusual for males, unusual for females. Alternative spellings: Bailie, Baillie, Baily, Bayley.

Bain English. From Bainbridge, Gaelic, "Fair bridge" or "direct bridge." Unusual.

Bainbridge English. Gaelic, "Fair bridge" or "direct bridge." Colby (secretary of state under Wilson, 1920). Unusual.

Baird Irish. Gaelic, "A bard" or "a traveling ballad singer." Unusual.

Baker English. Old English, occupational name used as a first name. Unusual.

Bal Unknown. Sanskrit, "A child born with lots of hair." Tilak (Indian nationalist who laid the foundation for India's independence). Unusual.

Balder English. Old Norse, "God of light" or "white god." According to myth, Balder was the son of the god Odin and was killed when touched by a sprig of mistletoe. Unusual. Alternative spelling: Baldur.

Baldwin German. Old German, "Bold friend." Name of five kings of Jerusalem; I (Emperor Constantinople, 1204–05); II (Emperor Constantinople, 1228–61). Unusual.

Bale French. From Basil, Greek, "Kingly." Unusual.

Bali Indo-Pakistani. From Balin. Unusual.

Balin Indo-Pakistani. Hindi, "Mighty soldier." According to myth, Balin is a tyrannical monkey king with the power to extract half the strength from anyone who challenges him. Unusual.

Ballabh Das Indo-Pakistani. Hindi, "Slave of Ballabh," a god. Unusual.

Ballas Hungarian. Hungarian, "Stammerer." Unusual.

Balta Hispanic. From Bartholomew, Aramaic, "Son of Tolmai." An alternate name for the apostle Nathaniel. Unusual.

Bambis Greek. From Henry, Old German (Heimerich), "Home ruler." Unusual.

Bandi Hungarian. From Andrew, Greek, "Manly." Unusual.

Bane Hawaiian. From Barnabas, Hebrew, "Son of consolation or exhortation." Unusual.

Bao Chinese. Chinese, "Treasure." Unusual for males, unusual for females.

Baram Hebrew/Israeli. From Abraham, Hebrew (Avraham), "Exalted father" or "father of a multitude." Genesis 17:4,5. Unusual.

Barclay Scottish. From Berkeley, English, surname and place name used as a first name; originally indicated someone living near a birch wood. Unusual.

Bard Irish. From Baird, Gaelic, "A bard" or "a traveling ballad singer." Unusual.

Bardo Danish. From Bartholomew, Aramaic, "Son of Tolmai." An alternate name for the apostle Nathaniel. Unusual.

Barker English. Old English, "Shepherd" or "tanner." Unusual.

Barn English. From Barnabas, Hebrew, "Son of consolation or exhortation." Unusual.

Barna Hungarian. From Barnabas. Unusual.

Barnabas English. Hebrew, "Son of consolation or exhortation." Apostle and saint; Collins (character in "Dark Shadows"); Sears (attorney). Unusual. Barney+.

Barnabe French. From Barnabas. Rich (British soldier and writer of short stories, military works, and commentaries on manners and morals); Barnes (British lyric poet); Googe (British poet). Unusual.

Barnaby English, Polish. From Barnabas; or from Bartholomew, Aramaic, "Son of Tolmai." An alternate name for the apostle Nathaniel. Ross (novelist, created detective Drury Lane; also published Ellery Queen's Mystery Magazine) (real name: Manfred Lee); Jones (television detective). Unusual.

Barnard English. From Bernard, Old German, "Bear-brave." Bee (soldier, gave General Thomas J. Jackson the nickname "Stonewall"). Unusual. Barney+.

Barnebas Hispanic. From Barnabas. Unusual.

Barnes English. Old English, surname and place name used as a first name. Originally indicated residence near barns. Unusual.

Barnett English. From Barnet. Newman (painter, abstract expressionist movement, known for paintings of simplified forms and large color areas). Unusual. Alternative spelling: Barnet.

Barney English. From Barnabas. Clark (first to receive artificial heart, the Jarvik 7; lived for 112 days after the operation); Barnato (British diamond speculator). Less popular. Alternative spellings: Barnie, Barny.

Baron English. Old English, "A warrior" or "baron." Unusual. Alternative spelling: Barron.

Barrett English. From Barret. Wendell (educator and writer on education). Unusual. Alternative spelling: Barret.

Barri See Barrie under Girls' Names.

Barrie See under Girls' Names.

Barrington English. English, surname used as a first name. Unusual.

Barry English. Irish, "Spear." Saint; Gibb (song writer, member of Bee Gees, has written or co-written 16 number-one hits); Manilow (singer and songwriter); Sanders (1988 Heisman trophy winner, running back for Detroit Lions); Fitzgerald (Irish actor, won Oscar, 1944). Less popular.

Barrymore English. English, surname used as a first name. Unusual.

Bart English. From Bartholomew. Starr (quarterback and coach of Green Bay Packers); Connor (gymnast). Less popular.

Barta Hungarian. From Bartholomew. Unusual.

Bartel English, German. From Bartholomew. Unusual.

Bartek Czech, Polish. From Bartholomew. Unusual.

Barth Dutch, from Bartholomew; and Hebrew/Israeli, Hebrew, "Farmer." Anthony van der Leck (Dutch artist, known for pottery and stained glass). Unusual.

Barthel German. From Bartholomew. Unusual.

Barthelemy Swedish. From Bartholomew. Boganda (African politician, laid groundwork for creation of the Central African Republic); Schérer (French Revolution general); Thimonnier (French tailor, patented first sewing machine in France); Faujas de Saint-Fond (French geologist). Unusual.

Barthélmy French. From Bartholomew. Unusual.

Bartholome French. From Bartholomew. Unusual.

Bartholomew English. Aramaic, "Son of Tolmai." An alternate name for the apostle Nathaniel. Apostle and patron saint of tanners and leatherworkers; of Farne (saint); Young (16th-century British translator); Warburton (Irish novelist, "Darien"); Legate (British, last person to die in London because of religious beliefs, 1612). Less popular. Bart.

Bartholomieu French. From Bartholomew. Unusual.

Bartle English. From Bartholomew. Unusual.

Bartlett English. From Bartholomew. Unusual.

Barto Czech, Hispanic. From Bartholomew. Unusual.

Bartol German. From Bartholomew. Unusual.

Bartoli Hispanic. From Bartholomew. Unusual.

Bartolo Hispanic. From Bartholomew. of Saxoferrato (14th-century Italian jurist and professor at Perugia). Unusual.

Bartolomé Hispanic. From Bartholomew. Murillo (Spanish painter of religious works); Mitre (president of Argentina, 1862–68); Ordóñez (Spanish sculptor, organizer of Spanish school of Renaissance sculpture); Bermejo (Spanish painter, "La Piedad"); de Carranza (Spanish theologian). Unusual.

Barton English. Old English, surname used as a first name; refers to a place where barley was grown. Stone (clergyman, led "New Light" Presbyterian movement, founded "Christian Messenger"); Booth (British actor); MacLane (actor, "The Outlaws"). Less popular. Bart.

Bartos Polish. From Bartholomew. Unusual.

Bartz Czech. From Bartholomew. Unusual.

Baruch Hebrew/Israeli. Hebrew, "Blessed." Friend of and secretary to the prophet Jeremiah; Spinoza (17th-century Dutch philosopher, regarded as leading developer of rational pantheism). Unusual.

Barzillai English. Hebrew, "Of iron." 2 Samuel 19:31. Unusual.

Bas English. From Basil. Unusual.

Basil English. Greek, "Kingly." Saint; Liddell Hart (British military strategist and historian); of Ancyra (Greek prelate and theologian); Spence (British architect, designed Coventry cathedral); Rathbone (actor, "The Adventures of Sherlock Holmes"). Unusual. Alternative spelling: Bazyl.

Basile French. From Basil. Unusual.

Basilio Hispanic, Italian, Portuguese. From Basil. Unusual.

Basilios Greek. From Basil. Unusual.

Basilius Swedish. From Basil. Unusual.

Basir Turkish. Turkish, "Intelligent and discerning." Unusual.

Basle German, Swedish. From Basil. Unusual.

Bassett English. Old English, surname used as a first name. Unusual.

Bat English. From Bartholomew, Aramaic, "Son of Tolmai." An alternate name for the apostle Nathaniel. Unusual.

Baudier French. From Balder, Old Norse, "God of light" or "white god." According to myth, Balder was the son of the god Odin and was killed when touched by a sprig of mistletoe. Unusual.

Baul Gypsy. English Gypsy, "Snail." Unusual.

Bavol Gypsy. English Gypsy, "Wind" or "air." Unusual.

Bay Vietnamese. Vietnamese, "Seventh-born child." Also given to a child born on Saturday or in July. Unusual.

Bayard French. Old French, "Bay horse." Unusual.

Bayley English. From Bailey, Old French, "Steward" or "bailiff." Unusual.

Bazek Polish. From Basil. Unusual.

Bazel Hungarian. From Basil. Unusual.

Bazil Czech. From Basil. Unusual.

Bearnard English. From Bernard, Old German, "Bear-brave." Unusual.

Beatham Scottish. From Benjamin, Hebrew (Benyamin), "Son of my right hand." Genesis 35:18. Unusual.

Beau English. French, "Handsome." Bridges (actor, "The Fabulous Baker Boys"). Unusual.

Beaumont English. French, "Beautiful hill or mountain." Unusual.

Beck Swiss. Middle English, "Brook." Unusual.

Bede English. Old English, "Prayer." Patron saint of scholars, known as "The Venerable." Unusual.

Bedford English. English, surname and place name used as a first name. Unusual.

Bedřich Czech. From Frederick, Old German, "Peaceful ruler." Smetana (Czech composer); Hrozný (Czech archaeologist and Orientalist). Unusual.

Bela Czech. From Blanche, French, "White." Name of four kings of Hungary, Arpad dynasty, 1060–1270; Matina (one of the shortest twins ever: 30 inches); Lugosi (actor, "Murders in the Rue Morgue"); Schick (physician, discovered test for diphtheria susceptibility); Imredy (Hungarian politician); Bartók (Hungarian modernist conductor). Unusual for males, unusual for females.

Beldon English. Old English, "Child of the beautiful glen." Unusual. Alternative spellings: Belden, Beldin.

Belen Greek. Greek, "An arrow." Unusual.

Bell English. Old English, surname used as a first name. Unusual for males, unusual for females.

Bello African. African, "Helper" (or promoter) of Islam. Unusual.

Bem African. Nigerian, "Peace." Unusual.

Ben English. From Benjamin. Hecht (actor); Moreell (WWII naval officer); Nicholson (British painter); Travers (British playwright, "The Bed Before Yesterday"); Greet, Sir (British Shakespearean actor). Less popular. Alternative spelling: Benn.

Ben-Ahmed Arabic. Arabic, "Son of Ahmed." Unusual.

Benci Hungarian. From Benedict. Unusual. Alternative spelling: Bence.

Bendek Polish. From Benedict. Unusual.

Bendix English. From Benedict. Unusual.

Benedek Hungarian. From Benedict. Unusual.

Benedetto Italian. From Benedict. da Maiano (Italian sculptor); Marcello (Italian composer, "Oboe Concerto in D Minor"); Pistrucci (Italian gem engraver and medalist); Zaccaria (Genoese merchant, diplomat and admiral); Ferrari (Italian poet and composer). Unusual.

Benedict English. Latin, "Blessed." Patron saint of monks and speleologists; Labre (patron saint of the homeless); of Biscop (patron saint of learning); name of 15 popes. Unusual. Alternative spelling: Benedick.

Benedicto Hispanic. From Benedict. Unusual.

Benedik Hungarian. From Benedict. Unusual.

Benedikt Bulgarian, Czech, German, Russian. From Benedict. Carpzov (17th-century Saxon jurist). Unusual.

Benedo Russian. From Benedict. Unusual.

Benek Polish. From Benedict. Unusual.

Bengt Scandinavian. From Benedict. Unusual.

Beni Hispanic. From Benedict. Unusual.

Beniamin Polish. From Benjamin. Unusual.

Beniamino Italian. From Benjamin. Gigli (Italian operatic tenor). Unusual.

Benitín Hispanic. From Benedict. Unusual.

Benito Hispanic. From Benedict. Lynch (Argentine novelist); Mussolini (Italian dictator); Pérez Galdós (Spanish novelist and playwright); Feijoo y Montenegro (18th-century Spanish Benedictine monk and scholar, led educational reawakening); Juárez (19th-century Mexican revolutionary, later president). Unusual.

Benja Hispanic. From Benjamin. Unusual.

Benjamin English. Hebrew (Benyamin), "Son of my right hand." Genesis 35:18. Twelfth son of Jacob, second with Rachel; Holt (invented tractor); Kubelsky (real name of entertainer Jack Benny); Britten (British composer, "Peter Grimes"); Franklin (invented bifocal lens, lightning rod); Harrison (23rd president); Spock (child-care expert). Popular. Ben, Benny. Alternative spellings: Benejaman, Benjamen, Banjamon, Benjiman, Benjimon.

Benjy English. From Benjamin. Unusual. Ben.

Benke Hungarian. From Benedict. Unusual.

Bennett English. From Benedict. Cerf (publisher and editor, regular panelist on game show "What's My Line?"). Less popular. Alternative spelling: Bennet.

Benny English. From Benjamin. Goodman (big-band leader); Leonard (1917 world lightweight champion); Davis (songwriter, "Baby Face"). Less popular. Alternative spelling: Bennie.

Beno Hungarian. From Benjamin. Gutenberg (seismologist). Unusual.

Benoist French. From Benedict. Unusual.

Benoît French. From Benedict. Fourneyron (19th-century French hydraulic engineer, built first water turbine, 1827). Unusual.

Benson English. Latin, surname used as a first name. Dubois (character in TV's "Benson"). Unusual. Alternative spelling: Bensen.

Bent Scandinavian. From Benedict. Unusual.

Bentley English. Old English, surname and place name used as a first name. Unusual.

Benton English. Old English, "Moor-dweller." Unusual.

Benyamin Hebrew/Israeli. Hebrew, "Son of my right hand." Genesis 35:18. Unusual.

Benzi Hebrew/Israeli. Hebrew, "Excellent son." Unusual.

Beppi German. From Joseph, Hebrew (Yosef), "God will add." Unusual.

Berdy Russian. From Hubert, Old German (Hugibert), "Mind" + "bright" or "shining." Unusual.

Berend German. From Bernard, Old German, "Bear-brave." Unusual.

Beresford English. English, surname and place name used as a first name. Unusual. Alternative spelling: Berresford.

Berg English. German, "Mountain." Unusual.

Berger English. French, "Mountain dweller" or "shepherd." Unusual.

Berk Turkish. Turkish, "Solid," firm," or "rugged." Unusual.

Berkeley English. English, surname and place name used as a first name; originally indicated someone living near a birch wood. Moynihan (British surgeon, author, and president Royal College of Surgeons, 1926–32). Unusual. Alternative spelling: Berkley.

Bern English. From Bernard. Unusual.

Bernabé Hispanic. From Barnabas, Hebrew, "Son of consolation or exhortation." Unusual.

Bernal English. Old German, "Bear-power." Díaz del Castillo (Spanish soldier and historian). Unusual.

Bernard English. Old German, "Bear-brave." Patron saint of bee-keepers; of Aosta (patron saint of mountain climbers); Malamud (author, "The Natural"); Goetz (New York subway vigilante); Rich (drummer) (real name of Buddy Rich); Schwartz (real name of actor Tony Curtis). Less popular. Bernie+. Alternative spelling: Burnard.

Bernardas Lithuanian. From Bernard. Unusual.

Bernardel Hispanic. From Bernard. Unusual.

Bernardin French. From Bernard. Unusual.

Bernardino Italian. From Bernard. Of Sienna (patron saint of advertisers, preachers, and weavers); Luini (16th-century Italian painter and fresco artist, "Birth of Christ"); Machado (Portuguese president, 1925–26); Ochino (Italian theologian and reformer); Rivadavia (Argentine politician). Unusual.

Bernardo Hispanic, Italian. From Bernard. Bertolucci (director, "The Sheltering Sky"); Sáda Bandeira (premier of Portugal, 1865, 68–69, 70–71); Rossellino (15th-century Florentine sculptor, especially of church facades); Strozzi (16th-century baroque Italian painter); Vittone (18th-century rococo Italian architect, especially churches). Unusual.

Bernardyn Polish. From Bernard. Unusual.

Bernarr English. From Bernard. Macfadden (physical culturist and publisher, founder of Cosmotorianism, "the happiness religion"). Unusual.

Bernat Hungarian. From Bernard. Metge (Catalan poet). Unusual.

Bernek Czech. From Bernard. Unusual.

Bernel English. From Bernal, Old German, "Bear-power." Unusual.

Berngards Latvian, Russian. From Bernard. Unusual.

Bernhard Latvian. From Bernard. Bolzano (Austrian mathematician); Malmstrom (Swedish poet, "Angelika"); Romberg (German cellist and composer); Schmidt (invented photographic telescope). Unusual.

Bernhards Latvian. From Bernard. Unusual.

Berno Czech. From Bernard. Unusual.

Berresford English. From Beresford, English, surname and place name used as a first name. Unusual.

Berry English. English, "Flower." Less popular for males, unusual for females.

Bersh Gypsy. English Gypsy, "One year." Unusual.

Bertalan Hungarian. From Bartholomew, Aramaic, "Son of Tolmai." An alternate name for the apostle Nathaniel. Unusual.

Bertel German. From Bartholomew, Aramaic, "Son of Tolmai." An alternate name for the apostle Nathaniel. Thorvaldsen (Danish sculptor); Gripenberg (Finnish poet). Unusual.

Berthold English. Old German, "Bright-power." Delbrück (Greek linguist); Schwarz (14th-century German alchemist and monk, sometimes credited with inventing gunpowder). Unusual.

Berti English, from Bertram; and Hungarian, from Bartholomew, Aramaic, "Son of Tolmai." An alternate name for the apostle Nathaniel. Unusual. Alternative spellings: Bertie, Birtie, Birty, Burty.

Bertín Hispanic. Spanish, "Distinguished friend." Unusual.

Berto Hispanic. From Albert, Old English (Aethelbeorht), "Noble-bright." Unusual.

Bertram English. Old German, "Bright-raven." Mills (British circus owner); Schrieke (Dutch social anthropologist); Boltwood (scientist, specialized in radioactivity); Goodhue (architect, designed several American cathedrals, the United States Military Academy, and West Point). Less popular. Bert.

Bertrand English. French, "Bright-shield." de Bar-sur-Aube (French poet); Malegue (holds record for 24-hour swim in a 50-meter pool: 54.39 miles, 1980); Russell (British mathematician and philosopher); Dawson (British physician). Less popular. Bert.

Berty Czech. From Bertram. Unusual.

Berwin English. Middle English, "Friend of the harvest." Unusual. Alternative spelling: Berwyn.

Besh Gypsy. From Bersh, English Gypsy, "One year." Unusual.

Bethel Hebrew/Israeli. Hebrew, "House of God." Unusual for males, unusual for females. Alternative spelling: Bethell.

Betto Italian. From Benedict, Latin, "Blessed." Unusual.

Beval Gypsy. English Gypsy, "Like the wind." Unusual.

Bevan Welsh. Welsh, surname used as a first name. Unusual. Alternative spelling: Bevin.

Beverley See Beverly under Girls' Names.

Bevis English. Old French, place name used as a first name. Unusual.

Biagio Italian. From Blaze, Latin, "Stammerer." Unusual.

Bilal Arabic. Arabic, "Chosen." Unusual.

Bill English. From William, Old German, "Will" + "helmet." Cosby (highest-paid TV performer: $92 million, 1987–88); Murray (actor, "Saturday Night Live" and many movies); Robinson (tap dancer, known as "Mr. Bo Jangles"); Bixby (actor, "The Incredible Hulk"). Less popular.

Billy English. From William, Old German, "Will" + "helmet." Crystal (comedian and actor); Martin (five-time manager of Yankees); Wilder (actor); Joel (pop-rock singer); Carter (brother of President Jimmy). Less popular.

Billy Joe English. English, combination of Billy (William, Old German, "Will" + "helmet") + Joe (Joseph, Hebrew (Yosef), "God will add"). Less popular.

Billy Ray English. English, combination of Billy (William, Old German, "Will" + "helmet") and + Raymond (Old German, "Wise protector"). Less popular.

Bing Created. Created, meaning and origin unknown. Crosby (most successful solo recording artist and actor: sold as many as 300 million records) (real name: Harry Lillis Crosby). Unusual.

Binh Vietnamese. Vietnamese, "Piece." Unusual.

Bink English. From Vincent, Latin, "Vincentius," from "vincere" ("to conquer"). Unusual.

Binkentios Greek. From Vincent, Latin, "Vincentius," from "vincere" ("to conquer"). Unusual.

Binns Unknown. Surname used as a first name; origin unknown. Unusual.

Binyamin Yiddish. From Benjamin, Hebrew (Benyamin), "Son of my right hand." Genesis 35:18. Unusual.

Birch English. Old English, "Birch tree." Bayh (senator). Unusual.

Birt English. From Bertram. Unusual.

Bjorn Scandinavian. Scandinavian, "Bear." Borg (greatest number of tennis singles wins: 5 consecutively); Lokken (longest distance skied in 48 hours: 319 miles, 205 yards, 1982); Healland-Hansen (Norwegian oceanographer). Unusual.

Blackburn English. English, place name used as a first name. Unusual.

Blaine English. Scottish, surname used as a first name. Unusual. Alternative spelling: Blain.

Blair See under Girls' Names.

Blaise English. Latin, "Crippled" or "stuttering." Patron saint of throat sufferers; Pascal (17th-century French scientist and philosopher, invented a mechanical calculator (forerunner of the digital computer), the syringe, and the hydraulic press). Unusual.

Blaisot French. From Blaze. Unusual.

Blake English. Old English, "Pale" or "black." Edwards (director, "Breakfast at Tiffany's," "10"); Carrington (character in TV's "Dynasty"). Popular. Alternative spelling: Blaike.

Blane Irish. Gaelic, "Lean." Saint. Unusual. Alternative spelling: Blayne.

Blas Hispanic. From Blaze. Unusual.

Blasi German. From Blaze. Unusual.

Blasius German. From Blaze. Unusual.

Blaz Serbian. From William, Old German, "Will" + "helmet." Unusual.

Blaze English. Latin, "Stammerer." Unusual. Alternative spelling: Blase.

Blazek Polish. From Blaze. Unusual.

Bly Native American. Native American, "High." Among some Native Americans, a child was given this name in the hopes he or she would grow tall. Unusual for males, unusual for females.

Bo English. Chinese, "Precious." Jackson (1985 Heisman Memorial trophy winner); Goldman (screenplay writer). Less popular for males, less popular for females.

Boaz English. Hebrew, "Fleetness." Unusual.

Bob English. From Robert, Old English (Hreodbeorht), "Fame-bright." Hope (comedian); Guccione (publisher, "Penthouse"); Dylan (rock singer); Barker (TV game show host, "The Price is Right"); Newhart (actor, "Newhart"). Less popular.

Bobbi See Bobbie under Girls' Names.

Bobbie See under Girls' Names.

Bobby English. From Robert, Old English (Hreodbeorht), "Fame-bright." Darin (singer, member of Rock-and-Roll Hall of Fame); Brown (singer, "My Prerogative"); McFerrin (singer, "Don't Worry, Be Happy"); Hull (hockey player, retired from Chicago Blackhawks); Ewing (character in TV's "Dallas"). Less popular for males, unusual for females.

Bobby Joe English. English, combination of Bobby (Robert, Old English, "Bright-fame") + Joe (Joseph, Hebrew (Yosef), "God will add"). Less popular.

Bobby Lee English. English, combination of Bobby (Robert, Old English, "Bright-fame") + Lee (English, "Wood," "clearing," or "meadow"). Less popular.

Bobby Ray English. English, combination of Bobby (Robert, Old English, "Bright-fame") + Ray (Raymond, Old German, "Wise protector"). Less popular.

Bobek Czech. From Robert, Old English (Hreodbeorht), "Fame-bright." Unusual.

Bodil Norwegian. Norwegian, "Commanding." Unusual.

Bódog Hungarian. From Felix, Latin, "Happy," "fortunate," or "lucky." Unusual.

Bodua African. African, "An animal's tail." Unusual.

Bogdan English. From Donald, Gaelic (Domhnall), "Mighty in the world." Hăsdeu (Romanian archivist and philologist). Unusual.

Bogdashka Ukrainian. From Donald, Gaelic (Domhnall), "Mighty in the world." Unusual.

Bogomir Serbian. From Geoffrey, Old German (Gottfried), "peace" (?). Unusual.

Bohdan Ukrainian. From Donald, Gaelic (Domhnall), "Mighty in the world." Khmelnytsky (17th-century Cossack leader who led Ukrainian uprising). Unusual.

Bolton English. English, place name used as a first name. Unusual.

Bonar Scottish. Old French, "Gentle." Unusual.

Bond English. Old English, "Tiller of the soil." Unusual. Alternative spelling: Bonde.

Bondon English. From Bond. Unusual.

Bonds English. From Bond. Unusual.

Boniface English. Latin, "Of good fate." Saint; of Savoy (saint, archbishop of Canterbury 1243–70); Pope (I, 418-422; IX, 1389–1404). Unusual.

Booth English. English, surname used as a first name; origin unknown. Tarkington (novelist, "Alice Adams"). Unusual.

Borg Scandinavian. Old Norse, "One who lives in a castle." Unusual.

Boris Slavic. Russian, "Battle," "fight." Saint and martyr; Rosing (Russian, invented "electric vision," predecessor to TV); Shakhlin (Russian, won most individual titles in World Championship gymnastics: 10 in 10 years); Karloff (actor); Yeltsin (Russian leader); Pasternak (novelist, "Doctor Zhivago"). Unusual.

Botan Japanese. Japanese, "Peony." Unusual.

Bour African. African, "Rock," implying strength. Unusual.

Bow Irish. From Bowen. Unusual.

Bowen Irish. Gaelic, "Small, victorious one." Unusual.

Bowie Irish. From Bowen. Kuhn (former baseball commissioner). Unusual.

Boy English. Middle English, the word used as a first name. Unusual.

Boyce French. French, "Wood." Unusual.

Boyd Scottish. Gaelic, "Yellow hair." Raeburn (jazz band leader). Unusual.

Brad English. From Bradley. Less popular. Alternative spelling: Bradd.

Bradburn English. Old English, "From the broad brook." Unusual.

Braden English. English, "A broad lea" (a meadow). Unusual. Alternative spellings: Bradon, Braeden, Brayden, Braydon.

Bradford English. English, a water crossing; place name used as a first name. Dillman (actor, "The Way We Were"). Unusual. Brad.

Bradley English. Old English, "Broad clearing." Fiske (invented electronic systems for warships). Very popular. Brad. Alternative spellings: Bradlee, Bradly.

Bradshaw English. Old English, "Large forest." Unusual.

Brady English. English, surname used as a first name. Unusual.

Bram Dutch. From Abraham, Hebrew (Avraham), "Exalted father" or "father of a multitude." Genesis 17:4,5. Stoker (Irish novelist, created Count Dracula). Unusual.

Bramwell English. English, "Broom well." Unusual.

Bran English. From Brandon. Unusual.

Brand Czech. From Brandeis. Whitlock (mayor of Toledo, Ohio, 1905–11). Unusual. Alternative spelling: Brandt.

Brandeis Czech. Czech, "Dweller on a burned clearing." Unusual.

Brandon English. Old English, "Sword" or "flaming hill." Stoddard (director, ABC network production); de Wilde (actor, "The Member of the Wedding"); Tartikoff (NBC network executive). Very popular. Alternative spellings: Brandan, Branden, Brandin, Brandun, Brandyn.

Brant Czech. From Brandeis. Unusual.

Branwell English. From Bramwell, English, "Broom well." Unusual.

Braxton English. Old English, "Brock's town." Bragg (general, military advisor to Confederate president Jefferson Davis). Unusual.

Brede Scandinavian. Scandinavian, "Glacier." Unusual.

Bren English. From Brendan. Unusual.

Brencis Latvian. From Laurence, Latin, "Crowned with laurel." Unusual.

Brendan English. Irish, "Stinking hair." the Navigator (saint); Gill (journalist and author, "Here at the New Yorker"); Behan (Irish playwright). Less popular. Alternative spellings: Brenden, Brendin, Brendon.

Brennan English. Irish, "Raven." Unusual. Alternative spelling: Brennen.

Brent English. English, "High place" (?). Tarleton (character in "Gone With the Wind"); Scowcroft (national security advisor); Mydland (keyboard player for the Grateful Dead); Musburger (sportscaster). Popular.

Brenton English. From Brent. Unusual.

Bret English. From Brett, Latin (Britto), "Briton." Harte (shortstory author); Hull (hockey player, St. Louis Blues); Easton Ellis (author, "Less than Zero"); Maverick (TV cowboy). Unusual. Alternative spelling: Brett.

Bretton English. From Brett, Latin (Britto), "Briton." Unusual.

Brewster English. English, surname used as a first name. Unusual.

Brian English. Celtic, "Strong," "virtuous," "honorable." Dennehy (actor, "F/X"); DePalma (director); Wilson (singer, Beach Boys); Piccalo (former running back, Chicago Bears); Boitano (1988 world figure skating champion). Popular. Alternative spellings: Brien, Brion, Bryan, Bryon.

Briano Italian. From Brian. Unusual.

Bridger English. From Bainbridge, Gaelic, "Fair bridge" or "direct bridge." Unusual.

Brigham English. English, place name used as a first name. Young (religious leader, first governor of Territory of Utah, 1849–57). Unusual.

Brighton English. English, place name used as a first name. Unusual.

Brinley English. Old English, "Burnt wood." Unusual. Alternative spellings: Brindley, Brinly, Brynley, Brynly.

Brishen Gypsy. English Gypsy, "Born during a rain." Unusual.

Britt See under Girls' Names.

Britton English. From Britannia, Latin, the feminine personification of Britain on coins, etc. Unusual.

Brock English. Old English, "Badger." Adams (secretary of transportation under Carter); Peters (actor, "The Adventures of Huckleberry Finn"). Unusual. Alternative spelling: Broc.

Broderick Scottish. Norse, "Brother." The name once given to a second son. Less popular.

Brodny Slavic. Slavic, "One who lives near a shallow stream crossing"; place name used as a first name. Unusual.

Brody Scottish. From Broderick. The name once given to a second son. Unusual. Alternative spellings: Brodi, Brodie.

Bron African. African, "Source." Unusual.

Bronson English. Old English, "Son of the dark-skinned one." Howard (playwright, "Peter Stuyvesant"); Pinchot (actor, "Perfect Strangers"). Less popular.

Bronwen Welsh. Welsh, "White breast." Unusual.

Brook English. Old English, "Dweller by the brook." Taylor (18th-century mathematician, established the calculus of finite differences). Unusual.

Brooks English. From Brook. Adams (historian and author); Stevens (modernistic product designer: Hiawatha railcar, 1950 Roadmaster bicycle). Unusual. Alternative spelling: Brookes.

Bruce English. Scottish, surname used as a first name. Springsteen (rock singer); Willis (actor, "Die Hard"); McLaren (youngest driver to win Formula I Grand Prix: 22 years old, 1959); Hornsby (musician); Catton (author, "A Stillness at Appomattox"). Less popular.

Bruno English. Old German, "Of dark complexion" or "brown." Saint; the Great (10th-century Greek prelate); Barreto (Brazilian director); Maderna (Italian avant-garde, electronic composer); Abakanowicz (19th-century Lithuanian mathematician, invented integraph); Walter (conductor). Less popular.

Bruns German. German, "Dark" or "brown-haired one." Unusual.

Bryant English. From Brian. Less popular. Alternative spelling: Briant.

Bryce English. Celtic, meaning unknown. Unusual. Alternative spelling: Brice.

Bryden English. Place name used as a first name; meaning and origin unknown. Unusual.

Brynmor Welsh. Welsh, "Great hill." Unusual.

Bryson English. English, "Son of a nobleman." Unusual.

Buck English. From Penelope, Greek, "Bobbin" or "weaver." Freeman (played 534 consecutive games for Boston Red Sox, a record prior to 1987, when the new record became 927); Henry (TV writer); Owens (country singer). Less popular.

Bud English. From Buddy. Abbott (comedian); Grant (former Minnesota Vikings football coach); Anderson (character in TV's "Father Knows Best"). Unusual.

Buddy English. Old English, "Friend" or "companion." Less popular. Bud.

Budington English. Meaning and origin unknown. Swanson (novelist, wrote on western Americana). Unusual.

Burke English. Old French, "One who lives at the stronghold or fortress." Marshall (former attorney general). Unusual. Alternative spellings: Birk, Birke, Burk.

Burnett English. From Burnet. Streeter (British theologian and biblical scholar). Unusual. Alternative spellings: Burnet, Burnitt.

Burr Scandinavian. Scandinavian, "Youth." Unusual.

Burt English. From Burton. Bacharach (songwriter); Lancaster (actor, "The Sweet Smell of Success"); Standish (writer of adventure stories) (real name: Gilbert Patten); Wilder (zoologist); Reynolds (actor, "The Longest Yard"). Less popular. Alternative spelling: Bert.

Burton English. English, "Farm near a fort." Wheeler (Montana senator, 1923–47); Hendrick (author, "Lincoln's War Cabinet"); Cummings (singer with the Guess Who); Lane (composer, "Finian's Rainbow"). Less popular. Burt.

Buster English. English, nickname for an active boy, used as a first name. Keaton (actor). Unusual.

Byron English. Old English, "Cow shed" or "barn." Nelson (won record 18 golf tournaments in one season, including a record 11 consecutively, 1945); "Whizzer" White (Supreme Court Justice, 1962-); Haskin (comedian); Johnson (baseball great); Allen (TV host). Less popular.

Cachi Hispanic. From Casimir, Old Slavic, "He announces [or "commands"] peace." Unusual.

Cadao Vietnamese. Vietnamese, "Folk song." Unusual.

Cade Welsh. From Cadel. Unusual.

Cadel Welsh. Welsh, "Battle." Unusual. Alternative spelling: Cadell.

Caesar English. Latin (Caesarius), "Hairy child." Rodney (attorney general under Jefferson). Unusual. Alternative spellings: Caezar, Cesar, Cesare, Seaser, Sezar.

Cahil Turkish. Turkish, "Young," "inexperienced," "naive." Unusual. Alternative spelling: Kahil.

Cai Welsh. From Gaius, Latin, "To rejoice." Unusual.

Cailean Scottish. From Nicholas, Greek, "Victorious people." Unusual.

Cain English. Hebrew, "Spear." Unusual.

Caio Welsh. From Gaius, Latin, "To rejoice." Unusual.

Caius Welsh. From Gaius, Latin, "To rejoice." Pope (283–296); Cibber (17th-century Danish sculptor). Unusual.

Cal English. From Caldwell. Less popular.

Calder English. From Caldwell. Unusual.

Caldwell English. Old English, "Cool, clear spring." Less popular.

Cale English. From Caleb. Unusual.

Caleb English. Hebrew, "Dog." Numbers 13:6. Unusual. Alternative spelling: Kaleb.

Callum Irish. From Columba, Latin, "Dove." Unusual. Alternative spelling: Calum.

Calvert English. Old English, "Calf herder." Vaux (19th-century landscape architect, assisted with Capitol grounds and Central Park). Unusual. Cal.

Calvin English. Latin, "Bald." Klein (fashion designer); Phillips (shortest male dwarf: 26-1/2 inches); Ripken (played record 927 consecutive baseball games through 1987); Coolidge (29th president); Bridges (geneticist, helped prove chromosome theory of heredity). Less popular. Cal. Alternative spelling: Kalvin.

Cam Gypsy. English Gypsy, "Beloved." Unusual.

Camden English. Old English, "Dweller in the winding alley." Unusual.

Cameron English. Scottish, surname and place name used as a first name. Possible meanings include "crooked stream" and "crooked nose." Mitchell (actor). Unusual for males, unusual for females. Cam, Cammie+.

Camillo Italian. From Camillus. Sitte (19th-century Austrian architect, advocated abundant greenery within cities). Unusual.

Camillus Latin. Latin, an attendant at religious services. Patron saint of nurses and patients. Unusual.

Camlo Gypsy. English Gypsy, "Lovely." Unusual.

Campbell Scottish. Gaelic, "Crooked mouth." Unusual.

Camron English. From Cameron, Scottish, surname and place name used as a first name. Possible meanings include "crooked stream" and "crooked nose." Unusual. Cam.

Canute English. From Knut, Old Norse, "Knot." Unusual.

Cappi Gypsy. English Gypsy, "Good fortune." Unusual.

Captain English. Latin, "caput" ("head"); a military title used as a first name. Unusual.

Car Irish. From Carney, Gaelic, "Victorious one." Unusual.

Caractacus Latin. From Caradog. Unusual.

Caradog Welsh. Welsh, "Love." Twelfth-century Welsh saint (also known as Caradoc). Unusual. Alternative spelling: Caradoc.

Carey English. From Katherine, Greek, "katharos" ("pure"). Unusual for males, less popular for females.

Carl English. From Charles, Old English, "ceorl" ("man" or "husbandman"). Reiner (actor); Severinsen (band leader) (real name of Doc); Lewis (won 100-meter dash, 1988 Olympics: 9.92 seconds); Liebermann (19th-century German chemist, developed first synthetic alizarin, a dye); Ludwig (19th-century German physiologist, developed pump to study blood pressure). Less popular.

Carlin Irish. Gaelic, "Small champion." Unusual.

Carling Irish. From Carlin. Unusual.

Carlino Italian. From Charles, Old English, "ceorl" ("man" or "husbandman"). Unusual.

Carlo Hispanic, Italian. From Charles, Old English, "ceorl" ("man" or "husbandman"). Levi (Italian physician, painter, and novelist); Lorenzini (19th-century Italian adventure writer, "Pinocchio"); Passaglia (19th-century Italian theologian, attacked power of pope); Sigonio (16th-century Italian, wrote history of Italy, 570-1200); Zeno (15th-century Venetian admiral). Unusual.

Carlos Hispanic. From Charles, Old English, "ceorl" ("man" or "husbandman"). Vieira (cycled for record 191 hours non-stop, traveling 1,496 miles, 1983); Mendieta (Cuban politician, president, 1934–35); Pereyra (Mexican historian, especially Hispanic-American topics); Santana (rock singer, "Oye Como Va"). Unusual.

Carlton English. English, place name used as a first name. Fisk (baseball player). Unusual. Alternative spelling: Carleton.

Carlyle English. From Carlisle, Old English, "From the castle tower." Unusual. Carl. Alternative spelling: Carlisle.

Carmel Hebrew/Israeli. Hebrew, "Garden." Unusual.

Carmelo Italian. From Carmel. Unusual.

Carmine English, Italian. From Carmel. Less popular.

Carney Irish. Gaelic, "Victorious one." Unusual. Alternative spellings: Carny, Karney, Karny.

Carol See under Girls' Names.

Carolo Italian. From Charles, Old English, "ceorl" ("man" or "husbandman"). Unusual.

Carr English. Old Norse, "From the marsh." Unusual.

Carroll English. From Charles, Old English, "ceorl" ("man" or "husbandman"). O'Connor (actor, "In the Heat of the Night"); Wright (first commissioner of the Bureau of Labor, 1885–1905). Less popular. Alternative spelling: Carrol.

Carson English. Surname used as a first name; origin unknown. McCullers (novelist, "The Member of the Wedding"); Drew (father of fictional character Nancy Drew). Unusual.

Carswell English. Old English, "Child from the watercress spring." Unusual.

Cartage English. From Caradog. Unusual. Alternative spelling: Cartagh.

Carter English. Old English, "Cart driver." Woodson (historian and author, "African Heroes and Heroines"); Glass (senator, 1920–46). Unusual.

Carthach Irish. From Caradog. Unusual.

Carthage English. From Caradog. Unusual.

Cartwright English. Old English, "Cart builder." Unusual.

Carvel French. Old French, "From the marshy estate." Unusual. Alternative spelling: Carvell.

Cary English. English, "Pleasant stream." Schuman (made longest drive in golf: 411 yards, 32-1/4 inches, 1989); Grant (actor); Elwes (actor, "The Princess Bride"); Middlecoff (golfer). Less popular.

Casar English. From Caesar, Latin (Caesarius), "Hairy child." Unusual.

Case English. From Casimir, Old Slavic, "He announces [or "commands"] peace." Unusual.

Casey English. From Casimir, Old Slavic, "He announces [or "commands"] peace." Jones (legendary engineer); Stengel (baseball player and manager of New York Mets); Kasem (radio disk jockey, "American Top 40"). Popular for males, popular for females.

Cash English. From Jasper, Persian, "Treasure-holder." Unusual.

Cashi Hispanic. From Casimir. Unusual.

Casimir Polish. Old Slavic, "He announces [or "commands"] peace." Saint; name of four rulers of Poland, 10th-15th centuries; Périer (19th-century French politician). Unusual.

Casimiro Hispanic. From Casimir. Unusual.

Caspar English. From Jasper, Persian, "Treasure-holder." Weinberger (secretary of defense under Reagan); Netscher (17th-century German portraitist and genre painter); Olevianus (16th-century German theologian, a founder of German Reformed church); Wessel (19th-century Norwegian mathematician); Wistar (18th-century, first American glass manufacturer). Unusual. Alternative spelling: Casper.

Cass English. From Jasper, Persian, "Treasure-holder." Gilbert (architect, Supreme Court Building). Unusual for males, less popular for females.

Cassidy See under Girls' Names.

Castel Hispanic. From Castle. Unusual.

Castimer English. From Casimir. Unusual.

Castle English. Latin, "One who worked in the castle." Unusual.

Cater English. English, "Caterer," the buyer of provisions for a large household. Unusual.

Catlin Irish. From Katherine, Greek, "katharos" ("pure"). Unusual.

Cato English. From Catón. Guldberg (19th-century Norwegian chemist, developed law of boiling points). Unusual.

Catón Hispanic. Latin, "Knowledgeable" or "wise." Unusual.

Caw Welsh. From Gaius, Latin, "To rejoice." Unusual.

Cearbhall Irish. From Charles, Old English, "ceorl" ("man" or "husbandman"). Unusual.

Cecil English. Latin, "Blind." Hepworth (British director of least expensive, successful short film, "Rescued by Rover," 1937: $37.40); Andrus (secretary of the interior under Carter); Taylor (jazz musician); Day-Lewis (British leftist poet; poet laureate, 1968–72). Less popular.

Cedric English. From Cedrych. Hardwicke, Sir (actor, "Nicholas Nickleby"); Maxwell (baseball player). Unusual. Alternative spelling: Cedrick.

Cedrych Welsh. Welsh, "Bounty" or "boon." Unusual.

Celestin Czech. Latin, "Heavenly." Unusual.

Cemal Arabic. Arabic, "Beauty." Unusual.

Cenón Hispanic. From Zēnōn, Greek, "Life from Zeus." Unusual.

Cephas Aramaic. Aramaic, "Rock." Unusual.

Cerdic Welsh. From Ceredig. Unusual.

Ceredig Welsh. Welsh, "Kind," "beloved." Unusual.

Ceretic Welsh. From Ceredig. Unusual.

Cerek Unknown. Meaning and origin unknown. Unusual.

Ceretic Welsh. From Ceredig. Unusual.

Ceri See under Girls' Names.

Cerri See Ceri under Girls' Names.

Cerrie See Ceri under Girls' Names.

Cesareo Hispanic. From Caesar, Latin (Caesarius), "Hairy child." Unusual. Alternative spelling: Cesario.

Cezar Hungarian, Polish. From Caesar, Latin (Caesarius), "Hairy child." Unusual.

Cezary Polish. From Caesar, Latin (Caesarius), "Hairy child." Unusual.

Cezek Polish. From Caesar, Latin (Caesarius), "Hairy child." Unusual.

Chad English. Celtic, "Defender." Saint; Stuart (singer with Jeremy Clyde, "Yesterday's Gone"); Everett (actor in TV's "Medical Center"). Popular. Alternative spelling: Chadd.

Chadwick English. Celtic, "Battle" or "warrior." Unusual. Chad.

Chago Hispanic. From Jacob, Hebrew (Yaakov), "Supplanter" or "heel." Genesis 25:26. Unusual.

Chaim Hebrew/Israeli. Hebrew, "Life." Vital (16th-century Palestinian Cabbalist, disciple of Isaac ben Solomon Luria); Bailik (leading modern Hebrew poet). Unusual.

Chaimek Polish. From Chaim. Unusual.

Chal Gypsy. English Gypsy, "Lad," "boy," or "son." Unusual.

Chalmer Scottish. From Chalmers. Unusual.

Chalmers Scottish. Scottish, "Head of the household." Unusual.

Cham Vietnamese. Vietnamese, "Hard worker." Unusual.

Chan English. From Chauncey. Unusual.

Chance English. From Chauncey, English, Middle English, "Chancellor"; or Middle English, "Good fortune." Unusual.

Chancey English. From Chauncey. Unusual.

Chandler English. Old French, "Candlemaker." Unusual.

Chane African. African, "Weaving leaf." Unusual.

Chaney English. Old French, "Oak wood." Unusual.

Chango Hispanic. From Jacob, Hebrew (Yaakov), "Supplanter" or "heel." Genesis 25:26. Unusual.

Channing English. English, "Knowing and wise." Unusual for males, unusual for females.

Chanoch Hebrew/Israeli. Hebrew, "Educated," "trained," or "dedicated." Unusual.

Chanti Hispanic. From Jacob, Hebrew (Yaakov), "Supplanter" or "heel." Genesis 25:26. Unusual.

Charles English. Old English, "ceorl" ("man" or "husbandman"). Borromeo (patron saint of bishops); Lwanga (saint); Walgreen (established drugstore chain); Darwin (19th-century British, developed theory of evolution); Babbage (British, designed "analytical engine," foundation of computers); Cornwallis (British Revolutionary War general). Popular. Charlie+, Chuck.

Charlie English. From Charles, Old English, "ceorl" ("man" or "husbandman"). Rich (singer); Chaplin (actor, called "The Little Tramp"); Murray (actor); Parker (jazz musician); Pride (country singer). Less popular for males, unusual for females. Alternative spelling: Charley.

Charlton English. English, "Settlement of free peasants." Heston (actor). Less popular. Charlie+. Alternative spelling: Charleton.

Chas English. From Charles. Unusual. Alternative spelling: Chaz.

Chase English. Old French, "Hunter." Benson (character in TV's "The Young and the Restless"); Gioberti (character in TV's "Falcon Crest"). Unusual.

Chaunce English. From Chauncey. Unusual.

Chauncey English. Middle English, "Chancellor." Dunn (holds altitude record in open-basket hot air balloon: 53,000 feet, 1979); Olcott (composer, "Wild Irish Rose"); Tinker (professor of English literature, Yale, early 1900s); Wright (19th-century, developed philosophy of science); Depew (lawyer, represented Vanderbilts). Unusual.

Chay English. From Charles. Unusual.

Che Hispanic. From Joseph, Hebrew (Yosef), "God will add." Unusual.

Checha Hispanic. From Caesar, Latin (Caesarius), "Hairy child." Unusual.

Cheche Hispanic. From Joseph, Hebrew (Yosef), "God will add." Unusual.

Chen Chinese. Chinese, "Vast" or "great." Unusual.

Chenche Hispanic. From Vincent, Latin, "Vincentius," from "vincere" ("to conquer"). Unusual.

Chencho Hispanic. From Laurence, Latin, "Crowned with laurel." Unusual.

Chepe Hispanic. From Joseph, Hebrew (Yosef), "God will add." Unusual.

Chepito Hispanic. From Joseph, Hebrew (Yosef), "God will add." Unusual.

Cheslav Russian. From Chester. Unusual.

Chesmu Native American. Native American, "Gritty." Unusual.

Chester English. Old English, "Camp" or "Roman site." Alan Arthur (21st president); Conklin (actor); Longwell (geologist and professor, studied western U.S.); Nimitz (battleship commander, later chief of naval operations); Barnard (businessman and sociologist, "Organization and Management"). Less popular. Chet.

Chet English. From Chester. Huntley (TV newscaster); Atkins (guitarist); Lemon (baseball player, formerly with the Chicago White Sox). Less popular.

Chev French. From Chevalier. Unusual.

Chevalier French. French, "Knight." Unusual.

Chevi French. From Chevalier. Unusual.

Chevy American. From Chevalier. Chase (comedian) (real name: Cornelius Crane Chase). Unusual.

Chi Nigerian. Nigerian, "God"; a personal guardian angel. Unusual.

Chick English. From Charles. Corea (jazz pianist); Webb (drummer). Unusual.

Chico Hispanic. From Francis, Latin, "Frenchman." Marx (actor, one of the Marx brothers) (real name: Leonard). Unusual. Alternative spelling: Chicho.

Chik Gypsy. English Gypsy, "Earth." Unusual.

Chilo Hispanic. From Francis, Latin, "Frenchman." Unusual.

Chim Vietnamese. Vietnamese, "Bird." Unusual.

Chip English. From Charles. Unusual.

Chito Hispanic. From Francis, Latin, "Frenchman." Unusual.

Chresta Swedish. From Christian, Greek, "christos" ("anointed"). Unusual.

Chris English. From Christopher. Evert-Lloyd (tennis champion); Lemmon (actor, son of Jack); Mullin (basketball player). Less popular. Alternative spellings: Cris, Kris, Kriss.

Christian English. Greek, "christos" ("anointed"). Saint; character in Bunyan's "Pilgrim's Progess"; Doppler (19th-century Austrian physicist, discovered sound, light change with motion); Lacroix (French clothing designer); Dior (clothing designer); Schenk (German, holds world record, and won 1988 Olympic gold medal, for decathlon). Popular for males, unusual for females. Chris, Christy+. Alternative spelling: Kristian.

Christianos Greek. From Christian, Greek, "christos" ("anointed"). Unusual.

Christmas English. Old English, "Christ's festival." Unusual for males, unusual for females.

Christofer Czech, Russian. From Christopher. Unusual.

Christoff Russian. From Christopher. Unusual. Alternative spelling: Christof.

Christoffer Danish. From Christopher. Unusual.

Christoforus German. From Christopher. Unusual.

Christoph German. From Christopher. Scheiner (17th-century German astronomer, invented pantograph); Wieland (18th-century German poet, wrote poem on which Mozart based "Magic Flute"); Clavius (17th-century Bavarian astronomer, developed algebraic notation); Demantius (17th-century German composer of sacred and secular music). Unusual.

Christophe French. From Christopher. Plantin (16th-century French bookbinder, printer, and publisher whose books were famous for their beauty and typographic excellence). Unusual.

Christopher English. Greek, "One who carries Christ in his heart." Patron saint of travelers; Polhem (17th-century Swede who invented early mass production by water power); Marlowe (16th-century British dramatist and poet, "Dr. Faustus"); Massey (Australian, fastest water skier: 143 mph, 1983); Plummer (Canadian actor). Extremely popular. Chris. Alternative spelling: Cristopher.

Christos Greek. From Christopher. Unusual. Alternative spelling: Kristos.

Chrystian Polish. From Christian, Greek, "christos" ("anointed"). Unusual. Alternative spelling: Krystian.

Chuck English. From Charles, Old English, "ceorl" ("man" or "husbandman"). Yeager (made first supersonic flight, 1947); Connors (actor); Berry (singer); Mangione (musician, pianist, and composer); Woolery (TV host, "The Love Connection"). Less popular.

Chul Korean. Korean, "Firmness." Unusual.

Chuma African. Rhodesian, "Bead." Unusual.

Chumin Hispanic. From Dominic, Latin, "Lord." Unusual.

Chuminga Hispanic. From Dominic, Latin, "Lord." Unusual.

Chumo Hispanic. From Thomas, Aramaic, "Twin." Unusual.

Cicero English. Latin, "vetch" or "chickpea," supposedly referring to the Roman orator's field of chick-peas. Noted first-century Roman orator and statesman. Unusual.

Cicerón Hispanic. From Cicero. Unusual.

Cid English. From Sidney, Old French, "From Saint-Denis." A Norman surname derived from a village named for a saint. Unusual. Alternative spellings: Sid, Syd.

Cilombo African. African, "Roadside camp," a welcome sight to a weary traveler in Africa. Unusual for males, unusual for females.

Cirillo Italian. From Cyril, Greek, "Lord" or "ruler." Unusual.

Cirilo Hispanic. From Cyril, Greek, "Lord" or "ruler." Unusual.

Ciro Hispanic. From Cyrus, Latin, "Throne." Alegría (Peruvian novelist, "La Serpiente De Oro"); Ferri (17th-century Italian painter and printmaker, worked on Pitti Palace, Florence). Unusual.

Cisco Hispanic. From Francis, Latin, "Frenchman." Unusual.

Clancy Irish. Irish, "Descendant of a red-haired warrior." Less popular.

Clarence English. Latin, "Bright," "shining," or "clear"; a place name used as a first name. Character in Mark Twain's "A Connecticut Yankee in King Arthur's Court"; Harvey (character in Maria Edgeworth's "Helen"); Darrow (lawyer in Scopes evolution trial); DeMar (won Boston marathon a record seven times). Less popular.

Clark English. Old French, surname used as a first name. Gable ("king" of Hollywood for nearly 30 years); Clifford (former secretary of defense); Mills (19th-century bronze sculptor, "Liberty" on Capitol dome); Shaughnessy (football coach, developed "T" formation); Wissler (anthropologist, especially concerned with American Indians). Less popular. Alternative spelling: Clarke.

Clarke English. From Clark. Hinkle (football fullback 1932–41, Hall of Fame). Less popular.

Claud English. From Claudius. Unusual.

Claude French. From Claudius. Debussy (French composer, "Claire de lune");

Monet (French impressionist painter); Dauphin (actor); Swanson (secretary of the navy, 1933); Simon (French, won Nobel Peace Prize, 1985). Unusual.

Claudio Italian. From Claudius. Abbado (orchestra conductor); Monteverdi (17th-century Italian composer); Merulo (16th-century Italian organist and composer); Aquaviva (16th-century Italian religious educator, promoted Jesuit scholarship); Coello (17th-century Spanish painter, known for his work at Toledo cathedral). Unusual.

Claudius Latin. Latin, "Lame." Ptolemy (2nd-century Alexandrian astronomer, proposed solar system revolves around earth); Mamertinus (4th-century Roman politician, governed Italy and Africa); Rich (19th-century British, laid foundation for Mesopotamian archaeology); Aelianus (3rd-century Roman rhetorician and author). Unusual.

Claus English, German. From Nicholas, Greek, "Victorious people." Sluter (14th-century Dutch sculptor, tomb of Philip of Bold, of Burgundy); Spreckels (19th-century sugar giant, monopolized West Coast production); Schenk von Stauffenberg (German soldier, leader of unsuccessful attempt to assassinate Hitler). Unusual.

Clay English. English, surname used as a first name. Felker (editor and publisher). Unusual.

Clayborne English. English, surname used as a first name. Unusual. Clay.

Clayton English. English, referring to someone living on a clay bed; a surname and place name used as a first name. Yeutter (secretary of agriculture, 1989); Moore (actor, "The Lone Ranger"); Farlow (character in TV's "Dallas"). Unusual. Clay. Alternative spellings: Clayten, Claytin.

Cledwyn Welsh. Welsh, the name of a river; occasionally used as a first name. Unusual.

Clem English. From Clement. Haskins (basketball coach). Unusual.

Cleme Hispanic. From Clement. Unusual.

Clemen Hispanic. From Clement. Unusual.

Clemens Danish, English. From Clement. Winkler (19th-century German chemist, discovered germanium, 1866); Brentano (19th-century German romantic dramatist and collector of folk songs); von Delbrück (Prussian minister of commerce, directed German recovery after WWI); Denhardt (19th-century German, explored Eastern Africa). Unusual.

Clement English. Latin, "Mild," "merciful." Patron saint of lighthouses; Moore (author, "'Twas the Night Before Christmas"); Haynsworth (federal judge); Attlee (British statesman, prime minister 1945–51); Marot (16th-century French allegorical, innovative poet). Unusual. Clem.

Clemente Hispanic, Italian. From Clement. Conte Solaro della Margarita (19th-century Piedmontese politician). Unusual.

Clemento Hispanic. From Clement. Unusual.

Clemmons English. From Clement. Unusual. Clem.

Clemmy English. From Clement. Unusual. Alternative spelling: Clemmie.

Cleveland English. Old English, "Cliff"; a place name used as a first name. Amory (author, "The Last Resorts"); Abbe (meteorologist, influenced founding of U.S. Weather Service, 1870). Unusual.

Cliff English. From Clifford. Richard (singer) (real name: Harry Webb); Arquette (actor) (real name: Charley Weaver); Robertson (actor); Huxtable (character in TV's "The Cosby Show"); Claven (character in TV's "Cheers"). Less popular.

Clifford English. Old English, "Ford near a slope." Odets (playwright, "Waiting for Lefty," "Golden Boy"); Curzon (concert pianist); Batt (Australian, oldest man to swim English Channel: 68 years old, 1987); Hardin (secretary of agriculture, 1969); Irving (author). Less popular. Cliff.

Clifton English. Old English, "Settlement near a cliff." Webb (actor) (real name: Webb Parmelee Hollenbeck); Fadiman (radio and TV critic); Davis (actor, "Amen"); Chenier (musician); Daniels (journalist). Unusual. Cliff.

Clint English. From Clinton. Walker (actor, "Cheyenne"); Eastwood (director and actor, "Dirty Harry"); Smith (hockey player, tied for most goals in one period: four, 1945); Howard (actor, "Gentle Ben"); Buchanan (character in TV's "One Life to Live"). Less popular.

Clinton English. Old English, "Settlement near a hill." Bailey (fastest time for tying six Boy Scout Handbook knots on individual ropes: 8.1 seconds, 1977); Anderson (secretary of agriculture, 1945); Frank (Heisman Memorial trophy winner, Yale, 1937); Merriam (naturalist and author, "Buffalo in North America"). Less popular. Clint.

Clive English. English, place name used as a first name. Brook (actor) (real name: Clifford Brook); Spate (scored highest competitive game of Scrabble: 979, 1988); Bell (British art critic and author, "Peace at Once"); Staples Lewis (British scholar and author, "The Chronicles of Narnia," "The Screwtape Letters"). Less popular.

Clyde English. Scottish, the name of a river. Beatty (dangerous-animal trainer, later circus owner); Pangborn (made first nonstop transPacific flight, 1931); Turner (football Hall of Fame, Chicago Bears, 1940–52); Kluckhohn (anthropologist and author, "Navaho Witchcraft"). Less popular.

Cob English. From Jacob, Hebrew (Yaakov), "Supplanter" or "heel." Genesis 25:26. Unusual. Alternative spelling: Cobb.

Cody English. Old English, "A cushion." Popular for males, less popular for females. Alternative spellings: Codey, Codie, Coty, Kody.

Cola Italian. From Nicholas, Greek, "Victorious people." Rienzo (Italian, led Roman revolution, 1347). Unusual.

Colan English. From Nicholas, Greek, "Victorious people." Unusual.

Colar French. From Nicholas, Greek, "Victorious people." Unusual.

Colby See under Girls' Names.

Cole English. From Nicholas, Greek, "Victorious people." Porter (composer, "Night and Day," "Kiss Me, Kate"). Less popular. Alternative spellings: Kohl, Kole.

Coleman Irish. From Colman. Livingston Blease (politician, senator 1925–31); Hawkins (jazz saxophonist). Unusual. Alternative spelling: Colman.

Colin English. From Nicholas, Greek, "Victorious people." Powell (chairman, Joint Chiefs of Staff, 1989-); MacLaurin (18th-century Scottish mathematician, youngest to hold full professorship: 19 years old); Macfarquhar (18th-century Scottish printer, co-founded Encyclopedia Britannica); Clive (actor, "Frankenstein"). Popular. Alternative spellings: Collin, Colyn.

Colley English. Old English, "Black-haired" or "swarthy." Cibber (British actor and playwright). Unusual.

Collingwood English, a wood of disputed ownership; origin unknown. Unusual.

Collins English. From Nicholas, Greek, "Victorious people." Unusual.

Collis English. From Colley. Potter Huntington (built transcontinental railroad, completed 1869). Unusual.

Colm Irish. From Columba, Latin, "Dove." Unusual.

Colonel English. English, military title used as first name. de Basil (Russian impresario, helped manage Russian opera and ballet companies) (real name: Vasily Grigoryevich Voskresensky). Unusual.

Colston English. English, settlement belonging to a little-known person; origin unknown. Unusual.

Colt English. From Colton. Unusual.

Colter English. From Colton. Unusual.

Colton English. Old English, "From a coal town." Unusual.

Colum Irish. From Columba. Unusual.

Columba Irish. Latin, "Dove." Patron saint of poets. Unusual.

Colville English. Old French, surname and place name used as a first name. Unusual. Alternative spellings: Colvile, Colvill.

Colvin English. Surname used as a first name; origin unknown. Unusual.

Colwyn Welsh. Welsh, the name of a river used as a first name. Unusual.

Coman Arabic. Arabic, "Noble." Unusual.

Con English. From Conrad. Unusual.

Conan Irish. Gaelic, "High." Saint; the Barbarian (character made famous by Arnold Schwarzenegger). Unusual.

Concetto American. From Concetta, Italian, a reference to the Immaculate Conception. Unusual.

Conn English. From Conrad. Cetchathach (2nd-century king of northern Ireland). Unusual.

Conni English. From Conrad. Gordon (taught largest art class: 2,500 first-time artists, 1965). Unusual.

Connor Irish. Irish, "High desire." Cruise O'Brien (former United Nations secretary general). Unusual. Alternative spellings: Conner, Conor.

Conny German. From Conrad. Unusual.

Conrad English. German, "Brave counsel." Hilton (founder of hotel chain that bears his name); Aiken (won Pulitzer Prize for poetry, 1930); Bain (actor); Janis (actor and musician); Nagel (movie industry mogul). Less popular.

Conrade French. From Conrad. Unusual.

Conrado Hispanic, Italian, Portuguese. From Conrad. Unusual.

Conroy English. English, surname used as a first name. Unusual.

Constance See under Girls' Names.

Constant English. From Constance, Latin, "constans" ("constant" or "unwavering"). Lambert (British composer of ballet "Romeo and Juliet"); Troyon (19th-century French painter, known especially for landscapes and studies of animals). Unusual.

Constantine English. From Constance, Latin, "constans" ("constant" or "unwavering"). Saint; the Great (1st-century, first Christian emperor of the Roman world); Lascaris (16th-century Greek grammarian, published first Greek-language grammar book, 1476); Manasses (12th-century Byzantine prelate and historian); Phaulkon (17th-century Greek politician in Siam). Unusual.

Constantinos Greek. From Constance, Latin, "constans" ("constant" or "unwavering"). Unusual.

Conway English. Welsh, "Holy river." Twitty (singer and guitarist) (real name: Harold Lloyd Jenkins). Unusual.

Cook English. Occupational surname; origin unknown. Unusual.

Cooper English. Occupational surname used as first name; origin unknown (refers to a barrel-maker). Unusual.

Corbet English. Surname used as a first name; origin unknown. Indicates an ancestor with raven-black hair. Unusual. Alternative spellings: Corbett, Corbitt.

Corbin English. From Corbet. Indicates an ancestor with raven-black hair. Bernsen (actor, "L.A. Law"). Unusual.

Cordell English. English, occupational surname used as a first name. Hull (former secretary of state, called "father of the United Nations"). Unusual.

Cordero Hispanic. Spanish, "Little lamb." Unusual.

Corey English. Irish, "From the hollow." Glover (rock and roll singer); Hart (Canadian singer, "Never Surrender"); Feldman (actor, "Stand by Me"); Haim (actor, "Lucas"). Very popular for males, less popular for females. Alternative spelling: Cory.

Cornall American. From Cornell. Unusual.

Cornelius Latin. Latin, "A horn." Acts 10: 1. Saint; Vanderbilt (railroad magnate); Bliss (secretary of the interior under McKinley); Bennett (football player); Tacitus (1st-century Roman historian, politician, and orator). Unusual. Alternative spellings: Cornelious, Cornilius.

Cornell American. English, surname and place name used as a first name. MacNeil (baritone); Green (football player). Unusual. Alternative spelling: Cornel.

Cornelus English. From Cornelius. Unusual.

Cornwallis English. English, surname and place name used as a first name, originally indicating one who came from Cornwall, England. Unusual.

Correy See under Girls' Names.

Corrye See Cori under Girls' Names.

Cort English. From Conrad. Adelaer (17th-century Norwegian naval commander, forced Turkish surrender, 1654). Unusual.

Cortez American. Spanish, surname and place name used as a first name. Unusual.

Cortney See Courtney under Girls' Names.

Corydon English. From Korudon, Greek, "Helmeted one" or "crested one." Wassell (WWII hero). Unusual.

Coryell English. From Korudon, Greek, "Helmeted one" or "crested one." Unusual.

Cosimo Italian. From Cosmo. Unusual.

Cosmo Italian. Greek, "kosmos" ("order"). Patron saint of Milan; Gordon Lang (archbishop of Canterbury, 1928); Innes (19th-century Scottish antiquarian and law professor, wrote "Scotland in the Middle Ages," 1860); Topper (character in "Topper"). Unusual.

Costa Greek. From Constance, Latin, "constans" ("constant" or "unwavering"). Unusual.

Coulson English. From Nicholas, Greek, "Victorious people." Unusual.

Courtland English. Old English, "From farmland" or "from court land." Unusual.

Cowan Irish. Gaelic, "A twin" or "hillside hollow." Unusual.

Coy English. English, "A wooded area." Unusual.

Craig English. Welsh, "Rock." Stevens (actor) (real name: Gail Shekles); Kennedy (character in Arthur B. Reeve's detective stories); Lucas (Broadway actor); McKay (film editor); Baumgarten (producer). Popular. Alternative spelling: Kraig.

Craven English. Surname and place name used as a first name; origin unknown. Unusual.

Crawford English. Scottish, "Ford where crows gather." Williamson Long (19th-century surgeon, first to use ether as anesthetic). Unusual.

Creighton English. "Rocky place"; origin unknown. Surname and place name used as a first name. Williams Abrams (WWII general). Unusual.

Crepin French. From Crispin, Latin, "crispus" ("curly"). Unusual.

Cresswell English. Old English, "Stream where cress grows." Unusual. Alternative spelling: Creswell.

Crispian English. From Crispin. Unusual.

Crispin English. Latin, "crispus" ("curly"). Patron saint of cobblers and leather workers. Unusual.

Crispino Italian. From Crispin. Unusual.

Crispo Hispanic. From Crispin. Unusual.

Crispus Latin. From Crispin. Attucks (18th-century patriot, possibly a runaway slave; killed in Boston Massacre, 1770); surname of a 4th-century Roman soldier, Flavius Julius, who ruled Gaul, 317. Unusual.

Cristao Portuguese. From Christian, Greek, "christos" ("anointed"). Unusual.

Cristian Hawaiian, Hispanic. From Christian, Greek, "christos" ("anointed"). Unusual.

Cristiano Hispanic, Italian, Portuguese. From Christian, Greek, "christos" ("anointed"). Unusual.

Cristino Hispanic. From Christian, Greek, "christos" ("anointed"). Unusual.

Cristóbal Hispanic. From Christabel, created, meaning unknown. de Morales (16th-century, first major Spanish composer); de Olid (16th-century Spanish soldier, with Cortés in conquest of Mexico, 1519–21); Virués (16th-century Spanish tragic poet); Balenciaga (Spanish couturier, especially known for elegant ball gowns). Unusual.

Cristoforo Italian. From Christopher, Greek, "One who carries Christ in his heart." Unusual.

Cristovão Portuguese. From Christopher, Greek, "One who carries Christ in his heart." Unusual.

Crofton English. Surname and place name used as a first name; origin unknown. Unusual.

Crosby English. "Living near the cross or crossroad"; origin unknown. Surname and place name used as a first name. Unusual. Alternative spelling: Crosbie.

Crosland English. English, a place where a public cross is located. Unusual. Alternative spelling: Crossland.

Crossland English. From Crosland. Unusual.

Crossley English. From Crosland. Unusual.

Crowther English. "Fiddle-player"; origin unknown. Unusual.

Crystek Polish. From Christian, Greek, "christos" ("anointed"). Unusual. Alternative spelling: Krystek.

Cullen English. Gaelic, "Handsome." Less popular.

Curcio Hispanic. From Curtis. Unusual.

Currito Hispanic. From Francis, Latin, "Frenchman." Less popular.

Curro Hispanic. From Francis, Latin, "Frenchman." Unusual.

Curt English. From Conrad, German, "Brave counsel." Sachs (musicologist, founder of modern organology); Carlson (business tycoon); Gowdy (sportscaster). Less popular. Alternative spelling: Kurt.

Curtis English. Old French, "Courteous." Mayfield (pop musician, "Freddy's Dead"); Wilbur (secretary of navy, 1924); LeMay (general); Strange (golfer). Popular. Curt. Alternative spelling: Kurtis.

Custance English. From Constance, Latin, "constans" ("constant" or "unwavering"). Unusual for males, unusual for females.

Cuthbert English. Old English, "Famous" or "bright." Patron saint of shepherds; Tunstall (16th-century British clergyman, a strict Catholic but refrained from persecuting Protestants); Collingwood (18th-century British naval commander, took command at Trafalgar after Nelson's death). Unusual.

Cy English. From Cyrus. Young (great baseball pitcher) (real name: Denton True Young); Coleman (composer). Unusual.

Cydney English. From Sidney, Old French, "From Saint-Denis." A Norman surname derived from a village named for a saint. Unusual. Cyd. Alternative spellings: Sidney, Sydney, Sydny.

Cymon English. From Simon, Hebrew (Shimon), "God heard." Genesis 29:33. Unusual. Alternative spellings: Cimon, Simeon, Simon, Symon.

Cyprian English. Latin, "Man from Cyprus." Saint; Norwid (19th-century Polish anti-romantic, free-verse poet); Southack (18th-century cartographer, mapped Northeast coast of North America). Unusual.

Cyril English. Greek, "Lord" or "ruler." of Alexandria (saint); Ritchard (actor and opera director); Newall (British general, governed New Zealand, early 1940s); Pearson, Sir (British publisher also known for work for blind); Scott (British pianist and composer); Tourneur (17th-century British tragic dramatist). Less popular. Alternative spelling: Cyrill.

Cyrille French. From Cyril. Unusual.

Cyrus English. Latin, "Throne." Vance (secretary of state under Carter); Field (promoted laying of first trans-Atlantic cable); McCormick (invented reaper); Adler (scholar and educator; founded American Jewish Committee, 1906); Alger (19th-century industrialist, invented cylinder stove). Unusual. Cy.

Dabir African. African, "Secretary" or "teacher." Unusual.

Dacey English. Gaelic, "A southerner." Unusual for males, unusual for females. Alternative spellings: Dace, Dacy.

Dacian Unknown. Latin, an inhabitant of the Roman province of Dacia. Unusual.

Dacso Hungarian. From Daniel, Hebrew, "God is my judge." Daniel 1:6. Unusual.

Dafydd Welsh. From David, Hebrew, "Beloved," "friend," or "darling." 1 Samuel 16:19. Ab Edmwnd (15th-century Welsh poet, defined Welsh poetic meter); ap Gruffydd (13th-century, last native Welsh prince); ap Gwilym (14th-century Welsh poet, known for fresh style). Unusual.

Dag Norwegian. From Dagny, Old Norse, "Day." Hammarskjöld (Swedish statesman, former United Nations secretary general). Unusual.

Dagon Hebrew/Israeli. From Dagan, Hebrew, "Corn" or "grain." Unusual.

Dakota American. Native American, tribal name used as a first name. Unusual for males, unusual for females.

Daksh Indo-Pakistani. Hindi, "Efficient." Unusual.

Dalal Indo-Pakistani. Sanskrit, "Broker." Unusual.

Dale English. Old English, "Dweller in the dale or valley." Nelson (holds record for most parachute jumps per hour from highest altitude: 301 in 24 hours, from 2,000 feet or more, 1988); Evans (actress); Cooper (character in TV's "Twin Peaks"); Carnegie (1920s writer, "How to Win Friends and Influence People"). Less popular. Alternative spelling: Dayle.

Daley English. From Daly, Irish, surname used as a first name. Thompson (British, decathlon gold medalist and world champion, 1984 Olympics). Less popular. Alternative spelling: Daly.

Dalibor Czech. From Dale. Unusual.

Dallas English. Scottish, surname and place name used as a first name. Green (baseball player and manager). Less popular for males, less popular for females.

Dallin English. From Dale. Unusual.

Dalton English. English, "Valley town"; a place name used as a first name. Less popular.

Damek Czech. From Adam, Hebrew, "Redness" or "man." Genesis 2:19. Unusual.

Damian Russian. Greek, "To tame." Patron saint of hairdressers; Forment (16th-century Spanish sculptor, influenced by Donatello). Less popular. Alternative spelling: Damyan.

Damiano Italian. From Damian. Unusual.

Damien French. From Damian. Karras (priest in "The Exorcist"); religious name of Joseph De Veuster, 19th-century Belgian priest who served Hawaiian leper colony for 16 years. Less popular.

Damion English. From Damian. Less popular. Alternative spelling: Dameon.

Damján Hungarian. From Damian. Unusual.

Damon English. From Damian. Runyon (sportswriter and author, "Guys and Dolls"); of Athens (5th-century B.C. philosopher, taught Pericles and Socrates). Unusual. Alternative spellings: Daemon, Daimen, Daimon, Daman, Damen, Damon.

Dan English. From Daniel, Hebrew, "God is my judge." Daniel 1:6. Fifth son of Jacob, the first with Rachel's maid, Bilha; Duryea (actor); Ayckroyd (actor); Dailey (actor and dancer); Golenpaul (created "Information Please" radio show and almanac); Râther (TV newscaster). Less popular.

Dana See under Girls' Names.

Danal English. From Daniel, Hebrew, "God is my judge." Daniel 1:6. Unusual. Alternative spelling: Danill.

Dane English. Old English, "Trickling stream." Unusual.

Daneil Hungarian. From Daniel, Hebrew, "God is my judge." Daniel 1:6. Unusual.

Danek Polish. From Daniel, Hebrew, "God is my judge." Daniel 1:6. Unusual.

Danforth English. Origin unknown. Less popular. Dan.

Dani See under Girls' Names.

Daniel English. Hebrew, "God is my judge." Daniel 1:6. Upright Hebrew leader during Judean exile (Bible); the Stylite (saint); Barenboim (classical pianist and conductor); Chester French (sculptor, Lincoln Memorial); Bernoulli (Swiss, advanced theory of kinetic gases and fluids); Day-Lewis (actor, "My Left Foot"). Extremely popular for males, unusual for females. Dan, Danny. Alternative spellings: Daneal, Danial.

Daniele Italian. From Daniel, Hebrew, "God is my judge." Daniel 1:6. de Bernard (French, Olympic silver medalist: slalom, 1972; missed gold by narrowest margin); Manin (19th-century Italian, defended Venice against Austria, 1849); Varè (Italian diplomat, minister to China, author of "The Maker of Heavenly Trousers"). Unusual.

Daniels Latvian. From Daniel, Hebrew, "God is my judge." Daniel 1:6. Unusual.

Danil Bulgarian. From Daniel, Hebrew, "God is my judge." Daniel 1:6. Unusual.

Danila See under Girls' Names.

Danilka See under Girls' Names.

Danilo Hispanic. From Daniel, Hebrew, "God is my judge." Daniel 1:6. Petrovic Njegos (name of two 17th-century and 18th-century ruling princes of Montenegro). Unusual.

Danior Gypsy. English Gypsy, "Born with teeth." Unusual.

Danko Czech. From Daniel, Hebrew, "God is my judge." Daniel 1:6. Unusual.

Danladi African. African, "Born on Sunday." Unusual.

Danny English. From Daniel, Hebrew, "God is my judge." Daniel 1:6. Aiello (actor); Kaye (comedian) (real name: David Daniel Kominski); DeVito (actor and director); Thomas (actor, "Make Room for Daddy"); White (quarterback, Dallas Cowboys). Less popular. Alternative spelling: Dannie.

Dano Czech. From Daniel, Hebrew, "God is my judge." Daniel 1:6. Halsall (Swiss, fastest swimmer in 25-meter pool: 5.5 mph). Unusual.

Dante English. Latin, "Enduring" or "obstinate." Gabriel Rossetti (19th-century British pre-Raphaelite painter and poet, especially sonnets); Laveill (football Hall of Fame, Cleveland Browns); Alighieri (13th-century Italian poet, "The Divine Comedy"). Unusual. Alternative spellings: Dontae, Donte.

Danukas Lithuanian. From Daniel, Hebrew, "God is my judge." Daniel 1:6. Unusual.

Danya Russian. From Daniel, Hebrew, "God is my judge." Daniel 1:6. Unusual.

Danyele See under Girls' Names.

Danylets Russian. From Daniel, Hebrew, "God is my judge." Daniel 1:6. Unusual.

Danylo Russian. From Daniel, Hebrew, "God is my judge." Daniel 1:6. Unusual.

Dar Hebrew/Israeli. Hebrew, "Pearl" or "mother-of-pearl." Robinson (highest-paid stuntman: $100,000 for 1,100-foot jump from Toronto's CN Tower, 1979, "High Point"). Unusual.

Dara See under Girls' Names.

Darb English. From Darby. Unusual.

Darby English. Old Norse, "One from the deer estate." Unusual.

Darcy English. Irish, "Dark man." Unusual for males, less popular for females. Alternative spellings: Darce, Darcey, Darse, Darsey, Darsy.

Dare English. From Darren. Unusual.

Dario Hispanic, Portuguese. From Darren. Unusual.

Darius Greek. Persian, "Wealthy." Milhaud (French composer, wrote shortest published opera ("Deliverance of Theseus," 1928): 7 minutes, 27 seconds); name of three Achaemenid kings of Persia, 550–330 B.C. Unusual. Alternative spelling: Darrius.

Darnall American. From Darnell. Unusual. Alternative spelling: Darnal.

Darnell American. Old English, "Hidden" or "secret nook." Unusual. Alternative spelling: Darnel.

Darren English. Gaelic, "Small great one." McGavin (actor, "Kolchak: The Night Stalker"). Unusual. Alternative spellings: Daran, Daren, Darin, Daron, Darran, Darrin, Darron, Darryn, Darun, Daryn.

Darrick English. From Theodoric, Old German, "Ruler of the people." Unusual. Alternative spellings: Darik, Darrik.

Darrie Irish. From Derry, Gaelic, "Red-haired." Unusual. Alternative spelling: Darry.

Darryl English. Surname used as a first name; origin unknown. Zanuck (film producer, introduced use of sound and foreign locations); Strawberry (baseball player, New York Mets). Less popular. Alternative spellings: Darel, Darell, Darrel, Darral, Darrell, Darrill, Darrol, Darryll, Daryl, Daryll, Derrell.

Darwin English. Old English, "A beloved friend." Unusual.

Dasan Native American. Native American, "Leader." Unusual.

Daudi African. Swahili, "Beloved one." Unusual.

Dave English. From David. Garroway (TV host); Barry (humorous author, "Dave Barry Slept Here"); Winfield (baseball player, New York Yankees); Brubeck (jazz pianist and composer). Less popular.

Daveed Russian. From David. Unusual.

Davi Portuguese. From David. Unusual.

David English. Hebrew, "Beloved," "friend," or "darling." 1 Samuel 16:19. Second king of Israel; saint; Sarnoff (established first radio network); Mamet (won 1984 Pulitzer Prize for drama, "Glengarry Glen Ross"); Brewer (Supreme Court Justice, 1889–1910); Bowie (pop musician, "Let's Dance"). Extremely popular. Dave, Davy.

Davide Italian. From David. Unusual.

Davidek Czech. From David. Unusual.

Davin Scandinavian. Scandinavian, "Brightness of the Finns." Unusual.

Davis English. Surname used as a first name; origin unknown. Unusual.

Davison English. From Davis. Unusual.

Davon English. From David. Unusual.

Davy English. From David. Crockett (legendary frontiersman). Less popular. Alternative spellings: Davey, Davie.

Dawid Polish, Yiddish. From David. Unusual.

Dawson English. Surname used as a first name; origin unknown. Unusual.

Dawūd Arabic. From David. Unusual.

Dax English. French, "Of the waters." Unusual.

Dayne English. From Daniel, Hebrew, "God is my judge." Daniel 1:6. Unusual.

Dayton English. Old English, "Bright town." Unusual.

De Chinese. Chinese, "Virtue." Unusual.

Dean English. Old English, "Valley." Rusk (former secretary of state); Martin (actor and singer) (real name: Dino Croccetti); Jagger (actor); Acheson (secretary of state, late 1940s); Stockwell (actor). Less popular. Alternative spelling: Dene.

Deandre Created. Created, African-American. Unusual.

Deangelo Created. Created, African-American. Unusual.

Decimus Latin. Latin, "Tenth." Maximus Ausonius (1st-century Gallic poet and rhetorician); Caelius Calvinus Balbinus (1st-century Roman emperor and Salian priest); Junius Brutus (1st-century Roman general, conspired against Caesar); Laberius (1st-century Roman knight, writer of farces, satires, and an epic on Gallic War). Unusual.

Declan Irish. Irish, meaning unknown. Saint (early 5th-century Irish bishop, established church of Ardmore). Unusual.

Deco Hungarian. From Dominic, Latin, "Lord." Unusual.

Dee See under Girls' Names.

Deedee Hebrew/Israeli. Hebrew, "Beloved." Unusual.

Dejuan Created. Created, African-American. Unusual. Alternative spellings: Dajuan, Dujuan.

Dekel Arabic. Arabic, "Palm tree" or "date palm." Unusual.

Del English. English, nickname for first names beginning with "Del." Shannon (singer, best known for "Runaway"). Unusual.

Delaney Irish. Gaelic, "Challenger's descendent." Unusual.

Delano Irish. Gaelic, "Healthy black man." Unusual.

Delbert English. Old English, "Bright day" or "sunny day." Unser (hit most consecutive home runs by a pinch-hitter: 3, 1979); Mann (film director, "Marty"); McClinton (singer). Unusual. Del.

Dell English. English, "Small valley." Unusual for males, unusual for females.

Delmar American. Spanish, "By the sea." Watson (film director). Unusual.

Delmer American. From Delmar. Unusual.

Delroy English. From Leroy, Old French, "The king." Unusual.

Delsin Native American. Native American, "He is so." Unusual.

Delsy Native American. From Delsin. Unusual.

Delvin English. Old English, "Friend from the valley." Unusual.

Dema Russian. From Damian, Greek, "To tame." Unusual.

Demarco Created. Created, African-American. Unusual.

Demarcus Created. Created, African-American. Unusual.

Demario Created. Created, African-American. Unusual.

Demeter English, Hungarian. From Demetrius. Unusual.

Demetre French. From Demetrius. Unusual.

Demetrio Hispanic, Italian. From Demetrius. Unusual.

Demetris English. From Demetrius. Unusual.

Demetrius English. Greek, "Lover of the earth" or "from Demeter," the earth mother. Second-century B.C. king of Bactria, conquered parts of India; name of three Seleucid kings of Syria, 187–88 B.C.; 4th-century B.C. Greek sculptor famed for realism; Triclinius (14th-century Byzantine scholar, known for annotated texts of Sophocles, Pindar, others). Unusual.

Demetrois Greek. From Demetrius. Unusual.

Demond Created. Created, African-American. Unusual.

Demothi Native American. Native American, "Talks walking." Unusual.

Demyan Russian. From Damian, Greek, "To tame." Bedny (Russian socialist poet who glorified revolution) (real name: Yefim Alekseyvich Pridvorov). Unusual.

Den English. From Dennis. Unusual.

Dénes Hungarian. From Dennis. Unusual.

Denham English. From Denham. Unusual.

Denholm English. Scottish, surname and place name used as first name. Elliott (British actor). Unusual.

Denies English. From Dennis. Unusual. Denny.

Denis French, Irish, Russian. From Dennis. Diderot (18th-century French encyclopedist of all knowledge); Savard (Chicago Black Hawks hockey player, scored goal a record 4 seconds after opening face-off, 1986); Papin (18th-century French physicist, invented pressure cooker); Petau (17th-century French theologian, advocated positivism). Less popular. Alternative spelling: Denys.

Deniz Turkish. Turkish, "Sea." Unusual.

Denka Russian. From Dennis. Unusual.

Dennes Hungarian. From Dennis. Unusual.

Dennis English. Greek, "Of Dionysos," the Greek name for the god of wine. Weaver (actor, "McCloud"); Day (singer); O'Keefe (actor); Vollmer (youngest author-illustrator ("Joshua Disobeys"): 6 years old); Barrie (film director). Less popular. Denny.

Dennison English. English, "Son of Dennis (Greek, "Of Dionysos," the Greek name for the god of wine)." Unusual.

Denny English. From Dennis. Rowe (British, fastest barber: shaved 1,994 men in 60 minutes, 1988); McLain (baseball player, Detroit Tigers). Less popular. Alternative spelling: Denney.

Dennys American. From Dennis. Unusual. Denny.

Dent English. From Denton. Unusual.

Denton English. English, "Settlement in a valley." Cooley (heart surgeon whose group has performed a record 75,000 open-heart surgeries); Young (pitched most complete baseball games: 751 over lifetime); Welch (British novelist, "Maiden Voyage"). Unusual.

Denver English. English, "Dane's crossing-place." Pyle (actor, "The Dukes of Hazzard"); Carrington (character in TV's "Dynasty"). Unusual.

Denya Russian. From Dennis. Unusual.

Denzil English. English, place name used as a first name. Unusual. Alternative spellings: Denzel, Denziel, Denzill, Denzyl.

Der English. From Theodoric, Old German, "Ruler of the people." Unusual.

Derby English. English, "Village with deer park." Unusual.

Derek English. From Theodoric, Old German, "Ruler of the people." de Lint (actor, "The Unbearable Lightness of Being"); Bond (British actor); Farr (British actor); Jacobi (British actor); Denniss (holds duo joketelling record: 60 hours, 1988). Popular. Alternative spellings: Dereck, Deric, Derick, Derik, Derreck, Derrek, Derrick, Derrik, Deryck, Deryek, Deryk, Deryke.

Dermod Irish. From Dermot. Unusual.

Dermot Irish. Irish, "Envy-free." Saint (6th-century Irish abbot, founded monastery on island of Inchcleraun, in Lough Ree); MacMurrough (12th-century Irish ruler, initiated Anglo-Norman involvement, which led to British conquest of Ireland). Unusual.

Deron English. From Deryn, Welsh, "Bird." Unusual for males, unusual for females. Alternative spelling: Derrin.

Deror Hebrew/Israeli. Hebrew, "Freedom," "free-flowing brook," or "swallow." Unusual.

Derori Hebrew/Israeli. From Deror. Unusual.

Derrie English. From Theodoric, Old German, "Ruler of the people." Unusual for males, unusual for females.

Derry Irish. Gaelic, "Red-haired." Unusual.

Derwin English. From Darwin, Old English, "A beloved friend." Unusual.

Deshawn Created. Created, African-American. Unusual.

Desire See under Girls' Names.

Desmond English. Irish (Deasmhumhnaigh), "From south Munster." Taylor (actor); Tutu (South African civil rights advocate); Morris (anthropologist). Less popular.

Dev Irish. From Devlin. Unusual.

Devland Irish. From Devlin. Unusual.

Devlin Irish. Gaelic, "Brave," "one of fierce valor." Unusual. Alternative spellings: Devlen, Devlyn.

Devon English. English, place name used as a first name. Less popular for males, unusual for females. Alternative spellings: Devan, Deven, Devin.

Dewayne Created. Created, African-American. Unusual.

Dewei Chinese. Chinese, "Highly virtuous." Unusual.

Dewey English. Surname used as a first name; origin unknown. Unusual.

Dewi Welsh. From David, Hebrew, "Beloved," "friend," or "darling." 1 Samuel 16:19. Jones (British, holds record for steering motorcycle facing backwards from atop 10-foot ladder: 1.5 hours, 1988). Unusual.

Dexter English. Old English, a female dyer. Gordon (tenor saxophonist); Manley (football player, Minnesota Vikings). Unusual.

Diarmuid Irish. From Dermot, Irish, "Envy-free." Unusual.

Dic Romanian. From Richard, Old German, "Strong ruler." Unusual.

Dichali Native American. Native American, "He speaks after." Unusual.

Dick English. From Richard, Old German, "Strong ruler." Clark (TV personality,

"American Bandstand"); Rutan (first nonstop flight around world, with Jeana Yeager, 1986); Van Dyke (actor, "The Dick Van Dyke Show"); Cheney (former secretary of defense); Tracy (character in comic strip, then movie). Less popular.

Dicken English. From Richard, Old German, "Strong ruler." Unusual.

Dickie English. From Richard, Old German, "Strong ruler." Less popular. Alternative spelling: Dicky.

Dickon English. From Richard, Old German, "Strong ruler." Unusual.

Didi See under Girls' Names.

Didier French. From Desire, French, "To crave." Unusual.

Diego Hispanic. From Jacob, Hebrew (Yaakov), "Supplanter" or "heel." Genesis 25:26. Hurtado de Mendoza (16th-century Spanish ambassador to England, Venice); Barros Arana (19th-century Chilean professor, especially wrote on history of Chile); de Torres Villarroel (18th-century Spanish, colorful writer of burlesques and memoirs); Rivera (Spanish, leftist muralist). Unusual.

Dieter German. German, "People-army." Unusual.

Digby English. English, "Settlement by a ditch." Unusual.

Dilwyn Welsh. English, "Secret or shady place." Unusual. Alternative spelling: Dillwyn.

Dima Russian. From Demetrius, Greek, "Lover of the earth" or "from Demeter," the earth mother. Unusual.

Dimitr Bulgarian. From Demetrius, Greek, "Lover of the earth" or "from Demeter," the earth mother. Unusual.

Dimitri Russian. From Demetrius, Greek, "Lover of the earth" or "from Demeter," the earth mother. Mitropoulos (unorthodox conductor, modernist composer); Tiomkin (composed music for over 140 films and TV productions, including theme from "Rawhide"). Unusual. Dimitre, Dimitry, Dmitri.

Dimitrios Greek. From Demetrius, Greek, "Lover of the earth" or "from Demeter," the earth mother. Unusual. Alternative spelling: Demetrois.

Dimka Russian. From Walter, Old German, "Ruling people." Unusual.

Dimos Greek. From Demetrius, Greek, "Lover of the earth" or "from Demeter," the earth mother. Unusual.

Dingbang Chinese. Chinese, "Protect the country." Unusual.

Dinh Vietnamese. Vietnamese, "Settle down." Tien Hoang (10th-century Vietnamese emperor, gained independence from China). Unusual.

Dino English. German, "Little sword." Buzzati (Italian surrealistic, symbolist writer); Compagni (Florentine historian, chronicled Florence's history from 1280, written 1310–12). Unusual.

Dinos Greek. From Constance, Latin, "constans" ("constant" or "unwavering"). Unusual.

Dion English. From Dennis, Greek, "Of Dionysos," the Greek name for the god of wine. Boucicault (19th-century playwright and leading New York actor); DiMucci (singer, "Run-Around Sue"); Cassius (2nd-century Roman senator, wrote history of Rome in Greek). Less popular. Alternative spelling: Deon.

Dione French. From Dennis, Greek, "Of Dionysos," the Greek name for the god of wine. Mother of Aphrodite by Zeus (per Homer), daughter of Oceanus (per Hesiod); in early Greek mythology, the supreme goddess, female counterpart to Zeus. Unusual.

Dionigi Italian. From Dennis, Greek, "Of Dionysos," the Greek name for the god of wine. Unusual.

Dionis Hispanic. From Dennis, Greek, "Of Dionysos," the Greek name for the god of wine. Unusual.

Dionisio Hispanic, Italian. From Dennis, Greek, "Of Dionysos," the Greek name for the god of wine. Anzilotti (Italian professor, judge, president of Permanent Court of International Justice, 1928–30); Herrera (Nicaraguan president of Honduras, 1824–27, and Nicaragua, 1830–33). Unusual.

Dionusios Greek. From Dionysius. Unusual.

Dionysius Latin. Latin, the Latin name for the god of wine. Acts 17:34. Name of several saints; name of two tyrannical leaders of Syracuse, a city in the Roman empire, 405–343 B.C.; Thrax (2nd-century B.C. Greek, wrote first Greek grammar book). Unusual.

Dionysus German. From Dennis, Greek, "Of Dionysos," the Greek name for the god of wine. Unusual.

Dirk English. From Theodoric, Old German, "Ruler of the people." Benedict (actor, "A-Team"); Brouwer (astronomer, pioneered using computers to understand orbits); Camphuysen (16th-17th-century Dutch painter, poet, and theologian; translated psalms); Bogarde (actor, "The Servant"). Less popular. Alternative spelling: Derk.

Diverous Unknown. From Dives. Unusual. Alternative spellings: Divarus, Diveros, Diverus, Divorus.

Divers Unknown. From Dives. Unusual.

Dives Unknown. "Rich man"; origin unknown. Unusual.

Dixon English. English, "Dick's son"; surname used as a first name. Denham (19th-century British explorer of Africa). Unusual.

Dmitrik Russian. From Demetrius, Greek, "Lover of the earth" or "from Demeter," the earth mother. Unusual.

Dob English. From Robert, Old English (Hreodbeorht), "Fame-bright." Unusual.

Dobry Polish. Polish, "Good." Unusual.

Doctor English. Latin, "docere" ("to teach"); the word used as a first name. Unusual.

Dodek Polish. From Donato, Latin, "Gift." Unusual.

Dodya Russian. From David, Hebrew, "Beloved," "friend," or "darling." 1 Samuel 16:19. Unusual.

Dohosan Native American. Native American, "Small bluff." Unusual.

Dolf English. From Rudolph, Old German (Hrudolf), "Fame-wolf." Unusual.

Dolfe Slavic. From Rudolph, Old German (Hrudolf), "Fame-wolf." Unusual. Alternative spellings: Dolfi, Dolphe.

Dolphus English. From Adolphus, Old German, "Noble wolf" or "hero." Unusual.

Dom English. From Dominic, Latin, "Lord." Joseph (French monk and musician; pioneered restoration of Gregorian chants); DeLuise (comedian and actor). Less popular.

Dome Hungarian. From Dominic, Latin, "Lord." Unusual.

Domek Czech. From Dominic, Latin, "Lord." Unusual for males, unusual for females.

Domenic English. From Dominic, Latin, "Lord." Less popular.

Domenico Italian. From Dominic, Latin, "Lord." Beccafumi (16th-century Italian painter and sculptor, known especially for scenes from Old Testament); Montagnana (18th-century Italian violinist and cello maker); Morelli (19th-century Italian painter, known especially for realistic historical scenes). Unusual.

Domicio Hispanic. From Dominic, Latin, "Lord." Unusual.

Domingo Hispanic. From Dominic, Latin, "Lord." Martínez de Irala (16th-century Spanish conquistador and explorer); Santa María (president of Chile, 1881–86); Sarmiento (educator and writer, Argentine president, 1868–74). Unusual.

Domingos Portuguese. From Dominic, Latin, "Lord." Unusual.

Dominick English. From Dominic, Latin, "Lord." Less popular. Alternative spelling: Domenic.

Dominik Czech, German, Polish. From Dominic, Latin, "Lord." Unusual for males, unusual for females.

Dominique French. From Dominic, Latin, "Lord." Wilkens (basketball great); Pire (Belgian cleric, humanitarian; won Nobel Peace Prize, 1958, for postwar aid to displaced persons); Denon (17th-18th-century French illustrator, first to organize Louvre collections); Larrey (19th-century French surgeon, invented field hospital). Less popular. Alternative spelling: Dominque.

Domó Hungarian. From Dominic, Latin, "Lord." Unusual.

Domokos Hungarian. From Dominic, Latin, "Lord." Unusual.

Domotor Hungarian. From Demetrius, Greek, "Lover of the earth" or "from Demeter," the earth mother. Unusual.

Don English. From Donald. Knotts (comedian and actor); Johnson (actor, "Miami Vice"); Henley (Grammy winner); Buell (19th-century army general, fought with Grant at Shiloh); Carlos (claimed Spanish throne as Charles VII, 1872). Less popular. Alternative spelling: Donn.

Donahue Hungarian. Gaelic, "Dark warrior." Unusual.

Donal English. From Donald. Heatley (New Zealander who fought and lost longest fight between man and fish: 32 hours, 5 minutes; a black marlin, about 1,500 pounds, escaped). Unusual.

Donald English. Gaelic (Domhnall), "Mighty in the world." Barthelme (modernist novelist); Trump (billionaire businessman); Sutherland (actor, "Klute"); O'Connor (actor and dancer). Popular. Don, Donny.

Donaldo Italian. From Donald. Unusual.

Donalt Norwegian. From Donald. Unusual.

Donat Polish. From Donato. Unusual.

Donatello Italian. From Donato. Innovative 15th-century Florentine sculptor, developed new Renaissance style, widely considered greatest sculptor of 15th century. Unusual.

Donati Italian. From Donato. Unusual.

Donato Italian. Latin, "Gift." Bramante (16th-century Italian architect, designed new basilica of St. Peter, begun 1506). Unusual.

Donatus English. From Donato. Saint. Unusual.

Donek Polish. From Dominic, Latin, "Lord." Unusual.

Donnell English. Irish, surname used as a first name. Unusual.

Donnelly English. Celtic, "Black man" or "brave dark man." Unusual.

Donny English. From Donald. Lalonde (Canadian boxing great); Osmond (singer and actor). Less popular. Don. Alternative spelling: Donnie.

Donohue Irish. From Donahue. Unusual.

Donois French. From Daniel, Hebrew, "God is my judge." Daniel 1:6. Unusual.

Donovan English. Irish, "Dark brown." Scottish pop singer, "Mellow Yellow" (real name: Donovan Leitch). Less popular. Don, Donny. Alternative spellings: Donavan, Donavon, Donoven, Donovon, Dunavan.

Dor Hebrew/Israeli. Hebrew, "Home" or "generation." Unusual.

Doran English. Greek, "Gift." Unusual. Alternative spellings: Dorran, Dorren.

Dorek Polish. From Theodore, Greek, "theodoros" ("God's gift"). Unusual.

Dorian See under Girls' Names.

Dorien See Dorian under Girls' Names.

Doron Hebrew/Israeli. Hebrew, "Gift from God." Unusual.

Dorri See Dory under Girls' Names.

Dorrien English. From Dorian, Greek, place name used as a first name. Unusual.

Dorry See Dory under Girls' Names.

Dory See under Girls' Names.

Dotan Hebrew/Israeli. Hebrew, "Law." Unusual.

Dothan Hebrew/Israeli. From Dotan. Unusual.

Doug English. From Douglas. McClure (actor, "The Virginian"); Flutie (quarterback, formerly with Chicago Bears); Wilson (hockey player, Chicago Blackhawks). Less popular.

Dougal Scottish. Gaelic (Dubhgall), "Black stranger." Unusual.

Douglas English. Gaelic, "Dark blue or black water." Moore (composer, wrote opera "The Devil and Daniel Webster"); Fairbanks (actor, "Robin Hood"); MacArthur (led Pacific forces in WWII); Lowe (British track star); Edwards (TV newscaster); Mawson (Australian explorer, especially of Antarctic). Popular. Doug. Alternative spelling: Douglass.

Dov Hebrew/Israeli. Hebrew, "Bear." Unusual.

Dovev Hebrew/Israeli. Hebrew, "Whispering" or "quietly speaking." Unusual.

Dovidas Lithuanian. From David, Hebrew, "Beloved," "friend," or "darling." 1 Samuel 16:19. Unusual.

Dowid Yiddish. From David, Hebrew, "Beloved," "friend," or "darling." 1 Samuel 16:19. Unusual.

Doyle English. Celtic, "Dark stranger." Alexander (baseball player). Unusual.

Drake English. Latin, "Dragon." Unusual.

Dreng Norwegian. Norwegian, "Hired farmhand" or "brave man." Unusual.

Drew English. From Andrew, Greek, "Manly." Pearson (newspaper columnist, "Washington Merry-Go-Round"); Barrymore (actress, "E.T.—The Extra-Terrestrial"). Less popular. Alternative spelling: Drewe.

Drummond Scottish. Scottish, surname used as a first name. Unusual.

Duane English. Irish, "Black"; surname used as a first name. Allman (musician with the Allman Brothers and the Doobie Brothers); Bickett (football player); Thomas (football player). Less popular. Alternative spellings: Duwayne, Dwain, Dwaine, Dwane, Dwayne.

Duarte Portuguese. From Edward, Old English, "Property guardian." Pacheco Pereira (Portuguese, explored southwest Africa, governed it 1520–22); Coelho Pereira (16th-century Portuguese soldier, built Pernambuco into thriving colony). Unusual.

Dudd English. From Dudley. Unusual.

Dudley English. English, surname or place name used as a first name. Pound (British admiral, commander-in-chief, 1936–39); DeChair (British naval officer during WWI); Moore (comedian and actor, "Arthur"). Less popular. Alternative spelling: Dudly.

Duff English. Celtic, "One with a dark face." McKagen (musician with Guns 'n' Roses). Unusual.

Dugald Scottish. From Dougal, Gaelic (Dubhgall), "Black stranger." Stewart (18th-century Scottish philosopher, supported Scottish "common sense" school); Clerk, Sir (engineer, invented two-cycle gas engine). Unusual.

Duke English. English, title and surname used as a first name. Ellington (musician during big-band era); Snider (baseball player); Lavery (character in TV's "General Hospital"). Unusual.

Dukker Gypsy. English Gypsy, "Fortune teller." Unusual.

Dumaka African. African, "Give me a helping hand." Unusual.

Duman Turkish. Turkish, "Misty" or "smoky." Unusual.

Dumichel Created. Created, African-American. Unusual.

Dumin Czech. From Dominic, Latin, "Lord." Unusual for males, unusual for females.

Duncan English. Gaelic (Donnchad), "Brown warrior." Armstrong (Australian, Olympic gold medalist, 200-meter freestyle swim, 1988); Phyfe (19th-century woodworker noted for excellent chairs, tables, and couches); Scott (Canadian poet influenced by Indians and nature); Renaldo (actor, "The Cisco Kid"). Less popular.

Dune English. From Duncan. Unusual.

Dunham English. Celtic, "Dark man." Unusual. Alternative spelling: Dunam.

Dunn English. From Duncan. Unusual. Alternative spelling: Dun.

Dunstan English. English, "Stony hill." Patron saint of blacksmiths, goldsmiths, locksmiths, and the blind. Unusual.

Duoc Vietnamese. Vietnamese, "Moral." Unusual.

Dur Hebrew/Israeli. Hebrew, "To stack up." Unusual.

Durand English. Latin, "Enduring." Unusual.

Durell Scottish. Scottish, "King's doorkeeper." Unusual. Alternative spelling: Durrell.

Durko Czech. From George, Greek, "Husbandman," "farmer," or "earthworker." Unusual.

Durriken Gypsy. English Gypsy, "Fortune teller." Unusual.

Durril Gypsy. English Gypsy, "Gooseberry." Unusual.

Dusan Serbian. From Daniel, Hebrew, "God is my judge." Daniel 1:6. Simovic (Yugoslavian cabinet official). Unusual.

Dust English. From Dustin. Unusual.

Dustin English. Old English, "Dusty place." Hoffman (actor and Oscar winner, "Rain Man"); Farnum (actor in silent movies). Popular. Alternative spelling: Dustyn.

Dusty English. From Dustin, Old English, "Dusty place." Springfield (British singer, "Wishin' and Hopin'," 1964); Farlow (character in TV's "Dallas"); Baker (baseball player, L.A. Dodgers). Less popular for males, unusual for females. Alternative spelling: Dustie.

Dwight English. From Dionysius, Latin, the Latin name for the god of wine. Acts 17:34. Eisenhower (33rd president); Davis (secretary of war, 1925); Gooden (baseball player, N.Y. Mets). Less popular.

Dyami Native American. Native American, "Eagle." Unusual.

Dyer English. English, surname used as a first name. Unusual.

Dylan English. Welsh, "Son of the waves." Thomas (Welsh poet and writer, "Under Milk Wood," 1953). Unusual. Alternative spellings: Dillan, Dillon.

Dymek Polish. From Demetrius, Greek, "Lover of the earth" or "from Demeter," the earth mother. Unusual.

Dymitry Polish. From Demetrius, Greek, "Lover of the earth" or "from Demeter," the earth mother. Unusual.

Dymoke Unknown. Place name used as a first name; origin unknown. Unusual.

Dyre Norwegian. Norse, "Precious." Unusual.

Dyson English. From Dennis, Greek, "Of Dionysos," the Greek name for the god of wine. Unusual.

Dyzek Polish. From Demetrius, Greek, "Lover of the earth" or "from Demeter," the earth mother. Unusual.

Eamonn Irish. From Edmund, Old English, "Rich protector." Coghlan (Irish track and field champion, ran one of 10 fastest indoor miles: 3 minutes, 46.31 seconds, 1985). Unusual. Alternative spelling: Eamon.

Ean English. From John, Hebrew (Yochanan), "God has been gracious." Unusual.

Eardley English. Surname and place name used as a first name; origin unknown. Unusual.

Earl English. English, title of nobility and surname used as a first name. Powell (pianist, be-bop jazz pioneer); Warren (Chief Justice of the U.S., 1953–69); Scruggs (bluegrass musician, especially known for playing five-string banjo); Biggers (writer, created "Charlie Chan"). Less popular. Alternative spellings: Earle, Erle.

Earnest English. From Ernest, English, "Vigor" or "earnestness." Unusual. Ernie.

Ebbaneza English. From Ebenezer. Unusual.

Eben English. From Ebenezer. Tourjee (19th-century musician, founded New England Conservatory of Music, Boston, 1867); Fardd (19th-century Welsh poet and collector of hymns). Unusual.

Ebenezer English. Hebrew, "Helping stone." Hoar (attorney general, 1869); Prout (19th-century British composer and musical theorist); Zane (18th-century pioneer, first to settle on Ohio River, at Wheeling Creek, Ohio, 1770); Elliott (romantic, activist 19th-century British poet); Scrooge (character in Dickens' "Christmas Carol"). Unusual. Alternative spellings: Ebeneezer, Ebenezar, Ebenezeer.

Ed English. From Edward, Old English, "Property guardian." Koch (former mayor of New York City); Asner (actor); Howe (journalist, edited Atchison, Kan. "Daily Globe"); Begley, Jr. (actor, "The Accidental Tourist"); Wynn (comedic actor, "The Absent-Minded Professor"); McMahon (TV host, "Star Search"). Less popular.

Edan English. Celtic, "Fire." Unusual.

Eddie English. From Edward, Old English, "Property guardian." Albert (actor); Olmos (actor); Murphy (comedian and actor, "48 Hours"); Foy (vaudevillian, "Earl and Girl"). Less popular. Alternative spelling: Eddy.

Edek Polish. From Edward, Old English, "Property guardian." Unusual.

Eden See under Girls' Names.

Edgar English. Old English, "Prosperity" + "spear." Allan Poe (poet and writer of stories, "The Raven"); Winters (singer and musician); Snow (author, journalist, and editor, wrote especially on China); Bergen (ventriloquist with dummy Charlie McCarthy); Degas (French impressionist painter). Less popular. Ed.

Edgard French, Hungarian, Russian. From Edgar. Varese (composer who pioneered arrythmic, atonal electronic music). Unusual.

Edgardo Hispanic, Italian. From Edgar. Unusual.

Edgars Latvian. From Edgar. Unusual.

Edik Russian. From Edward, Old English, "Property guardian." Unusual.

Edison English. Old English, "Son of Edward." Unusual. Alternative spelling: Edisen.

Edko Czech. From Edward, Old English, "Property guardian." Unusual.

Edmon English, Russian. From Edmund. Unusual.

Edmond Russian. From Edmund. Perrier (French zoologist, defended theory of evolution); Pressensé (19th-century French clergyman and politician, founded Protestant journal); Richer (17th-century French theologian, opposed Jesuit policies); Rostand (playwright, "Cyrano de Bergerac"). Unusual.

Edmondo Italian. From Edmund. De Amicis (19th-century Italian writer known for children's stories). Unusual.

Edmondson English. English, surname used as a first name. Unusual.

Edmund English. Old English, "Rich protector." Saint, 9th-century and 13th-century; Muskie (secretary of state under Carter); of Langley (first Duke of York, 14th-century; founded House of York); Ludlow (British parliamentary leader); Wilson (critic of literature and politics, essayist). Less popular. Ed, Eddie+, Ned, Ted.

Edmundo Hispanic. From Edmund. Unusual.

Edmunds Latvian. From Edmund. Unusual.

Edo Czech. From Edward. Unusual.

Édouard French. From Edward. Le Roy (French pragmatist philosopher); Manet (19th-century French painter, mixed realism and impressionism); Martel (French, considered founder of speleology (caving)); Belin (French engineer and inventor, invented first telephoto transmission, 1907). Unusual.

Edric English. Old English, "Powerful with property." Streona (11th-century British ruler of Mercia). Unusual. Alternative spelling: Edrick.

Edson English. From Edison. Unusual.

Eduardo Italian, Portuguese. From Edward. Santos (Columbian, owner of "El Tiempo" newspaper; president, 1938–42); Torroja Miret (Spanish architect, pioneered design of concrete shell structures). Unusual.

Edus Czech. From Edward. Unusual.

Edvard Czech, Danish, Hungarian, Swedish. From Edward. Beneš (Czech president, 1935–38); Brandes (Danish dramatist and critic). Unusual.

Edward English. Old English, "Property guardian." Saint; Albee (won Pulitzer Prize for drama, 1975, "Seascape"); Gibbon (British historian, "Decline and Fall of the Roman Empire"); Hopper (realistic painter, "Nighthawks"); G. Robinson (actor, "Little Caesar"); Woodward (actor, "The Equalizer"). Popular. Ed, Eddie+, Ned, Ted.

Edwin English. Old English, "Friend" or "prosperity." Saint; Landseer (19th-century British portraitist, painted Queen Victoria and other nobility); Armstrong (invented FM radio frequency, 1933); Aldrin, Jr. (second man on the moon, July 21, 1969); Porter (film-maker, early 1900s: "The Great Train Robbery"). Less popular. Ed, Eddie. Alternative spelling: Edwyn.

Edwy Unknown. Old English, "War" or "prosperity." Unusual.

Edzio Polish. Old English, "Property guardian." Unusual.

Egan Irish. Irish, "Little fire." Unusual. Alternative spelling: Egen.

Egbert English. Old English, "Bright sword." Saint; first English king, circa 830. Unusual.

Egerton English. English, place name used as a first name. Unusual.

Egidius Scottish. Scottish, from the Greek "aigidion" ("young goat"). Unusual.

Egor Russian. From George, Greek, "Husbandman," "farmer," or "earthworker." Unusual. Alternative spelling: Igor.

Eifion Welsh. English, place name used as a first name. Unusual.

Eilwyn Welsh. From Eilwen, Welsh, "Fair brow" or "white brow." Unusual.

Einar Norwegian. Old Norse, "Individualist." Kvaran (Icelandic spiritualist writer). Unusual.

Eion Irish. From John, Hebrew (Yochanan), "God has been gracious." Unusual.

Ejnar Danish. From Einar. Mikkelsen (Danish, thoroughly explored Greenland, 1900–32); Hertzsprung (Danish astronomer, demonstrated existence of giant and dwarf stars). Unusual.

Elah Hebrew/Israeli. From Alva, Hebrew, "Brightness" (?). Genesis 36:40. Unusual.

Elam English. Place name used as a first name; origin unknown. Unusual.

Elan Native American. Native American, "Friendly." Unusual.

Elba Italian. Italian, place name used as a first name. Unusual.

Elbert American. From Albert, Old English (Aethelbeorht), "Noble-bright." Gary (lawyer and businessman; chairman, U.S. Steel, 1903–27; opposed unions but improved steelworkers' conditions and wages). Unusual.

Eldon English. English, "Ella's mound." Joersz (achieved fastest air speed: 2,193.167 mph, in a Lockheed SR-71A, 1976). Unusual. Alternative spelling: Elden.

Eldred English. Old English, "Elderly counsel." Unusual.

Eldridge English. German, "Mature counselor." Less popular.

Eleazar Hebrew/Israeli. From Eliezer. López Contreras (president of Venezuela, 1936–41); Wheelock (18th-century clergyman; educated Indians; founded Dartmouth College, 1769). Unusual. Alternative spelling: Eliezer.

Elek Hungarian. From Alexander, Greek, "Defender of men" or "warding off men." Mark 16:21; Acts 4:6, 19:33. Unusual.

Eleutherios Greek. Greek, "Free man." Unusual.

Eli Hebrew/Israeli. Hebrew, "God is exalted." 1 Samuel 4:12. High priest (Bible); Phipps (one of longest-lived identical twins: died at 108 years, 9 days, 1911); Beeding (withstood highest "g" force: 82.6 g's, for 0.04 seconds, on rocket sled, 1958); Wallach (actor, "Magnificent Seven"); Terry (19th-century clock maker). Unusual.

Elia Native American. From Elijah. Kazan (actor). Unusual.

Elias Greek. From Elijah. Saint; Lönnrot (19th-century Finnish professor, collected and systematized Finnish folksongs, 1835); ParishAlvers (19th-century British harpist); Howe (19th-century, invented sewing machine, 1846); Ashmole (17th-century British antiquarian, collection is basis of Ashmolean Museum, Oxford). Unusual. Alternative spellings: Eliasz, Ilias.

Elice See Ellice under Girls' Names.

Elie English. From Elijah. Algranti (South African, holds record for longest hair-styling session: 415 hours); Lescot (Haitian president, 1941–46); Nadelman (sculptor known for humorous works); de Cyon (19th-century Russian physiologist, studied vasomotor nerves of the heart). Unusual.

Elihu Hebrew/Israeli. From Elijah. Washburne (secretary of state, 1869); Root (secretary of war, 1899); Thomson (engineer, holds over 700 patents, invented electric welding); Vedder (painter and illustrator, work based on dream, fantasy); Yale (British colonial administrator, founded Yale University, 1718). Unusual.

Elijah English. Hebrew (Eliyahu), "The Lord is my God." 1 Kings 17:1. Prophet; Levita (16th-century Italian Jewish scholar, wrote on Hebrew grammar and the Torah); Blue Allman (son of Cher and Gregg Allman); Muhammad (black nationalist leader); White (physician and pioneer, led 120 immigrants to Oregon country, 1842). Unusual. Alternative spelling: Elija.

Elisha See under Girls' Names.

Elisher English. From Elisha, Hebrew, "God is salvation." Unusual.

Elison English. From Elijah. 1 Kings 17:1. Unusual.

Eliyahu Hebrew/Israeli. Hebrew, "The Lord is my God." 1 Kings 17:1. Unusual.

Elkan Hebrew/Israeli. Hebrew, "He belongs to God." Unusual.

Elkanah Hebrew/Israeli. Hebrew, "God has created." Unusual.

Elki Native American. Native American, "To hang over the top of." Unusual.

Ellery English. Latin, surname used as a first name. Queen (wrote over 40 detective novels) (real name: Manfred Lee). Less popular.

Ellice See under Girls' Names.

Elliot English. Hebrew, "High." Springs (textile magnate and novelist, "Warbirds"); Richardson (secretary of defense under Nixon); Paul (author of short stories and screenplays); Coues (19th-century ornithologist, assisted with census of North American birdlife). Less popular. Alternative spellings: Eliot, Eliott, Elliott.

Ellis English. From Elijah. 1 Kings 17:1. Butler (humorous author, "Pigs is Pigs," 1906). Less popular.

Ellison English. Old English, "Ellis's son." Unusual.

Elman German. German, "Elm tree." Unusual. Alternative spelling: Elmen.

Elmer English. Old English (Aethelmaer), "Noble-famous." Trett (highest terminal velocity from a standing start on a motorcycle: 201.34 mph after 440 yards, 1983); Rice (playwright and author, won Pulitzer Prize for "Street Scene," 1929); Sperry (industrialist, invented gyroscopic compass); Layden (football player). Less popular.

Eloy Hebrew/Israeli. From Eli, Hebrew, "God is exalted." 1 Samuel 4:12. Alfaro (Ecuadoran president, 1897–1901, 1906–11). Unusual.

Elrad Hebrew/Israeli. Hebrew, "God rules." Unusual.

Elric English. From Aldrich, Old English, "Wise ruler." Unusual.

Elroy American. From Leroy, Old French, "The king." Hirsch (football player, nicknamed "Crazy Legs"). Unusual.

Elston English. Old English, "From the old farm." Brooks (author, "The Man Who Ruined Football"); Howard (baseball player). Unusual.

Elsu Native American. Native American, "Falcon flying in a circle." Unusual.

Elton English. English, "Ella's settlement." John (British singer and musician, "Crocodile Rock"). Unusual.

Elvet English. English, "Swan stream." Unusual.

Elvin English. From Alvin, Old English, "Elf-friend," "noble friend," "everyone's friend," or "old friend." Hayes (scored most points in a college basketball career: 358, 1966–68; later played for Houston). Unusual. Alternative spellings: Alven, Alvin, Alvyn.

Elvis English. Created, meaning unknown. Presley (singer and actor, "King of Rock and Roll"; more than 170 hit singles and 80 top-selling albums); Costello (singer, musician, and songwriter). Less popular.

Elwin Welsh. From Alvin, Old English, "Elf-friend," "noble friend," "everyone's friend," or "old friend." Saint; Christoffel (19th-century Swiss mathematician known for work in geometry). Unusual. Alternative spelling: Elwyn.

Ely Hebrew/Israeli. From Eli, Hebrew, "God is exalted." 1 Samuel 4:12. Culbertson (authority on contract bridge). Less popular.

Elya English. From Elijah. Unusual.

Eman Czech. From Emanuel. Unusual.

Emanuel English. Hebrew, "God is with us," referring to a child about to be born. Isaiah 7:14. Zacchini (flew record distance when shot from a cannon: 175 feet, 1940); Lasker (German, world champion chess master, 1894–1921); Leutze (19th-century painter known for historical works, "Washington Crossing the Delaware," 1851). Less popular. Manny+. Alternative spellings: Emmanuel, Emmanuil.

Ember English. Old English, "aemerge" ("ashes"); the word used as a first name. Unusual.

Emek English. From Emanuel. Unusual.

Emerson English. From Emery. Fittipaldi (Brazilian, won largest individual Indianapolis 500 prize: $1,001,604, 1989); Hough (author and advocate of preserving wildlife and national parks). Unusual. Alternative spelling: Emmerson.

Emile English. Latin, a clan name probably meaning "eager." Levassor (French, won first car race, 1895; average speed: 15.01 mph); Durkheim (developed sociology's rigor); Zola (19th-century French naturalist author, ardent defender of Dreyfus); Berliner (invented flat disk for music reproduction, circa 1880). Unusual. Alternative spelling: Emil.

Emilek Czech. From Emile. Unusual.

Emilian Polish. From Emile. Unusual.

Emilio Hispanic, Italian, Portuguese. From Emile. Marinetti (Italian futurist writer); De Bono (Italian general, opposed Mussolini, tried and executed for treason); Praga (19th-century Italian romantic poet); Aguinaldo (Filipino, led Filipino forces in rebellion against Spain, 1896–98). Unusual.

Emilo English. From Emile, Latin, a clan name probably meaning "eager." Unusual.

Emils English. From Emile, Latin, a clan name probably meaning "eager." Unusual.

Emlyn See under Girls' Names.

Emmett English. Surname used as a first name; origin unknown. Kelly (clown, created well-known character "Weary Willie"). Unusual for males, unusual for females. Alternative spellings: Emmet, Emmot.

Emory English. From Emery. Upton (19th-century army officer, wrote on tactics and military policy). Less popular. Alternative spellings: Emery, Emmery.

Emrick German. From Emery. Unusual. Alternative spelling: Emryk.

Emrys Welsh. From Ambrose, Greek, "Immortal." Unusual.

Enderby English. English, surname and place name used as a first name. Unusual.

Endre Hungarian. From Andrew, Greek, "Manly." Ady (Hungarian, considered greatest lyrical poet of 20th century). Unusual.

Eneas Hispanic. From Aeneas, Greek, "Praiseworthy." Unusual.

Engelbert English. Old German, "Bright as an angel." I (saint and archbishop of Cologne, 1216–25); Humperdinck (German composer, wrote opera "Hansel und Gretel," 1893); Humperdink (singer, "After the Loving"); Kämpfer (18th-century German physician and member of trade missions to Russia, Persia, and Japan). Unusual. Alternative spelling: Englebert.

Enli Native American. Native American, "The dog I saw." Unusual.

Ennis English. From Angus, Gaelic, "Unique choice." Also a Scottish place name, now called Forfarshire. Unusual.

Enoch English. Hebrew (Chanoch), "Educated," "trained," or "dedicated." Grandson of Adam and Eve; Wood (18th-century potter, created busts of Shakespeare, Milton, and others; a principal figure in British pottery); Crowder (army officer; ambassador to Cuba, 1923–27). Unusual. Alternative spelling: Enock.

Enos English. Hebrew, "Man." Cabell (baseball player); Slaughter (baseball player); Slate (character in TV's "The Dukes of Hazzard"). Unusual.

Enric Romanian. From Harold, Old English, "Army power." Unusual.

Enrico Italian. From Henry, Old German (Heimerich), "Home ruler." Caruso (superb Italian tenor, estate worth $9 million at death in 1921); Betti (19th-century Italian mathematician known especially for his work in topology); Cecchetti (Italian dancer and teacher). Unusual.

Enrikos Greek. From Henry, Old German (Heimerich), "Home ruler." Unusual.

Enrique Hispanic. From Henry, Old German (Heimerich), "Home ruler." Larreta (Argentine historical novelist); de Arfe (16th-century Spanish silversmith known for Gothic altarpieces); Peñaranda Castillo (Brazilian president, 1940–43); González Martínez (Mexican physician, poet, and diplomat; minister to Chile, 1920–22). Unusual.

Enzio Italian. From Henry, Old German (Heimerich), "Home ruler." Unusual.

Enzo Italian. From Vincent, Latin, "Vincentius," from "vincere" ("to conquer"). Unusual.

Eoghan Irish. From Eugene, Greek, "Well born." Irish ruler, 400–450. Unusual.

Ephraim Hebrew/Israeli. Hebrew, "Fruitful." Genesis 41:52. Joseph's second son; Shay (invented geared steam locomotive, used in logging and mining, circa 1877); McDowell (19th-century pioneer in abdominal surgery); Bull (19th-century horticulturist, developed the Concord grape); Williams (18th-century army officer, funded Williams College). Unusual.

Er English. Hebrew, "Watcher." Unusual.

Erasmus English. Greek, "Desired" or "beloved." Patron saint of sailors and sufferers of intestinal diseases; Reinhold (16th-century German astronomer, second only to Copernicus in importance). Unusual.

Erek English. From Eric. Unusual.

Eric English. Old Norse, "Ruler of all" or "always ruler." Ambler (suspense writer); Clapton (musician and singer, "Layla"); Severeid (newscaster); Dickerson (football player, L.A. Rams; set seasonal rushing record, 1984: 2,105 yards); Heiden (won record five Olympic gold medals for speed skating, 1980). Very popular. Alternative spellings: Erek, Erick.

Erich Czech, German. From Eric. Leinsdorf (conductor); Segal (novelist, "Love Story"); Mendelssohn (expressionist architect, internationally prolific); Maria Remarque (German author, "All Quiet on the Western Front," 1929); Fromm (psychoanalyst and social philosopher, "Art of Loving"). Unusual.

Erico Italian, Portuguese. From Eric. Unusual.

Erik Scandinavian. From Eric. the Red (10th-century Norwegian navigator, explored Greenland) (real name: Erik Thorvaldson); Estrada (actor, "CHiPS"); Satie (French avant-garde composer, "Trois Gymnopedies," 1888). Unusual.

Eriks Latvian, Russian. From Eric. Unusual.

Erin See under Girls' Names.

Ernest English. English, "Vigor" or "earnestness." Hemingway (author, "The Sun Also Rises"); Borgnine (actor, "The Dirty Dozen"); Swanson (fastest base runner: 13.3 seconds, 1932); Lawrence (physicist, invented cyclotron, 1929); Rutherford (British physicist, won 1908 Nobel Prize for chemistry). Less popular. Ernie.

Ernestino English. From Ernest. Unusual.

Ernesto English. From Ernest. Moneta (Italian journalist and advocate of international peace, shared Nobel Peace Prize, 1907); Guevara (Argentine physician turned leftist revolutionary leader) (also known as Che). Unusual.

Ernie English. From Ernest. Less popular.

Ernst English. From Ernest. Mach (Austrian physicist, studied flight of projectiles; his work led to the Mach scale to gauge aircraft speeds); Mensen (Norwegian seaman in British navy, ran from Istanbul to Calcutta and back in 59 days, 1836); von Wildenbruch (19th-century German writer, "Spartacus"). Unusual.

Errol English. Place name used as a first name; origin unknown. Flynn (actor, "The Adventures of Robin Hood"); Mann (football player); Garner (jazz pianist). Unusual.

Erskine English. Scottish, "Green pastures"; place name used as a first name. Holland, Sir (British professor of international law and diplomacy, Oxford); Caldwell (author, "Tobacco Road"). Unusual.

Ervin Czech. From Irvin, Gaelic, "Beautiful." Scottish place name. Johnson (basketball player, L.A. Lakers) (real name of "Magic"). Unusual.

Ervine English. From Irvin, Gaelic, "Beautiful." Scottish place name. Unusual. Alternative spelling: Irvine.

Erving English. From Irvin, Gaelic, "Beautiful." Scottish place name. Unusual. Alternative spelling: Irving.

Ervins Latvian. From Irvin, Gaelic, "Beautiful." Scottish place name. Unusual.

Erwin English. From Irwin, Old English, "Boar" + "friend." Panofsky (art historian, especially Renaissance and medieval art); Piscator (German expressionistic theater producer); Shaw (author, "Rich Man, Poor Man"); Allen (film producer, "Towering Inferno"); Schrödinger (Austrian physicist, developed basis of quantum physics). Unusual. Alternative spelling: Irwin.

Erwinek Polish. From Irwin, Old English, "Boar" + "friend." Unusual.

Eryl See under Girls' Names.

Esau English. Hebrew, "Rough," "hairy," or "thick-haired," referring to the biblical Esau's appearance at birth. Unusual. Alternative spelling: Esaw.

Esdras French, Hispanic. From Ezra, Hebrew, "Help." Ezra 7:1. Unusual.

Esme English. Latin, "Esteem." Stuart (16th-century British, first Duke of Lennox). Unusual for males, unusual for females.

Esmond English. Old English, "Rich protector." Unusual.

Esra German. From Ezra, Hebrew, "Help." Ezra 7:1. Unusual.

Essien African. African, "Sixth-born." Unusual.

Estéban Hispanic. From Stephen, Greek, "Crown" or "crowned." Acts 7:59. Villegas (17th-century Spanish poet, admired classical Roman poets); Echeverría (19th-century Argentine poet, introduced European romanticism to Latin America). Unusual.

Estevao Hispanic. From Stephen, Greek, "Crown" or "crowned." Acts 7:59. Unusual.

Etan English. From Ethan. Unusual.

Ethan English. Hebrew, "Consistency." Kings 4:31. Hitchcock (former secretary of the interior); Allen (soldier during American Revolution). Less popular.

Ethelbert Unknown. Old English, "Noble-bright." Saint; Nevin (19th-century composer and pianist, "Mighty Lak a Rose"). Unusual.

Ethelwyn English. Old English, "Noble friend." Unusual. Alternative spellings: Ethelwin, Ethelwyne, Ethelwynne.

Étienne French. From Stephen, Greek, "Crown" or "crowned." Acts 7:59. Marcel (14th-century French bourgeois leader, led Paris mob against the dauphin); Méhul (18th-century French composer, wrote more than 40 operas); de La Boétie (16th-century French poet, close friend of Montaigne); Pasquier (16th-century French lawyer, fought the Jesuits). Unusual.

Etu Native American. Native American, "The sun." Unusual.

Euclid Greek. Greek, surname used as a first name. Greek pioneer of geometry, circa 300 B.C. Unusual.

Eugen Czech, German. From Eugene. Langen (19th-century German, invented prototype car engine, 1877); Böhm-Bawerk (Austrian economist, developed theory of interest); Neureuther (19th-century German artist, illustrated Goethe's works); Steinach (Austrian physiologist, rejuvenated men with grafts of animals' sex organs). Unusual.

Eugene English. Greek, "Well born." Cernan (astronaut, longest on moon: 72 hours, 59 minutes, 1972); Ormandy (conductor, violinist); O'Neill (playwright, "Desire Under the Elms"); Delacroix (19th-century French painter); Field (poet, "Wynken, Blynken, and Nod"); Lockhart (football player, also known as "Spider"). Less popular. Gene.

Eugeni Russian. From Eugene. Unusual.

Eugenio Hispanic. From Eugene. Soler (Spanish, plays 50 instruments simultaneously, all mounted on a tricycle); de Ochoa (19th-century Spanish writer and scholar, translated complete works of Virgil); Montale (Italian poet noted for directness, won Nobel Prize for literature, 1975). Unusual.

Eugenius German. From Eugene. Unusual. Alternative spelling: Eugenios.

Eustace English. Greek, "Fruitful." Saint; name of four counts of Boulogne (1027–1153); Tilley (mascot of "New Yorker" magazine); Budgell (18th-century British writer, contributed to "The Spectator," a paper concerned with manners, morals, and literature). Unusual.

Ev Welsh. From John, Hebrew (Yochanan), "God has been gracious." Unusual.

Evagelos Greek. From Andrew, Greek, "Manly." Unusual.

Evan Welsh. From John, Hebrew (Yochanan), "God has been gracious." Shelby (18th-century soldier, served in Braddock's campaign, fought Chickamauga Indians); Evans (18th-century Welsh poet and scholar of poetry). Less popular for males, unusual for females. Alternative spelling: Evin.

Evans Welsh. From John, Hebrew (Yochanan), "God has been gracious." Unusual.

Evelyn See under Girls' Names.

Evelyne See Evelyn under Girls' Names.

Everard English. Old German, "Boar" + "hard." Unusual.

Everett English. From Everard. Sloane (actor, "Citizen Kane"); Dirksen (former senator). Unusual. Alternative spellings: Everet, Everitt.

Everild English. From Averil, Old English, "Boar" + "battle." May also be related to the month of April. Unusual.

Everitt English. From Everard. Unusual.

Everton English. English, place name used as a first name. Unusual.

Evgenios German. From Eugene. Unusual.

Ewan Scottish. Scottish, "Youth." Kennedy (Australian, drove greatest distance in a standard vehicle without refueling: 1,300.9 miles, 1988). Unusual.

Ewart English. English, "Home near a river." Unusual.

Ewen English. From Ewan. Cameron (17th-century Scottish highland chieftain, renowned for feats of strength). Unusual. Alternative spellings: Euan, Euen, Ewhen.

Eyota Native American. Native American, "The greatest." Unusual for males, unusual for females.

Ezekiel English. Hebrew (Yechezkel), "Strengthened by God" or "may God strengthen." Ezekiel 1:3. One of Saul's commanders; prophet; Moore, Jr. (football player). Unusual. Zeke.

Ezera Hawaiian. From Ezra. Ezra 7:1. Unusual.

Ezio Italian. Meaning and origin unknown. Unusual.

Ezra Hebrew/Israeli. Hebrew, "Help." Ezra 7:1. Fourth-5th-century B.C. Hebrew scribe, priest, reformer of religious practices; Cornell (19th-century businessman, organized Western Union Telegraph Co., endowed Cornell University); Pound (great imagist poet); Benson (former secretary of agriculture). Less popular.

Fabek Polish. From Fabian. Unusual.

Faber German. From Fabian. Unusual.

Fabert French. From Fabian. Unusual.

Fabi Russian. From Fabian. Unusual.

Fabian English. Latin, "Bean-grower." Saint; Forte (rock singer). Unusual. Alternative spelling: Fabyan.

Fabiano Italian. From Fabian. Unusual.

Fabien French. From Fabian. Unusual.

Fabio Italian. From Fabian. Unusual.

Fabius Latvian. From Fabian. Unusual.

Fabiyan Russian. From Fabian. Unusual.

Faddei Russian. From Thaddeus, Old Welsh, "Father." Unusual.

Fadey Ukrainian. From Thaddeus, Old Welsh, "Father." Unusual.

Fāḍil Arabic. Arabic, "Generous." Unusual.

Fairleigh English. Old English, "From the bull meadow." Unusual. Alternative spellings: Fairlay, Fairlee, Fairlie.

Faithful See under Girls' Names.

Farewell See under Girls' Names.

Farley English. Surname and place name used as a first name; origin unknown. Granger (actor, "Strangers on a Train"); Mowat (author, "Never Cry Wolf"). Unusual. Alternative spellings: Farlay: Farlee, Farly.

Farnham English. English, "River meadow with ferns." Unusual.

Faron English. English, surname used as a first name. Unusual for males, unusual for females.

Farquhar Scottish. Gaelic (Fearchar), "Very dear one." Unusual.

Farrar Irish. Irish, surname used as a first name. Unusual.

Farrell Irish. Irish, "Man of valor." Unusual.

Farrow Irish. Irish, surname used as a first name. Unusual.

Farruco Hispanic. From Francis, Latin, "Frenchman." Unusual.

Fath Arabic. Arabic, "Victory." Unusual.

Faxon German. Old German, "Long hair." Unusual.

Feargus Scottish. From Fergus, Gaelic, "Supreme choice." O'Connor (19th-century Irish Chartist leader, advocated violence) (Chartists worked for improved working and social conditions for the working classes). Unusual.

Featherstone English. English, place name used as a first name. Unusual.

Fedar Russian. From Theodore, Greek, "theodoros" ("God's gift"). Unusual. Alternative spelling: Fedir.

Federico Hispanic, Italian. From Frederick, Old German, "Peaceful ruler." Unusual.

Federoquito Hispanic. From Frederick, Old German, "Peaceful ruler." Unusual.

Fedinka Russian. From Theodore, Greek, "theodoros" ("God's gift"). Unusual.

Fedor Czech, Russian. From Theodore, Greek, "theodoros" ("God's gift"). Unusual.

Feeleep Russian. From Philip, Greek, "philippos" ("lover of horses"). Matthew 10:3. Unusual.

Feliks Bulgarian, Phoenecian, Russian. From Felix. Nowoweijski (Polish composer, wrote the Polish national hymn, "Rota"). Unusual.

Felipe Hispanic. From Philip, Greek, "philippos" ("lover of horses"). Matthew 10:3. Trigo (18th-century Spanish novelist); Pedrell (Spanish composer, led nationalist music movement). Unusual.

Felipino Hispanic. From Philip, Greek, "philippos" ("lover of horses"). Matthew 10:3. Unusual.

Felix English. Latin, "Happy," "fortunate," or "lucky." Saint; pope (I, 269-V, 1439); Adler (professor of ethics, established Ethical Culture Society); Mendelssohn (19th-century German classical composer); Timmermans (Flemish, known for regional novels); Vening Meinesz (Dutch geophysicist, measured gravity from submarine). Less popular.

Felo Hispanic. From Felix. Unusual.

Fenton English. English, "Settlement by a swamp." Hort (19th-century British theologian, produced critical edition of Greek New Testament). Unusual.

Fenwick English. English, "Dairy farm by the swamp." Unusual.

Feodor Bulgarian, Russian. From Theodore, Greek, "theodoros" ("God's gift"). Lynen (German biochemist, won 1964 Nobel Prize for his studies on the metabolism of fatty acids and cholesterol). Unusual.

Feodore Russian. From Theodore, Greek, "theodoros" ("God's gift"). Unusual.

Ferdinand English. Gothic, "Peace" or "travel" + "boldness." Saint; character in Shakespeare's "Love's Labour's Lost" and "Tempest"; Porsche (designed Volkswagen "Beetle"); Morton (jazz musician) (real name of Jelly Roll); de Lesseps (19th-century French diplomat, planned construction of Suez and Panama canals). Less popular.

Fergus Scottish. Gaelic, "Supreme choice." Unusual.

Ferguson Scottish. Gaelic, surname used as a first name. Unusual.

Fernando Hispanic. From Ferdinand, Gothic, "Peace" or "travel" + "boldness." Pessôa (greatest Portuguese modernist poet); de Rojas (Spanish writer, chief contributor to 15th-century national drama); Sor (19th-century Spanish composer and virtuoso guitarist); de Ávalos (16th-century Spanish soldier, commanded Spanish forces in Italy for Charles V). Unusual.

Fernleigh See Fernley under Girls' Names.

Fernley See under Girls' Names.

Fiance English. French, "Betrothed." Unusual. Alternative spelling: Fiancy.

Fico Hispanic. From Frederick, Old German, "Peaceful ruler." Unusual.

Fidel English. From Faith, Latin, "fides"; the word used as a first name. Castro Ruz (president of Cuba, made longest speech to the United Nations: 4 hours, 29 minutes, 1960). Unusual.

Fidelis English. From Faith, Latin, "fides"; the word used as a first name. Saint. Unusual.

Field English. Old English, "From the field." Unusual.

Fife Scottish. Scottish, name of a shire (county). Unusual.

Fil Polish. From Philip, Greek, "philippos" ("lover of horses"). Matthew 10:3. Unusual.

Filib Irish. From Philip, Greek, "philippos" ("lover of horses"). Matthew 10:3. Unusual.

Filip English. From Philip, Greek, "philippos" ("lover of horses"). Matthew 10:3. Unusual. Alternative spellings: Philip, Phillip, Phillipe, Phillipp, Phillippe.

Filipek Polish. From Philip, Greek, "philippos" ("lover of horses"). Matthew 10:3. Unusual.

Filipo Hispanic. From Philip, Greek, "philippos" ("lover of horses"). Matthew 10:3. Unusual.

Filipp Russian. From Philip, Greek, "philippos" ("lover of horses"). Matthew 10:3. Unusual.

Filippo Italian. From Philip, Greek, "philippos" ("lover of horses"). Matthew 10:3. Pacini (19th-century Italian anatomist, discovered cholera bacillus); Lippi, Fra (15th-century Italian painter); Marchetti (19th-century Italian opera composer, "Gentile da Varano"); Taglioni (19th-century Italian ballet master, choreographer); Turati (Italian, founded socialist party, 1892). Unusual.

Filips Latvian. From Philip, Greek, "philippos" ("lover of horses"). Matthew 10:3. van Montmorency (16th-century Dutch courtier to Emperor Charles V). Unusual.

Filya Russian. From Philip, Greek, "philippos" ("lover of horses"). Matthew 10:3. Unusual.

Finlay English. Gaelic (Fionnlagh), "Fair hero." Unusual. Alternative spelling: Findlay.

Finley English. From Finlay. Dunne (Chicago journalist and novelist, created Irish saloon-keeper and philosopher "Mr. Dooley" as a character). Unusual. Alternative spelling: Findley.

Finn English. From Finlay. Unusual. Alternative spelling: Fin.

Firth English. English, "Woodland." Surname used as a first name. Unusual.

Fischel Yiddish. From Philip, Greek, "philippos" ("lover of horses"). Matthew 10:3. Unusual.

Fisk English. Middle English, "Fish." Unusual. Alternative spelling: Fiske.

Fitz English. Latin, "Son." Unusual.

Fitzgerald English. Old English, "Son of the spear-mighty" or "son of the ruler with a spear." Unusual.

Fitzroy English. Latin, "King's son." Somerset (British, commanded British troops in Crimean War, 1850s). Unusual.

Flavian French. From Flavia, Latin, "Yellow," signifying blond hair. Patriarch of Constantinople, 446–49; Bishop of Antioch (I, 381-II,). Unusual. Alternative spelling: Flavien.

Flavio Italian. From Flavia, Latin, "Yellow," signifying blond hair. Biondo (15th-century Italian historian, first to suggest 1,000-year span of Middle Ages). Unusual.

Fletcher English. Anglo-Saxon, "Arrow-maker." Henderson (pianist and jazz band leader); Christian (British, led mutiny against Captain William Bligh on H.M.S. "Bounty," 1789; founded colony on Pitcairn Island). Unusual.

Flint English. Old English, "Stream" or "hard as flint." Unusual.

Flo See under Girls' Names.

Florence See under Girls' Names.

Florian English. From Flora, Latin, "Flower." Roman emperor for three weeks, died 276, half-brother to emperor Tacitus; de O'campo (16th-century Spanish historian to Charles V); Znaniecki (sociologist, analyzed immigrants' social disorganization); Cajori (mathematician and professor of history of mathematics). Unusual.

Florie See Florry under Girls' Names.

Floris See under Girls' Names.

Florrie See Florry under Girls' Names.

Florry See under Girls' Names.

Flory See Florry under Girls' Names.

Floyd English. Welsh, "Gray," "hoary." Also a surname used as a first name. Patterson (former heavyweight boxing champion); Beattie (rode unicycle 100 miles in record 7 hours, 18 minutes, 55 seconds, 1986); Rood (played golf from Pacific to Atlantic coasts, 1963–64); Richtmyer (physicist, expert in x-ray spectroscopy). Less popular.

Flurry Irish. From Florence, Latin, "Flourishing" or "blooming." Unusual.

Flynn English. Gaelic, "Red-head's son." Unusual. Alternative spellings: Flin, Flinn, Flyn.

Foma Russian. From Thomas, Aramaic, "Twin." Unusual.

Fomka Russian. From Thomas, Aramaic, "Twin." Unusual.

Fonya Russian. From Tanek, Greek, "Immortal." Unusual.

Forbes Scottish. Scottish, "Field," "headstrong," or "cold-brow." Unusual.

Ford English. From Oxford, Old English, "Where the oxen cross the river"; place name used as a first name. Sterling (actor); Brown (19th-century British pre-Raphaelite painter). Unusual.

Fordel Gypsy. English Gypsy, "Forgiving." Unusual.

Forrest English. Latin, "Woodsman." Originally a surname describing one who worked in a forest. Tucker (actor); Gregg (tackle, Green Bay Packers, member of Pro Football Hall of Fame); Allen (University of Kansas basketball coach, won 770 games, lost 223); Reid (Irish romantic and mystical novelist). Unusual. Alternative spelling: Forest.

Forster English. Occupational surname; origin unknown. Unusual. Alternative spelling: Forester.

Fortunatus Latin. Latin, "Fortune." Unusual.

Foster English. Latin, "Keeper of the woods." Unusual.

Fotfryd Polish. From Geoffrey, Old German (Gottfried), "peace" (?). Unusual.

Fran See under Girls' Names.

Franc Bulgarian. From Francis, Latin, "Frenchman." Unusual.

Francesco Italian. From Francis, Latin, "Frenchman." Landini (14th-century Italian virtuoso musician); da Laurana (15th-century Italian sculptor, especially known for busts of women); Zuccarelli (18th-century Italian landscape painter); Scipione (18th-century Italian playwright, advocated classical simplicity); Selmi (19th-century Italian toxicologist, named ptomaine poison). Unusual.

Franchot French. From Francis, Latin, "Frenchman." Unusual.

Francis English. Latin, "Frenchman." of Assisi (patron saint of animals, especially birds); of Sales (patron saint of writers); Drake (British explorer, first such to circumnavigate globe, 1577–80); Ford Coppola (film director, "Godfather" series); McClintock, Sir (19th-century British Arctic explorer). Less popular for males, unusual for females. Fran, Francie+, Frannie+.

Francisco Hispanic. From Francis, Latin, "Frenchman." de Rojas Zorrilla (17th-century Spanish playwright, introduced eccentrics as main characters); Rodrigues Alves (president of Brazil, 1902–06; eliminated yellow fever there); Bayeu (18th-century Spanish painter, decorated royal palace, Madrid). Unusual.

Franco Hispanic. From Francis, Latin, "Frenchman." of Cologne (13th-century German, systematized musical rules); Zeffirelli (Italian director, "Hamlet"); Leoni (Italian opera composer, "Rip Van Winkle"); Sacchetti (14th-century burlesque and serious Italian poet); Harris (Pittsburgh football great, holds record for lifetime points). Unusual.

François French. From Francis, Latin, "Frenchman." Villon (15th-century learned, lyrical French poet); Truffaut (French film director, won 1973 Oscar, "La Nuit Americaine"); Rude (19th-century French sculptor known for Paris monuments); Magendie (19th-century French physiologist, expert on nerves, medical drugs); Matthes (mapped western U.S.). Less popular.

Franek Polish. From Francis, Latin, "Frenchman." Unusual.

Franio Polish. From Francis, Latin, "Frenchman." Unusual.

Frank English. From Francis, Latin, "Frenchman." Sinatra (singer and actor); Woolworth (merchant, opened first 5-cent store); Lloyd Wright (architect, known for Prairie Style); Loesser (composer and lyricist, "Baby, It's Cold Outside"); Capra (Italian film director, "It Happened One Night"). Less popular.

Frankie English. From Francis. Valli (pop singer) (real name: Frank Castellaccio); character in pop song "Frankie and Johnny." Unusual for males, unusual for females. Alternative spellings: Frankey, Franki, Franky.

Franklin English. German, surname used as a first name. Pierce (14th president); Delano Roosevelt (32nd president); Pangborn (actor, "Hail the Conquering Hero"); Sanborn (journalist, helped establish Concord School of Philosophy, 1879–88); Pierce Adams (newspaper columnist, "Conning Tower"). Unusual. Frank. Alternative spelling: Franklyn.

Frans Finnish. From Francis, Latin, "Frenchman." Sillanpää (Finnish novelist, won 1939 Nobel Prize for literature); Snyders (17th-century Dutch painter, especially of hunting scenes); Blom (Danish archaeologist, discovered several lost Mayan cities); Hals (17th-century Dutch preeminent portraitist). Unusual.

Frants Danish. From Francis, Latin, "Frenchman." Unusual.

Franus Polish. From Francis, Latin, "Frenchman." Unusual.

Franz German. From Francis. Schubert (Austrian classical composer, "Unfinished Symphony"); Liszt (Hungarian pianist and composer, "Hungarian Rhapsodies"); Müller-Lyer (German sociologist and psychiatrist); Kafka (Austrian novelist, "Metamorphosis"); Rosenzweig (German Jewish existentialist). Unusual for males, unusual for females.

Franzen Scandinavian. From Francis, Latin, "Frenchman." Unusual.

Franzl German. From Francis, Latin, "Frenchman." Unusual.

Frasco Hispanic. From Francis, Latin, "Frenchman." Unusual.

Frascuelo Hispanic. From Francis, Latin, "Frenchman." Unusual.

Fraser English. French, place name used as a first name; origin unknown. Unusual. Alternative spellings: Frasier, Frazer, Frazier.

Fraze English. From Fraser. Unusual.

Fred English. From Frederick. Astaire (dancer and actor) (real name: Frederick Austerlitz); MacMurray (actor); Savage (child actor, "Wonder Years"); Allen (radio host, "Allen's Alley"); Noonan (navigator on first San Francisco–Honolulu flight, 1935). Less popular.

Freddie See under Girls' Names.

Freddy English. From Frederick. Less popular.

Fredek Polish. From Frederick. Unusual.

Frederick English. Old German, "Peaceful ruler." Loewe (composer, collaborated with lyricist Alan Lerner on "Gigi"); Taylor (efficiency engineer, invented time study); Weyerhauser ("lumber king," owns two million acres of timber); Archer (19th-century British jockey, best of his day). Unusual. Fred, Freddie+. Alternative spellings: Frederic, Frederich, Fredric, Fredrick.

Frederico Hispanic. From Frederick. Unusual.

Frederik Swedish. From Frederick. De Moucheron (17th-century Dutch landscape painter); Páludan-Müller (19th-century Danish poet, moralist and critic of romanticism). Unusual.

Fredo Hispanic. From Geoffrey, Old German (Gottfried), "peace" (?). Unusual.

Fredwick English. From Frederick. Unusual.

Free English. From Freeman. Unusual.

Freedom English. Old German, "fri" ("free"); the word used as a first name. Unusual. Alternative spelling: Freedham.

Freeman English. Old German, "fri" ("free") + Sanskrit, "manu" ("man"); the word used as a first name. Crofts (Irish writer of detective novels, "Inspector French's Greatest Case," 1925); Freeman-Thomas (British administrator, viceroy of India, 1931–36). Unusual.

Frida See Freeda under Girls' Names.

Fridrich Czech, Russian. From Frederick. Unusual.

Friedel German. From Frederick, Old German, "Peaceful ruler." Unusual.

Friedrich German. From Frederick. Löffler (19th-century German bacteriologist, developed serum against foot-and-mouth disease); Nietzsche (19th-century German philosopher, advocated perfectibility of man, glorified the superman); Plumpe (German expressionistic film director); Strohmeyer (German chemist, discovered cadmium, 1817). Unusual. Alternative spelling: Friederike.

Friend English. Old English, "Friend." Unusual.

Friendship English. From Friend. Unusual.

Fritz English, German, Swedish. From Frederick. Kreisler (violinist and composer); Pfleumer (German, developed tape recording, 1928); Lang (film director, "You Only Live Once"); Zwicky (Swiss astronomer, discovered 18 supernovas); Pregl (Austrian chemist, developed methods to measure atomic groups, won 1923 Nobel Prize). Less popular.

Fritzchen German. From Frederick. Unusual.

Fritzroy English. Created, meaning unknown. Unusual.

Fuller English. English, "One who shrinks and thickens cloth." An occupational surname used as a first name. Unusual.

Fülöp Hungarian. From Philip, Greek, "philippos" ("lover of horses"). Matthew 10:3. Unusual.

Fynn African. Ghanaian, "River Offin." Unusual.

Gab English. From Gabriel, Hebrew (Gavriel), "Hero of God" or "man of God." Daniel 8:16. Unusual.

Gabby English. From Gabriel, Hebrew (Gavriel), "Hero of God" or "man of God." Daniel 8:16. Unusual. Alternative spelling: Gabie.

Gabe English. From Gabriel, Hebrew (Gavriel), "Hero of God" or "man of God." Daniel 8:16. Less popular.

Gabi Hebrew/Israeli. From Gabriel, Hebrew (Gavriel), "Hero of God" or "man of God." Daniel 8:16. Less popular.

Gabko Czech. From Gabriel, Hebrew (Gavriel), "Hero of God" or "man of God." Daniel 8:16. Unusual.

Gabo Czech. From Gabriel, Hebrew (Gavriel), "Hero of God" or "man of God." Daniel 8:16. Unusual.

Gábor Hungarian. From Gabriel, Hebrew (Gavriel), "Hero of God" or "man of God." Daniel 8:16. Bethlen (prince of Transylvania, 1613–29; king of Hungary, 1620–21). Unusual.

Gabriel English. Hebrew (Gavriel), "Hero of God" or "man of God." Daniel 8:16. One of two archangels; patron saint of broadcasters and diplomats; Duval (Supreme Court Justice, 1811–35); Metsu (17th-century Dutch genre painter, "Music Lesson"); Prosser (American slave, planned rebellion to form black state, 1800); Voisin (French, established first airplane manufacturing plant). Unusual for males, less popular for females. Gabe, Gabby+.

Gabriele Italian. From Gabriel, Hebrew (Gavriel), "Hero of God" or "man of God." Daniel 8:16. D'Annunzio (Italian journalist, later sensational WWI aviator and political leader). Unusual.

Gabrielli Italian. From Gabriel, Hebrew (Gavriel), "Hero of God" or "man of God." Daniel 8:16. Unusual.

Gabriello Italian. From Gabriel, Hebrew (Gavriel), "Hero of God" or "man of God." Daniel 8:16. Chiabrera (16th-century Italian poet, introduced innovations in meter). Unusual.

Gabris Czech. From Gabriel, Hebrew (Gavriel), "Hero of God" or "man of God." Daniel 8:16. Unusual.

Gabys Czech. From Gabriel, Hebrew (Gavriel), "Hero of God" or "man of God." Daniel 8:16. Unusual.

Gadi Arabic. Arabic, "My fortune." Unusual.

Gadiel Arabic. From Gadi. Unusual.

Gael See Gail under Girls' Names.

Gail See under Girls' Names.

Gaius Welsh. Latin, "To rejoice." Saint; pope, 283–296; Caesar (Roman emperor, 37–41); 2nd-century Roman jurist, laid foundations of Roman law; Valerius Flaccus (1st-century Roman poet, wrote "Argonautica," based on legend of the golden fleece); Victorinus (4th-century Latin writer on philosophy, grammar). Unusual.

Gale See Gail under Girls' Names.

Galen English. Greek, "Healer" or "calm." Second-century Greek physician, founded experimental physiology. Unusual.

Galeno Hispanic. From Galen. Unusual.

Galt Norwegian. From Galt. Unusual.

Galvin English. Gaelic, "Sparrow" or "brightly white." Unusual. Alternative spellings: Galvan, Galven.

Galya See under Girls' Names.

Gan Vietnamese. Vietnamese, "To be near." Unusual.

Gannon English. Gaelic, "Fair-skinned." Unusual.

Garai African. African, "To be settled." Unusual.

Garald Russian. From Gerald, Old German, "Spear" + "ruler." Unusual. Alternative spelling: Garold.

Garek Polish. From Edgar, Old English, "Prosperity" + "spear." Unusual.

Gareth English. Welsh, "Gentle," "benign." Knight in Sir Thomas Malory's 14th-century poem "Le Morte d'Arthur" and Alfred, Lord Tennyson's 1872 poem "Gareth and Lynette"; Edwards (Welsh rugby star). Less popular.

Garfield English. English, "Field of spears." Oxnam (clergyman, president of World Council of Churches, 1948–54); Wood (boat builder and racer, designed WWII PT boat); St. Aubrun Sobers, Sir (British cricketer). Unusual. Gar.

Garner English. Old French, "Armed sentry." Unusual.

Garnet English. English, "Shelter," "protection." Also a jewel name. Wolseley, Sir (commander-in-chief of British army, 1895–1901). Unusual for males, unusual for females. Alternative spelling: Garnett.

Garolds Russian. From Gerald, Old German, "Spear" + "ruler." Unusual.

Garret English. From Gerard, Old German, "Spear" + "brave." Hobart (vice-president under McKinley). Unusual. Alternative spellings: Garett, Garrat.

Garrett Irish. From Gerard, Old German, "Spear" + "brave." Unusual.

Garrick English. English, "Spear" + "rule." Unusual.

Garridan Gypsy. English Gypsy, "You hid." Unusual.

Garrison English. Old French, "Fort." Unusual.

Garth English. English, "One in charge of a garden." Dalmain (character in Florence Barclay's "Rosary"); Brooks (country singer whose album "No Fences" went platinum in six weeks). Unusual.

Gary English. From Gerard, Old German, "Spear" + "brave." Puckett (and the Union Gap, musicians, "Young Girl"); Windebank (British, lifted most tires at once: 96 (1,440 pounds), 1984); Cooper (actor, won 1941 Oscar for "Sergeant York"); Adelson (movie producer, "Hook"). Popular. Alternative spellings: Garey, Gari, Garri, Garrie, Garry.

Gaspar English, Hispanic, Hungarian (Gáspár), Portuguese, Russian. From Jasper, Persian, "Treasure-holder." Núñez de Arce (19th-century Spanish poet, playwright); Gil Polo (16th-century Spanish poet); de Portolá (Spanish governor of the Californias, established San Diego and Monterey, 1769); de Zúñiga y Azevedo (Spanish colonialist, viceroy of New Spain, 1595–1603). Unusual. Alternative spelling: Gasper.

Gaspard French. From Jasper, Persian, "Treasure-holder." Tournachon (French, took first aerial photo from a balloon: 1858, over the outskirts of Paris); Monge (French mathematician, helped establish metric system, 1791); Poussin (17th-century French landscape painter); de Schomberg (16th-century French finance minister under Henry IV). Unusual.

Gauther French. From Walter, Old German, "Ruling people." Unusual.

Gautier French. From Walter, Old German, "Ruling people." d'Arras (12th-century French poet, wrote two verse romances); de Metz (13th-century French poet, wrote octosyllabic verse treatise on the universe, circa 1246); Sans Avoir (French knight, led Peasants' Crusade, 1096–97). Unusual.

Gav English. From Gawain. Unusual.

Gaven English. From Gawain. Unusual. Alternative spellings: Gavan, Gavyn.

Gavin Scottish. From Gawain. Maxwell (Scottish novelist, "Ring of Bright Water"); Hamilton (18th-century Scottish neoclassical painter, portraitist). Unusual.

Gavriel Hebrew/Israeli. Hebrew, "Hero of God" or "man of God." Daniel 8:16. Unusual.

Gavril Bulgarian, Russian. From Gabriel, Hebrew (Gavriel), "Hero of God" or "man of God." Daniel 8:16. Pribylov (18th-century Russian sea captain, first to land on Pribilof Islands, in Bering Sea). Unusual.

Gawain Welsh. Welsh, "White hawk." Unusual.

Gawen English. From Gawain. Unusual.

Gayle See Gail under Girls' Names.

Gaylord English. Old French, "One of high spirits." Unusual.

Gedeon Bulgarian, French. From Gidon, Hebrew, "Feller," "hewer," or "to cast down." Judges 6:11. Tallemant des Reaux (17th-century French writer of short biographies of public figures). Unusual.

Gellart Hungarian. From Gerald, Old German, "Spear" + "ruler." Unusual. Alternative spelling: Gellert.

Gencho Hispanic. From Eugene, Greek, "Well born." Unusual.

Gene English. From Eugene, Greek, "Well born." Tierney (actress); Hackman (actor, won 1971 Oscar for "French Connection"); Wilder (actor, "Young Frankenstein") (real name: Jerome Silberman); Kelly (actor and dancer, "Singing in the Rain"); Tunney (heavyweight boxing champion); Krupa (big-band drummer). Less popular for males, unusual for females.

Genek Polish. From Eugene, Greek, "Well born." Unusual.

Genio Polish. From Eugene, Greek, "Well born." Unusual.

Genka Russian. From Eugene, Greek, "Well born." Unusual.

Gent English. English, "Gentleman." Surname used as a first name. Unusual.

Gentle English. From Gent. Unusual.

Genty English. Irish, "Snow." Unusual.

Genya Russian. From Eugene, Greek, "Well born." Unusual.

Geoffrey English. Old German (Gottfried), "peace" (?). of Monmouth (12th-century British bishop and chronicler); O'Hara (composer, songwriter, "K-K-K-Katy"); Dawson (British, editor of London "Times," 1912–19, 1923–41); De Havilland, Sir (British aeronautical engineer, manufactured first commercial jet, the Comet). Less popular. Geoff. Alternative spellings: Geoffery, Geoffry, Geofrey, Jefferey, Jeffery, Jeffree, Jeffrey, Jeffry.

Geoffroy French. From Geoffrey. Tory (16th-century French printer and typographer, introduced accent marks into the French language). Unusual. Alternative spellings: Geoffroi, Jeoffroi.

Geofri Romanian. From Geoffrey. Unusual.

Geordie English. From George, Greek, "Husbandman," "farmer," or "earth-worker." Unusual.

Georg Bulgarian, Scandinavian. From George, Greek, "Husbandman," "farmer," or "earth-worker." List (19th-century economist, advocated protective tariff); von Reichenbach (19th-century German, designed astronomical instruments); Solti, Sir (conductor, Chicago Symphony Orchestra); Telemann (18th-century German, most prolific composer ever); Steller (18th-century German, described animals of Alaska). Unusual.

George English. Greek, "Husbandman," "farmer," or "earth-worker." Patron saint of archers, knights; Bingham (19th-century painter, "Fur Traders Descending the Missouri"); Sand (19th-century unconventional, feminist French novelist) (real name: Amandine Dudevant); Custer (general killed at Little Big Horn); Washington (first U.S. president); Herbert Walker Bush (41st president). Popular for males, unusual for females. Georgie+.

Georges French. From George, Greek, "Husbandman," "farmer," or "earth-worker." Schmidt (French linguist fluent in record 19 languages); Simenon (Belgian novelist, "Inspector Maigret" mysteries); de la Tour (17th-century French painter known for candlelit subjects); Leclanché (French, invented first dry cell battery, 1866); Legrain (19th-century French Egyptologist). Unusual.

Georgi Bulgarian. From George, Greek, "Husbandman," "farmer," or "earth-worker." Chicherin (Russian czarist, then Menshevik; later negotiated secret Treaty of Rapallo with Germany, 1922); Dimitrov (Bulgarian prime minister, 1946–49). Unusual.

Georgie See under Girls' Names.

Georgios Greek. From George, Greek,

"Husbandman," "farmer," or "earthworker." Papandreou (Greek premier, 1963–65); Akropolites (13th-century Byzantine historian and diplomat, wrote history of Byzantine empire from 1204–1261). Unusual.

Georgiy Russian. From George, Greek, "Husbandman," "farmer," or "earthworker." Buryanov (Russian, flew jet-powered flying boat at record altitude of 49,088 feet, 1961). Unusual.

Georgy English. From George, Greek, "Husbandman," "farmer," or "earthworker." Lvov (Russian prince, briefly premier after 1917 revolution); Plekhanov (Russian, established first Marxist revolutionary organization, 1883); Zhukov (Russian officer, led assault on Berlin, 1945); Dobrovolsky (Russian astronaut, in space a record 24 days). Unusual.

Gerahd Russian. From Harold, Old English, "Army power." Unusual.

Geraint English. Greek, "Old." Evans, Sir (British opera singer). Unusual.

Gerald English. Old German, "Spear" + "ruler." Saint; Ford (38th president); Massey (19th-century British poet especially interested in psychic aspects of ancient Egypt); Seligman (British glaciologist, researched glacier flow and structure); Tyrwhitt-Wilson, Sir (British composer and author). Less popular. Gerry+. Alternative spellings: Gerrald, Gerrold, Jerald, Jerold, Jerrold.

Geraldo Hispanic, Italian. From Gerald. Rivera (TV talk-show host). Unusual. Alternative spelling: Heraldo.

Gerard English. Old German, "Spear" + "brave." Majella (saint); Pierre Charles (Haitian economist); Labrunie (19th-century French symbolist and surrealist author) (real name of Gerard de Nerval); Swope (president of General Electric, 1922–39, 1942–44); Terborch (17th-century Dutch portraitist and painter of interiors). Unusual. Gerry+. Alternative spellings: Garrard, Gerhard, Gerrard.

Géraud French. From Gerald. de Cordemoy (17th-century French philosopher and historian, built on Descartes). Unusual.

Gerek Polish. From Gerald. Unusual.

Geremia Italian. From Jeremiah, Hebrew, "Jehovah is high" or "Jehovah exalts." Book of Jeremiah. Unusual.

Gerik Polish. From Edgar, Old English, "Prosperity" + "spear." Unusual.

Germain French. Latin, "A German." of Paris (6th-century French bishop, saint); Pilon (French, leading Renaissance sculptor); Sommeiller (19th-century French engineer, developed compressed-air drill to build tunnel between France and Switzerland); Boffrand (French architect to the king, 1690). Unusual for males, unusual for females.

Germaine English. From Germain. Greer (feminist writer and activist). Unusual for males, unusual for females. Alternative spellings: Jermain, Jermaine, Jermane, Jermayne.

German English. From Germain, Latin, "A German." Unusual.

Gerome English. From Jerome, Latin, "Sacred name." Unusual. Gerry+. Alternative spelling: Jerome.

Gerrie English. From Gerald. Unusual. Alternative spellings: Jerrie, Jerry.

Gerrit Dutch. From Gerald. Rietveld (Dutch architect and designer of furniture and jewelry); Smith (19th-century reformer, helped John Brown in fight against slavery, advocated abolition); Jensen (best-known 17th-century British furniture designer); van Honthorst (17th-century Dutch painter influenced by Caravaggio). Unusual.

Gerry See under Girls' Names.

Gershom English. Hebrew, "Exile." Exodus 2:22. ben Judah (11th-century French rabbi, developed Talmudic study in France and Germany). Unusual. Alternative spelling: Gersham.

Gershon English. From Gershom. Unusual.

Gerson English. From Gershom. Unusual.

Gervais French. From Gervase. Unusual.

Gervase English. Latin, meaning unknown. Saint; Markham (17th-century British writer on forestry, agriculture, veterinary medicine). Unusual.

Gerwyn Welsh. Welsh, "Fair love." Unusual. Alternative spelling: Gerwen.

Geth Welsh. From Gethin. Unusual.

Gethin Welsh. Welsh, "Dusky." Unusual. Alternative spelling: Gethen.

Ghassān Arabic. Arabic, family name of unknown meaning. Unusual.

Gi Korean. Korean, "Brave." Unusual.

Giacobbe Italian. From Jacob, Hebrew (Yaakov), "Supplanter" or "heel." Genesis 25:26. Unusual.

Giacomo Italian. From Jacob, Hebrew (Yaakov), "Supplanter" or "heel." Genesis 25:26. Puccini (Italian operatic composer, "Madama Butterfly," 1904); della Porta (Italian architect, completed cupola of St. Peter's, 1588–90); Serpotta (18th-century Italian stucco-worker). Unusual.

Giacopo Italian. From Jacob, Hebrew (Yaakov), "Supplanter" or "heel." Genesis 25:26. Unusual.

Giamo Italian. From Jacob, Hebrew (Yaakov), "Supplanter" or "heel." Genesis 25:26. Unusual.

Gian Italian. From John, Hebrew (Yochanan), "God has been gracious." Sforza (15th-century ruler of Milan); Malipiero (Italian contrapuntal composer); Poggio Bracciolini (15th-century Italian humanist, discovered many lost Latin classics in European monasteries); Trissino (16th-century Italian poet and author, proposed merging all Italian dialects into one language). Unusual.

Giancarlo Italian. Italian, combination of John (Hebrew (Yochanan), "Jehovah has been gracious") + Charles (Old English, "Husbandman"). Unusual.

Gianetto Italian. From John, Hebrew (Yochanan), "God has been gracious." Unusual.

Giannis Greek. From John, Hebrew (Yochanan), "God has been gracious." Unusual. Alternative spellings: Giannes, Giannos.

Gibor Hebrew/Israeli. Hebrew, "Hero." Unusual.

Gibson English. From Gibson, surname used as a first name; origin unknown. Unusual.

Gideon English. From Gidon. Welles (secretary of navy under Lincoln); von Laudon (commander-in-chief of Austrian armed forces, 1790); Mantell (19th-century British geologist, paleontologist; discovered four of the five types of dinosaurs). Unusual.

Gideone Italian. From Gidon. Unusual.

Gidon Hebrew/Israeli. Hebrew, "Feller," "hewer," or "to cast down." Judges 6:11. Ancient Hebrew hero and judge, destroyed altar of Baal. Unusual.

Gifford English. Old English, "Chubby-cheeked." Surname used as a first name.

Pinchot (first professional American forester); Beal (painter of landscapes and coastal scenes, "The Puff of Smoke"). Unusual.

Gig English. Middle English, "Horse-drawn carriage." Young (actor). Less popular.

Gil Hispanic. From Egidius, Scottish, from the Greek "aigidion" ("young goat"). de Siloé (considered greatest Spanish 15th-century sculptor); Vicente (16th-century Portuguese playwright, laid foundations of Portuguese drama); de Albornoz (14th-century Spanish prelate, codified laws of the Papal States); Eanes (Portuguese mariner, first to round fearsome Cape Bojador, off west Africa, 1434). Less popular.

Gilad Hebrew/Israeli. Arabic, "Camel hump." Unusual.

Gilbert English. Old German, "Pledge" + "bright." Saint; Chesterton (prolific British writer, "Father Brown" detective novels); Lewis (chemist, developed theories on nature of atomic bonds); Stuart (painted portraits of Washington, other presidents, King George III); Roberts, Sir (British, developed all-welded ships). Less popular. Bert, Gib, Gil.

Gilberto English. From Gilbert. Mendoza (Panamanian, president of World Boxing Association). Unusual.

Gildero English. From Gilroy. Unusual.

Gildray English. From Gilroy. Unusual.

Gildrey English. From Gilroy. Unusual. Alternative spelling: Gildri.

Gildroy English. From Gilroy. Unusual. Alternative spelling: Gilderoy.

Giles English. From Egidius, Scottish, from the Greek "aigidion" ("young goat"). Saint; of Assisi (13th-century Italian religious figure famed for pithy sayings); Smith (Civil War general, with Sherman through the Carolinas); Farnaby (prolific 16th-century British keyboard composer); Fletcher ("the Elder," 15th-century, and "the Younger," 16th-century, father and son British poets). Unusual for males, unusual for females. Alternative spelling: Gyles.

Gillean Scottish. Gaelic, "St. John's servant." Unusual.

Gilleasbuig Scottish. Scottish, "Servant of the bishop." Unusual.

Gilles French. From Egidius, Scottish, from the Greek "aigidion" ("young goat"). Ménage (17th-century French scholar of law and language); de Rais (15th-century French soldier, fought with Joan of Arc); de Roberval (17th-century French mathematician, invented a balance now named for him); Binchois (15th-century Flemish composer of church music, mixed French and English styles). Unusual.

Gillespie English. From Gilleasbuig. Unusual.

Gillie Gypsy. English Gypsy, "Song." Unusual.

Gilroy English. Celtic, "Red-head's servant." Unusual.

Gilson English. Surname used as a first name; origin unknown. Unusual.

Gino Italian. From John, Hebrew (Yochanan), "God has been gracious." Marchetti (Baltimore Colts defensive end, member of Pro Football Hall of Fame); Capponi (19th-century prime minister of Tuscany, senator); Severini (Italian pointillist, then cubist, then neoclassical painter). Unusual.

Ginton Hebrew/Israeli. Hebrew, "A garden." Unusual.

Gioffredo Italian. From Geoffrey, Old German (Gottfried), "peace" (?). Unusual.

Giona Italian. From Jonah, Hebrew (Yonah), "Dove." Book of Jonah. Unusual.

Giordana Italian. From Jordan, Hebrew (Yarden), "To descend." Also the name of a river. Unusual.

Giorgos Greek. From George, Greek, "Husbandman," "farmer," or "earthworker." Seferiades (Greek poet, won 1963 Nobel Prize for literature) (real name of George Seferis). Unusual. Alternative spelling: Georgis.

Giosia Italian. From Joshua, Hebrew (Yehoshua), "God is my salvation." Exodus 17:9. Unusual.

Giotto Italian. From Geoffrey, Old German (Gottfried), "peace" (?). di Bondone (Italian, sculptor, architect, and the principal 14th-century painter; painted altarpiece for St. Peter's cathedral, designed Florence's Duomo). Unusual.

Giovanni Italian. From John, Hebrew (Yochanan), "God has been gracious." Amadeo (16th-century Italian Renaissance sculptor, architect); de'Medici (wealthy Italian merchant, founded influential family, ruled Florence, 1421–29); de'Rossi (Italian archaeologist, discovered catacombs of St. Callistus, 1849); Sammartini (18th-century Italian composer, developed Classical style). Unusual.

Gipsy English. Old English, "Wanderer." Unusual.

Giraldo Italian. From Gerald, Old German, "Spear" + "ruler." Unusual. Alternative spelling: Geraldo.

Girisa See under Girls' Names.

Giuseppe Italian. From Joseph, Hebrew (Yosef), "God will add." Verdi (19th-century Italian operatic composer, "La Traviata," 1853); Piazzi (Italian astronomer; discovered Ceres, the first known asteroid, 1801); Mercalli (Italian geologist, revised scale for gauging earthquake intensity, 1902); Peano (Italian linguist, developed artificial language). Unusual.

Giustino Italian. From Justin, Latin, "Just." Unusual.

Givon Hebrew/Israeli. Hebrew, "Heights" or "hill." Unusual.

Gladstone English. Scottish, surname used as a first name. Unusual.

Glanvile English. English, surname taken from a Norman place name. Unusual.

Glasgow English. Scottish, place name used as a first name. Unusual.

Glendower English. From Glyndwr, Welsh, surname used as a first name. Unusual.

Glenn English. From Glen. Ford (actor) (real name: Gwyllyn Ford); Miller (big-band leader); "Fireball" Roberts (stock-car racer, won 32 races, set numerous records); "Pop" Warner (college football coach); Jepsen (paleontologist, studied Tertiary period (70 million years ago)). Less popular. Alternative spelling: Glen.

Glenton English. English, "Settlement in a valley." Unusual.

Glentworth English. From Glenton. Unusual.

Glenville English. English, place name used as a first name. Unusual. Alternative spelling: Glenvil.

Glyn English. Welsh, "Small valley." Unusual.

Glyndwr Welsh. Welsh, surname used as a first name. Unusual. Alternative spelling: Glyndor.

Godfrey English. Old German, "God" +

"peace." II (duke of Upper Lorraine, 1044–47, and Lower Lorraine, 1065–69); of Bouillon (duke of Lower Lorraine, 1082–1100; idealized as perfect Christian knight); of Fontaines (13th-century French philosopher, proponent of Aristotelian philosophy). Unusual.

Godofredo Hispanic. From Geoffrey, Old German (Gottfried), "peace" (?). Unusual.

Godoired Romanian. From Geoffrey, Old German (Gottfried), "peace" (?). Unusual.

Godwin English. Old English, "God" or "good" + "friend" or "protector." 11th-century, Earl of Wessex; helped place Edward the Confessor on throne, 1042. Unusual.

Goel Hebrew/Israeli. Hebrew, "The redeemer." Unusual.

Gofredo Hispanic. From Geoffrey, Old German (Gottfried), "peace" (?). Unusual.

Gogos Greek. From George, Greek, "Husbandman," "farmer," or "earth-worker." Unusual.

Golding English. English, surname used as a first name. Unusual.

Goliath English. Hebrew, "Exile." 1 Samuel 17. Philistine giant slain by David. Unusual. Alternative spelling: Golliath.

Gomer English. English, "Good" or "battle" + "famous." Genesis 10:2. Pyle (television character). Unusual.

Goran Scandinavian. From George, Greek, "Husbandman," "farmer," or "earth-worker." Unusual.

Gordan Scottish. From Gordon. Unusual. Alternative spelling: Gorden.

Gordon English. Anglo-Saxon, "Round hill." Lightfoot (singer and songwriter); Allport (psychologist, wrote "Nature of Personality"); Bottomley (British poet, "Chambers of Imagery"); Daviot (Scottish novelist and playwright, "The Singing Sands") (real name: Elizabeth Mackintosh). Less popular. Gordie.

Gorman English. Gaelic, "Little one with blue eyes" or "man of clay." Unusual.

Goro Japanese. Japanese, "Fifth one" (that is, fifth to be born). Unusual.

Gosheven Native American. Native American, "Great leaper." Unusual.

Gotfrid Russian. From Geoffrey, Old German (Gottfried), "peace" (?). Unusual.

Gotfrids Latvian. From Geoffrey, Old German (Gottfried), "peace" (?). Unusual.

Gottfrid Hungarian. From Geoffrey, Old German (Gottfried), "peace" (?). Unusual.

Gottfried German. From Geoffrey, Old German (Gottfried), "peace" (?). von Strassburg (13th-century German poet, "Tristan und Isolde"); Leibniz (17th-century German, laid foundations of calculus); Semper (19th-century German neo-Renaissance architect, Dresden Opera House); Treviranus (19th-century German naturalist, known especially for studies of invertebrate anatomy). Unusual.

Gowon Nigerian. Nigerian, "Rainmaker." Given to a child born during a storm. Unusual.

Gozal Hebrew/Israeli. Hebrew, "A bird." Unusual.

Grady Irish. Gaelic, "Noble," "illustrious." Unusual.

Graeme Scottish. From Graham. Unusual.

Graham English. English, "Granta's homestead." Nash (rock singer); Sutherland (British portraitist and surrealistic painter, "Crucifixion"); Wallas (British political scientist, helped bring scientific methods to the field); Greene (British novelist, "The Power and the Glory"). Less popular. Alternative spellings: Graeham, Grahame, Gram.

Grant English. French, "Tall" or "great." Wood (painter, "American Gothic"). Less popular.

Grantly English. English, "Granta's meadow." Dick-Read (19th-century British obstetrician, wrote "Natural Childbirth," 1933). Unusual. Alternative spelling: Grantley.

Granville English. French, "Large city." Leveson-Gower (19th-century British politician, foreign secretary under Gladstone); Sharp (18th-century British foe of slavery); Bantock, Sir (British operatic composer, "Pearl of Iran"). Unusual. Alternative spellings: Granvil, Granvile, Granvill.

Gray English. English, surname used as a first name. Originally referred to gray hair. Reisfield (niece of Greta Garbo, inherited multimillion dollar estate). Unusual for males, unusual for females. Alternative spelling: Grey.

Graydon English. From Gray, English, surname used as a first name. Originally referred to gray hair. Unusual.

Grayson English. Middle English, "Bailiff's son." Unusual. Alternative spelling: Greyson.

Green English. From Greenwood. Unusual.

Greener English. From Greenwood. Unusual.

Greenshaw English. From Greenwood. Unusual.

Greenwood English. English, surname and place name used as a first name. Unusual.

Greg English. From Gregory. Louganis (Olympic gold medalist in both platform and springboard diving, 1984 and 1988). Less popular. Alternative spellings: Gregg, Greig.

Grégoire French. From Gregory. Unusual.

Gregor Scottish. From Gregory. Mendel (19th-century Austrian botanist, discovered laws of segregation and of independent assortment in genetics); Piatigorsky (virtuoso Romantic cellist). Unusual.

Gregorio Italian, Portuguese. From Gregory. López y Fuentes (Mexican novelist, works involve Mexican Revolution and Indians); Martínez Sierra (Spanish modernist playwright, novelist); de Matos Guerra (17th-century, first native Brazilian poet); Ricci-Curbastro (Italian mathematician, developed absolute differential calculus). Unusual.

Gregorios Greek. From Gregory. Akindynos (14th-century Greek neoplatonic theologian and monk). Unusual.

Gregors Latvian. From Gregory. Unusual.

Gregory English. Greek, "Watchful." Saint; pope (I, 590-XVI, 1831); Peck (actor, "To Kill a Mockingbird"); Martin (16th-century British, translated Bible from Latin Vulgate into English, published as Douay Bible); Sturdza (19th-century Romanian, Russophile deputy in Romanian assembly). Very popular. Greg+. Alternative spelling: Greggory.

Grenville English. From Granville. Dodge (chief engineer, Union Pacific Railroad, 1866–70). Unusual. Alternative spelling: Grenvil.

Gresham English. English, surname and place name used as a first name. Unusual.
Greville English. Surname derived from a Norman place name, used as a first name. Unusual.
Gries Swedish. From Gregory. Unusual.
Griffin English. Latin, name of a mythical beast. Bell (attorney general under Carter). Unusual.
Griffith English. Welsh, "Strong," "powerful" + "chief" or "fighter." Unusual.
Grigoi Bulgarian. From Gregory. Unusual.
Grigor Bulgarian. From Gregory. Unusual.
Grigorios Greek. From Gregory. Unusual.
Grimshaw English. Surname used as a first name; origin unknown. The surname derives from a place name that refers to a sinister-looking thicket. Unusual.
Grover English. German, "One who lives in a grove" or "gardener." Cleveland (24th president); Cleveland Alexander (Hall of Fame baseball pitcher, record 374 wins); Cleveland Loening (aircraft manufacturer, invented an amphibious airplane). Unusual.
Guadalupe Hispanic. Spanish, "Valley of the wolf." Victoria (first president of Mexican republic, 1824–29) (real name: Manuel Félix Fernández). Unusual for males, unusual for females.
Gualberto Hispanic. From Walter, Old German, "Ruling people." Unusual.
Gualterio Hispanic. From Walter, Old German, "Ruling people." Unusual.
Gualtiero Italian. From Walter, Old German, "Ruling people." Unusual.
Guenther German. From Gunther. Unusual. Alternative spelling: Guenter.
Guido Hispanic, Italian. From Guy, German, "Woods" (?). Mazzoni (16th-century Italian sculptor, worked especially in terra cotta); of Arezzo (11th-century Italian monk, music theorist; designed four-line staff, allowed precise indication of pitch); di Pietro (15th-century Italian, an outstanding painter of the early Renaissance) (also known as Fra Angelico). Unusual.
Guildford English. "Ford with golden flowers"; origin unknown. Unusual.
Guilford English. From Guildford. Unusual.
Guillaume French. From William, Old German, "Will" + "helmet." de Poitiers (11th-century Norman chronicler of William the Conqueror); de Machaut (14th-century French composer in service of king of Bohemia); de Lorris (13th-century French poet, wrote part of allegory "Roman de la Rose," on courtly love); Amontons (17th-century French physicist, invented barometer). Unusual.
Guillaums French. From William, Old German, "Will" + "helmet." Unusual.
Guillermo Hispanic. From William, Old German, "Will" + "helmet." Unusual.
Gun English. From Gunther. Unusual.
Gunnar Scandinavian. From Gunther. Wennerberg (19th-century Swedish poet, politician, composer of patriotic songs: "Hor oss, Svea!"); Ekelof (Swedish modernist poet and essayist); Nelson (singer in group Nelson, son of singer Ricky Nelson). Unusual.
Guntar English. From Gunther. Unusual.
Gunter English, French, German. From Gunther. Unusual.
Guntero Italian. From Gunther. Unusual.
Gunthar English. From Gunther. Unusual.
Gunther English. Old Norse, "Warrior" or "battle army." Gebel-Williams (Polish circus-animal trainer). Unusual.
Gur Hebrew/Israeli. Hebrew, "Lion cub." Unusual.
Gurpreet Indo-Pakistani. Punjabi, "Devoted to a prophet or religious leader" (i.e., a guru). Unusual for males, unusual for females.
Gus English. From Augustus, Latin, "Venerable" or "majestic." Less popular.
Gussy English. From Gustaf. Unusual. Alternative spelling: Gussie.
Gustaf Swedish. Swedish, "God's staff" or "staff of the Goths." Armfelt (Swedish general and statesman, commanded forces in Pomerania, 1805–07); Bonde (17th-century Swedish politician, governed Sodermanland, 1648). Unusual.
Gustaff Dutch. From Gustaf. Unusual.
Gustav Czech, French, German, Romanian. From Gustaf. Mahler (19th-century Austrian composer, wrote longest single classical symphony: 1 hour, 40 minutes (No. 3 in D Minor)); Nachtigal (19th-century German explorer, first European to several West African cities); Rose (19th-century German mineralogist, developed system to classify crystals). Unusual.
Gustava English. From Gustaf. Unusual.
Gustave English. From Gustaf. Flaubert (19th-century French novelist, "Madame Bovary," 1857); Le Bon (French sociologist, studied psychological characteristics of crowds); Moreau (19th-century French symbolist painter); Schirmer (19th-century, founded music publishing house); Stickley (developed Mission Style furniture). Unusual. Gus.
Gustavo Hispanic, Italian. From Gustaf. Thoeni (Italian skier, won Alpine World Cup, 1971–73); Martínez Zuviría (Argentine novelist) (real name of Hugo Wast); Rojas Pinilla (president of Colombia, 1953). Unusual.
Gustavs Latvian. From Gustaf. Unusual.
Gustik Czech. From Gustaf. Unusual.
Gustus English. From Gustaf. Unusual.
Gusty Czech. From Gustaf. Unusual. Alternative spelling: Gusti.
Gutierre Hispanic. From Walter, Old German, "Ruling people." de Cetina (16th-century Spanish poet highly influenced by Petrarch). Unusual.
Guy English, German. German, "Woods" (?). Chamberlin (member, Pro Football Hall of Fame); de Maupassant (French short-story writer, novelist); Fawkes (17th-century British, plotted to blow up Parliament for laws against Catholics); Lombardo (band leader); German (climbed up, down 100-foot pole in record 25 seconds). Unusual.
Guyapi Native American. Native American, "Candid." Unusual.
Guyon English. From Guy. Unusual.
Gwilym Welsh. From William, Old German, "Will" + "helmet." Unusual.
Gwyn English. Welsh, "Fair," "blessed." Unusual.
Gwynfor Welsh. Welsh, "Fair," "good" + "lord." Evans (president of Plaid Cymru, the Welsh National Party). Unusual.
Gyasi African. African, "Wonderful child." Unusual.

Haakon Scandinavian. From Hakon, Old Norse, "Of the exalted race." King of Norway (I, 935-VII, 1905). Unusual. Alternative spelling: Hakon.

Ḥabīb Arabic. Arabic, "Beloved." Unusual.

Hadad Arabic. Arabic, the name of the Syrian god of virility. Unusual.

Haddon English. English, "Hill with heather." Unusual. Alternative spellings: Haddan, Hadden, Haden, Hadon, Hadyn.

Hadley English. Old English, "From the heather meadow." Unusual. Alternative spellings: Hadlee, Hadleigh.

Hadrian Swedish. From Adrian, Latin (Hadrianus), "Black earth" or "of Adria," a city in northern Italy. Roman emperor (117–38); built wall in England, suppressed Jews' rebellion under Bar Kochba, 132–135, erected many buildings in Rome, including Castel Sant'Angelo. Unusual.

Hagan English. From Henry, Old German (Heimerich), "Home ruler." Unusual.

Hahnee Native American. Native American, "A beggar." Unusual.

Hai Vietnamese. From Hai, Vietnamese, "Sea." Unusual.

Ḥaidar Arabic. Arabic, "Lion." Unusual.

Hakan Native American. Native American, "Fiery." Unusual.

Hakim Arabic, from Hakeem; and African, African, "Ruler." Unusual. Alternative spellings: Hakeem, Hakem.

Hako Scandinavian. From Hakon. Unusual.

Hal English. From Henry, Old German (Heimerich), "Home ruler." Wallis (film producer, "Maltese Falcon"); Linden (actor, "Barney Miller") (real name: Harold Lipshitz). Less popular.

Hale Hawaiian. From Harold, Old English, "Army power." Unusual.

Haley See Hayley under Girls' Names.

Halford English. English, "Ford in a valley." Mackinder, Sir (British geographer, holds that Eurasia is the world center of geopolitical power). Unusual.

Halian Native American. From Julius, Latin, a Roman clan name meaning "downy" or "bearded." Unusual.

Halil Turkish. Turkish, "Intimate friend." Unusual.

Halim Arabic. Arabic, "Gentle," "mild," or "patient." Unusual.

Hall English. Old English, "From the hall or manor." Caine, Sir (19th-century British novelist, "Shadow of a Crime"); Johnson (organized and directed Hall Johnson Negro choir). Unusual.

Hallewell English. From Helliwell, "Holy well"; origin unknown. Surname and place name used as a first name. Unusual.

Ham Hebrew/Israeli. Hebrew, "Hot." Genesis 5:32. Noah's son; Nghi (Vietnamese emperor, 1884–86). Unusual.

Hamal Arabic. Arabic, "Lamb." Also a star in the constellation Aires. Unusual.

Hamdrem Arabic. From Mohammed, Arabic, "Greatly praised." Unusual.

Hamdun Arabic. From Mohammed, Arabic, "Greatly praised." Unusual.

Hamid Arabic. From Mohammed, Arabic, "Greatly praised." Unusual.

Hamilton English. Old English, "Fortified castle." Fish (secretary of state under Grant); Armstrong (journalist, established and edited "Foreign Affairs"); Basso (novelist, "Cinnamon Seed"). Unusual. Ham.

Hamish Scottish. From Jacob, Hebrew (Yaakov), "Supplanter" or "heel." Genesis 25:26. Unusual.

Hamlet English. Old Norse, "Village." Indecisive title character in Shakespeare's 1603 play. Unusual.

Hamlin English. Old Norse, "Village." Surname used as a first name. Garland (won Pulitzer Prize, 1921, "Daughter of the Middle Border"). Unusual. Alternative spelling: Hamlyn.

Hammad Arabic. From Mohammed, Arabic, "Greatly praised." arRawiyah (2nd-century Persian anthologist and scholar). Unusual. Alternative spelling: Hammed.

Hammet English. Old Norse, "Village." Surname used as a first name. Unusual.

Hammond English. Old Norse, "Village." Surname used as a first name. Unusual.

Hamnet English. From Hamlet. William Shakespeare's son. Unusual.

Hanan Hebrew/Israeli. From John, Hebrew (Yochanan), "God has been gracious." Unusual.

Hananiah Unknown. Meaning and origin unknown. Unusual.

Handel English. German, surname of composer George Frederick Handel used as a first name. Surname is derived from John (Hebrew (Yochanan), "God has been gracious"). Unusual.

Handley English. "High-wood clearing"; origin unknown. Surname used as a first name. Unusual.

Hanif Arabic. Arabic, "True believer." Unusual.

Hank English. From Henry, Old German (Heimerich), "Home ruler." Aaron (baseball great, hit record 755 lifetime home runs) (real name: Henry Aaron); Williams (country singer and songwriter, "Your Cheatin' Heart") (real name: Hiram Hank Williams). Less popular.

Hanley English. From Handley. Unusual.

Hannes Finnish. From John, Hebrew (Yochanan), "God has been gracious." Hafstein (Icelandic politician and poet, first Icelander to serve as minister of state to Danish royalty). Unusual.

Hannibal English. Meaning and origin unknown. Carthaginian general, governor from 202–195 B.C., sworn enemy of Rome; Sehested (17th-century Danish politician, modernized administration); Goodwin (invented flexible photographic film, 1887); Hamlin (vice-president under Lincoln). Unusual.

Hannu Finnish. From John, Hebrew (Yochanan), "God has been gracious." Unusual.

Hanraoi Irish. From Henry, Old German (Heimerich), "Home ruler." Unusual.

Hans German, Swedish. From John, Hebrew (Yochanan), "God has been gracious." Langseth (Norwegian, had longest beard: 17-1/2 feet, now in Smithsonian); Stuck (German, set Le Mans lap record: 3 minutes, 22.5 seconds, 1988); Ahlmann (Swedish glaciologist); Christian Andersen (19th-century Danish author of children's tales, "The Ugly Duckling"). Less popular.

Hansel German, Swedish. From John, Hebrew (Yochanan), "God has been gracious." Unusual. Alternative spellings: Haensel, Hansl.

Hanson English. Surname used as a first name; origin unknown. Unusual.

Hanuman Indo-Pakistani. Hindi, "Monkey chief." Unusual.

Hanuš Czech. From John, Hebrew (Yochanan), "God has been gracious." Unusual.

Happy See under Girls' Names.

Harailt Scottish. From Harold, Old English, "Army power." Unusual.

Harald Scandinavian. From Harold, Old English, "Army power." Lander (Danish ballet master, choreographer); Sverdrup (Norwegian oceanographer, developed method to predict breakers); Kidde (Danish psychological novelist); Bohr (Danish mathematician); Hudak (German, member of world record 4 x 1,500-meter relay team, 1977). Unusual.

Haraldo Hispanic. From Harold, Old English, "Army power." Unusual. Alternative spelling: Geraldo.

Haralds Latvian. From Harold, Old English, "Army power." Unusual.

Haralpos Greek. From Henry, Old German (Heimerich), "Home ruler." Unusual.

Harb Arabic. Arabic, "War." Unusual.

Harcourt English. Old French, "Fortified dwelling." Surname used as a first name. Unusual.

Hardeep Indo-Pakistani. Punjabi, "Loves God" or "devoted to God." Unusual.

Hardy English. English, "Courageous." Surname used as a first name. Kruger (German actor); Cross (engineer, developed novel measuring methods). Unusual.

Harel Hebrew/Israeli. Hebrew, "God's mountain." Unusual.

Hargrave English. From Hargreaves. Unusual.

Hargreaves English. "Grove with hares"; origin unknown. Surname used as a first name. Unusual.

Hari Indo-Pakistani. Hindi, "Tawny." Another name for the Hindu god Vishnu. Krishen (17th-century Sikh guru). Unusual.

Ḥarith Arabic. Arabic, "Ploughman." Unusual.

Ḥarithah Arabic. From Ḥarith. Unusual.

Harlan English. Old German, "Army land." Stone (Chief Justice of the U.S., 1941–46). Less popular.

Harley English. Old English, "Rabbit pasture." Surname used as a first name. Granville-Barker (British actor, manager, and playwright). Unusual.

Harman English. From Herman, Old German, "Army" + "man." Unusual.

Harold English. Old English, "Army power." King of England (I, 1035-II, 1066); Vanderbilt (developed game of contract bridge and endowed Vanderbilt Cup); Wright (novelist, "Shepherd of the Hills"); Ross (founder and editor of "New Yorker" magazine); Urey (discovered heavy hydrogen). Less popular. Hal, Harry. Alternative spellings: Harrold.

Haroldas Lithuanian. From Harold. Unusual.

Haroldo Portuguese. From Harold. Unusual.

Harper English. Old English, "Harp player." Lee (author, "To Kill a Mockingbird"). Unusual for males, unusual for females.

Harpreet Indo-Pakistani. Punjabi, "Loves God" or "devoted to God." Unusual for males, unusual for females.

Harray English. From Henry, Old German (Heimerich), "Home ruler." Unusual.

Harrington English. Surname and place name used as a first name; meaning and origin unknown. Unusual.

Harris English. Old English, "Harry's son." Surname used as a first name. Less popular.

Harrison English. Old English, "Harry's son." Surname used as a first name. Otis (Civil War army officer and owner of Los Angeles "Times"); Ford (actor, "Indiana Jones" trilogy). Unusual. Alternative spelling: Harrisen.

Harry English. From Henry, Old German (Heimerich), "Home ruler." Truman (34th president); Belafonte (singer and actor); Lauder, Sir (Scottish music-hall comedian); Rosenbusch (German geologist, laid foundations of microscopic petrography); Sinclair (founder and president of Sinclair Oil, 1916–49). Less popular. Hal. Alternative spellings: Harrey, Harri, Harrie.

Hartley English. English, "Stag wood" or "stag hill." Shawcross, Sir (British jurist, chief prosecutor at Nuremberg Trials, 1945–46). Unusual.

Harun Arabic. From Aaron, Hebrew (Aharon), "Teaching" or "singing." Exodus 6:20. ar-Rashid (5th caliph, 786–809). Unusual. Alternative spelling: Haroun.

Harvey English. Celtic, "Battle-ardent." O'Higgins (novelist, "Smoke-Eaters"); Wiley (chief chemist, Department of Agriculture, 1883–1912, led campaign against food adulteration); Cushing (neurosurgeon, won Pulitzer Prize for biography, 1926, "Life of Sir William Osler"). Less popular.

Harwood English. "Hare wood"; origin unknown. Surname used as a first name. Unusual.

Hasad Turkish. Turkish, "To harvest or reap." Unusual.

Hāshim Arabic. Arabic, "Broker" or "destroyer" (of evil). ibn Ḥakīm (Muslim religious leader, preached combination of Islam and Zoroastrianism); al-Atasi (president of Syrian republic). Unusual.

Hasin Indo-Pakistani. Hindi, "Laughing." Unusual.

Haskel English. From Ezekiel, Hebrew (Yechezkel), "Strengthened by God" or "may God strengthen." Ezekiel 1:3. Unusual. Alternative spelling: Haskell.

Ḥassan Arabic. Arabic, "Handsome." ibn Thabit (Arab poet). Unusual.

Hassel English. Old German, "From Hassall" (the witches' corner). Unusual. Alternative spellings: Hassal, Hassall, Hassell.

Hastin Indo-Pakistani. Hindi, "Elephant." The name of a hero in Hindu mythology who was born in a lake frequented by elephants. Unusual.

Havelock English. Old Norse, "Sea port." Surname used as a first name. Ellis (British physician, researched and wrote seven-volume "Studies in the Psychology of Sex"). Unusual.

Haven See under Girls' Names.

Hawthorn English. English, surname and place name used as a first name. Refers to a place where hawthorns grow. Unusual. Alternative spelling: Hawthorne.

Haydn Welsh. Surname of Austrian composer Joseph Haydn used as a first name. Origin unknown; possibly a Welsh variant of Aidan (Celtic, "Fire"). Unusual. Alternative spellings: Hayden, Haydon.

Hayward English. "Bailiff," origin unknown. Surname used as a first name. Harvey (established Harvey Steel, 1886; invented hay cutter). Unusual.

Hayyim English. From Chaim, Hebrew, "Life." Unusual.

Hazael English. From Hazel, English, name of a tree. King of Damascus, 9th-century B.C. Unusual for males, unusual for females.

Heath English. Surname used as a first name; origin unknown. Unusual.

Heaton English. English, "High place." Unusual.

Heber English. Hebrew, "Fellowship." Judges 4:11. Curtis (astrophysicist, researched extragalactic nebulae); Grant (president of Church of Latter-Day Saints, 1918–45). Unusual. Alternative spelling: Hebor.

Hector English. Greek, "Holding fast." Trojan hero of Homer's "Iliad"; Munro (Scottish satirical author, "Reginald") (real name of Saki); Berlioz (French Romantic composer, "Symphonie Fantastique"); Boece (Scottish historian); Macdonald, Sir (British major general). Less popular.

Hedeon Russian. From Gidon, Hebrew, "Feller," "hewer," or "to cast down." Judges 6:11. Unusual.

Hedley English. English, "Clearing overgrown with heather." Unusual. Alternative spellings: Headley, Hedly.

Hedrick English. Meaning and origin unknown. Smith (wrote "The Russians," "The New Russians"). Unusual.

Heiner German. From Henry. Unusual.

Heinrich German. From Henry. Heine (German poet, many of whose poems were set to music by Schumann and Schubert); Schliemann (German archaeologist, excavated ancient Greek ruins); Magnus (German chemist and physicist, discovered several acids); Arrest (German astronomer). Unusual.

Heinz German. From Henry. Unusual.

Helaku Native American. Native American, "Sunny day." Unusual.

Helliwell English. "Holy well"; origin unknown. Surname and place name used as a first name. Unusual. Alternative spelling: Hellewell.

Heman Hebrew/Israeli. Hebrew, "Faithful." Unusual.

Henderson English. English, surname used as a first name. Unusual.

Hendrik English. From Henry. Lorentz (Dutch physicist, developed electronic theory of matter); Steen (Dutch painter, especially interiors of Gothic churches); Tollens (Dutch poet, author of national anthem, "Wein Neerlands Bloed"); de Keyser (Dutch architect and sculptor). Unusual.

Heneage Irish. Irish, surname used as a first name. Unusual.

Heniek Polish. From Henry. Unusual.

Henier Polish. From Henry. Unusual.

Henley English. English, surname and place name used as a first name. Unusual.

Henri Bulgarian, English, French. From Henry. Giffard (earliest flight in an airship: September 24, 1852); Massue (French soldier, zealous Protestant); Nestlé (Swiss, established chocolate factory); Sainte-Claire Deville (French chemist); Winkelman (Dutch general, defended against German invasion). Less popular.

Henrik Finnish, Hungarian. From Henry. Mohn (Norwegian meteorologist); Pontoppidan (Danish novelist); Porthan (Finnish scholar); Steffens (German physicist and philosopher); Wergeland (Norwegian poet and dramatist). Unusual.

Henrim Bulgarian. From Henry. Unusual.

Henrique Portuguese. From Henry. Dias (Brazilian soldier). Unusual.

Henry English. Old German (Heimerich), "Home ruler." II (saint); of Finland (saint); Wadsworth Longfellow (poet); Ford (auto manufacturer); Kissinger (former secretary of state); Fonda (actor). Less popular. Hal, Hank. Alternative spelling: Henery.

Henryk English. From Henry. Rzewuski (Polish novelist); Sienkiewics (Polish novelist, "Quo Vadis?," won Nobel Prize for literature, 1905; also known as Litwos); Wieniawski (Polish violinist and composer); Dembinski (Polish soldier, governor of Warsaw, 1830). Unusual.

Herald English. English, surname used as a first name. Unusual.

Herbert English. Old German, "Army" + "bright," "shining." of Derwentwater (saint); Hoover (31st president); Adams (sculptor, bronze doors of St. Bartholomew's, New York City); Wells (British novelist, "The Time Machine") (real name of H.G. Wells); Spencer (British philosopher). Less popular. Herb. Alternative spelling: Hurbert.

Hercule French. From Hercules. Unusual.

Hercules English. Latin, meaning unknown. Greek, mythological son of Zeus and Alkmene; Seghers (Dutch painter and etcher). Unusual.

Hereward English. Old English, "Army," "defense." Unusual.

Heriberto Hispanic. From Herbert. Unusual.

Herman English. Old German, "Army" + "man." Melville (author, "Moby Dick"); Schaefer (holds record: stole bases in reverse, 1910); Snellen (Dutch ophthalmologist, originated test for acuteness of vision); Portaas (Norwegian poet); Wedel-Jarlsberg (Norwegian count, helped draft constitution). Less popular. Alternative spellings: Hermann, Hermon.

Hermes Greek. Greek, name of the Greek mythological messenger of the gods, meaning unknown. Pan (late dancer and choreographer, collaborated with Fred Astaire on musicals). Unusual.

Heronim Polish. From Harold, Old English, "Army power." Unusual.

Herschel English. From Hersh. Unusual. Alternative spelling: Hirschel.

Hersh English. Yiddish, "Deer." Unusual. Alternative spellings: Hersch, Hirsch.

Hersz Yiddish. From Henry. Unusual.

Hervey English. From Harvey, Celtic, "Battle-ardent." Allen (biographer and poet). Unusual.

Herzl English. From Hersh. Unusual.

Hesutu Native American. Native American, "Lifting a yellow jackets' nest out of the ground." Unusual.

Hew Welsh. From Hugh, Old German, "Mind" or "thought." Unusual.

Hewitt English. English, surname used as a first name. Unusual.

Hewlett English. English, surname used as a first name. Unusual.

Hewson English. English, surname used as a first name. Unusual.

Hezekiah English. Hebrew, "The Lord has strengthened." King of Judah; Bateman (actor); Niles (editor, Baltimore "Evening Post," 1805–11). Unusual.

Hieu Vietnamese. Vietnamese, "Respect." Unusual.

Hilel Arabic. Arabic, "The new moon." Unusual.

Hilery See Hillary under Girls' Names.

Hillary See under Girls' Names.

Hillery See Hillary under Girls' Names.

Hilmar Scandinavian. Old Norse, "Famous noble." Unusual.

Hilton English. English, "Hill town"; place name used as a first name. Unusual. Alternative spelling: Hylton.

Himeronim Polish. From Harold, Old English, "Army power." Unusual.

Hinrich Czech, German. From Henry. Unusual.

Hinun Native American. Native American, "Gods of clouds and rain." Unusual.

Hippolyte French. From Hippolyta, Greek, "Horses." Langlois (French general, specialist on artillery); Fontaine; (French engineer, first to transmit electrical energy). Unusual.

Hiram Hebrew/Israeli. Hebrew, meaning unknown. 1 Kings 5:10. Stevens, Sir (British inventor, maximum recoil-operated machine gun, and mousetrap); Paulding (naval officer); Powers (sculptor); Bingham (missionary, translated Bible into Hawaiian); Revels (first black elected to senate). Unusual. Alternative spellings: Hirom, Hyrum.

Hiroshi Japanese. Japanese, "Generous." Oshima (holds record for throwing flying-disc: 303.9 feet, 1988). Unusual.

Hisoka Japanese. Japanese, "Secretive" or "reserved." Unusual.

Ho Chinese. Chinese, "The good." Yen (Chinese philosopher, founder Wei dynasty); Chi Minh (Vietnamese political leader). Unusual.

Hoang Vietnamese. Vietnamese, "Finished." Unusual.

Hobart English. From Hubert, Old German (Hugibert), "Mind" + "bright" or "shining." Unusual.

Hobson English. Surname used as a first name; origin unknown. Unusual.

Hod Hebrew/Israeli. Hebrew, "Vigorous" or "splendid." Unusual.

Hodding English. Dutch, "Bricklayer." Carter (won Pulitzer Prize for editorial journalism, 1946; author of "Lower Mississippi," "Winds of Fear," "Flood Crest"). Unusual.

Hodgson English. Surname used as a first name; origin unknown. Unusual.

Hogan Irish. Gaelic, "Youthful one." Unusual.

Hoho Native American. Native American, "Bear growling." Unusual.

Hoku Hawaiian. Hawaiian, "Star." Unusual for males, unusual for females.

Holden English. "Hollow valley," origin unknown. Unusual.

Holic Czech. Czech, "Barber." Unusual.

Holland English. English, place name used as a first name. Smith (Marine officer, nicknamed "Howlin' Mad"). Unusual.

Holleb Polish. "Like a dove" (?); origin unknown. The dove is the symbol of peace. Unusual. Alternative spellings: Hollub, Holub.

Hollis English. Old English, "From the grove of holly trees." Unusual.

Holmes English. Surname and place name used as a first name; origin unknown. Herbert (British actor) (real name: Edward Sanger). Unusual.

Holt English. Old English, "Child of the unspoiled woods." Unusual.

Homer English. Greek, "Hostage," "pledge." the Younger (3rd-century B.C. Greek tragic poet); Cummings (attorney general under F.D. Roosevelt); Lea (soldier and author, "The Valor of Ignorance"); Martin (painter); Swift (physician, author of many medical articles). Unusual.

Honok Polish. From Henry, Old German (Heimerich), "Home ruler." Unusual.

Honon Native American. Native American, "Bear." Unusual.

Honovi Native American. Native American, "Strong." Unusual.

Honza Czech. From John, Hebrew (Yochanan), "God has been gracious." Unusual.

Hopkin English. From Robert, Old English (Hreodbeorht), "Fame-bright." Unusual.

Horace English. From Horatio. Gray (Supreme Court Justice, 1882–1902); McCoy (author, "They Shoot Horses, Don't They?"); Wells (19th-century dentist, pioneered administration of nitrous oxide); Wilson (19th- century British Orientalist); Bixby (Mississippi River pilot, friend of Mark Twain). Less popular.

Horatio English. Latin, a Roman clan name. Nelson (British naval hero, Battle of Trafalgar); Hornblower, Capt. (character in C.S. Forester's stories); Palmer (church music composer and director); Phillips (British aviation pioneer); Wright (Civil War army officer). Unusual.

Hototo Native American. Native American, "Whistler." Unusual.

Houston English. "Hill town" or "Hugh's town"; origin unknown. Chamberlain (British publicist, married second daughter of Richard Wagner). Unusual.

Hovhannes Armenian. From John, Hebrew (Yochanan), "God has been gracious." Unusual.

Howard English. Surname used as a first name; origin unknown. Saint; Hughes (reclusive industrialist and aviator, designed and flew the "Spruce Goose"); Keel (singer and actor) (real name: Harold); Lindsay (playwright, "Sound of Music"); Dietz (songwriter). Less popular.

Howell English. From Hywel, Welsh, "Eminent," "conspicuous." Cobb (secretary of treasury under Buchanan); Jackson (Supreme Court Justice, 1893–95). Unusual. Alternative spelling: Howel.

Howi Native American. Native American, "Turtledove." Unusual.

Howin Chinese. Chinese, "A loyal swallow." Unusual.

Hu Chinese. Chinese, "Tiger." Unusual.

Hubbard English. From Hubert. Unusual.

Hube English. From Hubert. Unusual.

Huber English. From Hubert. Unusual.

Hubert English. Old German (Hugibert), "Mind" + "bright" or "shining." Patron saint of dogs; Wilkins, Sir (polar explorer); Opperman, Sir (set 24-hour cycling record behind pace motorcyle: 860 miles, 367 yards); Newton (astronomer); Davies (British playwright, "Cousin Kate"). Less popular. Bert, Hugh.

Hubertek Czech. From Hubert. Unusual.

Huberto Hispanic. From Hubert. Unusual.

Hubi Hispanic. From Hubert. Unusual.

Hubie English. From Hubert. Unusual.

Hudson English. From Hugh. Lowe, Sir (British soldier, 19th-century governor of St. Helene). Unusual.

Huey English. From Hubert. Long (governor of Louisiana, 1928–31, nicknamed "the Kingfish"). Unusual.

Hugh English. Old German, "Mind" or "thought." Of Cluny (saint); of Lincoln (saint); Hefner (publisher, "Playboy" magazine); Scott (British novelist, "Velvet Glove") (real name of Henry Seton Merriman); Williams (British actor); Wynne (character in Mitchell's novel "Hugh Wynne, Free Quaker"). Less popular.

Hughes English. From Hugh. Unusual.

Hughie English. From Hugh. Green (Canadian TV quiz-master and actor). Unusual. Alternative spellings: Hughey, Hughy.

Hugo English. From Hugh. Barraso (longest swim using butterfly stroke: 43.46 miles in 12 hours, 20 minutes); Black (politician and Supreme Court Justice, strong constitutionalist); Preuss (German jurist); de Vries (Dutch botanist and geneticist); Winckler (German archaeologist). Unusual.

Hulwema Native American. Native American, "Dead grizzly bear." Unusual.

Humayd Arabic. From Mohammed, Arabic, "Greatly praised." Unusual.

Humbert German. Old German, "Giant" + "famous." Benedictine monk, expert in Greek and Latin; Wolfe (British poet) (real name: Umberto Wolff). Unusual.

Humberto Portuguese. From Humbert. Castelo Branco (Brazilian soldier and politician, led military coup that overthrew President Goulart, 1964). Unusual.

Humphrey English. Old German, ? + "peace." Bogart (actor, "Casablanca"); Lyttleton (British musician); Stafford (first Duke of Buckingham); Gilbert, Sir (British navigator and soldier, half-brother of Sir Walter Raleigh); Repton (British landscape designer). Unusual. Alternative spelling: Humphry.

Hung Vietnamese. Vietnamese, "Spirit of hero" or "brave." Hsiuchuan (Chinese religious leader and rebel); Shen (Chinese dramatist and film maker); Vuong (legendary founder of Vietnam, 29th-century B.C. (?)). Unusual.

Hunt English. Old English, "The hunt." Unusual.

Hunter English. Old English, "Huntsman." Thompson ("gonzo" writer); Miller (lawyer, legal advisor at Paris Peace Conference, 1919). Unusual.

Huntington English. From Huntington, Old English, "Hunters' estate." Unusual.

Huntly English. Old English, "Hunting meadow." Unusual.

Huram Hebrew/Israeli. From Hiram, Hebrew, meaning unknown. 1 Kings 5:10. Unusual.

Hurley Irish. Gaelic, "Sea child." Unusual. Alternative spellings: Hurlee, Hurleigh.

Huslu Native American. Native American, "Hairy bear." Unusual.

Hussein Arabic. From Husain, Arabic, "Little beauty." Unusual. Alternative spelling: Husain.

Hutchinson English. From Hugh, Old German, "Mind" or "thought." Unusual.

Hute Native American. Native American, "Star." Unusual.

Huw Welsh. From Hugh, Old German, "Mind" or "thought." Morus (18th-century Welsh poet). Unusual.

Hux English. From Huxley. Unusual.

Huxley English. Old English, "From Hugh's meadow." Unusual.

Huy Vietnamese. Vietnamese, "Glorious." Unusual.

Hyacinth See under Girls' Names.

Hyam English. From Chaim, Hebrew, "Life." Unusual.

Hyman English. From Chaim, Hebrew, "Life." Rickover (advocate and admiral of the first nuclear submarine, "Nautilus"). Unusual.

Hywel Welsh. Welsh, "Eminent," "conspicuous." ab Owain Gwynedd (Welsh prince and poet); Dda (10th-century Welsh ruler). Unusual.

Iago Italian, Welsh. From Jacob, Hebrew (Yaakov), "Supplanter" or "heel." Genesis 25:26. Character in Shakespeare's "Othello." Unusual.

Iakobos Greek. From Jacob, Hebrew (Yaakov), "Supplanter" or "heel." Genesis 25:26. Unusual.

Iakov Greek. From Jacob, Hebrew (Yaakov), "Supplanter" or "heel." Genesis 25:26. Unusual.

Iakovos Greek. From Jacob, Hebrew (Yaakov), "Supplanter" or "heel." Genesis 25:26. Unusual.

Ian Scottish. From John, Hebrew (Yochanan), "God has been gracious." Fleming (author of James Bond novels); Woosman (British golfer); Maclaren (British clergyman and author) (real name: John Watson); Hamilton (British soldier, chief of staff to Kitchener, 1901–02); Holm (actor, "Hamlet"). Popular. Alternative spelling: Iain.

Iancu Romanian. From John, Hebrew (Yochanan), "God has been gracious." Unusual.

Ianos Czech. From John, Hebrew (Yochanan), "God has been gracious." Unusual.

Iban Hispanic. From John, Hebrew (Yochanan), "God has been gracious." Unusual.

Ibn-Mustapha Arabic. Arabic, "Son of Mustapha." Unusual.

Ibrāhīm Arabic. From Abraham, Hebrew (Avraham), "Exalted father" or "father of a multitude." Genesis 17:4,5. Kavrak (Turkish, developed smallest microphone: 0.06 x 0.03 inches, 1967); Muteferrika (18th-century Hungarian Ottoman printer, printed first Turkish-language books); Nazzam (9th-century Muslim theologian); Sinasi (19th-century Turkish writer, wrote first Turkish play). Unusual.

Icarus Greek. From Icarus, Greek, "Devoted to the moon goddess Car." Mythological son of Daedalus. Unusual.

Icek Yiddish. From Isaac, Hebrew (Yitzchak), "Laughter." Genesis 21:3. Unusual.

Ichabod English. Hebrew, "The glory has departed." 1 Samuel 4:21. Crane (schoolmaster in Washington Irving's "The Legend of Sleepy Hollow"). Unusual.

Idris Welsh. Welsh, "Lord" + "ardent" or "impulsive." Unusual.

Idwal Welsh. Welsh, "Lord" + "wall" or "rampart." Unusual.

Iestyn Welsh. From Justin, Latin, "Just." Unusual.

Ieuan Welsh. From John, Hebrew (Yochanan), "God has been gracious." Madlock, Sir (British physicist, former chief science advisor). Unusual.

Ifor Welsh. From Ivor, Old Norse, the name of a god. Unusual.

Igasho Native American. Native American, "Wanderer." Unusual.

Ignac Polish. From John, Hebrew (Yochanan), "God has been gracious." Unusual.

Ignace French. From Ignatious. Paderewski (Polish, highest-paid classical concert pianist: earned estimated $5 million in his lifetime). Unusual.

Ignatius English. From Ignatious. of Antioch (saint); of Loyola (patron saint of retreatants, founder of the Jesuits, 16th-century). Unusual. Alternative spelling: Ignatious.

Igor Russian. From Ingeborg, Old Norse, "Ing's protection." Ing is the Norse god of peace, prosperity, and fertility. Polyansky (Russian, set 1985 world record for 200-meter backstroke: 1 minute, 56.24 seconds); Sikorsky (aeronautical engineer, built and flew world's first multi-motor plane, 1913); Stravinsky (neoclassical composer, ballet "Petrouchka"). Unusual. Alternative spelling: Egor.

Ike English. From Isaac, Hebrew (Yitzchak), "Laughter." Genesis 21:3. Less popular.

Ikey English. From Isaac, Hebrew (Yitzchak), "Laughter." Genesis 21:3. Unusual. Alternative spelling: Ikie.

Ilan Hebrew/Israeli. From Ilana, Hebrew, "Tree." Unusual.

Ilias Greek. From Elijah, Hebrew (Eliyahu), "The Lord is my God." 1 Kings 17:1. Unusual. Alternative spellings: Elias, Eliasz.

Ilja Czech. From Elijah, Hebrew (Eliyahu), "The Lord is my God." 1 Kings 17:1. Unusual.

Illingworth English. Old English, "Illa's enclosure." Place name in Yorkshire, England. Unusual.

Ilom Nigerian. Nigerian, "I have many enemies." Unusual.

Immanuel Yiddish. From Emanuel, Hebrew, "God is with us," referring to a child about to be born. Isaiah 7:14. Kant (19th-century German philosopher); Fuchs (German mathematician); ben Solomon (Hebrew poet). Unusual.

Imran Arabic. Arabic, "Host." Unusual.

Imrich Czech. From Emery, German (Emmerich), "Home-power." Unusual.

Imrus Hungarian. From Emery, German (Emmerich), "Home-power." Unusual.

Inar English. From Einar, Old Norse, "Individualist." Unusual. Incencio Hispanic. From Kenneth, Gaelic, "Fair one" + "fire-sprung." Unusual.

Inek Polish. From Irwin, Old English, "Boar" + "friend." Unusual.

Ingemar Scandinavian. From Ingmar. Johansson (Swedish, heavyweight boxing champion, 1959); Stenmark (Swedish skier, won record 86 victories at Alpine World Cup, 1974–87). Unusual. Alternative spellings: Ingamar, Ingmar.

Inger Scandinavian. Old Norse, "Son's army." Unusual. Alternative spelling: Ingar.

Ingham English. English, surname and place name used as a first name. Unusual.

Inglebert German. From Engelbert, Old German, "Bright as an angel." Unusual. Alternative spelling: Ingelbert.

Ingram English. Old German, "Anglian raven." Unusual. Alternative spelling: Ingraham.

Ingvar Scandinavian. From Ingeborg, Old Norse, "Ing's protection." Ing is the Norse god of peace, prosperity, and fertility. Unusual.

Inigo Hispanic. From Ignatious, Greek, meaning unknown. Jones (British architect, 17th-century reconstruction of St. Paul's cathedral). Unusual.

Iniko Nigerian. Nigerian, "Troubled times." Unusual.

Innes Scottish. Gaelic, "Island." Unusual for males, unusual for females.

Innis Scottish. From Innes. Unusual for males, unusual for females.

Inocente Hispanic. From Kenneth, Gaelic, "Fair one" + "fire-sprung." Unusual.

Inteus Native American. Native American, "He is not ashamed." Unusual.

Ioakim Russian. Russian, "God will establish." Unusual.

Ioan Bulgarian, Romanian. From John, Hebrew (Yochanan), "God has been gracious." Rădulescu (Romanian writer, established and edited first Romanian periodical in Bucharest, 1829). Unusual.

Ioann Russian. From John, Hebrew (Yochanan), "God has been gracious." Unusual.

Ioannis Greek. From John, Hebrew (Yochanan), "God has been gracious." Metaxas (Greek general and politician); Kapodistrias (19th-century Greek politician). Unusual. Alternative spelling: Ioannes.

Iolo Welsh. From Iorwerth, Welsh, "Lord" + "worth." Unusual.

Ionel Romanian. From John, Hebrew (Yochanan), "God has been gracious." Unusual.

Iorwerth Welsh. Welsh, "Lord" + "worth." Unusual.

Iosif Greek, Russian. From Joseph, Hebrew (Yosef), "God will add." Dzhugashvili (Soviet political leader) (real name of Joseph Stalin); Gurko (Russian general). Unusual.

Iosua Romanian. From Joshua, Hebrew (Yehoshua), "God is my salvation." Exodus 17:9. Unusual.

Iov Russian. From Ioakim, Russian, "God will establish." Unusual.

Ira Hebrew/Israeli. Hebrew, "Watchful." 2 Samuel 23:26. Bowen (astronomer); Remsen (discovered saccharin, established "American Chemical Journal"); Allen (American Revolution politician, helped draft constitution, 1777); Gershwin (lyricist for brother/composer George, won first Pulitzer Prize awarded a lyricist, 1931). Less popular.

Iram English. From Alva, Hebrew, "Brightness" (?). Genesis 36:40. Unusual.

Irvin English. Gaelic, "Beautiful." Scottish place name. McDowell (army officer); Westheimer (banker and philanthropist, established Big Brother movement, 1903); Cobb (journalist and playwright). Unusual.

Irvine English. From Irvin. Unusual. Alternative spelling: Ervine.

Irving English. From Irvin. Berlin (composer, "White Christmas") (real name: Israel Baline); Caesar (songwriter, "Tea for Two"); Thalberg (movie executive); Babbitt (scholar and educator); Colburn (manufacturer, developed improved method for flat-sheet glass production). Less popular. Irv. Alternative spelling: Erving.

Irwin English. Old English, "Boar" + "friend." Edman (philosopher, author of "Adam, the Baby, and the Man from Mars"). Less popular. Irv. Alternative spelling: Erwin.

Isaac English. Hebrew (Yitzchak), "Laughter." Genesis 21:3. Son of Abraham; Newton, Sir (British physicist and mathematician, discovered laws of motion and gravity, 1685); Stern (violinist); Lewis (army officer, invented Lewis machine gun); Wise (rabbi); Stern (merchant and American Revolution patriot). Less popular. Ike, Izzy, Zack.

Isaak German, Greek, Yiddish. From Isaac. Dorner (19th-century German Protestant theologian); Jost (19th-century German historian). Unusual.

Isaiah English. Hebrew, "God is my help and salvation." Book of Isaiah. Prophet; Sellers (Mississippi River steamboat pilot, held record run from New Orleans to St. Louis, 1844); Thomas (printer, published "Massachusetts Spy"); Leopold (comedian and actor, "Mary Poppins") (real name of Ed Wynn). Less popular. Alternative spelling: Isiah.

Isak Scandinavian. From Isaac. Genesis 21:3. Dinesen (Danish author. Unusual.

Isak Bulgarian. From Isaac. Unusual.

Isak Russian. From Isaac. Unusual.

Isas Japanese. Japanese, "Meritorious one." Unusual.

Ishmael Hebrew/Israeli. Hebrew, "God will hear." Unusual.

Isidore English. Greek (Isidoros), "Gift of Isis." of Selville (saint); Ducasse (19th-century French poet) (real name of Le Comte de Lautreamont). Unusual. Izzy. Alternative spelling: Isador.

Iskandar Arabic. From Alexander, Greek, "Defender of men" or "warding off men." Mark 16:21; Acts 4:6, 19:33. Muda (sultan of Acheh, 1607–36). Unusual.

Iskemu Native American. Native American, "Gently running creek." Unusual.

Ismael Hebrew/Israeli. From Ishmael. Saint; Montes (president of Bolivia, 1904–09, 1913–17). Unusual.

Israel English. From Yisrael, Hebrew, "Wrestled with God." Name of the Jewish nation. Genesis 35:10. Putnam (commander in American Revolution); White (geologist); Zangwill (British playwright and novelist, "Children of the Ghetto"); Abrahams (British scholar, wrote "Jewish Life in the Middle Ages"); Davidson (Hebrew scholar). Unusual.

Isti Hungarian. From Stephen, Greek, "Crown" or "crowned." Acts 7:59. Unusual.

Istu Native American. Native American, "Sugar-pine sugar." Unusual.

István Hungarian. From Stephen, Greek, "Crown" or "crowned." Acts 7:59. Széchenyi (19th-century Hungarian reformer and writer); Werboczi (16th-century Hungarian statesman and jurist); Bethlen (Hungarian politician); Bocskay (17th-century Hungarian leader and prince of Transylvania); Gyöngyösi (18th-century Hungarian poet). Unusual.

Ithel Welsh. Welsh, "Generous lord." Unusual.

Iuana See under Girls' Names.

Iustin Russian. From Justin, Latin, "Just." Unusual.

Ivan Russian. From John, Hebrew (Yochanan), "God has been gracious." Lendl (Czech tennis great); Pavlov (Russian physiologist, won Nobel Prize, 1904); Mažuranić (Croatian poet and politician); Zajc (Croatian composer); Turgenev (19th-century Russian writer). Unusual.

Ivanchik Russian. From John, Hebrew (Yochanan), "God has been gracious." Unusual.

Ivano Russian. From John, Hebrew (Yochanan), "God has been gracious." Unusual.

Ivar Scandinavian. From Ivor. Aasen (19th-century Norwegian philosopher); Kreuger (Swedish financier). Unusual.

Ivas Russian. From John, Hebrew (Yochanan), "God has been gracious." Unusual.

Iver English. From Ivor. Unusual.

Ives English. From Ivo. Patron saint of St. Ives, Cornwall, and of St. Ives, Huntingdon, both in England. Unusual.

Ivo English. Teutonic, "Yew wood" or "archer." Yew wood was used to make bows. Andric (Serbo-Croatian novelist, won Nobel Prize for literature, 1961). Unusual.

Ivon English. From Ivo. Unusual.

Ivor English. Old Norse, the name of a god. Novello (British actor, composer, and playwright, "Keep the Home Fires Burning") (real name: David Ivor Davies); Richards (British literary critic). Unusual.

Ivory See under Girls' Names.

Ivy English. Old English, "ifig"; a plant name used as a first name. Lee (public relations consultant to John D. Rockefeller and Bethlehem Steel). Unusual for males, less popular for females.

Iwan Polish. From John, Hebrew (Yochanan), "God has been gracious." Gilkin (Belgian writer of verse and plays). Unusual.

Iye Native American. Native American, "Smoke." Unusual.

Izaak Hebrew/Israeli. From Isaac, Hebrew (Yitzchak), "Laughter." Genesis 21:3. Unusual.

Izak Czech. From Isaac, Hebrew (Yitzchak), "Laughter." Genesis 21:3. Unusual.

Izzy English. From Isidore, Greek (Isidoros), "Gift of Isis." Unusual. Alternative spelling: Issy.

Ja Korean. Korean, "Attraction" or "magnetism." Unusual.

Jaan Estonian. From Christian, Greek, "christos" ("anointed"). Tonnison (Estonian prime minister, 1919–20; president, 1927–28, 1933). Unusual.

Jace Created. Created, possibly from initials "J" and "C." Unusual.

Jacinto Hispanic. Spanish, "Hyacinth." Picón y Bouchet (Spanish novelist and art critic, "Sacramento"). Unusual.

Jack English. From John, Hebrew (Yochanan), "God has been gracious." Nicklaus (golf great, first person to win all five major titles twice); Nicholson (actor, "Prizzi's Honor"); Lemmon (actor, "The Apartment"); Teague (musician, member of Louis Armstrong's "All Stars") (real name: Weldon Leo). Less popular.

Jackie English. From Jacob, Hebrew (Yaakov), "Supplanter" or "heel." Genesis 25:26. Collins (novelist); Gleason (actor, "The Hustler"); Robinson (baseball great, elected to Baseball of Fame, 1962). Less popular for males, less popular for females.

Jackson English. Old English, "Jack's son." Browne (singer and guitarist); Pollock (abstract expressionist painter); Haines (dancer and ice skater, considered father of modern figure skating). Unusual.

Jaco Portuguese. From Jacob. Erasmus (South African, fastest time for one-mile wheelbarrow race: 4 minutes, 48.51 seconds, 1987); Vissier (South African, badminton endurance record: 83 hours, 25 minutes, 1988). Unusual.

Jacob English. Hebrew (Yaakov), "Supplanter" or "heel." Genesis 25:26. Second Hebrew patriarch, son of Isaac; Rils (urban reform crusader); van Ruisdael (17th-century Dutch landscape painter, "Jewish Cemetery"); Epstein, Sir (British sculptor, "Ecce Homo"); Shubert (theatrical manager and producer; with his brothers, built theaters in major cities). Very popular. Jack, Jake. Alternative spelling: Jakob.

Jacobo Hispanic. From Jacob. Arbenz Guzman (Guatemalan president, 1950–54). Unusual.

Jacoby English. From Jacob. Unusual.

Jacques French. From Jacob. Piccard (Swiss, achieved record ocean descent: 35,820 feet down, 1960); Mayol (French, set record for breath-held diving: 344 feet, 1983); Roux (French priest and revolutionary); Pradon (17th-century French dramatist); Necker (19th-century French financier). Less popular.

Jacquet French. From Jacob. Unusual.

Jacy Native American. Native American, "Moon." Unusual.

Jade See under Girls' Names.

Ja'far Arabic. Arabic, "A little stream." al-Askari (Iraq, first minister of defense); ibn Muḥammad (8th-century Islamic leader, sixth imam of Shiite Muslims). Unusual.

Jagger English. English, "To cart things around." Unusual.

Jago English. From Jacob. Unusual.

Jahi African. Swahili, "Dignity." Unusual.

Jaime English. From Jacob, Hebrew (Yaakov), "Supplanter" or "heel." Genesis 25:26. Ortiz-Patino (French art collector; Sotheby's sold his impressionist paintings for $67.8 million); Nuno (Catalan conductor and composer); Huguet (Spanish painter noted for altarpieces). Unusual for males, unusual for females.

Jaimito Hispanic. From Jacob. Unusual.

Jajuan American. Created, African-American. Unusual.

Jakab Hungarian. From Jacob. Unusual.

Jake English. From Jacob. Less popular.

Jakie English. From Jacob. Unusual.

Jakiv Russian. From Jacob. Unusual.

Jakov Russian. From Jacob. Unusual.

Jakub Czech. From Jacob. Unusual.

Jakubek Polish. From Jacob. Unusual.

Jal Gypsy. English Gypsy, "Wanderer." Unusual.

Jalu Polish. From Jacob. Unusual.

Jamaal Arabic. From Jamīl. Unusual. Alternative spellings: Jamahl, Jamal, Jamall.

Jamaine Arabic. From Germain, Latin, "A German." Unusual.

Jamar Created. Created, African-American. Unusual.

Jamarr Created. From Jamar. Unusual.

Jameel Arabic. From Jamīl. Unusual. Alternative spelling: Jamiel.

Jamel Arabic. From Jamīl. Unusual. Alternative spellings: Jamele, Jamelle.

James English. From Jacob, Hebrew (Yaakov), "Supplanter" or "heel." Genesis 25:26. the Deacon (saint); the Great (apostle, patron saint of rheumatism sufferers); the Less (apostle); Puckle (British, invented machine gun); McPherson (won Pulitzer Prize for fiction, 1978, "Elbow Room"); Taylor (musician, "You've Got a Friend"). Extremely popular. Jamie, Jim, Jimmy. Alternative spelling: Jaymes.

Jameson English. From Jacob, Hebrew (Yaakov), "Supplanter" or "heel." Genesis 25:26. Unusual. Alternative spellings: Jamieson, Jamison.

Jamie See under Girls' Names.

Jamīl Arabic. Arabic, "Handsome." Unusual.

Jan Czech, Dutch, Polish, Scandinavian. From John, Hebrew (Yochanan), "God has been gracious." Less popular.

Janco Czech. From John, Hebrew (Yochanan), "God has been gracious." Unusual.

Jancsi Hungarian. From John, Hebrew (Yochanan), "God has been gracious." Unusual.

Jandino Hispanic. From Alexander, Greek, "Defender of men" or "warding off men." Mark 16:21; Acts 4:6, 19:33. Unusual.

Jando Hispanic. From Alexander, Greek, "Defender of men" or "warding off men." Mark 16:21; Acts 4:6, 19:33. Unusual.

Janek Polish. From John, Hebrew (Yochanan), "God has been gracious." Unusual.

Janika Hungarian. From John, Hebrew (Yochanan), "God has been gracious." Unusual.

Jankiel Polish. From John, Hebrew (Yochanan), "God has been gracious." Unusual.

Janne Finnish. From John, Hebrew (Yochanan), "God has been gracious." Unusual.

Jano Hungarian, from Eugene, Greek, "Well born"; and Czech, from John, Hebrew (Yochanan), "God has been gracious." Unusual.

János Hungarian. From John, Hebrew (Yochanan), "God has been gracious." Mailáth, Count (Hungarian historian and poet); Garay (Hungarian poet and playwright); Damjanich (Hungarian general and patriot); Sylvester (16th-century Hungarian humanist, wrote first Hungarian poetry and grammar); Erdélyi (19th-century Hungarian scholar and author). Unusual.

Janson English. From John, Hebrew (Yochanan), "God has been gracious." Unusual. Alternative spellings: Jansen, Jantzen, Janzen.

Janus English. "Born in January"; origin unknown. Unusual.

Japheth Hebrew/Israeli. Hebrew, "May he expand." Genesis 9:27. Noah's oldest son. Unusual.

Jared English. Hebrew (Yared), "Descendent" or "to descend." Genesis 5:15. Sparks (historian, president of Harvard University, 1849–53). Popular. Alternative spellings: Jarad, Jarid, Jarod, Jarrad, Jarred, Jerrod, Jerryd, Jerad, Jered, Jerod, Jerrad, Jerrod.

Jarek Polish. From Janus. Unusual.

Jaron Hebrew/Israeli. Hebrew, "To sing" or "to cry out." Unusual. Alternative spelling: Jaren.

Jaroslav Slavic. Slavic, "Spring's glory." Seifert (Czech poet and journalist, won Nobel Prize for literature, 1984); Hasek (Czech writer); Heyrovsky (Czech physical chemist, won Nobel Prize, 1959, for his polarographic analysis); Vrchlický (Czech poet) (real name: Emil Frida). Unusual.

Jarrell English. From Gerald, Old German, "Spear" + "ruler." Unusual. Alternative spellings: Jarell, Jerel, Jerell, Jerrell.

Jarrett English. From Jared. Unusual. Alternative spellings: Jarett, Jarret.

Jarvis English. From Gervase, Latin, meaning unknown. Unusual.

Jas Polish. From John, Hebrew (Yochanan), "God has been gracious." Angelo (British, juggled three objects without dropping for record 6 hours, 26 minutes, 31 seconds, 1989). Unusual.

Jasha Russian. From Jacob, Hebrew (Yaakov), "Supplanter" or "heel." Genesis 25:26. Unusual.

Jasio Polish. From John, Hebrew (Yochanan), "God has been gracious." Unusual.

Jason English. From Joshua, Hebrew (Yehoshua), "God is my salvation." Exodus 17:9. Host to Paul at Thessalonica; leader of the Argonauts; Gould (child of Elliott Gould and Barbra Streisand); Robards (actor); Miller (playwright); Lee (pioneer and missionary, established the Oregon Institute, 19th-century). Popular. Alternative spellings: Jasen, Jayson.

Jaspal Indo-Pakistani. Punjabi, "Virtuous." Unusual.

Jasper English. Persian, "Treasure-holder." One of the three kings or wise men who worshiped the infant Jesus; Mayne (British dramatist and clergyman). Unusual.

Javan English. Meaning and origin unknown. Genesis 10:2. Son of Japheth. Unusual. Alternative spellings: Javin, Javon.

Javaris Unknown. From Gervase, Latin, meaning unknown. Unusual.

Javas Indo-Pakistani. Sanskrit, "Swift" or "quick." Unusual.

Jave English. From Jay. Unusual for males, unusual for females.

Javier Hispanic. Spanish, "Owner of the new house." Sotomeyer (Cuban, set 1988 high jump record: 7 feet, 11-1/2 inches). Unusual.

Jawhar Arabic. Arabic, "Jewel" or "essence." Unusual.

Jay English. Old French, "Blue jay." Leno (comedian and talk-show host); Farrar (singer and guitarist); "Dizzy" Dean (baseball great, elected to Hall of Fame, 1953); Gould (financier) (real name: Jason Gould); Darling (won Pulitzer Prize for editorial cartoons, 1923, 1943). Less popular for males, unusual for females.

Jayce Created. From Jace, Created, possibly from initials "J" and "C." Unusual.

Jayde See Jade under Girls' Names.

Jayme Hispanic, Portuguese. From Jacob, Hebrew (Yaakov), "Supplanter" or "heel." Genesis 25:26. Unusual.

Jaymee See Jamie under Girls' Names.

Jazeps Latvian. From Joseph, Hebrew (Yosef), "God will add." Unusual.

Jean English. From John, Hebrew (Yochanan), "God has been gracious." Bartel (Miss America, 1943); Lurcat (French painter and tapestry designer); Rhys (British novelist); Molinet (16th-century French poet); Tassaert (18th-century Dutch sculptor). Unusual for males, less popular for females.

Jean-François French. French, combination of Jean (John, Hebrew (Yochanan), "Jehovah has been gracious") + François (Francis, Latin, "A Frenchman"). Sarasin (17th-century French poet); Chalgrin (18th-century French architect, began Arc de Triomphe); Roberval (French soldier); Troy (17th-century French painter); Marmontel (18th-century French writer). Unusual.

Jean-Michel French. French, combination of Jean (John, Hebrew (Yochanan), "Jehovah has been gracious") + Michel (Michael, Hebrew, "Who is like God?"). Unusual.

Jean-Phillipe French. French, combination of Jean (John, Hebrew, "Jehovah has been gracious") + Phillipe (Philip, Greek, "Lover of horses"). Unusual.

Jeannot French. From John, Hebrew (Yochanan), "God has been gracious." Unusual.

Jeays English. From Jay. Unusual for males, unusual for females. Alternative spelling: Jeyes.

Jecis Lithuanian. From Jacob, Hebrew (Yaakov), "Supplanter" or "heel." Genesis 25:26. Unusual.

Jed English. From Jedidiah. Less popular.

Jedidiah English. Hebrew, "Beloved friend of God." Morse (clergyman, published "Geography Made Easy," 1784). Unusual. Alternative spelling: Jedediah.

Jedrek Polish. From Andrew, Greek, "Manly." Unusual.

Jedrus Polish. From Andrew, Greek, "Manly." Unusual.

Jeff English. From Geoffrey, Old German (Gottfried), "peace" (?). Tweedy (bassist); Chandler (actor) (real name: Iran Grossel). Less popular.

Jefferson English. From Geoffrey, Old German (Gottfried), "peace" (?). Davis (president of Confederate States of America, 1828–35). Unusual.

Jeffrey English. From Geoffrey, Old German (Gottfried), "peace" (?). Amherst, Baron (18th-century British soldier). Popular. Jeff. Alternative spellings: Geoffery, Geoffrey, Geoffry, Geofrey, Jefferey, Jeffery, Jeffree, Jeffry.

Jehan French. From John, Hebrew (Yochanan), "God has been gracious." Tabourot (16th-century French scholar); Bodel (13th-century French trouvère). Unusual.

Jehu Hebrew/Israeli. Hebrew, "The Lord is He." 2 Kings 9:20. King of Israel, 842–15 B.C. Unusual.

Jekebs Lithuanian. From Jacob, Hebrew (Yaakov), "Supplanter" or "heel." Genesis 25:26. Unusual.

Jeks Latvian. From Jacob, Hebrew (Yaakov), "Supplanter" or "heel." Genesis 25:26. Unusual.

Jem See under Girls' Names.

Jemmy English. From Jemima, Hebrew, "Dove." Job 42:14. Unusual. Alternative spelling: Jemmie.

Jena English. From John, Hebrew (Yochanan), "God has been gracious." Unusual.

Jenci Hungarian. From Eugene, Greek, "Well born." Unusual.

Jenda Czech. From John, Hebrew (Yochanan), "God has been gracious." Unusual.

Jenkin English. From John, Hebrew (Yochanan), "God has been gracious." Unusual. Alternative spelling: Jenkyn.

Jenoe Hungarian. From Eugene, Greek, "Well born." Unusual.

Jens Scandinavian. From John, Hebrew (Yochanan), "God has been gracious." Willumsen (Danish painter and sculptor); Jacobsen (19th-century Danish novelist and poet); Baggesen (19th-century Danish poet); Worsaae (19th-century Danish historian and archaeologist); Hansen (19th-century Danish journalist and politician). Unusual.

Jensi Hungarian. From Eugene, Greek, "Well born." Unusual.

Jeoffroi French. From Geoffrey, Old German (Gottfried), "peace" (?). Unusual. Alternative spellings: Geoffroi, Geoffroy.

Jeorg German. From George, Greek, "Husbandman," "farmer," or "earthworker." Unusual.

Jephtha Hebrew/Israeli. Hebrew, "Whom God sets free." Chief of the Gileadites. Unusual.

Jerald English. From Gerald, Old German, "Spear" + "ruler." Unusual. Jerry. Alternative spellings: Gerald, Gerrald, Gerrold, Jerold, Jerrold.

Jere English. From Jeremiah. Unusual.

Jeremia Swedish. From Jeremiah. Unusual.

Jeremiah Hebrew/Israeli. Hebrew, "Jehovah is high" or "Jehovah exalts." Book of Jeremiah. Prophet; Johnson (title character in 1972 movie); Black (attorney general under Buchanan); Clarke (18th-century British organist and composer); Dummer (18th-century British lawyer); Horrocks (17th-century British astronomer). Less popular. Alternative spelling: Gerimiah.

Jeremias Dutch, Finnish, German, Hispanic, Portuguese. From Jeremiah. Richter (19th-century German chemist, discovered law, which now bears his name, concerning combining acids and alkalies); Bitzius (19th-century Swiss novelist) (real name of Jeremias Gotthelf). Unusual.

Jeremie French. From Jeremiah. Unusual.

Jeremija Russian. From Jeremiah. Unusual.

Jeremy English. From Jeremiah. Bentham (19th-century British utilitarian philosopher); Collier (British clergyman, ordained a bishop, 1713); Irons (British actor, "Dead Ringers"). Popular. Alternative spellings: Jeramie, Jeramy, Jereme, Jeremey, Jermey, Jeromy.

Jerimiah English. From Jeremiah. Unusual. Jerry.

Jermane English. From Germain, Latin, "A German." Unusual. Alternative spellings: Germaine, Jermain, Jermaine, Jermayne.

Jerney Slavic. From Bartholomew, Aramaic, "Son of Tolmai." An alternate name for the apostle Nathaniel. Unusual.

Jerome English. Latin, "Sacred name." Patron saint of archaeologists and scholars; Emiliani (patron saint of orphans); Jerome (British novelist and playwright, "Three Men in a Boat"); Kern (composer, "Show Boat"); Robbins (choreographer) (real name: Jerome Rabinowitz). Less popular. Jerry. Alternative spelling: Jerrome.

Jeron English. From Jerome. Unusual.

Jerry English. From Gerald, Old German, "Spear" + "ruler." Rice (football great); Lewis (comedian) (real name: Joseph Levitz); Hall (model); Hoffman (actor); Van Dyke (actor). Less popular for males, unusual for females. Alternative spellings: Gerrie, Jerrie.

Jervis English. From Gervase, Latin, meaning unknown. Markham (17th-century British writer). Unusual.

Jeska Latvian. From Jacob, Hebrew (Yaakov), "Supplanter" or "heel." Genesis 25:26. Unusual.

Jess See under Girls' Names.

Jesse English. Hebrew, "Jehovah exists." Son of Obed, father of David; Jackson (politician); Owens (track and field great, won four Olympic gold medals, 1936); Lasky (movie producer, "Adventures of Mark Twain"); Elliot (naval officer). Popular for males, less popular for females. Alternative spellings: Jessey, Jessie, Jessy.

Jessie See under Girls' Names.

Jesús Hispanic. From Joshua, Hebrew (Yehoshua), "God is my salvation." Exodus 17:9. Founder of Christianity. Popular.

Jethro English. Hebrew, "Preeminence." Exodus 18:6. Father-in-law of Moses; Tull (British agriculturist, invented machine drill for sowing seed, 1701). Less popular.

Jibben Gypsy. English Gypsy, "Life." Unusual.

Jim English. From Jacob, Hebrew (Yaakov), "Supplanter" or "heel." Genesis 25:26. Henson (creator of the Muppets); Bakker (scandalridden TV evangelist); Tully (writer, publicist for Charlie Chaplin); Nabors (actor, "The Andy Griffith Show"); Backus (actor). Less popular. Jimmy.

Jimmy English. From Jacob, Hebrew (Yaakov), "Supplanter" or "heel." Genesis 25:26. Carter (39th president) (real name: James Earl Carter, Jr.); Dean (singer); Durante (comedian) (real name: James Francis). Less popular. Jim. Alternative spellings: Jimmie.

Jimoh African. From Jumah, Swahili, "Born on Friday." Unusual.

Jin Chinese. Chinese, "Gold." Unusual.

Jindra Czech. From Harold, Old English, "Army power." Unusual.

Jindřich Czech. From Henry, Old German (Heimerich), "Home ruler." Unusual.

Jing-Quo Chinese. Chinese, "To run the country." Unusual.

Jiři Czech. From George, Greek, "Husbandman," "farmer," or "earth-worker." Unusual.

Jiro Japanese. Japanese, "The second male." Unusual.

Jivin Indo-Pakistani. Hindi, "To give life." Unusual.

Jo English. From Joseph, Hebrew (Yosef), "God will add." Stafford (singer); Davidson (sculptor); Mielziner (theatrical designer, won Oscar for art direction, "Picnic," 1955). Unusual for males, less popular for females.

Joab Hebrew/Israeli. Hebrew, "Praise the Lord." Commander of David's army, son of David's half-sister Zeruiah. Unusual.

Joachim Hebrew/Israeli. Hebrew, "God will establish." Unusual.

Joah Hebrew/Israeli. Hebrew, "God [is] brother." Unusual.

Joannes Greek. From John, Hebrew (Yochanan), "God has been gracious." Unusual.

João Portuguese. From John, Hebrew (Yochanan), "God has been gracious." De Deus Ramos (19th-century Portuguese poet); Zarco (Portuguese navigator, discovered Madeira, 15th-century); Cabrillo (Portuguese explorer, discovered California, 1542); Castro (president of Costa Rica, 1847–49). Unusual.

Joaquim Portuguese. From Joshua, Hebrew (Yehoshua), "God is my salvation." Exodus 17:9. Nabuco de Araujo (Brazilian politician and diplomat); Machado de Assiz (Brazilian novelist). Unusual.

Joaquín Hispanic. From Joshua, Hebrew (Yehoshua), "God is my salvation." Exodus 17:9. Andujar (baseball, pitching great); Turina (Spanish composer); Prieto (president of Chile, 1831–41); Edwards Bello (Chilean journalist and novelist); Sorolla y Bastida (Spanish painter). Unusual.

Job English. Hebrew, possibly "afflicted" or "persecuted." Book of Job. Biblical sufferer; Charnock (British merchant, founder of city that became Calcutta, 17th-century). Unusual. Alternative spelling: Jobe.

Jobo Hispanic. From Joseph, Hebrew (Yosef), "God will add." Unusual.

Joby English. From Job, Hebrew, possibly "afflicted" or "persecuted." Book of Job.

Unusual for males, unusual for females. Alternative spelling: Jobie.

Jocelin See Jocelyn under Girls' Names.

Jocelyn See under Girls' Names.

Jock English. From John, Hebrew (Yochanan), "God has been gracious." Unusual.

Jockel German. From Jacob, Hebrew (Yaakov), "Supplanter" or "heel." Genesis 25:26. Unusual.

Jocko English. From John, Hebrew (Yochanan), "God has been gracious." Unusual.

Jodie See under Girls' Names.

Jody See Jodie under Girls' Names.

Joe English. From Joseph, Hebrew (Yosef), "God will add." Frazier (heavyweight boxing champion, 1968); Montana (football great); Eszterhas (screenplay writer, "Jagged Edge"). Less popular. Joey.

Joel English. Hebrew, "Jehovah is the Lord." Book of Joel. Hebrew prophet; Grey (actor, "Cabaret"); McCrea (actor); Spingarn (author, a founder of publisher Harcourt, Brace & Co. and the National Association for the Advancement of Colored People); Chandler Harris (author, "Uncle Remus" stories). Popular for males, unusual for females.

Joela See under Girls' Names.

Joergen Scandinavian. From George, Greek, "Husbandman," "farmer," or "earth-worker." Unusual.

Joey English. From Joseph, Hebrew (Yosef), "God will add." Heatherton (actress). Less popular.

Joffre English. French, surname used as a first name. Unusual.

Johan Dutch, English, Estonian. From John, Hebrew (Yochanan), "God has been gracious." Unusual.

Johana See under Girls' Names.

Johann German. From John, Hebrew (Yochanan), "God has been gracious." Molter (German, most prolific symphonist: 165); Lips (19th-century Swiss painter and engraver); Melchior (19th-century German porcelain modeler); Reiske (18th-century German philologist, authority on Greek literature); Uz (18th-century German poet). Unusual.

Johannes German. From John, Hebrew (Yochanan), "God has been gracious." Schönborn (German prince-prelate, bishop of Wurzburg, 1642); Stumpf (16th-century Swiss historian); Volkelt (German philosopher); Wislicenus (German chemist); Rydberg (Swedish physicist, discovered a constant that now bears his name, 1890); Sturm (19th-century French mathematician). Unusual.

John English. Hebrew (Yochanan), "God has been gracious." the Baptist (saint, apostle); pope (I, 523-XXIII, 1958); Adams (second president); Quincy Adams (sixth president); McEnroe (tennis great); Davis (17th-century British navigator); Updike (won Pulitzer Prize for fiction, 1982, "Rabbit is Rich"); Jay (first Chief Justice of the U.S. Supreme Court, 1789–95). Extremely popular. Johnny. Alternative spelling: Jon.

Johnny English. From John, Hebrew (Yochanan), "God has been gracious." Carson (long-time host of TV's "Tonight" show); Cash (country singer); Depp (actor, "21 Jump Street"); Marks (composer, "Rudolph, the Red-Nosed Reindeer"); Weissmuller (swimmer and actor, won three Olympic gold medals, 1924). Less popular for males, unusual for females. Alternative spellings: Johnie, Johnnie, Jonni, Jonnie, Jonny.

Johnson English. From John. Unusual.

Joji Japanese. From George, Greek, "Husbandman," "farmer," or "earth-worker." Unusual.

Jojo English. From Joseph, Hebrew (Yosef), "God will add." Unusual.

Jokubas Czech. From Jacob, Hebrew (Yaakov), "Supplanter" or "heel." Genesis 25:26. Unusual.

Jolly See under Girls' Names.

Jolon Native American. Native American, "Valley of the dead oaks." Unusual.

Jolyon English. From Julius, Latin, a Roman clan name meaning "downy" or "bearded." Forsyte (character in John Galsworthy's "Forsyte Saga"). Unusual.

Jonah English. Hebrew (Yonah), "Dove." Book of Jonah. Minor Hebrew prophet. Unusual.

Jonam Swedish. From John. Unusual.

Jonas English, French, Hispanic, Icelandic, Swedish. From Jonah. Mačiulis (Lithuanian poet); Lie (Norwegian novelist); Furrer (first president of Swiss Confederation, 19th-century); Basanavičius (Lithuanian scholar and politician). Unusual.

Jonathan English. Hebrew (Yonatan), "God has given" or "God's gift." Eldest son of King Saul (1 Samuel 13), friend of David; priest (Judges 18:30); Maccabeus (rebel against Romans); Edwards (preacher and theologian); Swift (17th-century British author, "Gulliver's Travels"); Trelawny, Sir (17th-century British bishop); Cummings (religious leader, organized Advent Christian Church, 1860). Very popular. Jon, Johnny+. Alternative spellings: Johnathan, Johnathon, Jonathen, Jonathon, Jonothan, Jonothon.

Jone Welsh. From John. Unusual.

Jonelis Lithuanian. From John. Unusual.

Jonukas Lithuanian. From John, Hebrew (Yochanan), "God has been gracious." Unusual.

Jonutis Lithuanian. From John. Unusual.

Joosef Finnish. From Joseph. Unusual.

Jooseppi Finnish. From Joseph. Unusual.

Jordan See under Girls' Names.

Jordy English. From Jordan, Hebrew (Yarden), "To descend." Also the name of a river. Unusual.

Jorge Hispanic. From George, Greek, "Husbandman," "farmer," or "earth-worker." Chamomo (Spanish, performed longest solo singing marathon in 1985: 200 hours, 20 minutes); Ubico Castañeda (president of Guatemala, 1931–44); Borges (Argentine writer, established Ultraist movement in South America); Chávez (Peruvian aviator, overflew Alps, 1910). Unusual.

Jörgen Scandinavian. From George, Greek, "Husbandman," "farmer," or "earth-worker." Moe (19th-century Norwegian poet). Unusual.

Jori English. From Jordan, Hebrew (Yarden), "To descend." Also the name of a river. Unusual. Alternative spelling: Jory.

Jorrín Hispanic. From George, Greek, "Husbandman," "farmer," or "earth-worker." Unusual.

José Hispanic. From Joseph. Feliciano (musician, "Light My Fire"); Ortega y Gasset (Spanish philosopher, advocated control by elite group); Azcona Hoyo (Honduran president, 1986-); Rivera (Colombian novelist); Silva (18th-century Portuguese playwright). Popular.

Josecito Hispanic. From Joseph. Unusual. Alternative spelling: Joseito.

Josef Czech, German, Portuguese, Scandinavian, Yiddish. From Joseph. Myslivečék (18th-century Czech composer); Zítek (Czech architect. Unusual.

Joselito Hispanic. From Joseph. Unusual.

Joseph English. Hebrew (Yosef), "God will add." Eleventh son of Jacob, by Rachel; chief steward to Pharaoh; saint, foster-father of Jesus and husband of Mary; of Arimathea (patron saint of funeral directors); Lister (invented antiseptics); Priestley (British, discovered oxygen); Smith (established Church of Jesus Christ of Latter-day Saints). Very popular. Joe, Joey.

Josephe French. From Joseph. Unusual.

Josephus English. From Joseph. Hermens (Dutch, ran 20,000 meters in record 57 minutes, 24.2 seconds); Daniels (secretary of navy under Wilson); Alberdingk Thijm (19th-century Dutch author and critic). Unusual.

Josh English. From Joshua. Billings (19th-century humorist) (real name: Henry Wheeler Shaw). Less popular.

Josha Indo-Pakistani. Hindi, "Satisfaction." Unusual.

Joshua English. Hebrew (Yehoshua), "God is my salvation." Exodus 17:9. Moses' commander and successor; Reynolds (18th-century British portraitist, "Mrs. Siddons as the Tragic Muse"); Alexander (secretary of commerce under Wilson); Giddings (19th-century politician, antislavery advocate); Cowen (invented batteries and electric fuses). Extremely popular. Josh. Alternative spelling: Joshuah.

Josiah English. Hebrew, "Jehovah supports." King of Judah, 640–09 B.C.; Wedgwood (18th-century British potter, invented jasperware); Meigs (lawyer and educator); Quincy (educator, president of Harvard, 1829–45); Tucker (18th-century British economist, argued against monopolies). Unusual.

Josip Serbian. From Joseph. Strossmajer (Croatian prelate and nationalist). Unusual.

Jóska Hungarian. From Joseph. Unusual.

Josua German, Swedish. From Joshua. Unusual.

Josue French, Hispanic. From Joshua. Unusual.

Jotham Hebrew/Israeli. Hebrew, "Jehovah is perfect." Judges 9:5. Youngest son of Gideon; king of Judah. Unusual.

Jourdain French. From Jordan, Hebrew (Yarden), "To descend." Also the name of a river. Unusual.

Jov Russian. From Ioakim, Russian, "God will establish." Unusual.

Jovan Slavic. From John, Hebrew (Yochanan), "God has been gracious." Ristić (19th-century Serbian politician); Avakumović (Serbian statesman, president of provisional government, 1903); Jovanović (Serbian journalist and author). Unusual.

Joyce See under Girls' Names.

Jozhe Serbian. From Joseph. Unusual.

Juan Hispanic. From John, Hebrew (Yochanan), "God has been gracious." Llorente (Spanish priest); Manuel (14th-century Spanish prince and author) (real name: Don Juan Manuel); Masip (16th-century Spanish painter); O'Donojú (soldier, acting viceroy of Mexico, 1821); Ríos (president of Chile, 1942–46). Popular.

Juanch Hispanic. From John, Hebrew (Yochanan), "God has been gracious." Unusual.

Juancho Hispanic. From John, Hebrew (Yochanan), "God has been gracious." Unusual.

Juanito Hispanic. From John, Hebrew (Yochanan), "God has been gracious." Unusual.

Jubal Hebrew/Israeli. Hebrew (Yubal), "Ram's horn," used as a trumpet. Early (Confederate army officer). Unusual.

Judah English. Hebrew (Yehuda), "Praise to the Lord." Genesis 29:35. Fourth son of Jacob and Leah; 2nd-century Jewish scholar in Palestine; Magnes (religious leader, led Society for Advancement of Judaism, 1912–20); Sommo (Italian Jewish playwright); Alkalai (rabbi and author); Benjamin (senator and lawyer). Less popular. Alternative spelling: Juda.

Judas Greek. From Judah. Maccabeus (purified Temple of Jerusalem circa 165 B.C., an occurrence now commemorated by Chanukah); Iscariot (one of original 12 apostles); Thaddaeus (one of original 12 apostles). Unusual.

Judd English. From Judah. Hubbard (psychologist and educator); Hirsch (actor, "Dear John"). Less popular.

Jude English. From Judah. Patron saint of hopeless cases; character in Beatles' song "Hey, Jude!"; Wanniski (editor, "Polyconomics, Inc."); character in Thomas Hardy's "Jude the Obscure." Less popular.

Judson English. From Judah. Adoniram (missionary to Burma, 1812); Harmon (attorney general under Cleveland); Arthur (manager of Philadelphia Orchestra); Edward (adventurer and writer). Less popular.

Juhana Finnish. From John, Hebrew (Yochanan), "God has been gracious." Unusual.

Juho Finnish. From John, Hebrew (Yochanan), "God has been gracious." Paasikivi (Finnish politician, negotiated end of Russo-Finnish War). Unusual.

Jukka Finnish. From John, Hebrew (Yochanan), "God has been gracious." Unusual.

Juku Estonian. From Richard, Old German, "Strong ruler." Unusual.

Julas American. From Julius. Unusual.

Jules English, French. From Julius. Verne (French author, "Around the World in Eighty Days"); Rimet (honorary president of FIFA, a soccer organization); Dassin (film director); Anethan (Belgian premier, 1870); Violle (French physicist). Less popular.

Julian Hispanic, Latin. From Julius. Saint; Roman emperor, 361–63; Lavon (chemist); Lennon (musician, child of John Lennon); Lincaw (fastest magician: performed 98 different tricks in 1 minute, 57.9 seconds). Less popular. Alternative spelling: Julion.

Julianus Latin. From Julius. Unusual.

Julias American. From Julius. Unusual. Alternative spelling: Julious.

Julien English, French. From Julius. Pierre (French sculptor); La Mettrie (French physician and philosopher); Benda (French writer and philosopher); Dubuque (pioneer, first white settler near Dubuque, Iowa). Unusual. Alternative spelling: Julyan.

Julio Hispanic. From Julius. Roca (president of Argentina, 1880–1904); Acosta Garcia (president of Costa Rica, 1920–24); González (Spanish sculptor and painter); Iglesias (Spanish singer). Unusual.

Julius Latin. Latin, a Roman clan name meaning "downy" or "bearded." Saint; pope (I, 337-III, 1550); Caesar (Roman general and statesman); Morton (secretary of agriculture under Cleveland);

Mayer (German physician and physicist); Nieuwland (chemist and botanist); Payer (Austrian explorer and painter). Less popular.

Jumah African. Swahili, "Born on Friday." Unusual. Alternative spelling: Juma.

Jun Chinese. Chinese, "Truth." Jun-ichiro Tanizaki (Japanese novelist). Unusual for males, unusual for females.

Junior English. Latin, "juvenis" ("young"); the word used as a first name. Unusual.

Jupp German. From Joseph, Hebrew (Yosef), "God will add." Unusual.

Jur Czech. From George, Greek, "Husbandman," "farmer," or "earth-worker." Unusual.

Juraz Czech. From George, Greek, "Husbandman," "farmer," or "earth-worker." Unusual.

Jurek Polish. From George, Greek, "Husbandman," "farmer," or "earth-worker." Unusual.

Jürgen German. From George, Greek, "Husbandman," "farmer," or "earth-worker." Schult (set 1986 world record for discus throw: 243 feet); Ovens (Danish painter); Wullenwever (Hanseatic politician). Unusual.

Jurgi Russian. From George, Greek, "Husbandman," "farmer," or "earth-worker." Unusual.

Jurgis Lithuanian. From George, Greek, "Husbandman," "farmer," or "earth-worker." Unusual.

Juri Estonian. From George, Greek, "Husbandman," "farmer," or "earth-worker." Unusual.

Jurik Czech. From George, Greek, "Husbandman," "farmer," or "earth-worker." Unusual.

Jurko Czech. From George, Greek, "Husbandman," "farmer," or "earth-worker." Unusual.

Juro Czech. From George, Greek, "Husbandman," "farmer," or "earth-worker." Unusual.

Jusa Czech. From Justin. Unusual.

Jussi Finnish. From John, Hebrew (Yochanan), "God has been gracious." Unusual.

Just German. From Justin. Fontaine (soccer player, scored record 13 goals in six games, 1958 World Cup). Unusual.

Justas Lithuanian. From Justin. Unusual.

Justek Polish. From Justin. Unusual.

Justin English. Latin, "Just." Saint; Greek philosopher and martyr; emperor of the eastern Roman Empire (I, 518-II, 565); M'Carthy (Irish novelist and politician); Morrill (politician, author of first protective tariff act, 1861); Perkins (19th-century missionary to Persia). Extremely popular. Alternative spellings: Justen, Juston.

Justinas Lithuanian. From Justin. Unusual.

Justino Hispanic. From Justin. Unusual.

Justins Latvian. From Justin. Unusual.

Justinus Scandinavian. From Justin. von Hontheim (18th-century German prelate and theologian) (real name of Justinus Febronius). Unusual.

Justis English. From Justin. Unusual.

Justo Hispanic. From Justin. Urquiza (Argentine soldier and politician); Barrios (Guatemalan general and president, 1873–85). Unusual.

Justs Latvian. From Justin. Unusual.

Justukas Lithuanian. From Justin. Unusual.

Justus German. From Justin. Saint; von Liebig (German chemist); Lipsius (Flemish humanist and philosopher); Möser (18th-century German jurist and historian); Byrgius (Swiss mathematician, invented logarithms); van Effen (18th-century Dutch essayist). Unusual.

Justyn Czech. From Justin. Unusual.

Kabil Turkish. From Cain, Hebrew, "Spear." Unusual.

Kacey English. From Casimir, Old Slavic, "He announces [or "commands"] peace." Unusual for males, unusual for females. Alternative spellings: Casey, Kasey.

Kadar Arabic. Arabic, "Powerful." Unusual.

Kade Arabic. From Kadar. Unusual.

Kadin Arabic. Arabic, "Friend" or "confidant." Unusual. Alternative spelling: Kadeen.

Kadir Arabic. Arabic, "Green" or "green crop." Unusual. Alternative spelling: Kadeer.

Kaese German. From Kass, German, "Like a blackbird." Unusual.

Kaga Native American. Native American, "Writer" or "chronicler." Unusual.

Kahil Turkish. From Cahil, Turkish, "Young," "inexperienced," "naive." Unusual. Alternative spelling: Cahil.

Kai Hawaiian. Hawaiian, "Sea" or "sea water." Unusual for males, unusual for females.

Kaiser Bulgarian. From Caesar, Latin (Caesarius), "Hairy child." Unusual.

Kakar Indo-Pakistani. Hindi, "Grass." Unusual.

Kala Indo-Pakistani. Hindi, "Black" or "time." Another name for the Hindu god Siva. Unusual.

Kalb Arabic. From Caleb, Hebrew, "Dog." Numbers 13:6. Unusual.

Kale Hawaiian. From Charles, Old English, "ceorl" ("man" or "husbandman"). Unusual.

Kaleb English. From Caleb, Hebrew, "Dog." Numbers 13:6. Unusual. Alternative spelling: Caleb.

Kalechi Nigerian. Nigerian, "Praise God." Unusual.

Kalen Unknown. Meaning and origin unknown. Unusual. Alternative spelling: Kalin.

Kalil Arabic. Arabic, "Good friend." Unusual.

Kalin Unknown. Meaning and origin unknown. Unusual.

Kaliq Arabic. Arabic, "Creative." Unusual.

Kalkin Indo-Pakistani. Hindi, the name of a god. Kalkin is held to be the tenth incarnation of the Hindu god Vishnu. Unusual.

Kalle Scandinavian. From Charles, Old English, "ceorl" ("man" or "husbandman"). Unusual.

Kálmán Hungarian. From Charles, Old English, "ceorl" ("man" or "husbandman"). Konyves (king of Hungary, 1095–1116); Mikszath (Hungarian novelist and member of national assembly); von Darányi (Hungarian president of legislature, 1938–39). Unusual.

Kaloosh Armenian. Armenian, "Blessed coming" or "blessed advent." Unusual.

Kalvin English. From Calvin, Latin, "Bald." Unusual. Alternative spelling: Calvin.

Kamāl Arabic. Arabic, "Perfect." Unusual.

Kameron Scottish. From Cameron, Scottish, surname and place name used as a first name. Possible meanings include "crooked stream" and "crooked nose." Unusual. Alternative spelling: Cameron.

Kāmil Arabic. From Kamāl. Pasa (19th-century grand vizier of Turkey). Unusual.

Kan Hebrew/Israeli. From Kaniel. Unusual.

Kane English. Celtic, "Beautiful." Unusual.

Kaniel Hebrew/Israeli. Hebrew, "Stalk" or "reed." Unusual.

Kanny Hebrew/Israeli. From Kaniel. Unusual. Alternative spelling: Kani.

Kanoa See under Girls' Names.

Kantu Indo-Pakistani. Hindi, "Happy." Another name for Kama or Kami, the Hindu god of love. Unusual.

Kapildev Indo-Pakistani. Hindi, the name of a god. Unusual.

Karal German. From Charles, Old English, "ceorl" ("man" or "husbandman"). Unusual.

Kardal Arabic. Arabic, "Mustard seed." Unusual.

Kareem Arabic. Arabic, "Generous" or "distinguished." Abdul-Jabbar (basketball great, scored 37,639 points from 1970–88) (real name: Lewis Ferdinand Alcindor). Unusual. Alternative spelling: Karim.

Karel Czech. From Charles, Old English, "ceorl" ("man" or "husbandman"). Sobota (Czech, made longest kabob: 885.87 feet long); Hynek (Czech poet and novelist); van Mander (Dutch painter and writer); van de Woestijne (Belgian poet and government official); Erben (Czech scholar, poet, and ethnologist). Unusual.

Karl Bulgarian, German, Russian. From Charles, Old English, "ceorl" ("man" or "husbandman"). I and II, dukes of Brunswick; Henize (oldest astronaut, flew 19th space shuttle mission in 1985 at 58 years old); Jansky (first man to detect extraterrestrial radio waves, 1932); Malden (actor); Marx (German political philosopher). Less popular.

Karlen Latvian, Russian. From Charles, Old English, "ceorl" ("man" or "husbandman"). Unusual.

Karlens Latvian. From Charles, Old English, "ceorl" ("man" or "husbandman"). Unusual.

Karlik Czech. From Charles, Old English, "ceorl" ("man" or "husbandman"). Unusual.

Karlin Russian. From Charles, Old English, "ceorl" ("man" or "husbandman"). Unusual.

Karlis Latvian. From Charles, Old English, "ceorl" ("man" or "husbandman"). Ulmanis (Latvian president, 1936–40). Unusual.

Karney Irish. From Carney, Gaelic, "Victorious one." Unusual. Alternative spellings: Carney, Carny, Karny.

Karol Czech, Polish. From Charles, Old English, "ceorl" ("man" or "husbandman"). Wojtyla (Polish, first non-Italian pope since 1522) (real name of Pope John Paul II); Szymanowski (Polish opera composer). Unusual.

Karolek Polish. From Charles, Old English, "ceorl" ("man" or "husbandman"). Unusual.

Károly Hungarian. From Charles, Old English, "ceorl" ("man" or "husbandman"). Huszár (Hungarian journalist and politician, head of Christian Social party); Kerenyi (Hungarian philologist and authority on primitive mythology); Khuen-Hédervár (established the pro-Hungarian Croatian Nationalist party). Unusual.

Karr Scandinavian. From Carr, Old Norse, "From the marsh." Unusual.

Karrel English. From Charles, Old English, "ceorl" ("man" or "husbandman"). Unusual.

Kasch German. From Kass, German, "Like a blackbird." Unusual.

Kase German. From Kass, German, "Like a blackbird." Unusual.

Kaseko African. Rhodesian, "To mock" or "to ridicule." A woman who is ridiculed for her barrenness may use this name for her first son. Unusual.

Kasib Arabic. Arabic, "Fertile." Unusual. Alternative spelling: Kaseeb.

Kasim Arabic. Arabic, "Divided." Unusual. Alternative spelling: Kaseem.

Kasimir Slavic. From Casimir, Old Slavic, "He announces [or "commands"] peace." Badeni (prime minister of Austrian half of dual monarchy of Austria-Hungary, 1895–97); Edschmid (German novelist, leader of expressionist movement) (real name: Eduard Schmid); Fajans (physical chemist, discovered protactinium-234). Unusual.

Kaspar Czech, German. From Jasper, Persian, "Treasure-holder." Schwenckfeld (German nobleman, leader of Protestant Reformation in Silesia); Hauser (German foundling adopted by Lord Stanhope). Unusual.

Kasper German. From Jasper, Persian, "Treasure-holder." Unusual.

Kass German. German, "Like a blackbird." Unusual.

Katóne Hungarian. From Jeremiah, Hebrew, "Jehovah is high" or "Jehovah exalts." Book of Jeremiah. Unusual.

Kayin Nigerian. Nigerian, "Celebrated." Unusual.

Kayle See under Girls' Names.

Kazek Polish. From Casimir, Old Slavic, "He announces [or "commands"] peace." Unusual. Alternative spelling: Kazik.

Kazimir Bulgarian, Czech, German, Russian. From Casimir, Old Slavic, "He announces [or "commands"] peace." Malevich (Russian painter, established school of suprematist abstract art). Unusual.

Kazio Polish. From Casimir, Old Slavic, "He announces [or "commands"] peace." Unusual.

Kázmér Hungarian. From Casimir, Old Slavic, "He announces [or "commands"] peace." Unusual.

Keahi Hawaiian. Hawaiian, "Fire." Unusual for males, unusual for females.

Kearney Irish. From Carney, Gaelic, "Victorious one." Unusual.

Keary Irish. From Kerry, Irish, "The place of Ciar's people"; also the name of a county. Unusual.

Keath English. From Keith, Scottish, "Wood" or "enclosed place." A Scottish place name and clan name. Unusual.

Keaton English. English, "From Ketton." Unusual.

Keb Egyptian. Egyptian, the name of an ancient earth god. Unusual.

Kedar Arabic. From Kadar, Arabic, "Powerful." Unusual.

Keddy Scottish. From Adam, Hebrew,

"Redness" or "man." Genesis 2:19. Unusual. Alternative spellings: Keady, Keddie. Kedem Hebrew/Israeli. Hebrew, "Old," "ancient." Unusual.

Keegan Irish. Gaelic, "Little fiery one." Unusual.

Keelby German. From Kelby, Old German, "From the farm by the spring." Unusual.

Keenan Irish. Gaelic, "Little ancient one." Ivory Wayans (actor, "In Living Color"). Unusual.

Keir English. Gaelic, "Swarthy." Also a place name. Dullea (actor); Hardie (British labor leader, established the miners' labor union and became secretary of the Scottish Miners' Federation). Unusual.

Keith English. Scottish, "Wood" or "enclosed place." A Scottish place name and clan name. Jarrett (jazz pianist); Richards (guitarist with Rolling Stones); Hernandez (New York Mets baseball captain); Douglas (British poet); Smith, Sir (Australian, served in Royal Flying Corps and made first flight from England to Australia, 1919). Popular.

Kekoa Hawaiian. Hawaiian, "Koa tree in Koolau mountains." Unusual.

Kelby German. Old German, "From the farm by the spring." Unusual. Alternative spellings: Kelbee, Kelbie, Kellby.

Kele Native American. Native American, "Sparrow hawk." Unusual. Alternative spelling: Kelle.

Kelemen Hungarian. From Clement, Latin, "Mild," "merciful." Unusual.

Kelii Hawaiian. Hawaiian, "The chief." Unusual.

Kell English. Old Norse, "From the spring." Unusual.

Kellen English. From Kelly, Gaelic (Ceallach), "A warrior." Surname used as a first name. Unusual.

Kelley See Kelly under Girls' Names.

Kelly See under Girls' Names.

Kelsey See under Girls' Names.

Kelvin English. Celtic, the name of a Scottish river. Thomson (British mathematician and physicist, invented Kelvin temperature scale). Unusual. Alternative spelling: Kelvyn.

Ken English. From Kenneth. Burns (producer and director of PBS's "Civil War" series). Less popular. Kenny. Alternative spelling: Kenn.

Kenaz Hebrew/Israeli. From Alva, Hebrew, "Brightness" (?). Genesis 36:40. Unusual.

Kendall English. English, "Valley of the river Kent." Surname and place name used as a first name. Less popular for males, less popular for females. Alternative spellings: Kendal, Kendell.

Kendrick English. Celtic (Cynwrig), "Chief hero." Unusual.

Kenelm English. Old English, "Brave" + "helmet." Digby, Sir (17th-century British courtier and naval commander); Digby (British writer of works on medieval customs). Unusual.

Kennedy English. Irish, "Head" + "ugly." Surname used as a first name. McKinney (won 1988 Olympic gold medal for bantamweight boxing). Unusual.

Kenneth English. Gaelic, "Fair one" + "fire-sprung." Thomson (Canadian, heads fourth-largest media conglomerate); Patchen (poet); Tynan (British drama critic); Anderson (British general, captured Tunis); Clark (British, created TV series "Civilization," 1969). Popular. Ken, Kenny. Alternative spelling: Kennith.

Kenny English. From Kenneth. Rogers (country singer); Loggins (pop singer). Less popular. Ken. Alternative spellings: Kenney, Kennie.

Kenrick English. Celtic (Cynwrig), "Chief hero." Unusual. Alternative spelling: Kenric.

Kent English. English, the name of a county. McCord (actor, "Adam 12"). Less popular.

Kentigern Scottish. Celtic, "Chief lord." Saint. Unusual.

Kenton English. Place name used as a first name; origin unknown. Unusual.

Kentrell Unknown. Meaning and origin unknown. Unusual.

Kenya Russian. From Kenneth. Unusual.

Keon Irish. Irish, "Well-born." Unusual.

Ker Gypsy. From Kerey. Unusual.

Kerby English. From Kirby, Anglo-Saxon, "Church village." Unusual.

Keree See Keri under Girls' Names.

Kerrey See Keri under Girls' Names.

Kerry See Keri under Girls' Names.

Kerel African. Afrikaans, "Young man." Unusual.

Kerem Turkish. Turkish, "Noble," "kind." Unusual.

Kerestel Hungarian. From Christian, Greek, "christos" ("anointed"). Unusual.

Kerey Gypsy. English Gypsy, "Homeward-bound." Unusual.

Kermit English. From Dermot, Irish, "Envy-free." Unusual.

Kern Irish. From Kieran, Irish (Ciaran), "Dark" or "black." Unusual. Alternative spellings: Kearn, Kerne.

Kerr Scottish. Scottish, surname and place name used as a first name. Unusual.

Kerrick English. From Kenrick, Celtic (Cynwrig), "Chief hero." Unusual.

Kers Indo-Pakistani. Hindi, "The wight plant." Unusual.

Kersen Indonesian. Indonesian, "Cherry." Unusual.

Kervin English. From Kerwin. Unusual.

Kerwaine English. From Kerwin. Unusual.

Kerwin English. Irish, "Dark" or "black." Unusual. Alternative spellings: Kerwen, Kerwinn.

Kes English. "Kestrel," a European falcon resembling the American sparrow hawk; origin unknown. Unusual.

Kesar Russian. From Caesar, Latin (Caesarius), "Hairy child." Unusual.

Kesha Created, from Lakeisha, Created, African-American; and Russian, from Kenneth, Gaelic, "Fair one" + "fire-sprung." Unusual.

Kesin Indo-Pakistani. Hindi, "Long-haired beggar." Unusual.

Kesse African. Ghanaian, "Born fat." Unusual.

Kester English. From Christopher, Greek, "One who carries Christ in his heart." Unusual.

Kev English. From Kevin. Unusual.

Keverne English. From Kevin. Saint. Unusual.

Kevin English. Irish, "Handsome." Saint; Costner (actor and director, "Dances With Wolves"); McEnroe (child of John and actress Tatum O'Neal); McCarthy (took longest shower: 340 hours, 40 minutes, 1985); Butler (Chicago Bears kicker, scored most points in his rookie season: 144, 1985). Very popular. Kev. Alternative spellings: Kevan, Keven, Kevyn.

Kevvy English. From Kevin. Unusual. Kev.

Khaim Russian. From Chaim, Hebrew, "Life." Unusual.

Khālid Arabic. Arabic, "Eternal." Ibn Saud (king of Saudi Arabia, 1975–82); al-Qasri (governor of Iraq, 724–38); ibn al-Walid (Arab general, won battle of the Yarmuk, 636). Unusual.

Khalīl Arabic. From Kalil, Arabic, "Good friend." Mamluk sultan of Egypt, 1290–93. Unusual. Alternative spelling: Khaleel.

Khambis Greek. From Henry, Old German (Heimerich), "Home ruler." Unusual.

Kharald Russian. From Gerald, Old German, "Spear" + "ruler." Unusual.

Kharlambos Greek. From Henry, Old German (Heimerich), "Home ruler." Unusual.

Kibbe Native American. Native American, "Night bird." Unusual.

Kier Irish. From Kieran. Unusual.

Kieran Irish. Irish (Ciaran), "Dark" or "black." Unusual. Alternative spellings: Keiran, Keiren, Keiron, Kiaran, Kieron, Kyran.

Kijika Native American. Native American, "Walks quietly." Unusual.

Kiki Hispanic. From Henry, Old German (Heimerich), "Home ruler." Vandeweghe (NBA basketball great, had .871 freethrow percentage). Unusual.

Kilab Arabic. From Caleb, Hebrew, "Dog." Numbers 13:6. Unusual.

Kiley English. From Kyle, Gaelic, "Strait" or "narrow piece of land." Unusual.

Killian English. Irish, "Strife." Unusual. Alternative spelling: Kilian.

Killy English. From Killian. Unusual. Alternative spelling: Killie.

Kim See under Girls' Names.

Kimball English. Celtic, "Chief-war." Unusual.

Kimberley See Kimberly under Girls' Names.

Kimberly See under Girls' Names.

Kin Japanese. Japanese, "Golden." Unusual.

King American. From Kingsley. Vidor (movie director, "War and Peace"); Gillette (developed safety razor, 1895–1901). Unusual.

Kingsley English. Old English, "King's wood" or "king's meadow." Wood, Sir (British politician, introduced "pay as you earn" income tax, 1944); Amis (British novelist). Unusual.

Kingston English. Old English, "King's estate." Unusual.

Kinston English. From Kingston. Unusual.

Kip English. From Kipp. Winger (musician). Unusual.

Kipp English. Old English, "From the pointed hill." Unusual.

Kipper English. From Kipp. Unusual.

Kippy English. From Kipp. Unusual. Alternative spelling: Kippie.

Kir Bulgarian. From Cyrus, Latin, "Throne." Unusual.

Kiral Turkish. Turkish, "King." Unusual.

Kirby English. Anglo-Saxon, "Church village." Less popular for males, unusual for females.

Kiril Bulgarian. From Cyril, Greek, "Lord" or "ruler." Unusual.

Kiritan Indo-Pakistani. Hindi, "Wearing a crown." Another name for the Hindu god Vishnu. Unusual.

Kirk English. Old Norse, "Church." Douglas (actor, "Spartacus") (real name: Issur Danielovitch Demsky); Cameron (actor, "Growing Pains"); Kerkorian (sold MGM/UA to Giancarlo Parretti); Bryan (geologist). Less popular.

Kirton English. English, "Settlement with a church." Unusual.

Kirwin English. From Kerwin, Irish, "Dark" or "black." Unusual.

Kiryl Russian. From Cyril, Greek, "Lord" or "ruler." Unusual. Alternative spelling: Kirill.

Kistna Indo-Pakistani. From Krishna, Hindi, "Delightful." Krishna is the Hindu incarnation of Vishnu, a god protecting all creation. Unusual. Alternative spelling: Kistnah.

Kistur Gypsy. English Gypsy, "A rider." Unusual.

Kit English. From Christopher, Greek, "One who carries Christ in his heart." Carson (19th-century scout, trapper, and Indian agent). Unusual. Alternative spelling: Kitt.

Kito African. Swahili, "Jewel." Unusual.

Kiva Hebrew/Israeli. From Jacob, Hebrew (Yaakov), "Supplanter" or "heel." Genesis 25:26. Unusual.

Kivi Hebrew/Israeli. From Jacob, Hebrew (Yaakov), "Supplanter" or "heel." Genesis 25:26. Unusual.

Kiyoshi Japanese. Japanese, "Quiet." Shiga (Japanese bacteriologist, developed serum for dysentery); Miki (Japanese philosopher). Unusual.

Kizza African. African, "Born after twins." Unusual.

Klaus German. From Nicholas, Greek, "Victorious people." Friedrich (German, set up record 320,236 dominoes in formation); Enders (German, won record six world speed titles with a motorcycle with a side car); Dibiasi (Italian, won Olympic gold medals for platform dives, 1968–76); Groth (19th-century German poet). Unusual.

Klema Czech. From Clement, Latin, "Mild," "merciful." Unusual.

Klemens Polish. From Clement, Latin, "Mild," "merciful." von Metternich (19th-century Austrian statesman and diplomat); von Droste zu Vischering (archbishop of Cologne, 1835–45); Hofbauer (established Redemptorist monasteries). Unusual.

Klement Czech. From Clement, Latin, "Mild," "merciful." Gottwald (president of Czechoslovakia, 1948–53). Unusual.

Klemet Russian. From Clement, Latin, "Mild," "merciful." Unusual.

Klemo Czech. From Clement, Latin, "Mild," "merciful." Unusual.

Klim Russian. From Clement, Latin, "Mild," "merciful." Unusual.

Klimek Polish. From Clement, Latin, "Mild," "merciful." Unusual.

Kliment Russian. From Clement, Latin, "Mild," "merciful." Voroshilov (Soviet politician, credited with reorganization of Russian general staff, mechanization of army, and development of air force). Unusual. Alternative spelling: Klyment.

Klimka Russian. From Clement, Latin, "Mild," "merciful." Unusual.

Knight English. Surname used as a first name; origin unknown. Unusual.

Knightly English. Surname used as a first name; origin unknown. Unusual. Alternative spelling: Knightley.

Knoton Native American. From Nodin, Native American, "The wind." Unusual.

Knowles English. From Nowles, Middle English, "A forested grassy slope." Unusual. Alternative spelling: Knolls.

Knox English. Old English, "From the hills." Unusual.

Knud Danish. Danish, "Kind." Rasmussen (Danish explorer and ethnologist); Rahbek (19th-century Danish poet); Kristensen (Danish prime minister, 1945–47). Unusual.

Knut Scandinavian. Old Norse, "Knot." Hamsun (Norwegian novelist, won

1920 Nobel Prize for literature) (real name: Knut Pedersen); Wallenberg (Swedish foreign minister, 1914–17); Wicksell (Swedish economist, originated theory of marginal productivity). Unusual.

Knute Danish. From Knut. Rockne (head football coach at Notre Dame, coached record 105 wins, 12 losses, 5 ties). Unusual.

Kobi Hungarian. From Jacob, Hebrew (Yaakov), "Supplanter" or "heel." Genesis 25:26. Unusual.

Kody English. From Cody, Old English, "A cushion." Unusual. Alternative spellings: Codey, Codie, Cody, Coty.

Kokudza African. African, "The child will not live long." This name is given to make the demons leave the child alone. Unusual.

Kola Latvian. From Nicholas, Greek, "Victorious people." Unusual.

Kolby English. From Colby, Old English, "From the black farm." Unusual.

Kolya Russian. From Nicholas, Greek, "Victorious people." Unusual.

Konane Hawaiian. Hawaiian, "Bright as moonlight." Unusual.

Konni German. From Conrad, German, "Brave counsel." Zilliacus (Finnish nationalist, established the underground revolutionary Activist Opposition party). Unusual.

Kono Native American. Native American, "Squirrel eating a pine nut." Unusual.

Konrad Czech, English, German, Hungarian, Russian, Swedish. From Conrad, German, "Brave counsel." Muth (16th-century German humanist); Pellicanus (Swiss scholar, first Christian to publish a Hebrew grammar); Witz (15th-century German painter, among first to introduce realistic landscapes in religious paintings); Bercovoci (writer on gypsies). Less popular.

Konstandinos Greek. From Constance, Latin, "constans" ("constant" or "unwavering"). Unusual.

Konstantinos Greek. From Constance, Latin, "constans" ("constant" or "unwavering"). Unusual.

Kontar African. Ghanaian, "Only child." Unusual.

Korb German. German, "Basket." Unusual.

Korey English. From Corey, Irish, "From the hollow." Unusual.

Korudon Greek. Greek, "Helmeted one" or "crested one." Unusual.

Kostas Greek. From Constance, Latin, "constans" ("constant" or "unwavering"). Kariotakis (Greek poet). Unusual.

Kosti Finnish. From Gustaf, Swedish, "God's staff" or "staff of the Goths." Unusual.

Kotsos Greek. From Constance, Latin, "constans" ("constant" or "unwavering"). Unusual.

Kovar Czech. Czech, "Smith." Unusual.

Kraig English. From Craig, Welsh, "Rock." Unusual. Alternative spelling: Craig.

Krischan German. From Christian, Greek, "christos" ("anointed"). Unusual.

Krishna Indo-Pakistani. Hindi, "Delightful." Krishna is the Hindu incarnation of Vishnu, a god protecting all creation. Unusual. Alternative spelling: Krishnah.

Krispin Czech, German, Hungarian. From Crispin, Latin, "crispus" ("curly"). Unusual.

Kris English, German, Latvian. From Christopher, Greek, "One who carries Christ in his heart." Unusual. Alternative spellings: Chris, Cris, Kriss.

Krister Swedish. From Christian, Greek, "christos" ("anointed"). Unusual.

Kristian English, Estonian, Russian, Slavic. From Christian, Greek, "christos" ("anointed"). Unusual. Alternative spelling: Christian.

Kristjan Estonian. From Christian, Greek, "christos" ("anointed"). Unusual.

Kristo Greek. From Christopher, Greek, "One who carries Christ in his heart." Markov (Bulgarian, won 1988 Olympic gold medal for the triple jump). Unusual.

Kristof Czech, Hungarian. From Christopher, Greek, "One who carries Christ in his heart." Unusual.

Kristofer English. From Christopher, Greek, "One who carries Christ in his heart." Uppdal (Norwegian author of proletarian novels); Janson (Norwegian novelist). Unusual. Kris. Alternative spellings: Christopher, Cristopher, Kristopher.

Kristoffer Swedish. From Christopher, Greek, "One who carries Christ in his heart." Eckersberg (19th-century Danish painter, established the national Danish school of painting). Unusual. Alternative spelling: Kristofor.

Kristoph English. From Christopher, Greek, "One who carries Christ in his heart." Unusual. Kris.

Kristos Greek. From Christian, Greek, "christos" ("anointed"). Unusual. Alternative spelling: Christos.

Krists Estonian, Latvian. From Christian, Greek, "christos" ("anointed"). Unusual.

Krisus Latvian. From Christopher, Greek, "One who carries Christ in his heart." Unusual.

Kruin African. Afrikaans, "Tree top" or "mountain peak." Unusual.

Krys Polish. From Christian, Greek, "christos" ("anointed"). Unusual.

Krystek Polish. From Christian, Greek, "christos" ("anointed"). Unusual. Alternative spelling: Crystek.

Krystian Polish. From Christian, Greek, "christos" ("anointed"). Unusual. Alternative spelling: Chrystian.

Kuba Czech. From Jacob, Hebrew (Yaakov), "Supplanter" or "heel." Genesis 25:26. Unusual.

Kubo Czech. From Jacob, Hebrew (Yaakov), "Supplanter" or "heel." Genesis 25:26. Unusual.

Kubus Polish. From Jacob, Hebrew (Yaakov), "Supplanter" or "heel." Genesis 25:26. Unusual.

Kuper Yiddish. Yiddish, "Copper." Suggests reddish hair. Unusual.

Kurt English. From Conrad, German, "Brave counsel." Russell (actor); Waldheim (former UN secretary general); Suckert (Italian journalist, assisted Allies in WWII) (real name of Curzio Malaparte); Alder (won 1950 Nobel Prize for chemistry). Less popular. Alternative spelling: Curt.

Kurtis English. From Curtis, Old French, "Courteous." Unusual. Kurt. Alternative spelling: Curtis.

Kuzih Native American. Native American, "Great talker." Unusual.

Kwako Nigerian. Nigerian, "Born on Wednesday." Unusual for males, unusual for females.

Kwaku African. African, "Born on Wednesday." Unusual for males, unusual for females.

Kwam Native American. From John, Hebrew (Yochanan), "God has been gracious." Unusual.

Kwamin African. African, "Born on Saturday." Unusual for males, unusual for females.

Kwan Korean. Korean, "Strong." Unusual.

Kwesi African. African, "Born on Sunday." Unusual.

Ky English. From Kyle, Gaelic, "Strait" or "narrow piece of land." Unusual.

Kyle English. Gaelic, "Strait" or "narrow piece of land." MacLachlan (actor, "Twin Peaks"). Very popular for males, less popular for females. Alternative spellings: Kiel, Kile, Kyele.

Kyler English. From Kyle, Gaelic, "Strait" or "narrow piece of land." Unusual.

Laban Hebrew/Israeli. Hebrew, "White." Genesis 24:32. Brother of Isaac's wife Rebecca. Unusual.

Labhras Irish. From Laurence, Latin, "Crowned with laurel." Unusual.

Labhruinn Scottish. From Laurence, Latin, "Crowned with laurel." Unusual.

Labrencis Latvian. From Laurence, Latin, "Crowned with laurel." Unusual.

Labrentsis Russian. From Laurence, Latin, "Crowned with laurel." Unusual.

Lachlan Scottish. From Lachlann. Macquarie (19th-century British soldier and colonial administrator); McIntosh (American Revolutionary soldier, wintered with Washington at Valley Forge). Unusual. Alternative spelling: Lachlann.

Lachunn Scottish. From Lachlann. Unusual.

Ladd English. Middle English, "Attendant." Unusual. Alternative spelling: Lad.

Laddy English. From Ladd. Unusual. Alternative spelling: Laddie.

Ladislaus Polish. From Walter, Old German, "Ruling people." Unusual.

Lado African. African, "Second-born son." Unusual.

Lafayette American. French, surname used as a first name. du Motier (general under George Washington). Unusual.

Lais Indo-Pakistani. East Indian, "Lion." Unusual.

Lal Indo-Pakistani. From Krishna, Hindi, "Delightful." Krishna is the Hindu incarnation of Vishnu, a god protecting all creation. Shastri (prime minister of India, 1964–66). Unusual.

Lamar English. Latin, "By the sea." Hunt (established the American Football League); Clark (boxer, knocked out record six opponents in one night, 1958). Unusual.

Lambard English. From Lambert. Unusual.

Lambert English. Old German, "Land-bright." Patron saint of Liege; Quételet (Belgian statistician and astronomer, established the Royal Observatory, Brussels); Winkel (19th-century Dutch philologist, founder of modern Dutch grammar). Unusual.

Lamont American. "Lawman"; origin unknown. Surname used as a first name. Unusual.

Lampard English. From Lambert. Unusual.

Lance English. German, "Land." Alworth (pro football wide receiver; member, Hall of Fame). Unusual.

Lancelot English. From Launcelot, Old French, "Servant." Andrewes (17th-century British prelate); Hogben (British scientist and writer, "Mathematics for the Millions"); Brown (18th-century British landscape gardener). Unusual. Lance. Alternative spellings: Lancelott, Launcelot.

Lando Hispanic. From Roland, Old German (Hrodland), "Famous land." Unusual.

Landon English. Old English, "From the grassy meadow." Unusual. Alternative spellings: Landan, Landen.

Lane English. Middle English, "One who lives near the lane." Unusual. Alternative spelling: Layne.

Lang Scandinavian. Old Norse, "Tall." Unusual.

Langdon English. Old English, "From the long town, hill, or valley." Unusual.

Langley English. Old English, "From the long meadow or forest." Unusual. Alternative spelling: Langly.

Langston English. Old English, "From the tall man's town or estate." Hughes (author and poet, "Shakespeare in Harlem"). Unusual.

Langundo Native American. Native American, "Peaceful." Unusual.

Lani Hawaiian. Hawaiian, "Sky" or "heavenly." Unusual for males, unusual for females.

Lanny English. From Leonard, Old German (Leonhard), "Strong as a lion." Budd (character in series of novels by Upton Sinclair). Unusual.

Lansar Unknown. Meaning and origin unknown. Unusual.

Lanty Irish. From Laurence. Unusual.

Lanu Native American. Native American, "Running around the pole" at a religious ceremony. Unusual.

Lao Hispanic. From Stanislaus, Latin, "Camp glory" (?). Unusual.

Lap Vietnamese. Vietnamese, "Independent." Unusual.

Laris Swedish. From Laurence. Unusual.

Larka Russian. From Laurence, Latin, "Crowned with laurel." Unusual.

Laron French. French, "Thief." Unusual.

Larrance English. From Laurence. Unusual. Larry.

Larry English. From Laurence. McMurtry (won Pulitzer Prize for fiction, 1986, "Lonesome Dove"); Woiwode (novelist, "What I'm Going to Do, I Think"). Popular. Alternative spellings: Larrie, Lary.

Lars Scandinavian. From Laurence. Nilson (Swedish physicist, discovered metallic element scandium); Onsager (awarded 1968 Nobel Prize for chemistry); Wivallius (17th-century Swedish poet and adventurer); Esbjörn (clergyman, helped organize independent Augustana Synod). Unusual. Alternative spelling: Larse.

Larya Russian. From Laurence. Unusual.

Lash Gypsy. From Louis, Old German (Hlutwig), "Famous warrior." Unusual.

Lashi Gypsy. From Louis, Old German (Hlutwig), "Famous warrior." Unusual.

Lasho Gypsy. From Louis, Old German (Hlutwig), "Famous warrior." Unusual.

Lasimonne French. From Solomon,

Hebrew, "Peace." Unusual.
Lathe English. From Lathrop. Unusual.
Lathrop English. Old English, "From the barn farmstead." Unusual.
Launce English. From Launcelot. Unusual.
Launclet English. From Launcelot. Unusual.
Laurel See under Girls' Names.
Lauren See under Girls' Names.
Laurence English. Latin, "Crowned with laurel." Saint; Sterne (18th-century British novelist, "Tristram Shandy"); Tribe (professor and constitutional law expert). Less popular. Larry. Alternative spellings: Laurance, Lawrance, Lawrence, Lorence.
Laurencio Hispanic. From Laurence. Unusual.
Laurens Dutch. From Laurence. Coster (14th-century Dutch, credited by some with invention of movable type). Unusual.
Laurent French. From Laurence. Delvaux (18th-century Flemish sculptor); de Gouvion Saint-Cyr (French minister of war, 1815, 1817–19). Unusual.
Lauri See Laurie under Girls' Names.
Laurie See under Girls' Names.
Lauris Swedish. From Laurence. Unusual.
Lauritz Danish. From Laurence. Melchior (opera singer, a highly regarded heldentenor in early 20th-century). Unusual.
Laurus English. From Laurence. Unusual.
Lavi Hebrew/Israeli. Hebrew, "My lion." Unusual.
Lavon See under Girls' Names.
Lavonne See Lavon under Girls' Names.
Lavr Russian. From Laurence. Kornilov (Russian WWI general). Unusual.
Lavrik Russian. From Laurence. Unusual.
Lavro Russian. From Laurence. Unusual.
Lawrie Scottish. From Laurence. Unusual.
Lawson English. English, "Son of Laurence." Surname used as a first name. Unusual.
Lawton English. English, "Settlement on a hill." Unusual.
Lay English. From Lathrop. Unusual.
Layton English. English, place name and surname used as a first name. Unusual. Alternative spellings: Leighton, Leyton.
Lázaro Hispanic. From Eliezer, Hebrew, "He whom God helps." Genesis 15:2. Cárdenas (president of Mexico, 1934–40); Chacón (president of Guatemala, 1926–30). Unusual.
Lazarus Greek. From Eliezer, Hebrew, "He whom God helps." Genesis 15:2. Unusual.
Leander English. Greek, "Lion man." Saint. Unusual for males, unusual for females.
Leão Portuguese. From Leo, Latin, "Lion." Unusual.
Leben Yiddish. Yiddish, "Life." Unusual.
Lee See under Girls' Names.
Lei Chinese. Chinese, "Thunder." Unusual.
Leib Hebrew/Israeli. From Lavi, Hebrew, "My lion." Unusual.
Leibel Hebrew/Israeli. From Lavi, Hebrew, "My lion." Unusual.
Leif Norwegian. Old Norse, "Beloved." Eriksson (11th-century Norwegian explorer, may have been first to visit North America). Unusual.
Leigh See Lee under Girls' Names.
Lekeke Hawaiian. Hawaiian, "Powerful ruler." Unusual.
Leks Estonian. From Alexander, Greek, "Defender of men" or "warding off men." Mark 16:21; Acts 4:6, 19:33. Unusual.
Leksik Czech. From Alexander, Greek, "Defender of men" or "warding off men." Mark 16:21; Acts 4:6, 19:33. Unusual.
Lekso Czech. From Alexander, Greek, "Defender of men" or "warding off men." Mark 16:21; Acts 4:6, 19:33. Unusual.
Lel Gypsy. English Gypsy, "He takes." Unusual.
Leland English. From Leland, surname or American place name used as a first name; origin unknown. Unusual.
Lemmie English. From Lemuel. Unusual. Alternative spellings: Lemmy, Lemy.
Lemuel English. Hebrew, "Devoted to God." Proverbs 31:1. Less popular.
Len English. From Leonard. Wickwar (British lightweight boxer, had record 463 documented fights). Less popular. Lenny.
Lencho Hispanic. From Laurence, Latin, "Crowned with laurel." Unusual.
Lenci Hungarian. From Laurence, Latin, "Crowned with laurel." Unusual.
Lenno Native American. Native American, "Man." Unusual.
Lennor Gypsy. English Gypsy, "Spring" or "summer." Unusual.
Lennox Scottish. Scottish, aristocratic surname and place name used as a first name. Originally referred to a large collection of elm trees. Lewis (Canadian boxer, won 1984 Olympic gold medal for super-heavyweight division); Robinson (Irish playwright, "Big House"). Unusual for males, unusual for females.
Lenny English. From Leonard. Bruce (comedian); Kravitz (rock singer). Less popular. Alternative spellings: Lennie, Leny.
Leo Latin. Latin, "Lion." Saint; pope (I, 440-XIII, 1878); Tolstoy (Russian author, "War and Peace"); Delibes (19th-century French operatic composer); Sayer (singer). Less popular.
Leon English. From Leo. Ames (actor, "Life With Father"); Vanderstuyft (Belgian cyclist, covered greatest distance in one hour: 76 miles, 604 yards); Russell (pianist, singer); Uris (novelist, "Trinity"); Trotsky (Russian communist, led Bolshevik seizure of power, 1917). Less popular.
Leonard English. From Leonard, Old German (Leonhard), "Strong as a lion." Patron saint of prisoners; Bernstein (composer and conductor, "West Side Story"); Lyons (columnist, "Lyons Den"). Less popular. Len, Lenny. Alternative spellings: Lenard, Lennard.
Leonardo Hispanic, Italian, Portuguese. From Leonard. da Vinci (15th-century Italian painter, "Mona Lisa"); Fibonacci (Italian mathematician, introduced Arab numerals to Europe in Middle Ages); Bruni (15th-century Italian humanist, translated Greek philosophers into Latin); Vinci (Italian classical composer). Unusual.
Leonas Lithuanian. From Leo, Latin, "Lion." Unusual.
Leone English. From Leo, Latin, "Lion." Leoni (16th-century Italian sculptor, bronze bust of Charles V); Ebreo (poet and physician, known as "Leo the Hebrew") (real name: Judah Leon Abrabanel). Unusual for males, unusual for females.
Leonek Polish. From Leonard. Unusual.
Leonel English. From Lionel, Latin, "Little lion." Power (15th-century British composer in chanson style). Unusual.

Leonhard German. From Leonard. von Blumenthal (Prussian general); Euler (Swiss mathematician, discovered law of quadratic reciprocity); Frank (German expressionist novelist); Hutter (German theologian, supported Lutheran orthodoxy). Unusual.

Leonhards Latvian. From Leonard. Unusual.

Leonid Russian. From Leonard. Andreyev (Russian writer of realist short stories, novels, and plays); Brezhnev (Russian communist leader); Kantorovich (Russian, awarded 1975 Nobel Prize for economics). Unusual.

Leonidas Greek. From Leo. Polk (Confederate army commander). Unusual.

Leons Latvian. From Leonard. Unusual.

Leontes Scandinavian. From Leonard. Unusual.

Leopold German. Old German (Luitpold), "Bold people." King of Belgium (I, 1831-III, 1934); Holy Roman Emperor (I, 1658-II, 1790); Stokowski (conductor, established the American Symphony Orchestra, 1962); Auer (Hungarian violinist). Unusual.

Leor Hebrew/Israeli. Hebrew, "I have light." Unusual.

Leos Polish. From Leo. Janáček (Czech classical composer, influenced by Moravian folk music). Unusual.

Leosko Czech. From Leo. Unusual.

Leron Hebrew/Israeli. Hebrew, "Song is mine." Unusual. Alternative spellings: Lerone, Liron, Lirone, Lyron.

Leroy English. Old French, "The king." Grumann (president of Grumann Aircraft Engineering Co., 1929–46). Less popular. Alternative spelling: Le Roy.

Les English. From Leslie, Scottish, "Low meadow." Also a Scottish clan name. Stewart (Australian record holder, typed numbers 1 to 548,000 in word format on 11,570 long sheets); Brown (band leader). Less popular.

Lesley See Leslie under Girls' Names.

Leslie See under Girls' Names.

Lester English. English, surname and place name (Leicester) used as a first name. Piggott (jockey); Pearson (Canadian prime minister, 1960s). Less popular. Les.

Leuel Unknown. Meaning and origin unknown. Unusual.

Lev Russian. From Leo. Sternberg (Russian anthropologist); Ivanov (19th-century Russian ballet dancer and choreographer); Kamenev (Russian communist leader, member of ruling triumvirate after Lenin's death). Unusual.

Levi Hebrew/Israeli. Hebrew, "Joined to" or "attached." Genesis 29:34. Jacob's son by Leah; Morton (vice-president under Harrison); Strauss (established company to manufacture denim jeans); Coffin (abolitionist); Woodbury (Supreme Court Justice, 1845–51). Unusual. Alternative spellings: Levey, Levy.

Levko Russian. From Leo. Unusual.

Lewi English. From Levi. Genesis 29:34. Unusual.

Lewin English. Old English, "Beloved friend." Unusual.

Lewis English. From Louis, Old German (Hlutwig), "Famous warrior." Carroll (British author, "Alice's Adventures in Wonderland") (real name: Charles Lutwidge Dodgson); Strauss (secretary of commerce under Eisenhower); Rutherfurd (19th-century astrophysicist); Waterman (patented improved fountain pen); Sayre (orthopedic surgeon). Less popular.

Lex English. From Alexander, Greek, "Defender of men" or "warding off men." Mark 16:21; Acts 4:6, 19:33. Barker (actor, Tarzan films). Unusual.

Leyland English. English, "Untilled land." Unusual.

Li See under Girls' Names.

Liam Irish. From William, Old German, "Will" + "helmet." Higgins (Irish, drove golf ball a record 634.1 yards on airport runway); O'Maonlai (member of rock band Hothouse Flowers). Unusual.

Liang Chinese. Chinese, "Good" or "excellent." Unusual.

Liberty See under Girls' Names.

Lico Hispanic. From Frederick, Old German, "Peaceful ruler." Unusual.

Lienard French. From Leonard, Old German (Leonhard), "Strong as a lion." Unusual.

Like Chinese. Chinese, "Protected by Buddha." Unusual.

Liko Chinese. Chinese, "Buddhist nun." Unusual.

Lin English. From Lyndon, Old English, "Hill with lime trees"; surname and place name used as a first name. Unusual.

Linc English. From Lincoln. Unusual. Alternative spelling: Link.

Lincoln English. Old English, "Roman colony at the pool." Ellsworth (polar explorer); Steffens (muckraking journalist). Unusual.

Lindsay See under Girls' Names.

Lindsey See Lindsay under Girls' Names.

Linek Polish. From Leonard, Old German (Leonhard), "Strong as a lion." Unusual.

Linfred German. Old German, "Gentle peace." Unusual.

Linus Greek. Greek, "Flax." Saint; Pauling (won two Nobel Prizes: Chemistry in 1954, Peace in 1962). Unusual.

Lio Hawaiian. From Leo, Latin, "Lion." Unusual.

Lionel English. Latin, "Little lion." Barrymore (actor). Less popular.

Lister English. "A dyer"; origin unknown. Surname used as a first name. Unusual.

Liu African. African, "Voice." Unusual.

Liutas Lithuanian. From Leo, Latin, "Lion." Unusual.

Liwanu Native American. Native American, "Growling bear." Unusual.

Llewellyn Welsh. Welsh, "Like a lion" or "leader." Unusual. Alternative spellings: Lewellen, Lewellin, Llewelin, Llewelleyn, Llywelyn.

Lloyd English. Welsh, "Gray" or "holy." Nolan (actor); Bridges (actor). Less popular. Alternative spelling: Loyd.

Loe Hawaiian. From Leroy, Old French, "The king." Unusual.

Logan English. Celtic, "Hollow-meadow." Clendening (medical author, "The Human Body"). Unusual for males, unusual for females.

Lokni Native American. Native American, "Raining through the roof." Unusual.

Loman Serbian. Serbo-Croatian, "Delicate." Unusual.

Lomas English. Surname and place name used as a first name; origin unknown. Unusual.

Lon Irish. Gaelic, "Fierce," "strong." Chaney (actor, "Hunchback of Notre Dame"). Unusual.

Lonato Native American. Native American, "Flint." Unusual.

Long Chinese. Chinese, "Dragon." Unusual.

Lonnie English. From Alphonso, Old German (Hildefuns), "Ready for battle." Donegan (singer). Unusual.

Lono Hawaiian. Hawaiian, the god of peace and agriculture. Unusual.

Loránd Hungarian. From Roland, Old German (Hrodland), "Famous land." Unusual.

Lóránt Hungarian. From Laurence, Latin, "Crowned with laurel." Unusual.

Lord English. Old English, "hlaf" ("loaf") + "weard" ("keeper"); the title used as a first name. Unusual.

Loree See Laurie under Girls' Names.

Loren See Lauren under Girls' Names.

Lorens Scandinavian. From Laurence, Latin, "Crowned with laurel." Unusual. Alternative spelling: Laurans.

Lorenz Polish. From Laurence, Latin, "Crowned with laurel." Oken (German philosopher and naturalist, strove to unify natural sciences). Unusual.

Lorenzo Hispanic, Italian. From Laurence, Latin, "Crowned with laurel." Character in Shakespeare's "Merchant of Venice"; Amato (baked largest pizza: diameter 100 feet, 1 inch); Tonti (17th-century French banker, developed tontine system of life insurance); Snow (Mormon apostle, established Brigham City, Utah); Lotto (16th-century Venetian painter). Unusual.

Loretto Italian. From Laurence, Latin, "Crowned with laurel." Unusual. Alternative spelling: Loreto.

Lorey See Laurie under Girls' Names.

Lorie See Laurie under Girls' Names.

Lorin English. From Laurence, Latin, "Crowned with laurel." Maazel (French conductor); Hollander (pianist). Unusual.

Lorinc Hungarian. From Laurence, Latin, "Crowned with laurel." Unusual.

Lorne Scottish. From Lorna, Scottish, place name (Lorn) used as a first name. Greene (actor, "Bonanza"). Unusual for males, unusual for females. Alternative spelling: Lorn.

Lorrie See Laurie under Girls' Names.

Lorry See Laurie under Girls' Names.

Lory See Laurie under Girls' Names.

Lot Hebrew/Israeli. Hebrew, "Covering." Nephew of Abraham. Unusual.

Lothar German. From Louis. Unusual.

Lou English. From Louis. Henry Hoover (wife of President Herbert); Ferrigno (actor, "The Incredible Hulk"); Rawls (singer); Reed (singer); Costello (comedian) (real name: Louis Cristillo). Less popular for males, unusual for females.

Love See under Girls' Names.

Loveday See under Girls' Names.

Lovey See under Girls' Names.

Lovie See Lovey under Girls' Names.

Loudon German. Old German, "From the low valley." Unusual. Louie English. From Louis. Less popular.

Louis French. Old German (Hlutwig), "Famous warrior." Saint; Farigoule (French, wrote longest novel: 2,070,000 words); Armstrong (jazz musician, invented scat-singing) (real name of Satchmo); Le Vau (French, designed parts of the Louvre); Pasteur (French chemist, developed vaccine against rabies). Less popular.

Loukas Greek. From Luke, Greek (Loukas), "From Lucania," a district in Southern Italy. Book of Luke. Unusual.

Lourenco Portuguese. From Laurence, Latin, "Crowned with laurel." Unusual.

Louvain English. The name of a Belgian city; origin unknown. The name has often been given to the sons of soldiers who fought there in WWI and WWII. Unusual.

Lovel English. From Lovell. Surname used as a first name. Unusual. Alternative spelling: Lovell.

Lowden English. From Loudon. Unusual.

Lowell English. Latin, "Little wolf." Elliott (returned to owners the largest amount of cash ever found: $500,000); Thomas (author of travel books); Mason (musician, established first music program in U.S. public schools). Less popular.

Luca English. From Luke. Marenzio (16th-century Italian composer); Pacioli (15th-century Italian mathematician, first to write description of double-entry bookkeeping); Signorelli (15th-century Italian painter of nudes and frescos); Cambiaso (16th-century Genoese painter of church frescos). Unusual.

Lucanus English. From Luke. Unusual. Luke.

Lucas English. From Luke. van Leyden (16th-century Dutch painter, among first to use aerial perspective); Vázquez de Ayllón (16th-century Spanish explorer of America); Alaman (19th-century Mexican politician, promoted industrialization); Cranach (16th-century German painter, originator of Protestant religious painting). Less popular.

Luce French. From Luke. Unusual.

Luchok Russian. From Luke. Unusual.

Lucian English. From Lucius. of Antioch (saint); of Beauvais (saint); Blaga (Romanian poet and playwright). Unusual.

Luciano Italian. From Lucius. Unusual.

Lucien French. From Lucius. Lévy-Bruhl (French sociologist, studied religion and mentality of primitive peoples); Bonaparte (president of Council of Five Hundred, ensured his brother Napoleon's election as French consul). Unusual.

Lucio Hispanic. From Lucius. Unusual.

Lucius English. Latin, "lux" ("light"). A Roman clan name. Saint; Septimius Severus (Roman emperor, 193–211, annexed Mesopotamia); Stilo Praeconinus (Roman, first teacher of Latin philology and literature); Accius (Roman tragic poet); Lamar (Supreme Court Justice, 1888–93). Unusual.

Ludovic English. From Louis, Old German (Hlutwig), "Famous warrior." Halévy (French dramatist, co-wrote libretti for Bizet's "Carmen"). Unusual.

Ludwig German. From Louis, Old German (Hlutwig), "Famous warrior." von Beethoven (composer); Wittgenstein (British philosopher especially concerned with linguistic analysis). Unusual.

Luigi Italian. From Louis, Old German (Hlutwig), "Famous warrior." Marsili (18th-century Italian naturalist and geographer, wrote first treatise on oceanography); Palmieri (19th-century Italian physicist, invented mercury tube seismograph); Pulci (15th-century Italian poet); Robecchi-Bricchetti (19th-century Italian explorer, crossed Somali peninsula). Unusual.

Luis Hispanic. From Louis, Old German (Hlutwig), "Famous warrior." de Vargas (16th-century Spanish painter); de Vasconcelos e Sousa (Portuguese governor, secured Portuguese independence from Spain, 1668); Milan (16th-century Spanish musician, played the viheula); Vaez de Torres (Spanish navigator, discovered Torres Strait, 1606). Popular.

Luister African. Afrikaans, "Listener." Unusual.

Luka Russian. From Luke. Bloom (Irish rock singer and songwriter, "Riverside"). Unusual.

Lukas Czech (Lukáš), Greek, Swedish. From Luke. Unusual.

Lukash Russian. From Luke. Unusual.
Lukasha Russian. From Luke. Unusual.
Lukass Latvian. From Luke. Unusual.
Lukasz Polish. From Luke. Unusual.
Luke English. Greek (Loukas), "From Lucania," a district in Southern Italy. Book of Luke. Patron saint of painters; Wright (secretary of war under T. Roosevelt); Wadding (17th-century Irish Franciscan, compiled history of the order); Hansard (British, printed journals of the House of Commons, still known as "Hansards"). Popular. Alternative spelling: Luc.
Lukyan Russian. From Luke. Unusual.
Lulani Hawaiian. Hawaiian, "Highest point in heaven." Unusual for males, unusual for females.
Lunt Scandinavian. Old Norse, "From the grove." Unusual.
Lusio Native American. From Luke. Unusual.
Luther English. Old German, "Fame-people." Martin (member of Continental Congress and federal Constitutional Convention); Weigle (clergyman, headed committee that produced Revised Standard Version of Bible); Burbank (horticulturist, developed strain of potato that now bears his name). Less popular.
Lutherum Gypsy. English Gypsy, "Slumber." Unusual.
Luyu Native American. Native American, "To shake the head sideways." Unusual.
Ly English. From Lyle. Unusual.
Lyle English. Old French, "From the island." Character in Dinah Craik's "Olive." Less popular. Alternative spelling: Lyell.
Lyman English. "From the valley"; origin unknown. Surname used as a first name. Gage (secretary of treasury under McKinley); Abbott (clergyman, wrote "Henry Ward Beecher"); Frank Baum (author of "Oz" books); Beecher (clergyman, father of Henry Ward Beecher and Harriet Beecher Stowe); Draper (Wisconsin historian). Unusual.
Lyndal English. English, "Lime-tree valley"; surname and place name used as a first name. Unusual. Alternative spelling: Lyndall.
Lyndon English. Old English, "Hill with lime trees"; surname and place name used as a first name. Baines Johnson (36th president). Unusual. Alternative spellings: Lindan, Linden, Lindon, Lynden.
Lyndsay See Lindsay under Girls' Names.
Lynn See Lynne under Girls' Names.
Lynsey See Lindsay under Girls' Names.
Lynton English. Place name derived from the River Lyn; origin unknown. Unusual. Alternative spelling: Linton.

Mac English. Celtic, "Son of." Also a nickname for any name beginning with "Mc" or "Mac." Less popular. Alternative spelling: Mack.
Macaulay Scottish. Scottish, "Son of (?)." Surname used as a first name. Culkin (child actor, "Home Alone"). Unusual.
Macdonald Scottish. Scottish, "Son of Donald." Surname used as a first name. Unusual. Alternative spelling: McDonald.
Macdougal Scottish. Scottish, "Son of the dark stranger." Surname used as a first name. Unusual.
Machas Polish. From Michael, Hebrew, "Who is like God?" Daniel 12:1. Unusual.
Mackenzie Irish. Gaelic, "Son of the wise leader." Surname used as a first name. Bowell (Canadian prime minister, 1894–96). Unusual for males, unusual for females.
Macmurray Irish. Gaelic, "Son of the mariner." Surname used as a first name. Unusual.
Maco Hungarian. From Emanuel, Hebrew, "God is with us," referring to a child about to be born. Isaiah 7:14. Unusual.
Madison English. Old English, "Son of the mighty warrior." Unusual.
Magnus English. Latin, "Great." Saint; Landstad (Norwegian pastor and poet, compiled national hymnal that included 50 of his own hymns); Mittag-Leffler (Swedish mathematician, derived theorem that bears his name); Stenbock (18th-century Swedish soldier); Ennodius (6th-century Roman bishop). Unusual. Alternative spelling: Magnes.
Maheesa See under Girls' Names.
Mahesa Indo-Pakistani. Hindi, "Great lord." Another name for the Hindu god Siva. Unusual for males, unusual for females.
Mahir Hebrew/Israeli. Hebrew, "Expert," "industrious," or "quick." Unusual.
Mahisa See Maheesa under Girls' Names.
Maḥmūd Arabic. From Mohammed, Arabic, "Greatly praised." Sevket Pasa (Ottoman general and politician); Ghazan (13th-century Mongol ruler of Persia, established Islam as official religion). Unusual. Alternative spellings: Mahmed, Mahmoud.
Mahomet Arabic. From Mohammed, Arabic, "Greatly praised." Unusual.
Maimun Arabic. Arabic, "Lucky." Unusual.
Maitland English. Surname and place name used as a first name; origin unknown. Unusual.
Major English. Latin, comparative form of "magnus" ("great" or "large"); a military title or surname used as a first name. Jack (character in Defoe's "Life of Colonel Jack"). Unusual.
Makani Hawaiian. Hawaiian, "The wind." Unusual for males, unusual for females.
Makimus Polish. From Maximilian, Latin, "Greatest in excellence." Unusual.
Makis Greek. From Michael, Hebrew, "Who is like God?" Daniel 12:1. Unusual.
Maks Hungarian. From Maximilian, Latin, "Greatest in excellence." Unusual.
Maksim Russian. From Maximilian, Latin, "Greatest in excellence." Litvinov (Russian diplomat, signed Kellogg Pact, 1928) (real name: Meir Walach); Gorky (Russian novelist, developed aesthetic of socialist realism) (real name: Aleksey Peshkov). Unusual. Alternative spelling: Maksym.
Maksimka Russian. From Maximilian, Latin, "Greatest in excellence." Unusual.
Maksymilian Polish. From Maximilian, Latin, "Greatest in excellence." Unusual.

Makszi Hungarian. From Maximilian, Latin, "Greatest in excellence." Unusual.

Mal English. From Mallory. Less popular for males, less popular for females.

Malachi English. Hebrew, "My messenger" or "messenger of the Lord." Book of Malachi. Prophet. Unusual.

Malachy Irish. From Malachi. Saint. Unusual.

Malcolm English. Gaelic, "Servant of St. Columba." King of Scotland (I, 943-IV, 1153); Campbell, Sir (British racer, set nine land speed records, peaking at 301.13 miles per hour); X (first black Muslim "national minister") (real name: Malcolm Little); Baldrige (secretary of commerce under Reagan). Unusual. Mal. Alternative spelling: Malcom.

Maldwyn Welsh. From Baldwin, Old German, "Bold friend." Unusual.

Málik Arabic. Arabic, "Master." al-Kāmil (13th-century Palestinian sultan, gave Jerusalem to Frederick II in sixth Crusade). Unusual.

Mallory See under Girls' Names.

Malory See Mallory under Girls' Names.

Malvern English. Welsh, "Bare hill"; place name used as a first name. Unusual.

Malvin English. From Malvina, created by James Macpherson in his Ossianic poems. Whitfield (won Olympic gold medals for 800-meter run, 1948, 1952). Unusual.

Mamo See under Girls' Names.

Manasseh Hebrew/Israeli. Hebrew, "Cause to forget." Genesis 41:51. Son of Joseph; Cutler (clergyman and botanist, helped organize Ohio Company for colonizing Ohio River valley). Unusual.

Manchu Chinese. Chinese, "Pure." Unusual.

Manco Native American. Inca, "King." Capac (13th-century, established Inca dynasty in Peru). Unusual.

Mandek Polish. From Herman, Old German, "Army" + "man." Unusual.

Mander Gypsy. English Gypsy, "From me." Unusual.

Mando Hispanic. From Herman, Old German, "Army" + "man." Unusual.

Manfred English. Old German, "Man-peace" or "man of peace." Schnelldorfer (German, won Olympic gold medal for men's figure skating, 1964); Lee (collaborated with Frederic Dannay on detective novels) (real name of Ellery Queen and Barnaby Ross); von Richthofen (German WWI aviator) (real name of the Red Baron); Mann (pop singer, "Doo Wah Diddy Diddy"). Unusual.

Mango Hispanic. From Emanuel, Hebrew, "God is with us," referring to a child about to be born. Isaiah 7:14. Unusual.

Manipi Native American. Native American, "Walking wonder." Unusual.

Manius Scottish. From Magnus, Latin, "Great." Curius Dentatus (Roman general, conquered Samnites in 290 B.C. after 50-year war). Unusual. Alternative spelling: Manyus.

Manley English. English, "Manly." Surname used as a first name. Hudson (judge, Permanent Court of International Justice, 1936–45). Unusual.

Manny Hispanic. From Emanuel, Hebrew, "God is with us," referring to a child about to be born. Isaiah 7:14. Unusual.

Mano Hungarian. From Emanuel, Hebrew, "God is with us," referring to a child about to be born. Isaiah 7:14. Unusual.

Manolón Hispanic. From Emanuel, Hebrew, "God is with us," referring to a child about to be born. Isaiah 7:14. Unusual.

Mansa African. African, "King." Musa (14th-century emperor of Mali, made opulent pilgrimage to Mecca via Cairo). Unusual.

Mansel English. French, surname and place name used as a first name. Unusual. Alternative spelling: Mansell.

Mansfield English. English, surname and place name used as a first name. Unusual.

Manṣūr Arabic. Arabic, "Divinely aided." Unusual.

Manu African. Ghanaian, "Second-born son." Unusual.

Manue Hispanic. From Emanuel, Hebrew, "God is with us," referring to a child about to be born. Isaiah 7:14. Unusual.

Manuel Hispanic. From Emanuel, Hebrew, "God is with us," referring to a child about to be born. Isaiah 7:14. Lisa (18th-century fur trader, established posts along Missouri River); Oribe (president of Uruguay, 1835–38); Lujan, Jr. (secretary of interior under Bush); de Arriaga (first elected president of Republic of Portugal, 1911–15); Quintana (president of Argentina, 1904–06). Less popular.

Manuil Russian. From Emanuel, Hebrew, "God is with us," referring to a child about to be born. Isaiah 7:14. Unusual. Alternative spelling: Manuyil.

Manus Scottish. From Magnus, Latin, "Great." Unusual.

Marar African. Rhodesian, "Dirt." Unusual.

Marara African. From Marar. Unusual.

Marcel See under Girls' Names.

Marcelle See Marcel under Girls' Names.

Marcello Italian. From Marcus. Malpighi (17th-century Italian anatomist). Unusual.

Marcellus Latin. From Marcus. Saint; Emants (Dutch poet, playwright, and novelist). Unusual.

March English. "Dweller by a boundary"; origin unknown. Surname used as a first name. Unusual.

Marci Hungarian. From Marcus. Unusual.

Marcilka Hungarian. From Marcus. Unusual.

Marcilki Hungarian. From Martin, Latin, "Warlike." Derived from Mars, the Roman god of war. Unusual.

Marcin Polish. From Martin, Latin, "Warlike." Derived from Mars, the Roman god of war. Bielski (16th-century Polish historian and poet). Unusual.

Marco Italian. From Marcus. Polo (Venetian explorer, found Kublai Khan, 1275); Vida (16th-century Italian poet); Soto (Honduran president, 1876–83); Gagliano (17th-century Italian priest, composer); Dominis (17th-century Italian prelate). Unusual.

Marcos Hispanic, Portuguese. From Marcus. Niza (16th-century missionary and explorer, discovered Arizona and New Mexico); Antônio da Fonseca (19th-century Portuguese composer). Unusual.

Marcus English. Latin, "Warlike one." Derived from Mars, the Roman god of war. Garvey (black nationalist leader); Allen (football player, won Heisman Memorial Trophy, 1981); Verrius (1st-century Roman grammarian and teacher);

Maximian (Roman Emperor 286–305, 306–308); Loew (film producer and theater owner). Popular. Marc.

Marek Czech. From Marcus. Unusual.

Marid Arabic. Arabic, "Rebellious." Unusual.

Marinos Greek. From Marcus. Unusual.

Mario English, Italian. From Marius. Andretti (race-car driver); Puzo (novelist); Nizzoli (Italian humanist); de Sa-Carneiro (Portuguese writer); Rapisardi (Italian poet). Unusual.

Marion See under Girls' Names.

Marius Latin. Latin, a Roman clan name derived from Mars, the god of war. Leblond (French novelist) (real name: George Athenas); Goring (British actor); Servius (4th-century Latin grammarian and scholar). Unusual.

Mark English. From Marcus. Patron saint of secretaries; Clark (led forces in WWII and Korea); Rothko (abstract painter, "Light, Earth, and Blue"); Twain (novelist, "Tom Sawyer") (real name: Samuel Clemens); Spitz (swimmer, won record seven gold medals at 1972 Olympics). Popular. Alternative spelling: Marc.

Marka Russian. From Marcus. Unusual.

Markham English. "Homestead on the boundary"; origin unknown. Unusual.

Marko Czech. From Marcus. Marulic (16th-century Croatian poet and philosopher); Kraljević (king of Servia, 1371–95). Unusual.

Markos Greek. From Marcus. Botsaris (19th-century Greek patriot); Eugenikos (15th-century Greek prelate). Unusual.

Márkus Hungarian. From Marcus. Unusual.

Markusha Russian. From Marcus. Unusual.

Marlin English. From Marlene, English, combination of Maria (Miriam, Hebrew (Miryam), "Bitterness," "rebellion," "wished-for child," or "sea" (?)) + Magdalene (Magdalen, Greek, "From Magdala," an ancient city on the Sea of Galilee). Fitzwater (White House press secretary under Bush). Unusual for males, unusual for females.

Marlon English. From Mervyn, Welsh, "Sea hill"; place name used as a first name. Brando (actor). Unusual.

Marlowe English. Surname used as a first name; origin unknown. Unusual.

Marmaduke English. Meaning and origin unknown. Unusual.

Marnin Hebrew/Israeli. Hebrew, "He creates joy" or "he sings." Unusual.

Marsden English. "Boundary valley"; origin unknown. An English surname and place name used as a first name. Unusual.

Marshall English. Old French, "Horse-servant." Jewell (postmaster general under Grant); McLuhan (Canadian communications theorist); Field (merchant, founded Marshall Field & Co.); Hall (19thcentury British physician and physiologist). Less popular. Alternative spelling: Marshal.

Marston English. "Dwelling by the marsh"; origin unknown. Surname and place name used as a first name. Bates (zoologist). Unusual.

Mart English. From Martin. Unusual.

Martel German. From Martin. Unusual.

Martin English. Latin, "Warlike." Derived from Mars, the Roman god of war. of Tours (patron saint of beggars); Porres (patron saint of the poor); pope (I, 649-V, 1417); Wegelius (Finnish educator and composer); Scorsese (film director); Tupper (British writer); van Buren (eighth president); Luther (16th-century German, founder of Protestantism). Less popular. Marty. Alternative spellings: Martan, Marten, Marton.

Martinas Lithuanian. From Martin. Unusual.

Martinho Portuguese. From Martin. Unusual.

Martiniano Hispanic. From Martin. Unusual.

Martinka Czech. From Martin. Unusual.

Martino Hungarian, Italian. From Martin. Unusual.

Martinos Greek. From Martin. Unusual.

Martins Latvian. From Martin. Unusual.

Marto Hispanic. From Martin. Unusual.

Marts Latvian. From Marcus. Unusual.

Marty English. From Martin. Less popular. Alternative spellings: Martey, Marti, Martie.

Martyn Russian. From Martin. Unusual.

Marv English. From Merfin, Old Welsh, the name of a 9th-century king. Unusual.

Marvin English. From Merfin, Old Welsh, the name of a 9th-century king. Hamlisch (pianist and composer); Gaye (singer). Less popular. Marv. Alternative spelling: Marvyn.

Marvine English. From Merfin, Old Welsh, the name of a 9th-century king. Unusual. Marv.

Marwan Arabic. Arabic, meaning unknown. Unusual.

Masaccio Italian. From Thomas, Aramaic, "Twin." Unusual.

Maska Native American. Native American, "Powerful." Unusual.

Maslin French. Old French, "Little twin." Unusual.

Mason English. Old French, "Stone-worker." Surname used as a first name. Weems (19th-century clergyman and author). Unusual.

Massey English. From Thomas, Aramaic, "Twin." Unusual.

Massimiliano Italian. From Maximilian, Latin, "Greatest in excellence." Sforza (Duke of Milan, 1512–15). Unusual.

Massimo Italian. From Maximilian, Latin, "Greatest in excellence." Taparelli (19th-century Italian author and politician); Bontempelli (Italian novelist and playwright). Unusual.

Masʿud Arabic. Arabic, "Fortunate." Unusual.

Mata Scottish. From Matthew. Unusual.

Máté Hungarian. From Matthew. Unusual.

Mateĭ Bulgarian. From Matthew. Unusual.

Matek Czech. From Matthew. Unusual.

Mateo Hispanic. From Matthew. Alemán (17th-century Spanish novelist); Alonso (Argentine sculptor, "Christ of the Andes"); Cerezo (17th-century Spanish painter). Unusual.

Mateus Portuguese. From Matthew. Unusual.

Matfei Russian. From Matthew. Unusual.

Mathe German. From Matthew. Unusual.

Mathia English. From Matthew. Unusual.

Mathias English, German, Swedish. From Matthew. Unusual.

Mathieu French. From Matthew. Molé (17th-century French jurist and politician); Dombasle (19th-century French agriculturist, invented plow). Unusual.

Matías Hispanic. From Matthew. Romero (19th-century Mexican economist and diplomat). Unusual.

Mato Native American. Native American, "Brave." Unusual.

Matope African. Rhodesian, "He will be the last child." Unusual.

Matt English, Estonian. From Matthew. Dillon (actor). Less popular. Alternative spelling: Mat.

Matteo Italian. From Matthew. Visconti (14th-century lord of Milan); Ricci (17th-century Italian missionary); Civitali (16th-century Italian sculptor and architect); Bartoli (Italian linguist); Boiardo (15th-century Italian poet). Unusual.

Matteus Norwegian. From Matthew. Unusual.

Matthaios Greek. From Matthew. Unusual.

Matthaus German. From Matthew. Merian (17th-century Swiss engraver and bookseller); Zell (16th-century German religious reformer); Pöppelmann (18th-century German architect, "Pavilion of the Zwinger," Dresden); Schiner (16th century Swiss prelate). Unusual.

Matthew English. Hebrew, "Gift of the Lord." Book of Matthew. Patron saint of accountants and bookkeepers; Arnold (British poet, "Thrysis"); Lewis (British novelist and dramatist); Perry (19th-century naval officer); Thornton (19th-century physician). Extremely popular. Matt. Alternative spelling: Mathew.

Matthia English. From Matthew. Unusual.

Matthias German. From Matthew. Saint; Weckmann (17th-century German organist and composer); Schleiden (19th-century German botanist); Jochumsson (Icelandic poet); Gheyn (18th-century Belgian composer). Unusual.

Matthieu French. From Matthew. Orfila (19th-century French chemist). Unusual.

Mattias English. From Matthew. Unusual.

Mattmias English. From Matthew. Unusual.

Matty English. From Matthew. Unusual. Alternative spelling: Mattie.

Matus Czech. From Matthew. Unusual.

Matvey Russian. From Matthew. Unusual.

Matyas Polish. From Matthew. Rakosi (Hungarian prime minister, 1952–53); Corvinus (king of Hungary, 1458–90); Bél (18th century Hungarian scholar and author); Dévay (16th-century Hungarian church reformer). Unusual.

Mauli Hawaiian. Hawaiian, "Dark-skinned." Unusual.

Maurice English. Latin (Mauritius), "Moorish" (i.e., dark-skinned). Patron saint of infantrymen; Tobin (secretary of labor under Truman); Utrillo (French painter); Ravel (French composer); Sterne (painter and sculptor); Gibb (musician in group The Bee Gees). Less popular. Morrie+. Alternative spelling: Morrice.

Maurie English. From Maurice. Unusual. Alternative spellings: Maurey, Maury, Morey, Morie, Morrie, Morry.

Maurizio Italian. From Maurice. Unusual.

Maury English. From Maurice. Unusual.

Max English. From Maximilian. Mallowan, Sir (British archaeologist, married Agatha Christie); Oertel (19th-century German physician); Pettenkofer (German hygienist, established experimental hygiene); Mason (mathematician); Waller (19th-century Belgian poet). Less popular.

Maxi Czech, Hispanic, Hungarian. From Maximilian. Unusual.

Maxie English. From Maximilian. Unusual.

Maxim Czech. From Maximilian. Unusual.

Maximalian German. From Maximilian. Unusual.

Maxime French. From Maximilian. Weygand (French minister of defense, 1940); Du Camp (19thcentury French journalist and traveler). Unusual.

Maximilian English. Latin, "Greatest in excellence." Saint; Schell (actor); Wolf (German astronomer, discovered comet, 1884); von Spee (German admiral). Unusual. Max. Alternative spelling: Maximillian.

Maximiliano Hispanic, Portuguese. From Maximilian. Herández Martínez (president of El Salvador, 1931–44). Unusual.

Maximino Hispanic. From Maximilian. Unusual.

Máximo Hispanic. From Maximilian. Santos (president of Uruguay, 1882–86); Alvear (president of Argentina, 1922–28); Gómez (Cuban patriot and general). Unusual.

Maxwell Scottish. Scottish, "Maccus's well." Surname and place name used as a first name. Anderson (playwright); Close (Irish geologist); Perkins (editor for Fitzgerald, Hemingway, Wolfe); Bodenheim (poet, novelist, and essayist). Less popular.

Maxy English. From Maximilian. Unusual.

Mayfey Russian. From Matthew, Hebrew, "Gift of the Lord." Book of Matthew. Unusual.

Maynard English. Old English, "Strength-hard." An English surname used as a first name. Unusual.

Māzin Arabic. Arabic, surname used as a first name. Unusual.

Mead English. Old English, "From the meadow." Unusual. Alternative spelling: Meade.

Mehemet Arabic. From Mohammed, Arabic, "Greatly praised." Unusual.

Mehetabel Hebrew/Israeli. Hebrew, "Whom God benefits." Unusual.

Mehmet Arabic. From Mohammed, Arabic, "Greatly praised." Unusual.

Mehtar Indo-Pakistani. East Indian, "Prince." Unusual.

Meir Hebrew/Israeli. Hebrew, "Light." Unusual.

Mel Male: English, from Malvina, Created by James Macpherson in his Ossianic poems; female: Portuguese, Portuguese, "Honey." Saint; Gibson (actor, "Lethal Weapon"); Brooks (film director and producer) (real name: Melvin Kaminsky); Harris (actress, "thirtysomething"); Torme (singer). Less popular for males, less popular for females.

Melbourne English. Surname and place name used as a first name; Australian city named after 18th-century English official Lord William Lamb Melbourne. Unusual.

Melvern Native American. Native American, "Great chief." Unusual.

Melville English. Anglo-Saxon, "Hill." A French place name and English surname used as a first name. Fuller III (Supreme Court Justice, 1888–1910); Post (lawyer, detective-story writer); Stone (journalist); Bissell (invented carpet sweeper, 1876); Herskovits (anthropologist). Unusual.

Melvin English. From Malvina, Created by James Macpherson in his Ossianic poems. Laird (secretary of defense under Nixon); Ott (baseball great, first to hit 500 home runs in National League). Less popular. Mel. Alternative spelling: Melvyn.

Menachem Hebrew/Israeli. Hebrew, "Comforter." 2 Kings 15:14. Begin (Israeli prime minister). Unusual.

Mendel Hebrew/Israeli. Hebrew, "Wisdom" or "knowledge." Unusual.

Mendeley Yiddish. From Menachem. Unusual.

Menico Italian. From Dominic, Latin, "Lord." Unusual.

Menz German. From Clement, Latin, "Mild," "merciful." Unusual.

Mered Hebrew/Israeli. Hebrew, "Revolt." Unusual.

Meredith See under Girls' Names.

Merfin Welsh. Old Welsh, the name of a 9th-century king. Unusual. Alternative spelling: Merfyn.

Merion Welsh. From Meirion, Welsh, place name. Unusual. Alternative spellings: Meirion, Merrion.

Merle English. French, "Blackbird." Haggard (country singer and songwriter); Tuve (physicist, verified the existence of neutrons, 1933). Unusual.

Merlin English. From Mervyn, Welsh, "Sea hill"; place name used as a first name. Olsen (defensive tackle, member of pro football Hall of Fame). Unusual for males, unusual for females.

Merrick English. From Maurice, Latin (Mauritius), "Moorish" (i.e., dark-skinned). Unusual. Alternative spelling: Meyrick.

Merrill English. From Muriel, Irish, "Sea-bright"; and Old French, "Small and famous." Unusual. Alternative spellings: Meril, Merill, Merrel, Merrell, Meryl.

Merripen Gypsy. English Gypsy, "Life" or "death." Unusual.

Mertin French. From Martin, Latin, "Warlike." Derived from Mars, the Roman god of war. Unusual.

Merton English. "Residence by the lake"; origin unknown. An English surname and place name used as a first name. Unusual.

Merville English. French, "Minor village"; surname and place name used as a first name. Unusual.

Mervyn English. Welsh, "Sea hill"; place name used as a first name. Peake (British novelist, "Mr. Pye"). Unusual. Alternative spelling: Mervin.

Meshach English. Meaning and origin unknown. One of Daniel's three friends in Bible; Taylor (actor, "Designing Women"). Unusual.

Mestipen Gypsy. English Gypsy, "Fortunate" or "lucky." Unusual.

Meurig Welsh. From Maurice, Latin (Mauritius), "Moorish" (i.e., dark-skinned). Unusual.

Meyer German. German, "Farmer." Guggenheim (industrialist, controlled American Smelting and Refining Co.); London (socialist and labor leader). Unusual. Alternative spelling: Mayer.

Michael English. Hebrew, "Who is like God." Daniel 12:1. Saint; Shaara (won Pulitzer Prize for fiction, 1975, "Killer Angels"); Jackson (musician, "Beat It"); Faraday (British chemist and physicist, discovered laws of electrolysis, 19th-century); J. Fox (actor, "Back to the Future"); Jordan (Chicago Bulls basketball great). Extremely popular for males, less popular for females. Mick, Micky+, Mike. Alternative spellings: Micael, Micheal, Mickel, Mikel.

Michail Russian. From Michael. Unusual.

Michak Polish. From Michael. Unusual.

Michal Czech, Polish. From Michael. Ogiński (19th-century Polish composer and politician); Bobrzyński (Polish historian and politician). Unusual.

Michalek Polish. From Michael. Unusual.

Michau French. From Michael. Unusual.

Micheil Scottish. From Michael. Unusual.

Michel French. From Michael. Trouillet (French, flew longest kite: 2,313 feet); Roset (17th-century Genovese politician); Montaigne (16th-century French essayist); Wohlgemuth (German painter, mainly of altars); Bibaud (19th-century French Canadian poet and historian). Unusual.

Michele Italian. From Michael. Mercati (16th-century Italian physician); Sanmicheli (16th-century Italian architect); Carafa (19th-century Italian composer); Giambono (15th-century Italian painter). Less popular.

Micho Hispanic. From Michael. Unusual.

Michon French. From Michael. Unusual.

Mick English. From Michael. Jagger (rock musician, Rolling Stones); Fleetwood (rock musician, Fleetwood Mac). Less popular. Micky+.

Mickey English. From Michael. Mantle (baseball great); Spillane (mystery writer); Rourke (actor); Rooney (actor) (real name: Joe Yule). Less popular. Alternative spellings: Mickie, Micky.

Micu Hungarian. From Nicholas, Greek, "Victorious people." Unusual.

Middleton English. English, "Middle farm"; surname and place name used as a first name. Unusual.

Mietek Polish. From Michael. Unusual.

Miguel Hispanic. From Michael. Legazpi (16th-century Spanish explorer); Unamuno (Spanish philosopher and writer); Miramón (19th-century Mexican soldier); Covarrubias (Mexican illustrator); Asturias (Guatemalan writer, awarded 1967 Nobel Prize for literature). Unusual.

Migui Hispanic. From Michael. Unusual.

Mihail Bulgarian, Greek, Romanian. From Michael. Sadoveanu (Romanian politician and novelist). Unusual.

Mihailo Ukrainian. From Michael. Unusual.

Mihal Hungarian. From Michael. Unusual.

Mihalje Swedish. From Michael. Unusual.

Mihály Hungarian. From Michael. Vörösmarty (19th-century Hungarian poet and dramatist); Károlyi (Hungarian politician); Csokonai (19th-century Hungarian poet); Babits (Hungarian writer); Horváth (19th-century Hungarian prelate and politician). Unusual.

Mihas Romanian. From Michael. Unusual.

Mihkel Estonian. From Michael. Unusual.

Mika Russian. From Michael. Waltari (Finnish novelist). Unusual.

Mikael Swedish. From Michael. Unusual.

Mike English. From Michael. Tyson (boxing great); Ovitz (movie producer and director); Myers (comedian, "Saturday Night Live"). Less popular.

Mikelis Latvian. From Michael. Unusual.

Mikhail Greek, Russian. From Michael. Gorbachev (Soviet president); Baryshnikov (ballet dancer and artistic director); Sholokhov (Russian novelist, awarded 1965 Nobel Prize for literature); Zagoskin (Russian novelist and playwright). Unusual.

Mikhalis Greek. From Michael. Unusual.

Mikhalka Russian. From Michael. Unusual.

Mikhos Greek. From Michael. Unusual.

Miki Hispanic, Hungarian. From Michael. Saint. Unusual.

Mikk Estonian. From Michael. Unusual.

Mikkel Norwegian. From Michael. Unusual.

Mikko Finnish. From Michael. Leinonen (hockey player, record six assists in one Stanley Cup game, 1982). Unusual.

Mikolai Polish. From Nicholas, Greek, "Victorious people." Unusual.

Miks Latvian. From Michael. Unusual.

Miksa Hungarian. From Maximilian, Latin, "Greatest in excellence." Unusual.

Mikus Latvian. From Michael. Unusual.

Milborough English. "Middle borough"; origin unknown. An English surname and place name used as a first name. Unusual.

Milbrough English. "Middle borough"; origin unknown. An English surname and place name used as a first name. Unusual.

Milek Polish. From Nicholas, Greek, "Victorious people." Unusual.

Miles English. From Milo. Coverdale (published first English translation of complete Bible, 1535); Davis (jazz trumpeter); Standish (colonist, arrived in America on the "Mayflower," 1620). Unusual. Alternative spelling: Myles.

Milkins Latvian. From Michael. Unusual.

Milko Czech. From Emile, Latin, a clan name probably meaning "eager." Unusual.

Millard English. "Caretaker of the mill"; origin unknown. Fillmore (13th president). Less popular.

Mills English. English, surname used as a first name. Unusual.

Milo German. Old German, "Generous" or "merciful." Jewett (19th-century educator, first president of Vassar College); 6th-century Greek athlete, wrestling champion six times each at Olympic and Pythian games. Unusual.

Milson English. "Son of Miles" or "son of Miller"; origin unknown. Surname used as a first name. Unusual.

Miltaiye Native American. Native American, "Water in waves." Unusual.

Milton English. "Settlement near a mill" or "middle settlement"; origin unknown. An English surname and place name used as a first name. Friedman (economist); Ager (songwriter, "Happy Days Are Here Again"); Avery (painter, "Mother and Child"); Bradley (publisher and manufacturer, helped popularize croquet); Bramlette (geologist); Berle (comedian) (real name: Mendel Berlinger). Less popular.

Mimis Greek. From Demetrius, Greek, "Lover of the earth" or "from Demeter," the earth mother. Unusual.

Mincho Hispanic. From Benjamin, Hebrew (Benyamin), "Son of my right hand." Genesis 35:18. Kichizan (15th-century Japanese painter and Buddhist priest). Unusual.

Minel Hispanic. From Emanuel, Hebrew, "God is with us," referring to a child about to be born. Isaiah 7:14. Unusual.

Mingan Native American. Native American, "Gray wolf." Unusual.

Mingo Hispanic. From Dominic, Latin, "Lord." Unusual.

Mique Hispanic. From Michael. Unusual.

Misa Czech. From Michael. Unusual.

Misha Russian. From Michael. Unusual. Alternative spelling: Mischa.

Mishka Russian. From Michael. Unusual. Alternative spelling: Mishca.

Misi Hungarian. From Michael. Unusual.

Miska Hungarian. From Michael. Unusual.

Misko Czech. From Michael. Unusual.

Miso Czech. From Michael. Unusual.

Misu Native American. From Misu, Native American, "Rippling water." Unusual.

Mitch English. From Michael. Miller (musician) (real name: Mitchell Miller). Less popular.

Mitchell English. From Michael. Popular. Mitch. Alternative spelling: Mitchel.

Mitsos Greek. From Demetrius, Greek, "Lover of the earth" or "from Demeter," the earth mother. Unusual.

Moe English. From Moses, Hebrew (Moshe), "Drawn from the water." Exodus 2:10. Unusual.

Mohamet Arabic. From Mohammed. Unusual.

Mohammadi Arabic. From Mohammed. Unusual.

Mohammed Arabic. Arabic, "Greatly praised." Unusual. Alternative spellings: Mohamad, Mohamed, Mohammad.

Mohan Indo-Pakistani. Hindi, "Delightful." Another name for the Hindu god Krishna. Unusual.

Moïse French. From Moses, Hebrew (Moshe), "Drawn from the water." Exodus 2:10. Amyraut (17thcentury French Protestant theologian). Unusual.

Moisei Bulgarian. From Moses, Hebrew (Moshe), "Drawn from the water." Exodus 2:10. Unusual.

Moises Portuguese, Yiddish. From Moses, Hebrew (Moshe), "Drawn from the water." Exodus 2:10. Unusual.

Moisey Russian. From Moses, Hebrew (Moshe), "Drawn from the water." Exodus 2:10. Unusual.

Moisis Greek. From Moses, Hebrew (Moshe), "Drawn from the water." Exodus 2:10. Unusual.

Mojag Native American. Native American, "Never quiet." Name for a baby who cries a lot. Unusual.

Momuso Native American. Native American, "Yellow jackets nesting in winter." Unusual.

Montague English. French, "Sharp mountain." Summers (British author, expert on witchcraft and demonology); James (British scholar, provost of Eton, 1918–36). Unusual. Alternative spelling: Montagu.

Monty English. From Montague. Less popular. Alternative spelling: Monte.

Mordechai Hebrew/Israeli. Hebrew, meaning unknown. Possibly from the Persian god Marduc. Esther 10:3. Cousin and foster-father of Esther. Unusual.

Morgan See under Girls' Names.

Morley English. "Moor clearing"; origin unknown. An English surname and place name used as a first name. Unusual.

Morris English. From Maurice, Latin (Mauritius), "Moorish" (i.e., dark-skinned). Katz (most prolific salable painter: sold 187,218 paintings through July 1989); Chalfen (established Holiday on Ice Productions, 1945); Badgro (member of pro football Hall of Fame); Cohen (philosopher and educator); Travers (British chemist). Less popular. Morrie+. Alternative spelling: Moris, Moriss, Morriss.

Morrison English. From Maurice, Latin (Mauritius), "Moorish" (i.e., dark-skinned). Waite (Supreme Court Justice, 1874–88). Unusual. Alternative spelling: Morrisson.

Mortimer English. French, "Still water"; surname and place name used as a first name. Less popular. Mort.

Morton English. "Village on the moor"; origin unknown. An English surname and place name used as a first name. Sahl (entertainer); Prince (neurologist and psychologist). Less popular. Mort.

Morven Scottish. Gaelic, "Big mountain peak." Unusual.

Mose English. From Moses. Unusual.

Moses English. Hebrew (Moshe), "Drawn from the water." Exodus 2:10. Hebrew leader and law-giver, brought the 10 Commandments down from Mt. Sinai; Rogers (19th-century mariner); Tyler (educator); Dropsie (lawyer); Cotsworth (British advocate of calendar reform); Gaster (British scholar). Unusual.

Moshe Hebrew/Israeli, Polish, Yiddish. Hebrew, "Drawn from the water." Exodus 2:10. Luzzato (18th-century Italian Cabbalist and poet); Sharett (Israeli politician); Dayan (Israeli soldier and politician). Unusual.

Mosi African. Swahili, "First-born." Unusual.

Moss English, from Moses; and Irish, from Maurice, Latin (Mauritius), "Moorish" (i.e., dark-skinned). Hart (playwright, won Pulitzer Prize, 1936, "You Can't Take It With You"). Unusual.

Mostyn Welsh. Welsh, "Fortress in a field"; surname and place name used as a first name. Unusual.

Moswen African. African, "Light in color." Unusual.

Mosya Russian. From Moses. Unusual.

Mosze Polish. From Moses. Unusual.

Moszek Polish. From Moses. Unusual.

Motega Native American. Native American, "New arrow." Unusual.

Motka Russian. From Matthew, Hebrew, "Gift of the Lord." Book of Matthew. Unusual.

Motya Russian. From Matthew, Hebrew, "Gift of the Lord." Book of Matthew. Unusual.

Moze Lithuanian. From Moses. Unusual.

Mózes Hungarian, Yiddish. From Moses. Unusual.

Muata Native American. Native American, "Nesting yellow jackets." Unusual.

Muḥammad Arabic. From Mohammed, Arabic, "Greatly praised." Prophet; Ali (world boxing champion); Nader Khan (king of Afghanistan, 1929–33); Amilial (17th-century Iranian theologian, astronomer, and writer); Rashid (Muslim theologian); Abduh (Egyptian scholar). Unusual. Alternative spelling: Muhammed.

Muir Scottish. Scottish, "Dweller by the moor." Surname used as a first name. Unusual.

Mundan African. Rhodesian, "Garden." Unusual.

Mundek Polish. From Edmund, Old English, "Rich protector." Unusual.

Mundo Hispanic. From Edmund, Old English, "Rich protector." Unusual.

Mungo Scottish. Gaelic, "Amiable." Saint, nickname of Kentigern; Park (19th-century Scottish explorer); Ponton (19th-century Scottish inventor, discovered that sunlight renders potassium dichromate insoluble, which is the basis for photoengraving). Unusual.

Munro Scottish. Scottish, surname used as a first name. Unusual.

Munroe Scottish. From Munro. Unusual. Alternative spellings: Monro, Monroe, Munro.

Muraco Native American. Native American, "White moon." Unusual.

Murdo Scottish. From Murdoch. Unusual.

Murdoch Scottish. Gaelic, "Mariner" or "sea warrior." Unusual.

Murray Scottish. From Moray, Scottish, surname and place name used as a first name. Rose (Australian swimmer, won Olympic gold medals for 400-meter freestyle, 1956, 1960). Less popular. Alternative spellings: Murrey, Murry.

Musenda African. African, "Nightmare." Unusual.

Mustapha Arabic. Arabic, "Chosen." Unusual.

Myer English. Surname used as a first name; origin unknown. May mean "physician," "bailiff," or "marsh dweller." Prinstein (won Olympic gold medals for long jump, 1904, 1906). Unusual.

Myers English. From Myer. May mean "physician," "bailiff," or "marsh dweller." Unusual.

Myron English. Greek, "Sweet-smelling oil." Greek sculptor, "Discus Thrower"; Herrick (diplomat, ambassador to France, 1912–14, 1921–29). Less popular.

Nabīl Arabic. Arabic, "Noble." Unusual.

Nagid Hebrew/Israeli. Hebrew, "Ruler" or "prince." Unusual.

Nahele Hawaiian. Hawaiian, "Forest" or "grove of trees." Unusual.

Nahma Native American. Native American, "Sturgeon." Unusual.

Nairne Scottish. Scottish, "From the narrow river glade." Unusual for males, unusual for females.

Najīb Arabic. Arabic, "Of noble descent." Unusual.

Nalren Native American. Native American, "He is thawed out." Unusual.

Namid Native American. Native American, "Star dancer." Unusual.

Namir Hebrew/Israeli. Hebrew, "Leopard." Unusual.

Nandin Indo-Pakistani. Hindi, "Destroyer." Another name for the Hindu god Siva. Unusual.

Napier Hispanic. From Neper, Spanish, "Of the new city." Unusual.

Napoleon English. Old German, meaning unknown. Popular interpretations relate the name to Naples, Italy, and to lions. Bonaparte (19th-century French emperor). Unusual.

Napthali Hebrew/Israeli. Hebrew, "My strife." Fifth son of Jacob. Unusual.

Narain Indo-Pakistani. Hindi, another name for the Hindu god Vishnu. Unusual.

Narcissus English. Greek, "Daffodil." Legendary Greek youth who fell in love with his own reflection; 2nd-century bishop of Jerusalem. Unusual.

Nard Persian. Persian, "Chess game." Unusual.

Nardek Polish. From Leonard, Old German (Leonhard), "Strong as a lion." Unusual.

Nasser Arabic. Arabic, "Victorious." Unusual.

Nassor African. From Nasser. Unusual.
Nat English. From Nathan. "King" Cole (singer). Unusual. Alternative spelling: Natt.
Natal Hispanic. From Natalie, Latin, "Birthday of the Lord." Unusual.
Natale Italian. From Natalie, Latin, "Birthday of the Lord." Unusual.
Natan Hebrew/Israeli, Hispanic, Hungarian, Polish, Russian. Hebrew, "Gift" or "God has given." 2 Samuel 7. Unusual.
Nataniele Italian. From Nathaniel. Unusual.
Nate English. From Nathaniel. Less popular.
Nathan English. From Nathaniel. Hebrew prophet; Clifford (Supreme Court Justice, 1858–81); Forrest (Confederate general); Meeker (19th-century journalist); Weinstein (novelist, "Day of the Locust") (real name of Nathanael West). Popular. Nate. Alternative spelling: Nathon.
Nathaniel English, French. Hebrew, "Gift of God." John 1:45. Saint; Pringsheim (19th-century German botanist); Culverwel (17th-century British philosopher and clergyman); Greene (American Revolution officer); West (novelist, "Day of the Locust") (real name: Nathan Weinstein); Hawthorne (novelist, "Scarlet Letter"); Currier (19th-century lithographer with James Ives, "Midnight Race on the Mississippi"); Rochester (pioneer, established city of Rochester, New York, 1811); Ward (17th-century British clergyman); Lyon (19th-century army officer). Popular. Nate.
Nathon English. From Nathaniel. Unusual. Nate.
Natty English. From Nathaniel. Unusual.
Nav Gypsy. Hungarian, "Name." Unusual.
Navin Indo-Pakistani. Hindi, "Novel" or "new." Unusual.
Nawat Native American. Native American, "Left hand." Unusual.
Nayati Native American. Native American, "The wrestler." Unusual.
Nayland English. Old English, "Island dweller"; surname and place name used as a first name. Unusual.
Ned English. From Edward, Old English, "Property guardian." Lud (18th-century British laborer who launched riots against labor-saving devices; rioters were called "Luddites"); Ward (British tavern-keeper and humorist); Kelly (Australian outlaw, became a symbol of protest against authority and the rich). Less popular.
Neddy English. From Edward, Old English, "Property guardian." Unusual.
Nehemiah Hebrew/Israeli. Hebrew, "God comforts." Book of Nehemiah. Hebrew prophet; Mosessohn (rabbi, established and edited "Jewish Tribune" in Portland, Oregon); Grew (British botanist, pioneer of plant anatomy); Persoff (actor). Unusual.
Nehru Indo-Pakistani. East Indian, "Canal." Unusual.
Neil English. Irish, "Champion." Diamond (pop singer); Armstrong (first astronaut on moon); McElroy (secretary of defense under Eisenhower); Simon (playwright); Munroe (Scottish novelist and journalist); Bush (son of President George). Less popular. Alternative spellings: Neal, Neale, Neill.
Neils English. From Neil. Unusual.
Neilson English. "Son of Neil"; origin unknown. An English surname used as a first name. Unusual.
Nelek Polish. From Cornell, English, surname and place name used as a first name. Unusual.
Nelo Hispanic. From Daniel, Hebrew, "God is my judge." Daniel 1:6. Unusual.
Nels English. From Neil. Unusual.
Nelson English. From Neilson. An English surname used as a first name. Riddle (composer and conductor); Miles (Civil War officer); Hunt (billionaire businessman; with his brother, owns the most valuable coin collection: $50 million+); Mandela (South African civil rights advocate); Rockefeller (vicepresident under Ford). Less popular.
Nen Egyptian. Egyptian, the name of a spirit. Unusual.
Neper Hispanic. Spanish, "Of the new city." Unusual.
Neptune Latin. Latin, the name of the Roman god of the sea. Unusual.
Nero Latin. Latin, "Strong" or "stern." Roman emperor, 54–68. Unusual.
Neron Bulgarian, French, Hispanic. From Nero. Unusual.
Nerone Italian. From Nero. Unusual.
Netis Native American. From Nitis, Native American, "Good friend." Unusual for males, unusual for females.
Neto Hispanic. From Ernest, English, "Vigor" or "earnestness." Unusual.
Nev Irish. From Nevin. Unusual.
Neville English. Old French, "New town"; surname and place name used as a first name. Brand (soldier and actor); Chamberlain (British prime minister, 1937–40); Patten (constructed smallest-wheeled rideable bicycle: 0.76-inch diameter wheels). Unusual. Alternative spellings: Nevil, Nevile, Nevill.
Nevin Irish. Irish, "Holy." Unusual. Alternative spelling: Nevan.
Nevins Irish. From Nevin. Unusual.
Newell English. From Newel, meaning and origin unknown. Surname used as a first name. Wyeth (illustrator and painter). Unusual. Alternative spelling: Newel.
Newlin Welsh. Old Welsh, "Son of the new pool." Unusual. Alternative spelling: Newlyn.
Newman English. Old English, "Newcomer." Surname used as a first name. Noggs (character in Charles Dickens' "Nicholas Nickleby"). Unusual.
Newton English. "New settlement"; origin unknown. An English surname and place name used as a first name. Baker (secretary of war under Wilson); Rowell (Canadian lawyer and politician); Winchell (geologist and archaeologist). Unusual.
Nial Irish. From Neil, Irish, "Champion." Unusual. Alternative spellings: Niall, Nialle, Niel.
Nibaw Native American. Native American, "I stand up." Unusual.
Nicabar Gypsy. Spanish Gypsy, "To steal." Unusual.
Nicanor Hispanic. From Nicholas. Unusual.
Nicho Hispanic. From Dennis, Greek, "Of Dionysos," the Greek name for the god of wine. Unusual.
Nichol See Nicole under Girls' Names.
Nicholas English. Greek, "Victorious people." of Tolentino (saint); of Flue (pa-

tron saint of Switzerland); pope (I, 858-V, 1447); Butler (president of Columbia University, 1901–45); II (czar of Russia, 1894–1917); Brady (secretary of treasury under Bush); Lanier (British composer, singer, and painter). Very popular. Nick, Nicki+. Alternative spelling: Nickolas.

Nicholson English. English surname used as a first name; origin unknown. Linked with Nicholas (Greek, "Victorious people"). Unusual.

Nick English. From Nicholas. Castle (film director). Unusual. Nicky. Alternative spellings: Nic, Nik.

Nicky English. From Nicholas, Greek, "Victorious people." Unusual for males, unusual for females. Alternative spelling: Nikky.

Nicodemus Greek. Greek, "Victory of the people." John 3:1. 18th-century Greek saint ("the Hagiorite"). Unusual.

Nicol English. From Nicholas, Greek, "Victorious people." Unusual for males, less popular for females. Nick, Nicky+.

Nicola Italian. From Nicholas. Unusual.

Nicolaas Dutch. From Nicholas. Louw (South African poet, dramatist, and literary theorist); Beets (Dutch clergyman and professor of theology). Unusual.

Nicolai Norwegian. From Nicholas. Hartmann (German philosopher and professor). Unusual.

Nicolás French, Hispanic. From Nicholas. Largillière (18th-century French portraitist); Leblanc (18th-century French chemist, manufactured soda from salt); Cugnot (invented a steam-powered, three-wheeled artillery tractor, 1770); Perrot (French explorer, claimed upper Mississippi for France, 1689). Unusual.

Nicolau Portuguese. From Nicholas. Tolentino de Almeida (Portuguese poet, satirized society). Unusual.

Nicolaus German. From Nicholas. Simrock (German music publisher, established firm in 1793); Copernicus (radical 16th-century Polish astronomer, discarded Ptolemaic system and developed heliocentric system). Unusual. Alternative spelling: Nikolaus.

Nicolò Italian. From Nicholas. Unusual.

Niel Irish. From Neil, Irish, "Champion." Gow (18th-century Scottish fiddler and composer). Unusual.

Niels Danish. From Nicholas. King of Denmark, 1104–34; Stenson (17th-century Danish anatomist, discovered parotid salivary duct); Bohr (Danish, awarded 1922 Nobel Prize for physics); Finsen (Danish, developed phototherapy technique for smallpox, awarded 1903 Nobel Prize for medicine). Unusual.

Nigan Native American. Native American, "Ahead." Unusual.

Nigel English. From Neil, Irish, "Champion." British bishop of Ely, 1133; Balchin (British novelist, "Mine Own Executioner"); Mansell (British race-car driver); Towning (British, holds duration record for ironing: 128 hours); Bruce (British actor); Davenport (British actor). Less popular. Alternative spellings: Nigal, Nigiel, Nigil.

Niki Hungarian. From Nicholas. Unusual.

Nikita Russian. From Nicholas. Khrushchev (Russian, first secretary of communist party, 1953–64); Minin (Russian prelate, patriarch of Moscow, 1652–58). Unusual.

Nikki See Nicki under Girls' Names.

Niklas Latvian, Swedish. From Nicholas. Unusual.

Niklos Hungarian. From Nicholas. Unusual.

Nikolai Estonian, Russian. From Nicholas. Abildgaard (Danish neoclassical painter); Andrievski (Russian, holds record for flying-boat speed: 566.69 miles per hour); Grundtvig (19th-century Danish theologian); Petrushenko (Russian colonel; member of Soyuz, group dedicated to preventing breakup of USSR). Unusual.

Nikolais Latvian. From Nicholas. Unusual.

Nikolaos Greek. From Nicholas. Politis (Greek jurist and diplomat). Unusual.

Nikolas Bulgarian. From Nicholas. Unusual.

Nikolos Greek. From Nicholas. Unusual.

Nikos Greek. From Nicholas. Kazantzakis (Greek novelist). Unusual.

Nikula Czech. From Nicholas. Unusual.

Nikulas Czech. From Nicholas. Unusual.

Nil Russian. From Neil, Irish, "Champion." Unusual.

Niles English. From Neil, Irish, "Champion." Unusual.

Nili Hebrew/Israeli. Hebrew, "The glory of Israel will not lie or repent." 1 Samuel 15:29. Unusual for males, unusual for females.

Nilo Finnish. From Neil, Irish, "Champion." Unusual.

Nils Swedish. From Nicholas. Nordenskjöld (Swedish geologist and explorer); Lied (holds record for longest golf drive: 2,640 feet across ice); Sefström (Swedish chemist and mineralogist, named element vanadium, 1830); Vogt (Norwegian novelist and playwright). Unusual.

Nilya Russian. From Neil, Irish, "Champion." Unusual.

Nimrod Hebrew/Israeli. Hebrew, "Rebel." Genesis 10:8. Great-grandson of Noah. Unusual.

Ninian Scottish. Scottish, meaning unknown. Wirt Edwards (first superintendent of public instruction in Illinois, 1854–57; at his house, Lincoln met and married Mary Todd). Unusual.

Nipton English. Place name referring to the Isle of Wight; origin unknown. Unusual.

Nissan Hebrew/Israeli. Hebrew, "Flight." Unusual.

Nissim Hebrew/Israeli. Hebrew, "Signs" or "miracles." Often given to children born on holidays that commemorate miracles, such as Purim or Chanukah. Unusual.

Nitis Native American. Native American, "Good friend." Unusual.

Niven Irish. From Nevin, Irish, "Holy." Unusual.

Nnamdi Nigerian. Nigerian, "My father is still alive." The name suggests reincarnation. Unusual.

Noach Czech, Hebrew/Israeli. Hebrew, "Rest," "long-lived," or "wandering." Unusual.

Noah English. Hebrew (Noach), "Rest," "long-lived," or "wandering." Old Testament patriarch who built an ark; Beery (actor); Swayne (Supreme Court Justice, 1862–81); Porter (clergyman and educator, president of Yale, 1871–86); Webster (lexicographer, wrote first spelling book). Less popular.

Noak Scandinavian. From Noah. Unusual.

Noble English. Latin, "noscere" ("to

know"); the word used as a first name. Unusual.

Nodin Native American. Native American, "The wind." Unusual.

Noe Czech, French (Noë), Greek, Hispanic, Hungarian, Italian, Romanian. From Noah. Unusual.

Noel See Noelle under Girls' Names.

Noga See under Girls' Names.

Noi Russian. From Noah. Unusual.

Nokonyu Native American. Native American, "Katydid's nose." Unusual.

Nolan English. Gaelic, "Noble" or "famous." Ryan (baseball pitching great, holds record for fastest pitch: 100.9 miles per hour). Unusual. Alternative spelling: Nolen.

Norbert English. Old German, "Famous in the north." Saint; Jokl (Czech linguist, studied Balkan language patterns). Less popular.

Norice English. From Norris. Unusual.

Norman English. Old English, "Man from the north." Mailer (novelist, "Tough Guys Don't Dance"); Rockwell (painter); Lindsay (Australian illustrator and novelist, "Magic Pudding"); Macleod (Scottish clergyman and author); Vincent Peale (clergyman); Hapgood (editor and writer, "Industry and Progress"). Less popular.

Norreys English. From Norris. O'Riodan (Irish dramatist and novelist) (real name: Norreys Connell). Unusual.

Norris English. Old English, "Northerner." Unusual. Alternative spellings: Noris, Norriss.

Norry English. From Norris. Unusual. Alternative spelling: Norrie.

Norton English. "Northern settlement"; origin unknown. Less popular.

Norval English. Scottish, meaning unknown. Baptie (world champion speed skater, 1905–07); character in John Home's play "Douglas." Unusual. Alternative spellings: Norvel, Norvell.

Norville English. From Norval, Scottish, meaning unknown. Unusual.

Noton Native American. From Nodin, Native American, "The wind." Unusual.

Nowell English. From Natalie, Latin, "Birthday of the Lord." Unusual.

Nowles English. Middle English, "A forested grassy slope." Unusual.

Noy Hebrew/Israeli. Hebrew, "Beauty." Unusual.

Numa Arabic. From Naomi, Hebrew, "Pleasantness," "delight." Ruth 1:2. Pompilius (second legendary king of Rome, 715–673); Droz (president of Swiss Confederation, 1881, 1887); Fustel de Coulanges (19th-century French historian, authority on ancient and medieval history). Unusual for males, unusual for females.

Numair Arabic. Arabic, "Panther." Unusual.

Nur Hebrew/Israeli. From Nuria, Hebrew, "Fire of the Lord." Unusual.

Nuri Hebrew/Israeli. From Nuria. as-Saʿīd (Iraqi politician, served as prime minister 14 times from 1930). Unusual for males, unusual for females.

Nuria See under Girls' Names.

Nuriel See under Girls' Names.

Nuru African. Swahili, "Light." Unusual.

Nusair Arabic. Arabic, "Vulture." Unusual.

Nwa Nigerian. Nigerian, "Son." Unusual.

Nwake Nigerian. Nigerian, "Son born on the market day Eke." Unusual.

Nye Welsh. From Aneurin, Welsh, "Honor" or "gold." Unusual.

Oalo Hispanic. From Paul, Latin, "paulus" ("small"). Unusual.

Obadiah Hebrew/Israeli. Hebrew, "Servant of God." Book of Obadiah. Hebrew prophet; Yareh ben Abraham (Italian rabbi, author of commentary on the Mishnah). Unusual.

Obed English. From Obadiah. Book of Obadiah. Hussey (invented reaper that competed with McCormick's). Unusual.

Oberon English. From Auberon, Old German, "Noble bear-like." Unusual.

Obie English. From Obadiah. Book of Obadiah. Unusual. Alternative spelling: Obe.

Ocean See under Girls' Names.

Oceanus English. From Ocean, Greek, "okeanos"; the word used as a first name. Unusual.

Octavius Latin. Latin, "Eighth." Given to the eighth-born child or to a child born on the eighth day or month. Family of five Roman soldiers and rulers; Frothingham (Unitarian minister, established the Boston Free Religious Association, 1867). Unusual.

Ode English. From Odell. Unusual.

Odell English. Middle English, "Wood hill"; surname and place name used as a first name. Unusual.

Odi Hungarian. From Edmund, Old English, "Rich protector." Unusual.

Odie English. From Odell. Unusual. Alternative spellings: Odey, Ody.

Odin Scandinavian. Scandinavian, the name of the chief Norse god. Unusual.

Odinan African. African, "Fifteenth-born child." Unusual.

Odion Nigerian. Nigerian, "First-born twin." Unusual.

Odissan African. African, "Thirteenth-born son." Unusual.

Odo Norwegian. From Otto, Old German, "Possessions." of Cluny (saint). Unusual.

Ödön Hungarian, from Edmund, Old English, "Rich protector"; and French, from Otto, Old German, "Possessions." von Horváth (German playwright and novelist). Unusual.

Ogden English. Old English, "Oak valley"; surname and place name used as a first name. Mills (secretary of treasury under Hoover); Nash (writer of humorous verse, "Hard Lines"); Reid (editor and publisher of New York "Tribune," 1913–47); Rood (physicist, developed flicker photometer for comparing color brightness). Unusual. Alternative spellings: Ogdan, Ogdon.

Ogun Nigerian. Nigerian, the name of the war god. Unusual.

Ogunkeye Nigerian. Nigerian, "Ogun has earned honor." Ogun is the god of war. Unusual.

Ogunsanwo Nigerian. Nigerian, "Ogun helps." Ogun is the god of war. Unusual.

Ogunsheye Nigerian. Nigerian, "Ogun

has performed honorably." Ogun is the god of war. Unusual.

Ohanko Native American. Native American, "Reckless." Unusual.

Ohannes Turkish. From John, Hebrew (Yochanan), "God has been gracious." Unusual.

Ohin African. African, "Chief." Unusual.

Oko Nigerian. From Ogun. Unusual.

Okon African. African, "Born at night." Unusual.

Olaf Scandinavian. From Olave. Patron saint of Norway; Kjeldsberg (introduced modern skiing to Switzerland, 1881); Bull (Norwegian poet); Gulbranson (Norwegian illustrator and caricaturist). Unusual.

Olafur Icelandic. From Olave. Thors (Icelandic prime minister, 1942–63). Unusual.

Olav Scandinavian. From Olave. Bjaaland (one of the first to visit the South Pole, 1911); Aukrust (Norwegian poet, helped develop Nynorsk as a literary language); Duun (Norwegian novelist). Unusual. Alternative spelling: Olave.

Olavus Scandinavian. From Olave. Unusual.

Olay Scandinavian. From Olave. Unusual. Alternative spelling: Ole.

Ole Scandinavian. From Olave. Rölvaag (educator and novelist, established the Norwegian-American Historical Association); Roemer (17th-century Danish astronomer, discovered light travels at a finite speed, which he estimated to be 140,000 miles per second); Worm (17th-century Danish physician, studied runes). Unusual. Alternative spelling: Olay.

Olef Scandinavian. From Olave. Unusual.

Olek Polish. From Alexander, Greek, "Defender of men" or "warding off men." Mark 16:21; Acts 4:6, 19:33. Unusual.

Oleksandr Russian. From Alexander, Greek, "Defender of men" or "warding off men." Mark 16:21; Acts 4:6, 19:33. Unusual.

Olery French. Old German, "Ruler of all." Unusual.

Olés Polish, Russian. From Alexander, Greek, "Defender of men" or "warding off men." Mark 16:21; Acts 4:6, 19:33. Unusual.

Olesko Russian. From Alexander, Greek, "Defender of men" or "warding off men." Mark 16:21; Acts 4:6, 19:33. Unusual.

Olin English. From Olave. Downes (music critic for the "New York Times," 1924–55). Unusual.

Olindo Italian. Italian, "From Olinthos," a Greek city. Guerrini (Italian poet, chief representative of verism) (real name of Lorenzo Stecchetti). Unusual.

Oliver English. From Olive, Greek, "elaia," the name of a fruit. Plunket (17th-century Irish prelate); Hardy (comedian, half of comic duo Laurel and Hardy, who made 200 films); Lodge, Sir (British physicist, first to suggest that the sun might be a source of radio waves); Winchester (19th-century industrialist, introduced repeating rifles). Less popular. Ollie+.

Olivier French. From Olive, Greek, "elaia," the name of a fruit. Favre (Swiss, holds record for world's highest high dive: 176 feet, 10 inches); Basselin (15th-century French poet and author of drinking songs); de Clisson (14th-century French soldier, fought for John IV); La Marche (15th-century French chronicler and poet). Unusual.

Olle Scandinavian. From Olave, Old Norse, "Forefather" or "ancestor." Unusual.

Ollie English. From Olive, Greek, "elaia," the name of a fruit. Unusual for males, unusual for females.

Olney English. Old English, place name used as a first name. Unusual.

Olo Hispanic. From Roland, Old German (Hrodland), "Famous land." Unusual.

Olorun Nigerian. Nigerian, "Belonging to the god Olorun." Unusual.

Olov Scandinavian. From Olave. Unusual.

Oluf Scandinavian. From Olave. Unusual.

Olufemi Nigerian. Nigerian, "God loves me." Unusual.

Olujimi Nigerian. Nigerian, "God gave me this." Unusual.

Olukayode Nigerian. Nigerian, "God brings me happiness." Unusual.

Olushegun Nigerian. Nigerian, "God is the victor." Unusual.

Olushola Nigerian. Nigerian, "God has blessed me." Unusual.

Omar Hebrew/Israeli. Hebrew, "Eloquent." Genesis 36:11. Khayyam (11th-century Persian poet, philosopher, mathematician, and astronomer); Sharif (actor, "Doctor Zhivago"); Tjokroaminoto (Indonesian nationalist, organized Sarekat Islam, 1912); Bradley (WWII army general, field commander of largest force ever). Unusual.

Omer Hebrew/Israeli. From Omar. Saint; 17th-century Ottoman poet (real name of Nef'i); Pasha (19th-century Turkish general). Unusual.

Onan Turkish. Turkish, "Prosperous." Unusual.

Onani African. African, "Look." Unusual.

Ondro Czech. From Andrew, Greek, "Manly." Unusual.

Onek Polish. From Otto, Old German, "Possessions." Unusual.

Onur Turkish. Turkish, "Dignity," "self-respect." Unusual.

Opanas Russian. From Tanek, Greek, "Immortal." Unusual.

Oran Irish. Irish, "Green." Unusual.

Orbán Hungarian. From Urban, Latin, "One from the city." Romans 16:9. Unusual.

Ordando Hispanic. From Roland, Old German (Hrodland), "Famous land." Unusual.

Oren Hebrew/Israeli. Hebrew, "Ash tree." Unusual.

Orestes Greek. Greek, "Mountain." Son of Agamemnon and Clytemnestra; 5th-century Roman soldier under Attila, placed his son Romulus Augustulus on the throne; Brownson (19th-century clergyman and writer). Unusual.

Orin Created. Created, possibly related to Orestes (Greek, "Mountain"). Unusual.

Orion Latin. Latin, "Dawn." Unusual.

Orji Nigerian. Nigerian, "Mighty tree." Unusual.

Orland English. From Roland, Old German (Hrodland), "Famous land." Unusual.

Orlando Hispanic, Italian. From Roland, Old German (Hrodland), "Famous land." Di Lasso (16th-century Flemish composer); Gibbons (17th-century British organist and composer). Unusual.

Orlo Hispanic. From Roland, Old German (Hrodland), "Famous land." Unusual.

Ormand English. From Herman, Old German, "Army" + "man." Unusual.

Ormerod English. "Orm's clearing"; origin unknown. An English surname and place name used as a first name. Unusual.

Ormond English. Irish, "Red." Surname used as a first name. Unusual. Alternative spelling: Ormonde.

Ormrod English. From Ormerod, "Orm's clearing"; origin unknown. An English surname and place name used as a first name. Unusual.

Orrin English. From Orin, Created, possibly related to Orestes (Greek, "Mountain"). Unusual.

Orris English. From Horatio, Latin, a Roman clan name. Unusual. Alternative spelling: Orriss.

Orsino Italian. From Orson. Unusual.

Orson English. Latin, "Little bear." Bean (actor); Welles (actor, director, producer, and screenwriter, "Citizen Kane") (real name: George Orson Welles). Unusual.

Orunjan Nigerian. Nigerian, "God of the midday sun." Unusual.

Orval English. French, surname and place name used as a first name. Unusual.

Orville English. French, "Gold town." Redenbacher (popcorn manufacturer); Wright (aviation pioneer, made first successful flight in a motor-powered airplane, near Kitty Hawk, N.C., 1903); Browning (secretary of interior under Johnson); Babcock (private secretary to Grant). Unusual.

Osbern English. From Osborn. Bokenam (15th-century British poet, "Legends of Holy Women"). Unusual. Ozzi+.

Osbert English. Old English, "God-bright." Unusual.

Osbon English. From Osborn. Unusual.

Osborne English. From Osborn. Mavor (Scottish physician and playwright, "Sunlight Sonata") (real name of James Bridie); Reynolds (British engineer and physicist, known for theory of lubrication, 1886). Unusual. Ozzi+. Alternative spellings: Osborn, Osbourn.

Osburn English. From Osborn. Unusual. Ozzi+.

Oscar English. Old English, "God-spear." Wilde (Irish playwright, "Importance of Being Earnest"); Straus (secretary of labor and commerce under T. Roosevelt); Levant (jazz pianist and composer); Hammerstein II (lyricist, won 1945 Oscar for "It Might as Well Be Spring" from "State Fair"). Less popular.

Osgood English. Old English, "Divinely good." Unusual.

Osip Russian. From Joseph, Hebrew (Yosef), "God will add." Unusual.

Osman English. From Osmond. Unusual.

Osmanek Polish. From Osmond. Unusual.

Osmen Polish. From Osmond. Unusual.

Osmond English. Old English, "God-protector." Unusual. Alternative spellings: Osmand, Osmund.

Osmundo Hispanic. From Osmond. Unusual.

Osten English. From Augustus, Latin, "Venerable" or "majestic." Unusual. Alternative spelling: Ostin.

Oswald English. Old English, "God-power." Saint; Jacoby (first bridge player to amass 10,000 points); Mosley, Sir (British politician, established British Union of Fascists, 1932); Heer (19th-century Swiss botanist and paleontologist). Unusual. Alternative spelling: Oswold.

Oswell English. From Oswald. Unusual. Alternative spelling: Oswall.

Oswin English. Old English, "God-friend." Unusual.

Osya Russian. From Joseph, Hebrew (Yosef), "God will add." Unusual.

Otadan Native American. Native American, "Plenty." Unusual.

Otek Polish. From Otto. Unusual.

Otello Italian. From Otto. Unusual.

Otfried German. From Otto. Unusual.

Otho German. From Otto. Unusual.

Othon French. From Otto. Friesz (French Fauvist painter). Unusual.

Otik Czech. From Otto. Unusual.

Otilio Hispanic. From Otto. Unusual.

Otis English. From Otto. Bowen (secretary of health and human services under Reagan); Redding (pop singer); Mason (ethnologist, curator of National Museum, 1884–92); Skinner (actor). Less popular.

Otman Hispanic. From Otto. Unusual.

Oto Czech, Hispanic. From Otto. Unusual.

Otón Hispanic. From Otto. Unusual.

Ottah Nigerian. Nigerian, "Thin one." Unusual.

Otto English. Old German, "Possessions." Preminger (film director and producer); Ludwig (19th-century German realist writer); Mencke (co-founder of first literary and scientific periodical in Germany, 1682); Bucher (Swiss, oldest golfer to shoot hole-in-one: 99 years, 244 days). Less popular.

Ottocar German. From Otto. Unusual.

Ottomar German. From Otto. Unusual.

Otton Polish. From Otto. Unusual.

Ottone Italian. From Otto. Visconti (archbishop of Milan, 1262–95). Unusual.

Ouray Native American. Native American, "Arrow." Unusual.

Owain Welsh. From Owen. Unusual.

Owen English. Greek, "Well-born." Morse (set record for 100-meter "joggling" (running + juggling) of five objects: 13.8 seconds); Roberts (Supreme Court Justice, 1930–45); Richardson, Sir (British physicist, awarded 1928 Nobel Prize); Edwards, Sir (Welsh writer and educator). Less popular.

Oxford English. Old English, "Where the oxen cross the river"; place name used as a first name. Unusual.

Oz English. From Osgood, Old English, "Divinely good." Unusual.

Ozzy English. From Osgood, Old English, "Divinely good." Osborne (rock singer). Unusual. Alternative spellings: Ozzi, Ozzie.

Pablo Hispanic. From Paul, Latin, "paulus" ("small"). Picasso (Spanish painter and sculptor); Neruda (Chilean poet and diplomat); Casals (Spanish violoncellist, conductor, and composer); Céspedes (17th-century Spanish painter, "Ascension of Christ"). Less popular.

Pace English. From Pascal, French, "Easter child." Unusual.

Paco Hispanic, from Francis, Latin, "Frenchman"; and Native American,

Native American, "Bald eagle." Unusual.

Pacorro Hispanic. From Francis, Latin, "Frenchman." Unusual.

Paddy English. From Patrick, Latin, "Noble man." Doyle (did record 37,350 push-ups in 24 hours); Chayefsky (screenplay writer, won 1976 Oscar for "Network") (real name: Sidney Chayefsky). Unusual.

Padget English. From Paige, French, "Young attendant." Unusual. Alternative spelling: Padgett.

Padraic Irish. From Patrick, Latin, "Noble man." Colum (Irish poet and playwright, "Miracle of the Corn"). Unusual.

Padraig Irish. From Patrick, Latin, "Noble man." Unusual.

Padruig Scottish. From Patrick, Latin, "Noble man." Unusual.

Page See Paige under Girls' Names.

Paget English. From Paige. Unusual for males, unusual for females.

Paige See under Girls' Names.

Painter English. English, occupational surname used as a first name. Unusual.

Paki African. African, "Witness." Unusual.

Pál Hungarian. From Paul, Latin, "paulus" ("small"). Teleki (premier of Hungary, 1920–41). Unusual.

Palani Hawaiian. From Francis, Latin, "Frenchman." Unusual.

Pali Hungarian. From Paul, Latin, "paulus" ("small"). Unusual.

Palika Hungarian. From Paul, Latin, "paulus" ("small"). Unusual.

Pall Icelandic. From Paul, Latin, "paulus" ("small"). Unusual.

Palladin English. From Pallaton, Native American, "Fighter." Unusual.

Pallaten English. From Pallaton. Unusual.

Pallaton Native American. Native American, "Fighter." Unusual.

Palmer English. Old English, "Crusader" or "pilgrim bearing palms." Cox (illustrator and author, series of "Brownie" books for children). Unusual.

Panas Russian. From Tanek, Greek, "Immortal." Unusual.

Panayiotos Greek. From Peter, Greek, "Stone," "rock." John 1:42. Unusual.

Panchito Hispanic. From Francis, Latin, "Frenchman." Unusual.

Pancho Hispanic. From Francis, Latin, "Frenchman." Villa (Mexican bandit and revolutionary leader) (real name: Doroteo Arango). Unusual.

Panos Greek. From Peter, Greek, "Stone," "rock." John 1:42. Unusual.

Paolo Italian. From Paul, Latin, "paulus" ("small"). Orsi (Italian archaeologist); Rolli (18th-century Italian poet and librettist); Ruffini (19th-century Italian mathematician and physician); Sarpi (16th-century Italian prelate, historian, and scientist, discovered function of venous valves). Unusual.

Paquito Hispanic. From Francis, Latin, "Frenchman." Unusual.

Paris English. Greek, meaning unknown. Bordone (16th-century Venetian painter). Unusual for males, unusual for females.

Parke English. From Parker. Thompson (holds record for most travel: visited 309 countries). Unusual. Alternative spelling: Park.

Parker English. Middle English, "Park keeper." Surname used as a first name. Stevenson (actor). Unusual.

Parlan Scottish. From Bartholomew, Aramaic, "Son of Tolmai." An alternate name for the apostle Nathaniel. Unusual.

Parnell English. Old French, "Little Peter." Unusual. Alternative spellings: Parnel, Parrnell.

Parry English. Welsh, "Son of Harry." Surname used as a first name. O'Brien (won Olympic gold medals for 16-pound shot-put, 1952, 1956). Unusual.

Parzival German. From Percival, French, "Pierce the vale." The implication is piercing a veil of mystery. Unusual.

Pascal French. French, "Easter child." Leclerc (successfully filled tallest column of champagne glasses: 24.7 feet); Taskin (18th-century French harpsichord maker). Unusual.

Pascoe English. From Pascal. Unusual. Alternative spelling: Pascow.

Pascual English. From Pascal. Ortiz (president of Mexico, 1930–32); Cervera (Spanish admiral, commander in the Spanish-American War). Unusual. Alternative spelling: Pasqual.

Pasha Russian. From Paul. Unusual.

Pashka Russian. From Paul. Unusual.

Pasko English. From Pascal. Unusual.

Pat English. From Patrick, Latin, "Noble man." Nixon (wife of President Richard) (real name: Thelma Catherine Ryan Nixon); Sajak (TV game-show host, "Wheel of Fortune"). Less popular for males, less popular for females. Patty+.

Patakasu Native American. Native American, "Biting ant." Unusual.

Patamon Native American. Native American, "Raging." Unusual.

Pate English. From Peyton, Old English, "Fighter's estate"; surname and place name used as a first name. Unusual.

Patek Polish. From Patrick, Latin, "Noble man." Philippe (made most expensive standard men's pocket watch 1922: purchased in 1989 for $1,275,000). Unusual.

Patrice French. From Patrick, Latin, "Noble man." Lumumba (first prime minister of Zaire, 1960); Mansel (opera singer). Less popular for males, unusual for females.

Patricio Hispanic, Portuguese. From Patrick. Unusual.

Patricius German. From Patrick. Unusual.

Patrick English. Latin, "Noble man." Patron saint of Ireland; Goldmark (invented LP record); Kelly (fashion designer); Swayze (actor, "Dirty Dancing"); Manson, Sir (Scottish parasitologist, discovered mosquito is the host of malaria); Miller (18th-century Scottish inventor of steamboat). Popular. Pat.

Patrin Gypsy. English Gypsy, "Leaf trail." Unusual.

Patrizio Italian. From Patrick. Unusual.

Patrizius German. From Patrick. Unusual.

Patsy See under Girls' Names.

Pattin Gypsy. English Gypsy, "Leaf." Unusual.

Patton English. Old English, "Warrior's estate." Unusual. Alternative spellings: Paten, Patin, Paton, Patten.

Patwin Native American. Native American, "Man." Unusual.

Paul English. Latin, "paulus" ("small"). Saint; Tillich (philosopher and theologian); Revere (patriot, warned countryside of British invasion on celebrated ride); McCartney (musician, the Beatles); Ehrlich (German immunology pioneer, awarded 1908 Nobel Prize for physiology). Very popular.

Paulin Polish. From Paul. Unusual.
Paulino Hispanic. From Paul. Unusual.
Paulis English. From Paul. Unusual.
Paulo Hispanic, Italian. From Paul. Dias de Novais (Portuguese official, established São Paulo de Luanda, 1576, first European city in southern Africa). Unusual.
Pauls Latvian. From Paul. Unusual.
Pavel Russian. From Paul. Geordiyenko and Senko (Russian, in party of first men to reach the North Pole on ground level, 1943); Milyukov (Russian, helped establish Constitutional Democratic party, 1905); Šafařik (Czech scholar, pioneered Slavonic philology and archaeology). Unusual.
Pavils Latvian. From Paul. Unusual.
Pavlik Russian. From Paul. Unusual.
Pavlo Russian. From Paul. Unusual.
Pavlos Greek. From Paul. Unusual.
Paweł Polish. From Paul. Unusual.
Pawl Russian. From Paul. Unusual.
Pax English. Old English, "Peaceful town"; surname and place name used as a first name. Unusual.
Paxon English. From Paxton. Unusual.
Paxton English. Old English, "Peaceful town"; surname and place name used as a first name. Unusual.
Pay Native American. From Payat. Unusual.
Payat Native American. Native American, "He is coming." Unusual. Alternative spelling: Payatt.
Paz Hispanic. Spanish, "Peace." Unusual for males, unusual for females.
Peadair Scottish. From Peter, Greek, "Stone," "rock." John 1:42. Unusual.
Pearcy English. From Percy, Old French, "Valley prisoner"; surname and place name used as a first name. Unusual. Alternative spelling: Pearcey.
Pearson English. "Son of Piers [Peter]"; origin unknown. Surname used as a first name. Unusual. Alternative spelling: Pierson.
Peat English. From Peter, Greek, "Stone," "rock." John 1:42. Unusual.
Peder Scandinavian. From Peter, Greek, "Stone," "rock." John 1:42. Schumacher (17th-century Danish politician and royal librarian). Unusual.
Pedrín Hispanic. From Peter, Greek, "Stone," "rock." John 1:42. Unusual.
Pedro Hispanic. From Peter, Greek, "Stone," "rock." John 1:42. Carrasco (boxer, won 83 consecutive fights, 1964–70); Delgado (Spanish, holds record for fastest average speed in the Tour de France: 24.18 miles per hour); de Mena (17th-century Spanish sculptor); de Sousa Holstein (Portuguese prime minister, 1842–46). Unusual.
Peers English. From Peter, Greek, "Stone," "rock." John 1:42. Unusual.
Peet Estonian. From Peter, Greek, "Stone," "rock." John 1:42. Unusual.
Peeter Estonian. From Peter, Greek, "Stone," "rock." John 1:42. Unusual.
Pelham English. "Peola's residence"; origin unknown. An English surname and place name used as a first name. Grenville Wodehouse, Sir (British novelist, "The Inimitable Jeeves"); Humfrey (British Baroque lutenist and composer). Unusual.
Pepa Czech. From Joseph, Hebrew (Yosef), "God will add." Unusual.
Pepe Hispanic. From Joseph, Hebrew (Yosef), "God will add." Unusual.
Pepi German. From Pepin. I (king of Egypt 24th century B.C., established 6th dynasty); II (king of Egypt, 2294–2200 B.C.; his 94-year reign is the longest in history). Unusual. Alternative spellings: Peppi, Peppie, Peppy.
Pepik Czech. From Joseph, Hebrew (Yosef), "God will add." Unusual.
Pepillo Hispanic. From Joseph, Hebrew (Yosef), "God will add." Unusual.
Pepin German. Old German, "One who perseveres" or "one who petitions"; and Hispanic, from Joseph, Hebrew (Yosef), "God will add." King of Aquitaine (I, 817-II, 845); Frankish mayor of the palace (I, 640-III, 741); king of Italy, 781–810. Unusual.
Pepito Hispanic. From Joseph, Hebrew (Yosef), "God will add." Unusual.
Peppe Italian. From Joseph, Hebrew (Yosef), "God will add." Unusual.
Peppo Italian. From Joseph, Hebrew (Yosef), "God will add." Unusual.
Pequin Hispanic. From Peter. Unusual.
Per Swedish. From Peter. Atterbom (19th-century Swedish Romantic poet, philosopher, and literary historian); Brahe (17th-century Swedish soldier and statesman); Hansson (Swedish prime minister 1932–46, maintained Swedish neutrality during WWII). Unusual.
Perceval French. From Percival. Gibbon (British short-story writer). Unusual.
Percival English. French, "Pierce the vale." The implication is piercing a veil of mystery. Lowell (astronomer, built observatory near Flagstaff, Ariz., 1893). Unusual.
Percy English. Old French, "Valley prisoner"; surname and place name used as a first name. Faith (conductor and composer); Paget (with Marconi, received the first wireless signals across the Atlantic, 1901); Pilcher (19th-century British aeronautical engineer, pioneer in glider construction); Bysshe Shelley (19th-century British Romantic poet, "Queen Mab"). Less popular. Alternative spelling: Percey.
Peredur Welsh. From Percival. Unusual.
Peregrine Latin. Latin, "Traveler" or "pilgrim." Saint; White (first child of British parents born on the "Mayflower"); Pickle (character in Tobias Smollet's novel). Unusual.
Perequin Hispanic. From Peter. Unusual.
Perico Hispanic. From Peter. Unusual.
Perka Russian. From Peter. Unusual.
Pernell English. From Parnell, Old French, "Little Peter." Roberts (actor, "Bonanza"). Unusual. Alternative spelling: Pernel.
Pero Italian. From Peter. Covilhã (15th-century Portuguese explorer, sent by John II to locate India). Unusual.
Perry English. Latin, "Traveler" or "pilgrim." Como (singer) (real name: Nick Perido); Mason (TV criminal lawyer played by Raymond Burr); Miller (scholar, wrote "The New England Mind"). Less popular.
Petar Romanian. From Peter. Preradović (19th-century Croatian poet); Hektorovic (16th-century Dalmatian poet, author of Latin and Italian verse). Unusual.
Pete English. From Peter. Rose (baseball great, had 4,256 lifetime base hits and 14,053 times at bat) (real name: Peter Rose); Seeger (folk singer); Townshend (musician, the Who). Less popular.
Peter English. Greek, "Stone," "rock." John 1:42. Apostle; saint; Taylor (Pulitzer Prize for fiction, 1987, "A Summons

to Memphis"); Paul Rubens (17th-century Flemish painter, "Mystic Marriage of St. Catherine"); Jennings (TV news anchor); Dowdeswell (British, ate record 38 soft-boiled eggs in 75 seconds). Popular. Pete. Alternative spellings: Peterr, Petre.

Petie English. From Peter. Unusual. Alternative spelling: Petey.

Petinka Russian. From Peter. Unusual.

Petr Bulgarian, Russian. From Peter. Bezruc (Czech poet) (real name: Vladimir Vasek). Unusual.

Petras Lithuanian. From Peter. Unusual.

Petrelis Lithuanian. From Peter. Unusual.

Petro Russian. From Peter. Unusual.

Petronio Hispanic. From Peter. Unusual.

Petros Greek. From Peter. Unusual.

Petru Romanian. From Peter. Unusual.

Petrukas Lithuanian. From Peter. Unusual.

Petruno Russian. From Peter. Unusual.

Petrusha Russian. From Peter. Unusual.

Petter Norwegian. From Peter. Dass (18th-century Norwegian clergyman and poet). Unusual.

Peyo Hispanic. From Peter. Kracholov (Bulgarian symbolist poet) (real name of Peyo Yavorov). Unusual.

Peyton English. Old English, "Fighter's estate"; surname and place name used as a first name. Randolph (lawyer and politician, first president of the Continental Congress, 1774). Unusual. Alternative spelling: Payton.

Pharaoh English. Egyptian, a title of the ancient kings. Unusual. Alternative spelling: Pharoah.

Phelan English. Irish, "Wolf." Surname used as a first name. Unusual.

Phil English. From Philip. Donahue (TV talk-show host); Collins (British pop singer); Spector (rock music producer, famed for his "wall of sound"); Joanou (film director, "State of Grace"); Stong (author of juvenile stories, "Return in August"). Less popular. Alternative spelling: Phill.

Philander Greek. Greek, "Fond of men" or "a woman fond of her husband." Character in Ludvico Ariosto's 1532 romantic epic "Orlando Furioso"; Knox (attorney general under McKinley and T. Roosevelt); von Sittewald (17th-entury German satirist); Chase (19th-century missionary in Ohio, established Kenyon College, 1824). Unusual.

Philemon English. Greek, "Kiss." Book of Philemon. Saint; Holland (17th-century British scholar and translator). Unusual.

Philip English. Greek, "philippos" ("lover of horses"). Matthew 10:3. Saint; Barbour (Supreme Court Justice, 1836–41); Murray (labor leader, president of United Steel Workers of America, 1942–52); Larkin (British poet, "North Ship"); de Laszlo de Lombos (British portraitist); Armour (19th-century industrialist, improved meat-packing methods). Popular. Phil. Alternative spellings: Filip, Phillip, Phillipe, Phillipp, Phillippe.

Philipp German. From Philip. Lenard (German physicist, discovered properties of cathode rays, awarded 1905 Nobel Prize); Spener (17th-century German theologian, leader of Lutheran Pietism); Veit (19th-century German painter, established the Nazarenes in Rome); Cluver (17th-century German historical geographer). Unusual.

Philippe French. From Philip, Greek, "philippos" ("lover of horses"). Matthew 10:3. Monet (French, sailed alone around the world in record 129 days, 19 hours, 17 minutes); Lebon (18th-century French chemist, patented engine that used coal gas); Panneton (Canadian novelist, described rural life); Quinault (17th-century French dramatist). Unusual for males, unusual for females.

Philippel French. From Philip. Unusual.

Phillipos Greek. From Philip. Unusual.

Phillips English. From Philip. van Almonde (17th-century Dutch admiral, commander of fleet that brought William of Orange to England). Unusual.

Phineas English. Hebrew, "Oracle" or "face of pity." 1 Samuel 1:3. Grandson of Aaron; Quimby (19th-century "mental healer," father of the New Thought movement); Taylor Barnum (opened "Greatest Show on Earth," 1871). Unusual.

Phthisis Greek. Greek, "Wasting," "consumption." Unusual.

Pias Gypsy. English Gypsy, "Fun." Unusual.

Pictrus Polish. From Peter, Greek, "Stone," "rock." John 1:42. Unusual.

Pierce English. From Peter, Greek, "Stone," "rock." John 1:42. Butler (Supreme Court Justice, 1923–39); Brosnan (Irish actor, "Remington Steele"); Egan (19th-century British sportswriter, provided slang phrases for Grose's "Dictionary of the Vulgar Tongue"). Unusual. Alternative spelling: Pearce.

Piercy English. "Pierce-hedge"; origin unknown. Surname used as a first name. Unusual. Alternative spelling: Piercey.

Piero Italian. From Peter, Greek, "Stone," "rock." John 1:42. di Lorenzo (15th-century Florentine painter, "Battle of the Centaurs and the Lapiths"); della Francesca (15th-century Italian painter, first humanist artist of the Quattrocento). Unusual.

Pierre French. From Peter, Greek, "Stone," "rock." John 1:42. Bonnard (French painter, leading member of the Nabis group of artists); Cardin (fashion designer); Fehlmann (holds record for fastest circumnavigation of globe by yacht: 117 days, 14 hours, 13 minutes); de Voyer (governor of New France, 1657–61). Less popular.

Pierrot French. From Peter, Greek, "Stone," "rock." John 1:42. Unusual.

Piers English. From Peter, Greek, "Stone," "rock." John 1:42. Gaveston (14th-century earl of Cornwall, companion of Edward II). Unusual. Alternative spelling: Pierse.

Pieter Dutch. From Peter, Greek, "Stone," "rock." John 1:42. van Loggerenberg (South African, played an accordion for record 85 hours, 1987); Lastman (17th-century Dutch painter, taught Rembrandt); Post (17th-century Dutch architect); Candid (17th-century Flemish painter of murals and altarpieces); van Bloemen (18th-century Flemish painter). Unusual.

Pietrek Polish. From Peter, Greek, "Stone," "rock." John 1:42. Unusual.

Pietro Italian. From Peter, Greek, "Stone," "rock." John 1:42. Mennea (Italian, set 1979 world record for 200-meter dash: 19.72 seconds); Liberi (17th-century Venetian painter, "Battle of the Dardanelles"); Locatelli (18th-century Italian violinist and composer); Verri (18th-century Italian economist). Unusual.

Pilar Hispanic. Spanish, "Pillar" or "fountain base." Unusual for males, unusual for females.

Pili African. Swahili, "Second-born son." Unusual.
Pilib Irish. From Philip. Unusual.
Pillan Native American. Native American, "Supreme essence." Araucanian Indian god of thunder and lightning. Unusual. Alternative spelling: Pilan.
Pinchas Hebrew/Israeli. Hebrew, "The Nubian" (i.e., dark of complexion). High priest, grandson of Aaron. Unusual.
Pino Italian. From Joseph, Hebrew (Yosef), "God will add." Unusual.
Piotr Bulgarian. From Peter, Greek, "Stone," "rock." John 1:42. Fijas (Polish, holds record for longest ski jump: 636 feet); Skarga (16th-century Polish preacher and writer, first Polish representative of the Counter-Reformation). Unusual.
Piotrek Polish. From Peter, Greek, "Stone," "rock." John 1:42. Unusual.
Pipo Hispanic. From Joseph, Hebrew (Yosef), "God will add." Unusual.
Piran English. Meaning and origin unknown. Possibly a form of Peter (Greek, "Stone," "rock"). Patron saint of miners. Unusual. Alternative spellings: Peran, Pieran.
Pirro Greek. Greek, "With flaming hair." Ligorio (16th-century Italian architect, built the Casino of Pope Pius IV in Vatican Gardens). Unusual.
Piti Hispanic. From Peter, Greek, "Stone," "rock." John 1:42. Unusual.
Pitin Hispanic. From Felix, Latin, "Happy," "fortunate," or "lucky." Unusual.
Pito Hispanic. From Felix, Latin, "Happy," "fortunate," or "lucky." Unusual.
Plato Greek. Greek, meaning unknown. Greek philosopher. Unusual.
Platón Hispanic. Spanish, "Broad-shouldered." Unusual.
Pol English, from Paul, Latin, "paulus" ("small"); and Greek, Greek, "Crown." Unusual.
Pollyam See under Girls' Names.
Porter English. Latin, "Gatekeeper"; surname used as a first name. Unusual.
Poul Danish. From Paul, Latin, "paulus" ("small"). Moller (19th-century Danish writer, a founder of poetic Realism in Denmark); Stemann (premier of Denmark, 1826–48). Unusual.
Pov Gypsy. English Gypsy, "Earth." Unusual.
Powa Native American. Native American, "Rich." Unusual.
Pramod Indo-Pakistani. Hindi, "Rejoicing." Unusual.
Precious See under Girls' Names.
Prem Indo-Pakistani. Hindi, "Love." Unusual.
Prent English. From Prentice. Unusual.
Prentice English. Middle English, "Apprentice." Unusual. Pren. Alternative spelling: Prentiss.
Prescott English. Old English, "Priest's cottage." Unusual. Scott+, Scotty+. Alternative spelling: Prescot.
Preston English. Old English, "Priest's settlement" or "priest's song." Place name and surname used as a first name. Sturges (screenplay writer and director, won 1940 Oscar for best original screenplay, "Great McGinty"). Unusual.
Price English. Old Welsh, "Ardent one's son" or "Rhys's son." Surname used as a first name. Unusual. Alternative spelling: Pryce.
Priestley English. "Priest's clearing"; origin unknown. An English surname and place name used as a first name. Unusual. Alternative spelling: Priestly.
Prince English. Latin, "princeps" ("one who takes the first part"); the royal title used as a first name. Rock musician, "Purple Rain" (real name: Prince Roger Nelson). Unusual.
Pry English. From Pryor. Unusual.
Pryor English. Latin, "Head of the monastery." Unusual. Alternative spelling: Prior.
Putnam English. Old English, "One who lives by the pond." Unusual.
Pyatr Russian. From Peter, Greek, "Stone," "rock." John 1:42. Unusual.
Pyotr Russian. From Peter, Greek, "Stone," "rock." John 1:42. Alekseyevich (I, "the Great," 17th-century Russian czar). Unusual.

Qabil Arabic. Arabic, "Able." Unusual.
Qadim Arabic. Arabic, "Ancient." Unusual.
Qadir Arabic. Arabic, "Powerful." Unusual.
Qamar Arabic. Arabic, "Moon." Unusual.
Quenby English. From Quimby, Old Norse, "From the woman's estate." Unusual.
Quennel French. Old French, "Dweller by the oak tree." Unusual.
Quentin English. From Quintin, Latin, "Fifth." Usually given to the fifth-born child or to a child born on the fifth day or month. Saint; Posthumus (South African, holds record for barefoot water ski jump: 67 feet, 3 inches); Massys (16th-century Flemish painter). Less popular.
Quico Hispanic. Spanish, a diminutive form for many Spanish names. Unusual.
Quillan Irish. Gaelic, "Cub." Unusual.
Quim English. From Quimby. Unusual.
Quimby English. Old Norse, "From the woman's estate." Unusual.
Quinby English. From Quimby. Unusual.
Quincy English. Old French, "From the fifth son's estate." Jones (composer); Porter (orchestral composer); Wright (political scientist, adviser to the State Department and Nurnberg Tribunal). Less popular for males, unusual for females.
Quinley Irish. From Quinlin. Unusual.
Quinlin Irish. Gaelic, "Strong one." Unusual.
Quinn Irish. Gaelic, "Intelligent" or "wise." Unusual. Alternative spelling: Quin.
Quint English. From Quintin. Unusual.
Quintin English. Latin, "Fifth." Usually given to the fifth-born child or to a child born on the fifth day or month. Brand (British aviator, served in Royal Flying Corps, WWI); Craufurd (Scottish author, helped arrange the escape of his friend Marie-Antoinette). Unusual. Alternative spellings: Quinten, Quinton.
Quinto Hispanic. From Henry, Old German (Heimerich), "Home ruler." Unusual.
Quiqui Hispanic. From Henry, Old German (Heimerich), "Home ruler." Unusual.
Quirin English. The name of a magic

stone said to cause a sleeping person to reveal his true thoughts; origin unknown. Unusual.

Quito Hispanic. From Quintin. Unusual.

Rab Scottish. From Robert, Old English (Hreodbeorht), "Fame-bright." Unusual.

Rabbi Hebrew/Israeli. Hebrew, "My master"; religious title used as a first name. Unusual.

Rabi Arabic. Arabic, "Breeze." Unusual for males, unusual for females.

Raby Scottish. From Robert, Old English (Hreodbeorht), "Fame-bright." Unusual. Alternative spellings: Rabi, Rabbie.

Rachamim Hebrew/Israeli. Hebrew, "Mercy" or "compassion." Often given to children born around Yom Kippur, the day of atonement. Unusual.

Rad English. English, a nickname for any name beginning with "Rad-." Unusual. Alternative spelling: Radd.

Radborne English. From Radburn. Unusual. Alternative spellings: Radborn, Radbourne.

Radburn English. Old English, "From the red stream"; surname and place name used as a first name. Unusual.

Radcliff English. Old English, "From the red cliff"; surname and place name used as a first name. Unusual. Alternative spelling: Radcliffe.

Radford English. Old English, "Reedy ford"; surname and place name used as a first name. Unusual.

Radman Slavic. Slavic, "Joy." Unusual.

Radolphus Latin. From Ralph, Anglo-Saxon, "Wolf-counsel." Unusual.

Radomil Slavic. Slavic, "Peace-lover." Unusual.

Rafael Hispanic, Romanian. From Raphael, Hebrew, "God heals" or "God cures." Job 4:17. Molina (president of Dominican Republic); Sabatini (Italian novelist, "Sea Hawk"); Núñez (president of Colombia, 19th-century); Altamira y Crevea (Spanish historian); Carrera (19th-century Guatemalan revolutionist). Unusual.

Rafe Irish. From Rafferty. Unusual.

Rafer Irish. From Rafferty. Unusual. Alternative spelling: Raffer.

Raff Irish. From Rafferty. Unusual.

Rafferty Irish. Gaelic, "Rich," "prosperous." Unusual.

Rafi Arabic, Arabic, "Exalting"; and Hispanic, from Raphael, Hebrew, "God heals" or "God cures." Job 4:17. Unusual.

Ragnar Scandinavian. Old Norse, "Mighty army." Östberg (Swedish architect, designed Stockholm Town Hall); Frisch (Norwegian, awarded first Nobel Prize in economic science, 1969). Unusual.

Ragnor English. From Ragnar. Unusual.

Rahman Arabic. Arabic, "Compassionate" or "merciful." Unusual.

Rahmet Turkish. From Rahman. Unusual.

Raiden Japanese. Japanese, "Thunder god." Unusual.

Raimondo Italian. From Raymond, Old German, "Counsel-protection." Unusual.

Raimund German. From Raymond, Old German, "Counsel-protection." Unusual.

Raimundo Hispanic, Portuguese. From Raymond, Old German, "Counsel-protection." Montecuccoli (Italian soldier in Austrian army, commanded imperial army in 17th-century war of empire). Unusual.

Rainer German. From Rayner, Old German, "Mighty army." Unusual.

Raini Native American. Native American, "Creator." The name of a god. Unusual.

Rainier French. From Rayner, Old German, "Mighty army." Unusual.

Rajmund Czech. From Raymond, Old German, "Counsel-protection." Unusual.

Raleigh English. Old English, "From the deer meadow"; surname and place name used as a first name. Less popular. Alternative spellings: Rawleigh, Rawley.

Ralph English. Anglo-Saxon, "Wolf-counsel." Waldo Emerson (poet, transcendental philosopher, "Nature"); Richardson, Sir (British actor); Lane, Sir (British colonist, to Virginia 1585); Upson (won International Balloon Race, 1913); Sadler (Henry VIII's secretary of state). Less popular. Alternative spelling: Ralf.

Ralphie English. From Ralph. Unusual.

Ralston English. Old Norse, "Settlement"; surname and place name used as a first name. Unusual.

Ramadan African. Arabic, the ninth month of the Moslem year. Unusual.

Ramón Hispanic. From Raymond, Old German, "Counsel-protection." Coffman (syndicated children's columnist, "Ray's Corner"); Llull (Catalan mystic and philosopher); Menéndez Pidal (Spanish professor of Roman philology); de la Sagra (Spanish sociologist, established first anarchist journal). Unusual.

Ramsay English. Old English, "Wooded island," "ram's island," or "raven island"; surname and place name used as a first name. Macdonald (British, first Labor prime minister). Unusual.

Ramsden English. Old English, "Valley with rams" or "valley where wild garlic grows"; surname and place name used as a first name. Unusual.

Ramsey English. From Ramsay. Clark (attorney general under LBJ). Unusual. Alternative spelling: Ramsy.

Ranald Scottish. From Reynold, Old English (Regenweald), "Counsel" + "power." Mackenzie (commander of Union cavalry during Civil War). Unusual.

Rance African. African, "Borrowed all." Unusual.

Rancel English. From Rance. Unusual. Alternative spellings: Rancell, Ransel, Ransell.

Rancie English. From Randolph. Unusual.

Rand English. From Randolph. Unusual.

Randall English. From Randolph. Davidson (British, archbishop of Canterbury, 1903–28, influenced ecumenical movement); Jarrell (writer, "Sad Heart at the Supermarket"). Less popular. Randy. Alternative spellings: Randal, Randel, Randell, Randle, Randol.

Randolph English. Old English (Randwulf), "Shield-wolf." Bourne (essayist, "History of a Literary Radical"); Caldecott (British illustrator of children's books, Caldecott Medal named for him);

Churchill (British author, son of Winston Churchill). Less popular. Randy.

Randy English. From Randolph, Old English (Randwulf), "Shield-wolf." Travis (country singer). Less popular for males, unusual for females. Alternative spellings: Randey, Randi, Randie.

Ranieri Italian. From Rayner, Old German, "Mighty army." Unusual.

Ranon Hebrew/Israeli. Hebrew, "To sing" or "to be joyous." Unusual. Alternative spelling: Ranen.

Ransom English. From Ransome. Olds (automobile inventor, established Olds Motor Works, which made the Oldsmobile). Unusual. Alternative spelling: Ransome.

Ranson English. From Ransom. Unusual.

Raoul French. From Ralph. Walsh (film director, "Strawberry Blond"); Dufy (French Fauvist painter); Feuillet (French dancer, choreographer); Valnay (French journalist, established "Le Soleil") (real name: Aimé Marie Édouard Hervé); Wallenberg (Swedish diplomat, saved Hungarian Jews). Less popular.

Raphael English. Hebrew, "God heals" or "God cures." Job 4:17. Saint; archangel mentioned in Book of Tobit; Abramowitz (Russian revolutionary, opposed Bolshevik Revolution); Holinshed (16th-century British chronicler, used as a historical source by Shakespeare); Meldola (British chemist, produced first oxazine dye). Less popular.

Rapier French. Middle French, "As strong as a sword." Unusual.

Rashid Turkish. Turkish, "Rightly guided." Unusual.

Raúl Hispanic. From Ralph, Anglo-Saxon, "Wolf-counsel." Julia (actor). Unusual.

Raulas Lithuanian. From Laurence, Latin, "Crowned with laurel." Unusual.

Raulo Lithuanian. From Laurence, Latin, "Crowned with laurel." Unusual.

Ravi Indo-Pakistani. Hindi, "Conferring." Also an alternate name for the Hindu sun god, Surya. Shankar (Indian sitar player); Batra (economist, "Downfall of Capitalism and Communism"). Unusual.

Raviv Hebrew/Israeli. Hebrew, "Rain" or "dew." Unusual.

Rawdon English. "Rough hill"; origin unknown. Surname and place name used as a first name. Crawley (character in Thackeray's "Vanity Fair"). Unusual.

Rawson English. Surname used as a first name; origin unknown. Unusual.

Ray English. From Raymond. Kroc (established McDonald's, 1955); Charles (jazz musician); Ewry (held Olympic record for high jump, 1900–08); Liotta (actor, "GoodFellas"); Baker (Pulitzer Prize-winning author, "Woodrow Wilson: Life and Letters") (real name of David Grayson). Unusual.

Rayhan Arabic. Arabic, "Favored by God." Unusual.

Rayment English. From Raymond. Unusual.

Raymond English. Old German, "Counsel-protection." Spruance (WWII admiral, won victory at Midway Island); Chandler (novelist, Philip Marlowe series); Hunthausen (liberal Seattle archbishop, defied pope); Burr (actor, "Perry Mason"); Hubbard (British, ran fastest three marathons in three days, 1988). Popular. Ray. Alternative spellings: Ramond, Raymund, Raymunde.

Rayner English. Old German, "Mighty army." Goddard, Baron (British, lord chief justice, 1946–58). Unusual. Alternative spellings: Rainor, Raynor.

Raz Hebrew/Israeli. From Razi. Unusual.

Razi Hebrew/Israeli. Aramaic, "My secret." Unusual.

Raziel Hebrew/Israeli. From Razi. Unusual.

Reagan English. From Regan, Irish, "Descended from the little king"; surname used as a first name. Unusual. Alternative spelling: Reagen.

Reave English. From Reeve. Unusual.

Redmond Irish. From Raymond. Barry, Sir (Irish colonial judge, founder and first chancellor of the University of Melbourne, Australia, 1853–80). Unusual.

Redvers English. Old French, surname and place name used as a first name. Buller (supreme commander of the British troops during the Boer War, 1899). Unusual.

Reed English. Old English, "Red-haired" or "ruddy-skinned"; surname used as a first name. Smoot (Utah senator, co-wrote the Smoot-Hawly Tariff Act, 1930). Less popular. Alternative spellings: Read, Reade, Reid.

Reese Welsh. From Rhys, Welsh, "Ardent." Unusual. Alternative spellings: Reece, Rees.

Reeve English. Middle English, "Bailiff." Unusual.

Reeves English. From Reeve. Unusual.

Reg English. From Reynold, Old English (Regenweald), "Counsel" + "power." Morris (British fire-eater, blew a flame a record 31 feet, 1986); Moores (British inventor of first radio-microphone, 1947). Less popular.

Regan English. Irish, "Descended from the little king"; surname used as a first name. Character in Shakespeare's "King Lear." Unusual for males, unusual for females. Alternative spelling: Regen.

Reginald English. From Reynold, Old English (Regenweald), "Counsel" + "power." Marsh (painter, "The Bowery"); Mitchell (British aircraft designer, designed Spitfire fighter, 1936); Pocock (British zoologist, classified animals by external features); Carey (British actor) (real name of Rex Harrison). Less popular. Reg, Reggie.

Reimond Romanian. From Raymond, Old German, "Counsel-protection." Unusual.

Reinold German. From Reynold, Old English (Regenweald), "Counsel" + "power." Unusual.

Reku Finnish. From Richard, Old German, "Strong ruler." Unusual.

Rem English. From Remington. Unusual.

Remington English. Old English, "From the raven's estate"; surname used as a first name. Steele (TV detective played by Pierce Brosnan). Unusual.

Remy English. From Remington. Saint; Belleau (16th-century French poet, "Petites inventions"); de Gourmont (19th-century French writer, "Le Latin mystique"). Unusual.

Renaldo American. From Reynold. Nehemiah (set 1981 world record for 110-meter hurdling: 12.93 seconds). Unusual. Alternative spelling: Rinaldo.

Renātus Latin. From Renata, Latin, "Reborn." Harris (18th-century British organ builder). Unusual.

Renauld American. From Reynold. Unusual.

Renault French. From Reynold. Unusual.

Rendor Hungarian. Hungarian, "Policeman." Unusual.

René French. From Renata, Latin, "Reborn." Bérenger (French politician, elected senator for life, 1875); Panhard (French automotive engineer); Descartes (17th-century French mathematician and philosopher, laid foundations of analytic geometry); Schick Gutierrez (president of Nicaragua, 1963–66). Unusual.

Renzo Italian. From Laurence, Latin, "Crowned with laurel." Unusual.

Reuben English. Hebrew (Reuven), "Behold a son." Genesis 29:32. First son of Jacob and Leah; Nakian (sculptor, bronze "Hiroshima"); Thwaites (historian, edited and wrote several historical novels). Unusual. Alternative spellings: Reuban, Reubin, Rubin, Rueben.

Reuven Hebrew/Israeli. Hebrew, "Behold a son." Genesis 29:32. Unusual.

Reuvin English. From Reuben. Unusual.

Rex English. Latin, "King." Harrison (British actor, "My Fair Lady") (real name: Reginald Carey); Stout (author of Nero Wolfe detective stories); Whistler (British illustrator, "Gulliver's Travels"); Reed (movie critic). Unusual.

Rey Hispanic. From Leroy, Old French, "The king." Unusual.

Reynaldo American. From Reynold. Hahn (Venezuelan classical composer). Unusual.

Reynold English. Old English (Regenweald), "Counsel" + "power." Nicholson (British Orientalist, wrote "Literary History of the Arabs"); Scott (16th-century British writer, "The Discoverie of Witchcraft"). Unusual. Alternative spelling: Renald.

Rez Hungarian. Hungarian, "With copper hair." Unusual for males, unusual for females.

Rezsö Hungarian. From Rudolph, Old German (Hrudolf), "Fame-wolf." Unusual.

Rhett Welsh. From Rhys. Butler (character in Mitchell's "Gone With the Wind"). Unusual.

Rhodes English. Latin, "Island of roses." Unusual. Alternative spelling: Rhoades.

Rhodri Welsh. Welsh, "Circle" + "ruler." Unusual.

Rhys Welsh. Welsh, "Ardent." Prichard (17th-century Welsh poet and clergyman). Unusual.

Ricard English. From Richard. Unusual.

Ricardo Hispanic. From Richard. Montalban (actor, "Fantasy Island"); Alfaro (president of Panama, 1931–32); Guiraldes (Argentine novelist); Jiménez (president of Costa Rica, 1910–14, 1924–28, 1932–36); Palma (Peruvian writer of prose sketches blending colonial Peruvian fact and fiction). Unusual. Alternative spelling: Riccardo.

Rice Welsh. From Rhys. Unusual.

Rich English. From Richard. Little (actor and impersonator). Less popular. Richie. Alternative spelling: Ritch.

Richard English. Old German, "Strong ruler." Saint; Hoe (invented rotary printing press, 1847); Sears (19th-century merchant, founded mail-order company); Feynman (physicist); Hofstadter (historian, "Age of Reform"); Steele (17th-century British playwright, "Conscious Lovers"); Cheney (secretary of defense under Bush). Popular. Dick, Rich, Richie, Rick, Ricky. Alternative spelling: Richerd.

Richards Latvian. From Richard. Unusual.

Richart German. From Richard. Unusual.

Richi Hispanic. From Richard. Unusual.

Richie Scottish. From Richard. Unusual.

Richmond English. French, "Hill richly covered in vegetation"; surname and place name used as a first name. Unusual.

Rick English. From Richard. Barry (basketball great, made 90% of all free throws attempted). Less popular. Ricky. Alternative spelling: Ric.

Rickard Swedish. From Richard. Unusual.

Rickert English. From Richard. Unusual.

Ricky English. From Richard. Nelson (singer and child actor). Less popular. Alternative spellings: Rickey, Ricki, Rickie.

Rico Hispanic. From Richard. Unusual.

Riczi Hungarian. From Richard. Unusual.

Riḍa See under Girls' Names.

Riel Hispanic. From Gabriel, Hebrew (Gavriel), "Hero of God" or "man of God." Daniel 8:16. Unusual.

Rihardos Greek. From Richard. Unusual.

Rihards Latvian. From Richard. Unusual.

Rikard Hungarian, Scandinavian. From Richard. Nordraak (19th-century Norwegian composer, wrote music for the national anthem). Unusual.

Riki Estonian. From Richard. Unusual.

Riks Estonian. From Richard. Unusual.

Riley English. Irish, "Valiant"; surname used as a first name. King (blues guitarist) (real name of B. B. King). Unusual. Alternative spelling: Reilly.

Rimon Hebrew/Israeli. Hebrew, "Pomegranate." Unusual.

Ringo Japanese. Japanese, "Apple." Starr (musician, the Beatles) (real name: Richard Starkey). Unusual.

Riobard Irish. From Robert. Unusual.

Rip Dutch. Dutch, "Ripe" or "full-grown." Torn (actor) (real name: Elmore Torn, Jr.). Unusual.

Ripley English. Old English, "From the shouter's meadow." Unusual.

Ripp English. From Ripley. Unusual.

Riqui Hispanic. From Richard. Unusual.

Risa Czech. From Richard. Unusual.

Risardas Lithuanian. From Richard. Unusual.

Risto Finnish. From Christopher, Greek, "One who carries Christ in his heart." Unusual.

Ritchie English. From Richard. Unusual. Alternative spellings: Richy, Ritchy.

Roald Scandinavian. Old German, "Famous ruler." Amundsen (Norwegian explorer, first to reach South Pole, 1911); Dahl (author of children's books). Unusual.

Rob English. From Robert. Roy (Scottish, designed Rob Roy canoe for river cruising) (real name: John MacGregor); Reiner (actor and director); Lowe (actor, "About Last Night"). Less popular. Alternative spelling: Robb.

Robbie See under Girls' Names.

Robby English. From Robert, Old English (Hreodbeorht), "Fame-bright." Benson (actor, "Ice Castles"). Less popular for males, unusual for females. Alternative spelling: Robbi.

Rober Hispanic. From Robert. Unusual.

Robers French. From Robert. Unusual.

Robert English. Old English (Hreodbeorht), "Fame-bright." Saint; Goddard (developed first liquid-fuel rocket); Benchley (humorist, "From Bed to Worse"); Penn Warren (first U.S. poet laureate); Redford (actor and director); Schumann (German classical composer); Taylor (actor) (real name: Spangler Brugh). Very popular. Bob, Bobby, Rob, Robbie.

Roberto Hispanic, Italian. From Robert. Rossellini (Italian film director); Ortiz (president of Argentina, 1938–40); Ardigò (Italian positivist philosopher); Bracco (Italian playwright); Ridolfi (Italian conspirator in England, 16th-century). Unusual.

Roberts English, Latvian. From Robertson. Surname used as a first name. Unusual.

Robertson English. "Son of Robert"; origin unknown. Surname used as a first name. Unusual.

Robi Hungarian. From Robert. Unusual.

Robin English. From Robert, Old English (Hreodbeorht), "Fame-bright." Williams (comic and actor, "Dead Poets Society"); Wright (actress); Collingwood (British philosopher and historian); Hood (British outlaw); Goodfellow (sprite) (real name of Puck). Less popular for males, less popular for females.

Robinet French. From Robert. Unusual.

Robinson English. From Robertson. Ellis (British, professor of Latin at Oxford); Jeffers (poet, "Be Angry at the Sun"); Crusoe (character in Daniel Defoe's novel). Unusual.

Robson English. From Robertson. Unusual.

Rocco Italian. German, "Repose." Unusual.

Rock English. Old English, "From the rock." Hudson (actor) (real name: Roy Fitzgerald). Unusual.

Rocky English. From Rock. Marciano (world heavyweight boxing champion, retired undefeated); Balboa (boxer played by Sylvester Stallone in movies); Graziano (boxer and author, "Somebody Up There Likes Me"). Unusual. Alternative spelling: Rockie.

Rod English. Created, a nickname for names beginning with "Rod-," like Roderick, Rodger, Rodman, and Rodney. Steiger (actor); Stewart (British rock singer); Sterling (creator of TV series "Twilight Zone"). Less popular. Alternative spelling: Rodd.

Rodas Hispanic. From Rhodes, Latin, "Island of roses." Unusual.

Roddy English. From Roderick. McDowall (British actor). Unusual. Alternative spelling: Roddie.

Roderich German. From Roderick. Benedix (19th-century German novelist). Unusual.

Roderick English. Old German (Hrodric), "Famous ruler." Last king of Visigoths in Spain, 710–11; Wallace (played pro baseball for 25 years, 1894–1918); Murchison (British geologist); character in Tobias Smollet's novel "Roderick Random"; character in Henry James' novel "Roderick Hudson." Unusual. Rod. Alternative spellings: Roderic, Rodric, Rodrich, Rodrick.

Rodge English. From Roger. Unusual.

Rodman English. Old English, "Famous" or "heroic." Unusual.

Rodney English. Anglo-Saxon, "Island clearing"; surname and place name used as a first name. Dangerfield (comic and actor); Porter (British biochemist, awarded 1972 Nobel Prize for physiology/medicine); character in Sir Arthur Conan Doyle's novel "Rodney Stone." Less popular. Rod.

Rodolfo Hispanic, Italian. From Rudolph, Old German (Hrudolf), "Fame-wolf." Graziani (Italian commander in Libya, 1940); character in Puccini's opera "La Bohème." Unusual.

Rodolph English. From Rudolph, Old German (Hrudolf), "Fame-wolf." Unusual.

Rodolphe French. From Rudolph, Old German (Hrudolf), "Fame-wolf." Töpffer (Swiss short-story writer); Bresdin (19th-century French etcher and lithographer); Kreutzer (French violinist and composer). Unusual.

Rodrigo Hispanic, Hungarian, Italian. From Roderick. de Bastidas (16th-century Spanish explorer in South America); Calderón (Spanish courtier); Cota de Maguaque (Spanish poet); Díaz de Bivar (11th-century Spanish military leader) (real name of El Cid). Unusual.

Rodriguez Hispanic. Spanish, "Son of Rodrigo"; surname used as a first name. Unusual. Alternative spelling: Rodrigues.

Rodrique French. From Roderick. Unusual.

Rog English. From Roger. Less popular.

Rogelio Hispanic. From Roger. Unusual.

Roger English. Old German (Hrodgar), "Fame-spear." of Ellant (saint); Bacon (British, invented telescopic lens, 13th-century); Kingdom (won Olympic gold medals for 110-meter hurdles, 1984, 1988); Moore (British actor in James Bond movies); Daltry (singer, the Who); Maris (baseball great). Less popular. Rog. Alternative spellings: Rodger, Rogar, Rogre.

Rogerio Hispanic. From Roger. Unusual.

Rogerios Hungarian. From Roger. Unusual.

Rogers English. "Son of Roger"; origin unknown. Surname used as a first name. Morton (secretary of interior under Nixon); Hornsby (baseball Hall of Famer, lifetime batting average .358). Unusual. Rog.

Rohan Irish. Irish, "Red"; surname used as a first name. Koda (Japanese writer) (real name: Koda Shigeyuki). Unusual.

Rohin Indo-Pakistani. East Indian, "On the upward path." Unusual.

Roi French, Indo-Pakistani. From Leroy, Old French, "The king." Adam (13th-century French trouvère, chief minstrel to Guy de Dampierre) (real name: Adenet le Roi). Unusual.

Rois Irish. From Rose, Latin, "rosa," a flower name used as a first name. Unusual.

Roisin Irish. From Rose, Latin, "rosa," a flower name used as a first name. Unusual.

Roland English. Old German (Hrodland), "Famous land." Dixon (anthropologist); Garros (French aviator, first to fly over Mediterranean); Perry (sculptor); Dorgelès (French writer) (real name: Roland Lecavele); Barthes (French critic). Less popular. Alternative spelling: Rolland.

Rolando Hispanic, Italian. From Roland. Unusual.

Roldán Hispanic. From Roland. Unusual.

Rolek Polish. From Roland. Unusual.

Rolf Scandinavian. From Rudolph, Old German (Hrudolf), "Fame-wolf." Boldrewood (Australian novelist) (real name: Thomas Browne). Unusual. Alternative spellings: Rolfe, Rolph.

Rolla English. From Roland. Unusual.

Rolle Swedish. From Roland. Unusual.

Rolli Estonian. From Richard, Old German, "Strong ruler." Unusual.

Rollie English. From Roland, Old German (Hrodland), "Famous land." Unusual for males, unusual for females. Alternative spelling: Rolly.

Rollin English. From Roland. Salisbury (geologist). Unusual.

Rollins English. From Roland. Unusual.

Rollo English. From Roland. Ogden (journalist); character in series of juvenile books by Jacob Abbott. Unusual.

Rolo Hispanic. From Rudolph, Old German (Hrudolf), "Fame-wolf." Unusual.

Rolon Hispanic. From Roland. Unusual. Alternative spelling: Rollon.

Romain French. French, "Roman." Gary (French novelist, "Roots of Heaven") (real name: Romain Kacew); Rolland (French, awarded 1915 Nobel Prize for literature). Unusual.

Romeo English. Italian, "Pilgrim who visited Rome." Montague (character in Shakespeare's "Romeo and Juliet"). Unusual.

Romney Welsh. Old Welsh, "River that curves." Unusual.

Ron English. From Reynold, Old English (Regenweald), "Counsel" + "power." Less popular. Alternative spelling: Ronn.

Ronald English. From Reynold, Old English (Regenweald), "Counsel" + "power." Reagan (40th president); McNair (first black astronaut); Gallagher (gave longest sermon: 120 hours, 1983); McKerrow (British publisher); Norrish (British chemist, won 1967 Nobel Prize); Colman (actor, won 1947 Oscar for "Double Life"). Popular. Ron, Ronnie.

Ronan Irish. Irish, "Little seal." Saint; Coghlan (Irish author, "Irish Christian Names"). Unusual.

Ronel Hebrew/Israeli. From Roni. Unusual.

Roni Hebrew/Israeli. Hebrew, "Joy is mine." Unusual for males, unusual for females.

Ronli See under Girls' Names.

Ronny English. From Reynold, Old English (Regenweald), "Counsel" + "power." Unusual. Alternative spellings: Ronney, Ronni, Ronnie.

Rory English. Gaelic, "Red." Calhoun (actor) (real name: Francis Durgin); Blackwell (one-man band with most instruments: 314); O'More (name of three Irish rebel chieftains). Less popular.

Rosario Italian. From Russell, French, "Red-haired" or "red-faced"; surname used as a first name. Unusual.

Rosertas Lithuanian. From Robert, Old English (Hreodbeorht), "Fame-bright." Unusual.

Ross English. Gaelic, "Cape" or "promontory"; surname and place name used as a first name. Harrison (biologist); Macdonald (writer, created detective Lew Archer, "Barbarous Coast") (real name: Kenneth Millar); Smith, Sir (Australian aviator, made first flight from Cairo to Calcutta, 1918); Hunter (movie producer). Less popular. Alternative spelling: Rosse.

Rossy English. From Ross. Unusual. Alternative spellings: Rosse, Rossie.

Rostik Russian. From Richard, Old German, "Strong ruler." Unusual.

Rostislav Russian. From Richard, Old German, "Strong ruler." Unusual.

Rostya Russian. From Richard, Old German, "Strong ruler." Unusual.

Rosy See Rosie under Girls' Names.

Roth English. Old German, "Red-haired" or "ruddy-skinned." Unusual.

Rousse French. From Rush, French, "Red-haired." Unusual.

Rouvin Greek. From Reuben, Hebrew (Reuven), "Behold a son." Genesis 29 : 32. Unusual.

Rowan English. Irish, "Red." Unusual.

Rowe English. From Roland, Old German (Hrodland), "Famous land." Unusual.

Rowland English. From Roland, Old German (Hrodland), "Famous land." Taylor (British Protestant martyr); Hill (reformed British postal system). Unusual.

Rowlands English. English, surname used as a first name. Unusual.

Rowlandson English. English, surname used as a first name. Unusual.

Rowley English. English, "Rough clearing." Unusual.

Roy English. Gaelic, "Red." Rogers (singing cowboy) (real name: Leonard Slye); Orbison (rock singer, "Pretty Woman"); "Dizzy" Carlyle (longest home run: 618 feet); Wilkins (civil rights leader); Andrews (explored Alaska and central Asia). Less popular.

Royal English. French, "Like a king." Cortissoz (art critic, opposed modernism); House (invented printing telegraph); Ingersoll (naval officer, commanded Atlantic fleet, 1942–44). Unusual.

Royce English. English, surname of uncertain origin. Possibly from Old German, "Fame-kind," or Old English, "King's son." Unusual.

Royd Scandinavian. Old Norse, "From the forest clearing." Unusual.

Royden English. English, "Hill where rye grows." Unusual. Alternative spelling: Roydon.

Royston English. English, surname and place name used as a first name. Unusual. Alternative spelling: Roystan.

Rube English. From Reuben, Hebrew (Reuven), "Behold a son." Genesis 29 : 32. Unusual.

Ruben German. From Reuben, Hebrew (Reuven), "Behold a son." Genesis 29 : 32. Darío (Nicaraguan poet) (real name: Félix García Sarmiento). Unusual.

Rubert Czech. From Robert, Old English (Hreodbeorht), "Fame-bright." Unusual.

Ruberto Italian. From Robert, Old English (Hreodbeorht), "Fame-bright." Unusual.

Ruby See under Girls' Names.

Ruda Czech. From Rudolph, Old German (Hrudolf), "Fame-wolf." Unusual.

Rudbert German. From Robert, Old English (Hreodbeorht), "Fame-bright." Unusual.

Rude Slavic. From Rudolph. Unusual.

Rudek Czech. From Rudolph. Unusual.

Rudi Hispanic. From Rudolph. Blesh (jazz historian). Less popular.

Rüdiger German. From Roger, Old German (Hrodgar), "Fame-spear." von der Goltz (German general, occupied Helsinki, 1918, and Riga, 1919). Unusual.

Rudland German. From Roland, Old German (Hrodland), "Famous land." Unusual.

Rudo African. African, "Love." Unusual.

Rudolf German. From Rudolph. Wolf (Swiss astronomer); Lotze (German philosopher); Abel (Russian spy in U.S.); Bartsch (Austrian novelist); Baumbach (German poet); Rassendyll (character in Anthony Hope's "Prisoner of Zenda"); Friml (light-opera composer, "Firefly"). Unusual.

Rudolfs Latvian. From Rudolph. Unusual.

Rudolph English. Old German (Hrudolf), "Fame-wolf." Valentino (actor, "Sheik") (real name: Rodolpho d'Antonguolla); Ackermann (German, invented method to waterproof paper and cloth); Reti (Serbian classical composer); Steiner (Austrian philosopher, invented anthroposophy). Unusual. Rudy.

Rudolpho Italian. From Rudolph. Unusual. Alternative spelling: Rudolfo.

Rudolphus English. From Rudolph. Unusual. Rudy.

Rudy English. From Rudolph. Vallee

(band leader and singer) (real name: Hubert Prior). Unusual. Alternative spelling: Rudie.

Rufo Hispanic. From Rudolph. Unusual.

Rufus English. Latin, "Red" or "red-haired." Saint; Greek physician; Avienus (Roman poet); Gilbert (invented elevated railway system); Isaacs (British ambassador to U.S.); Peckham (Supreme Court Justice, 1896–1909); Putnam (officer in American Revolution and pioneer); Jones (religious leader, established American Friends Service Committee). Unusual.

Ruggerio Italian. From Roger, Old German (Hrodgar), "Fame-spear." di Lauria (13th-century Italian naval commander, led Aragonese fleet against French). Unusual.

Ruggero Italian. From Roger, Old German (Hrodgar), "Fame-spear." Leoncavallo (Italian composer in verismo style, "Pagliacci"). Unusual.

Ruland German. From Roland, Old German (Hrodland), "Famous land." Unusual.

Rupert German. From Robert, Old English (Hreodbeorht), "Fame-bright." Saint; German king, 1400–10; Brooke (British poet); Hammerling (Austrian poet) (real name of Robert Hamerling); Murdoch (renegade Australian publisher); character in Anthony Hope's novel "Rupert of Hentzau." Unusual.

Ruperto Italian. From Robert, Old English (Hreodbeorht), "Fame-bright." Unusual.

Ruprecht German. From Robert, Old English (Hreodbeorht), "Fame-bright." Unusual.

Rurich Russian. From Roderick, Old German (Hrodric), "Famous ruler." Unusual.

Rurik Slavic. From Roderick, Old German (Hrodric), "Famous ruler." Scandinavian Varangian prince, established 16th-century Rurik dynasty in Russia. Unusual.

Rush English. French, "Red-haired." Unusual.

Russ English. From Russell. Less popular. Alternative spelling: Rus.

Russell English. French, "Red-haired" or "red-faced"; surname used as a first name. Alger (secretary of war under McKinley, 1897–99); Sage (financier); Varian (physicist, researched microwaves). Less popular. Russ. Alternative spelling: Russel.

Rusty English. From Russell. Less popular. Russ. Alternative spelling: Rustie.

Rutger English. From Roger, Old German (Hrodgar), "Fame-spear." Schimelpenninck (Dutch politician). Unusual. Alternative spelling: Ruttger.

Rutherford English. Scottish, "Red crossing." Hayes (19th president). Unusual.

Rutz German. From Rudolph, Old German (Hrudolf), "Fame-wolf." Unusual.

Ruvim Russian. From Reuben, Hebrew (Reuven), "Behold a son." Genesis 29:32. Unusual.

Ruy Hispanic. From Roderick, Old German (Hrodric), "Famous ruler." Lopez (Spanish bishop); González de Clavijo (Spanish diplomat). Unusual.

Ryan English. Irish, surname of unknown meaning, possibly "little king." White (heroic child AIDS victim); O'Neal (actor, "Love Story"). Very popular for males, less popular for females. Alternative spelling: Ryon.

Rye Polish. From Richard, Old German, "Strong ruler." Unusual.

Ryne English. From Ryan, Irish, surname of unknown meaning, possibly "little king." Sandberg (baseball player, Chicago Cubs). Less popular.

Rysio Polish. From Richard, Old German, "Strong ruler." Unusual.

Ryszard Polish. From Richard, Old German, "Strong ruler." Berwinski (19th-century Polish poet and revolutionary). Unusual.

Saburo Japanese. Japanese, "Third-born son." Ouchi (Japanese, drove record 167,770 miles across 91 countries, 1969–78). Unusual.

Sacha Russian. From Alexander, Greek, "Defender of men" or "warding off men." Mark 16:21; Acts 4:6, 19:33. Unusual.

Sachar Russian. From Zachariah, Hebrew, "The Lord has remembered." Unusual.

Sacharja German. From Zachariah, Hebrew, "The Lord has remembered." Unusual.

Saddam Arabic. Arabic, meaning unknown. Unusual.

Sadler English. English, "Maker of saddles"; occupational surname used as a first name. Unusual.

Sagar English. Old English, "Victory people." Unusual.

Sahale Native American. Native American, "Above." Unusual.

Sahen Indo-Pakistani. Hindi, "Falcon." Unusual.

Saʿīd Arabic. Arabic, "Happy." Halim Pasa (Turkish politician); ibn Sultan (ruler of Muscat, Oman, and Zanzibar, 1806–56); Pasha (Ottoman viceroy of Egypt, 1854–63). Unusual.

Sakari Finnish. From Zachariah, Hebrew, "The Lord has remembered." Yrjö-Koskinen (19th-century historian, wrote first history of Finland in Finnish) (real name: Georg Zachris Forsman). Unusual.

Sakarias Scandinavian. From Zachariah, Hebrew, "The Lord has remembered." Unusual.

Sakarja Scandinavian. From Zachariah, Hebrew, "The Lord has remembered." Unusual.

Sakima Native American. Native American, "King." Unusual.

Salamen Polish. From Solomon, Hebrew, "Peace." Unusual.

Salamon Hispanic (Salamón), Hungarian, Norwegian. From Solomon, Hebrew, "Peace." Unusual.

Salamun Czech. From Solomon, Hebrew, "Peace." Unusual.

Salaun French. From Solomon, Hebrew, "Peace." Unusual.

Sāliḥ Arabic. Arabic, "Right" or "good." Ayyub (13th-century Egyptian ruler). Unusual.

Salīm Arabic. Arabic, "Peace" or "safe." Unusual. Alternative spelling: Saleem.

Salmalin Indo-Pakistani. Hindi, "Taloned." Another name for Garunda, the Hindu god Vishnu's half-eagle, half-giant carrier. Unusual.

Salom English. From Solomon, Hebrew, "Peace." Unusual.

Salomo German. From Solomon, Hebrew, "Peace." Unusual.

Salomon French. From Solomon, Hebrew, "Peace." Maimon (German philosopher); van Ruysdael (Dutch Baroque landscape painter); Sulzer (Austrian composer, called "father of modern synagogue music"); Rothschild (Jewish financier); Gessner (18th-century Swiss poet and landscape painter). Unusual.

Salomone Italian. From Solomon, Hebrew, "Peace." Rossi (Italian composer at court of Mantua). Unusual.

Salvador Hispanic. From Salvatore. Dali (surrealist painter); Allende (elected president of Chile, 1970); de Madariaga y Rojo (Spanish writer). Unusual.

Salvatore Italian. Latin, "Savior." Marchesi (Italian baritone); Quasimodo (Italian poet); Vigano (Italian ballet dancer and choreographer); Cammarano (Italian librettist); Di Giacomo (Italian novelist). Unusual.

Sam English. From Samuel. Marx (movie producer); Kinison (comedian); Patch (daredevil: dived from cliffs, often with bear); Slick (Canadian humorist, created Sam Slick character) (real name: Thomas Haliburton); Weller (character in Dickens' "Pickwick Papers"); Spade (detective character). Unusual.

Samaru Japanese. From Samuel. Unusual.

Samein Arabic. From Simon, Hebrew (Shimon), "God heard." Genesis 29:33. Unusual.

Samie Hungarian. From Samuel. Unusual.

Samīr Arabic. Arabic, "Entertainer." Sawan al Aw (swam record 49.04 miles underwater in 24 hours with sub-aqua gear). Unusual.

Samko Czech. From Samuel. Unusual.

Samman Arabic. Arabic, "Grocer." Unusual. Alternative spelling: Sammon.

Sammel English. From Samuel. Unusual.

Sammy English. From Samuel, Hebrew (Shmuel), "His name is God" or "God has heard." 1 Samuel 1:20. Davis, Jr. (actor and singer, "Tap"). Less popular for males, unusual for females. Sam. Alternative spelling: Sammie.

Samo Czech. From Samuel. 7th-century Frankish merchant, controlled much of Austria. Unusual.

Samouel Greek. From Samuel. Unusual.

Samson English. Hebrew, "Sun." Judges 13. Saint; biblical man of strength; of Tottington (British abbot of Abbey of Bury St. Edmunds, 1182–1212, brought material and moral increase); Raphaelson (playwright, "Jazz Singer"); Hirsch (German theologian); François (French pianist). Unusual. Alternative spelling: Sampson.

Samu Hungarian. From Samuel. Unusual.

Samuel English. Hebrew (Shmuel), "His name is God" or "God has heard." 1 Samuel 1:20. One of Saul's commanders; Pepys (British writer on Navy and court); Blatchford (Supreme Court Justice, 1882–93); de Champlain (French, discovered Canadian interior); Cunard (led trans-Atlantic navigation); Eliot Morison (historian); Gompers (established AFL); Clemens (writer) (real name of Mark Twain). Popular. Sam, Sammy.

Samuele Italian. From Samuel. Unusual.

Samuelis Lithuanian. From Samuel. Unusual.

Samuil Bulgarian, Russian. From Samuel. Petrovsky-Sitnianovich (17th-century Byelorussian monk, tutored Czar Alexis's children). Unusual.

Samvel Russian. From Samuel. Unusual.

Sande English. From Alexander, Greek, "Defender of men" or "warding off men." Mark 16:21; Acts 4:6, 19:33. Unusual.

Sandeep See under Girls' Names.

Sander English. From Alexander, Greek, "Defender of men" or "warding off men." Mark 16:21; Acts 4:6, 19:33. Unusual.

Sanders English. From Alexander, Greek, "Defender of men" or "warding off men." Mark 16:21; Acts 4:6, 19:33. Unusual.

Sanderson English. From Alexander, Greek, "Defender of men" or "warding off men." Mark 16:21; Acts 4:6, 19:33. Unusual.

Sandford English. Old English, "Sandy crossing." Fleming, Sir (Canadian, chief engineer of Canadian Pacific railroad). Unusual.

Sándor Hungarian. From Alexander, Greek, "Defender of men" or "warding off men." Mark 16:21; Acts 4:6, 19:33. Ferenczi (Hungarian psychoanalyst); Kisfaludy (Hungarian writer of songs and poetry); Petőfi (Hungarian poet); Wekerle (Hungarian premier, 1892–95, 1906–10, 1917–18). Unusual.

Sandy See under Girls' Names.

Sanford English. From Sandford. Character on TV show "Sanford and Sons." Less popular. Sandy.

Sansao Portuguese. From Samson. Unusual.

Sanson English, Hispanic. From Samson. Unusual.

Sansone Italian. From Samson. Unusual.

Sansum English. From Samson. Unusual.

Santiago Hispanic. Spanish, "Saint." Liniers (Spanish naval officer); Pérez (Colombian politician); Ramón (Spanish history professor); Rusiñol y Prats (Spanish painter). Unusual.

Santo Hispanic, Italian. Spanish, "Sacred" or "saintly." Unusual.

Santosh Indo-Pakistani. Hindi, "Satisfaction." Unusual.

Sanyi Hungarian. From Alexander, Greek, "Defender of men" or "warding off men." Mark 16:21; Acts 4:6, 19:33. Unusual.

Sarad Indo-Pakistani. Hindi, "Born in the fall." Unusual.

Sargent English. English, a legal officer. Unusual. Alternative spellings: Sargant, Sargeant, Sarjent.

Sarito Hispanic. From Caesar, Latin (Caesarius), "Hairy child." Unusual.

Sarngin Indo-Pakistani. Hindi, "Archer." Another name for the Hindu god Vishnu, who carries a bow. Unusual.

Sarojin Indo-Pakistani. Hindi, "Like the lotus," a holy flower. Unusual.

Sascha Russian. From Alexander, Greek, "Defender of men" or "warding off men." Mark 16:21; Acts 4:6, 19:33. Unusual for males, unusual for females.

Sashenka Russian. From Alexander, Greek, "Defender of men" or "warding off men." Mark 16:21; Acts 4:6, 19:33. Unusual.

Sashka Russian. From Alexander, Greek, "Defender of men" or "warding off men." Mark 16:21; Acts 4:6, 19:33. Unusual.

Saul English. From Shaul, Hebrew, "Asked-for" or "requested of God". 1 Samuel 9:2. Bellow (novelist, "Rain King"); Tchernichowsky (Israeli poet); Alinsky (pioneer community organizer). Less popular.

Saunders English. From Alexander, Greek, "Defender of men" or "warding off men." Mark 16:21; Acts 4:6, 19:33. Unusual.

Saunderson English. From Alexander, Greek, "Defender of men" or "warding off men." Mark 16:21; Acts 4:6, 19:33. Unusual.

Saverio Italian. From Xavier, Spanish, "New house." Mercadante (19th-century Italian classical composer); Bettinelli (18th-century Italian writer and critic). Unusual.

Savil English. From Savilla. Unusual. Alternative spellings: Savile, Savill, Saville.

Savilla English. French, surname and place name used as a first name. Unusual.

Sawney Scottish. From Alexander, Greek, "Defender of men" or "warding off men." Mark 16:21; Acts 4:6, 19:33. Unusual. Alternative spellings: Sawnie, Sawny.

Saxon English. German, the name of an early Germanic tribe, possibly meaning "axe." Unusual.

Schmuel Yiddish. From Samuel, Hebrew (Shmuel), "His name is God" or "God has heard." 1 Samuel 1:20. Unusual.

Schuyler Dutch. Dutch, "Scholar." Colfax (vice-president under Grant, 1869–73). Unusual.

Scott English. Old English, "Native of Scotland." Joplin (composed ragtime music); Hamilton (1981 world champion figure skater); SorLokken (gave longest name to his daughter: 622 letters); Turow (novelist,"Presumed Innocent"); Glen (actor, "Urban Cowboy"). Very popular. Scotty. Alternative spelling: Scot.

Scotty English. From Scott. Less popular. Alternative spellings: Scotti, Scottie.

Seamus Irish. From Jacob, Hebrew (Yaakov), "Supplanter" or "heel." Genesis 25:26. Unusual.

Sean Irish. From John, Hebrew (Yochanan), "God has been gracious." O'Casey (Irish playwright, "Juno and the Paycock"); Connery (British actor, James Bond films); O'Kelly (president, Republic of Ireland, 1945–59); Slade (record producer); Penn (actor, "Fast Times at Ridgemont High"). Popular. Alternative spelling: Seann.

Seasar English. From Caesar, Latin (Caesarius), "Hairy child." Unusual. Alternative spellings: Caesar, Caezar, Cesar, Cesare, Sezar.

Seaton English. English, "Settlement by the sea"; surname and place name used as a first name. Unusual.

Sebastian English. Latin, "Man from Sebastia," a city in Asia Minor. Saint; character in Shakespeare's "Twelfth Night," "Tempest"; Coe (British, Olympic gold medal for 1500-meter run, 1980, 1984); Cabot (16th-century explorer, led Spanish expedition to South America); Münster (16th-century German scholar, wrote first description of world in German). Less popular.

Sébastien French. From Sebastian. de Vauban (French military engineer, invented socket bayonet); Bourdon (French painter, established Academy of Painting and Sculpture, 1648); Chamfort (18th-century French writer of comedies). Unusual.

Sebert English. English, "Sea-bright"; surname used as a first name. Unusual.

Sef Egyptian. Egyptian, "Yesterday." Also a lion god. Unusual.

Sefton English. English, "Settlement in the rushes"; a surname and place name used as a first name. Unusual.

Segel English. Hebrew, "Treasure." Unusual.

Seif Arabic. Arabic, "Sword of religion." Unusual.

Seifert German. From Sigfrid, Old German, "Victory-peace." Unusual.

Seifried German. From Sigfrid, Old German, "Victory-peace." Unusual.

Selah Hebrew/Israeli. Hebrew, musical term indicating a musical interlude or a change in the instrumentation of a psalm. Unusual for males, unusual for females.

Selby English. English, "Willow-farm"; a surname and place name used as a first name. Unusual.

Selim English. From Solomon, Hebrew, "Peace." Ottoman sultan (I, 1467-III, 1789); Palmgren (Finnish pianist and composer). Unusual.

Selvin English. From Selwyn. Unusual.

Selwyn English. Latin, "Of the woods" or "wild, savage." Lloyd (19th-century British bishop of New Zealand). Unusual.

Sem English. From Samuel, Hebrew (Shmuel), "His name is God" or "God has heard." 1 Samuel 1:20. Benelli (Italian dramatist). Unusual.

Semon Greek. From Simon, Hebrew (Shimon), "God heard." Genesis 29:33. Unusual.

Sen Japanese. Japanese, "Wood fairy." Suggests longevity. Unusual for males, unusual for females.

Senón Hispanic. Spanish, "Living" or "given by Zeus." Unusual.

Senwe African. African, "Dry grain stalk." Refers to child's appearance. Unusual.

Sepp German. From Joseph, Hebrew (Yosef), "God will add." Unusual.

Septimus Latin. Latin, "Seventh." Odaenathus (3rd-century prince of Palmyra); Winner (songwriter, "Oh Where, Oh Where Has My Little Dog Gone?"). Unusual.

Serg Polish. From Sergius. Unusual.

Serge French. From Sergius. Testa (French, sailed in smallest boat around the world: 11 feet, 10 inches); Lifar (French dancer, choreographer, and writer on dance); Poliakoff (French abstract painter); Koussevitzky (orchestra conductor; organized Berkshire Music Festival). Unusual.

Sergeant English. From Sargent, English, a legal officer. Unusual.

Sergei Russian. From Sergius. Rachmaninov (Russian; greatest finger span on the piano: 12 white keys); Ignatov (Russian, juggles record 11 rings); Eisenstein (film maker). Unusual.

Sergey Russian. From Sergius. Bubka (Russian, holds 8 of 10 longest pole vault records since 1989: around 19 feet, 10 inches); Yesenin (Russian poet); Aksakov (Russian novelist); Bulgakov (Russian theologian). Unusual. Alternative spellings: Sergi, Sergie.

Sergeyka Russian. From Sergius. Unusual.

Sergio Italian. From Sergius. Osmena (founder of Nationalist party in Philippines). Unusual.

Sergius German. Latin, "Servant"; a Roman clan name. Saint; name of four popes. Unusual.

Sergiusz Polish. From Sergius. Unusual.

Sergo Russian. From Sergius. Unusual.

Sergunya Russian. From Sergius. Unusual.

Serhiy Russian. From Sergius. Unusual.

Serhiyko Russian. From Sergius. Unusual.
Serzh Russian. From Sergius. Unusual.
Seth Hebrew/Israeli. Hebrew, "To put or "to set," or "substitute," "compensation," or "appointed." "She bore a son and called his name Seth, for she said, 'God has appointed for me another child'." Genesis 4:25. Son of Adam and Eve; Ward (British astronomer, debated Hobbes); Kalwitz (German composer); Thomas (clock maker); Warner (American officer during Revolution; present with Ethan Allen and Benedict Arnold at Ticonderoga). Popular.
Seton English. From Seaton, English, "Settlement by the sea"; surname and place name used as a first name. Unusual.
Seumas Scottish. From Jacob, Hebrew (Yaakov), "Supplanter" or "heel." Genesis 25:26. O'Kelly (Irish writer); O'Sullivan (Irish poet, founded "Dublin" magazine) (real name: James Starkey). Unusual.
Sevilen Turkish. Turkish, "Beloved one." Unusual.
Seward English. From Seward. Unusual.
Sewati Native American. Native American, "Curving of the bear's claws." Unusual.
Sewek Polish. From Sergius. Unusual.
Seymour English. French, place name (St. Maur) used as a first name. Hicks, Sir (British actor and writer). Less popular. Sy. Alternative spellings: Seamor, Seamore, Seamour.
Shad English. From Chad, Celtic, "Defender." Unusual.
Shadrach English. Babylonian, possibly a reference to Aku, the sun god. One of Daniel's three biblical companions; Babylonian name for Hananiah. Unusual. Alternative spelling: Shadrack.
Shaiming Chinese. Chinese, "Life of sunshine." Unusual.
Shaine English. From John, Hebrew (Yochanan), "God has been gracious." Unusual. Alternative spellings: Shane, Shayn, Shayne.
Shaka African. African, origin and meaning unknown. Founder of Zulu empire (19th-century), conquered most of South Africa. Unusual for males, unusual for females.
Shalom Hebrew/Israeli. Hebrew, "Hello," "good-bye," "peace." Abramovich (Russian Jewish writer); Aleichem (Russian Jewish humorist) (real name: Sholem Rabinowitz). Unusual. Alternative spelling: Sholom.
Shamir Hebrew/Israeli. Hebrew, a hard, precious stone possibly used in building Solomon's temple. Unusual.
Shamus Irish. From Jacob, Hebrew (Yaakov), "Supplanter" or "heel." Genesis 25:26. Unusual.
Shanahan Irish. Gaelic, "Wise one." Unusual.
Shanan See Shannon under Girls' Names.
Shandy English. Old English, "Little and rambunctious." Unusual. Alternative spelling: Shandie.
Shannan See Shannon under Girls' Names.
Shannon See under Girls' Names.
Shanon See Shannon under Girls' Names.
Sharad Indo-Pakistani. Hindi, "Autumn." Unusual.
Sharīf Arabic. Arabic, "Honest"; surname used as a first name. Unusual. Alternative spelling: Shariff.
Shaul Hebrew/Israeli. Hebrew, "Asked-for" or "requested of God." 1 Samuel 9:2. First king of Israel. Unusual.
Shaun English. From John, Hebrew (Yochanan), "God has been gracious." Unusual for males, unusual for females.
Shavar Unknown. Meaning and origin unknown. Unusual.
Shaw English. English, "Wood"; surname and place name used as a first name. Unusual.
Shawn American. From John, Hebrew (Yochanan), "God has been gracious." Weatherly (actress). Popular for males, less popular for females.
Shea English. Hebrew, "Asked-for." Less popular for males, unusual for females.
Sheehan Irish. Gaelic, "Peaceful little one." Unusual.
Shelah See Sheila under Girls' Names.
Shelby See under Girls' Names.
Sheldon English. English, "Steep-sided valley"; surname and place name used as a first name. Cheney (author and critic, established "Theater Arts" magazine); Glueck (criminologist and author); Jackson (missionary and educator); Harnick (lyricist, "Fiddler on the Roof"). Less popular.
Shelley See under Girls' Names.
Shelomoh Yiddish. From Solomon, Hebrew, "Peace." Unusual.
Shelton English. English, "Settlement on a high plateau"; surname and place name used as a first name. Unusual.
Shem English, Hebrew/Israeli, Hispanic. From Samuel, Hebrew (Shmuel), "His name is God" or "God has heard." 1 Samuel 1:20. Noah's oldest son; Ibn Shem Tov (Spanish Jewish theologian and philosopher, an ardent Cabbalist who opposed rationalist Judaism). Unusual.
Shemuel Yiddish. From Samuel, Hebrew (Shmuel), "His name is God" or "God has heard." 1 Samuel 1:20. Unusual.
Shen Chinese, Chinese; and Egyptian, Egyptian, "Sacred amulet." In the Egyptian "Book of the Dead," the amulet symbolizes eternal life. It was set near the feet of the dead. Yen-ping (Chinese realist novelist) (real name of Mao Tun); Shen-yueh (6th-century Chinese courtier, classified the four tones of the Chinese language); Chou (led Wu school of Chinese painting); Kua (Chinese official, engineer, and astronomer). Unusual.
Shepherd English. English, occupational surname used as a first name. Unusual. Shep. Alternative spellings: Shephard, Sheppard.
Sherborn English. Old English, "Out of the pure, clear brook." Unusual. Alternative spelling: Sherborne.
Sherburne English. From Sherborn. Burnham (astronomer, discovered 1,290 new double stars). Unusual. Alternative spelling: Sherburn.
Sheridan English. Irish, surname used as a first name. Le Fanu (Irish novelist, "Uncle Silas"); Morley (British writer and son of actor Robert); Downey (senator). Unusual. Alternative spelling: Sheridon.
Sherman English. Anglo-Saxon, "Cutter of cloth." Original form of the name was "Shearman." Minton (Supreme Court Justice, 1949–56); Adams (White House chief of staff, 1953–58); Hemsley (film actor). Less popular.
Shimon Hebrew/Israeli. Hebrew, "God heard." Genesis 29:33. Unusual.
Shing Chinese. Chinese, "Victory." Unusual.

Shiro Japanese. Japanese, "Fourth-born son." Tashiro (biochemist, invented biometer). Unusual.

Shlomo Hebrew/Israeli. Hebrew, "Peace." Yitzaqi (11th-century French rabbi, wrote commentaries on Talmud) (real name of Rashi). Unusual.

Shmuel Hebrew/Israeli. Hebrew, "His name is God" or "God has heard." 1 Samuel 1:20. Unusual.

Sholto Scottish. Gaelic, "Propagator" or "sower." A Scottish clan name. Unusual.

Shurik Russian. From Alexander, Greek, "Defender of men" or "warding off men." Mark 16:21; Acts 4:6, 19:33. Unusual.

Si French. From Sidney, Old French, "From Saint-Denis." A Norman surname derived from a village named for a saint. Unusual.

Siarl Welsh. From Charles, Old English, "ceorl" ("man" or "husbandman"). Unusual.

Sid English. From Sidney, Old French, "From Saint-Denis." A Norman surname derived from a village named for a saint. Grauman (theater magnate, Grauman's Chinese Theater); Sheinberg (Universal Film Studio executive); Vicious (rock musician); Caesar (comedian); Field (British entertainer). Unusual. Alternative spellings: Cyd, Syd.

Siddy English. From Sidney, Old French, "From Saint-Denis." A Norman surname derived from a village named for a saint. Unusual. Alternative spelling: Siddie.

Sidon French. From Sidney, Old French, "From Saint-Denis." A Norman surname derived from a village named for a saint. Unusual.

Sidonio Hispanic. From Sidney, Old French, "From Saint-Denis." A Norman surname derived from a village named for a saint. Da Silva (Portuguese politician; president, 1917–18). Unusual.

Sidwell English. English, "Wide stream"; surname and place name used as a first name. Saint. Unusual.

Siegfried German. From Sigfrid. Sassoon (British writer and biographer); Marcus (German inventor of autos and electric devices); Nadel (Austrian anthropologist, "Theory of Social Structure"); Ochs (German conductor, established Philharmonischer Chor, 1882); Passarge (German geographer). Unusual.

Siegmund German. From Sigmund. Unusual.

Siffre French. From Sigfrid. Unusual.

Sig English. From Sigfrid. Unusual.

Sigefriedo Italian. From Sigfrid. Unusual.

Sigfrid English. Old German, "Victory-peace." Saint (abbot of Wearmouth, 686); Karg-Elert (19th-century German composer, virtuoso organist at Leipzig Conservatory). Unusual.

Sigfrido Hispanic. From Sigfrid. Unusual.

Sigfroi French. From Sigfrid. Unusual.

Sigifredo Hispanic. From Sigfrid. Unusual.

Sigismund German. From Sigmund. Unusual.

Sigmund German. German, "Shield of victory." Mowinckel (Norwegian theologian and Old Testament scholar); Romberg (operetta composer, "Student Prince"); Spaeth (writer on music, "Fun with Music"); Freud (Austrian neurologist, founder of psychoanalysis). Unusual.

Siguefredo Portuguese. From Sigfrid. Unusual.

Sigurd Scandinavian. Old Norse, "Victorious guardian," a reference to a mythical hero. I and II (12th-century Norse kings); Hoel (Norwegian novelist). Unusual.

Sigvard Norwegian. From Sigfrid. Unusual.

Silas Latin. From Silva, Latin, "Woods." Saint (companion to Paul); Mitchell (19th-century physician and author of books and novels on medicine); Pratt (19th-century composer, wrote opera "Zenobia"); Talbot (18th-century naval officer, commanded U.S.S. Constitution); Deane (18th-century lawyer, member of Continental Congress). Unusual.

Sill English. From Silence, Latin, "silens." Puritan name, emphasizing learning in silence. Unusual for males, unusual for females.

Silvain French. From Silva, Latin, "Woods." Unusual.

Sim English. From Simon. Unusual.

Sima Hebrew/Israeli. Aramaic, "Treasure." Unusual.

Simao Portuguese. From Simon. Unusual.

Simen Gypsy. English Gypsy, "Alike" or "equal," referring to the comparative status of infant and parents. Unusual.

Simeon English, Russian. From Simon. Saint (4th-century, first of several to live in austerity atop pillars up to 60 feet high for 30 years); Poisson (French mathematician, specialized in magnetism and electricity); the Great (Bulgarian sovereign); of Durham (12th-century British monk and chronicler). Unusual. Sim.

Simion French, Romanian. From Simon. Unusual.

Simm English. From Simon. Unusual.

Simms English. From Simon. Unusual.

Simmy German. From Simon. Unusual.

Simon English. Hebrew (Shimon), "God heard." Genesis 29:33. Second son of Jacob and Leah; Saint (1st-century apostle); Colines (15th-century French printer, designed Garamond typeface); Mpadi (Congolese, fostered nationalism); Stevin (16th-century Dutch mathematician); Langham (archbishop of Canterbury, 1366); Bolívar (freed South America from Spanish rule). Less popular. Alternative spellings: Cimon, Cymon, Symon.

Simone See under Girls' Names.

Simpson Hebrew/Israeli. English, "Son of Simon"; surname used as a first name. Unusual.

Simson Swedish. From Samson, Hebrew, "Sun." Judges 13. Unusual.

Sinclair French. French, place name honoring St. Clair, also used as a surname. Lewis (novelist, "Babbitt," 1922); Weeks (secretary of commerce, 1953–58). Unusual.

Sinead See under Girls' Names.

Singefrid English. From Sigfrid. Unusual.

Sinjon English. From St. John, A title + the name of a saint (John, Hebrew (Yochanan), "God has been gracious"). Unusual. Alternative spelling: Sinjun.

Siôn Welsh. From John, Hebrew (Yochanan), "God has been gracious." Rhŷs (16th-century Welsh physician and grammarian, wrote grammar of the Welsh language). Unusual.

Sir English. Middle English, "sire"; a title used as a first name. Unusual.

Siurt Norwegian. From Sigfrid. Unusual.

Siva Indo-Pakistani. Hindi, the name of a Hindu god, Siva the Destroyer. Unusual.

Sivan Hebrew/Israeli. Hebrew, the ninth month of the Jewish year. Usually used as a name to refer to time of birth. Unusual.

Siwili Native American. Native American, "Fox's tail dragging along the ground." Unusual.

Skelly English. Gaelic, "One who tells stories." Unusual. Alternative spellings: Skelley, Skellie.

Skip English. Old Norse, "Master of a ship." Unusual. Alternative spelling: Skipp.

Skipper English. From Skip. Less popular. Skippy.

Skippy English. From Skip. Unusual. Alternative spelling: Skippie.

Skylar Dutch. From Schuyler, Dutch, "Scholar." Unusual. Alternative spelling: Skyler.

Slade English. Old English, "Child of the valley." Unusual.

Slane Czech. Czech, "Salty." Unusual.

Slava Russian. From Richard, Old German, "Strong ruler." Unusual.

Slaven English. From Slevin. Unusual.

Slavik Russian. From Stanislaus, Latin, "Camp glory" (?). Unusual.

Slavka Russian. From Richard, Old German, "Strong ruler." Unusual.

Slawek Polish. From Thomas, Aramaic, "Twin." Unusual.

Slevin English. Gaelic, "Mountaineer." Unusual.

Sloan English. Gaelic, "Fighter" or "warrior." Wilson (novelist). Unusual. Alternative spelling: Sloane.

Smith English. Occupational surname, referring to a blacksmith, sometimes used as first name; origin unknown. Thompson (secretary of navy, 1818; Supreme Court Justice, 1823); Tennant (British chemist, discovered osmium, 1803, and iridium, 1804). Unusual.

Socrates Greek. Greek, meaning and origin unknown. 5th-century B.C. Greek philosopher, examined virtue. Unusual.

Socratis Greek. From Socrates. Unusual.

Sofian Arabic. Arabic, "Devoted." Unusual.

Sol English. From Solomon. Less popular.

Solly English. From Solomon. Unusual. Sol. Alternative spelling: Sollie.

Solomon English. Hebrew, "Peace." Third king of Israel (1 Kings 4:30); Molcho (16th-century Portuguese Jew burned at stake during Inquisition); Plaatje (South African writer, politician); Bandaranaike (Ceylonese prime minister, 1956–59, established Sinhalese as official language); Alkabetz (wrote "Lecha Dodi," a traditional Hebrew song). Less popular. Sol. Alternative spellings: Solaman, Soloman.

Solomonas Lithuanian. From Solomon. Unusual.

Somhairle Irish. From Samuel, Hebrew (Shmuel), "His name is God" or "God has heard." 1 Samuel 1:20. Unusual.

Songan Native American. Native American, "Strong." Unusual.

Sonny English. Old English, "sunu" ("son"). Common affectionate form of address to young men. Rollins (jazz saxophonist); Bono (singer turned politician, formerly married to Cher); Stitt (jazz saxophonist). Less popular. Alternative spelling: Sonnie.

Sorrel English. Plant name, and description of light chestnut color; origin unknown. Bliss (character in Noël Coward's "Hay Fever," 1925). Unusual for males, unusual for females. Alternative spellings: Sorrell, Sorrelle.

Spangler English. meaning and origin unknown. Brugh (real name of TV's Robert Taylor). Unusual.

Spence English. From Spencer. Less popular.

Spencer English. Occupational surname referring to a dispenser of provisions; origin unknown. Tracy (Oscar-winning film star, frequently paired with Katharine Hepburn); Baird (zoologist, former secretary of Smithsonian Institute); Cavendish (eighth Duke of Devonshire, secretary of war, 1866); Compton (eighth Earl of Northampton, 17th-century). Less popular. Alternative spelling: Spenser.

Spoors English. Occupational surname referring to a maker of spurs; origin unknown. Unusual.

Squire English. Surname referring to a young gentleman or to the social title of large landholder; origin unknown. Whipple (civil engineer, wrote "Work on Bridge Building," 1847, first scientific book on bridge engineering). Unusual.

St. John English. A title + the name of a saint (John, Hebrew (Yochanan), "God has been gracious"). Unusual.

Stacey See Stacy under Girls' Names.

Stafford English. English, "Ford near a landing"; surname and place name used as a first name. Northcote (chairman of Hudson's Bay Co., 1860s); Cripps (British parliamentarian, lawyer, and diplomat; staunch advocate of peace during WWI). Unusual.

Stamford English. From Stanford. Unusual.

Stamos Greek. From Stephen, Greek, "Crown" or "crowned." Acts 7:59. Unusual.

Stan English. From Stanley. Musial ("The Man," baseball player); Laurel (half of comic duo Laurel and Hardy, who made 200 films). Unusual.

Stana English. From Stanislaus. Unusual.

Stanborough English. English, meaning unknown; surname used as a first name. Unusual.

Stancie English. English, meaning unknown; surname used as a first name. Unusual.

Stancio Hispanic. From Constance, Latin, "constans" ("constant" or "unwavering"). Unusual.

Stancombe English. English, meaning unknown; surname used as a first name. Unusual.

Stando English. From Stanislaus. Unusual.

Stane Serbian. From Stanislaus. Unusual.

Stanford English. English, "Stony ford"; surname used as a first name. White (19th-century architect, designed Madison Square Garden, 1889). Less popular.

Stanhope English. Old English, "Stony hollow." Unusual.

Stanislao Italian. From Stanislaus. Cannizzaro (19th-century Italian chemist, discovered a reaction that now bears his name, defined molecular and atomic weights). Unusual.

Stanislas French. From Stanislaus. Dupuy de Lôme (19th-century French naval engineer, designed and built first French screw steamship); Boufflers (French soldier and poet; governor of Senegal, 1785–88). Unusual.

Stanislau German. From Stanislaus. Unusual.

Stanislaus English. Latin, "Camp glory" (?). of Cracow (11th-century saint, bishop, and martyr); Kostka (16th-century saint; Jesuit novice); Hosius (16th-century Polish theologian; cardinal, 1561; opposed Protestant reformation). Unusual. Alternative spelling: Stanislus.

Stanislav Slavic. From Stanislaus. Neumann (Czech poet, "Nemesis, bonorum custos," 1895). Unusual.

Stanisław Polish. From Stanislaus. Leszczyński (Stanisław I, king of Poland, 1704–09, 1733–35); Moniuszko (Polish operatic composer, "Halka," 1848); Przybyszewski (Polish writer, "Androgyne," 1900); Wojciechowski (Polish politician and economist; president, 1922–26). Unusual.

Stanley English. English, "Stony clearing"; an aristocratic surname and place name used as a first name. Baldwin (British prime minister and Lord of Treasury, 1920s); Houghton (British playwright, "The Dear Departed," 1908); Ketchel (boxer, middleweight champion most of 1908–10); Kubrick (director, "2001: A Space Odyssey"); Spencer (British painter, "Resurrection"). Less popular. Stan.

Stannard English. English, "Stone-hard"; surname and place name used as a first name. Unusual.

Stano Czech. From Stanislaus. Unusual.

Stansfield English. English, "Stone field"; surname and place name used as a first name. Unusual.

Stanton English. English, "Settlement on stony ground"; surname and place name used as a first name. Macdonald-Wright (abstract painter, established synchronism, 1912). Unusual. Stan.

Starkie Unknown. Meaning and origin unknown. Unusual.

Stas Russian. From Stanislaus. Unusual.

Stashko Russian. From Stanislaus. Unusual.

Stasiek Polish. From Stanislaus. Unusual.

Stasio Polish. From Stanislaus. Unusual.

Staska Russian. From Stanislaus. Unusual.

Stavros Greek. From Stephen. Unusual.

Steele English. Sanskrit, "One who resists." Rudd (Australian novelist, "The Romance of Runnibede," 1927) (real name: Arthur H. Davis). Unusual. Alternative spelling: Steel.

Stefan Bulgarian, Czech, German, Polish, Russian, Swedish. From Stephen. Banach (Polish, developed theory of topological vector spaces, 1932); Lochner (German, of Cologne School; painted altar at Cologne cathedral); Stambolov (Bulgarian premier, 1887–94); Zeromski (Polish writer, advocated education for the masses). Less popular.

Stefano Italian. From Stephen. Casiraghi (husband of Princess Caroline); Bella (17th-century Italian designer and engraver); Francesco (also known as "Giuochi" or "Il Pesellino"; 15th-century Florentine painter). Unusual.

Stefans Latvian. From Stephen. Unusual.

Steffel German. From Stephen. Unusual.

Steffen English, Norwegian. From Stephen. Unusual.

Stefos Greek. From Stephen. Unusual.

Stenya Russian. From Stephen. Unusual.

Stepan Russian. From Stephen. Apraksin (18th-century Russian count, general in chief); Makarov (19th-century Russian admiral); Razin (17th-century Russian Cossack rebel, subject of folk songs and legends). Unusual.

Stepanya Russian. From Stephen. Unusual.

Steph English. From Stephen. Unusual. Alternative spelling: Stef.

Stéphane French. From Stephen. Peyron (one of two Frenchmen who traveled by sailboard from Africa to the U.S. in record 245 days, 1985); Mallarmé (19th-century French poet, leader in symbolist movement; "L'apres-midi d'un faune," 1876). Unusual.

Stephanos Greek. From Stephen. Unusual. Alternative spelling: Stefanos.

Stephanus Latin. From Stephen. Du Toit (19th-century South African cleric and politician, established language and identity of Boers). Unusual.

Stephen English. Greek, "Crown" or "crowned." Acts 7:59. Saint; first Christian martyr; popes (I, 254-X, 1057); Sondheim (Pulitzer Prize for drama, 1985, "Sunday in the Park with George"); Field (Supreme Court Justice, 1863–97); Benet (poet, novelist, "John Brown's Body"); Girard (financier, richest man in U.S. at death in 1831). Popular. Steve, Stevie. Alternative spellings: Stephan, Stephon, Stevan, Steven.

Stepka Russian. From Stephen. Unusual.

Sterling English. Middle English, "Of excellent quality"; surname used as first name. Hayden (actor); Holloway (actor); Morrison (musician, Velvet Underground); Price (19th-century politician, general in Confederate army). Unusual.

Steve English. From Stephen. Martin (TV and film actor, comedian, "Saturday Night Live"); Miller (musician); McQueen (film star); Guttenberg (film star); Cochran (film star). Less popular.

Steven See Stephen.

Stevens English. Surname based on Stephen (Greek, "Crown" or "crowned"). Unusual. Alternative spelling: Stephens.

Stevenson English. Surname based on Stephen (Greek, "Crown" or "crowned"). Unusual. Alternative spellings: Stephenson, Stevinson.

Stevie English. From Stephen, Greek, "Crown" or "crowned." Acts 7:59. Nicks (musician); Ray Vaughan (guitarist); Smith (poet). Less popular for males, unusual for females. Alternative spelling: Stevy.

Steward English. From Stuart. Unusual.

Stiggur Gypsy. English Gypsy, "Gate." Unusual.

Sting English. Greek, "stachys" ("spike of grain"). British rock singer (real name: Gordon Matthew Sumner). Unusual.

Stirling English. From Sterling, Middle English, "Of excellent quality"; surname used as first name. Moss (race-car driver). Unusual.

Stoffel German. From Christopher, Greek, "One who carries Christ in his heart." Unusual.

Stuart English. Old English, "Steward," "household caretaker." Merrill (American poet who wrote entirely in French, "Les Quatre Saisons," 1900); Cloete (South African writer, "Rags of Glory," 1963); Davis (artist, especially involved in cubism, collage, urban scenes). Less popular. Stu. Alternative spelling: Stewart.

Sudi African. Swahili, "Luck." Unusual.

Sugden English. Old German, "Valley containing sows"; surname and place name used as a first name. Unusual.

Sullivan Irish. Irish, "Black eyed" or "hawk-eyed"; surname used as a first name. Unusual.

Sultan African. Swahili, "Ruler." Unusual.

Sulwyn Welsh. Welsh, "Fair as the sun." Saint. Unusual.

Sundeep Indo-Pakistani. Punjabi, "Light" or "enlightened being." Unusual.

Sunny See under Girls' Names.

Sutcliffe English. Old English, "Southern cliff"; surname and place name used as a first name. Unusual.

Sven Scandinavian. Scandinavian, "Youth." Halvers (holds record, driving car farthest while tilted up on driver's side's two wheels: 97.2701 miles); Hedin (19th-century Swedish geographer and explorer of Asia); Fredriksson (claims he's Garbo's nephew, contesting her multi-million dollar will, 1991). Unusual.

Svend Danish. From Sven. Aagesen (earliest Danish historian: 12th-century). Unusual.

Swailey English. From Swaley. Unusual.

Swale English. From Swaley. Unusual.

Swales English. From Swaley. Unusual.

Swaley English. Old English, "Winding stream"; surname and place name used as a first name. Unusual.

Swinbourne English. Old English, surname and place name referring to "brook used by swine." Unusual. Alternative spelling: Swinborne.

Swinburne English. Old English, surname and place name based on Swinbourne (English, "Brook used by swine"). Unusual.

Swindel English. Old English, surname and place name based on Swinbourne (English, "Brook used by swine"). Unusual.

Swinfen English. Old English, surname and place name based on Swinbourne (English, "Brook used by swine"). Unusual.

Swinford English. Old English, surname and place name based on Swinbourne (English, "Brook used by swine"). Unusual.

Swinton English. Old English, surname and place name based on Swinbourne (English, "Brook used by swine"). Unusual.

Syarhey Russian. From Sergius, Latin, "Servant"; a Roman clan name. Unusual.

Sydney English. From Sidney, Old French, "From Saint-Denis." A Norman surname derived from a village named for a saint. Carton (character in Dickens' "Tale of Two Cities," 1859); Lady Morgan (Irish writer, "O'Donnel," 1814); Ringer (British physician, "Handbook of Therapeutics," 1869); Dobell (19th-century liberal British poet and critic, "Thoughts on Art, Philosophy and Religion"). Unusual for males, less popular for females. Syd. Alternative spellings: Cydney, Sidney, Sydny.

Syed Arabic. From Sa'īd, Arabic, "Happy." Unusual.

Sylvain English. From Silva, Latin, "Woods." Saudan (Swiss skier, holds record for steepest descent: 60 degrees, 1967); Levi (19th-century French Orientalist). Unusual.

Sylvanus English. From Silva, Latin, "Woods." Chararcter in Bible, 2 Cor. 1 : 19; Olympio (Togolese prime minister, 1958–60; first president, 1961–63); Thayer (army officer; superintendent, West Point, 1817–33); Urban (British printer and journalist, established "Gentleman's Magazine," 1731) (real name: Edward Cave). Unusual. Alternative spelling: Silvanus.

Sylvester English. From Silva, Latin, "Woods." Saint; bishop of Rome, 314; Stallone (star of "Rocky" films); Stone (rock musician) (real name of Sly Stone); Marsh (designed engines for ascending grades on cog railway, 1867). Less popular. Sly. Alternative spelling: Silvester.

Szigfrid Hungarian. From Sigfrid, Old German, "Victory-peace." Unusual.

Tab English. Old German, "Brilliant one among the people." Hunter (movie star). Unusual.

Tabib Turkish. Turkish, "Doctor." Unusual.

Tabo Hispanic. From Gustaf, Swedish, "God's staff" or "staff of the Goths." Unusual.

Tabor Hungarian. Hungarian, "From the fort." Unusual.

Tace See under Girls' Names.

Tad English. From Thaddeus, Old Welsh, "Father." Mosel (movie script writer). Less popular. Alternative spelling: Tadd.

Tadan Native American. From Otadan, Native American, "Plenty." Unusual.

Taddeo Italian. From Thaddeus, Old Welsh, "Father." Gaddi (14th-century Florentine painter, follower of Giotto). Unusual.

Taddy English. From Thaddeus, Old Welsh, "Father." Unusual.

Tade Hungarian. From Thaddeus, Old Welsh, "Father." Unusual.

Tadeas Czech. From Thaddeus, Old Welsh, "Father." Unusual.

Tadek Polish. From Thaddeus, Old Welsh, "Father." Unusual.

Tadeo Hispanic. From Thaddeus, Old Welsh, "Father." Unusual.

Tades Czech. From Thaddeus, Old Welsh, "Father." Unusual.

Tadeusz Polish. From Thaddeus, Old Welsh, "Father." Kościuszko (18th-century Polish military hero); Żeleński (Polish humorous writer); Brzozowski (19th-century Polish religious leader, first modern Jesuit general). Unusual.

Tadey Russian. From Thaddeus, Old Welsh, "Father." Unusual.

Tadi Native American. Native American, "Wind." Unusual.

Tadzi Native American. Native American, "Loon." Unusual.

Tadzio Polish. From Thaddeus, Old Welsh, "Father." Unusual.

Ṭāhir Arabic. Arabic, "Pure." Unusual.

Tai Vietnamese. Vietnamese, "Talent." Unusual.

Tait Native American, from Tate, Native American, "Great talker"; and Scandinavian, Swedish, "Cheerful." Unusual. Alternative spellings: Taite, Tate.

Takis Greek. From Peter, Greek, "Stone," "rock." John 1:42. Unusual.

Tal English. From Talia, Hebrew, "Dew" or "rain." Unusual for males, unusual for females.

Talbert English. From Talbot. Character in Shakespeare's "Henry V." Unusual.

Talbot English. Old German, "Bright valley"; surname used as first name. Unusual.

Talib Arabic. Arabic, "Seeker." Unusual.

Taliesin Welsh. Welsh, "Radiant brow." 6th-century Welsh poet, wrote of rulers in Wales. Unusual.

Talli Native American. Native American, meaning unknown. Unusual.

Tally English. From Talbot. Unusual. Alternative spelling: Tallie.

Talman Aramaic. Aramaic, "To injure" or "to oppress." Unusual. Alternative spelling: Talmon.

Talon Unknown. Meaning and origin unknown. Unusual.

Talor English. From Talia, Hebrew, "Dew" or "rain." Unusual for males, unusual for females.
Tam English. From Thomas, Aramaic, "Twin." O'Shanter (character created by Robert Burns). Unusual.
Taman Serbian. Serbo-Croatian, "Dark" or "black." Unusual.
Tamás Hungarian. From Thomas, Aramaic, "Twin." Unusual.
Tameas English. From Thomas, Aramaic, "Twin." Unusual.
Tammany English. From Thomas, Aramaic, "Twin." Unusual.
Tammas Scottish. From Thomas, Aramaic, "Twin." Unusual.
Tammen English. From Thomas, Aramaic, "Twin." Unusual.
Tammy See under Girls' Names.
Tanas Russian. From Tanek. Unusual.
Tanek Polish. Greek, "Immortal." Unusual.
Tani See under Girls' Names.
Tanix Hispanic. From Stanislaus, Latin, "Camp glory" (?). Unusual.
Tann English. From Tanner. Unusual. Alternative spelling: Tan.
Tanner English. Old English, "A leather worker." Unusual.
Tanney English. From Tanner. Unusual. Alternative spellings: Tannie, Tanny.
Tanno African. African, name of a river. Unusual.
Tano African, African, name of a river; and Hispanic, from Stanislaus, Latin, "Camp glory" (?). Unusual.
Tapani Finnish. From Stephen, Greek, "Crown" or "crowned." Acts 7:59. Unusual.
Ṭāriq Unknown. Meaning and origin unknown. Unusual.
Taro Italian. Japanese, "First-born male." Unusual.
Tarry English. From Terence, Latin, "Terentius," the name of a Roman clan. Unusual.
Tas Gypsy. English Gypsy, "A bird's nest." Unusual.
Tasida See under Girls' Names.
Tatiānus Latin. From Tatius. Unusual.
Tatius Latin. Name of a Sabine king, Titus Tatius; origin unknown. Unusual.
Tauno Finnish. From Donald, Gaelic (Domhnall), "Mighty in the world." Unusual.
Taurean English. Greek, "tauros" ("bull"). Unusual.
Tavares Unknown. Meaning and origin unknown. Unusual. Alternative spelling: Tavaris.
Tavis Scottish. From Thomas, Aramaic, "Twin." Unusual.
Tavish Scottish. From Thomas, Aramaic, "Twin." Unusual.
Tavo Slavic. From Gustaf, Swedish, "God's staff" or "staff of the Goths." Unusual.
Tawno Gypsy. From Tawnie, English Gypsy, "Little one." Unusual.
Tayib Arabic. Arabic, "Good" or "delicate." Unusual.
Taylor English. Middle English, occupational surname used as a first name. Unusual. Alternative spellings: Tayler, Taylour.
Tazio Italian. From Tatius. Unusual.
Teasdale English. Old English, place name (name of an English river) and surname used as a first name. Unusual.
Teb Hispanic. From Stephen, Greek, "Crown" or "crowned." Acts 7:59. Unusual.
Ted English. From Theodore, Greek, "theodoros" ("God's gift"). Less popular. Teddy. Alternative spelling: Tedd.
Teddy English. From Theodore, Greek, "theodoros" ("God's gift"). Less popular. Alternative spelling: Teddie.
Tedik Czech. From Theodore, Greek, "theodoros" ("God's gift"). Unusual.
Telek Polish. Polish, "Iron cutter." Unusual.
Telem Hebrew/Israeli. Hebrew, "Ford" or "furrow." Unusual.
Telford English. Old French, occupational surname referring to one who cuts and fits armor. Unusual.
Tem Gypsy. English Gypsy, "Country." Unusual.
Teman Hebrew/Israeli. Hebrew, "Right side." Unusual.
Temple English. Latin, "templum," a place marked for the observation of auguries. Unusual.
Tennant English. Latin, "tenere" ("to hold"); surname used as a first name. Unusual. Alternative spelling: Tenant.
Tennent English. From Tennant. Unusual.
Tennessee English. English, the name of the state used as a first name. Williams (playwright, "Streetcar Named Desire") (real name: Thomas Lanier Williams). Unusual.
Tenny English. From Dennis, Greek, "Of Dionysos," the Greek name for the god of wine. Unusual. Alternative spelling: Tennie.
Tennyson English. From Dennis, Greek, "Of Dionysos," the Greek name for the god of wine. Unusual.
Teodomiro Hispanic. From Theodore, Greek, "theodoros" ("God's gift"). Unusual.
Teodor Czech, Polish. From Theodore, Greek, "theodoros" ("God's gift"). Unusual.
Teodorek Polish. From Theodore, Greek, "theodoros" ("God's gift"). Unusual.
Teodoro Hispanic, Italian. From Theodore, Greek, "theodoros" ("God's gift"). Unusual.
Teodus Czech. From Theodore, Greek, "theodoros" ("God's gift"). Unusual.
Teos Polish. From Theodore, Greek, "theodoros" ("God's gift"). Unusual.
Teppo French. From Stephen, Greek, "Crown" or "crowned." Acts 7:59. Unusual.
Terell English. From Terence. Unusual. Alternative spellings: Terrel, Terrell, Terril, Terrill, Terryl.
Terence English. Latin, "Terentius," the name of a Roman clan. Rattigan (British playwright). Less popular. Terry. Alternative spellings: Terance, Terrence, Terrance.
Terry English. From Terence, Latin, "Terentius," the name of a Roman clan. Bradshaw (Pittsburgh Steelers quarterback); Meeuwsen (Miss America, 1973). Popular for males, less popular for females.
Tertius Latin. Latin, "Third." Given to the third-born child. Unusual.
Teva Hebrew/Israeli. Hebrew, "Nature." Unusual.
Tevis Scottish. From Thomas, Aramaic, "Twin." Unusual.
Tevish Scottish. From Thomas, Aramaic, "Twin." Unusual.
Tewdor German. From Theodore. Unusual.
Tex English. English, short form of "Texas" or "Texan." Ritter (singing cowboy, 1930s and 1940s) (real name: Woodward Ritter). Less popular.
Thad English. From Thaddeus. Less popular. Alternative spelling: Thadd.
Thaddaus German. From Thaddeus. Unusual.

Thaddeo Italian. From Thaddeus. Unusual.

Thaddeus English. Old Welsh, "Father." Less popular. Thad. Alternative spelling: Thaddius.

Thaddy English. From Thaddeus. Unusual.

Thadee French. From Thaddeus. Unusual.

Thane English. Old English, "Warrior" or "follower." Unusual. Alternative spellings: Thain, Thaine, Thayne.

Thanos Greek. From Arthur, Gaelic, "Rock," "noble," or "lofty hill." Unusual.

Theo English. From Theodore. Less popular.

Theobald English. German, "People-bold." Unusual.

Theodor German. From Theodore. Mommsen (19th-century German liberal scholar and historian, later politician; strongly opposed Bismarck); Curtius (German chemist, discovered hydrazine and hydrazoic acid); Billroth (19th-century German surgeon, pioneered use of antiseptics to advance abdominal surgery). Unusual.

Theodore English. Greek, "theodoros" ("God's gift"). Roosevelt (26th president); Dreiser (novelist). Less popular. Tad, Ted, Theo.

Theodoric German. Old German, "Ruler of the people." Anti-pope, 1100; "the Great," 5th-century king of the Ostrogoths (Italy). Unusual.

Theophilus Greek. Greek, "Loved by God." Ninth-century Greek ruler: builder, iconoclast, lover of pomp; Shepstone, Sir (19th-century South African politician, administered Transvaal and Zululand); Eaton (British, one of first emigrants to U.S., established colony at New Haven, 1638). Unusual.

Theron Greek. Greek, "Hunter." Unusual.

Thien Vietnamese. Vietnamese, "Smooth." Unusual.

Thoma German. From Thomas. Unusual.

Thomas English, French. Aramaic, "Twin." One of the 12 apostles; Savery (invented steam engine, 18th-century); Gainsborough (18th-century British portraitist, "Blue Boy"); Aquinas (13th-century Italian philosopher); Macauley (British historian and statesman); à Becket (12th-century British zealous defender of church rights). Very popular. Tom, Tommy.

Thomeson English. From Thompson. Unusual.

Thomison English. From Thompson. Unusual.

Thompson English. "Son of Tom"; origin unknown. Surname used as a first name. Unusual. Alternative spellings: Thomson, Tomson.

Thor Scandinavian. Old Norse, "Thunder." Heyerdahl (Norwegian explorer and author, "Kon-Tiki"). Unusual.

Thorald English. Old Norse, "Thor, the ruler" or "thunder ruler." Unusual.

Thorbert English. Old Norse, "Thor's brilliance." Unusual.

Thorbjorn Scandinavian. Old Norse, "Thor's bear" or "thunder bear." Unusual.

Thorburn English. From Thorbjorn. Unusual.

Thorleif Scandinavian. Old Norse, "Thor's beloved." Unusual.

Thorley English. Old Norse, "Thor's meadow." Unusual.

Thormond English. Old Norse, "Thor's protection." Unusual.

Thorne English. From Thornton. Smith (novelist, "Topper"). Unusual. Alternative spelling: Thorn.

Thornley English. From Thorley. Unusual.

Thornton English. Old English, "Settlement among thorns"; place name used as a first name. Wilder (Pulitzer Prize winner, "Our Town"); Burgess (author, "Peter Rabbit"). Unusual.

Thorpe English. Old English, "Dweller in the village." Unusual.

Thorvald Scandinavian. Old Norse, "Thunder ruler." Stauning (Danish premier, 1924–26, 1929–42). Unusual.

Thurlow English. Old Norse, "From Thor's hill." Weed (19th-century politician, strongly supported Lincoln's war policies). Unusual.

Thursday English. Old German, day name used as a first name. Unusual.

Thurstain English. From Thurston. Unusual.

Thurston English. Old Norse, "Thor's stone" or "Thor's jewel." Howell (character in TV's "Gilligan's Island"). Unusual. Alternative spellings: Thurstain, Thurstan.

Tiago Hispanic. From Jacob, Hebrew (Yaakov), "Supplanter" or "heel." Genesis 25:26. Unusual.

Ticho Hispanic. From Patrick, Latin, "Noble man." Unusual.

Tiennot French. From Stephen, Greek, "Crown" or "crowned." Acts 7:59. Unusual.

Tiimu Native American. Native American, "Caterpillar coming out." Unusual.

Tiktu Native American. Native American, "Bird digging up potatoes." Unusual.

Tilden English. Old English place name, "Fertile valley." Unusual.

Tilford English. Old English, "From the ford belonging to the good, liberal one." Unusual.

Tilo Hispanic. From Stanislaus, Latin, "Camp glory" (?). Unusual.

Tilton English. Old English, "From the good, liberal one's estate." Unusual. Alternative spellings: Tiltan, Tilten, Tiltin.

Tim English. From Timothy, Greek, "timotheos" ("honoring God"). Conway (TV comedian); Robbins (actor); Richmond (stock-car driver); Matheson (actor, "Animal House"). Unusual.

Tima Russian. From Timothy. Unusual.

Timin Arabic. Arabic, "Sea-serpent." Unusual.

Timka Russian. From Timothy. Unusual.

Timkin Slavic. From Timothy. Unusual.

Timmy English. From Timothy. Less popular. Alternative spelling: Timmie.

Timo Finnish. From Timothy. Unusual.

Timofey Russian. From Timothy. Sapronov (Russian, Bolshevik who agitated for more democracy in communist party). Unusual. Alternative spelling: Timofei.

Timok Russian. From Timothy. Unusual.

Timon English. From Timothy. Unusual.

Timót Hungarian. From Timothy. Unusual.

Timotei Bulgarian. From Timothy. Unusual.

Timoteo Hispanic, Italian, Portuguese. From Timothy. Unusual.

Timoteus Scandinavian. From Timothy. Unusual.

Timothee French. From Timothy. Unusual.

Timotheos Greek. From Timothy. Unusual.

Timotheus German. From Timothy. Unusual.

Timothey English. From Timothy. Unusual. Tim, Timmy.

Timothy English. Greek, "timotheos" ("honoring God"). Saint, companion to St. Paul; Dalton (British actor, James Bond) ("007"); Hutton (Oscar-winning actor, "Ordinary People"); Schmidt (member of pop group the Eagles); Cheeryble (character in Dickens' "Nicholas Nickleby"). Very popular. Tim, Timmy. Alternative spelling: Timmothy.

Timur Hebrew/Israeli. Hebrew, "Tall" or "stately." Unusual.

Tin Vietnamese. Vietnamese, "Think." Unusual.

Tino Hispanic. From Augustus, Latin, "Venerable" or "majestic." Unusual.

Tiomoid Irish. From Timothy. Unusual.

Tisha Russian. From Timothy. Unusual.

Tishka Russian. From Timothy. Unusual.

Tite French. From Titus. Unusual.

Titek Polish. From Titus. Unusual.

Tito Hispanic, Italian. From Titus. Puente (self-proclaimed "king of Latin music"); Ricordi (19th-century Italian music publisher and pianist). Unusual.

Titus Greek. Greek, "Of the giants." 2 Corinthians 2:13. Saint; Salt, Sir (19th-century British wool magnate); Petronius (Roman writer, director of entertainment at Nero's court); Plautus (creative, free-thinking Roman playwright); character in Longfellow's 1852 poem "The Golden Legend." Unusual. Alternative spelling: Titos.

Tivadar Hungarian. From Theodore, Greek, "theodoros" ("God's gift"). Unusual.

Tivon Hebrew/Israeli. Hebrew, "Naturalist" or "lover of nature." Unusual.

Tobal Hispanic. From Christopher, Greek, "One who carries Christ in his heart." Unusual.

Tobalito Hispanic. From Christopher, Greek, "One who carries Christ in his heart." Unusual.

Tobbar Gypsy. English Gypsy, "Road." Unusual.

Tobias English. Hebrew, "God is good." Furneaux (British explorer; first to cross South Pole: 1773); Lear (diplomat under Washington); Smollett (18th-century Scottish physician; later, translated Voltaire in 38 volumes and wrote complete history of England). Unusual. Toby.

Toby English. From Tobias, Hebrew, "God is good." Harrah (baseball player, holds record: played doubleheader at shortstop without once touching the ball); Veck (character in Dickens' "The Chimes"); Belch (character in Shakespeare's "Twelfth Night"); Philpot (character in 18th-century play "Poor Soldier"). Unusual for males, unusual for females. Alternative spellings: Tobey, Tobie.

Todd English. Scottish, "Fox" or "fox hunter." Matthewshikiza (South African writer and musician, wrote score for music "King Kong"); Worrell (pitcher). Less popular. Alternative spelling: Tod.

Todor Hungarian, Russian. From Theodore, Greek, "theodoros" ("God's gift"). Aleksandrov (19th-century Macedonian politician, directed terror campaigns against Bulgarian and Yugoslavian governments). Unusual.

Todos Russian. From Theodore, Greek, "theodoros" ("God's gift"). Unusual.

Tohon Native American. Native American, "Cougar." Unusual.

Tolek Polish. From Theodore, Greek, "theodoros" ("God's gift"). Unusual.

Toli Hispanic. From Barth, Hebrew, "Farmer." Unusual.

Tom English. From Thomas, Aramaic, "Twin." Cruise (actor); Seaver (pitching great); Petty (musician, member of Traveling Wilburys); Sayers (British boxing champion, 1857); Brokaw (TV newsman). Less popular. Alternative spellings: Thom, Tomm.

Tomáš Czech, Hispanic, Lithuanian, Portuguese, Russian, Scandinavian. From Thomas, Aramaic, "Twin." Masaryk (19th-century Czech statesman and philosopher; first president of Czechoslovakia, 1918–35); Mosquera (Columbian president, 1863–67); Gustafson (Swedish, holds record for 10K speed skating: 13 minutes, 48.20 seconds). Unusual.

Tomaso Italian. From Thomas, Aramaic, "Twin." Aniello (Italian fisherman, led successful tax protest in 17th-century Naples). Unusual.

Tomaz Portuguese. From Thomas, Aramaic, "Twin." Unusual.

Tomcio Polish. From Thomas, Aramaic, "Twin." Unusual.

Tome Portuguese. From Thomas, Aramaic, "Twin." Sousa (first governor of Brazil, 1549–53). Unusual.

Tomek Polish. From Thomas, Aramaic, "Twin." Unusual.

Tomelis Lithuanian. From Thomas, Aramaic, "Twin." Unusual.

Tomey English. From Thomas, Aramaic, "Twin." Unusual.

Tomi Hungarian, from Thomas, Aramaic, "Twin"; and Nigerian, Nigerian, "The people." Unusual.

Tomislaw Polish. From Thomas, Aramaic, "Twin." Unusual.

Tomkin English. From Tomlin. Unusual.

Tomlin English. Old English, "Little twin." Unusual.

Tommy English. From Thomas, Aramaic, "Twin." Burns (Canadian heavyweight boxing champion, 1906–08); Dorsey (big-band leader, 1930s and 40s); Tune (dancer and choreographer). Less popular. Tom. Alternative spellings: Tommey, Tommie.

Tonda Czech. From Anthony, Latin, a Roman clan name used as a first name. Unusual.

Tonek Polish. From Otto, Old German, "Possessions." Unusual.

Toni Hungarian, Slavic. From Anthony, Latin, a Roman clan name used as a first name. Unusual.

Tonik Czech. From Anthony, Latin, a Roman clan name used as a first name. Unusual.

Tonis Greek. From Anthony, Latin, a Roman clan name used as a first name. Unusual.

Tony English. From Anthony, Latin, a Roman clan name used as a first name. Curtis (actor, "Some Like It Hot") (real name: Bernard Schwarz); Orlando (entertainer and singer); Richardson (British director, won Oscar for "Tom Jones"); Kubek (baseball player in 1960s, now broadcaster); Randall (actor, "Odd Couple"). Less popular.

Toomas Estonian. From Thomas, Aramaic, "Twin." Unusual.

Topwe African. African, the name of a vegetable. Unusual.

Tor Nigerian, Nigerian, "King"; and English, Norwegian, from Thor, Old Norse, "Thunder." Unusual.

Torin Irish. From Torin, Gaelic, "Chief." Unusual.

Torquil Scottish. Old Norse, "Thunder" + "kettle" (?). Unusual.

Torrence Irish. From Terence, Latin, "Terentius," the name of a Roman clan. Unusual.

Torrey English. From Terence, Latin, "Terentius," the name of a Roman clan. Unusual.

Tory See under Girls' Names.

Toshi Japanese. From Toshio, Japanese, "Year-boy." Unusual for males, unusual for females.

Toshio Japanese. Japanese, "Year-boy." Unusual.

Tov Hebrew/Israeli. From Tovi. Unusual.

Tovi Hebrew/Israeli. Hebrew, "My good." Unusual.

Tracy See under Girls' Names.

Traver English. From Travis. Unusual.

Travers English. From Travis. Unusual.

Travis English. Old French, "From the crossroads." Tritt (country-western singer). Popular. Alternative spelling: Travus.

Trayton English. Old French, "Settlement near trees" (?); surname and place name used as a first name. Unusual.

Trefor Welsh. From Trevor. Unusual.

Tremain English. Celtic, "From the house by the rock." Unusual. Alternative spellings: Tremaine, Tremayne.

Trent English. English, the name of a river; surname and place name used as a first name. Unusual.

Trenton English. From Trent. Unusual.

Trev English. From Trevor. Unusual.

Trevor English. Old English, "Sea homestead." Howard (British actor); Mitchell (British, holds duration drumming record: 1,057 hours); Berbick (Canadian, 1986 heavyweight champion); Pinnock (British conductor). Popular. Alternative spellings: Trevar, Trever.

Trey English. Middle English, "Third-born." Unusual.

Tristan English. French, "Sad." de Luna y Arellano (16th-century Spanish explorer of Florida and New Mexico); Tzara (French poet and writer, founded Dada movement, 1916) (real name: Samuel Rosenfeld); Bernard (19th-century French comedic playwright) (real name: Paul Bernard); character in Wagner's opera "Tristan und Isolde." Unusual.

Tristram English. From Tristan. Speaker (baseball great; elected to Hall of Fame, 1937); character in Laurence Sterne's 18th-century novel "Tristram Shandy"; character in Matthew Arnold's 19th-century poem "Tristram and Iseult." Unusual.

Troy English. Gaelic, "Foot soldier." Aikman (NFL quarterback); Donahue (actor) (real name: Merle Johnson); Harris (holds record for jumping jacks: 50,482 in 12 hours). Unusual. Alternative spelling: Troi.

Tuan Vietnamese. Vietnamese, "Goes smoothly." Unusual.

Tucker English. Old English, "One who folds cloth." Unusual.

Tudor Welsh. From Theodore, Greek, "theodoros" ("God's gift"). Vladimirescu (19th-century Russian army officer and revolutionary against Greek-Turkish government). Unusual.

Tuketu Native American. Native American, "Bear raising dust as it runs." Unusual.

Tukuli Native American. Native American, "Insect crawling." Unusual.

Tull English. From Tully. Unusual.

Tully English. Gaelic, "Quiet and peaceful" or "devoted to God's will." Unusual. Alternative spellings: Tulley, Tullie.

Tulsidas Indo-Pakistani. Hindi, "Slave of Tulsi," a god. 16th-century Hindu poet, called the greatest poet of medieval Hindustan. Unusual.

Tung Vietnamese. Vietnamese, "Tree" or "calm and dignity." Cho (despotic 2nd-century Chinese general). Unusual.

Tunu Native American. Native American, "Deer eating onions." Unusual.

Tuomas Finnish. From Thomas, Aramaic, "Twin." Unusual.

Tuomo Finnish. From Thomas, Aramaic, "Twin." Unusual.

Tupi Native American. Native American, "To pull out or up," as in fishing. Unusual.

Turi Hispanic. From Arthur, Gaelic, "Rock," "noble," or "lofty hill." Unusual.

Turner English. Meaning and origin uncertain; surname used as a first name. Unusual.

Tuto Hispanic. From Justin, Latin, "Just." Unusual.

Ty English. From Tyrone. Cobb (baseball great; Hall of Fame, 1936; highest career batting average: 0.367) (real name: Tyrus). Unusual. Alternative spelling: Tye.

Tyee Native American. Native American, "Chief." Unusual.

Tyler English. Middle English, "Tile-maker." Dennett (historian, won Pulitzer Prize, 1933, for biography of John Hay). Very popular for males, less popular for females. Ty. Alternative spellings: Tylar, Tylor.

Tymek Polish. From Timothy, Greek, "timotheos" ("honoring God"). Unusual.

Tymon Polish. From Timothy, Greek, "timotheos" ("honoring God"). Unusual.

Tynek Czech. From Martin, Latin, "War-like." Derived from Mars, the Roman god of war. Unusual.

Tynko Czech. From Martin, Latin, "War-like." Derived from Mars, the Roman god of war. Unusual.

Tyree Unknown. Meaning and origin unknown. Unusual.

Tyrell English. From Terence, Latin, "Terentius," the name of a Roman clan. Unusual. Alternative spellings: Tyrel, Tyrrel.

Tyrone English. Gaelic, "From Owen's land." Power (actor, "Suez," "Blood and Sand," "Razor's Edge"); Guthrie (British theatrical director); Bogues (shortest basketball player ever in NBA: 5 feet, 3 inches). Unusual. Alternative spelling: Tyron.

Tyson English. French, meaning uncertain; surname used as first name. Unusual. Ty.

Tytus Polish. From Titus, Greek, "Of the giants." 2 Corinthians 2:13. Unusual.

Tzvi Hebrew/Israeli. Hebrew, "Deer" or "gazelle." Unusual.

Uhubitu Native American. Native American, "Foul water." Unusual.

Uilliam Irish. From William, Old German, "Will" + "helmet." Unusual.

Ulan African. African, "First-born twin." Unusual.

Ulbrecht German. German, "Noble splendor." Unusual.

Ulric English. Old German (Wulfric), "Ruler of all" or "wolf ruler." Unusual. Alternative spelling: Ulrick.

Ulrich German. From Ulric. Salchow (Swede, Olympic gold medalist, figure skating, 1908); Wille (Swiss military leader and commander of army, 1914–25); Boner (Swiss writer of one of first German books printed, 1461); von Cilli (Austrian prince, ruled Hungary 1453–56). Unusual. Alternative spelling: Ulrike.

Ulysses English. Latin form of Greek name "Odysseus" ("wounded in the thigh" or "wrathful"). Grant (Civil War general; 18th president). Unusual.

Uner Turkish. Turkish, "Famous." Unusual.

Upton English. Old English, "From the hill town." Sinclair (socialist writer and reformer, "Dragon's Teeth"; won Pulitzer Prize). Unusual.

Urbain French. From Urban. Leverrier (19th-century French astronomer, completely revised planetary theories). Unusual. Alternative spelling: Urbaine.

Urban English. Latin, "One from the city." Romans 16:9. Pope, elected in 222; Shocker (1920s baseball player). Unusual.

Urbane English. From Urban. Unusual.

Urbano Hispanic, Italian, Portuguese. From Urban. Rattazzi (Italian prime minister, 1862, 1867). Unusual.

Uri Hebrew/Israeli. Hebrew, "God is my light" or "God's light." Exodus 31:2. Leader of the tribe of Judah. Unusual. Alternative spelling: Urie.

Uriah English. Hebrew, "My light is the Lord." 2 Samuel 11:3. Bathsheba's husband; Levy (19th-century naval officer, bought Monticello); Stephens (labor leader, established Noble Order of the Knights of Labor, 1869); Heep (character in Dickens' novel "David Copperfield"). Unusual. Alternative spelling: Uria.

Urian Greek. Greek, "Heaven." Unusual.

Urias English. From Uriah. Unusual.

Uriel English. From Uriah. Costa (17th-century Portuguese Jew forcibly converted to Catholicism, wrote advocating faith based on natural reason). Unusual.

Ursan English. Latin, "Bear." Unusual. Alternative spelling: Urson.

Urvan Russian. From Urban. Romans 16:9. Unusual.

Ustin Russian. From Justin, Latin, "Just." Unusual.

Utatci Native American. Native American, "Bear scratching itself." Unusual.

Uzoma African. Nigerian, "Born during a journey." Unusual.

Uzziah Hebrew/Israeli. From Uzziel. King of Judah, 8th-century B.C. Unusual.

Uzziel Hebrew/Israeli. Hebrew, "God is strong." Unusual.

Vacys Lithuanian. From Walter, Old German, "Ruling people." Unusual.

Vadin Indo-Pakistani. Hindi, "Learned speaker." Unusual.

Vaino Finnish. From Wainwright, occupational surname indicating someone who built wagons; origin unknown. Tanner (Finnish prime minister, 1926–27). Unusual.

Val See under Girls' Names.

Valentine English. Latin, "To be strong." Saint; Dyall (British radio announcer during WWII); character in Shakespeare's "Two Gentlemen of Verona" and "Twelfth Night." Unusual for males, unusual for females. Val.

Valdemar Dutch. From Walter, Old German, "Ruling people." Poulsen (Danish, invented magnetic recording using steel wire, 1898); Rördam (Danish poet, especially known for verse narratives). Unusual.

Valery See Valerie under Girls' Names.

Valin Indo-Pakistani. From Balin, Hindi, "Mighty soldier." According to myth, Balin is a tyrannical monkey king with the power to extract half the strength from anyone who challenges him. Unusual.

Valter Latvian. From Walter, Old German, "Ruling people." Unusual.

Valters Latvian. From Walter, Old German, "Ruling people." Unusual.

Valtr Czech. From Walter, Old German, "Ruling people." Unusual.

Van English. From Vance. Johnson (actor); Morrison (Irish rock singer, "BrownEyed Girl," "Moondance"); Brooks (Pulitzer Prize-winning author, "Flowering of New England"); Heflin (actor). Less popular. Alternative spelling: Vann.

Vance English. English, "Lives near a marsh." Palmer (Australian author and novelist); Law (son of 1960 Cy Young winner Vern); Packard (author, "Hidden Persuaders"). Less popular.

Vancelo Unknown. Meaning and origin unknown. Unusual.

Vanda Lithuanian. From Walter, Old German, "Ruling people." Unusual.

Vandele Lithuanian. From Walter, Old German, "Ruling people." Unusual.

Vanek Russian. From John, Hebrew (Yochanan), "God has been gracious." Unusual.

Vanka Russian. From John, Hebrew (Yochanan), "God has been gracious." Unusual.

Vannevar English. Meaning and origin unknown. Bush (foresighted director of office of science research and development during WWII). Unusual.

Vansalo Unknown. From Vanslow. Unusual. Alternative spelling: Vanselow.

Vanslaw Unknown. From Vanslow. Unusual.

Vanslow Unknown. Meaning and origin unknown. Unusual.

Vanya Russian. From John, Hebrew (Yochanan), "God has been gracious." Unusual.

Varden English. Old French, "From the green hills." Unusual. Alternative spelling: Vardon.

Vartan Armenian. Armenian, "Rose." Unusual.

Vas Russian. From William, Old German, "Will" + "helmet." Unusual.

Vasil Czech. From Basil, Greek, "Kingly." Radoslavov (Bulgarian premier, 1913–18). Unusual.

Vasilak Russian. From William, Old German, "Will" + "helmet." Unusual.

Vasile Romanian. From Basil, Greek, "Kingly." Alecsandri (Romanian minister to France, 1885). Unusual.

Vasilek Russian. From Basil, Greek, "Kingly." Unusual.

Vasili Russian. From Basil, Greek, "Kingly." Alexeyev (Russian, broke record 80 records for weight-lifting, 1970s). Unusual. Alternative spellings: Vasiliy, Vassili, Vassily.

Vasilios Greek. From Basil, Greek, "Kingly." Unusual.

Vasilis Greek. From Basil, Greek, "Kingly." Unusual.

Vasilos Greek. From Basil, Greek, "Kingly." Unusual.

Vasily English. From Basil, Greek, "Kingly." Tikhon (Russian, bishop in Russian Orthodox church of U.S., 1898–1907); Zhukovski (wrote Russian national anthem, "God Save the Czar"); Dokuchayev (Russian geologist, classified soils); Kalinnikov (19th-century Russian composer of symphonies and more). Unusual.

Vasin Indo-Pakistani. Hindi, "Ruler" or "lord." Unusual.

Vaska Russian. From William, Old German, "Will" + "helmet." Unusual.

Vassos Greek. From William, Old German, "Will" + "helmet." Unusual.

Vasya Russian. From William, Old German, "Will" + "helmet." Unusual.

Vasyl Russian. From William, Old German, "Will" + "helmet." Unusual.

Vaughn English. From Vaughan. Shafer (jumped record 37 feet, 10 inches over five cars, using skateboard); Monroe (band leader). Less popular. Alternative spelling: Vaughan.

Vazul Hungarian. From Basil, Greek, "Kingly." Unusual.

Velvel Yiddish. From William, Old German, "Will" + "helmet." Unusual.

Vencel Hungarian. Hungarian, "Wreath" or "garland." Unusual.

Venedict Russian. From Benedict, Latin, "Blessed." Unusual. Alternative spelling: Venedikt.

Venka Russian. From Benedict, Latin, "Blessed." Unusual.

Venya Russian. From Benedict, Latin, "Blessed." Unusual.

Verdun French. French city; a place name used as a first name. Unusual. Alternative spellings: Verden, Verdon.

Vere English. French place name; later an aristocratic surname used as a first name. Unusual. Alternative spelling: Vear.

Vered Hebrew/Israeli. Hebrew, "Rose." Unusual.

Verlie French. French, place name used as a first name. Unusual. Alternative spelling: Verley.

Vern English. From Vernon. Law (pitcher; won Cy Young award, 1960); Taylor (Canadian, first skater to perform triple axel, a difficult jump). Less popular. Alternative spelling: Verne.

Vernon French. French, "Alder tree"; also a place name used as a first name. Castle (British dancer, originated one-step and turkey trot); Parrington (liberal scholar, wrote biography of Sinclair Lewis); Walters (diplomat under Eisenhower, Nixon, and Reagan; former UN ambassador); Watkins (Welsh mystic and visionary poet). Unusual.

Vian English. From Vivian, Latin, "Full of life." Unusual.

Vic English. From Victor. Morrow (actor "Twilight Zone," "Combat"); Damone (singer and entertainer). Less popular. Alternative spelling: Vick.

Vicente Hispanic. From Vincent, Latin, "Vincentius," from "vincere" ("to conquer"). Rocafuerte (Spanish, president of Ecuador, 1835–39); Alexandre (Spanish poet, won Nobel Prize for literature, 1977); Guerrero (Spanish; vice-president of Mexico, 1824–28); Blasco Ibáñez (Spanish novelist and ardent republican). Unusual.

Vicenzo Italian. From Vincent, Latin, "Vincentius," from "vincere" ("to conquer"). Campi (16th-century Italian painter, pupil and imitator of Boccaccino). Unusual.

Victoir French. From Victor. Unusual.

Victor English. Latin, "Conqueror." Saint; Adler (Austrian politician, established Social Democratic party, 1888); Borge (Danish entertainer); Hugo (French author, "Les Miserables"); Metcalf (Cabinet member under T. Roosevelt); Fleming (director, "Gone With the Wind"); Mature (actor). Less popular. Vic+.

Victorino Hispanic. From Victor. Unusual.

Victorio Hispanic. From Victor. Unusual.

Vida English. From David, Hebrew, "Beloved," "friend," or "darling." 1 Samuel 16:19. Ventsene (Russian, won gold medal in 1988 Olympics for skiing); Blue (baseball player). Unusual for males, less popular for females.

Vidor Hungarian. Latin, "Cheerful." Unusual.

Vijay Unknown. Meaning and origin unknown. Unusual.

Vika See under Girls' Names.

Vikas Indo-Pakistani. Hindi, "Growth." Unusual.

Vikent Russian. From Vincent. Unusual.

Vikenti Russian. From Vincent. Unusual.

Vikesha Russian. From Vincent. Unusual.

Viktor Bulgarian, Hungarian, Russian, Swedish. From Victor. Saneyev (Russian, won gold medal in track, 1968, 1972, and 1976 Olympics); Meyer (19th-century German chemist and researcher, led field of stereochemistry); Patsayev (Russian rocket designer); Chernov (Russian minister of agriculture, 1917). Unusual.

Vila Czech. From William, Old German, "Will" + "helmet." Unusual.

Vilek Czech. From William, Old German, "Will" + "helmet." Unusual.

Vilém Czech. From William, Old German, "Will" + "helmet." Unusual.

Vilhelm Bulgarian, Swedish. From William, Old German, "Will" + "helmet." Moberg (Swedish novelist, wrote on Swedish peasant life); Thomsen (Danish linguist); Bjerknes (Norwegian physicist, proposed theories essential to weather forecasting); Buhl (Danish prime minister, 1942, 1945); Ekelund (Swedish symbolist poet). Unusual.

Vili Hungarian. From William, Old German, "Will" + "helmet." Unusual.

Viliam Czech. From William, Old German, "Will" + "helmet." Unusual.

Viljo Finnish. From William, Old German, "Will" + "helmet." Revell (Finnish functionalist architect). Unusual.

Vilko Czech. From William, Old German, "Will" + "helmet." Unusual.

Ville Swedish. From William, Old German, "Will" + "helmet." Unusual.

Vilmos Hungarian. From William, Old German, "Will" + "helmet." Zsigmond (cinematographer). Unusual.

Vilous Czech. From William, Old German, "Will" + "helmet." Unusual.

Vin English. From Vincent. Scully (sports

broadcaster). Unusual. Alternative spelling: Vinn.

Vinay Indo-Pakistani. Hindi, "Politeness." Unusual.

Vince English. From Vincent. Lombardi (football coaching great); Edwards (actor, "Ben Casey"). Unusual.

Vincenc Czech. From Vincent. Unusual.

Vincent English. Latin, "Vincentius," from "vincere" ("to conquer"). Saint; Van Gogh (Dutch artist, "Irises," which sold for record $53.9 million, 1987); Price (actor); Wallace (19th-century Irish violinist, pianist, and composer); Alsop (17th-century British reformist clergyman); Auriol (first president of French Fourth Republic, 1947–54). Less popular. Vince.

Vincente Hispanic. From Vincent. Minnelli (movie director, husband of Judy Garland); Benedetti (19th-century French diplomat, indirectly launched Franco-Prussian War). Unusual.

Vincenz French, German. From Vincent. Unusual.

Vincenzo Italian. From Vincent. Monti (18th-century neoclassical Italian poet); Scamozzi (16th-century Italian architect, father of neoclassicism); Tommasini (Italian composer of operas and ballets); Vela (19th-century Italian, sculpted Donizetti's tomb); Viviani (17th-century Italian mathematician, assisted Galileo). Unusual.

Vinci Hungarian. From Vincent. Unusual.

Vinco Czech. From Vincent. Unusual.

Vine English. Occupational surname indicating a worker in a vineyard; origin unknown. Unusual.

Vinod Indo-Pakistani. Hindi, "Amusement." Unusual.

Vinson English. English, "Son of Vincent ("Vicentius," from "vincere" ("to conquer")." Unusual.

Vint English. From Vincent. Unusual.

Virgil English. Latin, "Vergilius"; a Roman clan name. Saint; Brand (owner of largest coin collection in world: 375,000 coins); Fox (organist); Grissom (one of first astronauts in U.S. space program). Less popular.

Vitalis English. Latin, "vita" ("life"). Saint. Unusual.

Vitenka Russian. From Victor, Latin, "Conqueror." Unusual.

Vitin Hispanic. From Victor, Latin, "Conqueror." Unusual.

Vitka Russian. From Victor, Latin, "Conqueror." Unusual.

Vito Hispanic. From Victor, Latin, "Conqueror." Volterra (Italian physicist, pioneered use of helium in airships). Unusual.

Vitor Portuguese. From Victor, Latin, "Conqueror." Unusual.

Vittore Italian. From Victor, Latin, "Conqueror." Carpaccio (15th-century Italian painter). Unusual.

Vittorio Italian. From Victor, Latin, "Conqueror." De Sica (Italian film director, won Oscar, 1946, "Shoeshine"); Orlando (Italian prime minister, 1917–19); Alfieri (18th-century Italian tragic poet, helped revive national spirit); Fossombroni (Italian prime minister, 1814–44). Unusual.

Vitus French. From Guy, German, "Woods" (?). Saint; Bering (Danish explorer, discovered Aleutian Islands and Bering Sea, 1728–41). Unusual. Vitya Russian. From Victor, Latin, "Conqueror." Unusual.

Vivian See under Girls' Names.

Vladimir Russian. From Walter, Old German, "Ruling people." Saint; Lenin (led Russian Revolution, 1917); Salnikov (Russian, won gold medals, 1980, 1988 Olympics); Chernyak (Ukrainian economist); Macek (Yugoslavian deputy prime minister, 1939–41); Horowitz (Russian pianist); Rebikov (Russian operatic composer, "The Thunderstorm"). Unusual.

Vladko Czech. From Walter, Old German, "Ruling people." Unusual.

Vladlen Russian. Russian, combination of Vladimir (Walter, Old German, "Ruling people") + Lenin (surname, meaning unknown). Unusual.

Vlas Russian. From Blaze, Latin, "Stammerer." Unusual.

Volya Russian. From Walter, Old German, "Ruling people." Unusual.

Vova Russian. From Walter, Old German, "Ruling people." Unusual.

Vovka Russian. From Walter, Old German, "Ruling people." Unusual.

Vyvyan English. From Vivian, Latin, "Full of life." Holland (British writer, son of Oscar Wilde). Unusual. Alternative spellings: Vivyan, Vyvian.

Waban Native American. Native American, "East wind." Unusual.

Wade English. Old English, a place to ford a river or stream; a place name used as a first name. Hampton (Confederate soldier, later brigadier general); Boggs (batting great); character in Margaret Mitchell's "Gone With the Wind." Unusual.

Wahoo Created. From Whoopi, Old French, "houpper," meaning unknown. McDaniels (wrestler). Unusual for males, unusual for females.

Wain English. From Wainwright. Unusual.

Wainwright English. Occupational surname indicating someone who built wagons; origin unknown. Unusual.

Wakiza Native American. Native American, "Desperate fighter." Unusual.

Wald English. From Walden. Unusual.

Waldemar Lithuanian. From Walter. Lindgren (geologist, created classification system for ores); Brögger (Norwegian geologist, specialized in native igneous rocks). Unusual.

Walden English. Old English, "Child of the valley." Unusual. Alternative spelling: Waldon.

Waldo English. German, "Strong." Pratt (music, professor of music and hymnology); Frank (writer, established "Seven Arts" magazine, 1916). Less popular.

Walford English. English, a place to cross a stream; place name used as a first name. Unusual.

Walker English. Occupational surname indicating someone who walked on cloth to cleanse it; origin unknown. Evans (Depression-era photographer). Unusual.

Wallace English. Scottish surname originally indicating a Celt or Welshman. Nutting (Congregationalist clergyman and painter); Sabine (physicist, developed science of acoustics); Stevens (poet, former lawyer; Pulitzer Prize, 1954, "Collected Poems"); Beery (actor, won Oscar for "The Champ," 1931); Fard (established Black Muslim movement in U.S.). Less popular. Alternative spelling: Wallis.

Waller English. Meaning and origin unknown. Unusual.

Walli German. From Walter. Unusual.

Wally English. From Walter. Cox (TV actor); Moon (baseball player, top rookie, 1954). Less popular. Alternative spelling: Wallie.

Walsh English. From Wallace. Unusual.

Walt English. From Walter. Disney (movie pioneer, won more Oscars than anyone else: 20); Whitman (poet, "I Sing the Body Electric") (real name: Walter); Rostow (economist); Kelly (cartoonist, "Pogo"). Less popular.

Walter English. Old German, "Ruling people." Saint; Payton (all-time football rushing leader); Reed (physician, discovered yellow fever transmission route, 1900); Adams (astronomer, determined distance and speed of thousands of stars); Smith (sportswriter and columnist, won Pulitzer Prize, 1976). Less popular. Walt, Wally.

Walther German. From Walter. Bothe (German physicist, won Nobel Prize, 1954; showed cosmic rays are particles); Flemming (19th-century German anatomist, studied genetics, coined word "mitosis"). Unusual.

Waltli German. From Walter. Unusual.

Walton English. Meaning and origin unknown. Unusual.

Waltr Czech. From Walter. Unusual.

Wapi Native American. Native American, "Lucky." Unusual.

Ward English. Old English, occupational surname indicating someone who worked as a watchman. Saint; Hunt (Supreme Court Justice, 1873–82); Bond (actor, "Gone With the Wind"). Less popular.

Warner English. Old French, "Keeper of the park." Unusual.

Warren English. German, "Protecting friend." Harding (29th president); Beatty (actor and director, "Reds"); de la Rue (19th-century British astronomer, invented device to photograph sun daily); Burger (Chief Justice of the U.S., 1969–86); Spahn (Hall of Fame pitcher); Littlefield (TV executive). Less popular.

Warrick English. From Warwick. Unusual. Alternative spelling: Warick.

Warwick English. Old English, "A dwelling near a dam." Deeping (prolific British novelist). Unusual.

Washington English. Meaning and origin unknown. Luiz Pereira de Souza (president of Brazil, 1926–30); Allston (romantic artist); Burpee (businessman, founded seed company); DePauw (19th-century banker and industrialist); Gladden (clergyman, preached applying religious principles to daily life); Irving (writer). Unusual.

Wat English. From Walter. Unusual.

Waterio Hispanic. From Walter. Unusual.

Watkin English. From Walter. Tench (18th-century British soldier and writer, chronicled settling of Australia). Unusual.

Watson English. "Son of Walter (Old German, "Ruling people")." Unusual.

Waylon English. Old English, "From the land by the road." Jennings (country-western singer). Unusual.

Wayne English. From Wainwright, occupational surname indicating someone who built wagons; origin unknown. Gretzky (Canadian hockey star, eight-time MVP); Wheeler (lawyer and reformer, led prohibition movement); Newton (singer and entertainer). Less popular. Alternative spelling: Wayn.

Wazir Arabic. Arabic, "Minister." Unusual.

Webb English. Old English, "A weaver." Unusual. Alternative spelling: Web.

Webster English. Old English, occupational surname referring to a female weaver. Saint; Booth (British singer). Unusual.

Wei-Quo Chinese. Chinese, "To run the country." Unusual.

Welby English. Old English, "Farm by the water." Unusual.

Welch English. From Wallace, Scottish surname originally indicating a Celt or Welshman. Unusual.

Welfel Yiddish. From William, Old German, "Will" + "helmet." Unusual.

Wellington English. Old English, "People in a clearing" (?). Unusual.

Wells English. Old English, "veallan" ("to bubble"—a source of water); place name used as a first name. Saint. Unusual.

Welsh Estonian. From Wallace, Scottish surname originally indicating a Celt or Welshman. Unusual.

Welvel Yiddish. From William, Old German, "Will" + "helmet." Unusual.

Wemilat Native American. Native American, "All will be given to him." Unusual.

Wemilo Native American. Native American, "All speak to him." Unusual.

Wen English. English Gypsy, "Born in winter." Unusual.

Wendell English. Old German, "Wanderer." Phillips (called for women's rights, advocated prohibition); Stanley (developed vaccine against influenza, won Nobel Prize, 1946); Willkie (politician, lost 1940 presidential election); Corey (actor). Unusual. Alternative spellings: Wendel, Wendle.

Wenford English. From Wynford, Old English, "White torrent." Unusual.

Wenutu Native American. Native American, "Sky clearing." Unusual.

Werner English. Old German, ? + "army." Munzinger (19th-century Swiss explorer, and later, governor, of parts of Africa); Forssmann (German physician, developed cardiac catheterization; won Nobel Prize, 1956); Heisenberg (German physicist; developed quantum physics and principle of indeterminacy). Unusual.

Wes English. From Wesley. Craven (director, "Nightmare on Elm Street"); Unseld (NBA MVP, 1969). Less popular.

Wesh English. English Gypsy, "Woods." Unusual.

Wesley English. English, "West meadow" or "west field." Snipes (actor, "Mo' Better Blues"); Merritt (army officer, headed West Point, 1882–87); Mitchell (economist). Popular. Wes. Alternative spellings: Wesly, Wessley.

West English. From Westbrook. Unusual.

Westbrook English. Old English, "From near the west brook." Pegler (journalist and sports commentator). Unusual. Alternative spelling: Westbrooke.

Westley English. From Wesley. Unusual.

Weston English. Old English, "Farm facing the west." Unusual.

Whalley English. Old English, "Woods near a hill." Unusual. Alternative spelling: Whallie.

Wharton English. Old English, "Settlement near the banks [of a body of water]." Unusual. Alternative spelling: Warton.

Wheatley English. From Wheatley. Unusual.

Whitney See under Girls' Names.

Whittaker English. Old English, "White field." Chambers (1950s journalist, exposed "communists" in State Department). Unusual. Alternative spelling: Whitaker.

Wicek Polish. From Vincent, Latin, "Vincentius," from "vincere" ("to conquer"). Unusual.

Wicent Polish. From Vincent, Latin, "Vincentius," from "vincere" ("to conquer"). Unusual.

Wichado Native American. Native American, "Willing." Unusual.

Wicus Polish. From Vincent, Latin, "Vincentius," from "vincere" ("to conquer"). Unusual.

Wiktor Polish. From Victor, Latin, "Conqueror." Unusual.

Wilanu Native American. Native American, "Pouring water on flour." Unusual.

Wilbert English. Old English, "Will-bright." Unusual. Alternative spelling: Wilburt.

Wilbur English. Old German, "Wilburg," meaning unknown. Wright (aviation pioneer); Cohen (Cabinet member under LBJ); Cross (educator, politician, and governor of Connecticut, 1931–39); Fisk (clergyman, first president of Wesleyan University, 1831–39); Shaw (won Indianapolis 500 three times). Less popular. Alternative spelling: Wilber.

Wilburt English. From Wilbert. Unusual.

Wildon English. Old English, "From the wild valley." Unusual.

Wiley English. Old English, "Water meadow" (?). Post (among first to fly around the world, 1933); Rutledge (Supreme Court Justice, 1943–49). Unusual.

Wilford English. Old English, "A crossing near willow trees." Woodruff (19th-century leader of Mormon Church). Unusual.

Wilfred English. English, "Will-peace." Saint (7th-century); Hardy (British, holds record for most tattoos: even on tongue and inner cheeks; only 4% of his body uncovered); Owen (British anti-war poet, WWI); Trotter (British surgeon to king, 1928–32); character in Sir Walter Scott's novel "Rob Roy." Unusual.

Wilfredo Hispanic. From Wilfred. Benítez (Puerto Rican, youngest boxer to be world champion: 17 years old). Unusual.

Wilfrid English. From Wilfred. Saint; Laurier (Canadian prime minister, 1896–1911); Meynell (British biographer of Disraeli); Blunt (British poet, advocated Muslim causes and anti-imperialism); Clark (British anthropologist, authority on primate evolution); character in Scott's novel "Rokeby." Unusual.

Wilhelm French, Swedish. From William, Old German, "Will" + "helmet." Roux (German zoologist, founded experimental embryology); Weber (German physicist, studied magnetics); Wundt (German psychologist, founded experimental psychology); Maybach (German, rode first motorcycle, in 1885). Unusual.

Wilkinson English. From William. Unusual.

Will English. From William. Smith (actor, "Fresh Prince of Bel-Air"); Rogers (actor and humorist); Cook (musician and composer); Fyffe (Scottish entertainer, especially popular during WWII); Cuppy (critic and humorist, "The Decline and Fall of Practically Everybody"). Less popular.

Willard English. Old English, "Bold resolve." Cravens (caught largest freshwater fish ever: a white sturgeon weighing 360 pounds, 1956); Wirtz (secretary of labor, 1962); Libby (chemist, Nobel Prize for carbon dating, 1960); Waller (founded sociology of knowledge); Wright (wrote detective stories, created character Philo Vance). Less popular. Will.

Willey English. From William. Unusual.

William English. Old German, "Will" + "helmet." Clinton (42nd president); Saint; Garrison (abolitionist); Thomson (British, discovered absolute 0); Kennedy (won Pulitzer Prize for fiction, 1984, "Ironweed"); Shakespeare (British playwright); Rogers (secretary of state under Nixon); Lear (businessman, founded company selling Lear jets). Very popular. Bill, Billy, Will, Willie.

Williamson English. From William. Unusual.

Willie English. From William, Old German, "Will" + "helmet." Nelson (country-western singer); Sutton (1920s and 1930s bank robber) ("Willie, why do you rob banks?" "'Cause that's where the money is!"); Mays (baseball great, hit 660 home runs); Dixon (blues singer). Less popular for males, unusual for females. Alternative spellings: Willi, Willy.

Willimar English. Old German, "Will-fame." Unusual.

Willis English. From William. Van Devanter (Supreme Court Justice, 1919–37); Carrier (invented air conditioning, then founded company to sell it); Hawley (congressman, 1907–33). Unusual.

Willoughby English. Old English, "A farm near willow trees." Unusual.

Wilmer English. From Willimar. Unusual.

Wilmott English. From William. Unusual. Alternative spelling: Wilmot.

Wilny Native American. Native American, "Eagle screaming." Unusual.

Wilson English. From William. Bissell (postmaster general under Cleveland); Wallis (anthropologist, studied religion and science among Indian tribes); Barrett (British actor, playwright, and theater owner); Collison (playwright and novelist, especially known for murder mysteries). Unusual.

Wilt English. From Wilton. Chamberlain (basketball legend, holds numerous records). Less popular.

Wilton English. Old English, "Farm with a spring." Unusual.

Wilu Native American. Native American, "Chicken hawk calling." Unusual.

Windsor English. From Windsor. Davies (British actor). Unusual.

Winfield English. Old German, "Friend of the field." Schley (naval officer during Spanish-American War, 1898); Scott (19th-century general, fought in Canada and Mexico, lost presidential election to Pierce, 1852); Hancock (general during Civil War, lost presidential election to Garfield, 1880). Unusual.

Winfred English. Old English, "Friend-peace." Unusual.

Wingi Native American. Native American, "Willing." Unusual.
Winny English. From Winfield. Unusual.
Winston English. Old English, "Wine's settlement"; surname and place name used as a first name. Churchill (British prime minister, 1940–45, 1951–55; won Nobel Prize for literature, 1953). Less popular. Alternative spelling: Winsten.
Winstone English. From Winston. Unusual.
Winthrop English. Old English, "Friend" + "village." Praed (19th-century British writer of witty skits and satire); Ames (theatrical producer, wrote "Snow White"); Sargent (first governor of Mississippi Territory, 1798–1801). Unusual.
Winward English. Old English, "Near my brother's forest." Unusual.
Wisdom See under Girls' Names.
Witek Polish. From Victor, Latin, "Conqueror." Unusual.
Wolf Yiddish. From William. Szmuness (epidemiologist, developed conclusive studies of hepatitis B vaccine); Baudissin (German literary critic and co-translator of nine Shakespeare plays); Huber (16th-century German painter, master of Danube school); Blitzer (author and journalist, 1991). Unusual.
Wolfe English. From Woolf. Tone (18th-century Irish revolutionary, founded Society of United Irishmen, 1791). Unusual.
Wolfgang German. Old German, "Wolf" + "strife." Saint; Mozart (18th-century Austrian composer of over 600 operas, symphonies, etc.); Müller (19th-century German writer on Rhine area); Pauli (physicist, won Nobel Prize, 1945; developed exclusion principle that now bears his name); Ratke (17th-century German educator, developed new way to teach languages). Unusual.
Wood English. From Woodrow. Unusual.
Woodfield English. Place name used as a first name; meaning and origin unknown. Unusual.
Woodfine English. Place name used as a first name; meaning and origin unknown. Unusual.
Woodford English. Place name used as a first name; meaning and origin unknown. Unusual. Alternative spelling: Woodforde.
Woodlock English. Place name used as a first name; meaning and origin unknown. Unusual.
Woodrow English. Old English, "Row of cottages in a wood." Wilson (28th president, 1913–21; signed constitutional amendments creating prohibition and women's voting rights; won Nobel Prize, 1919). Unusual. Woody.
Woodville English. Place name used as a first name; meaning and origin unknown. Unusual.
Woody English. From Woodrow. Allen (actor and director; "Annie Hall"); Harrelson (actor, "Cheers"); Hayes (college football coaching great); Guthrie (folk singer, "This Land Is Your Land"); Herman (big-band leader). Unusual.
Woolf German. Old German, "Wolf." Unusual.
Worth English. Old English, "From the farm." Unusual.
Worthy English. Old English, "Enclosure." Unusual. Alternative spelling: Worthey.
Wright English. Old English, a carpenter. Patman (congressman, helped create Small Business Administration, 1953). Unusual.
Wuliton Native American. Native American, "To do well." Unusual.
Wunand Native American. Native American, "God is good." Unusual.
Wuyi Native American. Native American, "Turkey vulture aloft." Unusual.
Wyatt English. Old French, "Little warrior." Earp (lawman, Kansas and Arizona, fought in "Gunfight at OK Corral"); Eaton (19th-century portraitist, founded Society of American Artists, 1877). Unusual. Alternative spellings: Wiatt, Wyat.
Wybert English. Old English, "Battle-bright"; surname used as a first name. Unusual.
Wylmer English. From Willimar, Old German, "Will-fame." Unusual.
Wyn English. From Winfield, Old German, "Friend of the field." Unusual. Alternative spellings: Win, Wynn, Wynne.
Wyndham English. Old English, "Wyman's settlement." Lewis (British writer and painter). Unusual.
Wynford English. Old English, "White torrent." Unusual.
Wynono Native American. Native American, "First-born son." Unusual.

Xaver German. From Xavier, Spanish, "New house." Unusual.
Xavier English. Spanish, "New house." Saint; Cugat (Spanish band leader); Montépin (popular 19th-century French novelist); Leroux (French opera composer). Unusual for males, unusual for females.
Xenos Greek. Greek, "A guest." Unusual.
Xerxes Persian. Persian, "Ruler." Name of three Persian kings, 519–400 B.C. Unusual.
Ximen Hispanic. Spanish, "Obedient." Unusual. Alternative spellings: Ximon, Ximun.
Xylon Greek. Greek, "Forest-dweller." Unusual.

Yaakov Hebrew/Israeli. Hebrew, "Supplanter" or "heel." Genesis 25:26. Stroganov (16th-century Russian businessman active in salt mining, fishing, and furs); Sverdlov (Russian revolutionary and high-ranking politician, 1917–19); Smirnoff (comedian). Unusual.
Yadid Hebrew/Israeli. Hebrew, "Friend" or "beloved." Unusual.
Yadin Hebrew/Israeli. Hebrew, "God will judge." Unusual.
Yadon Hebrew/Israeli. From Yadin. Unusual.
Yahoo English. Created by Jonathan Swift in "Gulliver's Travels" to describe a race of brutes. Serious (Australian actor). Unusual for males, unusual for females.

Yahya Arabic. Arabic, "Living." Unusual.
Yakecen Native American. Native American, "Sky song." Unusual.
Yakez Native American. Native American, "Heaven." Unusual.
Yale English. Old English, "From the hill." Lary (Hall of Fame football player, Detroit Lions, 1952–64). Unusual.
Yana Native American. Native American, "Bear." Unusual.
Yancy Native American. Native American, "Englishman." Unusual.
Yanka Russian. From John, Hebrew (Yochanan), "God has been gracious." Unusual.
Yannis Greek. From John, Hebrew (Yochanan), "God has been gracious." Unusual.
Yarb Gypsy. English Gypsy, "Herb." Unusual.
Yardan Arabic. Arabic, "King." Unusual.
Yarin Hebrew/Israeli. Hebrew, "To understand." Unusual.
Yasar Arabic. Arabic, "Wealth." Unusual. Alternative spellings: Yaser, Yassir, Yasser.
Yashko Russian. From Jacob, Hebrew (Yaakov), "Supplanter" or "heel." Genesis 25:26. Unusual.
Yates English. Old English, "Gate." Unusual.
Yazid Arabic. Arabic, "His power and influence will grow." Name of three Arab caliphs, 645–744. Unusual.
Yechezkel Hebrew/Israeli. Hebrew, "Strengthened by God" or "may God strengthen." Ezekiel 1:3. Unusual.
Yegor Russian. From George, Greek, "Husbandman," "farmer," or "earth-worker." Kankrin (German finance minister, 1823–44, had influence on Czar Nicholas I). Unusual.
Yehoshua Hebrew/Israeli. Hebrew, "God is my salvation." Exodus 17:9. Unusual.
Yehuda Hebrew/Israeli. Hebrew, "Praise to the Lord." Genesis 29:35. Unusual.
Yehudi Hebrew/Israeli. From Judah, Hebrew (Yehuda), "Praise to the Lord." Genesis 29:35. Menuhin (concert violinist; youngest person to appear in "Who's Who," at 15 years old). Unusual.
Yelutci Native American. Native American, "Bear traveling silently." Unusual.
Yemon Japanese. Japanese, "Guarding the gate." Unusual.
Yeremey Russian. From Jeremiah, Hebrew, "Jehovah is high" or "Jehovah exalts." Book of Jeremiah. Unusual.
Yerik Russian. From Jeremiah, Hebrew, "Jehovah is high" or "Jehovah exalts." Book of Jeremiah. Unusual.
Yeska Russian. From Joseph, Hebrew (Yosef), "God will add." Unusual.
Yestin Welsh. Welsh, "Just." Unusual.
Yesya Russian. From Joseph, Hebrew (Yosef), "God will add." Unusual.
Yevgenyi Russian. From Eugene, Greek, "Well born." Vuchetich (Russian, designed world's tallest statue: "Motherland," a 270-foot-tall woman with a sword in her hand). Unusual.
Yiannis Greek. From John, Hebrew (Yochanan), "God has been gracious." Unusual.
Yippee Created. Meaning and origin unknown. Unusual for males, unusual for females.
Yisrael Hebrew/Israeli. Hebrew, "Wrestled with God." Name of the Jewish nation. Genesis 35:10. Jacob's name after he struggled with God. Unusual.
Yitzchak Hebrew/Israeli. Hebrew, "Laughter." Genesis 21:3. Shamir (Israeli prime minister, 1988-). Unusual.
Yochanan Hebrew/Israeli. Hebrew, "God has been gracious." Unusual.
Yonah Hebrew/Israeli. Hebrew, "Dove." Book of Jonah. Unusual for males, unusual for females.
Yonatan Hebrew/Israeli. Hebrew, "God has given" or "God's gift." Unusual.
Yong Chinese. Chinese, "Courageous." Unusual.
Yorath English. From Iorwerth, Welsh, "Lord" + "worth." Unusual.
York English. Celtic, "Yew tree." Unusual. Alternative spelling: Yorke.
Yosef Hebrew/Israeli. Hebrew, "God will add." Unusual.
Yoshi Japanese. From Kiyoshi, Japanese, "Quiet." Unusual.
Yosif Bulgarian. From Joseph, Hebrew (Yosef), "God will add." Unusual.
Yotimo Native American. Native American, "Bee carrying food to its hive." Unusual.
Yottoko Native American. Native American, "Mud at water's edge." Unusual.
Young English. Old English, "geong"; surname used as a first name. Unusual.
Yousef Yiddish. From Joseph, Hebrew (Yosef), "God will add." Unusual.
Yov Russian. From Ioakim, Russian, "God will establish." Unusual.
Yoyi Hebrew/Israeli. From George, Greek, "Husbandman," "farmer," or "earth-worker." Unusual.
Yucel Turkish. Turkish, "Sublime." Unusual.
Yukiko Japanese. From Yuki, Japanese, "Snow." Unusual.
Yukio Japanese. From Yuki, Japanese, "Snow." Unusual.
Yul Chinese, Mongolian, "Beyond the horizon"; and English, from Yule. Brynner (actor, "The King and I"). Unusual.
Yule English. Old Norse, "jol"; a reference to Christmas. Unusual.
Yuma Native American. Native American, "Chief's son." Unusual.
Yunus Turkish. From Jonah, Hebrew (Yonah), "Dove." Book of Jonah. Unusual.
Yura Russian. From George, Greek, "Husbandman," "farmer," or "earth-worker." Unusual.
Yurchik Russian. From George, Greek, "Husbandman," "farmer," or "earth-worker." Unusual.
Yuri Russian. From George, Greek, "Husbandman," "farmer," or "earth-worker." Unusual.
Yurik Russian. From George, Greek, "Husbandman," "farmer," or "earth-worker." Unusual.
Yurko Russian. From George, Greek, "Husbandman," "farmer," or "earth-worker." Unusual.
Yusef Arabic. From Joseph, Hebrew (Yosef), "God will add." Unusual. Alternative spelling: Yusuf.
Yusha Russian. From George, Greek, "Husbandman," "farmer," or "earth-worker." Unusual.
Yusif Russian. From Joseph, Hebrew (Yosef), "God will add."
Yusts Russian. From Justin, Latin, "Just." Unusual.
Yustyn Russian. From Justin, Latin, "Just." Unusual.
Yusup Russian. From Joseph, Hebrew (Yosef), "God will add." Unusual.
Yutu Native American. Native American, "Coyote out hunting." Unusual.
Yuzef Russian. From Joseph, Hebrew (Yosef), "God will add." Unusual.
Yves French. From Ivo, Teutonic, "Yew wood" or "archer." Yew wood was used

to make bows. Saint-Laurent (French fashion designer); Polish (French, ran 3 miles backwards in record 22 minutes, 33 seconds); Tanguy (surrealist landscape painter); Delage (French zoologist, developed invertebrate anatomy); Kerguélen-Trémarec (18th-century French sub-antarctic explorer). Less popular.

Yvon French. From Ivo, Teutonic, "Yew wood" or "archer." Yew wood was used to make bows. Jolin (Canadian, holds ice skating barrel-jumping record: 29 feet, 5 inches, over 18 barrels, 1981); Delbos (French minister of foreign affairs, 1936–38, opposed capitulation to Germans). Unusual.

Zacarias Hispanic, Portuguese. From Zachariah. Unusual.

Zacchaeus Greek. From Zachariah. Unusual. Alternative spellings: Zacceus, Zaccheus.

Zacharia German. From Zachariah. Unusual.

Zachariah English. Hebrew, "The Lord has remembered." Prophet; king of Israel; Chandler (secretary of interior, 1875–78); Allen (invented first home heating system, 1821). Unusual. Alternative spellings: Zacariah, Zakaria.

Zacharias Hungarian, Latin. From Zachariah. Saint; Werner (18th-century German Catholic, religiously oriented poet and dramatist); Frankel (19th-century German rabbi, developed precursor to Conservative Judaism); Janssen (16th-century Dutch inventor of compound microscope, 1590, and telescope, 1608). Unusual.

Zacharie French. From Zachariah. Unusual.

Zachary English. From Zachariah. Saint; Taylor (12th president); Richard (rock singer); Boyd (17th-century Scottish minister and scriptural poet); Zzzzzzzzzzra (last name in San Francisco phone book). Very popular. Zack+. Alternative spellings: Zachery, Zackary, Zackery.

Zack English. From Zachariah. Unusual. Alternative spelling: Zach.

Zahid Arabic. Arabic, "Ascetic." Unusual.

Zahur African. Swahili, "Flower." Unusual.

Zaim Arabic. Arabic, "Brigadier general." Unusual.

Zakhar Russian. From Zachariah. Unusual.

Zaki Arabic. From Zakia, Arabic, "Bright" or "pure." Unusual.

Zako Hungarian. From Zachariah. Unusual.

Zakris Scandinavian. From Zachariah. Unusual.

Zamiel German. From Samuel, Hebrew (Shmuel), "His name is God" or "God has heard." 1 Samuel 1:20. Unusual.

Zamir Hebrew/Israeli. Hebrew, "Bird" or "song." Unusual.

Zane English. From John, Hebrew (Yochanan), "God has been gracious." Grey (novelist, mainly westerns, "Riders of the Purple Sage"); Smith (pitcher). Unusual.

Zareb African. African, "Protector." Unusual.

Zared Hebrew/Israeli. Hebrew, "Ambush." Unusual.

Zavier English. From Xavier, Spanish, "New house." Unusual.

Zayit See under Girls' Names.

Zayn Arabic. Arabic, "Beauty" or "ornament." Unusual.

Ze'ev Hebrew/Israeli. Hebrew, "Wolf." Unusual.

Zebulon Hebrew/Israeli. Hebrew, "To exalt." Jacob's tenth son by Leah; Pike (brigadier general, fought Canadian troops, discovered peak that now bears his name). Unusual.

Zechariah English. From Zachariah. Prophet, 5th-century B.C.; Chafee (lawyer and educator, authority on business practices). Unusual.

Zedekiah Hebrew/Israeli. Hebrew, "God is mighty." Last king of Judah, 597 B.C. Unusual.

Zeeman Dutch. Dutch, "Seaman." Unusual.

Zeheb Turkish. Turkish, "Gold." Unusual.

Zeke English. From Zachariah. Less popular.

Zeki Turkish. Turkish, "Intelligent." Unusual.

Zelimir Slavic. Slavic, "Wishes for peace." Unusual.

Zenda Czech. From Eugene, Greek, "Well born." Unusual.

Zeno French. From Zēnōn. Unusual.

Zēnōn Greek, Hispanic. Greek, "Life from Zeus." Unusual.

Zephaniah Hebrew/Israeli. Hebrew, "Protection." Prophet, 7th-century B.C. Unusual.

Zesiro African. African, "Older twin." Unusual.

Zeusef Portuguese. From Joseph, Hebrew (Yosef), "God will add." Unusual.

Zewek Polish. From Zēnōn. Unusual.

Zheka Russian. From Eugene, Greek, "Well born." Unusual.

Zhenka Russian. From Eugene, Greek, "Well born." Unusual.

Zhorka Russian. From George, Greek, "Husbandman," "farmer," or "earthworker." Unusual.

Zia Hebrew/Israeli. Hebrew, name occurring in 1 Chron. 5:13. Meaning and origin unknown. Unusual.

Zigfrid Hungarian. From Sigfrid, Old German, "Victory-peace." Unusual.

Zigfrids Latvian, Russian. From Sigfrid, Old German, "Victory-peace." Meierovics (first prime minister of independent Latvia, 1921–24). Unusual.

Zimraan Arabic. Arabic, "Celebrated." Unusual.

Zimri Hebrew/Israeli. Hebrew, "Celebrated in song." 1 Kings 16:9. Biblical king, 1 Kings 16:9. Unusual.

Zinon Russian. From Zēnōn. Unusual.

Ziv Slavic. From Ziven. Unusual.

Ziven Slavic. Slavic, "Lively." Unusual. Alternative spelling: Zivon.

Zoltán Hungarian. Greek, "Life." Tildy (Hungarian premier, 1945); Kodály (Hungarian composer of, and writer about, native folk music). Unusual.

Zorya Ukrainian. Slavic, "Star." Unusual.

Zowie Greek. From Zoë, Greek, "Life." Son of pop star David Bowie. Unusual for males, unusual for females.

Zygfryd Polish. From Sigfrid, Old German, "Victory-peace." Unusual.

Zygi Polish. From Sigfrid, Old German, "Victory-peace." Unusual. Alternative spelling: Ziggy.

Chapter Notes

NAMING CONSIDERATIONS

Full citations for the books and studies referred to below can be found in the reference section that follows.

Associations and Stereotypes:

Moldy skin: Rosenkrantz and Satran, 1988, 35

Popularity:

Popular and "strong": Lawson 1971
Popularity cycles: Hargreaves, Colman, and Sluckin 1983
Different kinds of "unusual": Zweigenhaft 1977
Boys eight to twelve: Johnson and Staffieri 1971
"Peculiar": Ellis and Beechley 1954
College success: Joubert 1983
High school academics: Zweigenhaft 1977
Teachers: Tompkins and Boor 1980
Five scales: Zweigenhaft, Hayes, and Haagen 1980
College women: Zweigenhaft 1981
Psychologists: Sadowski, Wheeler, and Cash 1983
Career choice: Gaffney 1971

Sound:

First and last sounds, rhyming names: Kelly 1985, 7–8
Last letter and "feeling": Rosenkrantz and Satran 1988, 22
Short and long syllables: Ames 1963, 20
Rhythmic patterns: Nurnberg and Rosenblum 1984, 48–49

Ethnic Naming Practices:

Browder 1974
Hanks and Hodges 1990
Rosenkrantz and Satran 1992
Ellefson 1987
McKinzie 1980
Withycombe 1960

Special Considerations:

"II": Zweigenhaft, Hayes, and Haagen 1980
Direction of change: Barry and Harper 1982

LANGUAGE/ETHNICITY BROWSER

Books and articles on first names, some broken down by language/ethnicity, are listed in the annotated bibliography. For an excellent guide to more sources for nearly every language/ethnicity, see Lawson 1987, listed in the references.

POPULARITY BROWSER

The source for the 1930s, 1940s, and 1950s popularity data is the Texas Department of Health records. For all other listings, Health Department records from some or all of the following states were consulted: California, Colorado, Florida, Georgia, Illinois, Indiana, Massachusetts, Missouri, New York, New Jersey, North Carolina, Ohio, Pennsylvania, Texas, and Virginia.

The source for the most popular baby names of 1990 is the Birth and Health Department records from Colorado, North Carolina, New York, Ohio, Pennsylvania, and Texas, plus Georgia for the male list. The year 1990 is the most recent for which statistics from this wide variety of states are available.

Popularity rankings throughout the book are based on these records. Names ranked "extremely popular" are among the top 10 names in those seven states. Names ranked "very popular" are in the top 11 through 25, while those ranked "popular" are in the top 26 through 50. The ratings "less popular" and "unusual" are subjective.

References

Barry, H., III, and Harper, A. S. 1982. "Evolution of Unisex Names." *Names* 30: 15–22.

Browder, S. 1974. *The New Age Baby Book.* New York: Warner Books.

Ellefson, C. L. 1987. *The Melting Pot Book of Baby Names.* Whitehall, Va.: Better Way Publications.

Ellis, A., and Beechley, R. M. 1954. "Emotional Disturbance in Children with Peculiar Given Names." *Journal of Genetic Psychology* 85: 337–339.

Gaffney, W. G. 1971. "Tell Me Your Name and Your Business; or, Some Considerations upon the Purposeful Naming of Children." *Names* 19: 34–42.

Hankes, P., and Hodges, F. 1990. *A Dictionary of First Names.* Oxford: Oxford University Press.

Hargreaves, D. J., Colman, A. M., and Sluckin, W. 1983. "The Attractiveness of Names." *Human Relations* 36: 393–402.

Johnson, P. A., and Staffieri, J. R. 1971. "Boys' Reactions to Unusual Names." *Developmental Psychology* 5: 176.

Joubert, C. E. 1983. "Unusual Names and Academic Achievement." *Psychological Reports* 53: 266.

Kelly, M. 1985. *Parents' Book of Baby Names.* New York: Ballantine Books.

Lawson, E. D. 1971. "Semantic Differential Analysis of Men's First Names." *Journal of Psychology* 78: 229–240.

———. 1987. *Personal Names and Naming: An Annotated Bibliography.* New York: Greenwood Press.

McKinzie, H. 1980. *Names from East Africa.* Self-published.

Nurnberg, M., and Rosenblum, M. 1984. *What to Name your Baby: From Adam to Zoë.* New York: Macmillan.

Rosenkrantz, L., and Satran, P. R. 1988. *Beyond Jennifer and Jason: An Enlightened Guide to Naming Your Baby.* New York: St. Martin's Press.

Sadowski, C. J., Wheeler, K. J., and Cash, M. 1983. "Unusual First Names and Achievement among Male Psychologists." *Journal of Social Psychology* 119: 181–185.

Tompkins, R. C., and Boor, M. 1980. "Effects of Students' Physical Attractiveness and Name Popularity on Student Teachers' Perceptions of Social and Academic Attributes." *Journal of Psychology* 106: 37–42.

Withycombe, E. G. 1950, 2nd ed. *The Oxford Dictionary of English Christian Names.* London: Oxford University Press.

Zweigenhaft, R. L. 1977. "The Other Side of Unusual Names." *Journal of Social Psychology* 103: 291–302.

———. 1981. "Unusual Names and Uniqueness." *Journal of Social Psychology* 114: 297–298.

Zweigenhaft, R. L., Hayes, K. N., and Haagen, C. H. 1980. "The Psychological Impact of Names." *Journal of Social Psychology* 110: 203–210.

Annotated Bibliography

Dozens of name books can be found in any bookstore, many of them retreads of each other. The following sources of information on names and naming include only the most important or unusual works. For a more complete listing, consult the *Books in Print* Subject volume under Names, Personal.

GENERAL

Naming and Language Generally

Shevoroshkin, V. 1990. "The Mother Tongue: How Linguists have Reconstructed the Ancestor of All Living Languages." *The Sciences,* May/June, 20–27.

Religiously oriented

Dunne, W. P. 1977. *Is It a Saint's Name?* TAN Books.

Farmer, D. H. 1987. *The Oxford Dictionary of Saints.* New York: Oxford University Press.

First names

Alford, R. D. 1988. *Naming and Identity: A Cross-Cultural Study of Personal Naming Practices.* New Haven: Hraf Press, 1988. In the author's words, "an attempt to (1) gender a systematic set of data on the naming practices of a sample of societies worldwide; (2) compare the data on naming practices with a variety of other sociocultural variables; and (3) offer preliminary hypotheses about the functions and significance of various naming practices."

Ashley, L. R. N. 1989. *What's in a Name?* Baltimore: Genealogical Publishing Co. Includes tips on naming babies. Reviewed favorably in *Names* 38: 143.

Bailey, S. B. 1983. *Big Book of Baby Names and Announcements.* HP Books.

Binswanger, B., and Mark, L. 1990. *Best Name for Your Baby.* New York: Henry Holt and Co. Well done.

Browder, S. 1974. *The New Age Baby Book.* New York: Warner Books.

Dunkling, L., and Gosling, W. 1973. *The New American Dictionary of First Names.* New York: Facts on File. Has 4,500 entries dealing with more than 10,000 names.

Ellefson, C. L. 1987. *The Melting Pot Book of Baby Names.* Whitehall, Va.: Better Way Publications, Inc. Offers an unusually wide selection of varied names.

Fields, M. 1985. *Baby Names from Around the World.* New York: Pocket Books. An unusual assortment.

Graye, M. B. 1987. *Celebrity Baby Names, or, Choosing the Perfect Baby Name.* Impossible Dream.

Hanks, P., and Hodges, F. 1990. *A Dictionary of First Names.* Oxford: Oxford University Press. An excellent, scholarly source.

Johnson, R., ed. 1974. *A Dictionary of Famous Names in Fiction, Drama, Poetry, History and Art.* Reprint of 1908 ed.

Kolatch, A. J. 1980. *Dictionary of First Names.* New York: G. P. Putnam's Sons. More than 10,000 names.

———. 1984. *The Best Baby Name Book in the Whole Wide World.* Deephaven, Minn.: Meadowbrook, Inc. More than 13,000 names.

Lansky, B. 1985. *10,000 Baby Names.* Deephaven, Minn.: Meadowbrook, Inc. Contains lists of the top 100 boys' and girls' names, used by permission of the National Baby Panel, a division of ParaTest Marketing, Inc., Eastchester, N.Y./Sinrod Marketing Group, Hicksville, N.Y.

Lansky, B., and Sinrod, B. 1990. *Baby Name Personality Survey.* Deephaven, Minn.: Meadowbrook, Inc.

———. 1990. *What People Will Think of Your Baby's Name: Personality Profiles of the 1,500 Most Popular Names.* New York: Simon and Schuster.

Lawson, E. D. *Personal Names: 100 Years of Social Science Contributions.* In two parts. Part 1 (1984): *Names* 32: 73; Part 2 (1986): *Names* 34: 89.

———, comp. 1987. *Personal Names and Naming: An Annotated Bibliography.* New York: Greenwood Press. A comprehensive listing of scholarly and popular books and journal articles on every imaginable aspect of names, including, for example, listings of names from Acadia and the Indo-Pakistani subcontinent, studies on the influence of "Jr." on its bearer, and "theoretical and linguistic aspects of the naming process."

Lempriere's Classical Dictionary of Proper Names Mentioned in Ancient Authors. 1986, 3d revised ed. New York: Routledge, Chapman & Hall.

Loughead, Flora Haines. 1950. *Dictionary of Given Names.* Glendale, Calif.: Arthur H. Clark Co.

Mawson, C. O. 1981. *International Book of Names.* Arden Lib. Reprint of 1934 ed.

Moody, Sophy. 1863, 1976. *What Is Your Name? A Popular Account of the Meanings and Derivations of Christian Names.* A classic, now out of print.

Names, a publication of the American Naming Society. A journal devoted exclusively to names, though not exclusively to first names. C/o Prof. Wayne H. Finke, Dept. of Romance Languages, Baruch College, New York, NY 10010.

Nurnberg, M., and Rosenblum, M. 1984. *What to Name Your Baby: From Adam to Zoë.* New York: Macmillan.

Rosenkrantz, L., and Satran, P. R. 1988. *Beyond Jennifer and Jason: An Enlightened Guide to Naming Your Baby.* New York: St. Martin's Press. Presents numerous impressionistic breakdowns that may be helpful — particular names are categorized, for example, as wimpy, beach boy, macho, or ultrafeminine.

Schwegel, J. 1988. *The Baby Name Countdown: Popularity and Meanings of Today's Baby Names.* Edmonton, Alberta, Canada: Personal Publishings.

Slovenko, R. 1983. "The Destiny of a Name." *Journal of Psychiatry and Law* 11: 227–260.

Smith, E. C. 1950. *The Story of Our Names.*

———. 1952. *Personal Names: A Bibliography.* Detroit: Gale. No longer in print.

———. 1953. "Books in English on Personal Names." *Names* 1: 197–202. Briefly reviews all the major English-language works on names' meanings.

———. 1956. *New Dictionary of American Family Names.* New York: Harper and Row.

Taylor, I. 1896. *Names and Their Histories.* Detroit: Gale. Reprint.

Wagner, L. 1968. *More about Names.* Detroit: Gale. Reprint of 1893 ed. Several other reprinted books by same author are also available.

Withycombe, E. G. 1950, 2nd ed. *The Oxford Dictionary of English Christian Names.* London: Oxford University Press. About 1,128 names. Very scholarly. A classic text.

Yonge, C. M. 1884. *History of Christian Names.* London: Macmillan and Co. A classic text. Withycombe calls it the "standard work." Fascinating histories.

Family Names

Autry, J. W., and Barker, D. G. 1970. "Academic Correlates of Alphabetical Order of Surname." *Journal of School Psychology* 8: 22–23.

Foss, K. A., and Edson, B. A. 1989. "What's in a Name? Accounts of Married Women's Name Choices." *Western Journal of Speech Communications* 53: 356–373.

Lebell, S. 1988. *Naming Ourselves, Naming Our Children: Resolving the Last-Name Dilemma.* Freedom, Calif.: Crossing Press. Reviewed in *Names* 37: 391.

BY LANGUAGE/ETHNICITY

African, African-American

Crane, L. 1982. *African Names: People and Places.* African Outreach Series No. 1. Urbana, Ill.: African Studies Program, University of Illinois at Champaign-Urbana.

Dillard, J. L. 1972. *Black English: Its History and Usage in the United States.* New York: Random House, 1972.

———. 1976. *Black Names.* The Hague: Mouton. Traces the survival of African naming patterns in America.

Freeman, R. F. 1990. "Philadelphia's African Americans: A Celebration of Life." National Geographic 178.

Jackson, C. M. 1989. Editorial, *Essence* magazine, April. Comes out against "created" African American names.

McKinzie, H. 1980. *Names from East Africa.* Self-published.

Puckett, N. M., and Heller, M. 1975. *Black Names in America: Origins and Usage.* Boston: G. K. Hall. Breaks down 340,000 black and 160,000 white names from 1619 to the mid-1940s. 75 references.

Sanyika, B. 1975. *Know and Claim Your African Name.* Dayton: Rucker Press. 540 male, 315 female names in Swahili, Yoruba, and other African languages.

Sontage, D. 1989. "What's in a Name? Many Young Black Mothers Think One-of-a-Kind Names Are Special." *Chicago Tribune,* June 21, sec. 7.

American

Johnson, E. D. 1956. "First Names in French Louisiana." *Names* 4: 49–53.

Lorenz, B. E. 1989. "Origins of Unusual Given Names from the Southern United States." *Names* 37: 201–207.

Loustalot, K. 1972. "Acadian Names and Nicknames." *Attakaps Gazette* 7: 170–181.

Schleuter, Paul. In press. *Names and American Literature.* International Library of Names. New York: Irvington.

Stewart, George R. 1979. *American Given Names — Their Origin and History in the Context of the English Language.* New York: Oxford University Press. Not terribly scholarly. No footnotes, but list of sources at end.

Anglo-Saxon

Barley, N. 1974. "Perspectives on Anglo-Saxon Names." *Semiotica* 11: 1–31. Analysis, discussion, and comment; more than 100 references.

Arabic

Muhammad, W. D. 1976. *Book of Muslim Names.* Chicago: Hon. Elijah Muhammad Mosque No. 2.

Qazi, M. A. 1974. *What's in a Muslim Name?* Chicago: Kazi Publications. 396 male, 220 female names; introduction to Muslim names.

Tushyeh, H. Y., Lawson, E. D., and Rishmawi, G. 1989. "Palestinian First Names: An Introduction." *Names* 37: 245–253.

Armenian

Atikian, M. B., and Atikian, H. 1973. *Armenians' Names.* N.p.; self-published. Meanings of about 620 names.

Hewsen, R. H. "Armenian Names in America." *American Speech* 38: 214–219.

British

Cunnington, C. W. 1959. "Fashions in Christian Names." In J. Hadfield, ed., *The Saturday Book,* vol. 18, pp. 285–291. London: Macmillan. Fashions in English naming associated with royalty, saints, Protestantism, and other influences.

Nightingale, J. L. 1959. "Puritans at the Font." *History Today* 9: 195–197. Naming practices of the periods before, during, and after the Commonwealth.

Rosenkrantz, L., and Satran, P. R. 1992. *Beyond Charles and Diana: An Anglophile's Guide to Baby Naming.* New York: St. Martin's Press.

Bulgarian

Nicoloff, A. 1983. *Bulgarian Folklore.* Cleveland: self-published. Covers first names and surnames, most with derivation and meaning.

Burmese

Khaing, M. H. 1958. "Burmese Names." *Atlantic Monthly,* February, 108. Brief description with a few examples.

Chinese

Zhu, B., and Millward, C. 1987. "Personal Names in Chinese." *Names* 35: 8–21.

Czech

Salzmann, Z. 1981, "Nicknaming in Bigar: A Contribution to the Anthroponymy of a Czech-Speaking Village in the Southern Romanian Banat." *Names* 29: 121–137. Patterns in a village of 340 people.

Danish

Sondergaard, G. 1979. "General Outline of a Computational Investigation of Danish Naming Practice." *Onoma* 23: 1–32. Sample of 10,000 names.

Dutch

Van Langendonck, W. 1982. "Socio-onomastic Properties of By-names." *Onoma* 26: 55–62. Using the French dialect of Dutch, discusses and evaluates combinations of first names, "by-names," and family names.

Eskimo

Guemple, D. L. 1965. "Saunik: Name Sharing as a Factor Governing Eskimo Kinship Terms." *Ethnology* 4: 323–335. Describes naming practices among the Qiqiktamiuk, a group of about 200 who inhabit the Belcher Islands in Hudson Bay, west of Quebec.

Estonian

Must, H. 1964. "Trends in Estonian Name-Giving from 1900 to 1945." *Names* 12: 42–51.

Hebrew/Israeli/Jewish

Diamant, A. 1988. *The Jewish Baby Book.* New York: Summit Books.

Jewish Language Review, a periodical published by the Assn. for the Study of Jewish Languages, 1610 Eshkol Tower, U. of Haifa, Mt. Carmel, Haifa, Israel.

Kaganoff, B. C. 1977. *A Dictionary of Jewish Names and Their History.* New York: Schocken Books. In the author's words, "attempts to trace the historical processes that created the name forms that appear today."

Kolatch, A. J. 1967. *Complete Dictionary of English and Hebrew First Names.* Middle Village, N.Y.: Jonathan David Publishers. 11,000 entries. Includes Hebrew spellings.

———. 1967. *The Name Dictionary — Modern English and Hebrew Names.* Middle Village, N.Y.: Jonathan David Publishers. Contains the results of several surveys by the author on what Jews take as English and Hebrew names, but with no attribution for etymology of names in listings and no list of sources.

Lawson, E. D. N.d. "Most Common Jewish Names in Israel." Unpublished ms.

Nissim, E. 1981. *"Names Survey in the Population Administration: State of Israel." Names* 29: 273–284. Analyzes and ranks (by frequency and otherwise) more than 4 million names, including Arab names.

Rosenkrantz, L., and Satran, P. R. 1992. *Beyond Sarah and Sam: An Enlightened Guide to Jewish Baby Naming.* New York: St. Martin's Press.

Sidi, S. S. *The Complete Book of Hebrew Baby Names.* San Francisco: Harper and Row.

Hindi

Mehrotra, R. R. 1982. "Impact of Religion on Hindi Personal Names." *Names* 30: 43–47.

Shanta, M. A. 1969. *Handbook of Hindu Names.* Calcutta: Arnica. Lists about 5,500 names, in English and Hindi, with meanings.

Hispanic

Fayer, J. M. 1988. "First Names in Puerto Rico: A Change in Progress." *Names* 36: 21–25.

Woods, R. D. 1984. *Hispanic First Names: A Comprehensive Dictionary of 250 Years of Mexican-American Usage.* Westport, Conn.: Greenwood press. Lists about 90 percent of all Hispanic names used in the United States.

Hungarian

Kalman, B. 1978. *The World of Names: A Study in Hungarian Onomatology.* Budapest: Akademiai Kiado. Extensive coverage of place names, first names, family names, and others. More than 100 references, most in Hungarian.

Icelandic

Tomasson, R. F. 1975. "The Continuity of Icelandic Names and Naming Patterns." *Names* 23: 281–289. Compares use of the most frequent 25 male and female names from 870 A.D. to 1970.

Irish

Coghlan, R. 1979. *Irish Christian Names.* London: Johnston and Bacon. Lists about 800 names with the derivation, pronunciation, meaning, and sometimes the location of name in Ireland, along with prominent namesakes.

Japanese

O'Neill, P. G. 1972. *Japanese Names.* New York: John Weatherhill. More than 36,000 names.

Javanese

Uhlenbeck, E. M. 1969. "Systematic Features of Javanese Personal Names."

Word 25: 321–335. Systematic description of the naming process and the six types of names in Java.

Norwegian

Stemshaug, O., ed. 1982. *Norsk Personnamnleksikon.* Oslo: Det Norske Samlaget.

Polish

Szajna, C. B. 1963. "Some Patterns in Polish First-Name Changes." *Polish American Studies* 20: 10–12. Examines patterns in 383 first-name changes.

Zand, H. S. 1950. "Polish Given Names in America." *Polish American Studies* 7: 34–38. Explores three trends in name-changes.

Russian

Davis, P. A. 1968. "Soviet Russian Given Names." *Names* 16: 95–104. Analyzes 11,000 Muscovite names.

———. 1970. "Modern Russian Given Names: An Historical and Statistical Study." *Dissertation Abstracts* 26: 7313. (University Microfilms No. 66-4610). Develops statistics on 26,000 Russian names.

Scandinavian

Jensen, G. F. 1968. *Scandinavian Personal Names in Lincolnshire and Yorkshire.* Copenhagen: Akademisk forlag. Lists 1,390 names; more than 100 references.

Scottish

Dunkling, L. A. 1978. *Scottish Christian Names: An A-Z of First Names.* London: Johnston and Bacon. Alphabetical listing; comments on current frequency; popular associations with names.

Swiss

Senn, A. 1962. "Notes on Swiss Personal Names." *Names* 10: 149–158. Many examples of German-Swiss first names and surnames; some attention to the transformation of Swiss names in the United States.

Turkish

Spencer, R. F. 1961. "The Social Context of Modern Turkish Names." *Southwestern Journal of Anthropology* 17: 205–218.

Ukrainian

Rudnyckyj, J. B. 1982. *An Entymological Dictionary of the Ukrainian Language.* Ottawa, Ontario, Canada: University of Ottawa Press. More than 3,000 first names and surnames. Hundreds of references.

Welsh

Davies, T. R. 1952. *A Book of Welsh Names.* London: Sheppard Press. About 480 entries that include etymology, meaning, and prominent namesakes.

Additional Sources

The following works provided some part of the information contained in this book.

Guinness Book of World Records, 1990 and 1991 eds.

Information Please Almanac, 1990 and 1991 eds.

Nite, N. N. 1989. *Rock On Almanac.* New York: Harper and Row

Premiere magazine

Time magazine

Rolling Stone magazine

Webster's New Biographical Dictionary

Webster's New Collegiate Dictionary

Family Tree

first: ________

middle: ________

last: ________

GRANDFATHER

GRANDMOTHER

GRANDFATHER

GRANDMOTHER

GRANDFATHER

GRANDMOTHER

GRANDFATHER

GRANDMOTHER

FATHER

MOTHER

FATHER

MOTHER

SPOUSE

YOU

Language / Ethnicity Worksheet

Mom's Choice	Dad's Choice

Popularity Worksheet

Mom's Choice	Dad's Choice

Meanings Worksheet

Mom's Choice

Dad's Choice

Occupations / Activities Worksheet

Mom's Choice	Dad's Choice

Girls' Names Worksheet

Rank	Mom's Choice	Rank	Dad's Choice
___	________________	___	________________
___	________________	___	________________
___	________________	___	________________
___	________________	___	________________
___	________________	___	________________
___	________________	___	________________
___	________________	___	________________
___	________________	___	________________
___	________________	___	________________
___	________________	___	________________

Boys' Names Worksheet

Rank	Mom's Choice	Rank	Dad's Choice
___	________________	___	________________
___	________________	___	________________
___	________________	___	________________
___	________________	___	________________
___	________________	___	________________
___	________________	___	________________
___	________________	___	________________
___	________________	___	________________
___	________________	___	________________
___	________________	___	________________